FoxPro Made Easy

FoxPro Made Easy

Edward Jones

Osborne McGraw-Hill
Berkeley New York St. Louis San Francisco
Auckland Bogotá Hamburg London Madrid
Mexico City Milan Montreal New Delhi Panama City
Paris São Paulo Singapore Sydney
Tokyo Toronto

Osborne **McGraw-Hill**
2600 Tenth Street
Berkeley, California 94710
U.S.A.

For information on translations and book distributors outside of the U.S.A., please write to Osborne **McGraw-Hill** at the above address.

A complete list of trademarks appears on page 769.

FoxPro® Made Easy

Copyright © 1990 by McGraw-Hill. All rights reserved. Printed in the United States of America. Except as permitted under the Copyright Act of 1976, no part of this publication may be reproduced or distributed in any form or by any means, or stored in a database or retrieval system, without the prior written permission of the publisher, with the exception that the program listings may be entered, stored, and executed in a computer system, but they may not be reproduced for publication.

1234567890 DOC 89

ISBN 0-07-881609-2

Acquisitions Editor: Cynthia Hudson
Technical Reviewer: Lisa Biow
Copy Editor: Kay Luthin
Word Processor: Judy Koplan, Carole Latimer
Composition: Bonnie Bozorg
Proofreaders: Julie Anjos, Barbara Conway
Production Supervisor: Kevin Shafer

Information has been obtained by Osborne **McGraw-Hill** from sources believed to be reliable. However, because of the possibility of human or mechanical error by our sources, Osborne **McGraw-Hill**, or others, Osborne **McGraw-Hill** does not guarantee the accuracy, adequacy, or completeness of any information and is not responsible for any errors or omissions or the results obtained from the use of such information.

CONTENTS AT A GLANCE

1	Getting Started with FoxPro	3
2	Creating and Displaying Databases	45
3	Changing Your Database	71
4	Sorting and Indexing a Database	107
5	Creating Entry Forms	153
6	Performing Queries	191
7	Introducing Reports	221
8	Managing Your Files	273
9	Automating Your Work with Macros	291
10	Advanced Report Topics	301
11	Using FoxPro's Relational Powers	327
12	Introduction to FoxPro Programming	367
13	Program Control	413
14	Programming for Data Entry and Editing	433
15	Programming for Data Retrieval	471
16	Advanced Programming Topics	489
17	Creating Applications with FoxView	533

18	Using FoxPro with Other Software	557
A	Glossary of FoxPro Commands	585
B	Glossary of FoxPro Functions	709
C	dBASE Commands Not Supported by FoxPro	767
	Index	771

TABLE OF CONTENTS

Introduction xix
Why This Book Is for You 1

1   Getting Started with FoxPro 3

    What Is a Database? 6
    Using a Database 8
    Relational Databases 9
    How You Will Use FoxPro 12
    System Requirements 14
    Designing a Database 15
        Data and Fields 16
    Three Phases of Database Design 17
        Data Definition 17
        Data Refinement 18
        Establishing the Relationships 19
    Installing FoxPro 23
        Hard-Disk Installation 23
        Creating a Batch File to Start the Program 25
    Starting FoxPro 26
    Selecting Menu Options 28
        Cancelling a Menu 28
    The Keyboard 28
    The Mouse 31
    Using FoxPro Commands 32
        Conventions 33
    Getting Help 33
    Windows 35
        Moving and Sizing Windows 36
        Changing Windows 37
        The Command Window 38
    Dialog Boxes 40
    Desktop Accessories 42

2 Creating and Displaying Databases......................... 45

Creating a Database... 46
    Correcting Mistakes... 52
    Saving the Database... 53
Adding Information to a File... 55
    Entering Data in a Memo Field 57
An Introduction to Browse... 59
Getting a Quick Report 63
Dot-Prompt Options for Displaying a Database 65
    Viewing a Database 66
Searching Within a Field.. 68
Keeping Track of Records 69

3 Changing Your Database 71

Editing a Database... 72
Editing in Browse Mode 78
    Browse Menu Options.. 81
    Manipulating the Window 83
    Using Edit in Browse... 85
    Unlinked Partitions 86
    Changing Field Sizes and Positions 87
Using Browse with Commands.. 89
Deleting Records 91
Deleting Files 96
Global Replacements with Commands 96
Modifying the Structure of a Database 99
    Moving Fields 101
    Saving the Changes 102
Creating the Rentals File 103

4 Sorting and Indexing a Database............................107

Sorting 108
    Sorting on Multiple Fields... 114
    Sorting a Subset of a Database 118
    Sorting Selected Fields to a File 119
    Why Sort? 120
Indexing.. 120
    Creating an Index.. 122
    Selective Indexing 125
    Indexing on Multiple Fields 126
    Indexing on Fields of Different Types 128

        Opening Databases and Index Files 130
        Using SET INDEX 130
        Open Index Files.. 132
        Using REINDEX 135
        Using CLOSE INDEX.. 137
    Searching for Specifics... 137
    Index Tips and Unusual Cases 139
        The Multiple Numeric Field Trap 139
        Indexing in Descending Order...................................... 142
        Descending Indexes on Character Fields 143
        Using Functions to Standardize Case 144
        Indexing on a Date Field 146
        Tips for Indexing 148
    Multiple Index Files and dBase IV Compatibility...................... 150

5   Creating Entry Forms 153

    Using FoxView... 154
        Commands Available in FoxView 155
    Using Forms View to Create a Form 157
    Moving Fields... 160
    Changing the Labels 162
    Adding Text.. 163
    Saving Screen Format Files 164
    Leaving FoxView 167
    Using a Screen Format File 167
    Modifying a Screen Form 168
    Drawing Boxes on a Form 169
    Changing Colors... 172
    Table View 176
    Moving Fields and Objects in Table View 182
    Using Picture 184
    Using Range 187
    FoxView and DOS 190

6   Performing Queries..191

    Performing Queries with the Menus 192
        Using GoTo... 192
        Using Locate 194
        Using Continue 200
        Using Seek 201
        Selecting Subsets of Data 202
    Reporting Needs... 205

Performing Queries with Commands 206
    Using LOCATE 207
    Using FIND and SEEK 210
    Comparisons, Comparisons: Find and Seek
        Versus Locate and Continue 211
Using Set Filter with Commands 214
Using View Files 218

7 Introducing Reports 221

The Report Dialog Box 225
Producing Selective Reports with Ease 228
Generating Reports with Commands 231
    Manual Margin Settings and Page Ejects 234
Designing Customized Columnar Reports 234
The Report Specification 235
    Making Changes to the Report's Design 238
    Applying Formats and Style Options to a Field 242
    Adding Text or Lines and Overlaying Objects 246
    Moving and Deleting Objects 247
    Saving and Running the Report 248
Practice Designing a Customized Report 249
Using the Group Menu Options 257
Adding Grouping by State to the Membership Report 260
Creating a Report with Multiple Groups 267
Report Design 272

8 Managing Your Files 273

Using the Filer 274
    Moving Around the Files List 275
    Deleting Files 276
    Renaming Files 276
    Finding Files 277
    Editing Files 277
    Moving and Copying Files 277
    Changing File Attributes 277
    Using Size and Tree 278
    Using Sort 278
Commands Used for Managing Files 279
    The RUN Command 279
    The COPY FILE Command 280
    The COPY Command 280
    Work Areas and Active Files 283

        The CLOSE DATABASES Command 286
        Combining Files.. 287
        Copying a Database Structure 289

9 Automating Your Work with Macros 291

    Creating Macros 292
    Saving Macros 294
    Command-Level Use and Macros.. 295
    Macro Menu Options 296
    Adding to Existing Macros 297
        Adding Pauses to Macros 298
    Rules and Limitations of Macros 299

10 Advanced Report Topics 301

    Using Expressions and Functions 301
        Using The IIF() Function in Expressions 303
        Other Useful Functions.. 305
    Designing Form Letters.. 306
    Designing Invoices 310
    Creating and Printing Mailing Labels.. 316
        Creating the Label... 316
        Adding Fields to the Design Area 319
        Saving the Label Design 321
        Printing Labels 321
    An Example Label 324
    Modifying Existing Labels.. 326

11 Using FoxPro's Relational Powers 327

    How to Relate Files 331
        A Warning About Index Files 336
        Using View Files to Store Relations 336
    Creating Relational Reports 338
        A Warning About SET FIELDS And dBASE 345
    Getting Selective Data from Related Files................................... 346
    Relating More Than Two Database Files 347
    Analyzing Types of Relationships 358

12 Introduction to FoxPro Programming 367

    Creating Command Files... 369
        Compiling 373
    Constants 374

- Memory Variables 375
- Expressions 380
- Operators 382
  - Mathematical Operators 383
  - Relational Operators 384
  - Logical Operators 384
  - String Operators 385
- Functions 385
  - EOF 386
  - BOF 387
  - DATE and TIME 388
  - UPPER 389
  - LOWER 390
  - CTOD and DTOC 390
  - DTOS 391
  - SPACE 391
  - TRIM 391
  - LTRIM 393
  - STR 393
- Commands Used in Command Files 393
  - SET TALK 394
  - SKIP 394
  - RETURN 395
  - ACCEPT and INPUT 395
  - COUNT 396
  - SUM 397
  - AVERAGE 399
  - @, ?,??, and TEXT 399
- Overview of a Program Design 401
  - Defining the Problem 402
  - Output Requirements 403
  - Input Requirements 403
  - Designing the Program 405
  - Writing the Program 408
  - Verifying the Program 409
  - Documenting the Program 410

13 Program Control 413

- Going in Circles 414
- SCAN and ENDSCAN 416
- IF, ELSE, and ENDIF 418
  - Nesting IF-ENDIFs 421
  - The Immediate If Function 421

Using CASE to Evaluate Multiple Choices 425
EXIT 428
CANCEL 429
WAIT 430
ZAP 431
Using Programming Macros 431

14 Programming for Data Entry and Editing 433

Putting Information on the Screen 435
    Using GET and READ with @ and SAY 437
    Working with Memo Fields 439
Customizing a Data-Entry Screen 440
    Using PICTURE 442
Using Format Files 446
    An Easier Way 447
Using Windows 452
    Defining the Window 453
    Activating and Using the Window 455
    Deactivating the Window 456
    An Example of the Window Use 456
Designing Light-Bar Menus with @PROMPT
    and MENU TO 458
Editing Records Under Program Control 460
Data Entry and Editing with Memory Variables 463
Deleting Records Under Program Control 466
Helpful Hints on Screen Design 469

15 Programming for Data Retrieval 471

Generating Reports from Stored Report Forms 472
Users' Choice: Reporting to the Screen or the Printer 474
Writing Reports with Program Code 475
Creating Columnar Listings 479
Controlling Your Printer 481
    Sending Escape Codes to the Printer 484

16 Advanced Programming Topics 489

Speeding Up Your Programs with Procedures 490
Hiding and Showing Variables 496
Debugging Techniques 499
    Using SET TALK 502
    Using SET ECHO 502
    Using SET STEP 502

Using SET ALTERNATE	503
Customizing FoxPro with SET Commands	503
SET BELL	504
SET CARRY	504
SET COLOR	504
SET CONSOLE	505
SET DATE	506
SET DECIMALS	506
SET ESCAPE	506
SET EXACT	507
SET NEAR	508
SET FUNCTION	508
SET INTENSITY	510
SET MEMOWIDTH TO	511
SET MESSAGE TO	512
SET SAFETY	513
Using User-Defined Functions	513
Enhancing FoxPro Power with LOAD and CALL	515
An Example of Using LOAD and CALL	517
Sources of Assembler Routines	518
Assembler Guidelines and a Warning	519
Drawing Bar Graphs	520
Using Modular Programming	523

17 Creating Applications with FoxView 533

Applications	534
Creating a Simple Application	536
Creating a More Complex Application	546
Adding Index-File Information to the Application	547
Creating an Advanced Application	554
About FoxPro Templates	556

18 Using FoxPro with Other Software 557

File Formats	557
ASCII Format	558
Delimited Format	558
SDF Format	559
DBMEMO3 or FOXPLUS Format	560
Data Sharing Options with the APPEND and COPY Commands	562
Examples of Transferring Files	563

        Transferring from FoxPro to WordStar and Other
            Word Processors 563
        Transferring Files from FoxPro to MailMerge
            and Other Database Managers 565
        Creating Files for Use with MailMerge Options 568
        WordStar 568
        Microsoft Word 570
        An Export Program for WordPerfect 572
        Transferring Between FoxPro and
            Lotus 1-2-3 or Symphony 575
        Transferring Files from FoxPro to
            Non-dBASE-Compatible Spreadsheets 578
        Transferring from Other
            Spreadsheets to FoxPro 579
        Transferring Files from WordStar and Other
            Word Processors to FoxPro 581
        Notes About FoxPro and Other
            dBASE Compatibles 584

A   **Glossary of Commands** **585**

B   **Glossary of Functions** **709**

C   **dBASE Commands Not Supported**
      by FoxPro **767**

      Index 771

ACKNOWLEDGMENTS

As with any detailed book, this one exists due to the combined work of many individuals. I would like to offer sincere thanks to the following persons: Liz Fisher and Cindy Hudson, who guided the project to completion during the height of the "busy season"; Lisa Biow, who does the best tech review of dBASE books in this hemisphere; Kevin Shafer, for his skillful management of production and for (yet again!) dealing with balky artwork; Kay Luthin, for her work in the trying field of copy edit; and the technical folks at Fox Software, whose helpful suggestions and fast answers during the beta software stage smoothed over the hills naturally encountered in working with new software.

INTRODUCTION

FoxPro is, technically, a "relational database manager." However, that term doesn't tell the full story regarding what FoxPro has to offer. FoxPro provides speed, dBASE IV compatibility, and an outstanding environment for the development of business applications. Multiple windows, pull-down menus, mouse support, and more are all here within FoxPro.

About This Book

This book is designed to present the features of FoxPro, in an easy-to-learn format. At the same time, easy-to-learn does not mean that you will be shortchanged in terms of depth; this book delves well into the more advanced uses of FoxPro, detailing programming techniques and concepts you'll need for effective development of your business applications. Most exercises throughout this book are presented in a step-by-step tutorial format, so that you can follow along with your copy of FoxPro.

How This Book Is Organized

This book is divided into 18 chapters. The first two thirds of the book cover the use of FoxPro in building databases, performing queries and generating reports, and working with multiple files. The last third of the book primarily covers the topic of programming in FoxPro, providing skills that will be necessary in building complete applications.

Chapter 1 gets you started with the software. It explains the concepts of relational databases, illustrates how you will use FoxPro, and provides instructions for installing FoxPro, for using the keyboard and (optional) mouse, for choosing menu selections, and for entering FoxPro commands. In Chapter 2 you begin creating databases, entering data, and using various FoxPro options and commands to get information from a database.

Chapter 3 provides details on changing databases. In this chapter, you'll learn how to edit records, how to make effective use of the Browse mode, how to delete unwanted records, and how to change the structure (or overall design) of a database. Chapter 4 provides details on how to sort or index a database to place records in any order you desire.

In Chapter 5 you'll learn to create data-entry forms using FoxView, a design tool that is built into FoxPro. By creating screen forms, you can provide users with various ways to view the records in a database. Chapter 6 covers the important area of performing queries. In a nutshell you'll learn how to get the precise data you want out of a database. And Chapter 7 introduces the topic of reports. You'll learn how to produce customized reports with the Report Generator built into FoxPro. And you will also learn to use various commands for creating quick listings of data with a minimum of hassle.

Chapter 8 covers file operations, such as copying, erasing, and renaming files. Here, you'll learn to use the Filer feature of FoxPro to easily perform file operations. In Chapter 9 you'll learn to use the macro features of FoxPro to automate often-used tasks.

Chapter 10 builds on the topics introduced in Chapter 7 by covering advanced reporting needs. In Chapter 10 you'll learn how the Report Generator can be used for more varied reporting tasks such as form letters and invoices. You will also learn how to create and modify mailing labels, and how various parts of commands (called expressions) can be used to enhance the flexibility of the reports that you create. Chapter 11 provides coverage of the relational capabilities of FoxPro. Here you'll learn to manage multiple files simultaneously, and how to produce reports based on more than one database file at a time.

Chapter 12 starts off the portion of the book on programming with FoxPro. In Chapter 12 you'll learn to create command files (or programs) to perform tasks in FoxPro. You will also learn how functions, variables, expressions, and operators can be used within a FoxPro program. Chapters 13 through 16 build on this programming knowledge, by covering various aspects of programming in detail. In Chapter 13, you will become familiar with various commands that control the flow of execution inside a FoxPro program. Chapter 14 covers how programs can be written specifically for data-entry and editing needs. Chapter 15 examines the specifics of programming for data retreival or the generation of reports. And Chapter 16 covers an assortment of advanced programming topics you will find useful when designing your own applications.

Chapter 17 details the use of FoxPro's ability to create complete applications, using the FoxView utility that is built into FoxPro. With FoxView, you can create moderately complex applications to manage a database and produce reports, without writing any program code. Chapter 18 provides tips on using FoxPro with other popular software packages, including Lotus 1-2- 3 and WordPerfect. The appendixes provide a detailed listing of FoxPro commands and functions, and a list of dBASE IV commands that are not compatible with FoxPro.

Conventions Used In This Book

Throughout this book you will be instructed to enter various commands. Each of these entries will either appear in boldface or will be visually set apart from the text. Menu selections you should make will be detailed within the text in a step-by-step format.

Disk Offer

The database and program files used in this book, including the sample applications in Chapter 17 and additional sample applications, are available on disk. The disk also contains a collection of useful FoxPro utilities and user-defined functions, including a notepad, phone dialer (requires modem), and other desktop utilities written in FoxPro. The complete cost of the disk package is $20.00, which covers the costs of duplication, postage, and handling. (Add $3.00 for Canadian or $5.00 for other foreign orders; foreign orders should be payable in U.S. funds.) To order the disk package, use the form on the following page.

Please send me the disk that accompanies *FoxPro Made Easy*. My payment of $20.00 ($23.00 Canadian or $25.00 foreign) is enclosed.

Type of disk _____ 5.25-inch   _____ 3.5-inch
Name_____
Address_____
City_____State_____ZIP___
_____

To order, send payment to:

J.E.J.A. Software
P.O. Box 1834
Herndon, VA 22070-1834

This offer is solely the responsibility of J.E.J.A. Software. Osborne/McGraw-Hill takes no responsibility for the fulfillment of this offer.

WHY THIS BOOK IS FOR YOU

Because it is likely that you'll want to utilize the full capabilities of FoxPro in the minimum amount of time, this book is for you. The book's format is designed to get you up and running in FoxPro quickly, managing and retrieving data by the end of the second chapter. At the same time, the later chapters in the book will delve into the more advanced features of FoxPro, so that no vital topics are omitted in the process of learning to put FoxPro to use in your applications.

If you are an experienced dBASE user just switching to FoxPro, you will find this book to be of significant help in discovering the features of FoxPro which are not available in current versions of dBASE, such as mouse support of windows within applications. If you have been using FoxPro, FoxBase, or dBASE through the menus or the command level and have stayed away from programming, this book will help you become familiar with the programming concepts needed to build sophisticated applications. And once you have become familiar with FoxPro, the detailed Command Reference provided as part of the appendixes will provide a useful dictionary-style listing which you can refer to when needed.

Because FoxPro provides many enhancements over current versions of dBASE, if you have made the switch to FoxPro or are seriously considering making the switch, you'll need an effective guide that specifically covers FoxPro. This book is designed from the ground up to provide just such a guide.

1
GETTING STARTED WITH FOXPRO

What Is a Database?
Using a Database
Relational Databases
How You Will Use FoxPro
System Requirements
Designing a Database
Three Phases of Database Design
Installing FoxPro
Starting FoxPro
Selecting Menu Options
The Keyboard
The Mouse
Using FoxPro Commands
Getting Help
Windows
Dialog Boxes
Desktop Accessories

Welcome to FoxPro, a high-powered relational database manager for the IBM PC and compatibles. You can use FoxPro to create database files that contain the necessary categories (fields) for your data. And you can display information in a format that best meets your needs with the custom form and report capabilities built into FoxPro. FoxPro displays information in a tabular format (known as Browse mode) or in a screen format (known as Edit or Change mode). The commonly used Browse mode is shown in the example in Figure 1-1.

Creating a database to store your data is a straightforward process. After choosing the New option from the File menu, you define the names and types of fields you will use. Seven different data types can be used in FoxPro: character (combinations of alpha and numeric characters), numeric, floating, date, logical (true or

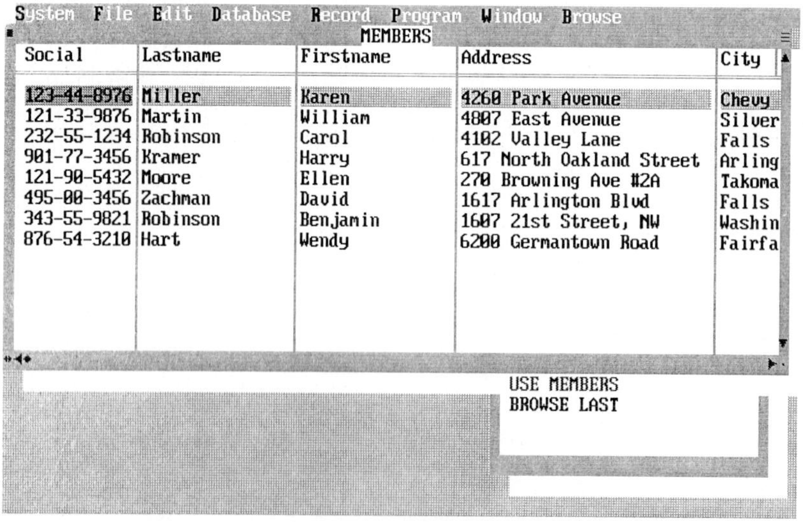

FIGURE 1-1. FoxPro in use (Browse mode)

false), and memo (which contain characters in varying lengths). Figure 1-2 shows the process of creating a database in FoxPro.

Once you have created a database, you can enter data by using on-screen forms that resemble the paper forms used in an office. You can also design custom forms with fields at locations you desire, along with borders or descriptive text.

To get more detailed information from your FoxPro databases, you will want to build detailed reports. For maximum flexibility in reporting, you can use the powerful Report Generator built into FoxPro to design custom reports in either a columnar or a free-form format. The Report Generator has a Quick Report option that lets you quickly design and produce a report.

If you are an advanced user, you will find that FoxPro has the power to match your complex database management needs. Using the relational capabilities of FoxPro, you can draw complex relationships between multiple database files. You can make use of

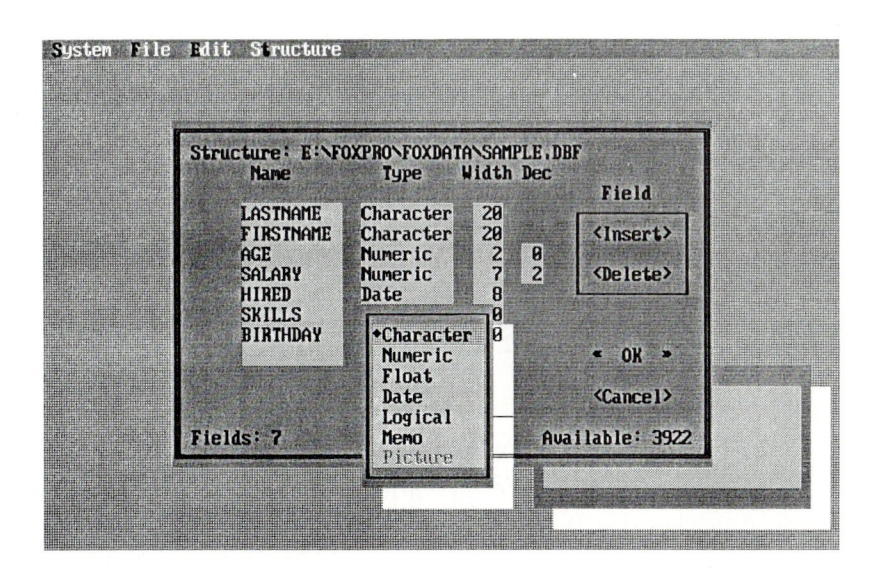

FIGURE 1-2. Creating a FoxPro database

Name	Address	City	State	ZIP	Phone No.	Cust. No.
J. Billings	2323 State St.	Bertram	CA	91113	234-8980	0005
R. Foster	Rt. 1 Box 52	Frink	CA	93336	245-4312	0001
L. Miller	P.O. Box 345	Dagget	CA	94567	484-9966	0002
B. O'Neill	21 Way St. #C	Hotlum	CA	92346	555-1032	0004
C. Roberts	1914 19th St.	Bodie	CA	97665	525-4494	0006
A. Wilson	27 Haven Way	Weed	CA	90004	566-7823	0003

FIGURE 1-3. A simple database

macros, which are automated actions that FoxPro carries out as if individual commands had been entered at the keyboard. You can also write programs that perform complex tasks, using the command language that is an integral part of FoxPro. If you have existing programs written for dBASE III, dBASE III Plus, or dBASE IV, you can use these programs with FoxPro. FoxPro is command-compatible with dBASE IV.

WHAT IS A DATABASE?

Although *database management* is a computer term, it can also apply to the ways in which information is catalogued, stored, and used. At the center of any information management system is a *database*. Any collection of related information grouped together as a single item, like Figure 1-3, is a database. Metal filing cabinets with customer records, a card file of names and phone numbers, and a notebook with a penciled listing of a store inventory are all databases. However, a file cabinet or a notebook does not make a database; the way information is organized makes it a database. Objects like cabinets and notebooks only aid in organizing information, and FoxPro is one such aid to organizing information.

Information in a database is usually organized and stored in the form of tables, with rows and columns in each table. As an example, in the mailing list shown in Figure 1-3, each row contains a name, an address, a phone number, and a customer number. Each row is related to the others because they all contain the same types of information. And because the mailing list is a collection of information arranged in a specific order—a column of names, a column of addresses, a column of customer numbers—it is a table. One or more tables containing information arranged in an organized manner is a *database*, as you saw in Figure 1-3. The multiple tables used to manage your data within FoxPro are also referred to as *database files*.

Rows in a table are called *records,* and columns are called *fields*. Figure 1-4 illustrates this idea with a comparison of a simple one-table database to an address filing system kept on 3X5 file

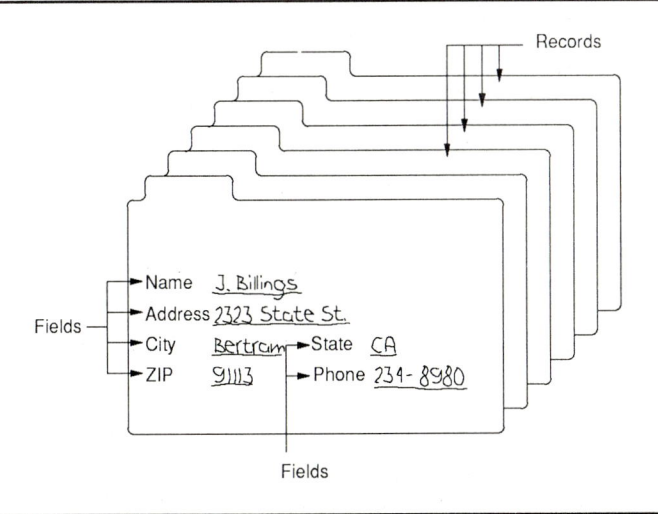

FIGURE 1-4. Each card represents a record; information is separated into fields

8   FoxPro Made Easy

	Name	Address	City	State	ZIP	Phone No.	Cust. No.
	J. Billings	2323 State St.		Bertram	CA	91113	234-8980
Record	R. Foster	Rt. 1 Box 52		Frink	CA	93336	245-4312
	L. Miller	P.O. Box 345		Dagget	CA	94567	484-9966
→	B. O'Neill	21 Way St. #C		Hotlum	CA	92346	555-1032
	C. Roberts	1914 19th St.		Bodie	CA	97665	525-4494
A. Wilson	27 Haven Way	Weed		CA		90004	566-7823

Field → Phone No.

FIGURE 1-5.   A record and a field of a database

cards. Each card in the box is a single record, and each category of information on a card is a field. Fields can contain any type of information that can be categorized. In the card box, each record contains six fields: a name, address, city, state, ZIP code, and phone number. Since every card in the box has the same type of information, the card box is a database. Figure 1-5 identifies a record and a field in the mailing-list database.

USING A DATABASE

In theory, any database is arranged in such a way that information is easy to find. In Figure 1-5, for example, names are arranged alphabetically. If you want to find the phone number of a customer, you simply locate the name and read across to the corresponding phone number.

You are already interested in how a computerized filing, or database, system can make information storage and retrieval more efficient than a traditional filing system, and you will find that FoxPro offers many advantages. A telephone book, for example, is fine for finding telephone numbers, but if all you have is an address and not the name of the person who lives there, the telephone directory becomes useless for finding that person's telephone number. A similar problem plagues conventional office filing systems: if the information is organized by name and you want to find all the clients located in a particular area, you could be in for a tedious search. In addition, organizing massive amounts of information into written directories and filing cabinets can consume a great deal of space. A manual database can also be difficult to modify. For example, adding a new phone number to the list may mean rearranging the list. If the phone company were to assign a new area code, someone would have to search for all phone numbers having the old area code and replace it with the new one.

When a database is teamed with a computer, many of these problems are eliminated. A computerized database provides speed: finding a phone number from among a thousand entries, or putting the file in alphabetical order, takes just seconds with FoxPro. A computerized database is compact: a database with thousands of records can be stored on a single floppy disk. A computerized database is flexible: it has the ability to examine information from a number of angles, so you could search for a phone number by name or by address.

Tasks that would be time-consuming to accomplish manually are more practical with the aid of a computer. In principle, a database in a computer is no different from a database recorded on paper and filed in cabinets. But the computer does the tedious work of maintaining and accessing a database, and it does it fast. A computerized database that can do all of this is known as a *database management system,* or *DBMS* for short.

RELATIONAL DATABASES

There are a number of ways to store information in a computer, but not all of these are relational database management systems. A word processing program can be used to organize data in the form of a list; however, it will offer only limited flexibility. You must still sort, rearrange, and access the information.

Move a level above word processors, and you get to the simple file managers, and the spreadsheets with simple database management capabilities. Most file managers (and spreadsheets with data management capabilities) can also perform sorting and other data management tasks.

Relational database managers can also store information in database files. In addition to being more sophisticated than file managers, however, they can access two or more database files simultaneously. By comparison, file managers can access only one database file at a time, which can be a severely limiting constraint. If the file manager is accessing information from one database file but needs three pieces of information from a second file, the file manager can't continue unless the second file is available. Only after the file manager is finished with first file can it proceed to the second file. But what good is this when the file manager needs information from both files simultaneously? The only solution is to duplicate the three fields from the second file in the first file. Fortunately, this is not a problem with a relational database manager like FoxPro.

Let's look at an example. Suppose the mailing list stores customer information for a warehouse that distributes kitchen appliances. The warehouse would also have a separate table within the database for customer orders, which would include fields for customer number, merchandise number, price per unit, quantity ordered, and total cost. The mailing list and customer order tables comprise a relational database because they have the customer number field in common (Figure 1-6). By searching for the customer number in the mailing list and matching it to the customer number in the order form, the database manager can determine who the purchaser is and where the purchaser is located from one table, and what the purchaser ordered and the total cost of the purchase from the other table. A database manager that draws information from different tables (or database files) linked by a common field is known as a *relational database manager*.

Mailing List

Name	Address	City	State	ZIP	Phone No.	Cust. No.
J. Billings	2323 State St.	Bertram	CA	91113	234-8980	0005
R. Foster	Rt. 1 Box 52	Frink	CA	93336	245-4312	0001
L. Miller	P.O. Box 345	Dagget	CA	94567	484-9966	0002
B. O'Neill	21 Way St. #C	Hotlum	CA	92346	555-1032	0004
C. Roberts	1914 19th St.	Bodie	CA	97665	525-4494	0006
A. Wilson	27 Haven Way	Weed	CA	90004	566-7823	0003

Customer Order

Cust. No.	Merchan-dise No.	Price per Unit	Quantity	Total Price
0001	15A	1500.00	5	7500.00
0001	15B	1750.00	10	17500.00
0002	311	500.00	3	1500.00
0003	555	1000.00	4	4000.00
0004	69	650.00	7	4550.00
0005	1111	300.00	2	600.00
0006	15A	1500.00	1	1500.00

FIGURE 1-6. Mailing List and Customer Order Dataases

To handle the same task with a file manager would be very difficult, since the file manager could not access the mailing list when it was time to find out where the merchandise should be shipped. The only alternative would be to combine the two tables, but this would result in a clumsy and inefficient database. For example, to represent both of R. Foster's purchases, you would have to duplicate his name, address, and phone number (Figure 1-7). If R. Foster had purchased 100 items instead, the extra typing would take far longer and use up valuable disk space.

Name	Address	Phone No.	Merch- andise No.	Price per Unit	Quan- tity	Total Price
J. Billings	2323 State St. Bertram CA 91113	234-8980	1111	300.00	2	00600.00
R. Foster	Rt. 1 Box 52 Frink CA 93336	245-4312	15A	1500.00	5	7500.00
R. Foster	Rt. 1 Box 52 Frink CA 93336	245-4312	15B	1750.00	10	17500.00
L. Miller	P.O. Box 345 Dagget CA 94567	484-9966	311	500.00	3	1500.00
B. O'Neill	21 Way St. #C Hotlum CA 92346	555-1032	69	650.00	7	4550.00
C. Roberts	1914 19th St. Bodie CA 97665	525-4494	15A	1500.00	1	1500.00
A. Wilson	27 Haven Way Weed CA 90004	566-7823	555	1000.00	4	4000.00

FIGURE 1-7. Combined customer-order invoice and mailing-list database; unnecessary customer number field was eliminated

HOW YOU WILL USE FOXPRO

Figure 1-8 shows the relationship between the database, the user, and the database software. At the core is the database from which you will retrieve, add, and delete information. The database must somehow be accessible to the user, and that is accomplished by the available menu options and commands provided within FoxPro. FoxPro lets you carry out operations in one of two ways: by

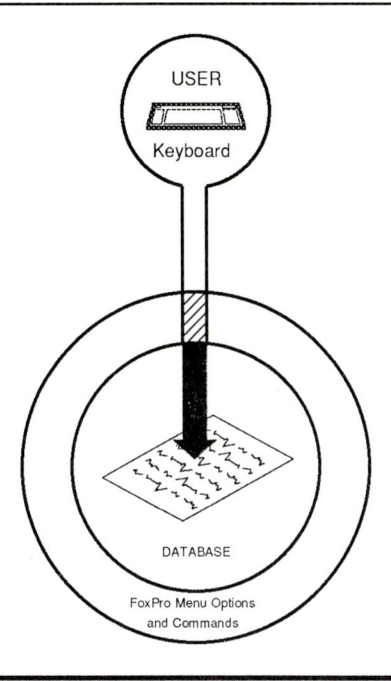

FIGURE 1-8. Simplified layout of database manager

choosing the options from a series of menus that appear at the top of the screen or by typing in a series of commands within the Command window. Whatever you want done to the database has to be communicated to the computer by means of the correct command or menu option.

FoxPro's commands and menu options offer you a host of ways to manage information. Among all these commands and menu options, however, you won't find a single command that creates a database, enters information into it, and prints the database on the printer. In any application, you probably won't be able to use only one command or make one menu choice that will perform the entire task. Instead, you will have to divide the task into smaller chores that FoxPro will handle. For example, to create a mailing list, you will need to perform the following steps:

1. Create the database structure.

2. Enter information into the database.

3. Print the contents of the database.

Even after breaking down the problem this far, you will need to segment the process further, since, for example, there is no single command that inputs information into the database. How does one know when the task is divided into sufficient steps for FoxPro to cope with it? Experience. You have to know the program, and you have to know what you can and can't get away with. This book is designed to provide that knowledge.

SYSTEM REQUIREMENTS

To use FoxPro, you will need an IBM XT or XT-compatible computer, such as the IBM XT, AT, or PS/2; the Compaq Portable, Plus, Deskpro, Portable II, Portable III, or Compaq 386; or any other 100%-compatible computer. Any personal computer that is software-compatible with the IBM XT should be able to use FoxPro. Your computer must have a minimum of 512K of memory, and it must be equipped with one floppy-disk and one hard-disk drive. A mouse is not required but is recommended for ease of use. You must be using DOS 2.1 or a newer version, or OS/2 version 1.0 or above.

FoxPro can be used with either a monochrome or a color monitor and with any compatible printer. FoxPro is designed to take advantage of extra memory and can use the AST RAMPage, Intel Above Board, or any other memory board meeting the LIM (Lotus-Intel-Microsoft) specifications.

To use FoxPro on a local area network, you will need workstations with a minimum of 640K of memory, any combination of disk drives (or no drives), and DOS 3.1 or above, or OS/2 version 1.0 or above. The operating system can be any of the following:

- Novell Advanced NetWare

- IBM PC network or Token Ring network with IBM PC Local Area Network program

- 3Com 3Plus network with 3Com 3Plus operating system

- Any other network configuration that is 100% NETBIOS compatible with DOS 3.1 or above, and with the networks just listed

DESIGNING A DATABASE

At this point, you may be anxious to load FoxPro into your computer and begin using the program. Resist the temptation to use FoxPro if you are new to the task of database design; there's an excellent reason for approaching the job of designing a database with patience. Planning is vital to effective database management. Many a buyer of database management software has gotten started with the software, created a database, and stored data within that database only to discover to his or her disappointment that the database does not provide all of the needed information. Although powerful databases like FoxPro let you make up for the mistakes you make during the design process, correcting such errors can nevertheless become a tedious job. To avoid such time-consuming mistakes, much of the remainder of this chapter will focus on database design. If you are experienced at database design but new to FoxPro, you may want to skip ahead to the "Installing FoxPro" later in this chapter.

Database design requires that you think about how the data should be stored and how you and others will ask for data from the database file. During this process, your problem (which FoxPro was purchased to help solve) will be outlined on paper.

Just as you would not haphazardly toss a bunch of files into a filing cabinet without designing some type of filing system, you cannot place information into a database file without first designing the database. As you do so, you must define the kinds of information that should be stored in the database.

Data and Fields

Data and *fields* are two important terms in database design. Data is the information that goes into your database. An individual's last name (Smith, for example) is data. Fields are the types of data that make up the database. A field is another name for an attribute or category, so an entire category of data, such as a group of names, is considered to be a field. Names, phone numbers, customer numbers, descriptions, locations, and stock numbers are common fields that your database might contain.

In addition to thinking about what kinds of information will go into the database, you must give careful consideration to the ways in which information will come out of the database. Information comes from a database in the form of *reports*. When you ask the computer for a list of all homes in the area priced between $100,000 and $150,000, or for a list of employees earning less than $15.00 per hour, you are asking for a report. When you ask for John Smith's address, you are also asking for a report. A report is a summary of information. Whether the computer displays a few lines on the screen or hundreds of lines on a stack of paper, it is providing a report based on the data contained within the database file.

To practice the techniques of database design, the example sessions in this text will demonstrate how you can design and utilize a database with various hypothetical examples. Throughout much of this text, the database needs of a video rental store, Generic Videos, will be used to illustrate many of the basics behind database management with FoxPro. From time to time, successive chapters of this text will show how the staff at Generic Videos successfully used FoxPro to manage information. By following along with these examples, you will learn how to put FoxPro to work within your particular application.

THREE PHASES OF DATABASE DESIGN

Designing a database file, whether it is for Generic Videos or for your own purposes, involves three major steps:

1. Data definition (an analysis of existing data)

2. Data refinement (refining necessary data)

3. Establishing relationships between the attributes (fields)

Data Definition

During the first phase, data definition, you must make a list on a piece of paper of all the important attributes, or fields, involved in your application. To do this, you must examine your application in detail to determine exactly what kinds of information must be stored in the database.

In discussing the design for the database, the staff at Generic Videos determined that certain things must be known about each member: the name of the member, the member's address, date of birth, and the date the membership expires. The resulting list of fields is as follows:

1. Member name

2. Member address

3. Date of birth

4. Expiration date

An important point to remember is that during this database design phase, you should list all possible fields of your database. You may list more fields than are actually needed by your particular application, but this isn't a problem, because unnecessary fields will be eliminated during the data refinement stage.

Data Refinement

During this phase, you will refine the list of fields on your initial list so that the fields form an accurate description of the types of data that will be needed in the database. At this stage, it is vital to include suggestions from as many other users of the database as possible. The people who use the database are likely to know what kinds of information they want to get from the database.

When the staff of Generic Videos took a close look at their initial list of fields, they realized that most of the refinements were obvious. The address field, for example, should be divided into street address, city, state, and ZIP code. This will make it a simple matter to sort or select records based on a specific category, such as all persons living in a particular ZIP code. In your own case, some refinements may quickly become evident and others may not be as evident, but going over your written list of fields will help make any necessary refinements more obvious. For example, when the staff of Generic Videos further examined the initial field list, they realized that the index-card system of members contained multiple occurrences of members with the same last name. To avoid confusion, the "name" field was further divided into last name and first name. Also, the managers wanted a field indicating whether the member rented tapes in the older beta format, and a comments field for member preferences. The following shows the refined list of fields:

1. Member last name

2. Member first name

3. Street address

4. City

5. State

6. ZIP code

7. Date of birth

8. Expiration date

9. Beta?

10. Preferences

Establishing the Relationships

During the third phase, drawing relationships between the fields can help determine which fields are important and which are not so important. One way to determine such relationships is to ask yourself the same questions that you will ask your database. As an example, suppose that a personnel agency develops a database to track its employees and their work assignments. If the personnel manager of the agency wishes to know how many different employees worked on a particular job for Mammoth Telephone & Telegraph, the database must draw a relationship between a member identifier (such as the social security number) and the types of jobs that the employees worked.

Relationships can be more complex. A company vice-president, using the same database, might want to know how many employees who are data-entry operators worked for Mammoth Telephone between July and October. The database management system must compare fields for the type of job worked with fields for the time at which the job was performed. These types of questions can help reveal which fields are unimportant so that they can be eliminated from the database. During this phase, it is particularly important that you determine which, if any, relationships between data will call for the use of multiple databases, keeping in mind the fact that FoxPro is a relational database. In a nutshell, relational capability means that the data within one database can be linked or "related" to the data in another. When designing a database, it is important not to lose sight of that fact. Too many users take relational database management software and proceed to create bulky, non-relational databases, an approach that drastically increases the amount of work involved.

As an example, the proposed staff database to be used by Generic Videos has fields that will be used to describe each member. A major goal of computerizing the records at the store is to support automated billing; by creating another database showing which tapes are checked out to a particular member, the store can quickly generate rental receipts and track needed inventory. If we take the nonrelational approach of adding another field for the name of a tape, we could store all of the information needed in each record. However, we would also have to fill in the name, address, and other information for each tape rental, every time a member rents tapes. The better solution is to create two databases, one containing the fields already described detailing each member, and the other containing a listing of rented tapes and a way of identifying the member.

When establishing the relationships, you may determine that an additional field is necessary. For Generic Videos, the method of member identification is by social security number, so this field was added to the proposed list of fields, resulting in the finalized list of fields shown here:

1. Member social security number

2. Member last name

3. Member first name

4. Street address

5. City

6. State

7. ZIP code

8. Date of birth

9. Expiration date

10. Beta?

11. Preferences

The sample database created in the next chapter is based on this list. A social security number is needed because in a relational database, the field you will use to link the files must be unique in at least one of the files. Since under normal circumstances no two social security numbers are the same, the social security number serves as a unique method of identification. Using fields like last-name and first-name fields for linking files could provide problems later, because the data might not always be unique. If two persons with the same name joined the video club, confusion between records could result if a relational link were based on name only.

During the design phases, it is important that potential users be consulted to determine what kinds of information they will expect the database to supply. Just what kinds of reports are wanted from the database? What kinds of queries will members make of the database? By continually asking these types of questions, you'll think in terms of your database, and this should help you determine what is important and what is unimportant. It often helps to consider examples of the data you will store while you design the database. For example, if your database contains many names that include salutations like "Dr." or "Honorable", you may need to create a separate title field to allow selections based on such information; you might, for example, want to provide a mailing to all doctors based on the contents of a sales database.

Keep in mind that even after the database design phases, the design of the database file is not set in stone. Changes to the design of a database file can be made later if necessary. But if you follow the systematic approach of database design for your specific application, the chances are better that you won't create a database that fails to provide much of the information you need and must then be extensively redesigned. FoxPro lets you change the design of a database at any time, although such changes are often inconvenient to make once the database is designed. Here is an example. If you were to create a database file using FoxPro to handle a customer mailing list, you might include fields for names, addresses, cities, states, and ZIP codes. At first glance this might seem sufficient. You could then begin entering customer information into the database and gradually build a sizable mailing list. However, if your company later decides to begin telemarketing with the same mailing list, you may suddenly realize that you have not included a field for telephone numbers. Using FoxPro, you could easily change the design to include such a field, but you would still face the mammoth task of going back and adding a telephone number for every name currently in the mailing list. If this information had been added as you developed the mailing list, you would not face the inconvenience of having to enter the phone numbers as a separate operation. Careful planning and time spent during the database design process can help avoid such pitfalls.

INSTALLING FOXPRO

FoxPro comes in the form of assorted manuals and quick reference guides and 5.25-inch floppy disks. At the time of this writing, FoxPro provides a phone number to call if you need 3.5-inch disks. (The phone number is on a sheet packed with the documentation.) If you are not sure whether all your disks are present, refer to your FoxPro documentation to be sure that you have the correct number of disks.

Hard-Disk Installation

Installing FoxPro on a hard disk is a simple matter, thanks to the installation program contained on the Installation Disk and the detailed instructions contained in the "Getting Started" booklet packaged with your software. If you do not have the "Getting Started" booklet, you should locate it now. Because versions of FoxPro change and the instructions may change along with software updates, this text will provide only some general tips regarding installation. You should refer to your latest FoxPro documentation for detailed specifics on installing the program.

The installation program supplied as a part of FoxPro will create the necessary subdirectory on your hard disk and then copy the needed files into that subdirectory. Before installing FoxPro, you should make sure that you have at least three megabytes (Mb) of free disk space remaining on your hard disk. (You can tell the amount of free space by using the DIR command; the description "*xxxxx* bytes free" that appears at the bottom of the directory listing indicates the amount of free space remaining.) The program itself requires between one and two megabytes of disk space for installation; however, you will certainly need adequate space for storing your databases and sorting files.

Note: If you are using FoxPro for the first time, you should also be aware of the memory requirements of the program. FoxPro requires 512K (kilobytes) of installed memory. While your machine may be equipped with 512K or more, some memory is consumed by DOS, and memory-resident programs like Sidekick or Superkey will also consume available memory. Also, although FoxPro may operate with some small memory-resident programs loaded, it will need to access the disk much more often when working with files of any size than when it has more memory to work with. For best performance, you should have 640K of memory in your machine, and you should avoid memory-resident programs while using FoxPro (unless those programs are designed to use other extended or expanded memory, which you may also have installed above 640K).

To install the program, turn on your computer and get to the DOS prompt in the usual manner. It is a good idea to create a separate subdirectory in which to store the program and data files; this will keep your data separate from the variety of program files that come with FoxPro. For example, if your hard disk is C, you could use the following commands to create a program directory and a data directory:

```
CD\
MD\FOXPRO
MD\FOXPRO\FOXDATA
CD\FOXPRO
```

The last line makes the FOXPRO subdirectory the current directory. You can then install FoxPro in that directory by performing the following steps:

1. Insert the Installation Disk into drive A.

2. Change the default drive to A by typing **A:** and then pressing the ENTER key.

3. Enter the following command:

   INSTALL C:

   where C is the drive on which you want to install FoxPro. (If your hard disk uses a letter other than C, substitute that letter for your hard disk in this example.) Refer to the "Getting Started" booklet supplied with your FoxPro documentation, and follow the instructions within to complete the installation process.

Creating a Batch File To Start the Program

You can create a batch file to make starting FoxPro and changing to the desired subdirectory an easier task. If you have installed FoxPro in a subdirectory named FoxPro on drive C of your hard disk, the commands shown here can be used to accomplish this task. If your hard disk is not C substitute your hard-disk letter in the following commands. If you installed FoxPro in a subdirectory named something other than FOXPRO, refer to your DOS manual for specifics on creating batch files.

To create the batch file, first enter the following commands from the DOS prompt, pressing ENTER at the end of each line:

CD\
COPY CON FOXPRO.BAT

When you complete the second command, the cursor will move down a line and will wait for additional entries. Type the following lines, pressing ENTER after each line:

```
PATH=C:\FOXPRO;C:\DOS
CD\FOXPRO\FOXDATA
FOXPRO
```

Then press the F6 key followed by the RETURN key. You should see the message "1 file(s) copied." From this point on, you can always start FoxPro and switch to the FOXPRO\FOXDATA subdirectory simply by entering **FOXPRO** at the DOS prompt.

STARTING FOXPRO

Start your computer in the usual manner. OS/2 users should note that if you are using FoxPro for DOS, you will need to run the program through the DOS Compatibility Box of OS/2; see your OS/2 documentation for details. If you created a batch file by following the directions in the previous paragraphs, you can enter **FOXPRO** and press ENTER to switch to the proper directory and load the program.

If you are not an OS/2 user and have not set up the batch file, first set a path to the FoxPro directory with the DOS PATH command. Next, switch to the subdirectory that will contain your data files and enter **FOXPRO** from the DOS prompt. For example, if your hard disk is drive C, the program is stored in a subdirectory named FOXPRO, and your data files will reside in a subdirectory named C:\FOXPRO\FOXDATA, you could start the program by entering the following commands from the DOS prompt:

```
PATH=C:\FOXPRO
CD\FOXPRO\FOXDATA
FOXPRO
```

Once the program starts, you will briefly see an introductory screen and a copyright message. Within a moment, the FoxPro menus and Command window will appear, as shown in Figure 1-9. The screen contains a *menu bar* with seven menu options, a *Command window,* and the working surface (the remainder of the screen). You can enter FoxPro commands, or you can select menu options that have the same results as entering FoxPro commands. Both methods for using FoxPro—through menus and through the use of commands—will be covered in detail throughout this text.

The top line of the screen shows the menu bar, which contains seven choices. You can open any of the menus by pressing the ALT key and the first letter of the menu name; for example, pressing ALT-F opens the File menu. Mouse users can point to any menu name and click and hold the left mouse button to open a menu. An

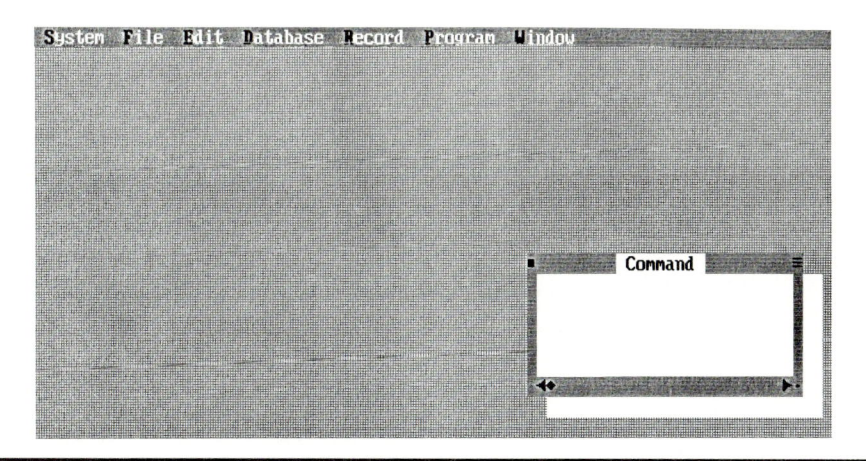

FIGURE 1-9. FoxPro menus and Command window

alternative method of opening a menu is to press F10, use the LEFT and RIGHT ARROW keys to highlight the desired menu, and then press ENTER to open the menu. When a menu is open, the appropriate menu options appear in a rectangular box called a *pull-down menu*.

SELECTING MENU OPTIONS

Once a menu has been opened, any option on that menu can be chosen by pressing the UP ARROW or DOWN ARROW key to highlight the option and then pressing ENTER. (An alternative is to press the highlighted letter in the desired menu option; this is usually, but is not always, the first letter of the option.) As an example, if you open the System menu with ALT-S, you will see the letter H highlighted within the Help option. Pressing H will cause the Help window to appear (you can close the Help window by pressing the ESC key). Note that not all of the menu options are available at all times. For example, you cannot access the Record menu until you open a database file.

Cancelling a Menu

You can use the ESC key to close a menu without selecting any option. In a similar fashion, the ESC key can be used to exit from many options within FoxPro without performing the operation. However, you should be aware that some operations (like copying files) cannot be cancelled once the process has actually begun.

THE KEYBOARD

If you're already familiar with the PC keyboard, you should skip this section and begin reading at the next section. FoxPro will use

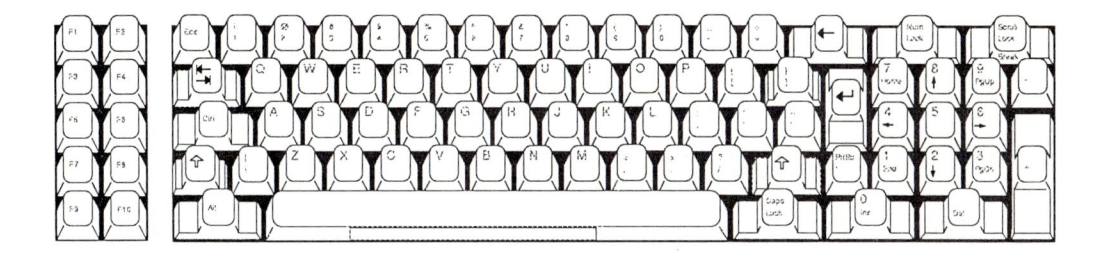

FIGURE 1-10. The IBM PC keyboard

a number of special-purpose keys for various functions. In addition to the ordinary letter and number keys, you'll use the function keys often. On most IBM PCs and compatible computers, the function keys are the double row of gray keys at the left side of the PC keyboard, as shown in Figure 1-10. On newer IBM PCs and some compatibles, the function keys are placed in a horizontal row at the top of the keyboard, as shown in Figure 1-11. The function keys on the older PCs are labeled F1 through F10, for Function 1 through Function 10. The newer machines have 12 function keys. Usually grouped on the left side of the keyboard are four often-used keys: the ESC (Escape) key, the TAB key (it may have the double arrows on it), the SHIFT key (it may have the hollow upwards-pointing arrow), and the ALT (Alternate) key. Some keyboards have the ESC key in a different location. Find these keys before going further; they will prove helpful for various operations.

You should locate the template supplied with your package of FoxPro and place it where you can refer to it for the uses of the

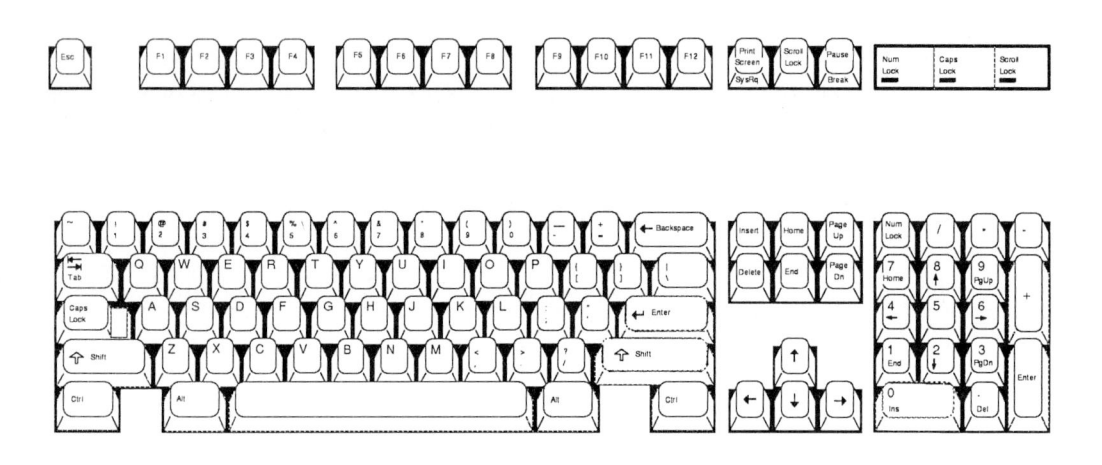

FIGURE 1-11. The enhanced IBM PC keyboard

function keys. The uses for the various function keys will be detailed in later chapters as pertinent operations are discussed.

Towards the right side of the keyboard is another SHIFT key. Located below it on some keyboards is a key labeled CAPS LOCK; it is used to change all typed letters to uppercase. Newer IBM PCs and many compatible keyboards will have the CAPS LOCK key above the left SHIFT key. (The CAPS LOCK key does not change the format of the numbers in the top row of the keyboard.) Just above the right SHIFT key is the ENTER or RETURN key; it performs a function that is similar to the Return key of a typewriter. Above the ENTER key is the BACKSPACE key.

On the right side of the keyboard, in the numeric key area, is a key labeled DEL. The DEL (Delete) key can be used to delete characters. Finally, the far right side of the keyboard has two gray keys with plus (+) and minus (−) labels. These keys will produce the plus and minus symbols when pressed.

The far right side of the keyboard contains a numeric keypad. On some computers, this area can serve a dual purpose. The keys in this area containing the up, down, left, and right arrows can be used to move the cursor in these directions. By pressing the NUM LOCK key, you can then use the same keys to enter numbers. Some keyboards will have a separate area with arrow keys and a separate area with a numeric keypad.

THE MOUSE

Although FoxPro is designed to be operated without a mouse, you can make good use of a mouse if one is installed on your system. There are three basic operations you will perform with the mouse: pointing, clicking, and selecting (also called dragging). The mouse controls the location of a special cursor called the *mouse pointer*. In FoxPro, the mouse pointer takes on the shape of a small, rectangular block.

To *point* at an object with the mouse, simply roll the mouse in the direction of the object. As you do so, the mouse pointer will move in the same direction on the screen. The term *clicking* refers to pressing the left mouse button. By pointing to different objects and clicking on them, you can select many of the objects while in FoxPro. The term *dragging* refers to pressing and holding down the left mouse button while moving the mouse. This is commonly done to choose menu options within FoxPro.

If you have just purchased your mouse for use along with FoxPro, a few hints are in order. Most mice require software drivers to be installed before they will work properly; refer to the instructions packed with your mouse for details on installing the mouse software. Obviously, you'll need a clear surface on your desk to manipulate the mouse. What is not so obvious is the fact that some desk surfaces work better than others. A surface with a small amount of friction seems to work better than very smooth desks. Commercial pads are available if your desktop is too smooth to obtain good results. Also, the mouse will probably require cleaning from time to time. (Some mice do not require regular cleaning, so check your manual to be sure.) If you turn the mouse upside down, you will probably see instructions that indicate how the ball can be removed for cleaning. A cotton swab dipped in alcohol works well for cleaning the ball. If your mouse uses an optical sensor design instead of a large ball underneath, you should refer to the manual that accompanied the mouse for any cleaning instructions.

USING FOXPRO COMMANDS

The menus provide one way in which you can use FoxPro, but another method is to enter commands directly in the Command window. The options you can choose from a menu have equivalent commands that can be entered in this window. You will get acceptable results from FoxPro regardless of which method you choose, but it does help to know a little about both methods of use.

If you do not use an ALT-key combination or F10 to open a menu, FoxPro assumes that any entry you type is a command, and it will appear within the Command window. FoxPro's basic command structure becomes obvious after you try a few commands. To print information on the screen, you use the question mark. As an example, type

? "Using FoxPro"

Once you press ENTER, the response

Using FoxPro

appears on the screen, outside of the Command window. The ? command prints everything between the quotation marks. To clear the entire screen of information, enter

CLEAR

Note that you can go from Command mode back to the menus at any time simply by pressing the ALT-key combination for the desired menu.

FoxPro also accepts commands in abbreviated form. Only the first four letters of any command are necessary, so you could use CLEA instead of CLEAR to clear the screen. However, all commands in this book will be used in their complete form.

Conventions

Before you start working with FoxPro, you need to know some conventions that will be used throughout the book.

All commands are printed in UPPERCASE, but you can type them in either uppercase or lowercase. Any part of a command surrounded by left ([) and right (]) brackets is optional, and any command followed by ellipses (...) can be repeated. Parameters in the command are in *italics*. Every command that you enter will be terminated by pressing ENTER (or RETURN). Pressing ENTER indicates to FoxPro that you have finished typing the command and that you want it to execute. So whenever you are asked to enter a command, finish it by pressing ENTER unless you are instructed otherwise.

GETTING HELP

Should you need help, FoxPro provides information on subjects ranging from basic database concepts to the use of programming commands and functions. This information is stored in a file that is always accessible to FoxPro, so you can get help at any time by pressing F1. For example, let's suppose you are working with FoxPro from the dot prompt and need information on the CLEAR command. Press F1 now, and a menu of help topics will appear.

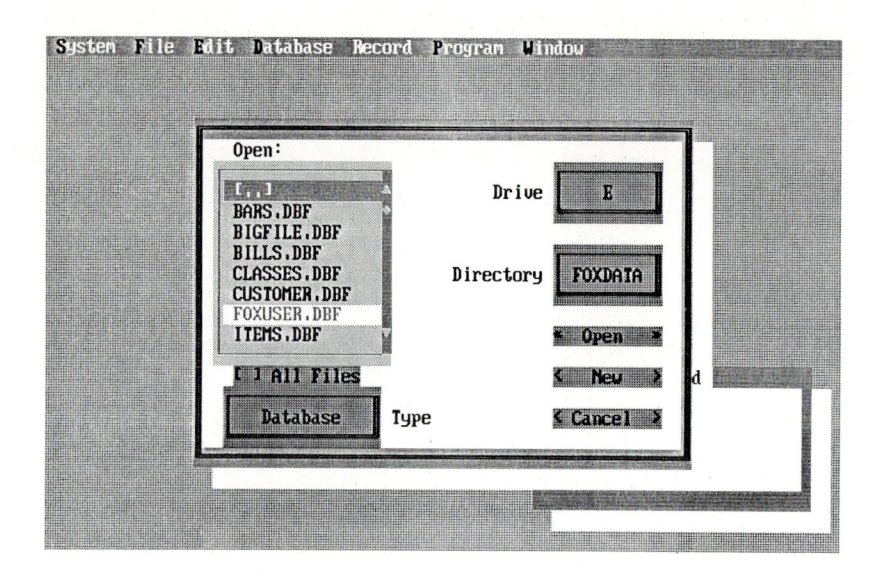

FIGURE 1-12. Help screen for CLEAR command

Since you want to know about the CLEAR command, type **CL** for CLEAR, and the CLEAR command will appear in a highlighted list. Press ENTER, and a description of the CLEAR command, along with the command's variations, will be displayed on the screen (Figure 1-12). If you already know the name of the command, you can circumvent the menus and go directly to the explanation by entering **HELP** followed by the command name within the command window, such as in **HELP CLEAR**.

The help file is quite extensive, so by all means take some time to rummage through it, view the different options, and understand how it is set up. Knowing where to locate information about a particular operation or command can be a great aid when you work with some of the more difficult operations in this book.

WINDOWS

FoxPro makes extensive use of *windows*. In FoxPro, you can manipulate windows with either the keyboard or the mouse. If the Help window is not currently open, press F1 now to display it; you may want to take a few moments to try various window operations using the Help and Command window.

With the Help window open, there are currently two windows on your screen: the Help window, and the Command window. Although FoxPro can display as many windows as you can comfortably work with at the same time, only one window can be *active*. Whichever window contains the cursor is the active window; since the last window you opened was the Help window, it is currently active. On most monitors, you can also tell which window is active by noting that the top line of the window is highlighted.

If you press ALT-W now, the Window menu will open, as shown in Figure 1-13. This menu contains various commands that let you manipulate windows. The first option, Hide, will hide the active window. The window remains open, but it is not visible. Once hidden, a window appears by name in the Window menu; you can open the Window menu and choose the window by name to unhide or redisplay it. If you choose Hide from the Window menu now, the Help window will vanish; open the Window menu again with ALT-W, and you will see the window name, HELP, added to the bottom of the Window menu. Choose HELP from the menu now, to redisplay the Help window.

Note that hiding a window and closing a window are two different things. If you hide a window, it is still open in memory. If you close a window, it is no longer active, and you have to reopen the window (by pressing F1 in the case of the Help window) to redisplay it. Windows can be closed by opening the File menu with ALT-F and choosing Close, or by mouse-clicking on the *close box*

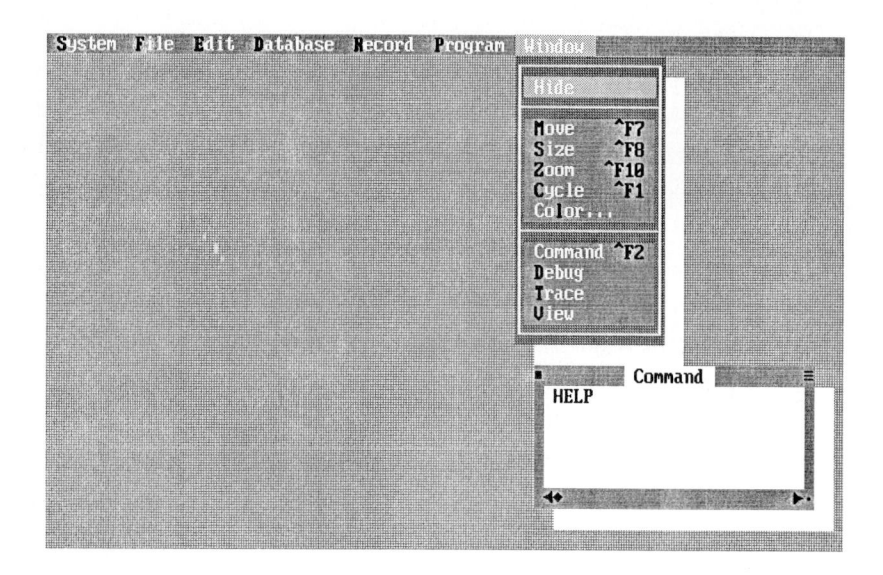

FIGURE 1-13. Window menu

within the window. (The close box is the small rectangle in the upper-left corner of the window.)

Moving and Sizing Windows

Windows can be moved around the screen and resized at will. If you open the Window menu with ALT-W, you will note two options for these tasks: the Move option and the Size option. Both of these options also have CTRL-key equivalents; pressing CTRL-F7 is the equivalent of choosing Move, and pressing CTRL-F8 is the equivalent of choosing Size.

To move a window, choose Move, and the window frame will start flashing. Use the cursor keys to move the window to its desired location, and then press ENTER or the spacebar to complete the movement. You may want to try this technique now with the

Help window. As you move the window around, you will note that you can move it anywhere on the screen, including over other windows such as the Command window.

To change a window's size, use the Size option of the Window menu. If you open the Window menu with ALT-W and select Size, the active window will start flashing. You can then use the cursor keys to change the window to its desired size and press ENTER or the spacebar to complete the resizing. You may want to try this technique now with the Help window.

Mouse users can quickly move and resize windows. To move a window, simply click anywhere on the *title bar* (the top bar of the window containing its name) and drag the window to the desired location. To resize a window, click on the size control dot at the lower-right corner of the window, and drag the window frame to its desired size.

The Zoom option can be used to expand a window so that it fills the entire screen. If you open the Window menu and choose Zoom (try it now with the Help window), you will see the window expand to fill the screen. The CTRL-F10 key combination can be used as a shortcut for the Zoom option. In this case, the key combination also serves as a *toggle;* that is, CTRL-F10 will expand the window, and CTRL-F10 again will contract the window to its previous size. Once the window has been expanded, you can also contract it to its previous size by opening the Window menu and again choosing Zoom. Mouse users can use the *zoom control,* which is the broken rectangle at the upper-right corner of the window frame. Clicking on the zoom control will alternately expand and contract the window.

Changing Windows

When more than one window is displayed, you can switch between windows with the Cycle option of the Window menu. The CTRL-key equivalent for this option is CTRL-F1. If you open the Window menu now and choose Cycle, you will see that the Command window becomes the active window. The Cycle option moves through all displayed windows currently on the screen; if you have more than two windows displayed, using Cycle will cause each window to be activated in the sequence in which the windows were opened. Press CTRL-F1 now until the Command window becomes the active window.

The Color option of the Window menu can be used to change the colors of the windows. The use of this option, as well as the dialog box that appears when you select it, is covered in detail in Chapter 15.

The Command Window

As mentioned earlier, the Command window is where FoxPro commands normally appear when you enter them. If you open the Window menu and choose the Command option, the Command window will be made the active window. (CTRL-F2 is the shortcut key for this menu option.) The Command option and its CTRL-F2 equivalent can also be used to display the Command window if it has been hidden.

All commands that you type appear in the Command window. By means of the Command window, you can control FoxPro operations when in the "interactive" or Command mode. Try entering the following commands now:

? 2 * 4

DIR *.*

HELP

When the Help window appears, press CTRL-F2 to again make the Command window the active window. In response to each of your commands, FoxPro performed some sort of action: displaying the result of 2 times 4 on the screen, showing a directory of files in response to the DIR *.* command, or bringing forward the Help window. With the Command window now active, you can see that the commands you just entered are still displayed within the window.

You can scroll through the Command window by using the UP ARROW or DOWN ARROW keys. Mouse users can scroll by clicking on the up or down arrows in the *scroll bar* at the right edge of the window. All the commands you see in the Command window are remembered by FoxPro, so you can repeat a command by moving the cursor up to that command and pressing ENTER. For example, if you now move the cursor back up to the command ? 2 * 4 and press ENTER, the calculation is again performed and the result displayed in the lower-left corner of the screen.

This capability of remembering commands can be quite useful for correcting mistakes. If you make an error when entering a command, simply move the cursor back up to that line; then use BACKSPACE, DEL, and the cursor keys to correct the error. When done with the correction, press ENTER to repeat the command.

Like all windows, you can resize the Command window. You may find this helpful, as many of the more complex commands that you enter will extend beyond the visible width of the default Command window size. Note that you are not restricted by the size of the Command window as to the length of the command you type; when you enter a long command, it simply scrolls to the right when you reach the right side of the window. Mouse users who make a mistake in entering a long command can go back to the incorrect line, and use the left or right arrow in the scroll bar at the bottom edge of the window to scroll horizontally in the window. Keyboard users will have to settle for the use of the cursor keys; however, you can use CTRL-LEFT ARROW and CTRL-RIGHT ARROW to move left or right a word at a time.

If you hide the Command window (or close it by mouse-clicking on the close box or choosing Close from the File menu), you can still enter commands. However, you will in a sense be "flying blind," because you will not be able to see the commands you enter.

The CTRL-F2 key combination can be used to quickly restore the Command window to view.

The remaining options available in the Window menu are Debug, Trace, and View. The Debug and Trace options are used for programming in FoxPro, and the View option lets you manipulate files and set many FoxPro options. These are more advanced options that will be covered in later sections of this text.

DIALOG BOXES

FoxPro also makes extensive use of *dialog boxes,* which are boxes designed to accept various responses. Many menu options and some commands will result in the appearance of a dialog box. Although different dialog boxes contain different options, navigating through the dialog boxes is similar in all cases. If you now open the File menu with ALT-F and choose Open, you will see the File Open dialog box, as shown in Figure 1-14. The use of this dialog box will be detailed in the next chapter, but you should become familiar with the overall design of a dialog box.

A dialog box contains various objects, including buttons, menus, a check box, and a pick list. The rectangles next to the words "Drive," "Directory," and "Type" are menus. You can open menus by mouse-clicking on them or by tabbing to the item and pressing ENTER. You can move in the reverse direction through the choices with SHIFT-TAB. For example, if you now tab over to the Drive menu and press ENTER, a pull-down menu listing all available disk drives will appear. Menu options can be selected by highlighting the desired one and pressing ENTER or by mouse-clicking on the desired one. For now, just press ESC to close the menu.

Check boxes can be selected by tabbing to them and pressing the spacebar or by mouse-clicking in between the brackets. The line in the dialog box currently labeled

[ ] All Files

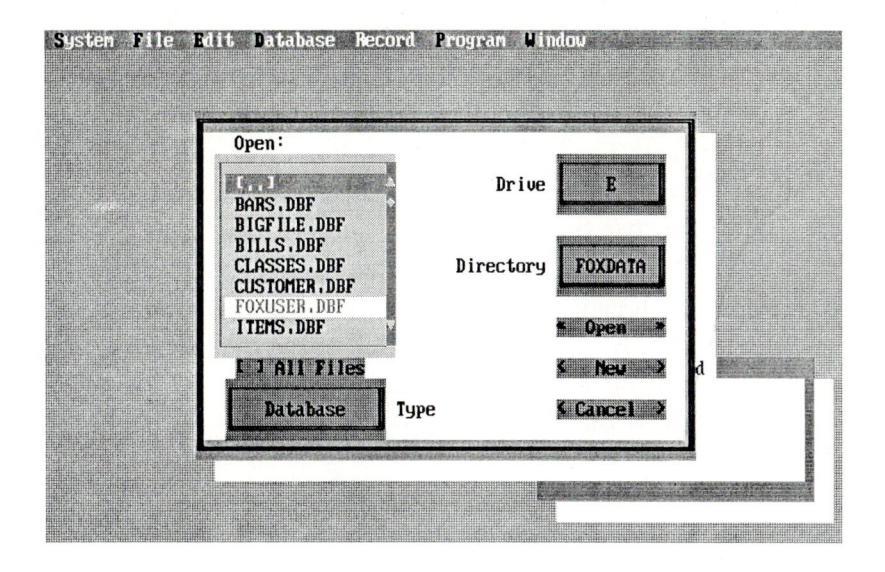

FIGURE 1-14.   A dialog box

is a check box. If you tab down to this entry and press the spacebar, an "X" will appear in the brackets, and the *list box* (just above) will change to view all files in the current directory. You can again tab to the All Files check box and press the spacebar (or just mouse-click on the box) to change back to viewing only database files.

A list box, like that occupying most of the left side of this dialog box, contains a list of items that is sometimes called a *pick list*. In this example, a list of database files appears; if none have been created yet, the list will be empty. Depending on how you set up your directories, there may be database files like ARCHIVE.DBF, FOXHELP.DBF, and FOXUSER.DBF in your list that were created by FoxPro during the installation process. These are used by FoxPro, and you should not try to change the data in these files unless your documentation suggests it. You can use the UP ARROW and DOWN ARROW keys to scroll among items in the list box, and you can select an item by pressing ENTER. Mouse users can click on an item in a list box to select it. If more items are in the list box than are visible at one time, mouse users can use the scroll bar, which then appears at the right edge of the window, to scroll in the list.

Buttons are used to perform a particular action, such as opening the selected file or cancelling the use of the dialog box. In this dialog box, the available buttons are labeled Open, New, and Cancel. Keyboard users can select a button by tabbing to it and pressing ENTER. Mouse users can select a button by clicking on it. For now, tab over to the Cancel button and press ENTER to cancel this operation and close the dialog box.

DESKTOP ACCESSORIES

FoxPro offers some desktop accessories, which are available from the System menu. Since most of these accessories don't deal specifically with database management, they won't be covered in detail in this book. However, you should be aware of their existence. The following paragraphs provide a brief description; you can learn more details on the accessories from the FoxPro documentation.

If you open the System menu with the mouse or with ALT-S, you will see options for a filer, a calculator, a calendar/diary, special characters, an ASCII chart, a capture, and a puzzle. The filer can be used for DOS file management, such as erasing and renaming files. Its operation will be covered further in Chapter 8.

The Calculator option, when selected, provides a desktop calculator. Modeled after a pocket calculator, its operation is fairly obvious. You can use the numeric pad (after pressing NUM LOCK) to enter numbers, or you can use the numbers on the top row of the keyboard. The ENTER key can be used to complete the entry of numbers or math symbols.

The Calendar/Diary option, when chosen, displays the current month (based on the computer's clock) along with a Diary area in which you can type notes of your choosing. To enter a note, press TAB and begin typing. When you close the calendar (by clicking on the close box at the upper-right corner with the mouse or by choosing Close from the File menu), the note will be saved automatically. You can repeatedly press the UP ARROW or DOWN ARROW keys to move from month to month, and you can press T (for Today) to return from anywhere to the current date.

The Special Characters option displays a chart of foreign characters and special graphics characters. The ASCII Chart option displays a chart of all ASCII characters in the ASCII character set. These options are of interest to programmers, who may need to refer to the list from time to time. If you do not know what an ASCII character set is, don't worry; you will not need it for performing database management tasks.

The Capture option lets you capture a block of information on the screen and paste it into the Editor. (Among other things, the Editor is used for writing and debugging FoxPro programs.) The use of Capture may come in handy for certain programming tasks, but it will not be needed for any operations covered in this text.

The Puzzle option displays an entertaining puzzle on the screen resembling a child's number puzzle. You can use either the cursor keys or click on the numbers with the mouse to move them around. Pressing S or clicking on Shuffle will cause the numbers to be remixed in a random order. The object of the game is to align the numbers in order from 1 through 15.

2

CREATING AND DISPLAYING DATABASES

Creating a Database
Adding Information to a File
An Introduction to Browse
Getting a Quick Report
Dot-Prompt Options for Displaying a Database
Searching Within a Field
Keeping Track of Records

This chapter assumes that you have installed FoxPro and know how to start the program. It also assumes that you know how to make selections within dialog boxes, move and resize windows, and use the keyboard (and the mouse, if a mouse is installed). If you are unfamiliar with any of these areas, you should review the latter half of Chapter 1 before proceeding.

CREATING A DATABASE

FoxPro gives you two ways to create a database. In the Command window, you can enter **CREATE** *filename,* where *filename* is the name for the new database you wish to create. Or you can open the File menu, choose New, and then select Database from the dialog box that appears. Either method has the same result: the appearance of the Database Structure dialog box in which you define the database by entering the field names, types, and widths. For an example, you can create the sample database used throughout this chapter now by opening the File menu with ALT-F, and selecting the New option. When you do this, the dialog box shown in Figure 2-1 appears.

The various options in the dialog box allow for the creation of new databases, programs, text files, index files, reports, labels, or

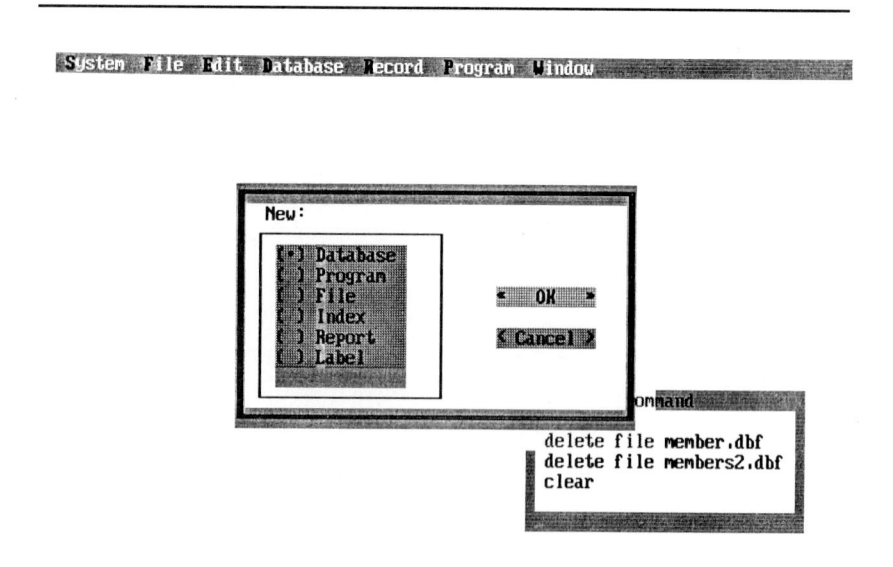

FIGURE 2-1. Dialog box for a new file

screen forms. If you have already created a database, there will be additional options in the dialog box. Unless an existing database has already been opened for use, the Index, Report, Label, and Form options are unavailable; hence, they are dimmed.

Once you select the Database option and choose OK (or simply press ENTER while the Database option is chosen), FoxPro will display a screen with highlighted blocks for the entry of field names, types of fields, field widths, and the number of decimal places. This box, known as the Database Structure dialog box, is shown in Figure 2-2.

When naming a field, use a name that best describes the contents of the field. Field names can be made of letters, numbers, and underscores but must start with a letter, and spaces are not allowed. Field names can contain up to 10 characters. FoxPro will not allow the entry of field names that are too long or that contain illegal characters.

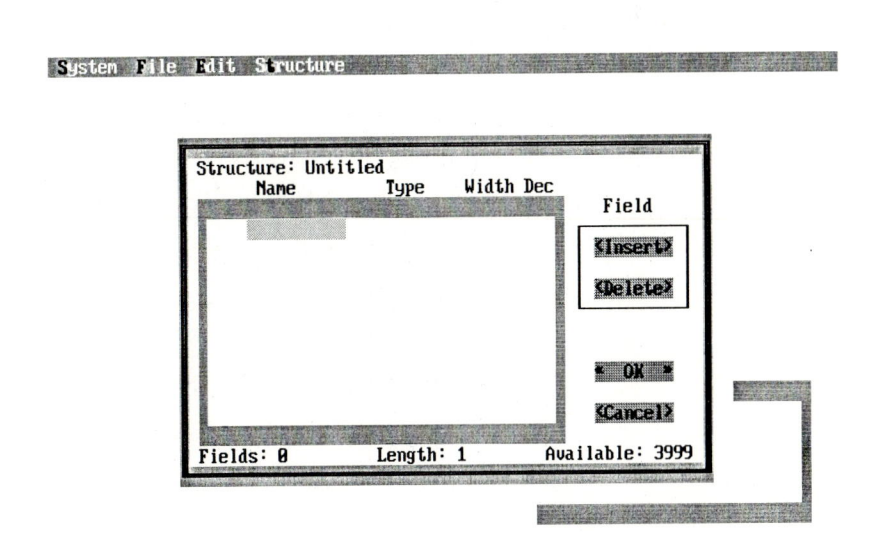

FIGURE 2-2. Database Structure dialog box

The first field on the list for the example database is the member's social security number. If you are following the example, enter **Social** for the field name. Once you press the ENTER key, the cursor will automatically move to the field-type column. FoxPro allows for the entry of six types of fields:

- *Character fields*. These are used to store any characters, including letters, numbers, special symbols, or blank spaces. A character field has a maximum size of 254 characters.

- *Date fields*. You'll use date fields to store dates. The default format for entering dates is MM/DD/YY, but this format can be changed with the SET command. FoxPro automatically inserts the slashes if you enter all six digits of a date into a date field. You must include any leading zeros for the day and month; if you do not, you must type in the slashes.

- *Numeric fields*. These use numbers, with or without decimal places. Only numbers and the minus sign (the hyphen) can be entered; FoxPro does *not* use commas in numbers larger than 1000, although you can format reports so that the commas appear. You can enter numbers of up to 20 digits in length, and FoxPro is accurate to 15 digits, so unless you are performing scientific calculations, you shouldn't have a problem with numeric accuracy.

- *Float fields*. These are numeric fields with a floating decimal point. As with numeric fields, you can enter numbers or the minus sign, and accuracy extends to 15 digits.

- *Logical fields*. These consist of a single letter representing a true or false value. T or Y represents true, and F or N represents false.

- *Memo fields*. FoxPro can store large blocks of text for each record in the form of memo fields. An unlimited amount of text can be stored in a memo field (you are limited only by available hard-disk space).

- *Picture fields.* Depending on your version of FoxPro, you may also see an option for picture fields. This field type is planned as a later addition to FoxPro. When available, it will allow for the storage of graphic images.

Most fields in a database are of the character or numeric type, although there may be times when you need all of the different field types that FoxPro offers.

When the cursor is in the Type column of the Database Structure dialog box, you can either enter the first letter of the desired field type or press ENTER to display a pull-down menu showing the available field types. When this menu is visible, you can press the first letter of the desired field type followed by ENTER, or you can mouse-click in the desired field type.

The social security numbers in our example database consist of numbers, so at first it might seem sensible to use a numeric field. However, this is not practical. If you include the hyphens that normally appear as part of a social security number, FoxPro will ignore everything typed after the first hyphen, and the result will be an incorrect entry. You will never use a social security number in a numerical calculation, so it makes sense to store entries such as social security numbers and phone numbers as character fields rather than numeric fields. A number stored in a character field cannot be used directly in a numerical calculation, although you could convert the value to a number with a FoxPro function.

Since the social security field will contain characters in the form of hyphens, the next step in the example is to choose Character. When this is done, FoxPro asks for the field width. Remember, character fields can be up to 254 characters in length, while numeric and float fields are limited to 20 digits. Logical fields are fixed at 1 character, and date fields are fixed at 8 characters. Earlier, in Chapter 1, the example structure for the videos database indicated that the social security field would require 11 characters, so enter **11** as the field width and press ENTER. The cursor will move to the next field description.

For this example, enter **Lastname** for the second field name. In the field-type area, enter **Character** for the field type, and **15** for the field width. The cursor will move to the third field definition. For the third item in the list of specified fields, enter **Firstname** as the field name. Again, when the cursor moves to the field-type area, enter **Character** (or press the ENTER key to accept the existing entry), and enter **15** for the field width.

To follow the example, enter **Address** for the fourth field definition, **Character** for the field type, and **25** for the field width. For the fifth field, enter **City**, enter **Character** for the field type, and enter **15** for the width. For the next field enter **State**, enter **C** for the field type, and enter **2** for the field width.

The next field will be ZIP code. While ZIP codes contain numbers, the same reasoning used with the social security field applies, because ten-digit ZIP codes also contain hyphens. Enter **Zipcode** as the field name, **Character** as the field type, and **10** as the width.

You may recall from Chapter 1 that two of the field attributes take the form of dates: the date of birth and the date the membership expires. FoxPro lets you use date fields to enter dates. By using date fields to store dates, you can perform date arithmetic (as in subtracting one date from another to come up with the difference in days between the two). You can also arrange records chronologically based on date fields.

Enter **Birthday** for the name of the next field, and type **D** in the field-type column. Note that FoxPro automatically supplies a width of 8 for this type of field.

Enter **Expiredate** for the name of the next field, and type **D** in the field type column to indicate a date field. For the next field name, enter **Tapelimit**. For the field type, enter **N** (for numeric). For the field width, enter **2**. This will create a numeric field with a maximum width of two digits. You will be able to store numbers from 0 to 99 in this field. (Generic Videos assumes it will never need to rent more than 99 tapes to one member.) When you specify a numeric field, the cursor moves next to the decimal heading. You could, if desired, specify a number of decimal places for the numeric field. In this example, whole numbers are used to describe the number of tapes, so you can press ENTER to bypass the decimal entry.

Whenever you are using numeric fields to track dollar or other currency amounts (such as salaries or costs), you should include one digit in the width to contain the decimal point. For example, to track salaries of up to $999.99, you would need a numeric field with a width of 6; 3 for the dollar amount, 1 for the decimal point, and 2 for the cents values. Whenever you include decimal amounts, allow one digit for the decimal, and if you are working exclusively with decimal numbers, include one digit so the decimal point can be preceded by a zero (for example, 0.1). Thus, the minimum field width for a decimal number is 3. Note that an additional space will be needed for the minus symbol if you plan to enter negative numbers in a numeric field.

If you are following the example, enter **Beta** as the next field name and choose Logical as the field type. After choosing a logical field, you will note that a width of 1 is assigned automatically by FoxPro.

Depending on the member's tastes, the Preference field may need to store a lengthy series of comments. The most economical way of storing any large group of information is to use a memo field, and Preference is designated as a memo field. Enter **Preference** as the next field name and then enter **M** (for memo) as the field type. FoxPro will automatically supply 10 as the field width.

While you are creating a database, you may notice the statistics listed at the bottom of the dialog box, as shown in Figure 2-3. In the lower-right corner of the dialog box is the number of available bytes remaining in the current record. This number is calculated by adding together the numbers in the field-width column and subtracting the total from the maximum of 4000 bytes (characters) per record. Memo fields count as 10 spaces, but since the actual text of a memo field is stored in a different file, the limit of 4000 characters per record will not affect the amount of text you can store in memo fields.

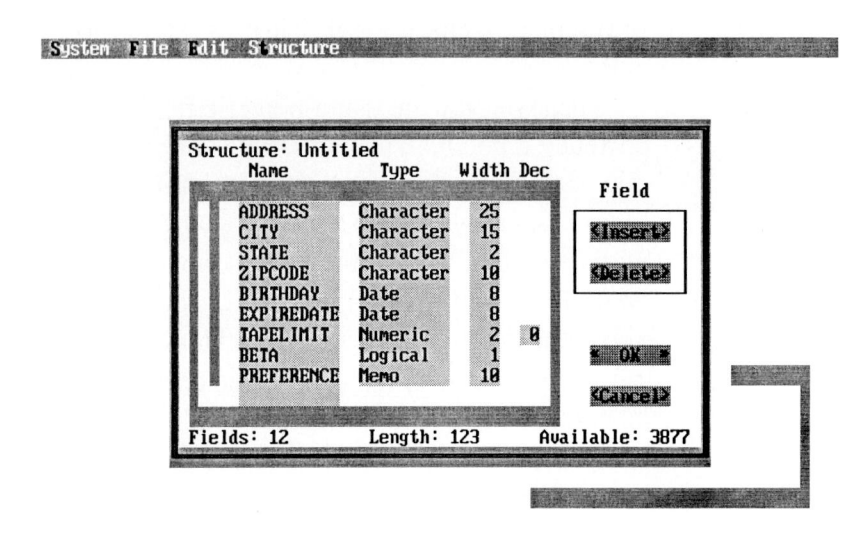

```
┌─────────────────────────────────────────────────────────────┐
│ System  File  Edit  Structure                               │
└─────────────────────────────────────────────────────────────┘
    ┌──────────────────────────────────────────────┐
    │ Structure: Untitled                          │
    │    Name         Type       Width  Dec        │
    │                                      Field   │
    │   ADDRESS     Character     25               │
    │   CITY        Character     15     <Insert>  │
    │   STATE       Character      2               │
    │   ZIPCODE     Character     10     <Delete>  │
    │   BIRTHDAY    Date           8               │
    │   EXPIREDATE  Date           8               │
    │   TAPELIMIT   Numeric        2   0           │
    │   BETA        Logical        1       < OK >  │
    │   PREFERENCE  Memo          10               │
    │                                    <Cancel>  │
    │ Fields: 12    Length: 123   Available: 3877  │
    └──────────────────────────────────────────────┘
```

FIGURE 2-3. Dialog box with statistics

The number shown in the lower-left corner of the dialog box indicates the number of fields created so far. Both figures, the number of bytes remaining and the number of fields, will change as you add fields to the database. The figure at the bottom center of the dialog box shows the combined length of all of the fields created thus far.

Correcting Mistakes

If you make any mistakes while defining the structure of the database, you can correct them before completing the database definition process. To correct mistakes, use the cursor keys to move to the field name or field type containing the offending characters, and use the BACKSPACE key, along with the character keys, to make any desired corrections. You can use the arrow keys

LEFT ARROW	Cursor left one character
RIGHT ARROW	Cursor right one character
UP ARROW	Cursor up one line or one field
DOWN ARROW	Cursor down one line or one field
INS	Insert mode on/off
DEL	Delete character at cursor
BACKSPACE	Delete character to left of cursor
CTRL-T	Delete word at cursor
CTRL-Y	Delete line at cursor
ESC	Abort operation
TAB	Move cursor right one field
SHIFT-TAB	Move cursor left one field
CTRL-W	Save changes and exit

TABLE 2-1. FoxPro Editing Keys

to move left, right, up, or down in the form. To insert new characters between existing characters, place the cursor at the desired location and then type the correction. Pressing the INS key takes you out of Insert mode. When you are not in Insert mode, any characters that you type will write over existing characters. A more complete list of FoxPro editing keys is shown in Table 2-1. These editing keys also work with the Editor when you are editing memo fields.

Saving the Database

To tell FoxPro that you have finished defining the database structure, you can tab over to the OK button in the dialog box and press ENTER, or you can mouse-click on the OK button. If you just leave the field name blank and press ENTER, the cursor will automatically move to the OK button and you can press ENTER. (An alternative

54   FoxPro Made Easy

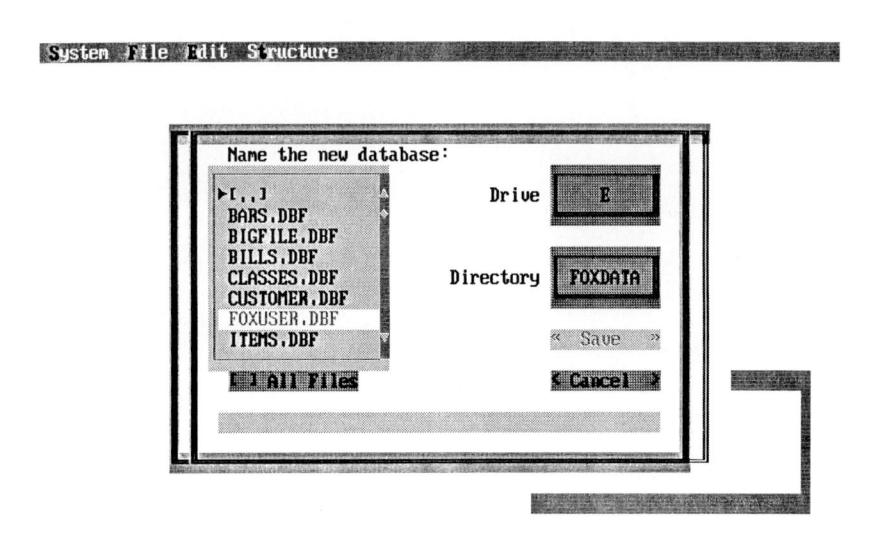

FIGURE 2-4.   Dialog box for naming a database file

is to press CTRL-W.) The screen will display the dialog box shown in Figure 2-4. In this box, you are prompted for a name for the file. Each database file must have a name, and the name must not contain more than eight characters. FoxPro automatically assigns an extension of .DBF to the name. Database files that include memo fields will also have a corresponding file with an .FPT extension created automatically by FoxPro.

If you have been following the example, enter **MEMBERS** as the name of the file. To save the new file structure, you must next tab over to the Save button in the dialog box and press ENTER (or mouse-click on the Save button). Once you have done this, you will see the following message in a new dialog box:

Input data records now? (Y/N)
< OK >   < Cancel >

You can choose OK or Cancel. Choosing Cancel completes the database definition process, and choosing OK completes the process and leaves the file open for adding new records. If you are following the example, choose OK, and FoxPro will enter Append Mode.

ADDING INFORMATION TO A FILE

As with nearly all operations in FoxPro, you can add data by using a menu choice or by using a command. From the Command window, the command you use is APPEND. (Note that a database file must first be opened with the USE command before you can use APPEND to add data.) From the menus, you can open the File menu, select the Open option, and then choose the file by name from the dialog box that appears. Once the file has been opened, you open the Record menu and choose the Append option to begin adding data.

Whether you enter **APPEND** in the Command window or choose Append from the Record menu, the result is the same: the screen will change to reveal a simple on-screen form (Figure 2-5), with blank spaces beside each corresponding field name. In FoxPro, this is the default screen used for adding and editing records. Its layout matches the structure of the database currently in use. The default form for adding data may not be precisely to your liking; in Chapter 5 you will learn to create forms that differ in design from the default form.

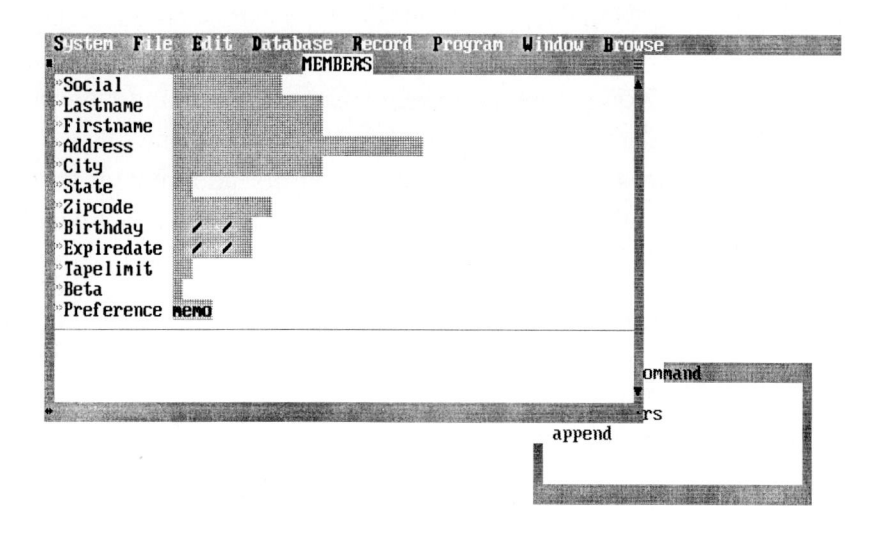

FIGURE 2-5. On-screen data-entry form

If you are following the example, enter the following information, pressing ENTER after each entry is completed.

Social: 123-44-8976
Lastname: Miller
Firstname: Karen
Address: 4260 Park Avenue
City: Chevy Chase
State: MD
Zipcode: 20815-0988
Birthday: 03/01/54
Expiredate: 07/25/92
Tapelimit: 6
Beta: F

If you make a mistake during the data-entry process, you can reach the offending field with the cursor keys and use the BACKSPACE key to correct and retype the entry. When you have entered all of the information, the cursor should be at the start of the memo field.

Entering Data in A Memo Field

Entering data in a memo field is different from entering data in other fields. Whenever the cursor is in a memo field (as it is now), you are at the entry point for a Memo window that can hold a theoretically unlimited amount of text. (In practice, you are limited only by the available hard-disk space.) You can enter the Memo window by pressing ENTER whenever the cursor is in the memo field. You can also enter a Memo window by double-clicking on the field with the mouse. Once you use either method, the entry form will be covered by a window, and you will be editing the memo field with the FoxPro Editor.

The FoxPro Editor lets you type text as you would with any word processing software. It isn't necessary to press the ENTER key at the end of every line; the Editor will automatically move the cursor to the next line. The BACKSPACE key will erase any mistakes, and you can use the arrow keys to move the cursor around the screen for editing.

The various menu options present in the Editor deserve more detailed treatment in a later chapter. For now, you'll use just the text-entry capabilities and the simple editing possible with the BACKSPACE and DEL keys to add a few comments in the memo fields. As an example, type the following:

Prefers science fiction, horror movies. Fan of Star Trek films.

When you have finished typing the text, you'll need to get back to the data-entry screen. You can do so either by choosing Close from the File menu or by mouse-clicking on the close box at the upper-left corner of the window. Another faster method is to use the CTRL-W key combination. Use any of these methods now to get back to the data-entry screen.

You can continue adding records by using the PGDN key or the DOWN ARROW key to move to the next (blank) record. To follow the example, fill in the following additional records for the video members' database, using CTRL-W to complete each memo field entry, and the PGDN or DOWN ARROW key to move to each new record as the prior one is completed.

Social: 121-32-9876
Lastname: Martin
Firstname: William
Address: 4807 East Avenue
City: Silver Spring
State: MD
Zipcode: 20910-0124
Birthday: 5/29/61
Expiredate: 07/04/91
Tapelimit: 4
Beta: F
Preference: Enjoys Clint Eastwood, John Wayne films.

Social: 232-55-1234
Lastname: Robinson
Firstname: Carol
Address: 4102 Valley Lane
City: Falls Church
State: VA
ZIPcode: 22043
Birthday: 12/22/55
Expiredate: 09/05/93
Tapelimit: 6
Beta: F
Preference: Likes comedy, drama films.

Social: 901-77-3456
Lastname: Kramer
Firstname: Harry
Address: 617 North Oakland Street
City: Arlington
State: VA
Zipcode: 22203
Birthday: 08/17/58
Expiredate: 12/22/90
Tapelimit: 4
Beta: T
Preference: Big fan of Eddie Murphy. Also enjoys westerns.

When you finish the last record, use CTRL-W (or mouse-click on the close box in the upper-left corner of the window) to close the Memo window. Then press CTRL-W again to leave Append mode.

AN INTRODUCTION TO BROWSE

Viewing and entering records in this manner gets the job done, but as you can see, it is impossible to view more than one record on the screen at a time. FoxPro can also display information in table form, an important advantage because most users find it easier to grasp the concept of a database when it is shown in a tabular manner. It is easy to see a number of records, and the records and fields are clearly distinguished. There will be times when you prefer to see the information in the form of a table, and there will be times when you find a form like the one you have been using until now to be the best approach.

If you are following the example, open the Database menu with ALT-D and choose Browse. (You can also choose Browse from the Browse menu; however, unless you are already appending to or editing a file, the Browse menu does not appear as a menu option.)

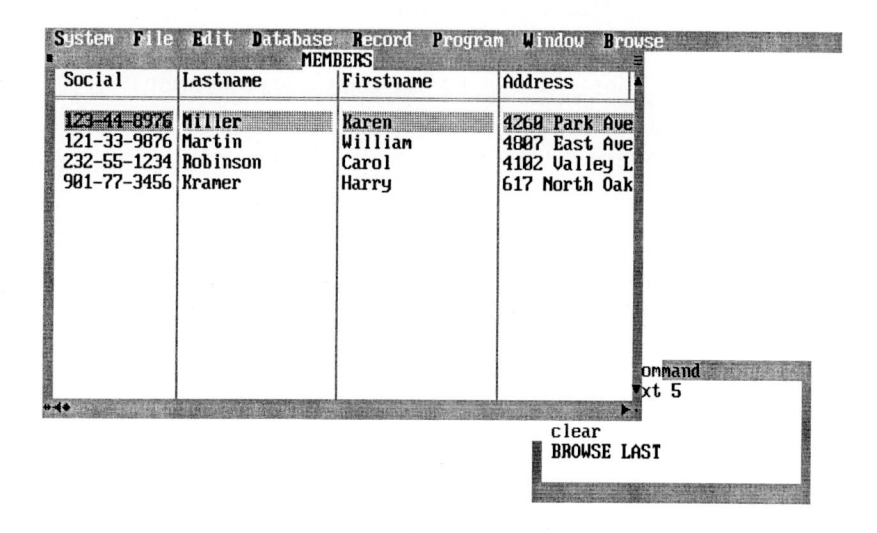

```
 System  File  Edit  Database  Record  Program  Window  Browse
                        MEMBERS
 Social      Lastname    Firstname    Address
 123-44-8976 Miller      Karen        4260 Park Ave
 121-33-9876 Martin      William      4807 East Ave
 232-55-1234 Robinson    Carol        4102 Valley L
 901-77-3456 Kramer      Harry        617 North Oak




                                              ommand
                                              xt 5
                                         clear
                                         BROWSE LAST
```

FIGURE 2-6.   Tabular view of record (Browse mode)

When you select the Browse option from either the Database or the Browse menu, the database in use appears in table form, as shown in Figure 2-6. This style of display is known as Browse mode. Another way to display data in this format is to enter the BROWSE command in the Command window.

Moving around in the database is different when you are in Browse mode than when you are in Append or Edit mode on the data-entry form. Try PGUP and PGDN, and then try using the UP ARROW and DOWN ARROW keys. Where previously (in Edit mode) PGUP and PGDN would have moved you up and down by a record at a time, they now move you up and down by a screenful of records. Also, the UP ARROW and DOWN ARROW keys now move the cursor between records, instead of between fields. You can use the TAB and SHIFT-TAB keys to move the cursor between fields. Mouse users can click on any desired field or record to place the cursor at that location. Mouse users can also use the scroll bars to navigate within the window; by clicking on the left, right, up, or down arrows in the window's scroll bars, you can move in those respective directions. You can also add new records to a database while in Browse mode with the Append Record option of the Browse menu.

There are a number of options for using Browse mode, and these will be covered in detail in the next chapter. Remember, you can press ALT-R at any time for the Records menu, and then choose Append from the menu to continue adding records to the database. A quicker shortcut is to press CTRL-P. If you are following along with the example, use CTRL-P, or the Append Record option of the Browse menu to add the remaining records to the table now.

Social: 121-90-5432
Lastname: Moore
Firstname: Ellen
Address: 270 Browning Ave #3C
City: Takoma Park
State: MD
Zipcode: 20912
Birthday: 11/02/64
Expiredate: 11/17/94
Tapelimit: 6
Beta: F
Preference: drama, comedy.

Social: 495-00-3456
Last name: Zachman
Firstname: David
Address: 1617 Arlington Blvd
City: Falls Church
State: VA
Zipcode: 22043
Birthday: 09/17/51
Expiredate: 09/19/90

Tapelimit: 4
Beta: T
Preference: science fiction, drama.

Social: 343-55-9821
Lastname: Robinson
Firstname: Benjamin
Address: 1607 21st Street, NW
City: Washington
State: DC
Zipcode: 20009
Birthday: 06/22/66
Expiredate: 09/17/91
Tapelimit: 2
Beta: T
Preference: westerns, comedy. Clint Eastwood fan.

Social: 876-54-3210
Lastname: Hart
Firstname: Wendy
Address: 6200 Germantown Road
City: Fairfax
State: VA
Zipcode: 22025
Birthday: 12/20/55
Expiredate: 10/19/92
Tapelimit: 2
Beta: T
Preference: drama, adventure. Likes spy movies, including all 'James Bond' series.

After the last memo field entry has been made, you can use CTRL-W or mouse-click on the close box to close the window.

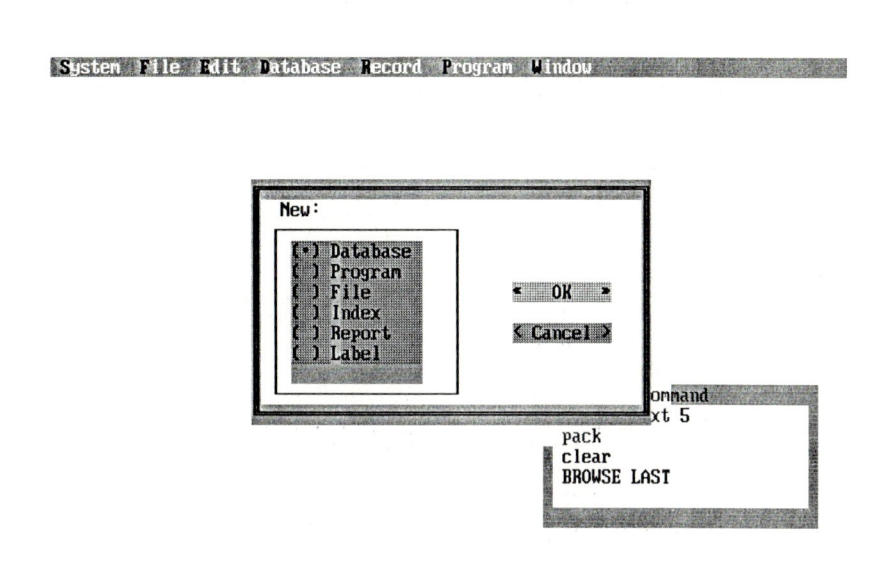

FIGURE 2-7. New File dialog box

GETTING A QUICK REPORT

You can create *quick reports* by selecting a few menu options. The options you'll use are part of the report creation process that is described in detail in Chapter 7. However, to show you how easily this can be done, the following paragraphs will demonstrate an example.

To create a quick report, you open the File menu with ALT- F and choose New. The New File dialog box that appears (Figure 2-7) offers a choice of different types of files to create. Select Report now by pressing the R key. Then, tab over to the OK box and press ENTER.

Once you have selected the OK button, the report design screen will appear. This screen can be used to create custom reports, a

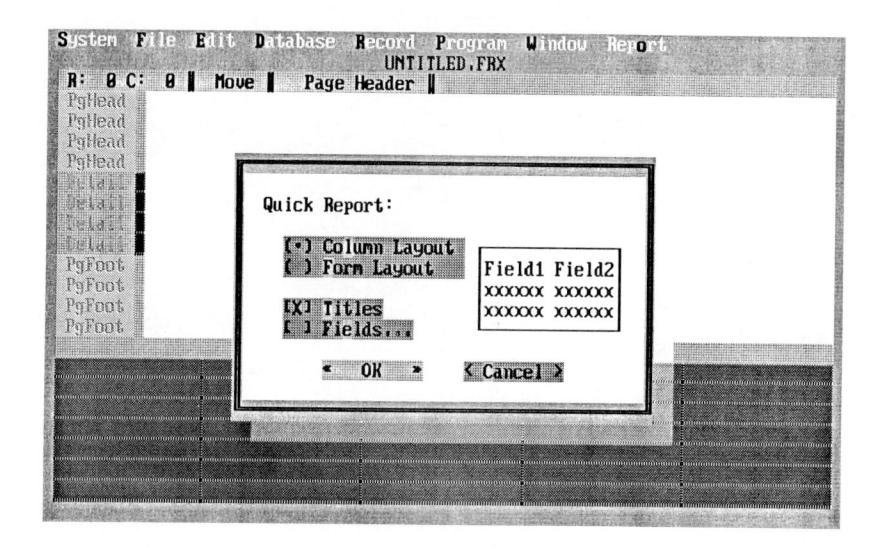

FIGURE 2-8. Quick Report dialog box

process detailed in Chapter 7. For a quick report, you simply choose Quick Report from the Report menu, and the report is designed automatically for you. Open the Report menu (note that the hot key here is ALT-O, not ALT-R), and choose Quick Report from the menu. The Quick Report dialog box appears, as shown in Figure 2-8.

The Column Layout and Form Layout options allow you to select either a columnar layout, with data appearing in columns, or a form layout, where each record appears with one field under another. For the purposes of this example, choose Form by pressing F. (The Title option can be used to turn on or off the appearance of field names as titles, and the Field option is used to select specific fields for inclusion in the report. You can ignore these options if all fields are desired in the report, as is the case here.)

Tab over to OK and press ENTER. You will see a report design appear, with field names laid out in a form fashion. Open the File menu with ALT-F, and choose Save.

You must now enter a name for the report file. Enter **RSAMPLE** and then tab over to the Save button and press ENTER. Finally, choose Close from the File menu to exit the report design process.

To run the report, you use the Report option of the Database menu. Open the Database menu with ALT-D, and choose Report. When the Report dialog box appears, enter **RSAMPLE**. If you would like the report printed as well as displayed on your screen, tab down to the To Print check box, and press the spacebar to check the box. (The remaining options in this dialog box are explained in Chapter 7.) Finally, tab over to OK and press ENTER. Don't forget to turn on your printer if you choose this option. The report will appear on the screen, and if you checked the To Print box, the report will be printed.

You can produce far more detailed reports in FoxPro. Such reports can include customized headers and footers, customized placement of fields, word-wrapping large amounts of text, and numeric results based on calculations of fields. These report features are covered in detail in Chapters 7 and 10.

DOT-PROMPT OPTIONS FOR DISPLAYING A DATABASE

A few shortcuts for displaying your data with commands may prove useful. While using the commands from the Command window requires a precise recall of how the commands should be entered, many users find commands to be faster than menu options.

When you first start FoxPro, you must choose a database file for use. This action can be performed with the USE command. The syntax for this command is

USE *filename*

If you now enter

USE MEMBERS

FoxPro opens the MEMBERS database file. (Since the file was previously open, this step was unnecessary; however, if you were just starting FoxPro, you would need the USE command or its menu to open a file before working with that file.)

Viewing a Database

You can use the LIST or DISPLAY command to examine the contents of a database. Typing **LIST** by itself will show the entire contents of a database unless you specify otherwise, but you can limit the display to certain fields by including the field name after the word "LIST." If you specify more than one field, separate them by a comma. For example, if you are using the example database and you enter

LIST LASTNAME, EXPIREDATE

FoxPro shows only the last names and expiration dates contained in the database, as shown below. If you had entered **LIST** without any field names, you would have seen a list of all the fields.

Record#	LASTNAME	EXPIREDATE
1	Miller	07/25/92
2	Martin	07/04/91
3	Robinson	09/05/93
4	Kramer	12/22/90
5	Moore	11/17/94
6	Zachman	09/19/90
7	Robinson	09/17/91
8	Hart	10/19/92

The DISPLAY command lets you view selected information. By default, the LIST command shows you all records, while the DISPLAY command shows only the current record. To see more than one record with DISPLAY, you must add an optional clause, such as ALL or NEXT 5. Enter the following:

GO 3
DISPLAY

You will see the third record in the database. (The GO command, followed by a record number, tells FoxPro to move to that record.) Note that the record may be partially hidden by the Command window. You can move the Command window; to do so, open the Window menu with ALT-W, choose Move, and use the cursor keys to drag the window to its desired location; then press ENTER to anchor the window. (Mouse users can drag the window in the usual manner, as outlined in Chapter 1.) If you try the following commands, you will see three records, beginning with record number 2:

GO 2
DISPLAY NEXT 3

You see an entire database by entering

DISPLAY ALL

There is one significant difference between DISPLAY ALL and LIST. If the database is large, the LIST command will cause the contents to scroll up the screen without stopping. If you use the DISPLAY ALL command, the screen will pause after every 20 lines, and you can press any key to resume the scrolling.

The DISPLAY command can also be used to search for specific information, if it is followed by a specific condition. For example, you could display only the name, city, state, and tape-limit fields for all members with a tape limit of four or more by entering

DISPLAY FIELDS LASTNAME, FIRSTNAME, CITY, STATE, TAPELIMIT FOR TAPELIMIT > 3

(This command appears on two lines here, but you must enter it all on one line in the Command window.)

You can find more detailed coverage on performing selective queries in Chapter 6, "Using Queries."

SEARCHING WITHIN A FIELD

There may be occasions when you want to search for information that is contained within a field, but you know only a portion of that information. This can cause problems, because FoxPro does not search "full text," or within a field, unless you give it specific instructions to do so. To demonstrate the problem, if one of the Generic Videos managers calls and asks for the name of "that member who lives on North Oakland Street," how do you find "that" record? The manager can't recall the member's name.

Try searching for a member who lives on North Oakland Street by entering the following:

DISPLAY FOR ADDRESS = "North Oakland"

Don't feel that you've done something wrong when the record does not appear. FoxPro normally begins a search by attempting to match your characters with the first characters of the chosen field. In our database, there is no record that begins with the characters "North Oakland" in the Address field. As a result, FoxPro failed to find the data.

To get around this problem, you can search within a field. The normal layout, or syntax, for the necessary command is

DISPLAY FOR "*search text*" $ *fieldname*

where *search text* is the actual characters that you want to look for and *fieldname* is the name of the specific field that you wish to search. To try an example, enter the following command:

DISPLAY FOR "North Oakland" $ ADDRESS

This time, FoxPro will find the desired information.
 You can use this technique to search for data within the text of a memo field. For example, the command

DISPLAY LASTNAME, PREFERENCE FOR "comedy" $ PREFERENCE

would display all records containing the word "comedy" anywhere in the Preference field.

KEEPING TRACK OF RECORDS

Whenever FoxPro looks at a database, it examines one record at a time. Even when you list all of the records in the database, FoxPro starts with the first record in the file and then examines each additional record, one by one. The program keeps track of where it is by means of a pointer. The FoxPro pointer is always pointing to a particular record whenever you are using a database. You can move the pointer to a specific record with the GO command.
 Enter **GO TOP**, and then enter **DISPLAY**. The pointer will be at the first record in the file:

1 123-44-8976 Miller   Karen   4260 Park Avenue...

To move the pointer to the fourth record, enter **GO 4**. Enter **DISPLAY**, and you will see the fourth record:

4 901-77-3456 Kramer   Harry   617 North Oakland Street...

You can go to the first record by entering **GO TOP**, or you can go to the end of a database by entering **GO BOTTOM**. If you don't know the record number but need to find a particular record, you can use the LOCATE command to find it. The use of the LOCATE command is detailed in the following chapter.

If this is a good time for a break, enter **QUIT**. The QUIT command saves any work in progress and exits the program. For your reference, the menu alternative to leave FoxPro is to open the File menu and choose Quit.

Now that you have a file containing data, you'll want to know how you can manipulate that data to better obtain the results you want. The next chapter covers this area in more detail.

3

CHANGING YOUR DATABASE

Editing a Database
Editing in Browse Mode
Using Browse with Commands
Deleting Records
Deleting Files
Global Replacements with Commands
Modifying the Structure of a Database
Creating the RENTALS File

FoxPro has a number of menu options and commands that you can use to change records and fields. You can edit information in a record, such as a person's name or phone number on a mailing list, and you can change the structure of a database, adding fields for items that you did not plan for or deleting fields that you no longer use. You can also shorten or expand the width of a field. Let's begin by editing records in the Generic Videos database.

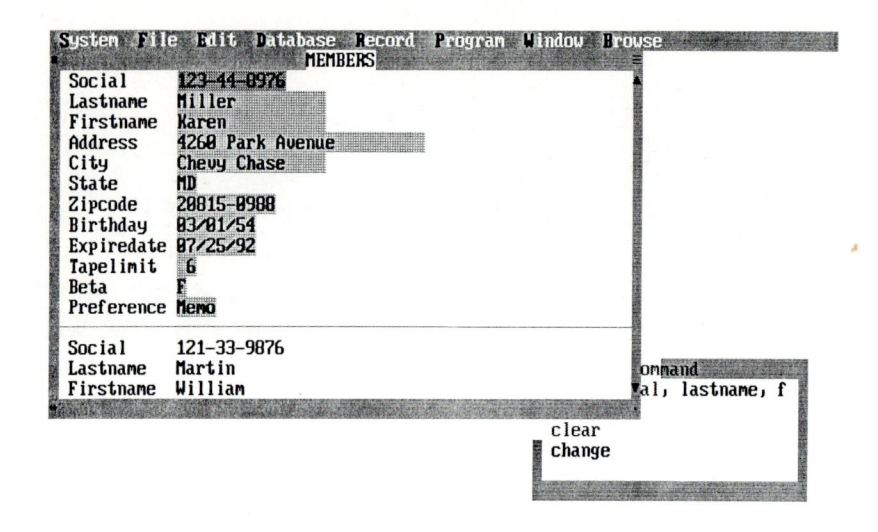

```
System File Edit Database Record Program Window Browse
              MEMBERS
Social      123-44-8976
Lastname    Miller
Firstname   Karen
Address     4260 Park Avenue
City        Chevy Chase
State       MD
Zipcode     20815-0900
Birthday    03/01/54
Expiredate  07/25/92
Tapelimit   6
Beta        F
Preference  Memo

Social      121-33-9876
Lastname    Martin
Firstname   William
                                          ommand
                                          al, lastname, f
                                    clear
                                    change
```

FIGURE 3-1.   Result of Change option or CHANGE command

EDITING A DATABASE

From the menus, you can use the Change option of the Record menu to make changes to records. (This assumes that you are already at the desired record, but there are many ways to find a record you wish to change; you will learn more about that later.) After opening a database for use, you open the Record menu and select Change. This menu option is equivalent to entering **CHANGE** at the command level. With either method a record in the database appears within the default form, as shown in Figure 3-1.

At this point you are in Change mode, and you can make changes to the data within the chosen record. If you repeatedly press the arrow keys, you will note that each keypress moves the cursor either one character or one row at a time. If you keep pressing the

DOWN ARROW key, FoxPro will take you to the next record in the file. Pressing the UP ARROW key repeatedly will eventually take you to the prior record in the file, unless you are already at the first record. You can use the arrow keys to move the cursor to any location in the record.

While you are in Change mode, you can also use the PGUP and PGDN keys to move around in the database. The PGDN key takes you one record forward, and the PGUP key takes you one record back. At the first record in the file, PGUP has no effect, and at the last record in the file, PGDN has no effect.

As an example of changing a file, an address change might be needed for Ms. Ellen Moore, a member of the video club. You could open the MEMBERS file with the Open option of the File menu or by entering **USE MEMBERS** in the Command window. You could then enter **CHANGE** or choose the Change option from the Record menu. You would next use the PGDN key to find the record for Ms. Ellen Moore. The final step in the correction would be to place the cursor in the Address field, use the RIGHT ARROW key to move to the apartment number, and use the BACKSPACE key to delete the old apartment number. You would then enter **#2A** as the new apartment number.

Once you make changes you can save them either by pressing CTRL-W or by moving to another record (with either the mouse, the arrow keys, or the PGUP and PGDN keys). For now, consider the menu options available for changing records.

If you press ALT-R, the Record menu opens (Figure 3-2). This menu contains options that are useful when you are changing a database. The Append option puts you in the Append mode, allowing the addition of new records as detailed in the previous chapter. The Change option puts you in Change (or Edit) mode, allowing records to be edited. The GoTo and Locate options can be used to quickly find a record for editing. GoTo can take you to a specific record by record number, and Locate can perform a search based on the contents of a particular field. The GoTo and Locate options are covered in more detail in Chapter 6; however,

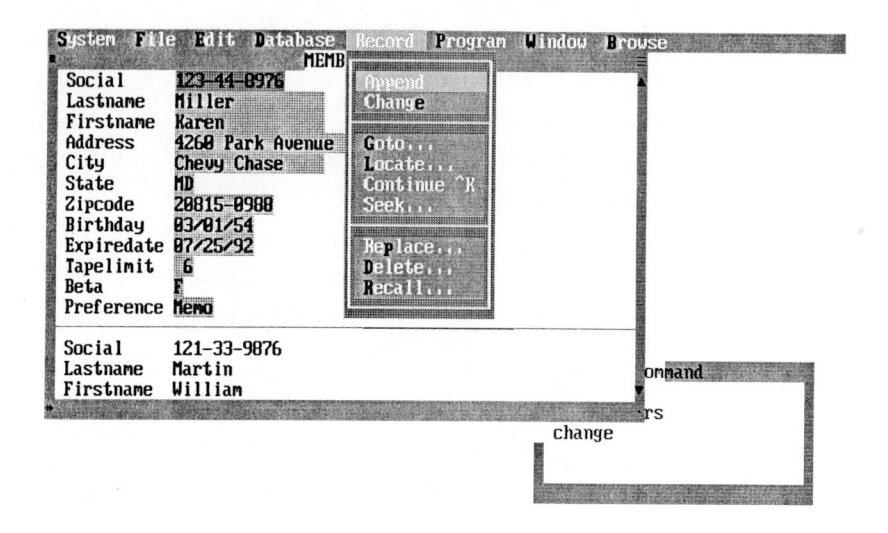

FIGURE 3-2. Record menu

a brief introduction to the Locate option is useful for the task of finding records to edit.

When you select Locate from the Record menu, another dialog box appears. It contains three options: Scope, For, and While. For your basic search, all you'll need is the For option (Scope and While are covered in Chapter 6). When you select For, another dialog box appears (Figure 3-3). The use of all the options in this dialog box are covered in detail in Chapter 6. For the purposes of a simple search, you should know that you can enter a *search expression* in the For Clause window, and then tab to or click on the OK button. A search expression is simply a combination of field name, operator (usually an equal sign), and search term you

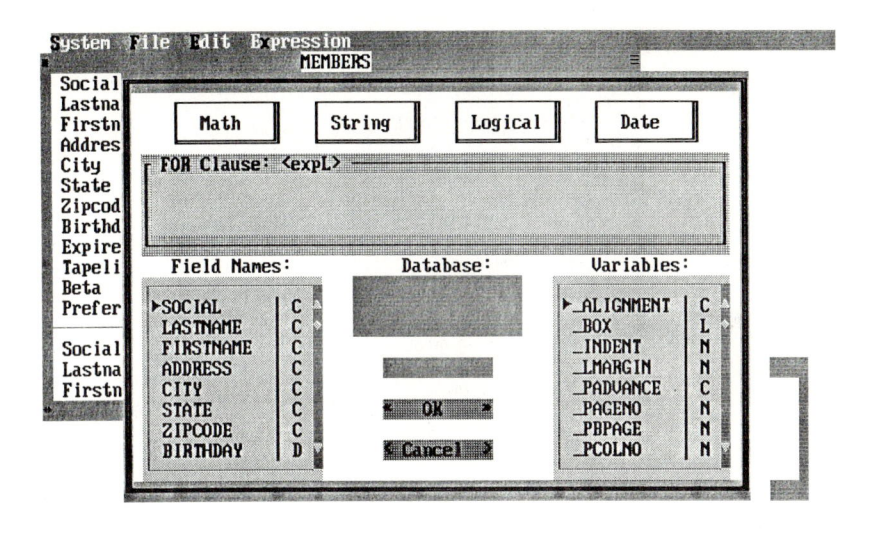

FIGURE 3-3. For Clause dialog box

are looking for. For example, say you are seeking the record for Mr. Robinson. Enter the expression

LASTNAME = "Robinson"

in the For Clause window, and then tab to the OK button and press ENTER. The For Clause dialog box disappears, and the previous dialog box (with the Scope, For, and While choices) is again visible. You next tab over to the Locate button in this dialog box and press ENTER to begin the Locate operation. Assuming you are still in Change mode, the desired record appears, as shown in Figure 3-4.

76   FoxPro Made Easy

```
 System  File  Edit  Database  Record  Program  Window  Browse
                      MEMBERS
  Social     232-55-1234
  Lastname   Robinson
  Firstname  Carol
  Address    4102 Valley Lane
  City       Falls Church
  State      VA
  Zipcode    22043
  Birthday   12/22/55
  Expiredate 09/05/93
  Tapelimit  6
  Beta       F
  Preference Memo

  Social     901-77-3456                    ommand
  Lastname   Kramer
                                            rs
                                  change
                                  LOCATE ALL FOR LASTNAME
```

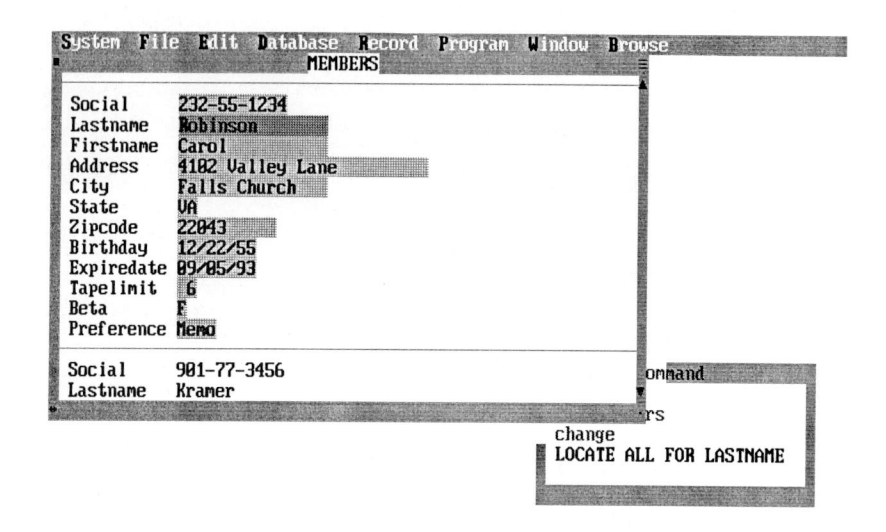

FIGURE 3-4.   Results of search

Note that the cursor stays in the field it was in when you initiated the search. If the cursor was in the Address field, for example, after you edited Ellen Moore's address, it would move to the Address field of Robinson's record, and you would need to press the UP ARROW key twice to see the name.

You can use similar search expressions to find any desired record. For example, within the For Clause window you could enter

TAPELIMIT = 4

to find the first record in the database with a value of 4 in the Tapelimit field. And you could use an expression like

LASTNAME = "Smith" .AND. FIRSTNAME = "Susan" .AND. CITY = "Raleigh"

to find a person with that name living in that specific city. (Chapter 6 offers more details on the use of the .AND. clause in expressions.)

The Locate option finds the first occurrence of the search term; if you wish to look for additional records meeting your search criteria, choose Continue from the Record menu to find additional records. For example, after the previous Locate operation, you could use the Continue option from the Record menu to find each successive record in which the value of Tapelimit was 4. If FoxPro could not find any records meeting the search criteria, you would see the message "End of Locate scope" on the screen.

If you know the record number of the desired record, you can use the GoTo option of the Record menu to find the desired record. For example, if you want to edit record number 6, press ALT- R to open the Record menu. Select the GoTo option, and from the dialog box that next appears, choose Record and enter **6** in response to the prompt. Tab to the GoTo button in the dialog box, and press ENTER. You will see that FoxPro jumps to record 6, which happens to be the record for Mr. David Zachman.

As with all menu operations, you can also perform these tasks with commands. From the Command window, once you have opened a file for use with the USE command, you can edit records by using the command CHANGE *n,* where *n* is the record number of the record you want to edit. Users who are familiar with the dBASE language may know that EDIT is an equivalent command. Entering **EDIT 5** accomplishes the same result as entering **CHANGE 5**: record number 5 appears, ready for editing.

You can also use the command GO *n,* where *n* is the record number of the record you wish to edit, and then enter the CHANGE or EDIT command without any record number after the command. For example, you could enter

GO 3
CHANGE

to edit the contents of record number 3. Once in Change mode, you can save your changes by using CTRL-W or by mouse-clicking on the close box.

From the Command window, you can also use the LOCATE command to perform a search in a manner similar to the search options of the menus. By default, LOCATE starts its search from the top of the file rather than from the current record. However, you can conduct a forward search by using the CONTINUE command after the LOCATE command. For example, if you use the command

LOCATE FOR LASTNAME = "Robinson"

and the name you find is not the Robinson you want, you can then enter

CONTINUE

to find additional occurrences of the same last name.

EDITING IN BROWSE MODE

Another useful way of editing data is from Browse mode, which was introduced in the previous chapter. Browse mode displays more than one record at a time on the screen, so you can conveniently access a number of records for editing. To use Browse mode, enter **BROWSE** at the command level or choose the Browse option of the Database menu. You'll see a screen full of records, as shown in Figure 3-5.

Browse mode displays as many fields as will fit on the screen and can display up to 20 records in a horizontal format. If there are

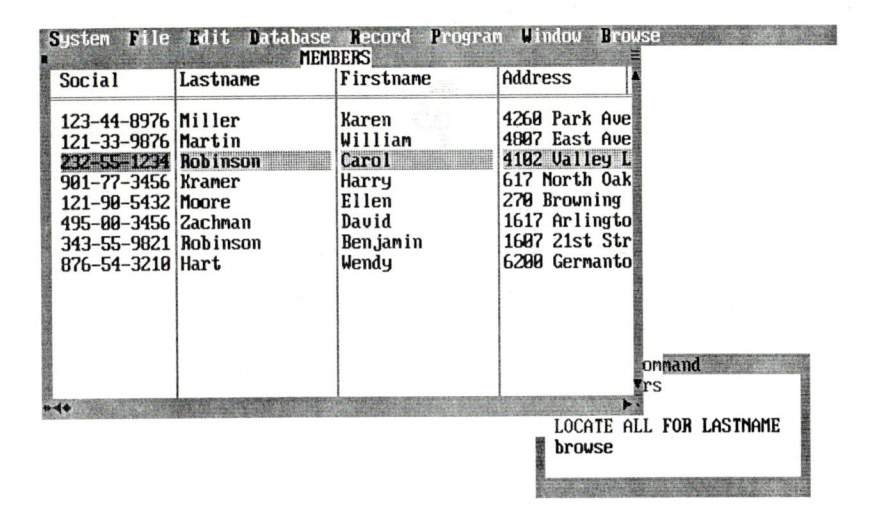

FIGURE 3-5. Browse mode

more fields in a record than will fit on a screen, only the first fields will appear, as is the case with the Generic Videos database. With the default Browse window size, fields after the Address field are hidden from view. Even if you resize the window to the full width of the screen, you won't see past the City field. All that the Browse mode can show you in this case is the Social, Lastname, Firstname, and Address fields, and part of the City field. The other fields are to the right of the display. When in Browse mode, you can scan across the database to bring the other fields into view by using the TAB and SHIFT-TAB key combinations.

Mouse users have quite a bit of flexibility, thanks to the scroll bars at the right and bottom edges of the window. Using the scroll bar at the right edge, you can click on the up and down arrows (they are triangular in shape) to scroll the database vertically. You can also drag the diamond-shaped indicator anywhere in the scroll box; this provides a vertical movement relative to the location of the indicator. For example, if you drag the indicator three-fourths of the way down the scroll bar and release it, you will be positioned about three-fourths of the way down the database.

The scroll bar at the bottom edge works in a similar manner for horizontal movement. Clicking on the triangular-shaped left and right arrows moves the database columns horizontally, and dragging the diamond-shaped indicator within the scroll box provides a horizontal movement relative to the location of the indicator. Other mouse features work the same with Browse as they do with other windows; you can resize the window by dragging on the size indicator (lower-right corner), and you can zoom the window to full screen and back by repeatedly clicking on the zoom indicator (upper-right corner).

Press the TAB key four times. The fields shift from right to left, with the Social field disappearing off the left side of the screen and the State field coming into view on the right side of the screen. If you continue to press the TAB key, fields on the screen will disappear as remaining fields come into view.

Press SHIFT-TAB repeatedly, and you'll notice the opposite effect. The fields that disappeared at the left of the screen reappear, the fields on the right side disappear. Continue pressing SHIFT-TAB until the Social field returns to the screen.

Try using the PGUP and PGDN keys. These two keys move the cursor through the database one screenful at a time. Since Generic Videos' list of members is rather short, pressing PGDN will move the cursor to the end of the database. To move the cursor up or down by one record, use the UP ARROW and DOWN ARROW keys.

You can also edit the records while in Browse mode. You can type changes in a field, and they will take effect just as they did when you were using Edit mode. However, since Browse mode displays a screenful of records and not just one record at a time, it is easier to access a particular field when in Browse mode.

In Browse mode records can be added to a database in one of two ways. You can add records to the end of the file by opening the Browse menu with ALT-B, and choosing Append Record. Note that there is a shortcut key, CTRL-P, for this menu option. When you choose the option (or press CTRL-P), a new, blank record appears at the end of the file, and the cursor appears in the first field of that record. You can enter the desired information and exit Browse mode when you are done by choosing Close from the File menu, by pressing CTRL-W, or by mouse-clicking on the close box.

The other way to add a record in Browse mode is with the INSERT command, which lets you place a new record anywhere in the database. There is no equivalent menu option; you simply enter **INSERT** as a command (you will have to switch to the Command window with CTRL-F1 to enter it). This will cause a new record to be inserted into the database at the present cursor location, and all existing records will be pushed down by one record.

Browse Menu Options

While in Browse mode, note that a new option, Browse, has been added to the menu bar at the top of the screen. Press ALT- B to open the Browse menu.

Its options are covered in detail in the following pages, and here is a brief overview of them.

- *Edit.* This option shows the database in the Browse window but in full-screen (edit) format, similar to the display that appears with the CHANGE or EDIT command.

- *Grid Off.* This option hides the vertical lines that normally appear between columns. Once selected, the name of this option changes to Grid On, and it can be reselected to restore the lines.

- *Unlink Partitions.* When a window is split into two parts or partitions, this option "unlinks" the two portions of the window, allowing independent movement in each.

- *Change Partitions.* When a window is split into two partitions, this makes the active partition of the window inactive and the inactive partition active.

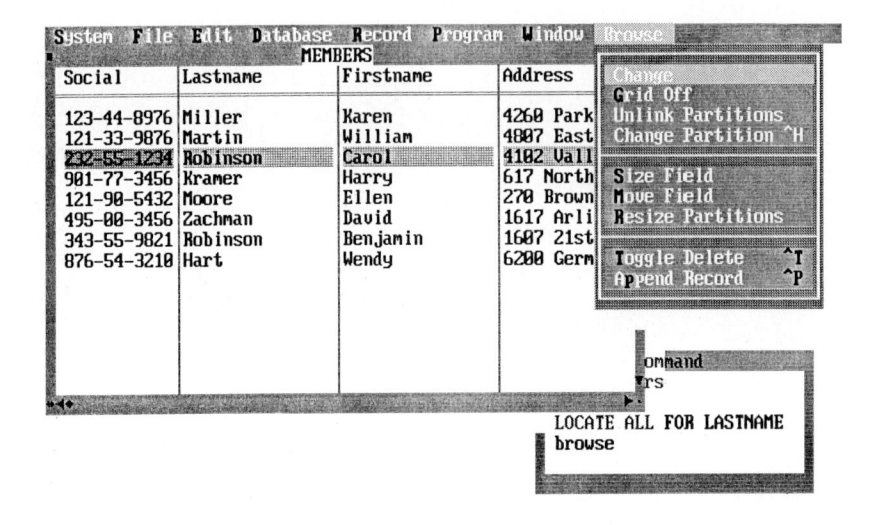

```
  System  File  Edit  Database  Record  Program  Window  Browse
                          MEMBERS                        Change
   Social     Lastname     Firstname    Address          Grid Off
                                                         Unlink Partitions
  123-44-8976 Miller      Karen        4260 Park         Change Partition ^H
  121-33-9876 Martin      William      4807 East
  232-55-1234 Robinson    Carol        4102 Vall
  901-77-3456 Kramer      Harry        617 North         Size Field
  121-90-5432 Moore       Ellen        270 Brown         Move Field
  495-00-3456 Zachman     David        1617 Arli         Resize Partitions
  343-55-9821 Robinson    Benjamin     1607 21st
  876-54-3210 Hart        Wendy        6200 Germ         Toggle Delete   ^T
                                                         Append Record   ^P

                                                    ommand
                                                   rs
                                              LOCATE ALL FOR LASTNAME
                                              browse
```

FIGURE 3-6. Browse menu

- *Size Field.* This resizes the field containing the cursor. Tab to the desired field, select the option, and use the arrow keys to change the size; then press any key (except the arrow keys) to complete the resizing.

- *Move Field.* This moves a field to a new location. Tab to the desired field, select the option, and use the LEFT or RIGHT ARROW keys to relocate the field. When done, press any key except the LEFT or RIGHT ARROW key.

- *Resize Partitions.* This lets you split a window into two parts, or if it is already split, lets you change the size of the partitions. You also use this option to restore a split window back to a single window. Choose the option, and then use the LEFT and RIGHT ARROW keys to open, close, or change the size of the partitions.

When done, press any key except the LEFT or RIGHT ARROW key.

- *Toggle Delete.* This lets you mark a record for deletion while in Browse mode. Place the cursor at the desired record, and then choose Toggle Delete to mark the record for deletion.

- *Append.* This adds a blank record to the end of the database.

Before proceeding, you will find it helpful to have a database to work with that contains more records than the sample one you created earlier. There is a simple way to create such a database: you can create a new file based on the existing one and copy records from the existing Videos file into the new file a number of times. Press ESC to exit the Browse window, and use the following commands now to create a larger database for use with Browse:

```
COPY STRUCTURE TO BIGFILE
USE BIGFILE
APPEND FROM MEMBERS
APPEND FROM MEMBERS
APPEND FROM MEMBERS
```

This will create a file with 24 records, enough to fill a screen while in Browse mode. Enter **BROWSE** to get back into Browse mode now.

Manipulating the Window

A significant plus of FoxPro's implementation of Browse is the ability to manipulate the size and contents of the Browse window. Open the Window menu and choose Zoom (or mouse-click on the zoom indicator) now to open the window to full-screen size (Figure 3-7), which allows the display of a maximum of 20 records at a time. You can now try the PGUP and PGDN keys to move throughout the database.

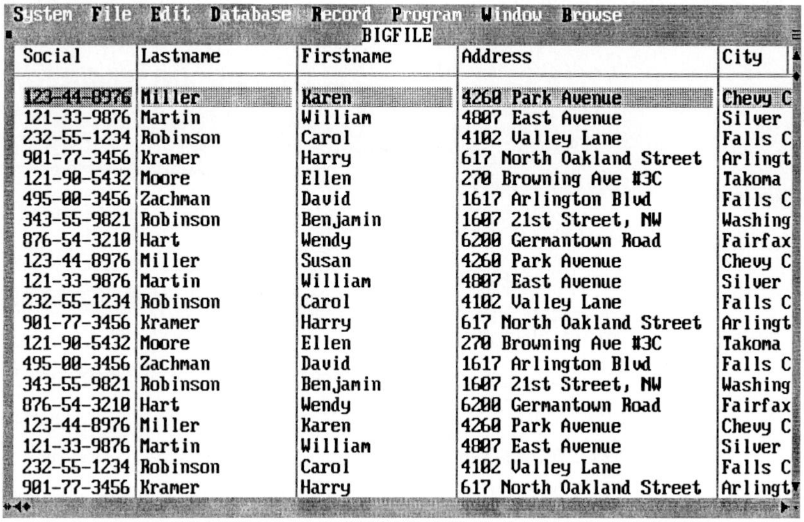

84   FoxPro Made Easy

System File Edit Database Record Program Window Browse				
BIGFILE				
Social	Lastname	Firstname	Address	City
123-44-8976	Miller	Karen	4260 Park Avenue	Chevy C
121-33-9876	Martin	William	4807 East Avenue	Silver
232-55-1234	Robinson	Carol	4102 Valley Lane	Falls C
901-77-3456	Kramer	Harry	617 North Oakland Street	Arlingt
121-90-5432	Moore	Ellen	270 Browning Ave #3C	Takoma
495-00-3456	Zachman	David	1617 Arlington Blvd	Falls C
343-55-9821	Robinson	Benjamin	1607 21st Street, NW	Washing
876-54-3210	Hart	Wendy	6200 Germantown Road	Fairfax
123-44-8976	Miller	Susan	4260 Park Avenue	Chevy C
121-33-9876	Martin	William	4807 East Avenue	Silver
232-55-1234	Robinson	Carol	4102 Valley Lane	Falls C
901-77-3456	Kramer	Harry	617 North Oakland Street	Arlingt
121-90-5432	Moore	Ellen	270 Browning Ave #3C	Takoma
495-00-3456	Zachman	David	1617 Arlington Blvd	Falls C
343-55-9821	Robinson	Benjamin	1607 21st Street, NW	Washing
876-54-3210	Hart	Wendy	6200 Germantown Road	Fairfax
123-44-8976	Miller	Karen	4260 Park Avenue	Chevy C
121-33-9876	Martin	William	4807 East Avenue	Silver
232-55-1234	Robinson	Carol	4102 Valley Lane	Falls C
901-77-3456	Kramer	Harry	617 North Oakland Street	Arlingt

FIGURE 3-7.   Browse window after Zoom

You can split the window into two portions with the Resize Partitions option. If you open the Browse menu and choose Resize Partitions, the small rectangle at the lower-left corner of the window will begin flashing. Begin pressing the RIGHT ARROW key repeatedly, and the window will split in two. Continue pressing the right arrow key until the Social, Lastname, and Firstname fields are visible. Then press any key (other than the arrow keys) to complete the operation.

Mouse users can split a window by dragging on the *split indicator* in the bottom scroll bar to the desired location. The split indicator is normally shaped like an arrow with two heads; when you choose the Resize Partitions option from the menu, it temporarily changes to a flashing rectangle.

With the window split, the portion of the window containing the cursor is the active portion. Try repeatedly using TAB and SHIFT-TAB now, and you will see that the active partition switches between the left and right sides. You can change partitions by choosing Change Partition from the Browse menu. Note that there is a shortcut key (CTRL-H) for this menu option. Mouse users can change partitions simply by clicking anywhere in the desired partition.

Using Edit in Browse

The Change option of the Browse menu can be used to display a record in Edit mode while you are still in a Browse window. This can be particularly useful for seeing records in both a tabular form and a full-record form at the same time (which you can do once you split a window). Make the right partition active now by mouse-clicking anywhere in the right partition or by pressing CTRL-H. Next, choose Change from the Browse menu. Note that the screen display in the right partition changes to Edit mode, as shown in Figure 3-8.

A major advantage of this type of display is that you can easily find records in the left partition, and see all of the fields for that corresponding record in the right partition. Press CTRL- H to make the left partition the active one, and try using the UP ARROW and DOWN ARROW keys to view different records. As you do this, you will see the same record appear in the right partition. Note that once you are using the Edit style of display in Browse, the first option on the Browse menu changes to "Browse." (This is only the case if the Change partition is the active partition.) You can then use the menu option to change the display back to a browse-style display.

The Grid Off option of the Browse menu can be used to remove the vertical lines that normally appear between fields when you use the browse style of display. Once the lines have been removed, you can restore them at any time by choosing Grid On from the Browse menu.

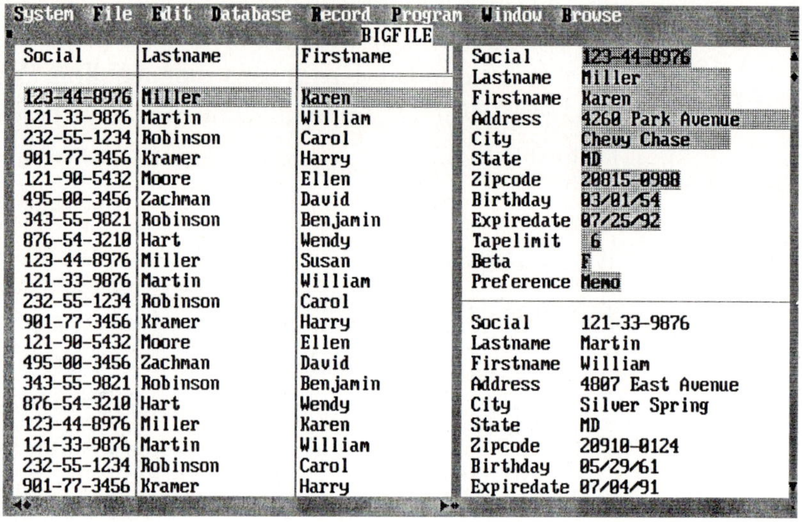

```
System File Edit Database Record Program Window Browse
                        BIGFILE
Social       |Lastname |Firstname |  Social      123-44-8976
                                     Lastname    Miller
                                     Firstname   Karen
123-44-8976  |Miller   |Karen     |  Address     4260 Park Avenue
121-33-9876  |Martin   |William   |  City        Chevy Chase
232-55-1234  |Robinson |Carol     |  State       MD
901-77-3456  |Kramer   |Harry     |  Zipcode     20815-0988
121-90-5432  |Moore    |Ellen     |  Birthday    03/01/54
495-00-3456  |Zachman  |David     |  Expiredate  07/25/92
343-55-9821  |Robinson |Benjamin  |  Tapelimit   6
876-54-3210  |Hart     |Wendy     |  Beta        F
123-44-8976  |Miller   |Susan     |  Preference  Memo
121-33-9876  |Martin   |William   |
232-55-1234  |Robinson |Carol     |
901-77-3456  |Kramer   |Harry     |  Social      121-33-9876
121-90-5432  |Moore    |Ellen     |  Lastname    Martin
495-00-3456  |Zachman  |David     |  Firstname   William
343-55-9821  |Robinson |Benjamin  |  Address     4807 East Avenue
876-54-3210  |Hart     |Wendy     |  City        Silver Spring
123-44-8976  |Miller   |Karen     |  State       MD
121-33-9876  |Martin   |William   |  Zipcode     20910-0124
232-55-1234  |Robinson |Carol     |  Birthday    05/29/61
901-77-3456  |Kramer   |Harry     |  Expiredate  07/04/91
```

FIGURE 3-8.   Edit mode in Browse window

Unlinked Partitions

As you move the cursor between records, both partitions display a corresponding movement. This happens because partitions are normally *linked,* or tied together with respective records. There may be times when you prefer to maintain independent control over the partitions. You can do so by choosing Unlink Partitions from the Browse menu. Once you do so, you can switch between partitions with CTRL-H or the mouse and move around in each partition independently. Mouse users will note that when partitions are unlinked, a second vertical scroll bar appears. The center scroll bar now controls movement in the left partition, and the right scroll bar controls movement in the right partition.

Open the Browse menu again, and you will note that the Unlink Partitions option has changed to Link Partitions. Choose it now to

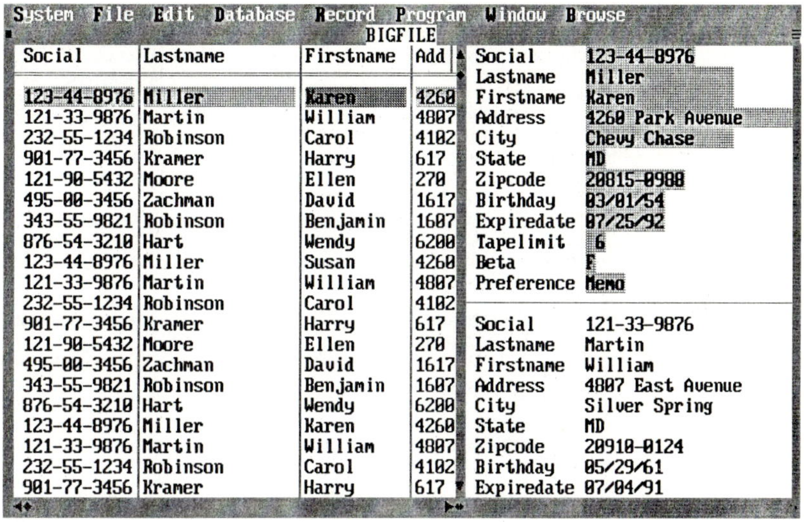

FIGURE 3-9. Fields after resizing

restore the link before proceeding. Then use CTRL-H or the mouse to make the left partition the active one.

Changing Field Sizes and Positions

You can change field widths and rearrange the position of the fields while you are in Browse mode. (Changing the position of the field does not affect the field's position in the database; only the screen display is affected.) You change field widths with the Size Field option of the Browse menu, and you change field locations with the Move Field option. Place the cursor in the Firstname field now, and choose Size Field from the Browse menu. Use the LEFT ARROW key to narrow the field size to roughly ten characters, and

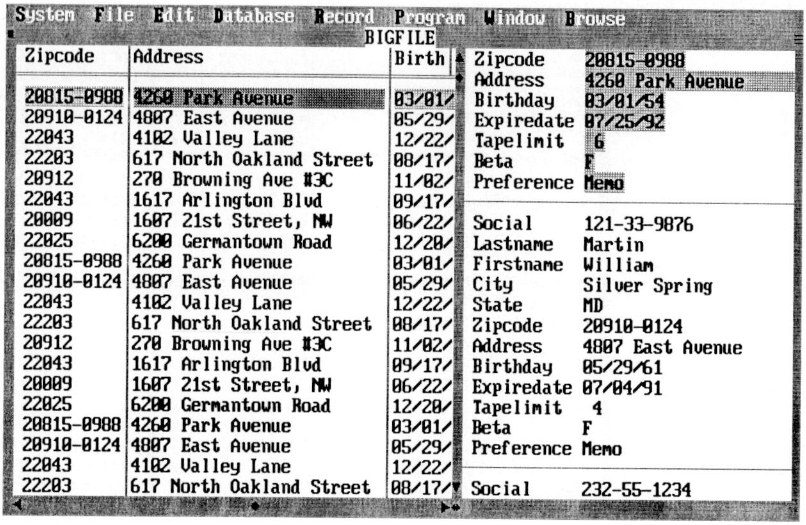

FIGURE 3-10. Fields after movement

then press any key (other than the arrow keys) to complete the resizing. The results will resemble those shown in Figure 3-9.

The normal procedure for moving a field is to tab over to the desired field, choose Move Field from the Browse menu, and relocate the field with the LEFT or RIGHT ARROW key. You can try this by placing the cursor in the Address field, choosing Move Field from the Browse menu, and pressing the RIGHT ARROW key three times. This will place Address between Zipcode and Birthday. Finally, press any key (other than the arrow keys) to end the process. If your window is still split between a browse-style display and an edit-style display, you will note that the field position has changed in both, as shown in Figure 3-10.

Before proceeding, press ESC to exit Browse mode.

USING BROWSE
WITH COMMANDS

You can enter the BROWSE command at the command level to get into Browse mode, and the same Browse menu options and key combinations described earlier can then be used to update records. There are also options that can be specified along with the BROWSE command when entered at the command level. These options provide ways to lock certain fields in place so that they are not lost from view when you pan with the CTRL and cursor keys. Other command-level options let you show or edit selected fields when using BROWSE.

Using the FIELDS option of the BROWSE command, you can name the fields that you want to display with BROWSE. This option is particularly helpful when you want to edit specific information while using BROWSE. The syntax for this form of the command is

BROWSE FIELDS *field1, field2,...field3*

As an example, you might wish to change the tape limit amounts to reflect new tape limits among some video club members. You only want to see the names and tape-limit amounts. Use ESC to get to the command level, and then try this command:

BROWSE FIELDS LASTNAME, FIRSTNAME, TAPELIMIT

The resulting display (Figure 3-11) shows only those fields that you named within the command. Since these are the only fields that are displayed, they are the only fields that can be edited at the present time.

```
 System File Edit Database Record Program Window Browse
                     BIGFILE
   Lastname     Firstname      Tapelimit
   Miller       Karen              6
   Martin       William            4
   Robinson     Carol              6
   Kramer       Harry              4
   Moore        Ellen              6
   Zachman      David              4
   Robinson     Benjamin           6
   Hart         Wendy              2
   Miller       Susan              6
   Martin       William            4
   Robinson     Carol              6
   Kramer       Harry              4
   Moore        Ellen              6
   Zachman      David              4
                                            ommand
                                            le
                                       browse
                                       browse fields lastname,
```

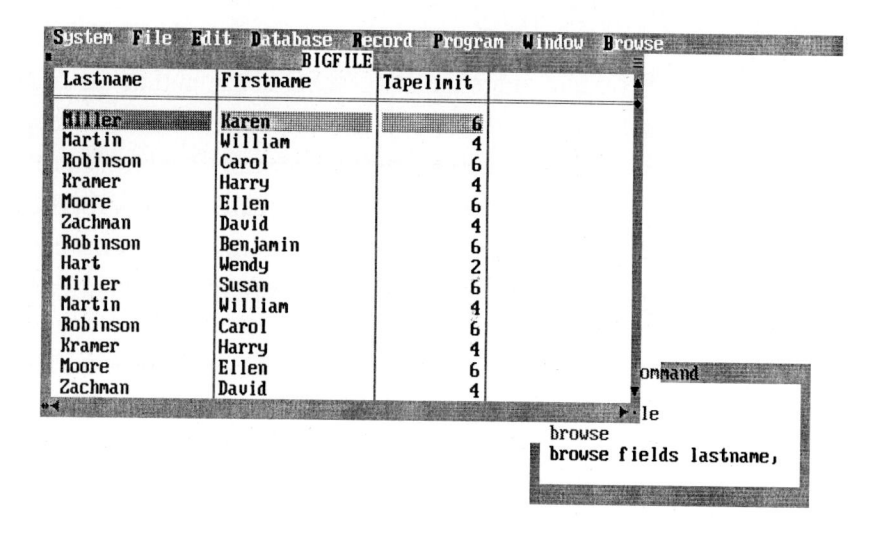

FIGURE 3-11. Selected fields within BROWSE

The FREEZE option of the BROWSE command lets you limit any editing to a specific field. This is a useful command to know, because there is no equivalent from the Browse menu. The FREEZE option comes in particularly handy when you must change one field in a number of records; when you do not use the option, ENTER moves you to the next column rather than the next field. When you use FREEZE, other fields are displayed, but only the specified field can be changed. The syntax for the command is

BROWSE FREEZE *fieldname*

To try the effect of this option, press ESC to exit the current Browse window, and then enter

BROWSE FREEZE EXPIREDATE

You will see that only the Expiredate field can be edited.

You can use the command-level options of the BROWSE command in combination with each other. For example, the command:

BROWSE FIELDS LASTNAME, CITY, STATE, EXPIREDATE
FREEZE EXPIREDATE

results in a display with the Lastname, City, State, and Expiredate fields visible, and just the Expiredate field available for editing.

Before proceeding, press ESC to close the Browse window. Then enter **USE MEMBERS** as a command to close the larger file you created earlier and get back into the video database.

DELETING RECORDS

FoxPro uses a combination of two menu options, or equivalent commands, to delete records. From the menus, these are the Delete option of the Record menu and the Pack option of the Database menu. From the command level, the two commands are DELETE and PACK.

The Delete option of the Record menu (or its command-level equivalent, the DELETE command) prepares a record for deletion but does not actually delete the record. This method allows you to mark as many records as you wish at one time for later deletion. By identifying records in this manner, FoxPro provides you with a built-in safeguard: you have the opportunity to change your mind and recall the record.

To mark a single record for deletion, first find the desired record with any of the search techniques discussed previously. Then open the Record menu with ALT-R and choose the Delete option. A dialog box appears, as shown in Figure 3-12. If you just want to mark the current record for deletion, you can ignore all of the options, tab over to the Delete button, and then press ENTER to

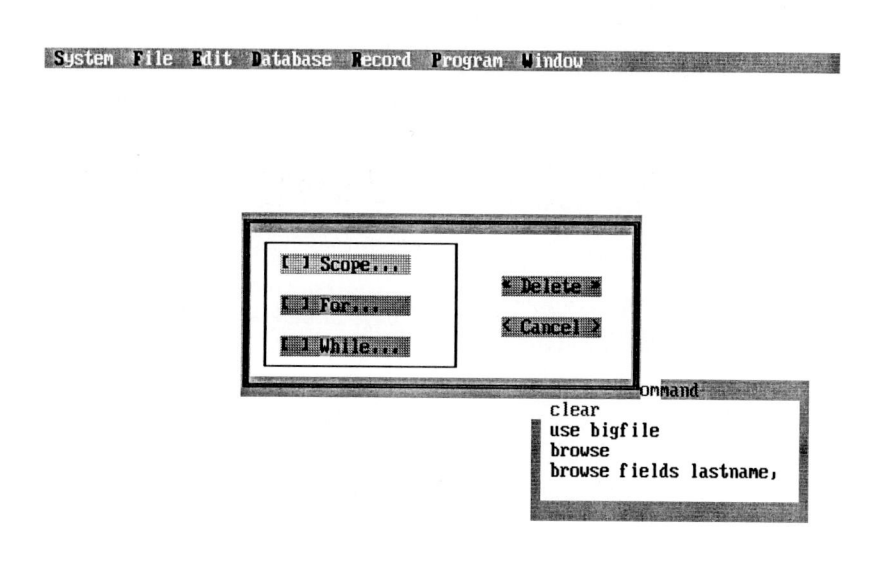

FIGURE 3-12. Delete dialog box

delete the record. For your information, the Scope option lets you choose a larger group of records for deletion; you can choose All records, Next *n,* where *n* is a number (such as the next five records), Record n where *n* is the record number of the record to be deleted, or Rest, which deletes all records from the current record to the end of the file. The While option of the dialog box is used with indexed files; it is discussed in Chapter 6, but it is actually not appropriate for use with simple deletions.

You can repeat the technique just described as often as necessary, deleting unwanted records. The records will remain in the database until you use the Pack option of the Database menu to make the deletions permanent. (If you are using the example database, *do not* permanently remove any records with Pack—they are used in additional examples later in the text.) Because the Pack option involves copying all records not marked for deletion to a temporary file, it can be quite time-consuming with large databases.

Command users can use the LOCATE command to find desired records, followed by the DELETE command to mark the records for deletion. To see how this works, press CTRL-W to exit Change mode. You may recall from earlier in the chapter that the format of the LOCATE command, when used with a simple search, is

LOCATE FOR *fieldname* = "*search-term*"

If you are searching a character field, you must surround the search term with quotes. Capitalization must also match inside the quotes; you will not find the desired record if you enter **Jackson** when what's really stored within the field is "jackson." If you are searching a numeric field, enter the number alone without any quotes. (The syntax for searching dates and memo fields will be discussed in Chapter 6.) As an example, if you are working with the video database, try the following:

LOCATE FOR LASTNAME = "Hart"

FoxPro should respond with the message "Record = 8." If you instead see an error message or the message "End of Locate scope," recheck your spelling of the command or the last name, and try the command again. Then, since record 8 is the one you want to mark for deletion, enter

DELETE

You will see the confirmation "1 record(s) deleted."

If you know the record number, you can specify the command DELETE RECORD *n,* where *n* is the number of the record to be deleted. Suppose that Mr. Kramer, listed in record 4, also needs to be removed from the list. Enter the command

DELETE RECORD 4

Again, the "1 record(s) deleted" message appears. Now enter the command

LIST LASTNAME, FIRSTNAME

and you will see that the marked records have not been removed from the database. When the LIST command is used, an asterisk appears beside the marked records, indicating that the records are marked for deletion.

If you decide that deleting a record is not the thing to do, you can use the RECALL command to undo the damage. For example, enter the following command to recall the fourth record:

RECALL RECORD 4

The confirmation "1 record recalled" appears. Now reenter the LIST LASTNAME, FIRSTNAME command. A shortcut is available here: by pressing the UP ARROW key, you can move the cursor within the Command window to the commands you entered earlier. When you see the desired command (in this case, LIST LASTNAME, FIRSTNAME), just press ENTER to repeat the command. Once you do so, the database will show that only record 8 is still marked for deletion. Note that the RECALL ALL command can be used to recall all records marked for deletion. (For now, leave record 8 marked for deletion.)

When a record has been marked for deletion, it remains in the database, and operations like SUM and COUNT (which will be covered later) can still use the record in calculations as if it had never been deleted. Also, the deleted record will still appear in your reports, which may not be what you had in mind. To avoid displaying and using records that have been marked for deletion, you can use the SET DELETED command. Enter

SET DELETED ON

Now repeat the LIST LASTNAME, FIRSTNAME command by pressing the UP ARROW key until you are at the command and then pressing ENTER. You will see that record 8, which is still marked for deletion, does not appear. To make the record visible again, enter

SET DELETED OFF

When you try the LIST command again, the record marked for deletion will be visible in the database.

There is no need to delete records one by one with the DELETE command. You can mark more than one record for deletion by specifying the number of records to be deleted. For example, enter the commands

GO 5
DELETE NEXT 2
LIST LASTNAME, FIRSTNAME

GO 5 moves the pointer to record 5; then DELETE NEXT 2 marks records 5 and 6 for deletion.

The RECALL command can be used in the same manner. Enter

GO 5
RECALL NEXT 2
LIST LASTNAME, FIRSTNAME

and records 5 and 6 will be unmarked. Before proceeding, enter the command

RECALL ALL

to recall any records that are still marked for deletion. Remember that after deleting records in your files, you must enter **PACK** (or choose the Pack option of the Database menu) to make your deletions permanent.

DELETING FILES

You can also delete files from within FoxPro. From the command level, you can use the DELETE FILE command. For example, the command

DELETE FILE NAMES2.DBF

would erase a file called NAMES2.DBF from the disk. Use such options for deleting files with care, because once a file has been deleted, you cannot recall it without special programs or techniques that are beyond the scope of this book.

GLOBAL REPLACEMENTS WITH COMMANDS

Suppose that you wanted to replace the five-digit ZIP codes with the new nine-digit ZIP codes for both members named Robinson. You can change the ZIP code for every Washington, DC, entry by adding options to the CHANGE command. With these options, you only need to use CHANGE once because it becomes a *global* command. A global command performs the operation of the command on the entire database, not just on a single record.

When used with the global options, the CHANGE command consists of a two-step process: first, CHANGE finds the proper field, and then it asks you to enter the correction. The format of the command is

CHANGE FIELDS *fieldname* FOR *keyfield* = "*keyname*"

where *fieldname* is the field where you want the changes to occur, and *keyfield* is the field where CHANGE searches for the occurrence of *keyname*. You must surround keyname with quotes.

In the following example you will use the CHANGE command to change the Zipcode field for each occurrence in the database that has the word "Robinson" within the Lastname field. Enter the following:

CHANGE FIELDS LASTNAME, ZIPCODE FOR LASTNAME = "Robinson"

The first record containing Robinson in the Lastname field appears. Notice that FoxPro only displays the fields that you named as part of the CHANGE command.

The cursor is flashing in the Lastname field, so you can move down to the Zipcode field and enter **22043-1234** as the new ZIP code for this record. After you fill the field, you will see the next record with Robinson in the Lastname field. Enter **20009-1010** and the screen form will vanish. To see the results, enter

LIST LASTNAME, CITY, ZIPCODE

The new ZIP codes you entered will be displayed, as shown here:

Record#	LASTNAME	CITY	ZIPCODE
1	Miller	Chevy Chase	20815-0988
2	Martin	Silver Spring	20910-0124
3	Robinson	Falls Church	22043-1234
4	Kramer	Arlington	22203
5	Moore	Takoma Park	20912
6	Zachman	Falls Church	22043
7	Robinson	Washington	20009-1010
8	Hart	Fairfax	22025

REPLACE operates very much like CHANGE, except that REPLACE won't ask you to type in the change after it finds the field. Instead, you specify the change within the command and it will be made automatically. The format of the command is

REPLACE [*scope*] *fieldname* WITH *field-replacement* FOR *condition*

The *scope* parameter is optional and is used to determine how many records REPLACE will look at. If ALL is used as the scope, REPLACE will look at all records; but if NEXT 5 is used as the scope, REPLACE will only look at the next five records from the pointer's current position. NEXT is always followed by the number of records REPLACE will look at. The *fieldname* parameter is the field where the change will occur, and *field-replacement* is what will be inserted if *keyfield,* which is the field REPLACE is searching for, matches *keyword*.

There is plenty going on with REPLACE, so it might be best described by an example. Enter the following:

REPLACE ALL CITY WITH "Miami" FOR CITY = "Falls Church"

This means "Search for all City fields containing the words 'Falls Church' and then replace those fields with the word 'Miami'." Next, enter

LIST LASTNAME, CITY

You'll see that the Falls Church members have been relocated to Miami. They probably would not enjoy the commute to work, so let's move them back. Enter the command

REPLACE ALL CITY WITH "Falls Church" FOR CITY = "Miami"

Again, enter

LIST LASTNAME, CITY

Now the City field is correct. The REPLACE command is very handy for updating salaries or prices on a global basis. If every employee in a personnel file is to receive a 50-cent per hour increase, do you really want to manually update each record? It would be much faster to use the REPLACE command to perform the task. Assuming a field named Salary in a personnel file, you could use a command like

REPLACE ALL SALARY WITH SALARY + .50

to quickly increase all salary amounts by 50 cents.

As you work with FoxPro, you'll find that REPLACE is a handy command for changing area codes, dollar amounts, and other similar applications. But you should be careful: REPLACE can wreak havoc on a database if used improperly. If you doubt whether REPLACE will have the desired effect, make a copy of the database file under a different name and experiment on the copy instead of the original. Or, you can use the CHANGE command as described earlier. CHANGE is a better command to use when you want to see the data and exercise some discretion regarding the changes.

MODIFYING THE STRUCTURE OF A DATABASE

You'll often use a database for a while, and then decide to enlarge a field, delete a field, or add a field for another category. You can make these changes in the structure of a database. From the command level, this is done with the MODIFY STRUCTURE command. From the menus, you choose the Setup option of the Database menu; when the dialog box appears, you select Structure—Modify. When you change the structure of a database, FoxPro creates a new, empty database according to your instructions, and then copies the old database into the new database.

If the manager at Generic Videos suddenly decides that the database should include all of the members' phone numbers, you can add a field for them. To make this change, from the command level enter

MODIFY STRUCTURE

or open the Database menu with ALT-D, and choose the Setup option. When the dialog box appears, select Structure—Modify. With either approach, you will see the structure of the Generic Videos database (Figure 3-13).

Since you want to add a field, move the cursor to the Birthday field with TAB and the DOWN ARROW key. You will enter the field name, type, and width exactly as you did when you created the database in Chapter 2, but before you do, you need room to add a new field. While it is easiest to add new fields at the end of the existing list of fields, you can add them anywhere you desire by using the double arrows that appear just to the left of the field names. You mouse-click or tab to the double arrow at the desired location; then you press the INS key to insert a field or the DEL key to delete a field.

Use TAB or SHIFT-TAB to go to the double arrow to the left of the Birthday field and press the INS key, and a new field will appear above the Birthday field. Since you want to enter phone numbers, the word "phone" would be a good title for the field. Enter **Phone**. Once you press ENTER, the cursor will move to the field type category. You want to use C for the character types (since phone numbers are never used in calculations, they need not be numeric), so press TAB to move on to the next category.

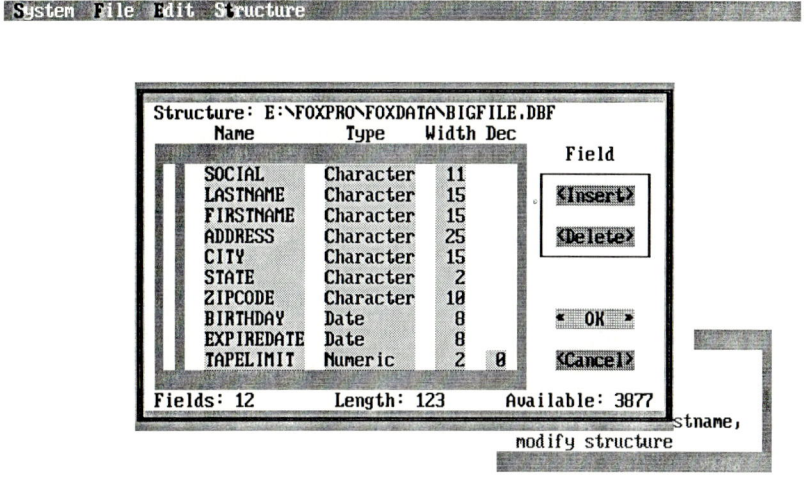

```
┌─System─File─Edit─Structure──────────────────────────────────┐

        ┌─Structure: E:\FOXPRO\FOXDATA\BIGFILE.DBF──────────┐
        │     Name          Type      Width Dec             │
        │                                         Field     │
        │    SOCIAL        Character    11                  │
        │    LASTNAME      Character    15       <Insert>   │
        │    FIRSTNAME     Character    15                  │
        │    ADDRESS       Character    25       <Delete>   │
        │    CITY          Character    15                  │
        │    STATE         Character     2                  │
        │    ZIPCODE       Character    10                  │
        │    BIRTHDAY      Date          8       ◄  OK  ►   │
        │    EXPIREDATE    Date          8                  │
        │    TAPELIMIT     Numeric       2    0   <Cancel>  │
        │                                                   │
        │  Fields: 12     Length: 123    Available: 3877    │
        └───────────────────────────────────────────────────┘stname,
                                              modify structure
```

FIGURE 3-13. The Generic Videos database structure

At the Width category, enter **12**. This will leave room for a ten-digit phone number and two hyphens. You could, if needed, change any of the field widths for the existing fields by moving to the desired field and entering a new value in the Width column.

Moving Fields

While it is not necessary in this example to move a field to a different location in the structure, you can easily do so if you desire. To move an existing field, delete the field at its old location, and then insert the same field name and specifications at the new location.

Saving the Changes

When you modify a database, data will be returned from the fields of the temporary file to the fields in the modified database automatically only if the field names and field types match. If you change the type of a field, FoxPro may not restore the data in that particular field, since it doesn't always know how to convert the data type. FoxPro will make the conversion when it can. For example, if you change a character field into a numeric field, all valid numeric entries will be converted. However, if you were to change a numeric field into a logical field, the data in the numeric field would be lost because the two field types have nothing in common.

Once you have completed your desired changes to the database structure, tab to or click on the OK button in the dialog box. You will see the following confirmation prompt:

Copy old records to new structure?
<< OK >>   << Cancel >>

This indicates that FoxPro is ready to copy the data from the old file into the modified database. Select OK from the prompt, and after a short delay (during which FoxPro automatically rebuilds the database), the Structure dialog box will disappear. You can tab to the OK button in the remaining dialog box to exit the operation. Now enter the command

BROWSE FIELDS LASTNAME, FIRSTNAME, PHONE FREEZE PHONE

Press PGUP, and you'll see that all of the Phone fields are present but empty. To complete the database, type in the phone numbers for the members as shown here:

Lastname	Firstname	Phone
Miller	Karen	301-555-6678
Martin	William	301-555-2912
Robinson	Carol	703-555-8778
Kramer	Harry	703-555-6874
Moore	Ellen	301-555-0201
Zachman	David	703-555-5432
Robinson	Benjamin	202-555-4545
Hart	Wendy	703-555-1201

Had this field been planned in advance during the database design stage outlined in Chapter 1, you wouldn't have the inconvenience of returning to each record to type in a phone number.

Note: If you rename a field and change its location in the database structure at the same time by inserting or deleting fields, FoxPro will not restore the data in that particular field because it doesn't know where to find the data. FoxPro uses either the field name or the position of the field in the database structure to transfer existing data. If both are changed, the existing data is discarded. If you need to change both the name of a field and its location in a database structure, perform the task in two steps. Change the field name and exit the Modify Structure process; then repeat the MODIFY STRUCTURE command and make any other changes to the file structure.

CREATING THE RENTALS FILE

Before proceeding to the next chapter, you should create an additional database. This database, called RENTALS, will contain a listing of videotapes rented by the members of Generic Videos. Later chapters will make use of this file along with various examples for working with more than one database file.

To create the file, enter the command

CREATE RENTALS

When the Database Structure window appears, enter the following field information.

Field	Field Name	Type	Width
1	Social	Character	11
2	Title	Character	30
3	Dayrented	Date	8
4	Returned	Date	8

Once the fields have been entered in the structure, save the new database structure by pressing CTRL-W. When the "Add new records now?" message appears, choose OK to begin adding new records to the file. Add the following records, and then press CTRL-W to exit Append mode when you are done.

Social	Title	Day rented	Returned
123-44-8976	Star Trek IV	03/05/90	03/06/90
121-33-9876	Lethal Weapon II	03/02/90	03/06/90
232-55-1234	Who Framed Roger Rabbit	03/06/90	03/09/90
901-77-3456	Beverly Hills Cop II	03/04/90	03/05/90
121-90-5432	Dirty Rotten Scoundrels	03/01/90	03/06/90
495-00-3456	Young Einstein	03/04/90	03/09/90
343-55-9821	When Harry Met Sally	03/06/90	03/12/90
876-54-3210	Lethal Weapon II	03/07/90	03/08/90
123-44-8976	Friday 13th Part XXVII	03/14/90	03/16/90
121-33-9876	Licence To Kill	03/15/90	03/17/90
232-55-1234	When Harry Met Sally	03/17/90	03/19/90
901-77-3456	Coming To America	03/14/90	03/18/90

121-90-5432	When Harry Met Sally	03/16/90	03/17/90
495-00-3456	Star Trek V	03/18/90	03/18/90
343-55-9821	Young Einstein	03/19/90	03/20/90
876-54-3210	Licence To Kill	03/16/90	03/18/90

4

SORTING AND INDEXING A DATABASE

Sorting
Indexing
Searching for Specifics
Index Tips and Unusual Cases

When you want to produce reports from your data, you will seldom want the data coming out to be in the same order as the data going in. Most databases contain records entered in a random manner; as different customers sign up or as different employees are hired, new records are added to the database. When you want a report, on the other hand, you usually want it in a specific order; perhaps alphabetically by name or by expiration date. With an inventory database, you may want to see the records arranged by part number. For a mailing list, a database might need to generate labels by order of ZIP code.

Databases can be arranged in a number of ways, with the SORT and INDEX commands. The first portion of this chapter teaches you how to sort and discusses some disadvantages that accompany the sorting process. The second portion of the chapter covers indexing, which offers some advantages over sorting while accomplishing the same overall result.

Most of the commands in this chapter will be executed at the command level, rather than through the menus. You can perform sorting and indexing tasks with either method, but many of the more complex sorting and indexing operations can be performed more quickly with commands. Once you are familiar with the syntax of the commands, you can use them within your own FoxPro programs. Because it is good to have an idea of both methods, the chapter will include both methods; use whichever method you are comfortable with for your own use.

SORTING

When FoxPro sorts a database, it creates a new file with a different filename. If you were to sort a database of names in alphabetical order, the new file would contain all the records that were in the old file, but they would be arranged in alphabetical order as shown in Figure 4-1.

The format for the SORT command is

SORT ON *fieldname* [/A/C/D] TO *new-filename*

From the menus, you open the Database menu, choose the Sort option, and then fill in the desired fields for the sort order. A new file by the name of *new filename* is created, sorted by the field that you specify. If you specify the /A option, the file will be sorted in *ascending order*. This order places character fields in alphabetical order, numeric fields in numerical order, and date fields in chronological order (earliest to latest). If you use the /D option, character fields are sorted in *descending order* (Z to A), numeric fields from highest to lowest, and date fields in reverse chronological order (from latest to earliest). You cannot sort on memo fields. If you do

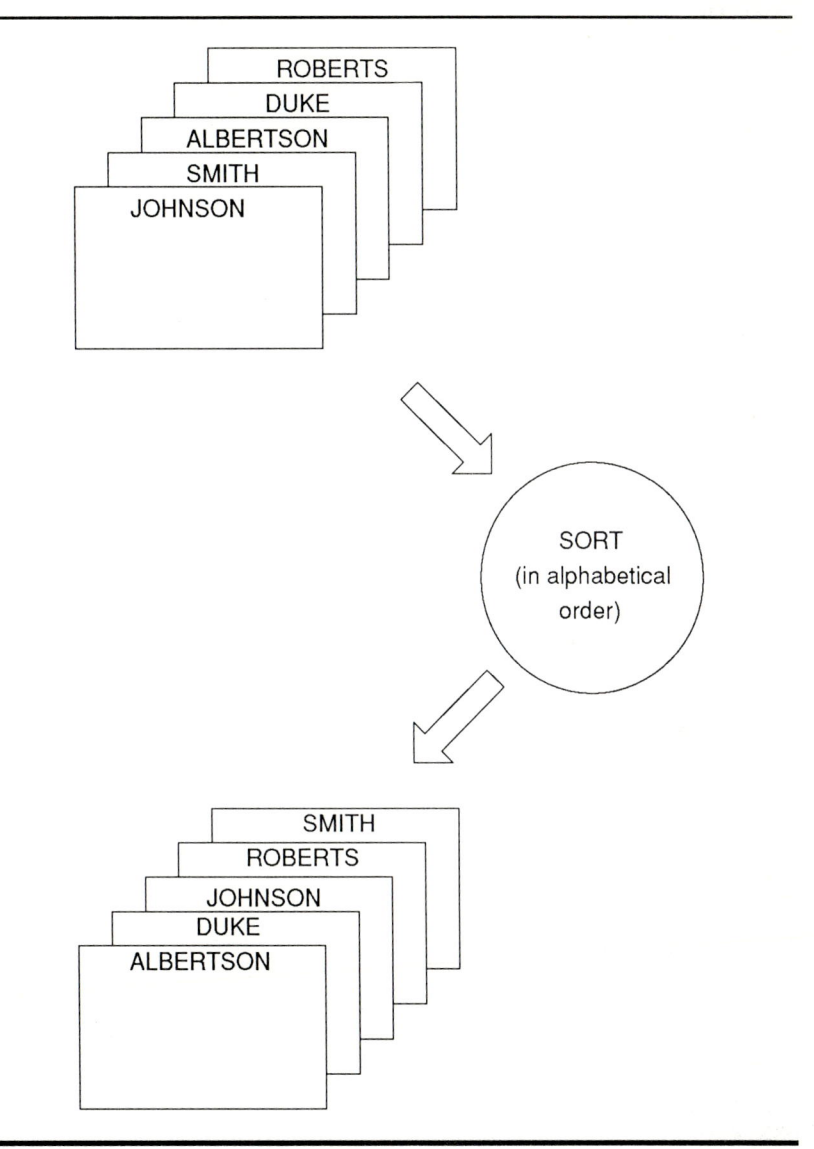

FIGURE 4-1. Sorting records in a database

not use either /A or /D, FoxPro assumes that ascending order is your preference. Sorts are also normally in ASCII order, with uppercase letters treated differently than lowercase letters. ASCII order ascending specifies A through Z, then a through z. ASCII order descending specifies Z through A, then z through a. If you want uppercase and lowercase letters to be treated equally in the sorting order, include the /C option for character/dictionary.

Use the SORT command to alphabetize the Generic Videos database by members' last names. Enter the following:

USE MEMBERS
SORT ON LASTNAME TO MEMBERS2

The file has been sorted, but you are still using the original MEMBERS file at this point. To see the results, you must open the new file. Try the following commands:

USE MEMBERS2
LIST LASTNAME

The results are shown here:

Record#	LASTNAME
1	Hart
2	Kramer
3	Martin
4	Miller
5	Moore
6	Robinson
7	Robinson
8	Zachman

The old file, MEMBERS, still exists in its unchanged form. The sorting operation has created a new file (called MEMBERS2) that is in alphabetical order. Remember, a file cannot be sorted into itself in FoxPro; each time a sort is performed, a new file must be created. Enter **USE MEMBERS** to switch back to the original file.

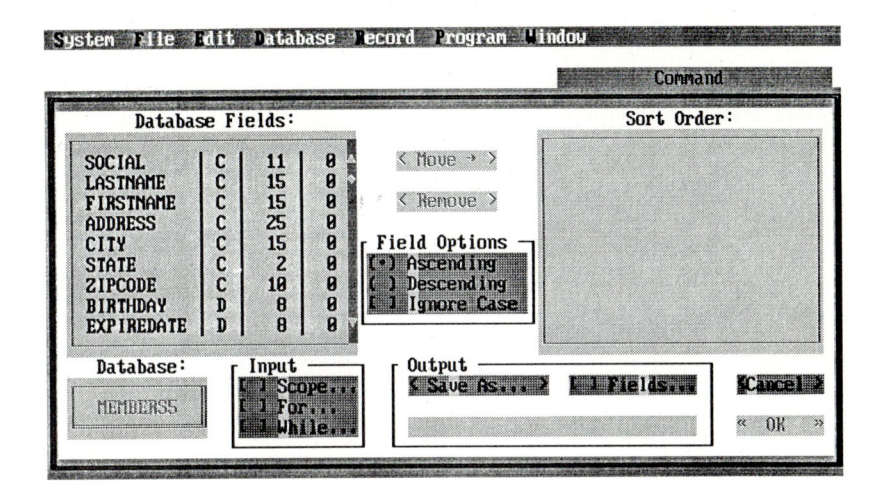

FIGURE 4-2. Sort dialog box

Now try a sort option from the menus. Open the Database menu with ALT-D, and choose Sort. The Sort dialog box will be displayed (Figure 4-2). In the upper-left part of the dialog box is the Database Fields list box, which lets you choose desired fields on which the sort will be based. The center portion of the dialog box contains a Field Options box; this lets you select ascending or descending order, and whether FoxPro should ignore case (sorting upper- and lowercase letters together) or sort uppercase before lowercase. As you select fields from the Database Fields list box, they are added to the Sort Order box on the right side of the dialog box.

The Input box at the bottom center of the dialog box lets you add a Scope, For, or While clause to limit records included in the sorted file. The Output box at the lower-right corner of the dialog box contains a Save As entry for the filename to be assigned to the sorted file, along with a Fields option. When chosen, the Fields option lets you specify a list of fields that will be included in the sorted file. When this option is chosen, all fields are included in the sorted file (the default).

For this example, a sort is needed on the expiration-date field. Tab to the Database Fields list box, and select Expiredate with the cursor and ENTER keys. Once selected, the field name, preceded by the database name (MEMBERS->), appears in the Sort Order list box. Ascending order, which is the default shown in the Fields Option box, is fine for this example. No Scope or For clauses are needed, since all records are desired. Tab to the entry space after the Fields button, and enter **MEMBERS3** as the filename. Then select OK from the dialog box.

In a few moments, you'll see a message indicating the completion of the sorting process. Enter

```
USE MEMBERS3
LIST LASTNAME, EXPIREDATE
```

You will then see the following:

Record#	LASTNAME	EXPIREDATE
1	Zachman	09/19/90
2	Kramer	12/22/90
3	Martin	07/04/91
4	Robinson	09/17/91
5	Miller	07/25/92
6	Hart	10/19/92
7	Robinson	09/05/93
8	Moore	11/17/94

It shows that the records in this new file are arranged in the order of expiration date, with the earliest dates first.

Enter **USE MEMBERS** and try the SORT command with the /D option (for descending order) on the Lastname field by entering

SORT ON LASTNAME /D TO MEMBERS4

To see the results, you need to list the new file you created. Enter this:

USE MEMBERS4
LIST LASTNAME

The results should be as follows:

Record#	LASTNAME
1	Zachman
2	Robinson
3	Robinson
4	Moore
5	Miller
6	Martin
7	Kramer
8	Hart

Return to MEMBERS by entering **USE MEMBERS**. For an example of numerical sorting, enter

SORT ON TAPELIMIT TO MEMBERS5

When the sorting process is complete, enter

USE MEMBERS5
LIST LASTNAME, TAPELIMIT

You should then see the following:

Record#	LASTNAME	TAPELIMIT
1	Robinson	2
2	Hart	2
3	Martin	4
4	Kramer	4
5	Zachman	4
6	Miller	6
7	Robinson	6
8	Moore	6

This shows the records arranged by the contents of the Tapelimit field, in ascending order.

Before going on to consider the topic of sorting on multiple fields, you may want to perform some housekeeping by deleting the example files you just created. This can easily be done from the command level. First, enter

USE MEMBERS

to close the file you are currently working with and open the original MEMBERS database. (Database files must be closed before you can erase them.) Then enter these commands to erase the database and accompanying memo field files:

DELETE FILE MEMBERS2.DBF
DELETE FILE MEMBERS3.DBF
DELETE FILE MEMBERS4.DBF
DELETE FILE MEMBERS5.DBF

DELETE FILE MEMBERS2.FPT
DELETE FILE MEMBERS3.FPT
DELETE FILE MEMBERS4.FPT
DELETE FILE MEMBERS5.FPT

Sorting on Multiple Fields

Sometimes you may need to sort on more than one field. For example, if you alphabetize a list of names that is divided into

Firstname and Lastname fields, you would not want to sort only on the Lastname field if there were three people with the last name of Williams. You would also have to sort on the Firstname field to find the correct ordering of the three Williamses. Fortunately, FoxPro can sort on more than one field. From the command level, this can be done by listing the fields as part of the SORT command, separating them with commas. The field that is sorted first would be listed first. From the menus, you can sort on multiple fields by choosing more than one field name from the dialog box for the database fields. You can also sort on a combination of different types of fields, such as a numeric field and a character field, at the same time.

As an example, consider the recent sort shown by tape limit. While the tape limits were in order, there were a large number of members with the same tape limit, and the members within the tape-limit group fall in random order. Sorting the file in order of tape limit, and within equal tape-limit groups by order of their last names, would provide a more logical listing.

First try it from the menus. Open the Database menu, and choose Sort. When the dialog box appears, tab to the Database Fields list box, highlight Tapelimit, and press ENTER. Then highlight Lastname, and press ENTER. The Tapelimit and Lastname fields will appear in the Sort Order list box at the right side of the dialog box. This indicates that the sort will take place by tape limit, and where the tape limits are the same, by last name.

Tab to the output portion of the dialog box, and enter **MEMBERS2** as the filename. Then select OK. When the sorting process is complete, choose Open from the File menu, and choose MEMBERS2 as the name of the new file to open. Next, open the Database menu and choose Browse. You will see the data sorted in order of tape limit and last name, as shown in Figure 4-3. (In the figure, the Browse window has been split to allow the Lastname and Tapelimit fields to be viewed at the same time.) When you're done viewing the data, press ESC to get out of Browse mode.

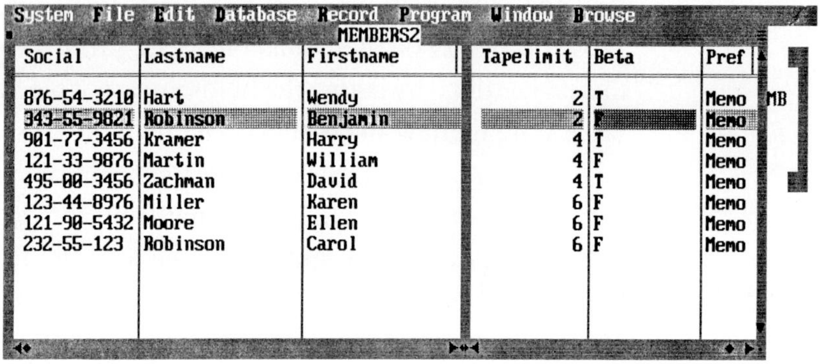

116   FoxPro Made Easy

```
System File Edit Database Record Program Window Browse
                         MEMBERS2
Social       Lastname   Firstname   Tapelimit  Beta  Pref
876-54-3210  Hart       Wendy            2     T     Memo   MB
343-55-9821  Robinson   Benjamin         2     F     Memo
901-77-3456  Kramer     Harry            4     T     Memo
121-33-9876  Martin     William          4     F     Memo
495-00-3456  Zachman    David            4     T     Memo
123-44-8976  Miller     Karen            6     F     Memo
121-90-5432  Moore      Ellen            6     F     Memo
232-55-123   Robinson   Carol            6     F     Memo
```

FIGURE 4-3.   File sorted by Salary and Lastname fields

To do this type of sort from the command level, the format for the command would be

SORT ON *1st-field* /A/C/D,*2nd field* /A/C/D...
last-field /A/C/D TO *new-filename*

so you could perform the same sort by getting to the command level and entering commands like this:

USE MEMBERS
SORT ON TAPELIMIT, LASTNAME /C TO MEMBERS2

The database would be sorted on both fields, in ascending order because the /D option has not been specified. The /C option was included, so the sort would be in character/dictionary rather than ASCII order.

To see the results of a descending-order sort on multiple fields, enter these commands:

USE MEMBERS
SORT ON TAPELIMIT /D, LASTNAME /D TO MEMBERS2

Because you are now trying to overwrite a file you already created (MEMBERS2.DBF), you will see a dialog box warning you that the file exists. Select Yes from the dialog box to tell FoxPro that you want to overwrite the previous file, and the sort will occur. To see the results, enter

USE MEMBERS2
LIST LASTNAME, TAPELIMIT

The results this time resemble the following:

Record#	LASTNAME	TAPELIMIT
1	Robinson	6
2	Moore	6
3	Miller	6
4	Zachman	4
5	Martin	4
6	Kramer	4
7	Robinson	2
8	Hart	2

The file is sorted in descending order by tape limit; and where the entries in the Tapelimit field are equal, in descending order by last names. In this sort, the Tapelimit field is the *primary field*. A primary field is the field that will be sorted first by the SORT command. After the database has been sorted by the primary field, if there is any duplicate information in the first field, SORT will sort the duplicate information by the second field listed in the command, known as the *secondary field*. It is possible to sort further with additional secondary fields; you can, in fact, sort with all fields in the database. For example, the commands:

```
USE MEMBERS
SORT ON STATE, CITY, TAPELIMIT, LASTNAME TO MASTER
```

would create a database called MASTER that would alphabetize records by states, sort each state by city, and sort each city by tape-limit amounts. If there were any duplicate entries at this point, the last names will be sorted in ascending order. In this example, State is the primary sort field, while City, Tapelimit, and Lastname are secondary sort fields.

Sorting a Subset of a Database

Adding a qualifying FOR statement to a SORT command lets you produce a sorted file that contains only a specific subset of the records in the database. The format for the SORT command when used in this manner is

SORT ON *fieldname* [A/C/D] TO *new-filename* FOR *condition*

For an example, let's produce a new database sorted by last names and containing only those records with Virginia addresses. Enter the following commands:

```
SORT TO VAPERSON ON LASTNAME FOR STATE = "VA"
USE VAPERSON
LIST LASTNAME, STATE
```

The results are shown here:

Record#	LASTNAME	STATE
1	Hart	VA
2	Kramer	VA
3	Robinson	VA
4	Zachman	VA

This display shows the result of the qualifying FOR condition. The new database contains only the records of members located in Virginia.

More examples of conditional use of the SORT command include the following:

SORT TO MYDATA ON LASTNAME, TAPELIMIT FOR TAPELIMIT < = 4

SORT TO PACIFIC ON ZIP FOR ZIP >="90000"

Once you know the syntax of these commands, using them can be much faster than using the menus. To do this type of selective sort from the menus, you would have to select various field names and For clauses from the pick lists within the dialog box. In the time it takes to get through half the options, you could have entered the entire command from the command level to do the job.

Sorting Selected Fields to a File

You can create a sorted file that includes selected fields from a database by including a list of fields with the SORT command. This can be quite useful for creating files that will be used by other software, such as a word processor for creating form letters. You might want to create a file in alphabetical order, containing only names and addresses and excluding all other fields. The syntax of the SORT command, when used in this manner, is

SORT TO *filename* ON *expression* FIELDS *list-of-fields*

As an example, you could create a file with only the names and addresses from the MEMBERS database with a command like the following:

SORT TO MYFILE ON LASTNAME, FIRSTNAME FIELDS LASTNAME, FIRSTNAME, ADDRESS, CITY, STATE, ZIPCODE

The resultant sorted file, called MYFILE, would contain only the Lastname, Firstname, Address, City, State, and Zipcode fields.

Why Sort?

Once you've learned all about sorting with FoxPro, you should know why you should *not* sort a database—at least not very often. Sorting can be very time-consuming, particularly when you are sorting large files. Sorting also uses a lot of disk space. Each time a sort occurs, FoxPro creates a new file that will be as large as the original, unless you limit the fields included or the records processed with a For clause. For this reason, you must limit the database to no more than half the free space on the disk if you are going to sort it.

Adding records to a database merely complicates matters. After you add records, chances are that the database must be sorted to maintain the desired order. If you are sorting multiple fields, the sorting time can become noticeable. However, there is a more efficient way of arranging a database alphabetically, numerically, or chronologically: by using index files.

INDEXING

An *index file* consists of at least one field from a database. The field is sorted alphabetically, numerically, or chronologically, and with each entry in the field is the corresponding record number

Sorting and Indexing a Database

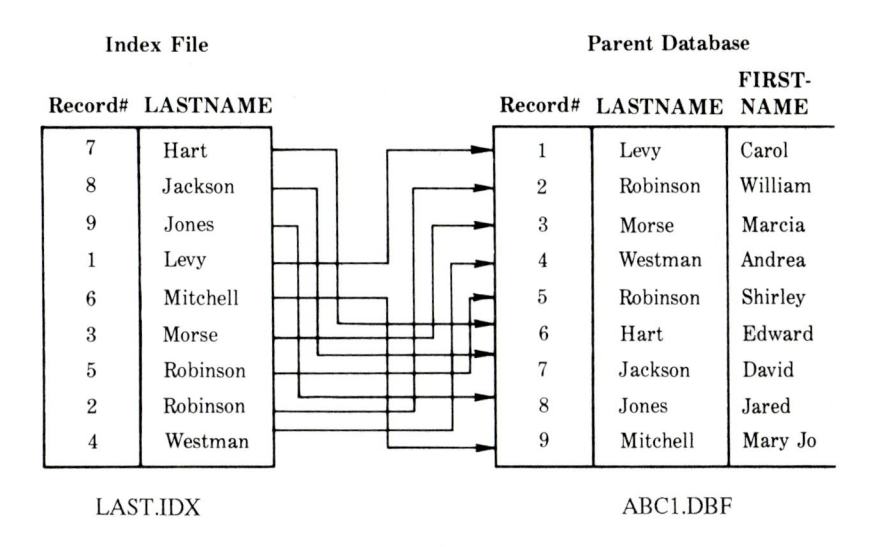

Index File			Parent Database	
Record#	LASTNAME	Record#	LASTNAME	FIRST-NAME
7	Hart	1	Levy	Carol
8	Jackson	2	Robinson	William
9	Jones	3	Morse	Marcia
1	Levy	4	Westman	Andrea
6	Mitchell	5	Robinson	Shirley
3	Morse	6	Hart	Edward
5	Robinson	7	Jackson	David
2	Robinson	8	Jones	Jared
4	Westman	9	Mitchell	Mary Jo

LAST.IDX   ABC1.DBF

FIGURE 4-4. Index file alphabetized by last name and parent directory that is organized by ZIP code

used to reference the record in the *parent* database (Figure 4-4). In effect, an index file is a virtual sort of the parent database, since none of the records in the parent database are sorted.

Just as a book index is a separate section that indicates where information is located, a FoxPro index file is a separate file that contains information regarding the location of individual records in the parent database. When the database file is opened along with the index file, the first record to be retrieved is not the first record in the parent database; instead, it is the first record listed in the index. The next record retrieved will be the second record listed in the index, and so on. Remember, indexing does not affect the order of the parent database.

From the command level, the general format of the INDEX command is similar to the format of the SORT command:

INDEX ON *expression* TO *index-filename*
[FOR *condition*] [UNIQUE]

The index command produces a single .IDX index file containing the index information. FoxPro appends the extension .IDX to all index files. Note that Ashton-Tate's dBASE III and III PLUS products use an .NDX extension for index files. dBASE IV can use index files with either an .NDX extension or an .MDX extension. If you attempt to open a dBASE database and accompanying .NDX index file under FoxPro, FoxPro will immediately rebuild the index, using its own .IDX extension.

A simple use of the syntax, INDEX ON *fieldname* TO *index-filename,* creates an index file based on the named field, with all records included in the index. The UNIQUE clause, if added, causes a *unique index* to be constructed. Such an index will not contain any duplicates of the index expression. You would use this type of index to intentionally hide any accidental duplicate records. For example, if a social security field were used to build the index and two records contained the same social security number, the second occurrence would be omitted from the index. The FOR expression lets you build a selective index, which contains only those records that meet a specified condition.

Creating an Index

Suppose you need to arrange the membership list in order by city for Generic Videos. You can create an index file by entering the following commands:

```
USE MEMBERS
INDEX ON CITY TO TOWNS
```

Enter **LIST LASTNAME, CITY** and you will see the result of the new index file:

Record#	LASTNAME	CITY
4	Kramer	Arlington
1	Miller	Chevy Chase
8	Hart	Fairfax
3	Robinson	Falls Church
6	Zachman	Falls Church
2	Martin	Silver Spring
5	Moore	Takoma Park
7	Robinson	Washington

Notice that the record numbers that indicate the order of the records in the database itself are not in order. The command you entered creates an index file, TOWNS.IDX, containing the index information. Any index file you create is automatically made active immediately after its creation; so the order of the records displayed with the LIST command is now controlled by the new index.

It's good practice to give index files a name related in some manner to the field that has been indexed. This helps you and others keep track of how the file was indexed and what field was used.

From the menus, you can index a file by choosing the New option of the File menu. When the dialog box appears, choose Index, and then choose OK. This causes the Index On dialog box to appear, as shown in Figure 4-5. It contains a field list from which you can select a field to base the index on. If you need to base the index on an expression (such as a combination of fields), you can manually enter the expression in the Expr window. Or you can tab over to Expr and press ENTER to bring up the Expression Builder to create the index expression. Expressions can be complex and can include field names, functions, and operators. (Examples of indexing with complex expressions are provided later in this chapter.) After you enter the expression used to build the index, you choose OK from the dialog box to exit the Expression Builder and return to the Index On dialog box.

The Unique check box lets you select a unique index, in which duplicate entries of the indexed field or expression are ignored. (This is equivalent to the UNIQUE clause used with the INDEX

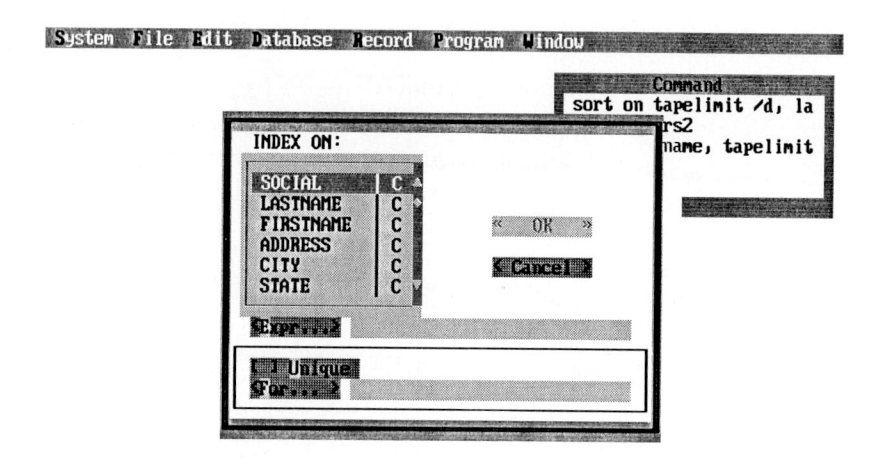

FIGURE 4-5. Index on dialog box

ON command.) The For entry lets you specify an expression to limit records that are stored in the index; this is the equivalent of adding a FOR clause to the INDEX ON command. For example, entering an expression like

STATE = "MD"

in the For window would limit the resultant index to those records with MD in the STATE field.

To try indexing from the menus, select New from the File menu. When the dialog box appears, choose Index, and then choose OK. In a moment, the Index On dialog box will appear. Choose Lastname from the Field Names list box. Once you select Lastname, it will appear in the Expr window. Tab to the OK button and press ENTER to accept the index expression. The dialog box will vanish, and another dialog box will appear, prompting you for a filename.

Enter **BYNAMES** as the filename for the index, and select OK to create the index. When the indexing is completed, choose Browse from the Database menu to view the file. It will appear in order by last name. Before continuing, press ESC to leave Browse mode.

Selective Indexing

You can use the FOR clause with the INDEX ON command (or the For expression window of the Index On dialog box) to add a clause that limits the records stored in the index. When used from the command level, the syntax for this INDEX command is

INDEX ON *expression* TO *filename* FOR *condition*

where the condition used with FOR is any expression that evaluates to a logical true or false.

This is a powerful FoxPro option that can, in effect, filter unwanted records from the database and place records in order at the same time. The SET FILTER command along with a simple use of the INDEX command would accomplish the same result, but assuming an updated index already exists, using FOR with INDEX ON is faster than using SET FILTER. As an example, if you wanted to produce a report of members in the videos database who lived in Maryland or Virginia, indexed in ZIP code order, you could use a command like this to accomplish such a task:

INDEX ON ZIPCODE TO ZIPS FOR STATE = "MD" .OR. STATE = "VA"

Indexing on Multiple Fields

You can index files based on several fields. The process is similar to sorting on multiple fields. There is a limitation, however; you cannot directly index on multiple fields that are not of the same field type. For example, you could not index by Lastname and Tapelimit, because Tapelimit is a numeric field and Lastname is a character field. However, there is a way to do this; you use special operators known as functions. (This technique will be discussed shortly.)

To see how indexing on multiple fields works and to be sure the BYNAMES index file that you created earlier is still active, take a look at the Lastname and Firstname fields by entering **LIST LASTNAME, FIRSTNAME**. Now notice that Carol Robinson is listed before Benjamin Robinson, which is not correct. Because you indexed the file on last names only, the order of the first names was ignored. To correct the situation, enter

INDEX ON LASTNAME + FIRSTNAME TO ALLNAMES

Records having the same last name are now indexed by last names and then by first names. To see the results, enter

LIST LASTNAME, FIRSTNAME

The listing should be as follows:

Record#	LASTNAME	FIRSTNAME
8	Hart	Wendy
4	Kramer	Harry
2	Martin	William
1	Miller	Karen
5	Moore	Ellen
7	Robinson	Benjamin
3	Robinson	Carol
6	Zachman	David

You can use this technique to create an index file on any number of fields within a record. The plus symbol (+) is always used with the INDEX command to tie the fields together. For example, the command

INDEX ON ZIPCODE + LASTNAME + FIRSTNAME TO ZIPNAMES

would result in a database that is indexed three ways: by ZIP codes, by last names for records having the same ZIP code, and by first names for records having the same last name. As you might expect, multiple indexes are valuable aids when you are dealing with a large database and must organize it into comprehensible subgroups.

INDEXING ON MULTIPLE FIELDS FROM MENUS You'll need to use the same plus symbol (+) to build a list of multiple index fields if you use the menu options to index your files. To see how this works, select New from the File menu. When the dialog box appears, choose Index, and then choose OK. In a moment, the Index On dialog box will appear. You cannot simply pick multiple field names from the Index On list box. If you try to, each selection will overwrite the previous entry. You can, however, enter the expression manually by typing it in the Expr window, or you can use the Expression Builder. Try tabbing over to Expr and pressing ENTER, to bring up the Expression Builder.

The Expression Builder works as described in Chapter 3. In this case, tab over to the Field Names list box, highlight Lastname, and press ENTER. Next, you can manually type the plus symbol, or you can use the mouse to open the Math pick list and choose the plus symbol from the pull-down menu. Then choose Firstname from the Field Names list box. Note that you should *not* press ENTER at the end of the expression; if you do, you will get an error message later. Tab to the OK button, and then press ENTER to accept the index expression; the dialog box will vanish, displaying the previous dialog box.

Tab to OK and press ENTER. In the File Name dialog box that next appears, enter **NEWNAMES** as the index file name, and then select OK to create the index. The new index file, arranged in order of the fields that you specified, will be created. When the indexing is complete, you can examine the results by entering **BROWSE** to view the file. When you are done, press ESC to exit Browse mode.

Indexing On Fields Of Different Types

One limitation of the basic use of the INDEX command, as noted earlier, is the inability to directly index on combinations of fields that are of different types. For example, you cannot index on a combination of the Lastname and Tapelimit fields in the Generic Videos database. To see the problem, at the command level, try either of the following commands:

```
INDEX ON LASTNAME + TAPELIMIT TO TEST
INDEX ON LASTNAME + BIRTHDAY TO TEST
```

The resulting error message, "Operator/operand type mismatch," tells you that FoxPro cannot index on a combination of fields that are of differing data types (such as date and character fields). The secret to indexing on fields that are not of the same type is to use *functions* to convert fields that are not character fields into character fields. Functions are used to perform special operations that supplement the normal FoxPro commands. They will be explained in greater detail in the programming portion of this text. For now, it is sufficient to know about two functions; the DTOS (Date-To-String) function, and the STR (String) function.

The DTOS function will convert the contents of a date field into a string of characters that follow a year-month-day format. The STR function will convert the contents of a numeric field into a string of characters. You can use the DTOS and STR functions in combination with your INDEX commands to accomplish the same results as indexing on combinations of different types of fields.

The normal format for an *index* command, when combined with these functions, is

INDEX ON *character-field* + STR(*numeric-field*) + DTOS(*date field*) TO *index-filename*

As with all indexing commands, you can use a combination of additional fields, in whatever order you prefer, to build the index. For an example of using these functions to build an index file that is indexed in alphabetical order by state and in numeric order by tape limit within each group of states, enter this command:

INDEX ON STATE + STR(TAPELIMIT) TO TEST

Enter **LIST LASTNAME, STATE, TAPELIMIT** to see the results of the index file; they should resemble the following.

Record#	LASTNAME	STATE	TAPELIMIT
7	Robinson	DC	2
2	Martin	MD	4
1	Miller	MD	6
5	Moore	MD	6
8	Hart	VA	2
4	Kramer	VA	4
6	Zachman	VA	4
3	Robinson	VA	6

Note that you can also use these functions within the menus by manually entering the functions along with the field names in the index Expr window.

Opening Databases
And Index Files

When opening databases with the USE command, you can simultaneously open one or more index files by adding the word "INDEX" and the index filenames after the USE *filename* portion of the command. The syntax for the USE command, when used with the INDEX option, becomes

USE *filename* INDEX *index-name1* [,*index-name2*]

You could simultaneously open the MEMBERS database along with the TOWNS and ALLNAMES index files with a command like

USE MEMBERS INDEX TOWNS, ALLNAMES

Note that the first index file you list is the controlling index, so in this example the TOWNS index file would control how the records were displayed or printed in a report.

Using SET INDEX

In many cases you'll create and work with more than one index for a database, but the order in which the records appear or are printed are controlled by only one index. For an index to control the order of the records, it must be *active*. An index that has just been created is active, and the SET INDEX command makes a dormant index active. The SET INDEX command is the command-level equivalent of choosing Open from the File menu and then selecting Index from the Type button in the dialog box that appears.

Suppose that you need three lists from the MEMBERS database. The first list must be in order by tape limit, another list by last name, and a third list by ZIP codes. Create the indexes from these three fields now with the following commands:

INDEX ON LASTNAME TO NAME
INDEX ON TAPELIMIT TO TAPES
INDEX ON ZIPCODE TO ZIP

These commands create three indexes on your hard disk: NAME, TAPES, and ZIP. Each index file contains the appropriate field from each record and the corresponding record numbers. NAME, for example, contains last names in alphabetical order and the matching record numbers for each last name.

Since ZIP was the last index created, it is the active index. By using the SET INDEX command, you can activate any index. For example, to activate and display the database organized by tape limit instead of by ZIP code, enter

SET INDEX TO TAPES
LIST LASTNAME, TAPELIMIT

The display should appear as follows:

Record#	LASTNAME	TAPELIMIT
8	Hart	2
2	Martin	4
4	Kramer	4
6	Zachman	4
1	Miller	6
3	Robinson	6
5	Moore	6
7	Robinson	6

Now try the same method to activate and display the ZIP file:

SET INDEX TO ZIP
LIST LASTNAME, ZIPCODE

The display should appear as follows:

Record#	LASTNAME	ZIPCODE
7	Robinson	20009-1010
1	Miller	20815-0988
2	Martin	20910-0124
5	Moore	20912
6	Zachman	22043
8	Hart	22025
3	Robinson	22043-1234
4	Kramer	22203

Remember, ZIP codes are stored as characters, so they will be indexed "alphabetically," which explains why the nine-digit ZIP codes are not at the bottom of the list.

Open Index Files

Although only one index can be active at a time, you can have up to seven *open files*. You can easily tell which indexes are in use at any time by using the LIST STATUS or DISPLAY STATUS commands. If an index file is open, any changes you make to the parent database will be updated automatically in that index file. For example, adding a record to MEMBERS will place the Lastname field of the new record and the record number in the NAMES index and then realphabetize the index file, provided that the NAME.IDX index file is open.

You can also open an index file with either the USE *filename* INDEX *index-names* command, and the SET INDEX command. You can open a database and index files at the same time with USE *filename* INDEX *index-names*. For example, the command

USE MEMBERS INDEX NAME, ZIP

will open the MEMBERS database, along with the NAME.IDX and ZIP.IDX index files. SET INDEX TO NAME, ZIP will also open the NAME.IDX and ZIP.IDX files if they are not already open. (You do not have to supply the .IDX extension to the command.) An active index file is also an open index file, so using SET INDEX will open a file that is closed. If you list more than one file with SET INDEX, all files will be opened, but only the first will be active.

Once you have opened index files, an alternative method of making any particular index active is the SET ORDER command. With SET ORDER, you use numbers, as in SET ORDER TO 3. The number indicates the order in which the index file was originally opened. If, for example, you entered **USE MEMBERS INDEX NAME, ZIP** to open the files, the ZIP index would be the second index opened; therefore, entering **SET ORDER TO 2** would make ZIP the active index file.

In general, use the USE *filename* INDEX *index-names* command to open your databases along with as many index files as needed; once they are open, use the SET INDEX command to make different index files active. For example, if you need three lists, one in order of name, one in order of ZIP code, and one in order of tape limit, you could use commands like these:

```
USE MEMBERS INDEX NAME, ZIP, TAPES
SET INDEX TO NAME
LIST LASTNAME, FIRSTNAME, CITY, ZIP, TAPELIMIT
SET INDEX TO ZIP
LIST LASTNAME, FIRSTNAME, CITY, ZIP, TAPELIMIT
SET INDEX TO TAPES
LIST LASTNAME, FIRSTNAME, CITY, ZIP, TAPELIMIT
```

To get an idea of why it is important to keep needed index files open, you can use the index files you created earlier, NAMES and TAPES. Use the SET INDEX command to open these files by entering this command:

SET INDEX TO TAPES, NAME

The two index files (TAPES.IDX, containing Tapelimit, and NAME.IDX, containing Lastname) are now open. Now enter **LIST LASTNAME, TAPELIMIT**. The display shows that the index you specified by naming the TAPES file first is the active index, but NAMES.IDX is also open. This is important if you add or edit records in the database because as long as the index files are open, they will be updated automatically. See how this works by entering

APPEND

When the new blank record appears, enter this data:

Social:	111-22-3333
Lastname:	Roberts
Firstname:	Charles
Address:	247 Ocean Blvd
City:	Vienna
State:	VA
Zipcode:	22085
Tapelimit:	3

The remaining fields in the record may be left blank for now. Press CTRL-W to store the new record and get back to the command level. Now enter this command again:

LIST LASTNAME, TAPELIMIT

The index file now includes the new entry, in the proper order of tape limits, as shown here:

Record#	LASTNAME	TAPELIMIT
8	Hart	2
7	Robinson	2
9	Roberts	3
2	Martin	4
4	Kramer	4
6	Zachman	4
1	Miller	6
3	Robinson	6
5	Moore	6

This brings up an important point: speed. Whenever you make changes or add records to a database, FoxPro automatically updates all open index files. This may slow down the entire operation, particularly if more than one index file is open at once. If you wish, you can close all open index files without closing the database with the CLOSE INDEX command.

Using REINDEX

If you changed a database and didn't remember to open an index file, you can update the index with the REINDEX command. You will want to do this with the ZIP index file, for example; because you did not open the ZIP index file, it does not include the newly added record. You can verify this by using the ZIP index and looking at names in the database. Enter the following:

SET INDEX TO ZIP, NAME, TAPES
LIST LASTNAME

As you can see, the name Roberts does not appear in the database because the ZIP index was not open when you added the record:

Record#	LASTNAME
7	Robinson
1	Miller
2	Martin
5	Moore
8	Hart
6	Zachman
3	Robinson
4	Kramer

To update an index that was not open at the time you added or edited records, you can use the REINDEX command. Try the command now by entering

REINDEX

To display the updated result, enter **LIST LASTNAME**. The results are shown here:

Record#	LASTNAME
7	Robinson
1	Miller
2	Martin
5	Moore
8	Hart
6	Zachman
3	Robinson
9	Roberts
4	Kramer

The Roberts entry is now in the indexed ZIP file. Mr. Roberts is no longer needed in the database. Enter **DELETE RECORD 9** and then enter **PACK** to remove him from the list. Since the ZIP, NAME, and TAPELIMIT index files are open, the entry for Roberts will be removed from each of the index files.

Using CLOSE INDEX

If you decide that you do not want to use any index file, the CLOSE INDEX command will close the index file and leave the associated database open. To execute the command from the command level, you enter

CLOSE INDEX

Note that the REINDEX command is available from the menus, while the CLOSE INDEX command is not. To rebuild an index file while at the menus, open the Database menu and choose the Reindex option. To close an index file through the menus, you could choose the Open option of the File menu and open the same database a second time, without opening the corresponding index file.

SEARCHING FOR SPECIFICS

You can use two additional FoxPro commands with indexed files: FIND and SEEK. These commands quickly find information in an indexed file. The commands will be discussed briefly here, since they do pertain to indexed files. Chapter 6, which deals with querying your database, will cover these commands in additional detail.

Both commands operate only on the active index. The format for the FIND command is FIND *character-string*, where *character-string* is a group of characters that do not have to be surrounded by quote marks. The format for SEEK is SEEK *expression*. Here, *expression* can be a number, a character string (which must be surrounded by single or double quotes), or a variable (variables are discussed in the programming portion of this text).

FIND and SEEK will search the active index file and find the first record that matches your specifications. The record itself will not be displayed; the FIND and SEEK commands will simply locate the record pointer at the desired record. If no match is found, FoxPro will respond with a "Find not successful" error message. To try the FIND command, enter

```
SET INDEX TO NAME
FIND Moore
DISPLAY
```

The result is as follows:

Record #	SOCIAL	LASTNAME	FIRSTNAME	ADDRESS...
5	121-90-5432	Moore	Ellen	270 Browning Ave...

To try the SEEK command, enter

```
SET INDEX TO TAPES
SEEK 4
DISPLAY
```

The result is as follows:

Record #	SOCIAL	LASTNAME	FIRSTNAME	ADDRESS...
2	121-33-9876	Martin	William	4807 East Avenue...

    The FIND and SEEK commands offer the advantage of speed over the LOCATE command (introduced in Chapter 3). LOCATE is simple to use, but slow. In a database containing thousands of records, a LOCATE command can take several minutes. A FIND or SEEK command can accomplish the same task in a matter of seconds.

    When you are searching for a character string, both FIND and SEEK allow you to search on only the beginning of the string. However, you should keep in mind that both the FIND and SEEK commands search for an exact match, in terms of capitalization. For example, if the Generic Videos database index is set to NAME, the two commands

FIND Mo

FIND Moore

would both find the record for Moore. However, the command

FIND mo

would not find the record, because FoxPro considers uppercase and lowercase letters to be different characters. As far as FoxPro is concerned, "Moore" and "moore" are different names. One way of preventing problems with the case-significance of FoxPro is to design entry forms that store your character data as all uppercase letters. Another method is to use a FoxPro function called the UPPER function. The use of this function will be discussed in a later chapter.

INDEX TIPS AND UNUSUAL CASES

With all the different ways to arrange a file, you may occasionally run into some unusual requests relating to indexing. The following sections cover some of the more unusual areas of indexing, along with hints for making your indexing as efficient as possible.

The Multiple Numeric Field Trap

With multiple numeric fields, things may not always turn out as you expect because of the way FoxPro builds an index expression.

Consider a database of department store sales, with fields for customer name, high credit amounts, and balance amounts. You are preparing a mailing, and you want to target customers who have high credit lines and low account balances; they are likely prospects for heavy spending. You'd like to get an idea of who these customers are, so you prepare a report showing records sorted by high credit amounts. Where the high credit amounts are the same, you'd like to order the records by outstanding balance. If you use the INDEX command to do something like

```
USE SALES
INDEX ON HIGHCREDIT + BALANCE TO MAILER
LIST STORE, CUSTNAME, CUSTNUMB, HIGHCREDIT, BALANCE
```

The results will look like this:

STORE	CUSTNAME	CUSTNUMB	HIGHCREDIT	BALANCE
Collin Creek	Artis, K.	1008	1200.00	0.00
Oak Lawn	Jones, C.	1003	900.00	350.00
Galleria	Johnson, L.	1002	1200.00	675.00
Six Flags	Keemis, M.	1007	2000.00	0.00
Collin Creek	Williams, E.	1010	2000.00	0.00
Prestonwood	Smith, A.M.	1009	2000.00	220.00
Prestonwood	Allen, L.	1005	2000.00	312.00
Downtown	Walker, B.	1006	1300.00	1167.00
Prestonwood	Smith, A.	1001	2000.00	788.50
Downtown	Jones, J.	1011	2000.00	875.00
Collin Creek	Jones, J.L.	1004	2000.00	1850.00

Rather than concatenating the two numbers, FoxPro has added them and indexed in the order of the sum, which may not be what you had in mind. The plus symbol means different things to FoxPro for numeric expressions, as opposed to string (character-based) expressions. The plus symbol adds numbers, but combines character expressions. If you instead use the SORT command, with commands like

```
USE SALES
SORT ON HIGHCREDIT,BALANCE TO SALES1
USE SALES1
LIST STORE, CUSTNAME, CUSTNUMB, HIGHCREDIT, BALANCE
```

You will get these results

STORE	CUSTNAME	CUSTNUMB	HIGHCREDIT	BALANCE
Oak Lawn	Jones, C.	1003	900.00	350.00
Collin Creek	Artis, K.	1008	1200.00	0.00
Galleria	Johnson, L.	1002	1200.00	675.00
Downtown	Walker, B.	1006	1300.00	1167.00
Six Flags	Keemis, M.	1007	2000.00	0.00
Collin Creek	Williams, E.	1010	2000.00	0.00
Prestonwood	Smith, A.M.	1009	2000.00	220.00
Prestonwood	Allen, L.	1005	2000.00	312.00
Prestonwood	Smith, A.	1001	2000.00	788.50
Downtown	Jones, J.	1011	2000.00	875.00
Collin Creek	Jones, J.L.	1004	2000.00	1850.00

What you get is what was expected: a file in numeric order by high credit, and where high credit is the same, in order of the outstanding balance. The unexpected results when using INDEX occur because the INDEX command, when used with multiple fields, depends on a math expression. In this case, FoxPro is adding the amounts, building the index on a value that is the sum of the amounts. To index on the combined numeric fields and get the desired results, you would have to first convert the numeric expressions into string values and then use the plus symbol to combine the string values. In the previous example, you could issue a command like

```
INDEX ON STR(HIGHCREDIT) + STR(BALANCE) TO CSALES
```

to accomplish the same result as the SORT command.

Indexing in Descending Order

There is no Descending option in the dialog boxes for indexing, and there is no /D option available with the INDEX command as there is with the SORT command. This does not mean you cannot index in descending order. The trick to indexing in descending order is to use an index key that always results in negative values. As an example, consider these commands and results for the same department store database mentioned earlier:

```
USE SALES
INDEX ON -(BALANCE) TO DUEDEBTS
LIST CUSTNAME, BALANCE
```

Record #	CUSTNAME	BALANCE
4	Jones, J.L.	1850.00
6	Walker, B.	1167.00
11	Jones, J.	875.00
1	Smith, A.	788.50
2	Johnson, L.	675.00
3	Jones, C.	350.00
5	Allen, L.	312.00
9	Smith, A.M.	220.00
7	Keemis, M.	0.00
8	Artis, K.	0.00
10	Williams, E.	0.00

An alternative for accomplishing the same result would be to index on an expression that subtracts the value from some arbitrarily large value. To do this, you use a command like

```
INDEX ON 10000-BALANCE TO DUEDEBTS
```

As long as no customer has an account balance of over $10,000, the results are correct. Since FoxPro always builds an index in ascending order, and negative numbers in ascending order resemble a descending order to humans, you get an index that is arranged in descending order.

Be aware that this works well for generating lists of values in descending order, and not so well for finding records with FIND and SEEK. Since the index in the first example is built on negative values, you would need to enter something like

FIND −58.50

to find a balance in the amount of $58.50. If you used the second method described, you are in worse shape; you would need to enter something like

FIND 9941.50

because 10000−58.50 provides the actual index entry value of 9941.50. Usually this is not a problem, because most users don't want to find a record based purely on the cost of an item. If you need to search on a combination of fields within an index created in this manner, remember to include the necessary expressions to make the search on the negative values present in the index.

Descending Indexes On Character Fields

With character fields, descending order gets much trickier. You cannot use a negative expression on a character field. Assuming that a field called Lastname is a character field, an expression like

INDEX ON −(LASTNAME) TO CNAMES

would result in nothing more than an "Invalid function argument" error. You can use the ASC function to convert part of a character string to its equivalent numeric ASCII code, and index on that numeric value. For example, commands like

```
USE TEMP
INDEX ON –ASC(LASTNAME) TO CNAMES
LIST LASTNAME, FIRSTNAME
```

provide the results shown here:

1	Smith	Allen
9	Smith	Allen M.
7	Keemis	Martin
2	Johnson	Lonnie
3	Jones	Charisse
4	Jones	Judie Lynn
11	Jones	Judith
5	Allen	Larry
8	Artis	Kelvin

By using the ASC function, which converts the first character in a text string to its numeric ASCII value, you build an index in descending order based on only the first character of the Lastname field. As shown by the example, this is not a very orderly index. This is probably a good example of when you must ask yourself whether you would be better off using the descending option of the SORT command. Fortunately, the reverse-order alphabetic index is a rare requirement.

Using Functions To Standardize Case

The UPPER function and, less commonly, the LOWER function are often used to avoid problems arising from the case-sensitive nature of FoxPro. These functions can also be used as part of an index expression, resulting in an index containing characters which are all uppercase or all lowercase. The potential problem that can arise when the data-entry people are not consistent with methods of data entry is shown in the following example. In this database of names, some of the names start with initial capital letters, some are entered as all caps, and some are all lowercase:

```
USE SAMPLE
INDEX ON NAME TO NAMES
LIST
```

Record#	NAME	AGE
1	ADDISON, E.	32
2	Addison, a.	28
3	Carlson, F.	45
4	McLean,R.	28
5	Mcdonald, s.	47
7	Smith, S.	55
8	Smith, b.	37
10	adams, j.q.	76
6	de laurentis, m.	25
9	edelstien, m.	22

Unless told otherwise, FoxPro puts lowercase letters after uppercase letters in the index, and the results are probably not what you had in mind. If you use the UPPER function to build the index, you get acceptable results, as shown with the following commands:

```
USE SAMPLE
INDEX ON UPPER(NAME) TO NAMES
LIST
```

Record#	NAME	AGE
10	adams, j.q.	76
2	ADDISON, A.	28
1	Addison, E.	32
3	Carlson, F.	45
6	de laurentis, m.	25
9	edelstien, m.	22
5	Mcdonald, s.	47

4	McLean,R.	28
8	Smith, b.	37
7	Smith, S.	55

To find such records in the index, simply enter all uppercase letters in the expression used along with the FIND or SEEK command. For example, the command

SEEK "ADDISON"

would find the record in this database, irregardless of the case of the letters in the actual record.

Indexing on a Date Field

When you need an index based partially on a date field, FoxPro can present a bit of a challenge. It's no problem when you want to see the database in order by just one date field. Consider the example of a small medical database, containing patient names and a field with the date of admission to a hospital. You can use commands like these, with the results shown:

USE PATIENT
INDEX ON ADMITTED TO DATESIN
LIST PATIENT, ADMITTED

Record#	PATIENT	ADMITTED
1	Smith, A.	04/05/85
2	Johnson, L.	04/15/85
3	Jones, C.	04/15/85
4	Jones, J.L.	04/15/85
5	Allen, L.	05/20/86
6	Walker, B.	05/20/86
7	Keemis, M.	05/20/86
8	Artis, K.	05/20/86
9	Smith, A.M.	05/20/86
10	Williams, E.	06/14/86
11	Jones, J.	06/22/86

You get a database indexed in the order of the entries in the date field. Things get more complex, however, when you want a database indexed on a combination of fields, and one of the fields is a date field.

Since FoxPro doesn't let you index directly on multiple fields of different types, you must use functions to convert the date into a character string. Assuming the database contains a date field named Diagnosed and a character field named Patient, and you want it indexed by date and then by the name of the patient, you would use the DTOS function. This function is specifically designed to store date values in true chronological order. It converts a date value to a character value of YYYYMMDD, where YYYY is the year, MM the month, and DD the day. When an index is built with the DTOS function, the result comes out in true chronological order. Using the sample database just described, the commands:

```
USE PATIENT
INDEX ON DTOS(DIAGNOSED) + PATIENT TO COMBO
LIST PATIENT, DIAGNOSED
```

provide an index based on date and patient name, in the correct chronological order:

Record#	PATIENT	DIAGNOSED
3	Jones, C.	02/08/85
4	Jones, J.L.	03/02/85
2	Johnson, L.	03/06/85
1	Smith, A.	03/17/85
9	Smith, A.M.	02/03/86
7	Keemis, M.	02/23/86
8	Artis, K.	04/19/86
5	Allen, L.	05/12/86
6	Walker, B.	05/16/86
10	Williams, E.	06/01/86
11	Jones, J.	06/13/86

INDEXING ON DATES IN DESCENDING ORDER If you need a file indexed in reverse chronological order (from the latest date to the earliest), you can use the index on negative values technique to build an index file based on negative date values. Simply subtract the actual dates from any date that is larger (that is, later) than the latest date in the database. Some arbitrary date far in the future works well for this. The technique is shown in this example:

```
USE PATIENT
INDEX ON CTOD("12/31/99")-DIAGNOSED TO REVERSE
LIST PATIENT, DIAGNOSED
```

Record#	PATIENT	DIAGNOSED
11	Jones, J.	06/13/86
10	Williams, E.	06/01/86
6	Walker, B.	05/16/86
5	Allen, L.	05/12/86
8	Artis, K.	04/19/86
7	Keemis, M.	02/23/86
9	Smith, A.M.	02/03/86
1	Smith, A.	03/17/85
2	Johnson, L.	03/06/85
4	Jones, J.L.	03/02/85
3	Jones, C.	02/08/85

Here, the index is built on a number that represents the difference in the number of days between 12/31/99 and the date field (Diagnosed) in the database. As the dates get earlier, this number increases, causing the position of the date to be further down in the index file.

Tips for Indexing

A few tips when you are using index files will help speed things along in FoxPro.

Use short keys when you don't need long ones. Most indexes are directly based on a series of character fields, and in real life, most character fields get unique around the tenth character, if not sooner. If you can get by with indexing on fewer characters, do so. FoxPro will manage the index in less time. Let's look at a real-world example. You are building a customer file for a store in a medium-sized city of about 100,000 people, so you do not need to deal with the duplicity of names that you get in New York or Los Angeles. The customer base is manageable: you might see a maximum of 5000 to 10,000 records in the file over the next ten years. The store manager despises labels with names cut off for lack of field width, so you've specified a width of 30 characters each for the Lastname and Firstname fields. You are going to index on a key field of customer number as the primary index, but you also want an index based on a combination of last and first names so you can quickly find a record when a customer is on the phone and does not have his or her customer number handy.

In this situation, do you really need an index based on the Lastname and Firstname fields? Quite likely not, but this is often done out of force of habit, and FoxPro must work harder for it. If you instead do something like

INDEX ON LEFT(LASTNAME,10) + LEFT(FIRSTNAME,10)

the use of the LEFT function will result in an index that contains 20 characters per entry, as opposed to an index that contains 60 characters per entry. Given the customer base, having the first ten characters of the last and first names should be more than enough to keep the records in order and find a given record. Also, the index file will use considerably less disk space.

Store numbers in character fields if you are never going to perform calculations on those numbers. If you use numbers as unique identifiers (as in part numbers, employee numbers, invoice numbers, and so on) and you plan to use this data as a part of the index, don't store it in a numeric field. Use a character field instead. It makes a difference to FoxPro, because FoxPro does a better job of indexing on character fields than on numeric fields. When you try indexing with very large files, it becomes apparent that FoxPro takes longer to index a numeric field than a character field of equivalent size. Assuming you are not going to calculate such fields, they don't need to be numeric fields.

Perform routine maintenance often. When FoxPro must perform sequential operations while your index files are open, it has to work harder. You can cut down processing times by regularly putting your database files back in their natural order. To do this, open the file along with the index you most often use for sequential reporting or processing, and use the COPY TO *filename* command to copy the contents of the file to another file. Then delete the original database, give the new database the same name as the original database, and rebuild the necessary indexes. In applications using large files that are regularly updated, this simple step can make a dramatic difference to users in terms of response time when they are performing any reporting or processing based on sequential operations in FoxPro. Part of the speed-up may also be due to the fact that the creation of a new database with the COPY command results in a new file under DOS, which may have its data arranged in sectors located side by side on the hard disk. Often, when a file has been updated over months of time, it is arranged in sectors that are scattered all over the hard disk. You can use the technique just described to reduce such fragmentation of files over a hard disk, or you can use one of the many "disk optimizer" software packages available to clean up your hard disk and make all of your files more accessible to your software.

Multiple Index Files and dBASE IV Compatibility

FoxPro is command-compatible with dBASE IV; however, FoxPro does use a different style of index file than versions of dBASE use. If you write programs or make use of both products, you should know that dBASE IV can maintain its index information in one of two ways, although either method will accomplish the same result of keeping things in order. The first method is to use a multiple index file with an extension of .MDX. The multiple index file maintains information on the different indexes that dBASE IV creates within a single file. The second method of indexing files is to create individual index files for each index desired, just as you have done with FoxPro throughout this chapter. Individual index files created with dBASE have an .NDX extension and are not directly usable under FoxPro. If you attempt to open a dBASE database and its corresponding index file with an .NDX extension, FoxPro will automatically create its own index file with an .IDX extension.

Although the initial version of FoxPro (FoxPro 1.0) does not support the multiple index file scheme used by dBASE IV, later versions of FoxPro will probably provide support for the multiple index file concept. The two methods of indexing will be provided for compatibility with dBASE IV procedures and programs. However, FoxPro 1.0 and earlier versions of FoxBase do not support multiple index files. FoxPro therefore provides menu options and commands that let you work with .IDX index files, which are the style of index files used by FoxBase. If you work with data created by dBASE users, you will want to recreate any needed index files once you are in FoxPro.

If your version of FoxPro supports multiple index files, you can make use of an additional syntax for the INDEX command. This syntax is

INDEX ON *expression* TAG *index-tag-name*

The index file in which the tags are stored is called the *production* index file; this file has the same name as the database, but with an .MDX extension. It is automatically opened whenever you open the corresponding database. Therefore, you could store three indexes, based on last-name, ZIP code, and state fields, in the same index file with commands like these:

```
INDEX ON LASTNAME TAG NAMES
INDEX ON ZIPCODE TAG ZIPS
INDEX ON STATE TAG STATES
```

Assuming that a database named MEMBERS.DBF was in use, the index data for all three files would be stored in a multiple index file named MEMBERS.MDX. Once the index has been created, you can make different index tags active with the SET ORDER command. With the previous example, the command

```
SET ORDER TO STATES
```

would make the STATES index tag within the MEMBERS.MDX index file the controlling index. The other index tags would remain open and would be updated if records were added, modified, or deleted.

Keep in mind that the TAG variations of the INDEX command, and the SET ORDER TO command used with tag names instead of numeric values, only operate if your version of FoxPro supports the multiple index file scheme. If you are not sure of this point, check your FoxPro documentation.

5
CREATING ENTRY FORMS

Using FoxView
Using Forms View to Create a Form
Moving Fields
Changing the Labels
Adding Text
Saving Screen Format Files
Leaving FoxView
Using a Screen Format File
Modifying a Screen Form
Drawing Boxes on a Form
Changing Colors
Table View
Moving Fields and Objects in Table View
Using Picture
Using Range
FoxView and DOS

When you are using APPEND, CHANGE, or EDIT and you add data or make changes to a database, you are presented with a simple on-screen entry form that lists the various field names, alongside highlighted areas that contain the actual data. For demonstrating how to add or change data within a database, this has been sufficient; but there can be problems with such a straightforward approach to adding data to a database. One drawback is in the unfriendly screen that this presents to the computer user. If a Generic Videos employee does not know what is meant by the word "Preference" on the screen, the help screens or the FoxPro manual won't offer any assistance. Another drawback is the lack of control during editing. If for any reason you wish to restrict the editing of a particular field, you cannot do so with CHANGE or EDIT.

To overcome such limitations, FoxPro provides a means of designing flexible entry forms. An entry form is simply a form that appears on the screen that is used for data display and data entry. Using the Forms View mode of FoxView, you can build forms that resemble the printed forms commonly used in an office. You can also restrict entry by omitting certain fields and including other fields in the data-entry form. You can limit fields to accept certain types of data, such as amounts that fall within a predefined range. And you can tell FoxPro to use a specific form when working with a database, so that the form automatically appears when you add or edit records. The forms you create can be used for the entry or the display of data in a database.

USING FOXVIEW

To create data-entry forms, you use the Forms View mode of FoxView. FoxView is a combination screen-design utility and application generator. You will learn more about the application

```
<D:\>                              Friday 09/01/89  9:00
Welcome to FoxView 3.0
Press F1 for HELP

FoxView D:>
```

FIGURE 5-1. FoxView shell

generator capabilities of FoxView in a later chapter; this chapter covers how to use Forms View to create data-entry forms.

To start FoxView, you enter **FOXVIEW** from the command level or choose FoxView from the Program menu. Use either method now to start FoxView. An introduction screen will appear, and you must now press ENTER to continue. In a moment, you will see the FoxView shell, shown in Figure 5-1.

Because FoxView is a stand-alone program, you must load a database from the FoxView shell before you can begin creating a data-entry screen. This is true even if you previously opened the MEMBERS file while in FoxPro. When you start FoxView, FoxPro transfers program control to FoxView through a DOS shell, so FoxPro no longer has control of your system.

Commands Available in FoxView

While you are at the prompt in the FoxView shell, you can use commands for such purposes as loading database files to create forms, saving existing form designs, and displaying the structure of a database. The following list provides some of the more commonly used FoxView commands. The first four commands listed here perform the same functions as they do in DOS; see your DOS manual for more details about the purpose of these commands.

Command	Purpose
drive:	Change default drive
CD*path*	Change directory
DIR	Directory listing
DIR /W	Directory listing in wide format
LIST	List database structure for file in use
LOAD *filename*	Load an existing table (previously saved with a screen form's design)
SAVE *filename*	Save a current form and the underlying table on which it is based
USE *filename*	Load a database file to be used in designing a new form
VIEW FORMS	Show Forms View; same as pressing F10
VIEW TABLE	Show Table View; same as pressing F10

You can also use certain keys for specific tasks while in FoxView. The F10 key serves as a toggle to switch between Forms View and Table View. Forms View is a mode that displays a screen design that you are working with as a form, and Table View displays an underlying table that the screen form is based upon. You'll learn more about Forms View and Table View later in the chapter.

The SCROLL LOCK key exits either the Forms View or the Table View and returns you to the FoxView shell. The ESC key is used to toggle a series of menus on or off. Regardless of where you are in FoxView, remember that you can use the SCROLL LOCK key to get back to the FoxView shell.

Let's look at a general scenario for using FoxView to create forms. You enter the USE *filename* command to open a database and simultaneously load the database fields into FoxView. (An alternate way of opening a file is to press ESC for the menus and choose Use Datafile from the Load menu.) You then enter **VIEW FORMS** (or press the F10 key) to switch to Forms View mode; here you see a form much like the one used so far for entry and editing, based on the database you opened with the USE command.

You next revise the form as desired, moving fields to new locations and changing the names of fields to more descriptive labels where necessary. You can also add lines and boxes and change colors within the form. When the form changes are complete, you save the form and the underlying table it is based on either by pressing SCROLL LOCK to get back to the shell and entering **SAVE** *filename* or by pressing ESC to display the menus, and choosing Save Table form the Load menu. You must also use the menus to generate a format file, which is used by FoxPro to display the data in your modified screen form. To do this, you press ESC to display the menus, and you choose Select From Template List from the Gen menu. From the next menu to appear, choose Format File Generator to create the format file.

When you want to modify an existing screen form, you can use the LOAD *filename* command from the FoxView shell to load the existing file. (An alternative method is to press ESC for the menus and choose Load Table from the Load menu.) Once the existing form has been loaded, you can then enter **VIEW FORMS** (or press the F10 key) to switch to Forms View mode. You next revise the form as desired, and then save the changes using the same save techniques as discussed in the previous paragraph.

USING FORMS VIEW TO CREATE A FORM

In FoxView, you can load a database with the same USE command as is used in FoxPro. Enter

USE MEMBERS

and you will see the message

13 field(s) loaded.

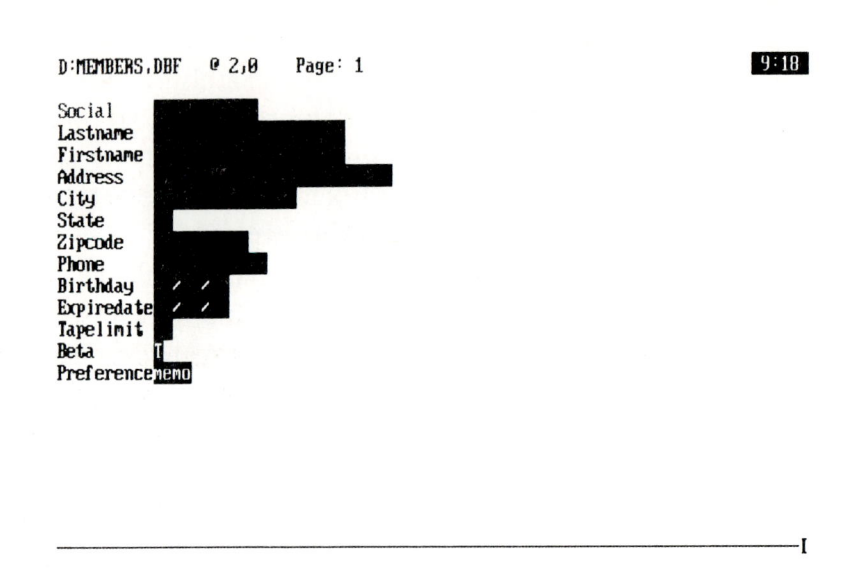

```
D:MEMBERS.DBF    @ 2,0    Page: 1                                    9:18
         Social
         Lastname
         Firstname
         Address
         City
         State
         Zipcode
         Phone
         Birthday      / /
         Expiredate    / /
         Tapelinit
         Beta
         Preference memo
```

                                                                    I

FIGURE 5-2.   Forms View mode

Next, you press F10 to enter the Forms View mode of FoxView. Press F10 now, and your screen should resemble the example shown in Figure 5-2. If you accidentally press F10 too many times, you may instead see a tabular chart containing data about the fields. This is Table View mode, and its use is covered in detail later in the chapter. If you accidentally get into Table View mode, just press F10 again and you will switch back to Forms View.

When inside the work area of Forms View, as you are now, you can draw your data-entry form. Fields can be moved around, boxes can be added, colors can be changed, and more descriptive names can be entered to describe the fields. The function keys are used for specific tasks in Forms View mode of FoxView; Table 5-1 outlines the uses for the function keys for Forms View.

Key	Action
F1 (Help)	Displays help screen.
F3 (Drag)	Used to drag (move) the currently selected area to a different location. Use cursor keys to highlight desired object, press F3, drag the item to the new location with the cursor keys, and press ENTER.
F4 (Size)	Used to resize the currently selected field or box. Use cursor keys to highlight desired object, press F4, use the cursor keys to resize the item, then press ENTER. Note that changing the size of a field in a form does not alter the field size in the database.
F5 (Resequence)	Lets you resequence, or change the data-entry order, of the fields in the form.
F6 (Extend Select)	Lets you select more than one field at a time, to apply other changes to. For example, you could simultaneously move the Lastname and Firstname fields in a form to a new location by moving the cursor to the Lastname field, pressing F6, moving the cursor down to the Firstname field, and pressing ENTER. Both fields would then be highlighted, and you could use Drag (F3) to move them to a new location.
F8 (Copy Fields)	Copies the selected field or fields to a new location, one row down and eight columns across.
F10 (Toggle Forms View/Table View)	Switches between Forms View and Table View.

TABLE 5-1. Function Key Assignments in Forms View

When you first load a database and begin using the Forms View mode, the field names appear at the left side of the screen. The highlighted areas that appear to the right of the field names represent the actual fields and are called *field templates*. On your screen, the word "Lastname" is a field name, not a field. The shaded area to the right of the Lastname label marks the start of the actual field, as represented by the field template. The "@ 2, 0" indicator at the top of the screen tells you the row and column position of the cursor while you are working within the screen. Cursor movement is performed with the same editing keys as you use in Edit or Change Mode.

Try pressing the INS key repeatedly. As you do so, note that "Ins" appears and disappears from the lower-right corner of the screen. Pressing the INS key moves you in and out of Insert mode. When you are in Insert mode, all characters that you type are added to the existing text at the cursor location. When you are out of Insert and in Overwrite mode, all characters that you type replace any existing characters. Press INS now until you are back in Insert mode.

MOVING FIELDS

The cursor is currently at the letter "S" in "Social." The form would look less cluttered if the text and fields were moved to a more central position in the screen. You can move fields with the F3 (Drag) key. In FoxView, F3 lets you drag the currently highlighted area to a different location. However, in this case, you want to drag all the fields. To do this, you will also need to use the F6 (Extend Select) key. You use Extend Select to highlight as many fields as you wish by pressing F6 and moving the cursor keys until the fields you want to select are highlighted; you then press ENTER to complete the selection.

With the cursor still at the "S" in "Social," press F6 (Extend Select) now. The message at the bottom of the screen offers help by displaying

SELECT: extend selection with the cursor keys; RETURN finishes.

Press the DOWN ARROW key until all the fields are highlighted, and then press ENTER. You can now drag the fields to a new location as a group.

Press F3 (Drag). The help message at the bottom of the screen now indicates

DRAG: move selection with the cursor keys; RETURN finishes.

Press the RIGHT ARROW key 15 times, and press the DOWN ARROW key 4 times. Then press ENTER to complete the movement of the fields. The fields will still appear highlighted as a block because of the Extend Select operation; however, as soon as you press any of the cursor keys, the extended selection will be cancelled.

From this movement, it may be obvious that Forms View considers both the actual field (the shaded area) and the text label containing the field's name as single objects. You can see this by moving the State field to a new location, to the right of the City field. Use the cursor keys to highlight the State field, and press F3 (Drag). Press the RIGHT ARROW key 28 times, and press the UP ARROW key once. The cursor should now be at row 10, column 43. The State field (both the text label and the field itself) will be repositioned to a location just to the right of the City field. Press ENTER to complete the operation.

Move the cursor down to the Zipcode field. Press F3, and press the UP ARROW key once to move the Zipcode field directly underneath the City field. Press ENTER to complete the operation.

When moving fields to new locations, you must be careful to measure whether there is sufficient room to fit the entire field at the screen location that you choose. If, for example, you attempt to place a field that is 20 characters long at column 62, you will cut off the display of the last two characters because the screen ends at the character position 80.

CHANGING THE LABELS

You can change the field labels by moving to the desired field and pressing the spacebar. Pressing it puts you in Edit mode, where you can add or delete characters and insert spaces or remove spaces at the end of the label. Adding spaces at the end of the label will increase the distance between the label and the field and removing spaces will shorten the distance between the label and the field.

As an example, the Birthday and Expiredate labels need to be changed to "Birth Date" and "Date of Expiration." Use the cursor keys to move the Birthday field, and press the spacebar. You will see the label "Birthday" appear at the bottom of the screen; the corresponding help message indicates that you can enter label names of up to 80 characters. Move the cursor to the "d" in "Birthday," and press the spacebar once. As you do this, you will see that the Birthday field near the center of the screen automatically shifts to the right to allow room for the inserted space. Change the word "day" to "date," and then press ENTER to complete the change to the label.

Move the cursor down to the Expiredate field, and press the spacebar to begin editing the label. Change the label to

Date of Expiration

and add a space at the end of "Expiration," so that a space appears between the end of the label and the start of the field. Then press ENTER to complete the change in the label.

To reduce the visual clutter in the form still further, let's move the memo field, Preference, one line down and to the left slightly. Place the cursor at the Preference field, and press F3. Press the DOWN ARROW key once and the LEFT ARROW key five times. Then press ENTER to complete the movement.

You may notice that the word "Preference" runs up against the start of the field. This can be corrected with the addition of a space at the end of the label. Press the spacebar to begin editing the label. Move to the end of the label and add a space, and then press ENTER to complete the change.

ADDING TEXT

You can add text, such as headings or comments, at any location in a form. Text objects can be inserted by pressing CTRL- N. Once a text object is inserted with CTRL-N, it is automatically placed in Drag mode. You can then use the cursor keys followed by the ENTER key to place the text where desired.

One benefit of designing a custom form is that it allows you to add descriptive messages that may help novice users. Generic Videos employees may not instinctively understand how to enter data in a memo field. To add an explanation, press CTRL-N. A new text object will appear just below the cursor location at the existing Preference field. Move the cursor to row 19, column 30 (slightly to the right of the Preference field), and press ENTER to complete the movement. With the text object currently selected, press the spacebar. Enter the message

CTRL-PGDN to change data; CTRL-W saves.

Once you press ENTER to complete the text, your screen should resemble the example shown in Figure 5-3.

```
E:MEMBERS.DBF    @ 6,15  Page: 1                                9 29 am


                    Social
              Lastname
              Firstname
              Address
              City                    State
              Zipcode

              Phone
              Birth date      / /
              Date of Expiration  / /
              Tapelimit
              Beta

         Preference memo    CTRL-PG DN to change data; CTRL-W saves.

─────────────────────────────────────────────────────────────────Ins
```

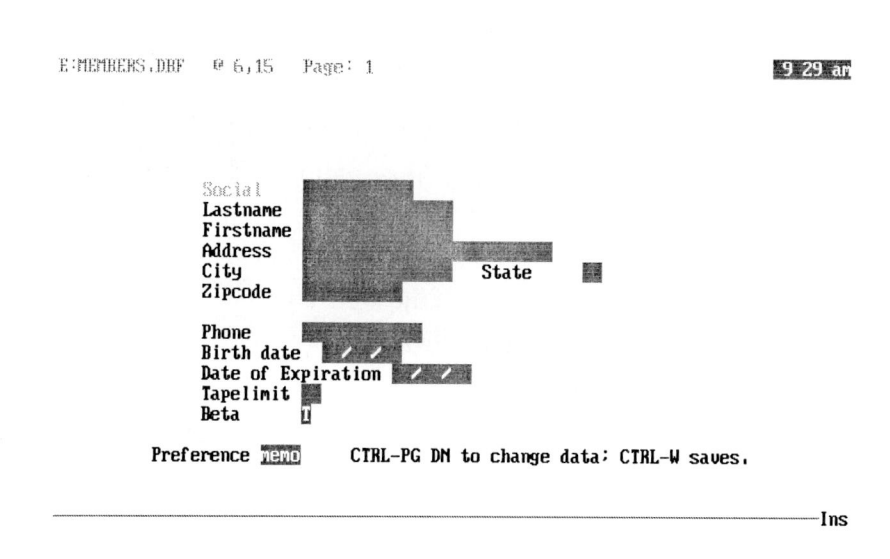

FIGURE 5-3. Completed form

SAVING SCREEN FORMAT FILES

To use the data-entry screen when you are back in FoxPro, you will need to save the file as a *screen format file*. You should also save the table, which contains the locations FoxView uses to create the screen format file. You could save just the screen format file and use the file to add or edit data; however, if you ever wanted to change the design of the screen, you would have to redo the entire screen from scratch. By saving both the screen format file and the table on which the screen's design is based, you can later modify the screen design without starting from scratch.

In FoxView, you can save screens, tables on which screens are based, and other objects related to applications design with various menu options that are available in FoxView. You can display and

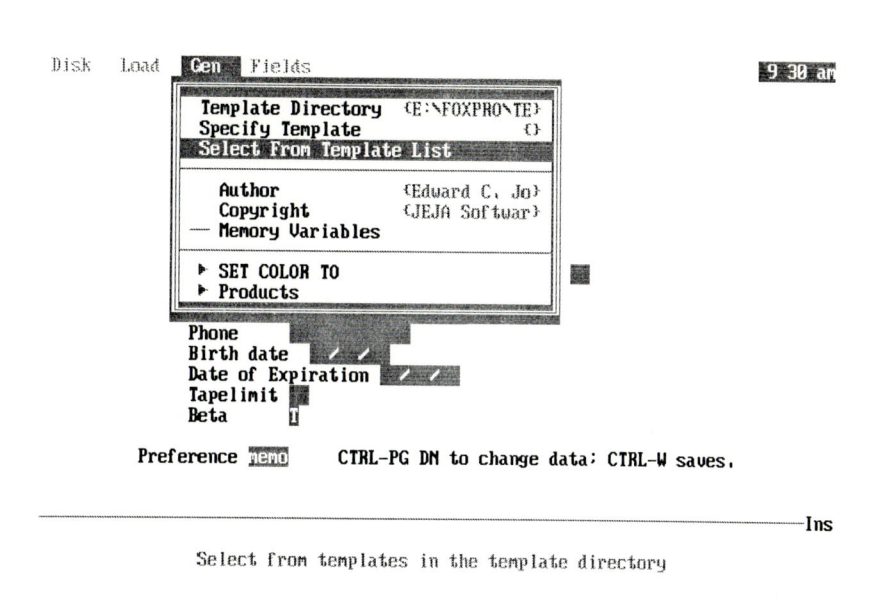

```
Disk   Load   Gen   Fields                                    9 30 am
            Template Directory    {E:\FOXPRO\TE}
            Specify Template              {}
            Select From Template List

            Author              {Edward C. Jo}
            Copyright           {JEJA Softwar}
           ─ Memory Variables

            ▶ SET COLOR TO
            ▶ Products

            Phone
            Birth date       /  /
            Date of Expiration   /  /
            Tapelimit
            Beta

            Preference  memo    CTRL-PG DN to change data; CTRL-W saves.
                                                                    ─Ins
                    Select from templates in the template directory
```

FIGURE 5-4. FoxView menus

hide the menus at any time by repeatedly pressing the ESC key. Press ESC now, and the menus will appear (Figure 5-4).

There are a number of menu options in the four menus, and most of them apply to more advanced uses of FoxView, such as generating complete applications. These will be covered in more detail in a later chapter; for this chapter, only the Select From Template List option of the Gen Menu and the Save Table option of the Load menu are appropriate. Using the Select From Template List option, you can select the Format File option from a list of possible templates; doing so will tell FoxView that you wish to create a screen format file based on the screen design you have completed.

If the Gen menu is not currently open, press the LEFT or RIGHT ARROW key until the Gen menu opens. Highlight the Select From Template List option, and press ENTER. In a moment, you will see a list of available templates (Figure 5-5).

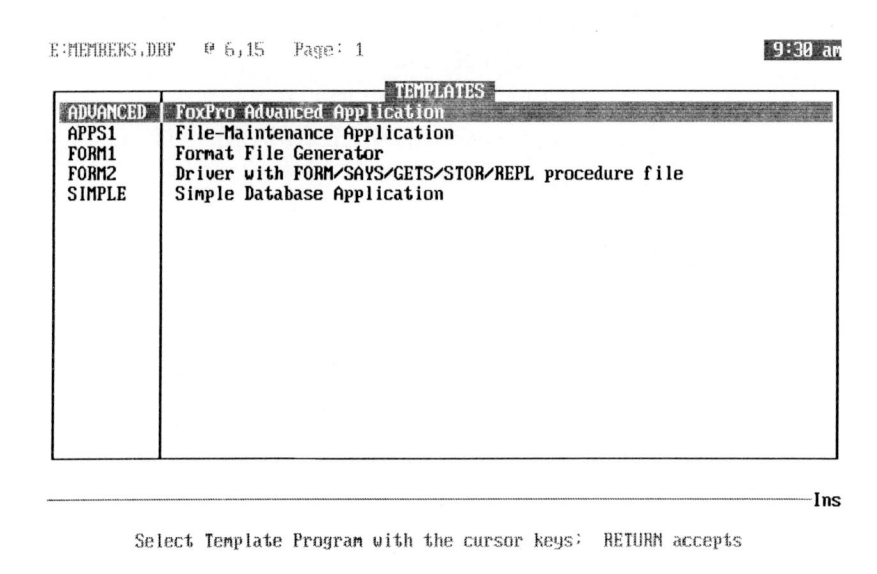

```
E:MEMBERS.DBF    @ 6,15   Page: 1                                    9:30 am
                         ┌──────TEMPLATES──────┐
          ┌─ADVANCED─┬ FoxPro Advanced Application ──────────────────┐
          │ APPS1    │ File-Maintenance Application                  │
          │ FORM1    │ Format File Generator                         │
          │ FORM2    │ Driver with FORM/SAYS/GETS/STOR/REPL procedure file │
          │ SIMPLE   │ Simple Database Application                   │
```

Select Template Program with the cursor keys; RETURN accepts

FIGURE 5-5. List of templates

Select Format File Generator from the list. At the bottom of the screen, FoxPro will now ask for a DOS filename to be assigned to the format file. Enter **MEMBERS**. You will briefly see programming commands flash on the screen as FoxPro creates a format file based on your screen design. When the process is complete the menu will reappear, and a message similar to

C:\FOXPRO\FOXDATA\MEMBERS.FMT
Program File(s) Created

will appear at the bottom of the screen.

You should now save the table on which the screen is based, so it can be modified later. To do this, you use the Save Table option of the Load menu. Press the LEFT ARROW key until the Load menu opens, and choose Save Table. Again, a prompt for a filename will appear at the bottom of the screen. Press ENTER to accept the default name of MEMBERS.FV for the file. Tables are saved with an .FV extension, and screen format files are saved with an .FMT extension. Hence, by choosing these commands you have added two new files—MEMBERS.FV and MEMBERS.FMT—to your hard disk.

LEAVING FOXVIEW

To leave FoxView, you can select Quit FoxView from the Disk menu. An alternate method of leaving FoxView is to press ESC to close any menus that are open, press SCROLL LOCK to exit Forms View mode, and enter **QUIT** at the FoxView prompt.

Open the Disk menu now, and choose Quit FoxView. In a moment, you will be returned to FoxPro.

USING A SCREEN FORMAT FILE

To use a screen format file, you first open the database with the USE command. Then you enter the command

SET FORMAT TO *filename*

where *filename* is the name of the format file you created while using FoxView. Once this is done, any full-screen operations (such as APPEND, EDIT, or CHANGE) will use the data-entry screen you designed, rather than the default data-entry screen.

To see the results of your work, enter the following commands:

USE MEMBERS
SET FORMAT TO MEMBERS
CHANGE

```
                                          Command
                                     foxview
                                     use members
                                     set format to members
          Social    121-33-9876     change
          Lastname  Martin
          Firstname William
          Address   4807 East Avenue
          City      Silver Spring    State  MD
          Zipcode   20910-0124

          Phone           301-555-2912
          Birth date      05/29/61
          Date of Expiration 07/04/91
          Tapelimit       4
          Beta            F

          Preference Memo    CTRL-PG DN to change data; CTRL-W saves.
```

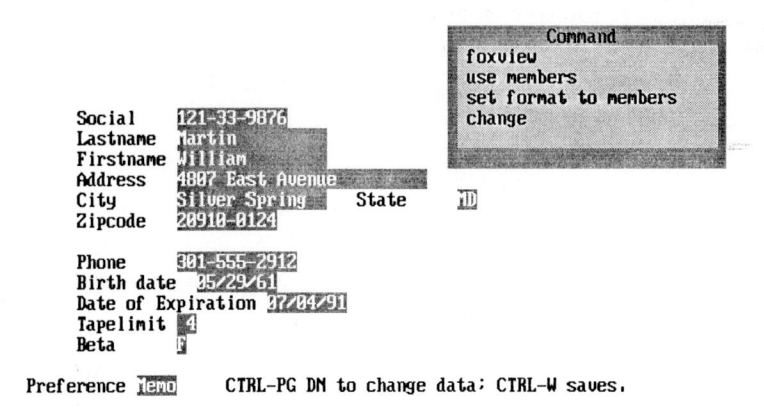

FIGURE 5-6. New form containing data

Your screen should resemble the example shown in Figure 5-6, with a record of the MEMBERS database shown within the new data-entry screen. Press ESC when you are done viewing data in the form.

MODIFYING A SCREEN FORM

To change an existing screen form, you enter FoxView by entering **FOXVIEW** as a command or choosing FoxView from the Program menu. When the FoxView shell appears, you enter the command

LOAD *filename*

where *filename* is the name of the table you saved when previously in FoxView. Once the file has been loaded, you can use F10 to get into Forms View mode. If you did not save a table while in FoxView, you will not be able to load the existing screen, even if you did save the format file.

Start FoxView now by entering **FOXVIEW** at the command level. When the FoxView shell appears, enter

LOAD MEMBERS

to load the existing table. You should see the message "14 field(s) loaded" and the cursor will reappear at the FoxView prompt. While your database contains just 13 fields, FoxView counts other objects, such as boxes and text, as fields. Hence, the addition of the text object results in the "14 fields" message that you see.

Note the difference here between the command you used when starting from scratch at the beginning of the chapter. When you first started, you entered **USE MEMBERS** to load the database file into FoxView. This time, you entered **LOAD MEMBERS** to load an existing table into FoxView. Press F10 to enter Forms View mode. Your existing form, shown earlier in Figure 5-3, should appear.

Note that while you can use the Drag key (F3) to relocate fields and the DEL key to remove fields and labels, you cannot insert an existing field into a table from Forms View mode. You can, however, insert fields while in Table View mode. This will be covered shortly.

DRAWING BOXES ON A FORM

You can draw boxes on a form with the Box (CTRL-B) key. The procedure for doing this is as follows:

1. Place the cursor at the object nearest the spot where you want to position one corner of the box. A precise location is not necessary, since you can drag the box to the desired location later.

2. Press CTRL-B to display the Select Box menu.

3. Pick one of the six available types of boxes from the menu.

4. Press ENTER to create the box, and automatically enter Drag mode.

5. Use the cursor keys to drag the box to the desired location, and press ENTER.

6. If you wish, use F4 (Size) to change the size of the box. With the box selected, press F4, and then use the cursor keys to change the box size. Press ENTER when yo are done.

To try this now, press CTRL-B to display the Select Box menu (Figure 5-7). The menu provides you with a choice of six different box types, all displayed within the menu. Choose a double line box by highlighting the choice and pressing ENTER. A double line box will appear over the form. At the same time, a message at the bottom of the screen warns you that the current shape of the box causes it to cover some of the fields in the form.

Press the UP ARROW key once and the LEFT ARROW key eight times. Then press ENTER to complete the movement. The box will still cover some fields, but you can now use the Size key (F4) to increase the size of the box.

Press F4. Use the RIGHT ARROW and DOWN ARROW keys to increase the size of the box until it measures 17 lines down and 65 characters across. You can easily tell the dimensions by examining

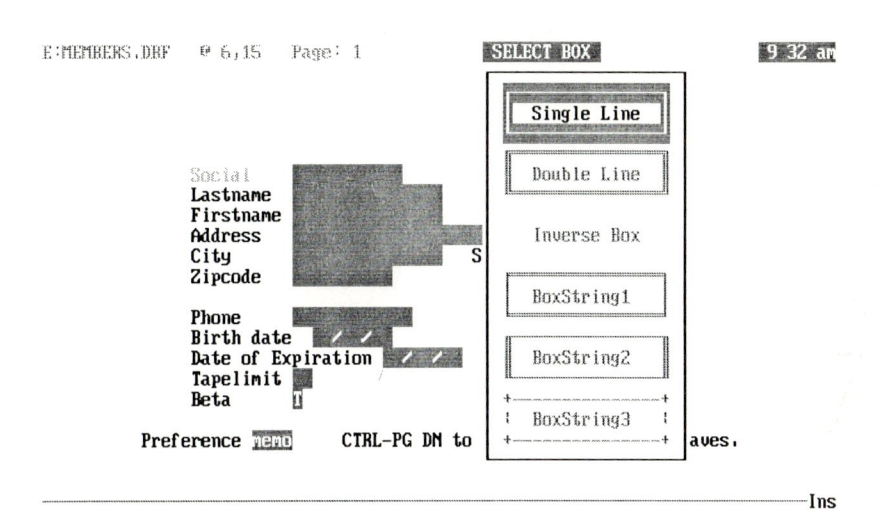

FIGURE 5-7. Select Box menu

the object name that appears at the bottom of the screen once you stretch the box past all overlapping objects. When you reach the correct size, this phrase will read

BOXOBJECT-B-65-17

The numbers 65 and 17 indicate a box size of 65 characters in width and 17 lines in height. Press ENTER to complete the resizing of the box (Figure 5-8).

If you place a box and later decide that you don't want the box, you can select it with the cursor keys and press CTRL-U to delete it. In Forms View, the CTRL-U key deletes the selected object.

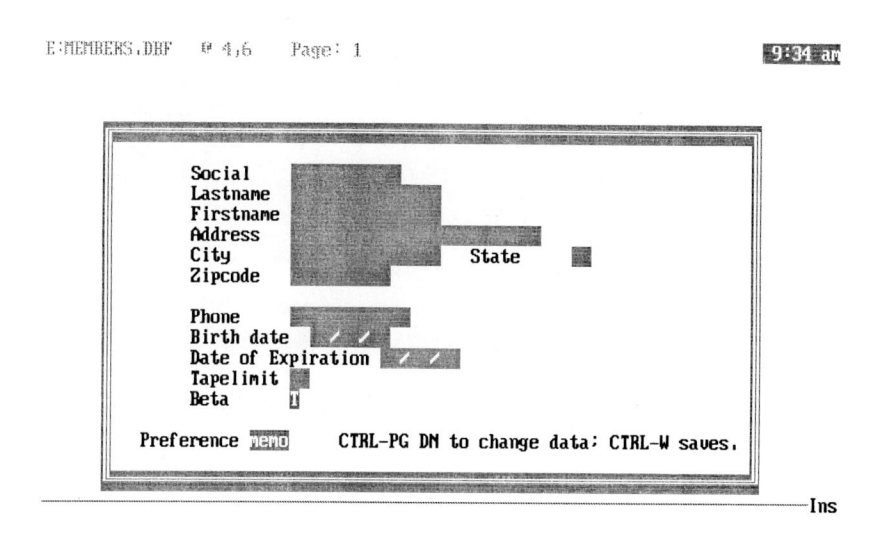

```
E:MEMBERS.DBF    # 4,6   Page: 1                                    9:34 am

        ┌─────────────────────────────────────────────────┐
        │    Social      ▬▬▬▬▬▬▬▬▬                        │
        │    Lastname    ▬▬▬▬▬▬▬▬▬▬▬▬▬                    │
        │    Firstname   ▬▬▬▬▬▬▬▬▬▬                       │
        │    Address     ▬▬▬▬▬▬▬▬▬▬▬▬▬▬▬▬▬                │
        │    City        ▬▬▬▬▬▬▬▬▬▬   State   ▬▬          │
        │    Zipcode     ▬▬▬▬▬▬                           │
        │                                                 │
        │    Phone       ▬▬▬▬▬▬▬▬▬▬▬▬                     │
        │    Birth date    /  /                           │
        │    Date of Expiration   /  /                    │
        │    Tapelimit   ▬▬                               │
        │    Beta        ▬                                │
        │                                                 │
        │    Preference  memo     CTRL-PG DN to change data; CTRL-W saves. │
        └─────────────────────────────────────────────────┘
                                                                      Ins
```

FIGURE 5-8.   Form with box added

CHANGING COLORS

If you are using a system with a color monitor, you can change the color of selected objects. The procedure for doing this is as follows:

1. Select the object(s) with the cursor keys. Extend Select (F6) may be used if more than one object will have the same color change.

2. Press the Palette key (CTRL-P) to display the color palette. If the color palette covers the fields or objects you are changing, you can move the color palette with the CTRL-LEFT ARROW and CTRL-RIGHT ARROW keys.

3. If you are working with fields, press the SLASH key (/) to switch back and forth between labels and the actual fields or shaded areas of the form.

4. Use the cursor keys to move among the different foreground and background choices of the color palette. Once the cursor highlights the desired color choice, press ENTER to assign the color to the selected object.

As an example, perhaps the Generic Videos staff wants to see the name of the member highlighted in a different color. Move the cursor to the Lastname field. Press F6 (Extend Select), and move the cursor down one line to the Firstname field; then press ENTER to complete the selection.

Press CTRL-P to display the color palette (Figure 5-9). Try pressing the slash key (/) repeatedly. As you do so, you will notice

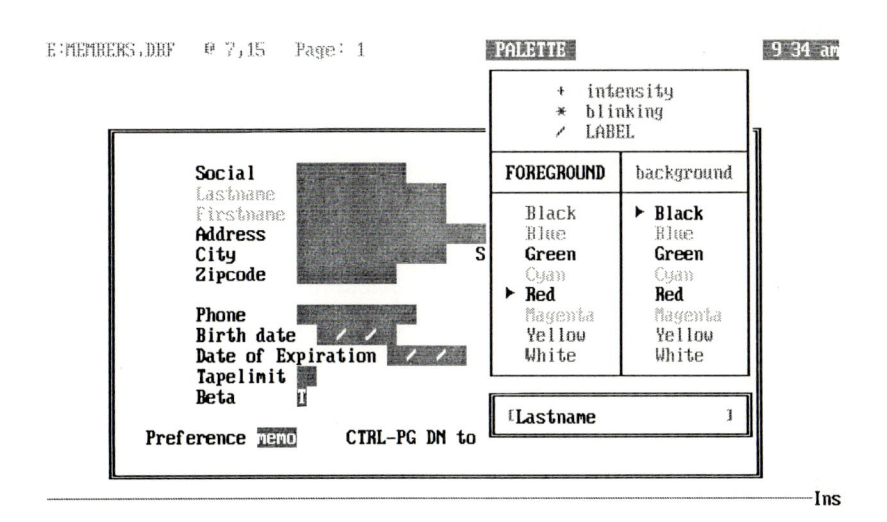

FIGURE 5-9. Color Palette

that the bottom of the palette changes between the label and the actual field. Pressing the slash key until the label appears applies successive color changes to the label, while pressing the slash until the field appears applies successive color changes to the field.

Press the slash key until the actual field, and not the label, appears at the bottom of the palette. You can now use the LEFT and RIGHT ARROW keys to move between foreground and background colors. The UP ARROW and DOWN ARROW keys may be used to move among the different available colors. As you move among the choices, you will see the results displayed at the bottom of the color palette.

Select a color combination that is appealing to you, and then press ENTER. You will not see any immediate change in the screen design, because the fields are still selected. Press the DOWN ARROW key a few times to move the selection, and you will see the new background color in the Lastname and Firstname fields. Later, when the form is used in FoxPro, you will see both the foreground and background colors with any data that is displayed in those fields.

Again, you can save the completed form as a screen format file, and you can save the underlying table. Press ESC to display the Forms View menus. Open the Gen menu, and choose Select From Template List. From the next menu to appear, choose Format File Generator. Enter **MEMBERS** as the filename when prompted for a filename, and answer Y to the prompt warning you that the old file will be overwritten.

When the menu reappears, open the Load menu and choose Save Table. Press ENTER to accept the default name of MEMBERS.FV, and answer Y to the prompt warning you that the old file will be overwritten. The modified table will be saved, and you can now exit FoxView.

Open the Disk menu and choose Quit FoxView to return to FoxPro. To see the results of the latest changes, you will first need to quit FoxPro completely and then restart the program. This is necessary because FoxPro speeds up its internal workings by keeping as much data in RAM as possible. You did change the screen's design, but because the filename is still the same, FoxPro will retrieve it from RAM rather than from disk.

Exit FoxPro and then restart the program. Enter the following commands:

USE MEMBERS
SET FORMAT TO MEMBERS
CHANGE

Your screen should resemble the example shown in Figure 5-10, with a record of the MEMBERS database shown in the modified data- entry screen.

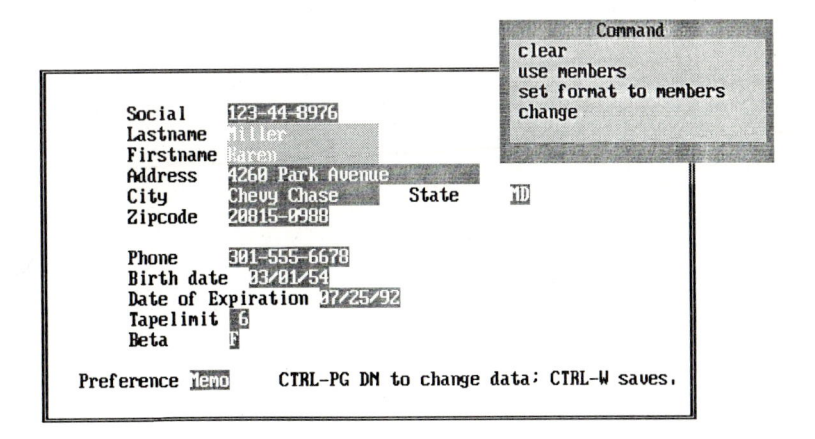

FIGURE 5-10. Modified form containing data

TABLE VIEW

FoxView lets you work with data-entry screens using either Table View or Forms View. Forms View displays the form as it will appear on the screen during data entry or editing. However, all of the underlying data that controls the appearance of the form is contained in a table. The table can be seen in Table View. By pressing F10 repeatedly, you can switch between Table View and Forms View. In effect, Table View is a kind of chart used by FoxPro to contain field characteristics, colors, sizes, locations, and so on. You can make changes to a screen form while in Table View or while in Forms View.

Table View may be visually more confusing than Forms View, but it offers significant advantages over Forms View. In Table View mode, you can limit the ways in which data is accepted into the fields. You can set rules, such as a maximum amount in the Tapelimit field. You can set formats for a field, such as a format that specifies that entries in the State field will appear as all uppercase letters.

It is important to realize is that Table View and Forms View are different visual representations of the same thing. Since the underlying table you see in Table View controls the screen appearance, any changes you make in Table View appear in the form when you are in Forms View. Likewise, the additions and changes you make to a form when in Forms View are stored (and visible in the table's columns when you switch modes) in Table View.

If you are still viewing data from within the form, press ESC to get out of Change mode. Enter **FOXVIEW** to get back into FoxView. When the FoxView shell appears, enter

LOAD MEMBERS

to load the existing table back into memory. Press F10, and you will switch to the Forms View mode of FoxView.

Creating Entry Forms   177

```
E:MEMBERS.DBF                                                    9:37 am
 #. Als Field       Typ Wid Dec  Label       Hue Row Col Pag (Fld) (Atr) Place
 1.  A  Social       C   11      [Social   ]  4   6  15   1  GET   112  SIDE
 2.  A  BOXOBJECT    B   65  17  [┌─┐│││└─┘]  4   4   6   1  SAY   112  HOR
 3.  A  Lastname     C   15      [Lastname ]  4   7  15   1  GET    48  SIDE
 4.  A  Firstname    C   15      [Firstname]  4   8  15   1  GET    48  SIDE
 5.  A  Address      C   25      [Address  ]  4   9  15   1  GET   112  SIDE
 6.  A  City         C   15      [City     ]  4  10  15   1  GET   112  SIDE
 7.  A  State        C    2      [State    ]  4  10  43   1  GET   112  SIDE
 8.  A  Zipcode      C   10      [Zipcode  ]  4  11  15   1  GET   112  SIDE
 9.  A  Phone        C   12      [Phone    ]  4  13  15   1  GET   112  SIDE
10.  A  Birthday     D    8      [Birth date] 4  14  15   1  GET   112  SIDE
11.  A  Expiredate   D    8      [Date of Exp]4  15  15   1  GET   112  SIDE
12.  A  Tapelimit    N    2      [Tapelimit ] 4  16  15   1  GET   112  SIDE
13.  A  Beta         L    1      [Beta     ]  4  17  15   1  GET   112  SIDE
14.  A  Preference   M   10      [Preference] 4  19  10   1  GET   112  SIDE
15.  A  TEXTOBJECT   T   40      [CTRL-PG DN] 4  19  30   1  SAY   112  HOR
                                                                          Ins
        FIELD: can be up to 10 alphanumeric characters and underscore
```

FIGURE 5-11.   Table View

Press F10 again until the Table View appears (Figure 5-11). There are 20 columns in Table View. You can view the various columns by using TAB and SHIFT-TAB. As you press TAB repeatedly, the eight rightmost columns are replaced with six additional columns. You can keep pressing TAB to view all the available columns in Table View mode. The columns within the table, and their purposes, are described here.

This first column contains the field numbers. They determine the order of data entry in the form; the cursor appears in field 1 first, in field 2 second, and so on. You can move fields to a new position in the table with the Move key (F7). If you do so, the field is renumbered in accordance with its new position.

Als This is the work area (or "alias") that the file is opened in. (Technically, work areas and aliases are not quite the same thing; this is covered in more detail in Chapter 11.) FoxPro can have up to ten database files opened in ten work areas, labeled A through J. By default, any file you open is opened in work area A unless you use the SELECT command (detailed in Chapter 11) to change work areas. For the purposes of this chapter, all fields in the form will use work area A.

Field This contains the field name, taken directly from the database structure when you used the USE command to load a database into FoxView.

Typ This is the field type, which can be C (character), N (numeric), F (float), D (date), L (logical), or M (memo). Two other designations can also appear in this column: B, for boxobject, and T, for textobject. Boxes you draw are designated as boxobjects in the table, while text that you add is designated as textobjects.

Wid This column indicates the width of the entry area in the form. Note that this is not necessarily the same as the actual width of the field in the database structure. For example, you might have a 20-character field, but in the form you might want to limit the visible width of the entry area to 15 characters.

Dec This column indicates the number of decimal places in a numeric field. Note that with box objects, the width and decimal columns contain the dimensions of the box. For example, the box you added has a width of 65 and a depth of 17, as indicated by the Wid and Dec columns.

Label This contains the name of the label that appears above or to the left of the actual field data-entry area. When you enter the

USE command in FoxView to open a database file, the default form uses the names of the fields as labels. You can modify these labels as desired to better reflect the purposes of the fields.

Hue This column controls the color, intensity, and blinking (if any) of the label. Different numeric values between 0 and 255 determine the exact color and whether it is displayed steadily or flashing. Because of the large number of color values, direct entry of the values into the Hue column of the table isn't recommended; it is usually much easier to select colors in Forms View mode by displaying the color palette with CTRL-P. Once you pick a desired color for a label from the color palette, you can switch back to Table View mode with F10, and the corresponding color code will appear in the Hue column.

Row This column indicates the row number where the field is located, from row 0 (the top row) to row 24 (the bottom row) of the screen.

Col This column indicates the column number where the field begins, from column 1 (the leftmost column) to column 80 (the rightmost column) on the screen.

Page This column indicates which page of the form a field appears on. You can create multiple-page data-entry forms, where certain fields appear on the first page, certain fields on the second page, and so on. Up to 16 pages are permitted on a data-entry form. When in Forms View mode, you can use the PGUP and PGDN keys to move between pages. To drag a field to a new page while in Table View, change its page number in this column. (You can move fields to another page in Forms View by highlighting the field, pressing Drag (F3), and pressing PGUP or PGDN). Note that fields can only be moved as far as the next available empty page.

Fld This column indicates whether the actual field is a GET, SAY, or hidden (HIDE) field. Once the cursor is in this column, you can press the spacebar to toggle between the three available options: GET, SAY, and HIDE. In a GET-type field, the data appears in reverse video, and it can be edited. In a SAY-type field, the data appears but cannot be edited. Contents of hidden fields do not appear in the form, but the field is shown in the table. Hidden fields are useful when you want certain fields to be available for your use but hidden from other users. As an example, you might want to include a salary field in a table so it can be used in calculations, but you might not want users to know that the salary field was present.

Atr This column controls the color, intensity, and blinking (if any) of the selected field's GET or reverse-video area (the actual field, as opposed to the label). (What this column does for the field's GET, the Hue column does for the field's label.) Different numeric values between 0 and 255 determine the exact color and whether it is displayed steadily or flashing. As with the Hue column, direct entry of the values into the Atr column of the table isn't recommended; it is easier to select colors in Forms View mode by displaying the color palette with CTRL- P. Once you pick a desired color for a field from the color palette, you can switch back to Table View mode with F10, and the corresponding color code will appear in the Atr column.

Place This column controls whether the field's GET (the reverse-video area denoting the actual field) appears beside the label or below the label. Once the cursor is in this column, you can press the spacebar to toggle between the available options: BESIDE and BELOW. Note that the Place column can also be used with text objects. With text objects, you are offered two choices: VERTICALLY (for vertical placement of the text) or HORIZONTALLY (for horizontal placement of the text).

Picture   This column lets you specify a Picture clause that will limit data entry to a specific type or format. You enter a template into this area, and the template limits how data is accepted in the field. As an example, you could restrict entries in the Zipcode field to numbers only, with a hyphen between the first five and the last four digits, by entering **99999-9999** in this column.

Range   This column defines an upper and lower boundary for a particular field. You could, for example, limit a numeric entry in a salaries field to no less than 3.50 and no more than 20.00. Any values outside of the proper range are rejected, and FoxPro displays an error message.

Valid   This column lets you enter an expression that validates the data entered. It differs from the Range column in that you can limit the data to specific values. As an example, perhaps only certain states should be accepted in a State field in a database. You could enter an expression such as

STATE $ MD VA DC

to limit the field to accept entries as only those three states. You could also include such complex expressions as LEN(TRIM(SOCIAL)) > 0, which would force an entry in the Social field, or >= DATE( ) + 366, which would force entries in a date field to be more than one year ahead of the current date. (The symbols used to define such expressions are covered in detail in the programming portion of this text.)

Note that the fields are not checked for validity until the cursor is moved out of the final field in the form. At that point, if a field entry does not meet a condition specified by the Valid option, an error message will appear and the cursor will move back to that field.

Init This column contains an optional expression, used to fill a blank field with initial data.

Calc This column defines a field as a calculated field, or a field whose contents are dependent on calculations based on other fields or memory variables.

User This column can contain any string of up to 254 characters. It is not normally used by FoxView, and you can store notes about a field in this column. However, if you use the Valid option, any text string in the User column will appear as the error message if the data entered does not meet the conditions specified by the Valid option.

MOVING FIELDS AND OBJECTS IN TABLE VIEW

You can move fields and labels around in Table View just as you can in Forms View. You can also add fields, delete fields, and change the data-entry order of fields. You must use Table View if you want to add any database fields you previously deleted from the form, or if you want to add calculated fields. If you attempt to add a field in Forms View, FoxView assumes you wish to add a text object.

To add a new field to the table, place the cursor at the desired location and press CTRL-N. A new field will be inserted below the cursor position. It will be called Noname, and its row and column positions will be directly below the prior field in the table. You can then change the name as desired. You can position the field on the resultant form by changing the Row and Col entries for the new field, or you can switch to Forms View with F10 and drag the field to the desired location. Note that adding a field to the table does not cause a new field to be added to any database. You must use

MODIFY STRUCTURE to add a corresponding field to the database.

To delete a field from the table, highlight the desired field and press CTRL-U. The field will be deleted from the table (and from its location in Forms View). Using this option does *not* delete the field from the corresponding database; it only means that the field will not be used in the form.

To change the data-entry order of fields, you can either move fields to new locations or you can resequence the fields. As an example, in the current form, when the cursor leaves the Zipcode field, it moves to the Birthday field. If you wanted the cursor to enter the Birthday field before the Zipcode field, you could move the Zipcode field underneath the Birthday field in the table. You move a field in the table by highlighting the field, pressing Move (F7), moving the cursor to the field that you want to come right before your relocated field (in this case, the State field), and pressing ENTER. Even though the fields would still appear at the same place in the form, the cursor would move to the Birthday field before moving to the Zipcode field. This is because field movement always occurs from the top of the table to the bottom. Field location in the form, however, is controlled by the row and column entries.

You can also use the Resequence key (F5) to resequence the data-entry order of all the fields. When you press F5, a prompt appears containing the following question:

RESEQUENCE fields by Row, Col, or Attribute (R/C/A)?

Choosing Row causes the fields in the table to be rearranged based on the row number of each field. The lower the row number, the earlier in the table the field appears. (If there is more than one object on a row, they are arranged by column number.) Choosing Column causes the fields in the table to be rearranged based on column positions of each field. The lower the column number, the earlier in the table the field appears. (If there is more than one object in a column, they are arranged by row number.)

Choosing Attribute causes the fields to be placed in order based on whatever attribute in the table the cursor is presently highlighting. For example, if you move the cursor to the Label column, press F5, and choose Attribute, the fields will be arranged in the table in alphabetical order based on what's in the Label column. If you move the cursor to the Typ column, press F5, and choose Attribute, the fields will be arranged in the table in groups of field type, with box objects first, character fields second, date fields third, floating fields fourth, logical fields fifth, memo fields sixth, and text objects last. You may want to try the Resequence key now, using the various options, to see the effects on the table. When you are done, press F5 and choose Row to resequence the table by row order.

USING PICTURE

The Picture column can be used to format the manner in which data is displayed or accepted into the fields of a form. By using certain functions and templates in the Picture column of the table, you can display all characters as uppercase letters, or you can display the dates in American (MM/DD/YY) or European (DD/MM/YY) date format. You can also use these options to restrict the way data can be entered into the system. You can specify that only letters or only numbers will be accepted, and with numeric fields you can specify a range of acceptable numbers. You can enter picture functions or picture templates into the Picture column.

Picture functions are used to restrict entries to all letters, to identify any lowercase-to-uppercase conversion of data from the database, and to format an entry. Picture templates let you choose what types of data users of the form will see and be allowed to enter. They are represented by an @ symbol followed by the characters that represent the desired function.

Templates also let you format a field by adding special characters. As an example, you could use a picture template to cause all phone numbers in a database to be displayed with parenthesis and hyphens, as in (202) 555-1212. The parenthesis and hyphens would be stored in the database, and they would appear automatically within the form. Templates consist of one character for every character that the user can enter into the field. The main difference between picture functions and picture templates is that picture functions affect the entire field, while picture templates allow you to restrict and format data one character at a time. Table 5-2 shows the possible picture functions and templates you can use.

As an example, you might wish to convert all characters entered

Symbol	Meaning
	Functions:
!	Converts letters to uppercase
A	Displays alphabetic characters only
S	Allows horizontal scrolling of characters
M	Allows multiple choice
T	Trims trailing spaces
B	Left alignment of entry
I	Center alignment of entry
C	Positive credits followed by CR
X	Negative credits followed by DB
(	Uses () around negative numbers
L	Displays leading zeros
Z	Displays zeros as blanks
$	Displays numbers in financial format
^	Displays numbers in exponential format
R	Allows use of literals within a template without having those literals stored in the database
	Templates:
A	Allows only letters
L	Allows only logical data (true/false, yes/no)
N	Allows only letters or digits
X	Allows any character
Y	Allows Y or N
#	Allows only digits, blanks, periods, or signs
9	Allows only digits for character data, or digits and signs for numeric data
!	Converts letters to uppercase
other	Used to format the entry; for example, with hyphens and parentheses to format a phone number, as in (999) 999-9999

TABLE 5-2. Picture Functions and Templates

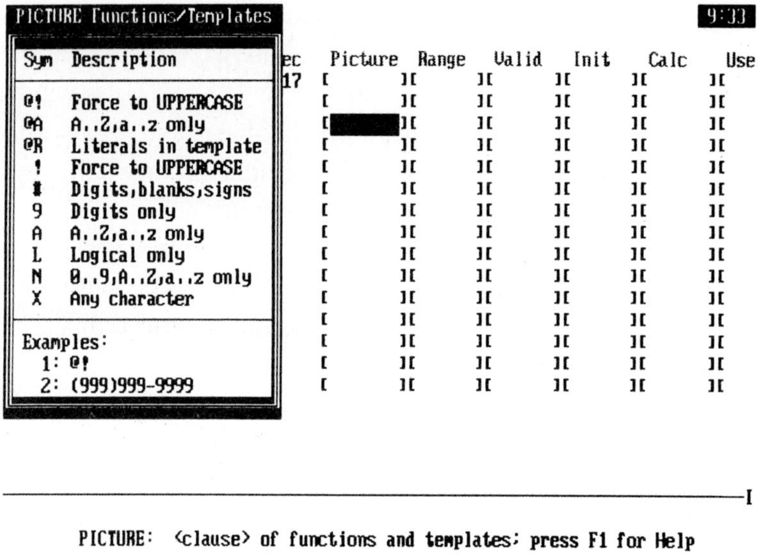

```
┌─────────────────────────────────────────────────────────────────────────┐
│ PICTURE Functions/Templates                                        9:33 │
│ ┌──────────────────────────────┐                                        │
│ │ Sym  Description             │ ec  Picture  Range  Valid  Init  Calc  Use │
│ │                              │ 17  [    ][    ][    ][    ][    ][    ] │
│ │ @!   Force to UPPERCASE      │     [    ][    ][    ][    ][    ][    ] │
│ │ @A   A..Z,a..z only          │     [█   ][    ][    ][    ][    ][    ] │
│ │ @R   Literals in template    │     [    ][    ][    ][    ][    ][    ] │
│ │  !   Force to UPPERCASE      │     [    ][    ][    ][    ][    ][    ] │
│ │  #   Digits,blanks,signs     │     [    ][    ][    ][    ][    ][    ] │
│ │  9   Digits only             │     [    ][    ][    ][    ][    ][    ] │
│ │  A   A..Z,a..z only          │     [    ][    ][    ][    ][    ][    ] │
│ │  L   Logical only            │     [    ][    ][    ][    ][    ][    ] │
│ │  N   0..9,A..Z,a..z only     │     [    ][    ][    ][    ][    ][    ] │
│ │  X   Any character           │     [    ][    ][    ][    ][    ][    ] │
│ │                              │     [    ][    ][    ][    ][    ][    ] │
│ │ Examples:                    │     [    ][    ][    ][    ][    ][    ] │
│ │   1: @!                      │     [    ][    ][    ][    ][    ][    ] │
│ │   2: (999)999-9999           │     [    ][    ][    ][    ][    ][    ] │
│ └──────────────────────────────┘                                        │
└─────────────────────────────────────────────────────────────────────────┘

PICTURE: <clause> of functions and templates; press F1 for Help
```

FIGURE 5-12. Help screen for Picture functions and templates

in the Lastname field to uppercase letters. Move the cursor to the Lastname field of the table, and use TAB or SHIFT- TAB to get over to the Picture column. You could refer to Table 5-2 for help with the possible functions and templates. However, note that FoxPro also offers specific help for the Picture and Range columns; whenever you are in Table View and the cursor is in the Picture column, pressing F1 displays a help screen with suggestions for functions and templates for that particular type of field.

If you press F1 now, you will see the help screen shown in Figure 5-12. This help screen varies according to field types. If the cursor is in a character field, you see the help screen that is visible now. If the cursor is in a date field, you see a help screen showing functions and templates that apply to date fields.

As the help screen shows, the ! template forces letters to uppercase. Press ESC to exit the help screen, and enter **@!** in the Picture column of the Lastname field now. The @ symbol denotes that this is a function, and it will therefore apply to the entire field and not just to one character. You could accomplish the same thing by entering the picture template

!!!!!!!!!!!!!!

in the field, and this would force each character position in the field to uppercase letters.

USING RANGE

You can use the Range column to define an upper and lower boundary for a particular field. As an example, you could limit a numeric entry in a salary field to no less than 3.50 and no more than 20.00. Any values outside of the proper range are rejected, and FoxPro displays an error message. To define a range, you enter an appropriate expression into the Range column of the desired field. Note that the use of the Range column is not limited to numeric fields; you can establish ranges of dates, or even of alphabetic values (such as from A to M).

Move the cursor down to the Tapelimit field. In the Range column, you can enter a range of acceptable values for this numeric field. Once you move the cursor into the Range column of the Tapelimit row, press F1. The help screen that appears, shown in Figure 5-13, shows how you can enter data in the Range column.

As the help screen shows in its second example, it is possible to enter just one value as a range. If the value follows the comma, it indicates an upper limit. If the value precedes the comma, it indicates a lower limit. As an example, entering

188   **FoxPro Made Easy**

in the Tapelimit field would set a maximum of 8 tapes with no set minimum, and entering

2,

in the Tapelimit field would set a minimum of 2 tapes with no set maximum. For this example, enter

2,10

in the Tapelimit column now. You can also use expressions, as demonstrated in the help screen. In the last example from the help screen, the expression

CTOD('01/01/86'),CTOD('12/31/86')

```
RANGE Expressions                                                 9:04
┌─────────────────────────────────────────┐  Range  Valid  Init  Calc  Use
│ Select a LOWER and/or UPPER boundary    │[   ][    ][    ][    ][    ]
│ expression for Numeric or Date fields.  │[   ][    ][    ][    ][    ]
│                                         │[   ][    ][    ][    ][    ]
│ Examples:                               │[   ][    ][    ][    ][    ]
│   1: 1000,75000                         │[   ][    ][    ][    ][    ]
│   2: ,49.95                             │[   ][    ][    ][    ][    ]
│   3: (12 * 4),(12 * 80 - 6)             │[   ][    ][    ][    ][    ]
│   4: CTOD('01/01/87'),                  │[   ][    ][    ][    ][    ]
│   5: CTOD('01/01/86'),CTOD('12/31/86')  │[   ][    ][    ][    ][    ]
└─────────────────────────────────────────┘[   ][    ][    ][    ][    ]
 10. A  Birthday    D   8     [   ][   ][    ][    ][    ][    ]
 11. A  Expiredate  D   8     [   ][   ][    ][    ][    ][    ]
 12. A  Tapelimit   N   2     [   ][███][    ][    ][    ][    ]
 13. A  Beta        L   1     [   ][   ][    ][    ][    ][    ]
 14. A  Preference  M  10     [   ][   ][    ][    ][    ][    ]
 15. A  TEXTOBJECT  T  35     [   ][   ][    ][    ][    ][    ]

            RANGE: <lower exp>,<upper exp>; press F1 for Help
```

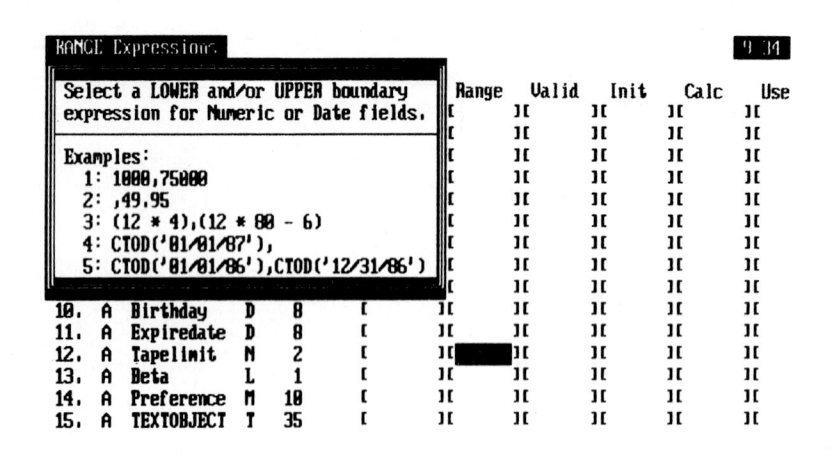

FIGURE 5-13. Help Screen for Range column

limits a date-type field to any date between 1/1/86 and 12/31/86. Another way to do this would be to enter

{1/1/86},{12/31/86}

because FoxPro lets you express date values by surrounding them with a set of curly braces. The help screen shows the older FoxBase+/dBASE III+ format, which must use the CTOD expressions.

Again, you can save the completed form as a screen format file, and you should also save the underlying table. (If you save the form as a format file but do not save the table, you will be able to use the form to edit data, but if you ever want to modify the form you will have to build it from scratch.)

Press ESC to display the Forms View menus. From the Gen menu, choose Select From Template List. From the next menu to appear, choose Format File Generator. Enter **MEMBERS** as the filename when prompted for a filename, and answer Y to the prompt warning you that the old file will be overwritten.

When the menu reappears, open the Load menu and choose Save Table. Press ENTER to accept the default name of MEMBERS.FV, and answer Y to the prompt warning you that the old file will be overwritten. The modified table will be saved, and you can now exit FoxView.

Open the Disk menu and choose Quit FoxView to return to FoxPro. To see the results of the latest changes, you will first need to quit FoxPro completely and then restart the program. Again, if you don't exit FoxPro completely, FoxPro will retrieve it from RAM rather than from disk. Exit FoxPro, and then restart the program. Enter the following commands:

```
USE MEMBERS
SET FORMAT TO MEMBERS
APPEND
```

Try entering a new record, noting the effects of the Picture and Range limits to the Lastname, Tapelimit, and State fields. When done, you may want to delete the extra record by entering

GO 9
DELETE
PACK

so it does not appear in examples of reports in later chapters.

FOXVIEW AND DOS

Because FoxView is a stand-alone program, you do not have to be in FoxPro to run it. You can run it directly from the DOS prompt, if desired. Just switch to the subdirectory containing your program files and enter **FOXVIEW** at the DOS prompt to load FoxView.

6

PERFORMING QUERIES

Performing Queries with the Menus
Reporting Needs
Performing Queries with Commands
Using SET FILTER with Commands
Using View Files

This chapter covers an important subject: getting the desired data out of your database. Performing *queries,* or the fine art of asking questions, is the most common task done with computer databases. With so much time spent in this area, it pays to know the best ways to query a database in FoxPro. There are many ways to get desired data out of a database in FoxPro. Some are faster than others, and different ways are often best suited to different tasks.

As with most activities in FoxPro, data can be retrieved with the menus and with commands. When it comes to queries, you're likely to see a distinct advantage the use of commands over menus. The commands, once learned, tend to be faster to implement; querying a database through the menus often involves a large number of menu selections. Also, the command structure can be used as an integral part of programs written in FoxPro, and the programming language (which you will begin to learn about in

Chapter 12) is a major resource of FoxPro. The first portion of this chapter highlights queries performed through menu selections, and the second half covers queries performed with commands.

PERFORMING QUERIES WITH THE MENUS

All of your data retrieval tasks will involve one of two scenarios: either you will need to select a single record or you will need to isolate a subgroup of records (a process often followed by the printing of a report). If a single record is all you need, the GoTo, Locate, and Seek options, found on the Record menu, are what you are after.

Using GoTo

The GoTo option lets you move to the top or bottom of the file, move by a set number of records, or move to a specific record (by record number). For example, if you know that record #7 needs to be edited, you can (after opening the database with a USE command or with the Open option of the File menu) open the Record menu and choose GoTo. When you do this, the dialog box shown in Figure 6-1 appears. Four options are provided: Top, Bottom, Record, and Skip. You must choose an option, then Tab over to the GoTo button in the dialog box, and press ENTER (or mouse-click on the button) to implement your choice.

Choosing Top will move the record pointer to the top of the database, while the Bottom option will move the record pointer to the last record in the database. The Skip option lets you move the record pointer by a certain number of records. If you choose Skip, the number 1 will appear in an entry field, because the Skip option assumes you want to skip forward by one record. You can enter any other number you want, including negative numbers; for

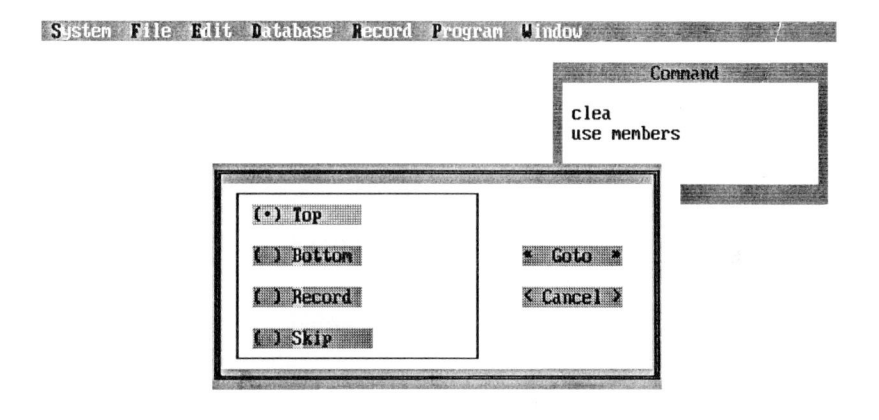

FIGURE 6-1. GoTo dialog box

example, entering − 5 would move you back five records in the database, and entering **42** would move you forward 42 records. If you choose the Record option, the number 1 appears in an entry field, and you can enter the record number of the desired record. Once you make your choice of ways to move the record pointer, you can tab over to the GoTo button and press ENTER, and the pointer will move to the desired record.

These methods are fine when you know by its record number where a record is located. Unfortunately, this is usually not the case; most users performing queries have no idea where a desired record may be. Thus, you need some sort of search operation. Searches can be performed with the Locate, Continue, and Seek option, also found on the Record menu. The Seek option assumes the use of an index, and the resulting search must be performed based on the field or fields used to build the index. Therefore, if

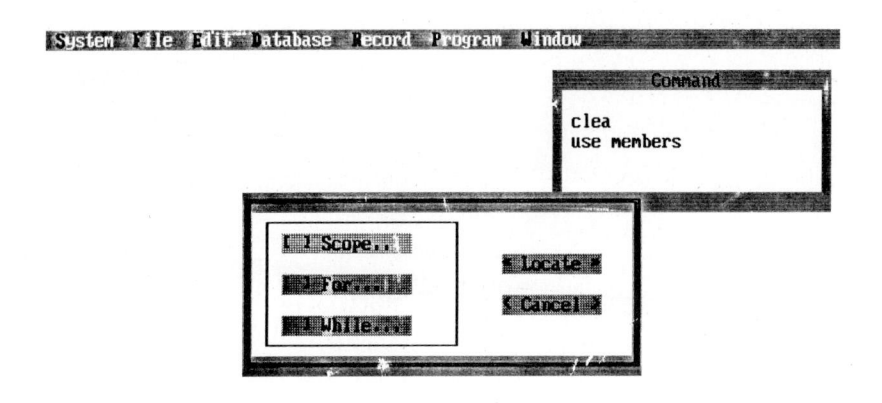

FIGURE 6-2. Locate dialog box

you wanted to perform a seek based on the last name, the database would need to be indexed on the Lastname field (or on a combination of fields that begins with the Lastname field). Locate and Continue do not need an index, but with large databases, they are considerably slower than Seek.

Using Locate

To find a record without an index in use, open the Record menu and choose Locate. The dialog box shown in Figure 6-2 appears. This dialog box provides you with three options: Scope, For, and While.

The Scope option reveals yet another dialog box with four options: All, Next, Record, and Rest. The optional use of a scope lets you define a further limit to the operation of the Locate option. You can choose All to specify that the use of Locate should span all records; this is the default. You can choose Next and then enter a number that specifies a group of records starting with wherever the pointer is now located; for example, entering **10** would tell FoxPro to limit its use of Locate to the next ten records. You can choose Record and enter a number, which again selects a specific record by its record number. (In the case of Locate, this is a useless option, since if you knew the record number, you wouldn't need a search.) Or you can choose Rest, which limits the use of Locate to all records located between the pointer and the end of the file. Again, none of these options will be of much help unless you know something about where the desired record is located.

The For and While options that appear after you choose Locate are the options likely to prove most useful. The While option works best with an index, but the For option can easily be used on any field, whether an index exists or not. Choose For from the dialog box, and the Expression Builder containing a For Clause window next appears (Figure 6-3). In this window, you enter the expression

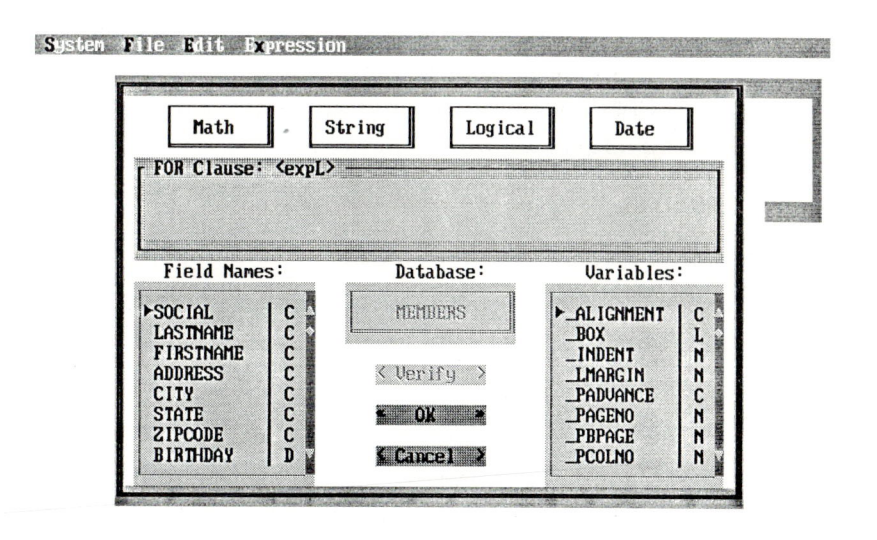

FIGURE 6-3. Expression Builder with For Clause window

that will locate the record you want. An *expression* is a combination of field names, operators, and constants that evaluate to a certain value. The term

LASTNAME = "Morris"

is an expression, as is

TAPELIMIT > 3

which evaluates to a tape limit of more than 3. If the parts of the expression do not make sense at this point, don't be too concerned; they will be explained in more detail later in this chapter.

Field names, which are normally used to build search expressions, can be selected from the Field Names box in the lower-left corner of the dialog box. Once a name is selected, it appears in the For Clause window. (As an alternative, you may choose to enter the field name in the For Clause window by typing it.) The next step is usually to enter an operator, such as an equal sign. You can choose most of the commonly used operators by mouse-clicking on the Logical box and selecting the operator from a pull-down menu; however, it is usually faster just to type the symbol into the For Clause box. Finally, enter the desired search value. Text expressions are always entered with quotes surrounding them; numbers are entered exactly as they are stored in the numeric field; and dates may be entered with the CTOD function. For example, CTOD("12/20/90") would be evaluated as a date value of 12/20/90. You can also use memo fields within your conditions when searching for a value.

You will make use of logical operators (covered in more detail in later chapters) to apply multiple conditions to a search. Two common logical operators are .AND. and .OR., which specify whether all conditions must be met (.AND.) or whether either condition can be met (.OR.). For example, the condition

LASTNAME = "Robinson" .AND. TAPELIMIT = 2

specifies that the last name must be Robinson, and the tape limit must contain a value of 2. The condition

CITY = "Falls Church" .OR. CITY = "Arlington"

specifies that the City field must contain either Arlington or Falls Church. Note that the logical operators are always surrounded by periods.

You can check your expression for correct syntax, if desired, by tabbing to or clicking on the Verify button. If the expression is a valid one, FoxPro will display an "Expression is valid" message. Finally, tab to or click on the OK button to finish your entry. The Locate dialog box will reappear, with the For option selected. You can now tab to or click on the Locate button to implement the search. Remember, the process only locates the record—it does not display it. You can now choose the Change option of the Record menu to view the record.

Consider a simple example, which you can duplicate if you've created the MEMBERS database outlined in Chapter 2. Perhaps you need to locate Mr. Kramer, a member of the video club. Assuming the MEMBERS file is open, you can open the Record menu with ALT-R, choose Locate, and select the For option when the Locate dialog box (shown in Figure 6-2) appears. The For Clause dialog box next appears (Figure 6-3); your desired expression will be LASTNAME = "Kramer". You can simply type this into the For Clause window, or you can select Lastname from the list of fields, type an equal sign or choose one from the pull-down menu that appears when you tab to the Logical menu and press the spacebar (or mouse-click on the Logical menu), and then type **"Kramer"** (you must include the quotation marks). For mouse users, an alternative to typing the quotation marks is to click on the String box and select Text from the pull-down that appears,

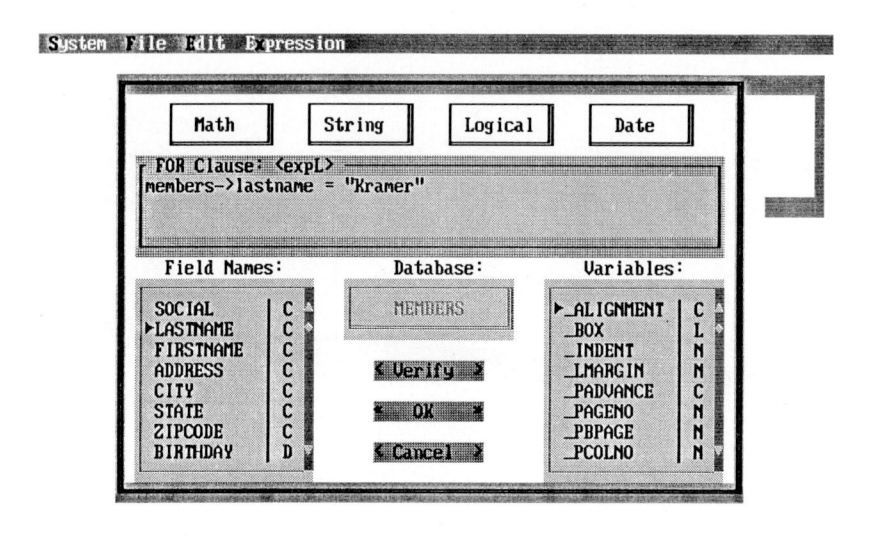

FIGURE 6-4. Filled-in For Clause dialog box

and then type the name; but again, it is usually faster to just type in the quotation marks manually.

Once all this is done, the For Clause dialog box resembles the example shown in Figure 6-4. (If you entered the field name manually, you probably won't have the filename prefix (MEMBERS->) in your example; it is added if you select the field name from the list box. Such prefixes are needed for working with multiple files, as covered in Chapter 11; when you are working with just one file, it does not matter whether they are included or not.

You next select the OK button, and the Locate dialog box reappears. Finally, click on the Locate button in the Locate dialog box to implement the search. If you then choose Change from the Record menu, the desired record appears.

Probably the strongest argument for using commands in place of the menu options appears in the Command window after you've completed the operation just described. These two commands are shown in the window:

LOCATE ALL FOR members->lastname = "Kramer"
CHANGE

They could have been entered from Command mode to perform the same task. Even the "members->" could have been omitted, as this combination of the database name, greater-than symbol, and hyphen identifies the file, and such identifiers are optional when you only have one file open. Hence, the command

LOCATE ALL FOR LASTNAME = "Kramer"

would have worked just as well as the menu options.

When you use Locate, FoxPro searches by examining the characters in your search term from left to right, so you need only enter as much of the term as necessary to find the record. For example, the command

LOCATE FOR LASTNAME = "Jo"

would be enough to find a person named Jones if there were no other names with "Jo" as the first two letters of the name.

When selected, the While option in the Locate dialog box (see Figure 6-2) causes the same Expression Builder to appear; the only difference is the window that will contain the expression is labelled "While Clause." Figure 6-5 shows an example of the Expression Builder containing the While Clause window. Using the While option takes a little more planning than using the For option, because the While clause is only effective "while" a condition exists. For example, if you were to enter **LASTNAME = "Kramer"** as an expression in the While Clause dialog box, FoxPro would only locate the record while the condition was true; in other

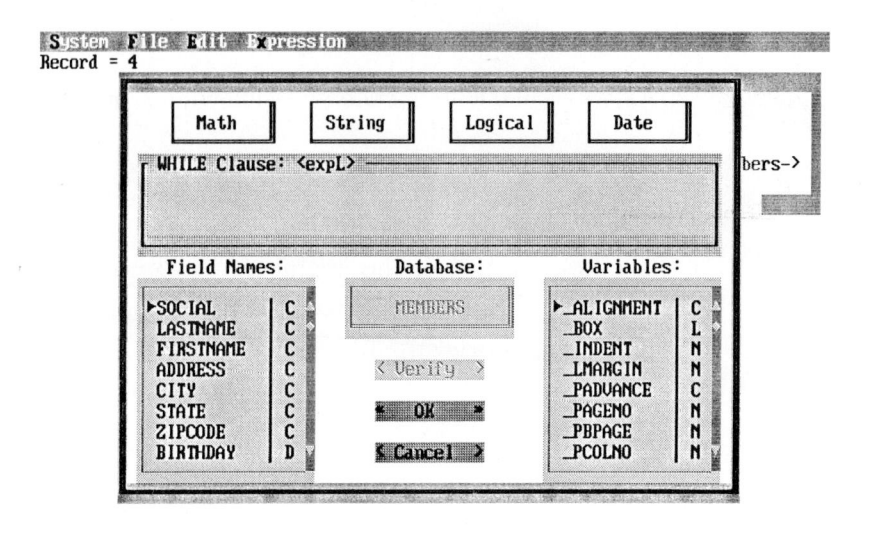

FIGURE 6-5. Expression Builder with While Clause window

words, the database pointer would need to already be at a record with Kramer in the Lastname field.

While clauses are normally used with indexed files, where you want to locate all records while a certain condition is true. For example, with a database indexed by tape limit, you could find the first record with a tape limit of 6, and then perform a Locate operation while the tape limit was 6.

Using Continue

The Locate option finds the first occurrence of what you are looking for. If there is more than one occurrence, you can use the Continue option to find successive records with the same search term. For example, your database might contain two persons with a last name of Robinson, and the use of Locate might turn up the wrong one. You can again open the Record menu with ALT-R and choose Continue. The Continue option is available from the menu only after you have used the Locate option. It will continue the search, seeking the next record that meets the condition you specified when using Locate. If no further records meet the specified condition, you will see an "End of Locate scope" message on the screen. (You will see the same error message if an initial use of Locate fails to find a record.)

Using Seek

If a file has been indexed, you can search the index with the Seek option. When you open the Record menu and choose Seek, the Expression Builder appears, containing a Value to Seek window (Figure 6-6). Again, the operation of the Seek option's Expression

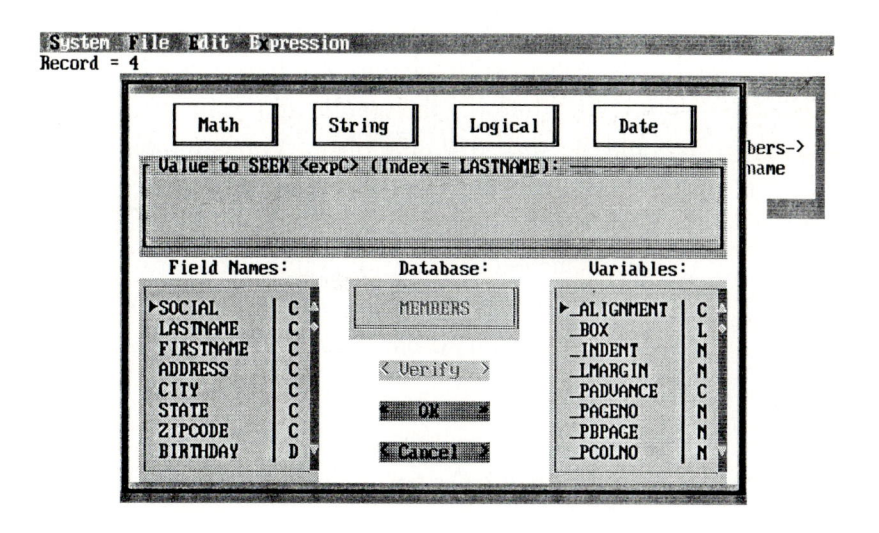

FIGURE 6-6. Expression Builder with Value to Seek window

Builder is like that used with the For and While options of Locate. Seek simply works much faster with large files, because it takes less time to search an indexed file.

You enter the desired expression into the Value to Seek window. However, you only need enter the expression itself, since FoxPro knows which field (or fields) the index is based on. For example, instead of entering LASTNAME = "Kramer" as was done with Locate, you would only enter **"Kramer"** in the Value to Seek window, assuming the active index is based on Lastname. Remember that since Seek is designed to work with an index, you must search for data based on the index. (You could not, for example, use Seek to search for a last name if the database was indexed only by social security number.)

Text expressions are always entered surrounded by quotes; numbers are entered exactly as they are stored in the numeric field; and dates may be entered with the CTOD function. As an example of Seek, if the video database were indexed on the Tapelimit field, you could enter **4** in the Value to Seek window, and the Seek option would find the first record with a value of 4 in the Tapelimit field. If the database were indexed on the Expiredate field, you could enter **CTOD("12/20/90")** in the Value to Seek window to find the first record with the expiration date of 12/20/90.

After entering the search value, tab to or click on the OK button, and the seek will take place. You can then use the Change option of the Record menu to view the desired record. Keep in mind that the Seek option finds the first occurrence in the index. If there are duplicate occurrences of that index expression (such as more than one last name of Robinson in a file indexed on Lastname only), you may want to use Browse to aid you in finding the desired record.

Selecting Subsets of Data

Often, a query involves selecting a group of records. For example, you may want to see all members who live in Maryland or Virginia.

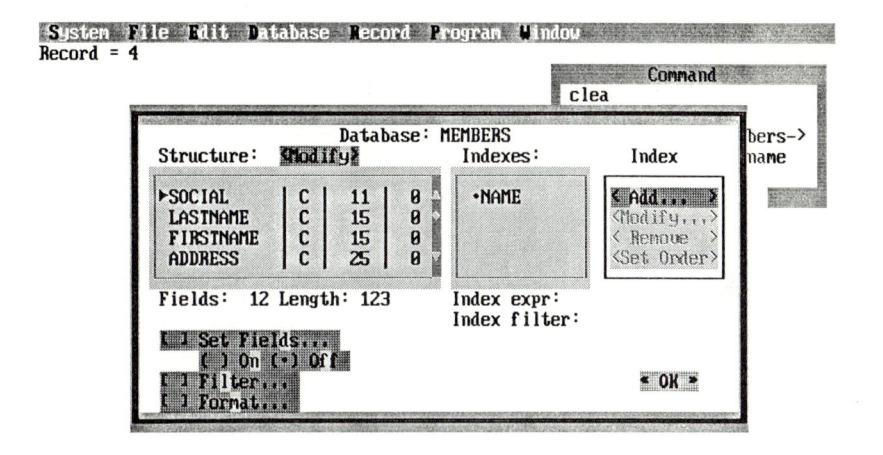

FIGURE 6-7. Setup dialog box

From the menus, this can be done with the Setup option of the Database menu. This option will, among other things, let you set a filter that restricts the available records; in effect, the records shown must meet the conditions of the filter that you specify.

When you open the Database menu and choose Setup, the Setup dialog box appears (Figure 6-7). This dialog box is used for many tasks; the one this chapter is concerned with is the Filter option, shown in the lower-left corner of the dialog box. If you choose Filter (by pressing the highlighted letter "L" or by tabbing to it or mouse-clicking on the option), the Expression Builder containing a Set Filter Expression window appears (Figure 6-8). By now, the design of the Expression Builder should be quite familiar; you enter an expression in the same manner as with the For option of the Locate command. Field names can be selected from the Field Names box in the lower-left corner of the dialog box. Once a name

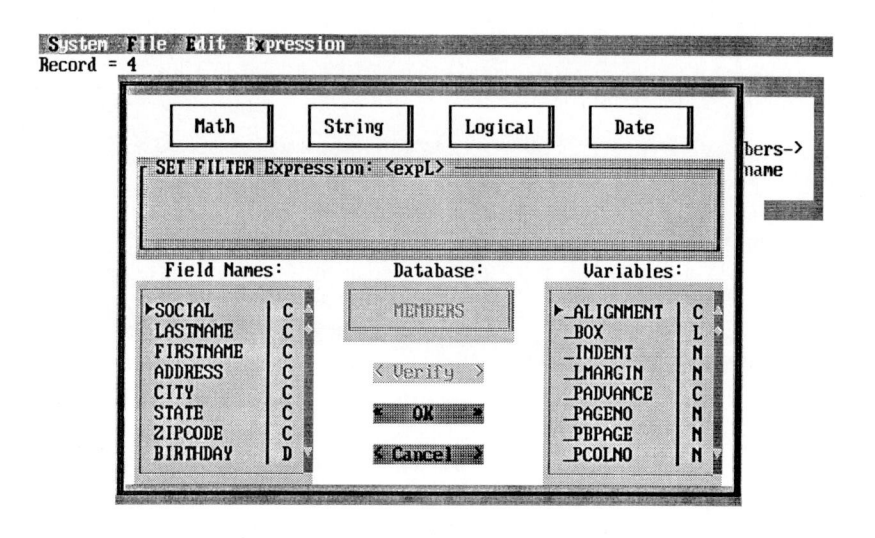

FIGURE 6-8. Expression Builder with Set Filter Expression window

is selected, it appears in the Set Filter Expression window. (As an alternative, you can enter the name in the For Clause window by typing it.) Next, you enter the desired operator, such as the equal sign. Finally, enter the desired search value. Remember to surround text expressions with quotes and enter any dates with the CTOD function. As an example, the expression

TAPELIMIT = 6

would select a group of records with a value of 6 in the Tapelimit field. The expression,

STATE = "MD" .OR. STATE = "VA"

would select records with either Maryland or Virginia in the State field.

Once you enter the expression and choose the OK button, the Database Structure dialog box reappears. Choose the OK button in this dialog box, and the needed SET FILTER command appears in the Command window. You must press ENTER to execute the command. You can then proceed to perform a browse to see your records meeting the condition, or you can use the LIST command to produce a simple on-screen report.

Again, consider a simple example. Perhaps you need a list of all customers in the video database who live in Maryland or Virginia. You would open the Database menu with ALT-D, choose Setup, and select Filter from the dialog box that appears. The Expression Builder would next appear, as shown in Figure 6-8. You would next enter the following expression in the Set Filter Expression window:

STATE = "MD" .OR. STATE = "VA"

Then you would select the OK button, and again select the OK button in the next dialog box that appears. The resultant command, which is

SET FILTER TO STATE = "MD" .OR. STATE = "VA"

now appears in the Command window, with the cursor flashing at the end of the line. You press ENTER to implement the command, and the filter is set. At this point, you could choose Browse from the Database menu to see the records meeting your filter condition.

REPORTING NEEDS

If you need a report based on a select group of data, one method is to use the menu options just described for setting a filter as a part of a three-step process. First, design and save a report, as detailed in Chapters 7 and 10 (this only needs to be done once). Then use the menu options just described to set the desired filter conditions. Finally, select the Report option from the Database menu to print the report.

Another method works well if a simple columnar report with no fancy headings will suffice. Set the filter as described earlier, then use the LIST command with the desired fields, and add the TO PRINT option to route the output to the printer. For example, after setting the filter condition described in the prior example, you could enter the command

LIST LASTNAME, FIRSTNAME, STATE, EXPIREDATE TO PRINT

to produce a columnar listing of the above named fields at the printer. Such a list would resemble the example shown here:

Record#	LASTNAME	FIRSTNAME	STATE	EXPIREDATE
1	Miller	Karen	MD	07/25/92
2	Martin	William	MD	07/04/91
3	Robinson	Carol	VA	09/05/93
4	Kramer	Harry	VA	12/22/90
5	Moore	Ellen	MD	11/17/94
6	Zachman	David	VA	09/19/90
8	Hart	Wendy	VA	10/19/92

You will find additional details on the use of the LIST command with the TO PRINT option in Chapter 7.

PERFORMING QUERIES WITH COMMANDS

There are four commands you can use to search for items in FoxPro: LOCATE, CONTINUE, FIND, and SEEK. The LO-

CATE and CONTINUE commands perform a sequential search (checking one record at a time) and will work with any database. The FIND and SEEK commands perform a much faster search than LOCATE, but work with indexed files only.

Using LOCATE

The LOCATE command can be used to find the first occurrence of a record. The syntax for the command is

LOCATE [*scope*] FOR *condition*

where *condition* is a logical expression (such as LASTNAME = "Morris") that defines your search. The scope, which is optional, can be used to limit the number of records searched. If the scope is omitted, FoxPro assumes that you want to search all of the records in the file. You can enter **ALL** to specify that the use of LOCATE should span all records; this is the default. You can enter **NEXT** and then enter a number that specifies a group of records starting with wherever the pointer is now located; for example, entering **NEXT 10** as the scope would tell FoxPro to limit its use of LOCATE to the next ten records, starting with the current record. Or you can enter **REST**, which limits the use of LOCATE to all records from wherever the pointer is located to the end of the file.

Note that LOCATE does not find all matches, or even the second match—only the first match. Its companion command, CONTINUE, is used to continue the search as many times as desired, assuming the first record found was not the one you really wanted. LOCATE and CONTINUE will carry on a sequential search until (a) a record is found or (b) you reach the end of the database. If a LOCATE or CONTINUE command is unsuccessful, you get the message, "End of LOCATE scope."

For an example, a simple search can be entered in the Command window to search the Tapelimit field of the video database:

```
LOCATE FOR TAPELIMIT = 4
DISPLAY
```

The result, shown partially here, shows that the record found indeed contains a value of 4 in the Tapelimit field:

121-33-9876   Martin   William   4807 East Avenue...

If this is not the desired record, the search can be continued with the CONTINUE command. By entering as examples the commands

```
CONTINUE
DISPLAY
```

the result shows that the CONTINUE command found the next occurrence of the desired record:

901-77-3456   Kramer   Harry   617 North Oakland Street..

You can add the logical conditions .AND. and .OR. to get closer to the precise data you want. (The periods must be included around the words AND and OR when used as part of an expression.) The .AND. condition specifies that both conditions on each side of the word "AND" must be true, while .OR. specifies that either one or the other condition must be true. As an example, if you needed to find a record where the last name was Miller and the tape limit was 6, you could try the command

```
LOCATE FOR LASTNAME = "Miller" .AND. TAPELIMIT = 6
```

If you were seeking a record with an expiration date of 12/31/90 or 1/1/91, you could try the following command:

LOCATE FOR EXPIREDATE = CTOD("12/31/90") .OR. EXPIREDATE = CTOD("01/01/91")

When using LOCATE, keep in mind that FoxPro searches by examining the characters in your search term from left to right. Therefore, you only need to enter as much of the term as necessary to find the proper record. For example, the command

LOCATE FOR LASTNAME = "Jon"

would be enough to find a person named Jones if there were no other names with "Jon" as the first three letters of the name. Sometimes, this left-to-right tendency of a search may be troublesome; for example, the command

LOCATE FOR LASTNAME = "Mills"

would locate names like Millson or Millsap, which might not be what you had in mind. If you want FoxPro to look for your precise search term, you can first enter the command

SET EXACT ON

and then enter the desired LOCATE command. The SET EXACT command tells FoxPro to execute any LOCATE, FIND, or SEEK operation using the same length for the search term and the actual data. You can later enter **SET EXACT OFF** to disable this effect.

Using FIND and SEEK

FIND and SEEK work very differently than LOCATE and CONTINUE. Both FIND and SEEK make use of index files to perform a very fast search. (FoxPro may not find anything, but you will know about it very quickly!) Either a record matching the condition supplied is found or the end of the database is reached. This type of search is common with database management software; it is popular, because it is extremely fast. Even with a very large database, FoxPro can usually find a record in this manner in well under two seconds. The time that a LOCATE command takes, by comparison, grows progressively worse as the database grows in size.

The syntax for both commands is similar:

FIND *character-string*
SEEK *expression*

where *character-string* is a group of characters that do *not* need to be surrounded by quotation marks.

The expression can be a number, a character string (which *must* be surrounded by quotation marks), or a variable (variables are covered in Chapter 12). The expression can also be a combination of constants, variables, and operators (including functions).

The FIND and SEEK commands will search the active index file and find the first record matching your specifications. The record itself will not be displayed; the FIND and SEEK commands will simply move the record pointer to the desired record. Try the commands with the sample video database, entering the following:

USE MEMBERS
INDEX ON LASTNAME TO NAMES
FIND Moore
DISPLAY

The result is as follows:

#5   121-90-5432 Moore   Ellen   270 Browning Ave #2A...

To try the SEEK command, enter

```
USE MEMBERS
INDEX ON TAPELIMIT TO TAPES
SEEK 4
DISPLAY
```

The result is shown here:

#2   121-33-9876 Martin   William   4807 East Avenue...

Note that the index need not be created in every case; if an index already exists, you need only ensure that it is opened before you attempt to use FIND or SEEK.

Comparisons, Comparisons: Find And Seek Versus Locate and Continue

Since FIND and SEEK are usually so much faster than LOCATE, why not use FIND or SEEK in every case? Simplicity sometimes plays a part. First, remember that none of these commands is guaranteed to find what you really want. In many cases, it is easier for novice users to get close with LOCATE and CONTINUE than with FIND or SEEK, because FIND and SEEK will find only the first matching record. If you're searching for Jim Smith in a 12,000-name mailing list with 75 Jim Smiths, a FIND command will find the first one. It's then up to you to figure out how to find the one you want. This can be done by using a WHILE qualifier along with the LOCATE command, which will then tell FoxPro to start its search at the current position in the database. As an example, you could use commands like these, assuming that the database is indexed by last names:

```
FIND "Smith"
LOCATE WHILE LASTNAME = "Smith" FOR FIRSTNAME = "Jim"
.AND. CITY = "New York"
```

This will help you narrow the search down to the desired record without wasting a great deal of time. An inherent advantage to LOCATE and CONTINUE is that these commands will find every matching record (and, sooner or later, the desired one).

Another advantage of LOCATE is its ability to search within a field, using the $ operator. For example, the statement

```
LOCATE FOR "East Avenue" $ ADDRESS
```

would search for the words "East Avenue" inside the Address field. If you are using FIND or SEEK, you must know the starting characters or values in the index key; you cannot search for something in the middle of a field with FIND or SEEK.

One more problem with FIND and SEEK is the index file requirement. Logically, for reasons of efficiency, you want to index your files on something. The problem arises when you need to make a search based on something different. You index by social security number as well as by a combination of last and first name, and pride yourself for being efficient. Then a co-worker comes along and wants to find "this customer I spoke with last week, and I can't remember her name, and I don't know her social security number, but she lives somewhere on Myterra Avenue." Armed with this knowledge, your index files are fairly worthless. And FoxPro spends ten minutes on a command like

```
LOCATE ALL FOR "Myterra Ave" $ ADDRESS
```

while you mutter under your breath, thinking there must be a better way. This is brought out to emphasize one point: the LOCATE and CONTINUE commands are in the language because there may be times you would need them. There are times you will need FIND and SEEK, and there are times you may need LOCATE and CONTINUE (although with good planning, you can minimize those times). Knowing how to effectively use all of the available commands will reduce the amount of time that FoxPro must spend searching for your data.

The secret to a quick find, if one can be said to exist, is to use an index file and a FIND or SEEK rather than a LOCATE. This may seem like elementary knowledge to some, but it is surprising how many users of the dBASE language are still using LOCATE when it isn't necessary. When indexing on one field, using FIND or SEEK is rarely a problem. If, for example, a personnel list is indexed by last names and you are looking for Ms. Samuels, you simply use

FIND Samuels
CHANGE

and unless the database is a sizeable one, you're probably at the record or close enough to use PGDN to get to it. The problem arises when you have large databases and you index on multiple fields to get a more precise match.

Let's say you're working with a large mailing list, and you index on a combination of Lastname + Firstname + City. The Lastname and Firstname fields are each 15 characters long. This means that the records in the index get stored like this:

Smith	Art	Raleigh
Smith	Louise	Tampa
Smith	Louise	Washington
Sodelski	Thomas	St. Louis

The contents of the index precisely match the structure of the field, spaces and all. To use FIND or SEEK from the Command window with such an index and be assured of finding the correct record, you would have to enter something like

FIND Smith   Louise   Washington

including the exact number of spaces to match the index; otherwise, you get a "no find." There are ways to get around this when writing programs that find records. However, if you do much of your work from the command level, you should be aware of this potential problem. One simple way around it is to search the first field in the index (in this case, Lastname) with a FIND command; when the first matching record is found, use BROWSE to visually scan for the exact record desired.

USING SET FILTER WITH COMMANDS

The SET FILTER command is a popular one in the dBASE language, and it is one that has its advantages and disadvantages. SET FILTER hides records that do not meet the condition described. The syntax for the command is

SET FILTER TO *condition*

where *condition* is a logical expression (such as LASTNAME = "Morris") that defines your search. Once the command is entered, other database commands that would normally use records from the entire database will instead use only records that meet the condition specified by the filter. In effect, this lets you work with a subset of a database as though it were the entire database. A command like

SET FILTER TO CITY = "Washington" .AND. STATE = "DC"

limits a database to those records located in Washington, DC. In effect, this is the equivalent of the Filter option available from the Database/Setup menu choices. You can isolate a group of records by issuing a SET FILTER command; then you can use the LIST or BROWSE command to view the data, or the REPORT FORM command (covered in the next chapter) to produce a printed report.

As an example, consider the following commands, used with the video database:

USE MEMBERS

SET FILTER TO EXPIREDATE >= CTOD("01/01/91") .AND. EXPIREDATE <= CTOD("12/31/91")

LIST LASTNAME, FIRSTNAME, SOCIAL, EXPIREDATE

(The second line appears on two lines here due to printing limitations, but you enter the entire command on a single line.) The SET FILTER command in this example restricts the listed records to only those with expiration dates that fall in the year 1991. You can enclose parts of the expression in parentheses to build very complex expressions. For example, the command

SET FILTER TO (EXPIREDATE >= CTOD("01/01/91") .AND. EXPIREDATE <= CTOD("12/31/91")) .OR. STATE = "MD"

would limit the records available to those with an expiration date sometime in 1991, or with the letters "MD" in the state field.

You can see whether a filter is in effect at any time by using the LIST STATUS or DISPLAY STATUS command. The listing that results from either of these commands will include the filter condition for any filter that is in effect. And you can cancel the effects of an existing filter by entering

SET FILTER TO

without including a condition in the command, as shown here.

One point sometimes overlooked, until you get used to this abnormality, is that when you set a filter, the current record is not immediately affected by the filter. The filter does not take effect until you move the record pointer. If the next command causes the record pointer to move before data is displayed or printed, fine. If not, you may wind up with a record you don't really want. This problem can be illustrated by the use of a large personnel database containing a Lastname field. When the following commands are entered, note the result:

```
SET FILTER TO LASTNAME = "Robinson"
LIST LASTNAME NEXT 10
```

Record#	LASTNAME
1	Miller
3	Robinson
7	Robinson
11	Robinson
15	Robinson
19	Robinson
23	Robinson
27	Robinson
31	Robinson
52	Robinson

The first name in the display obviously isn't Robinson—it is the name in the record that was current when the LIST command was entered. Once any action that causes movement of the record pointer is taken, the invalid record disappears.

You'll have to think about whether the commands you use immediately after the SET FILTER command will move the record pointer before displaying any data. The REPORT FORM and LABEL FORM commands will move the pointer to the top of the database before printing any reports or labels, so you will get the proper results if no NEXT or WHILE clauses are included in the REPORT FORM or LABEL FORM command. Similarly, a LIST command will normally move the pointer before a display of data, but it won't if you include a NEXT or WHILE scope along with the command. It you try a command like LIST NEXT 20 immediately after a SET FILTER command, you will get 19 records that meet the condition, and one that may not. The solution, simple enough, is to move the record pointer with a GO TOP command immediately after the SET FILTER command. This will move the record pointer to the first record meeting the filter condition, and you can then use the desired commands.

Before you become too fond of the SET FILTER command, you should be aware of its disadvantages. The SET FILTER command appears to perform a rapid sequential qualification of every record in the database, starting from record 1 and moving to the highest record number. Because FoxPro performs a rapid internal search during this process, it is not a problem if the record numbers happen to be in sequential order (which means that no index files are open). If an index file is open, and one usually is, FoxPro examines each record sequentially in index order. Since this involves checking both the index and the database for each record, any operation that uses SET FILTER will be terribly slow or a large, indexed database. Understandably, the larger the database, the more interminable the delays with an indexed file gets.

You can avoid opening the index files while using SET FILTER, which is fine if you don't mind the problems of trying to keep the indexes updated after changes have been made. Then, too, what happens when you want a report with an odd selection of certain records? You probably want it in some kind of sorted order, and the alternative of sorting the database and then setting a filter is about as appealing as the slow index.

The answer, like so many things in life, is a compromise. When using indexes, stay away from filters wherever possible; when using filters, stay away from indexes wherever possible. If you want to find records for editing and updating, don't use filters. Open indexes and use FIND or SEEK instead. Save the SET FILTER command for showing lists of data and for serving your reporting needs. It is less annoying to see a delay during reporting; most users turn on the printer, choose the report, and go off to do something else while FoxPro does all the work. Also, in reporting needs, often a large percentage of your records may meet the filter criteria, and performance improves as more records match the criteria outlined with the SET FILTER command. An alternative to the use of SET FILTER is to use the FOR clause with the INDEX command to build a selective index file. This topic is covered in detail in Chapter 4.

USING VIEW FILES

The conditions placed in effect with a SET FILTER command can be stored in the form of a *view file* for additional use at a later time. A view file will also contain a record of any open database and index files, as well as any screen format file in use at the time the view file was created. You can think of a view file as a "snapshot" of your open database files, index files, a filter condition, and any screen format file in use. The view file can be created with the command CREATE VIEW *filename* FROM ENVIRONMENT. Once you have opened your database and index files, placed any desired format file into use, and set a filter condition with a SET FILTER command, you enter

CREATE VIEW *filename* FROM ENVIRONMENT

where *filename* is the name for the view file. Once you have done this, you no longer need to repeat the same set of commands for the opening of files and the setting of the filter during a later session with FoxPro. Instead, you can simply use the SET VIEW command, using the following syntax:

SET VIEW TO *filename*

Filename is the name of the view file saved earlier, and FoxPro will open the same database, index files, and screen format file (if any). Any filter condition that was in effect when the view file was created will be placed back into effect.

Not only is this useful for saving yourself the tedious entry of a number of commands, but it can also be used with reports. As Chapter 7 will show, an Environment option of the REPORT FORM command will automatically open and place into effect the settings in a view file before a report is produced. And a view file will also contain any relations that have been established between multiple files. (Relations between multiple files are covered in Chapter 11.)

7

INTRODUCING REPORTS

The Report Dialog Box
Producing Selective Reports with Ease
Generating Reports with Commands
Designing Customized Columnar Reports
Practice Designing a Customized Report
Using the Group Menu Options
Adding Grouping by State to the Membership Report
Creating a Report with Multiple Groups
Report Design

Creating reports is, for many users, what database management is all about. You can readily perform queries to gain immediate answers to specific questions, but much of your work with FoxPro will probably involve generating reports. Detailed reports are easy to produce with FoxPro, thanks in part to the program's Quick Report option, which can be combined with selective commands such as SET FILTER and SET FIELDS to obtain reports of selective data.

FoxPro also provides several ways to print reports. You can design and print quick reports with a few steps. From the command level, you can also use a combination of the LIST and DISPLAY commands to print information. You can use FoxPro's sophisticated Report Generator to create customized reports. And you can print form letters or mailing labels.

This chapter will provide an introduction to the many ways you can produce reports. More advanced reporting topics, including mailing labels and form letters, are covered in Chapter 10. Before going any further, be sure that your printer is turned on and ready; otherwise, you may lock up your system when you try to print.

Reports available using the Report Generator in FoxPro can be divided into two overall groups: *quick reports* and *customized reports*. FoxPro creates quick reports immediately, when you start the Report Generator and choose the Quick Report option from the Report menu. Quick reports normally contain all of the fields in the file. (You can limit the fields available in the report with the SET FIELDS command, covered later in this chapter.) The field names supplied during the database design phase are used as headings for the fields.

Custom reports, by comparison, are reports that you create or modify to better fit your specific needs. A significant plus of the Report Generator is that it doesn't force you to design custom reports from scratch, starting with a blank screen. You can use the Quick Report option to create a report layout containing all fields, and then proceed to modify that layout as you wish, deleting fields, moving the location of fields, changing headings, or adding other text. Custom reports that you design with the Report Generator can contain any data you desire from the fields of the database. They can include numeric information, such as totals or other calculations based on numeric fields. Reports can also include headings that contain the specified title of the report, the date (as determined by the PC's clock), and the page number for each page. Such headings are commonly used with columnar reports. The following shows an example of a report in a *columnar* layout. Columnar layouts contain the data arranged in columns.

SOCIAL	TITLE	DAYRENTED	RETURNED
123-44-8976	Star Trek IV	03/05/90	03/06/90
121-33-9876	Lethal Weapon II	03/02/90	03/06/90
232-55-1234	Who Framed Roger Rabbit	03/06/90	03/09/90
901-77-3456	Beverly Hills Cop II	03/04/90	03/05/90
121-90-5432	Dirty Rotten Scoundrels	03/01/90	03/06/90
495-00-3456	Young Einstein	03/04/90	03/09/90
343-55-9821	When Harry Met Sally	03/06/90	03/12/90
876-54-3210	Lethal Weapon II	03/07/90	03/08/90
123-44-8976	Friday 13th Part XXVII	03/14/90	03/16/90
121-33-9876	Licence To Kill	03/15/90	03/17/90
232-55-1234	When Harry Met Sally	03/17/90	03/19/90
901-77-3456	Coming To America	03/14/90	03/18/90
121-90-5432	When Harry Met Sally	03/16/90	03/17/90
495-00-3456	Star Trek V	03/18/90	03/18/90
343-55-9821	Young Einstein	03/19/90	03/20/90
876-54-3210	Licence To Kill	03/16/90	03/18/90

Here is an example of a report in a *form* layout. Form layouts often resemble paper-based forms.

```
RENTAL: Record No. 1
SOCIAL       123-44-8976
TITLE        Star Trek IV
DAYRENTED    03/05/90
RETURNED     03/06/90

SOCIAL       121-33-9876
TITLE        Lethal Weapon II
DAYRENTED    03/02/90
RETURNED     03/06/90

SOCIAL       232-55-1234
TITLE        Who Framed Roger Rabbit
DAYRENTED    03/06/90
RETURNED     03/09/90

SOCIAL       901-77-3456
TITLE        Beverly Hills Cop II
DAYRENTED    03/04/90
RETURNED     03/05/90

SOCIAL       121-90-5432
TITLE        Dirty Rotten Scoundrels
DAYRENTED    03/01/90
RETURNED     03/06/90
```

One of the fastest ways to produce printed reports in FoxPro is to enter the Report Generator and use the Quick Report option, since this report needs no designing in advance. To produce a quick report, simply open the desired database, and enter **CREATE REPORT** *filename* as a command. (This command starts the Report Generator and is equivalent to choosing New from the File menu and then selecting Report.) When the Report Generator design screen appears, open the Report menu with ALT-O and choose Quick Report. From the dialog box that next appears, select Column Layout (if a columnar-style report is desired) or Form Layout (if a form-style report is desired). Select the OK button, and then choose Save from the File menu (or press CTRL-W). Exit the Report Generator by choosing Close from the File menu, and the stored report is ready for use. You can display the report on the screen or print it at any time with the REPORT FORM command. Entering **REPORT FORM** *filename* as a command will display the report on the screen, while entering **REPORT FORM** *filename* **TO PRINT** will send the report to the screen and printer at the same time. The menu equivalents for generating the report is to open the Database menu and choose Report; then enter the name of the stored report in the dialog box, check any desired options in the dialog box that appears (see the next section), and select the OK button to produce the report.

The first report shown was produced from the RENTALS database created in Chapter 5 by means of the Quick Report option. It illustrates the design of a columnar-style quick report. Field names appear as column headings, and the data appears in single-spaced rows beneath the headings.

If you generate your own quick report by opening the MEMBERS file (not the RENTALS file) and following the procedure described in the preceding paragraphs, you may notice one trait of a quick report which may not be very appealing to you. Depending on the number of fields in the file, one or more columns of data may be cut off at the right margin. You could solve this problem by changing widths or moving the locations of columns in a customized report. The right margin is set at 80, so you can't fit more data in the report by printing in compressed mode or using wide paper. You can, however, change the right margin as described later in this chapter.

If you don't want all the fields in the report, you can obtain a quick report with the selected fields you desire using the SET FIELDS command. Briefly, the syntax of this command is

SET FIELDS TO *field1*, *field2*, *field3*,...*fieldx*

This command makes the database appear to contain only the fields you specify in the list of fields. Therefore, if you wanted a quick report of the MEMBERS database with only the name, city, state, and expiration date fields in the report, you could first open the database and use the command

SET FIELDS TO LASTNAME, FIRSTNAME, CITY, STATE, EXPIREDATE

and then proceed to create and save the report; the report would contain only the fields named in the command. After you have created the report, you can make the rest of the fields available for use again by closing and reopening the database or by entering **SET FIELDS TO** without any list of fields after the command.

THE REPORT DIALOG BOX

When you choose the Report option of the Database menu to print a report, the default selections that appear on the Report dialog box (Figure 7-1) cause the data to be displayed on the screen only. You can choose instead to direct the output of a report to the printer or to a disk file as *ASCII* (American Standard Committee for Information Interchange) text.

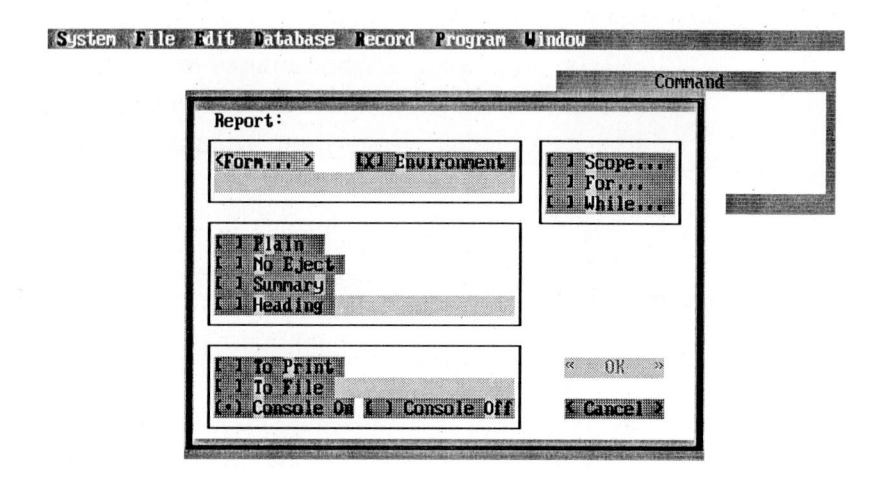

FIGURE 7-1.   Report dialog box

In the Form... window you enter the name of the report, which was created and saved earlier with the Report Generator. The Environment check box tells FoxPro to use any environmental settings that were in effect while the report was being designed. When you create and save a report, FoxPro automatically saves the environment settings to a view file with the same name as the report (see Chapter 6 for more on view files).

The Scope, For, and While options let you limit the records that will appear in the report. Scope can be used to limit the number of records that qualify for the operation. If the scope is omitted, FoxPro assumes that you want to use all records in the file. You can enter **ALL** (to specify the use of all records; this is the default scope). You can enter **NEXT** and then enter a number, which specifies a group of records starting with the current pointer position; for example, entering **NEXT 10** as the scope would tell

FoxPro to limit its selections to the next ten records. Or you can enter **REST**, which limits the operation to all records from the current pointer position to the end of the file.

The For and While options are used to further limit your records, as described in Chapter 6. The While option works best with an index, but the For option can easily be used on any field, whether an index exists or not. When you choose For from the dialog box, the Expression Builder (discussed in Chapter 6) appears. Using the Expression Builder, you can enter an expression that will limit the records available to the report. The use of the While option will also result in the display of the Expression Builder, which can be used in the same manner.

Checking the Plain box produces a plain report with no headings. The No Eject option tells FoxPro not to send a page-eject code before printing the report. The Summary option tells FoxPro to produce a summary report only; individual records do not appear in the report, only summary totals appear. (This option makes sense when you have included summary fields in your report, a subject covered later in the chapter.) Checking the To Print option routes the report to the printer, while checking the To File option and entering a filename in the corresponding text box stores the report output in the form of an ASCII text file. Such files can be read by most word processors and all popular desktop publishing packages.

The Heading option, when chosen, causes the Expression Builder to appear, this time containing a window for a heading, as shown in Figure 7-2. You can use this window to enter a custom heading of your choice, or you can build an expression that results in a desired heading. If you want to enter text in your heading, surround the text in quotes. Fields are normally used as headings with multiple groupings in reports, a topic covered later in the chapter.

Once you enter the name of the report form, check the desired options and select the OK button. The report will be produced in accordance with your chosen options.

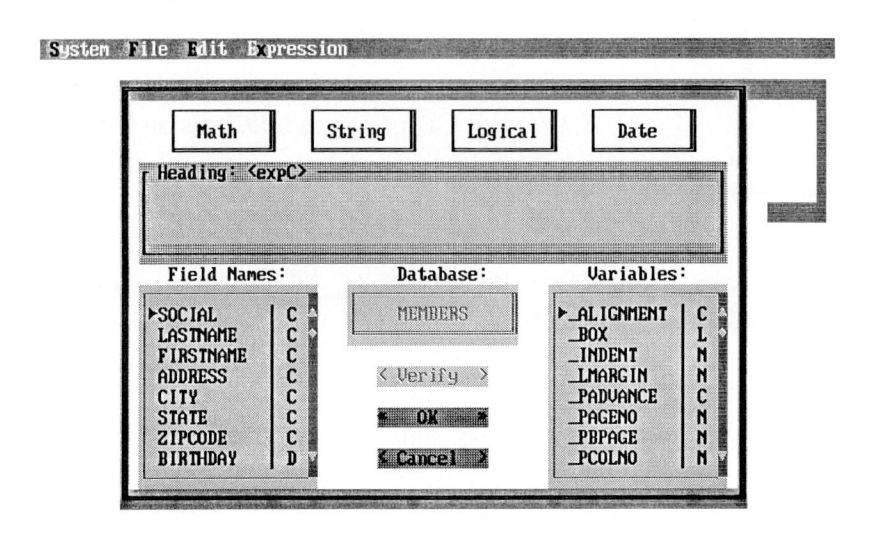

FIGURE 7-2. Expression Builder containing report heading window

PRODUCING SELECTIVE REPORTS WITH EASE

If you want maximum results in a minimum amount of time, keep in mind the flexibility that FoxPro provides with the SET FIELDS, INDEX ON...FOR, and SET FILTER commands; these can be used to provide selective views of data. You can use the SET FILTER command, described in Chapter 6, or you can add a FOR clause to the REPORT FORM command, to limit the records included in your reports. (An alternative way to do this is to produce the report using the menu options rather than commands;

when you use the menu option, the dialog box appears, and you can use the For clause to specify which records will appear in the report.) With large databases, you may find it less time-consuming to limit available records by building a selective index with the INDEX ON...FOR command. Details of this technique are found in Chapter 4.

In many cases, you can solve formatting problems by including selected fields and omitting unwanted fields with the SET FIELDS command. Take the quick report produced if you use the MEMBERS file, create a report, and choose the Quick Report option from the Report menu. Obviously, there are far too many fields to fit on a standard sheet of paper. Perhaps all you are really interested in are the Lastname, Firstname, City, and Tapelimit fields, and you know that these will comfortably fit on a standard sheet of paper. To create a Quick Report with only these fields, enter **USE MEMBERS** if the file is not already open, and enter the following SET FIELDS command:

SET FIELDS TO LASTNAME, FIRSTNAME, CITY, TAPELIMIT

Next, create a new report by entering the command

CREATE REPORT SAMPLE

to get into the Report Generator. Open the Report menu with ALT-O, and choose Quick Report. Select OK, and notice that the report that is produced contains only those fields listed with the SET FIELDS command, as shown in Figure 7-3.

Save the report with CTRL-W, and enter the command

REPORT FORM SAMPLE

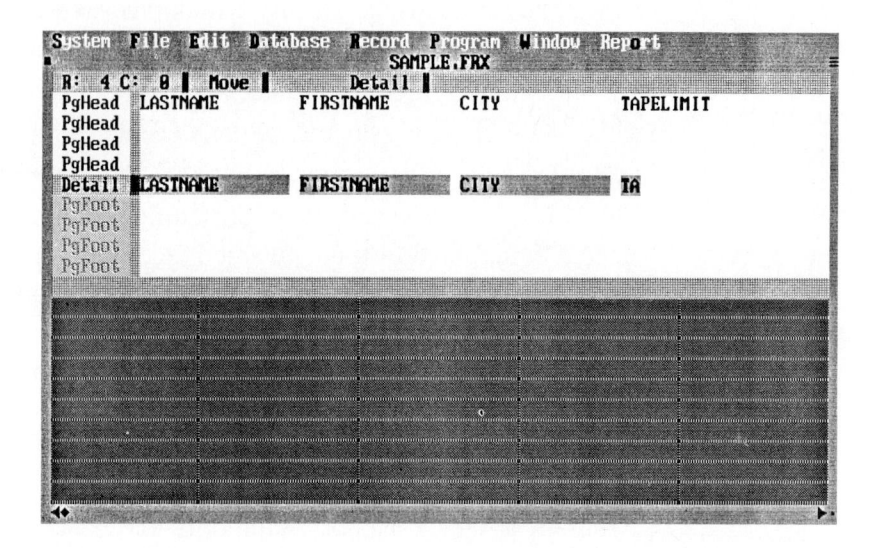

```
System File Edit Database Record Program Window Report
                        SAMPLE.FRX
R: 4 C: 0 | Move |        Detail |
PgHead  LASTNAME      FIRSTNAME      CITY          TAPELIMIT
PgHead
PgHead
PgHead
Detail  LASTNAME      FIRSTNAME      CITY          TA
PgFoot
PgFoot
PgFoot
PgFoot
```

FIGURE 7-3.   Report design resulting from SET FIELDS

to display the report on the screen. The resulting report should contain all of the records from the MEMBERS database, but only the desired fields, as shown here:

LASTNAME	FIRSTNAME	CITY	TAPELIMIT
Miller	Karen	Chevy Chase	6
Martin	William	Silver Spring	4
Robinson	Carol	Falls Church	6
Kramer	Harry	Arlington	4
Moore	Ellen	Takoma Park	6
Zachman	David	Falls Church	4
Robinson	Benjamin	Washington	6
Hart	Wendy	Fairfax	2

Before proceeding, be sure to enter

SET FIELDS TO

to restore the use of all fields in the database for subsequent operations.

If you wanted specific records in the report, you could use the methods described in Chapter 6 to produce a subset of records available to the report. Also, if you wanted to see the records within the quick report in some specific order, you could use the indexing or sorting techniques covered in Chapter 4, apply any desired filter conditions, and print the report. Using these techniques, you can generate detailed reports based on complex conditions with little or no custom report designing.

GENERATING REPORTS WITH COMMANDS

From the command level, the LIST command is useful for printing data as well as examining data on the screen. To direct output to the printer, use the TO PRINT option with the LIST command. This avoids having all your command words print on the page along with the desired data. The normal format of the command with this option is

LIST [*field1*, *field2*...*fieldx*] TO PRINT

To try this command, enter

LIST LASTNAME, CITY, STATE TO PRINT

to print all the Name, City, and State fields for each record in the database. If you are using a laser printer, you may also need to enter an EJECT command to cause the printed sheet to feed out of the printer.

You can be selective by specifying a FOR condition with the LIST command, and still send output to the printer with TO PRINT. For example,

LIST LASTNAME, FIRSTNAME, CITY FOR LASTNAME = "Robinson" TO PRINT

prints the last names, first names, and cities of both members named Robinson. The command

LIST LASTNAME, CITY, STATE, TAPELIMIT FOR TAPELIMIT < 6

provides a printed listing like the one shown here, with the last names, cities, states, and tape limits for all members with a tape limit of less than 6.

Record#	LASTNAME	CITY	STATE	TAPELIMIT
2	Martin	Silver Spring	MD	4
4	Kramer	Arlington	VA	4
6	Zachman	Falls Church	VA	4
8	Hart	Fairfax	VA	2

You can use the curly braces surrounding a date to tell FoxPro that the enclosed set of characters should be read as a date value. The date value can then be used to form a conditional command for printing a report. This is a very handy tool for printing reports that indicate activity within a certain time period. For example, the command

REPORT FORM SAMPLE FOR EXPIREDATE <= {10/01/87} TO PRINT

will produce a report of all records with expiration dates earlier than November 2 of 1987. A report of all members with expiration dates within a particular month could be produced with a command like this one:

REPORT FORM SAMPLE FOR EXPIREDATE > {09/30/87} .AND. EXPIREDATE < {10/31/87} TO PRINT

You can also generate stored reports with commands. The REPORT FORM command uses the following syntax:

REPORT FORM *filename* [*scope*]
       [FOR *expression*]
       [WHILE *expression*]
       [TO PRINT / TO FILE *filename*]
       [PLAIN] [SUMMARY] [NOEJECT]
       [HEADING *character-expression*]
       [ENVIRONMENT]

The SCOPE, FOR, and WHILE options work as discussed earlier in this text; see Chapter 6 for a full discussion on these options. If the TO PRINT clause is added to the command, the report is routed to the printer and to the screen. If TO PRINT is omitted, the report is displayed only on the screen.

    If the TO FILE option is included, the report will be sent to a file in the form of ASCII text. You can use either TO PRINT or TO FILE, but you cannot use both options in the same REPORT FORM command.

    The PLAIN option prints a plain report without the standard headings. The SUMMARY option prints a report with summary fields only. The NOEJECT option suppresses the normal page ejects (form-feed codes) that are sent to the printer. The HEADING option lets you add a custom heading; character expressions must be enclosed in quotes.

    The ENVIRONMENT option can be used to specify a view file that will control the records available for processing, which fields appear, and any relationships between other files. (View files are covered in Chapter 6.) When you save a report, FoxPro automatically saves the current environment to a view file with the same name as the report. Adding this clause to the REPORT FORM command therefore saves you the trouble of opening a database and index file if they are not already open. For example, you could load FoxPro from DOS or OS/2, and enter one command such as

REPORT FORM MYFILE ENVIRONMENT

to open the database and any index files, and to produce the report.

Manual Margin Settings And Page Ejects

You can change your printer's left margin with the SET MARGIN command. FoxPro normally defaults to a printer margin value of 0. Entering **SET MARGIN TO 12**, for example, would cause the printer to indent 12 spaces at the beginning of each line. (This command affects only the left margin. The right margin cannot be set with a command in FoxPro.) The EJECT command, as mentioned earlier, causes the printer to perform a form feed, which advances you to the top of the next sheet. The EJECT command is not available from the menus; it must be entered as a command. An alternative is to use the Form Feed button on your printer to accomplish the same task.

DESIGNING CUSTOMIZED COLUMNAR REPORTS

When you prefer to place fields in various locations, add custom headers and footers, and change formatting attributes, you can design customized reports. Depending on how complex your needs

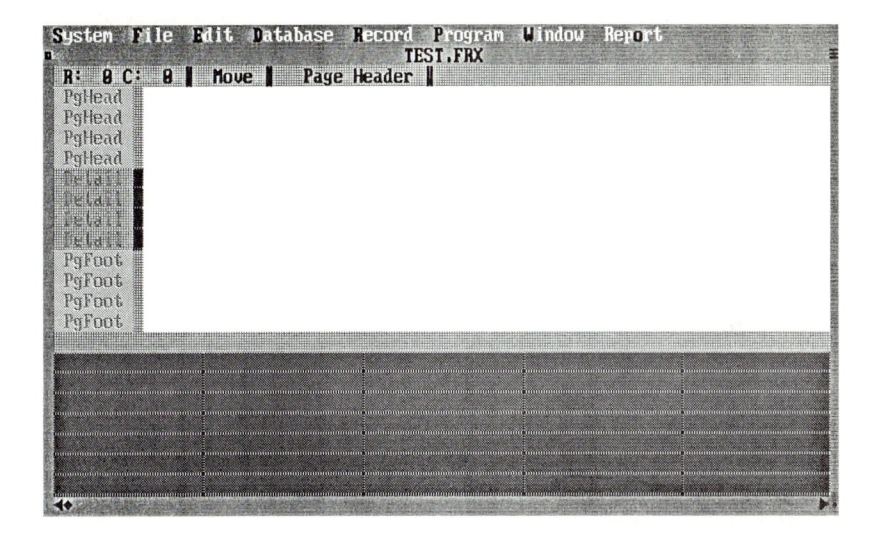

FIGURE 7-4. Report specification

are, the precise steps involved in the report's design will vary in complexity. The description that follows illustrates the basic process in creating a customize report with a columnar format.

To start the process, open the database in question, and then enter **CREATE REPORT** *filename* (or choose New from the File menu and select Report). In a moment, the design screen of the Report Generator will appear (Figure 7-4). The screen contains the menu bar, which includes one new option titled "Report," and the *report specification,* or layout of the report.

The Report Specification

The report specification is made up of several parts, as illustrated in Figure 7-5. FoxPro views each portion of the report as a horizontal area known as a *report band.* Every report contains a

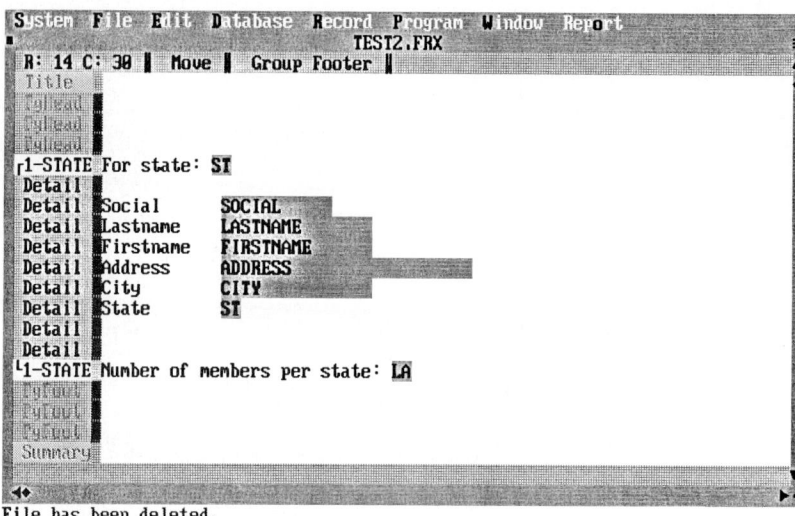

```
 System  File  Edit  Database  Record  Program  Window  Report
                              TEST2.FRX
 R: 14 C: 30 | Move | Group Footer |
 Title
 [Phead]
 [Phead]
 [Phead]
 ┌1-STATE For state: ST
 Detail
 Detail  Social      SOCIAL
 Detail  Lastname    LASTNAME
 Detail  Firstname   FIRSTNAME
 Detail  Address     ADDRESS
 Detail  City        CITY
 Detail  State       ST
 Detail
 Detail
 └1-STATE Number of members per state: LA
 [Pfoot]
 [Pfoot]
 [Pfoot]
 Summary

 File has been deleted.
```

FIGURE 7-5. Parts of a report specification

Page Header band, a Page Footer band, and a Detail band. There can also be an optional Title band or Summary band, and there can be optional Group bands; in the figure, the band containing the name of a field, State, is a Group band.

The Page Header band appears once for each page of the report. In many cases, you'll place such information as the date or time of the report and a report title in this area. The Page Footer band at the bottom of the report specification has the same purpose as the header but is for footers, the information that typically appears at the bottom of each page.

Title bands, when used, contain any information that should appear only at the start of the report (as opposed to at the start of each page). Summary bands, when used, contain information that should appear at the end of the report. You'll usually use Summary bands for totals of numeric fields.

The Detail band is used to define the actual information (usually fields) that will appear in the body of the report. The values in the Detail band are represented by highlighted blocks containing the name of the field or expression. While fields are common, expressions can also be used; such expressions might contain a function representing the current date, or a calculated value based on a numeric field.

Group bands, which are optional, are printed once for each group of records in a report. Group bands provide a means of grouping records in a report. Such grouping often includes some type of header identifying the group, along with subtotals of numeric data. You may or may not want to group records in a report; as an example of grouping, you might decide to print a list of members of the video database by state. If you decide to include groups, FoxPro lets you add an unlimited number of groups to a single report.

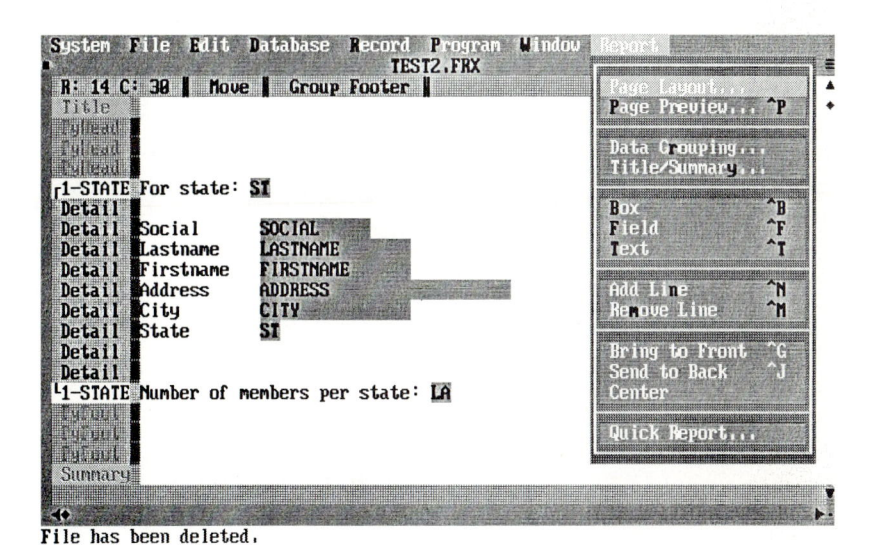

FIGURE 7-6. Report menu

Making Changes
To the Report's Design

Once the report specification appears on the screen, you can use various options of the Report menu to add, rearrange, or remove fields; to add new lines, boxes, or text; and to change the layout or format of the report in general. If you press ALT-O while the report specification is visible, the Report menu will open (Figure 7-6).

The Page Layout option of this menu lets you change specifications that affect the layout of the printed page. When you choose this option, the Page Layout dialog box appears (Figure 7-7). Use the Page Length option to change the length of the printed page. The default value of 60 allows 6 blank lines at the end of a normal 8.5- by 11-inch sheet of paper. Legal-size (14-inch long) paper works well with a setting of 82. For the various European paper sizes, you may need to experiment to obtain the best results.

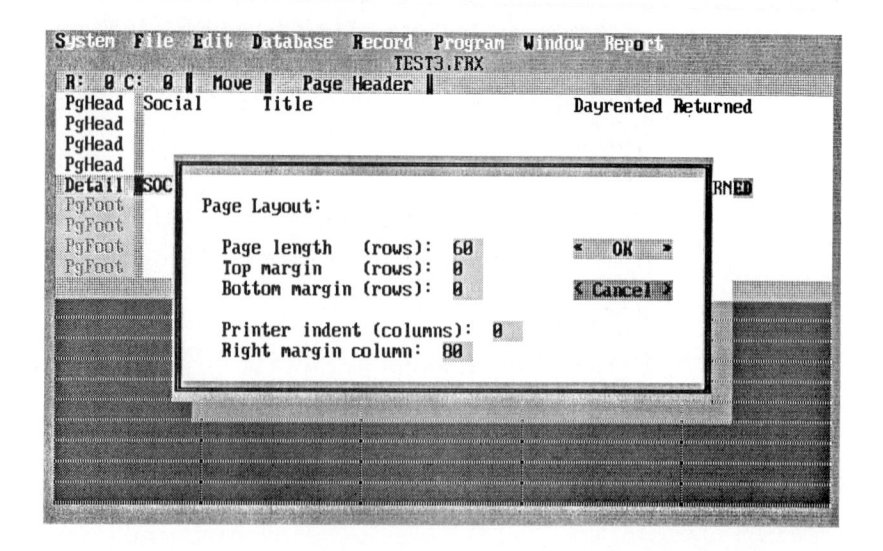

FIGURE 7-7. Page Layout dialog box

The Top Margin option lets you specify a top margin, or the number of lines down from the top edge where printing will begin. Laser-printer users should note that this will be in addition to the default top margin set internally by your printer; see your printer manual for details on the printer's default top margin. In a similar fashion, the Bottom Margin option provides a setting for the bottom margin, or the number of lines up from the bottom edge. Data will not appear beyond this setting.

The Printer Indent option lets you enter the number of spaces by which all data in the report should be indented. The Right Margin Column option lets you specify a number for the right margin. This is particularly useful with printers that allow compressed print. When using the compressed-print mode of most dot-matrix printers, you can enter 132 as a margin when using 8.5-inch wide paper, and you can enter 240 as a margin when using

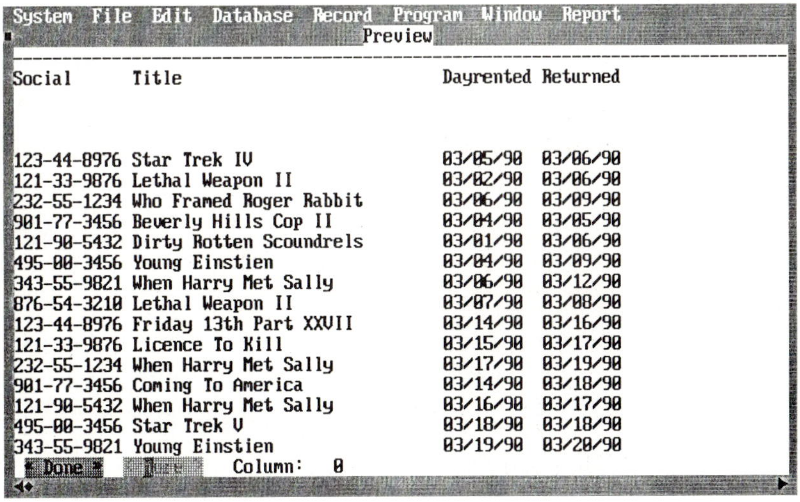

```
 System   File   Edit   Database   Record   Program   Window   Report
                                 Preview
 Social       Title                       Dayrented  Returned

 123-44-8976  Star Trek IV                03/05/90   03/06/90
 121-33-9876  Lethal Weapon II            03/02/90   03/06/90
 232-55-1234  Who Framed Roger Rabbit     03/06/90   03/09/90
 901-77-3456  Beverly Hills Cop II        03/04/90   03/05/90
 121-90-5432  Dirty Rotten Scoundrels     03/01/90   03/06/90
 495-00-3456  Young Einstien              03/04/90   03/09/90
 343-55-9821  When Harry Met Sally        03/06/90   03/12/90
 876-54-3210  Lethal Weapon II            03/07/90   03/08/90
 123-44-8976  Friday 13th Part XXVII      03/14/90   03/16/90
 121-33-9876  Licence To Kill             03/15/90   03/17/90
 232-55-1234  When Harry Met Sally        03/17/90   03/19/90
 901-77-3456  Coming To America           03/14/90   03/18/90
 121-90-5432  When Harry Met Sally        03/16/90   03/17/90
 495-00-3456  Star Trek V                 03/18/90   03/18/90
 343-55-9821  Young Einstien              03/19/90   03/20/90
   Done                    Column:    0
```

FIGURE 7-8. Screen preview of report

the larger computer-fanfold paper. Once all your desired options have been entered, select the OK button to exit the dialog box.

The Page Preview option of the Report menu lets you see what a report will look like before you save the report and exit the Report Generator. After laying out the desired fields and other data, choose Page Preview from the Report menu, and a visual representation of the printed report will appear on the screen (Figure 7-8). Two options, Done and More, appear at the bottom of the screen. Choose More to view successive pages of the report (if there are any); choose Done to exit back to the report specification. This option is quite useful for checking your design; you can go back into the report specification, make changes to the report, and try Page Preview again until you are satisfied with the design of the report.

The Data Grouping option of the Report menu lets you add groups to a report. This topic is covered later in this chapter. The Title/Summary option lets you add Title bands or Summary bands to a report. When you choose this option, the Title/Summary dialog box appears (Figure 7-9). You can check the boxes that affect both the Title band and the Summary band. Selecting Title Band adds the Title band, while selecting Summary Band adds the Summary band. The bands, once added, are empty; you must then add any desired text or fields to the bands. The New Page option tells FoxPro to start the band on a new page. Once you check the desired boxes and choose OK, you are returned to the report specification.

The Box, Field, and Text options are used to add boxes, fields, and text to the report. The added items will then appear in the report, in accordance with the band where you add them. For example, adding an item in the Detail band will cause it to appear once for each record of the report; adding an item in the Page Head band will cause it to appear once each time the Page Head prints, and so on.

Selecting Box from the Report menu causes another menu to be displayed, offering a choice of Single, Double, or Char (for Character). You can add boxes composed of a single line, a double line,

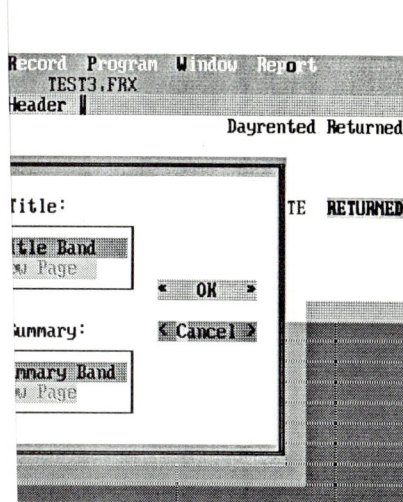

ary dialog box

u select. (If you choose Char, a pull-
ssible characters.) Keyboard users can
er-left corner for the box, choose Box
 select the box type), stretch the box
ss ENTER to complete the box. Mouse
 type of box, click at the upper-left
corner of the box, and drag to the desired lower-right corner.

Use the Field option of the Report menu (or its shortcut key, CTRL-F) to place fields or expressions (such as combinations of fields or calculations based on fields) at the cursor location. Choosing Field from the menu causes the dialog box shown in Figure 7-10 to be displayed. In the expression box, you enter the name of the field or expression that you want to place at the cursor location. If you need help in building the expression, tab to Expr and press ENTER to bring up the Expression Builder. As an

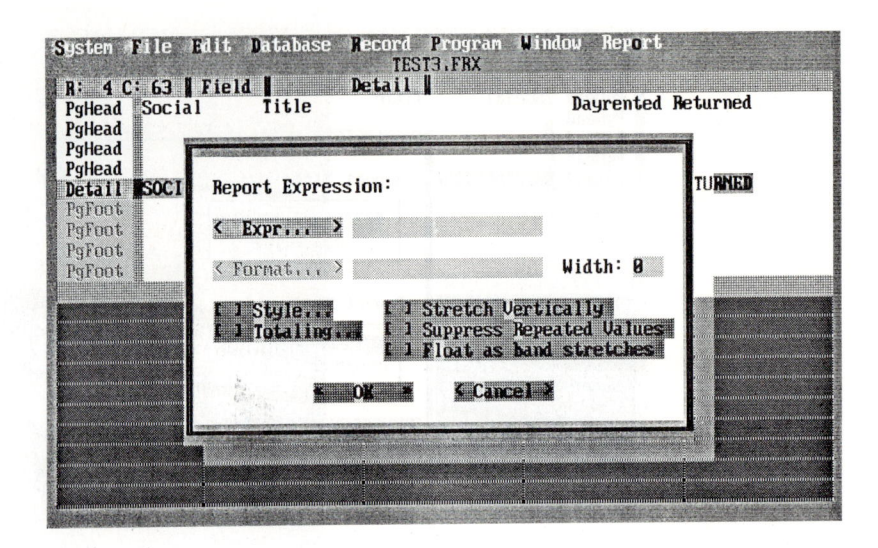

FIGURE 7-10. Report Expression dialog box

expression, you can enter a calculation based on a field; an example, in the case of a numeric field named Cost, might be

COST * .06

which would result in a "sales tax" figure that is 6% of the value contained in the Cost field.

Applying Formats and Style Options to a Field

At Format you can press ENTER to display the Format dialog box (Figure 7-11). This provides various formatting options that you can select by checking the boxes. One of the Character, Numeric, Date, and Logical options will be chosen based on the field type;

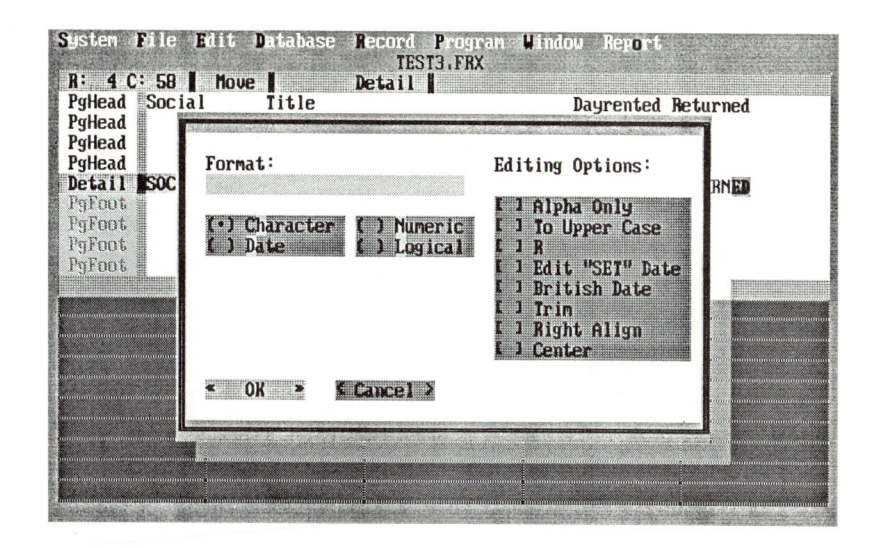

FIGURE 7-11. Format dialog box

however, if your field is based on an expression, you may want to change this option according to your preference. The list of available formatting options that you see will vary, depending on the data type. The editing options may be checked according to your wishes for that field. Table 7-1 shows the results of the various formatting options. Once you choose the desired options and select the OK button, the Report Expression dialog reappears.

In the Width box of the Report Expression dialog box (see Figure 7-10), you can enter a maximum width for the field. This is useful if you have a long field and you want to restrict its length in a particular report.

The Style option, when chosen, displays another dialog box with choices for any of eight printing styles: Normal, Bold, Italic, Underline, Superscript, Subscript, Condensed, and Double. Choose any of these as desired by checking the desired box and

Option	Result
For character data	
Alpha Only	Only alphabetic characters permitted
To Upper Case	All characters converted to uppercase
R	Characters are displayed but not stored
Edit SET date	Prints data as date that follows the current SET DATE format
British Date	Prints data following the British (European) date format
Trim	Removes leading and trailing blanks
Right Align	Prints data flush right in field
Center	Prints data centered in field
For numeric data	
Left justify	Aligns numeric data flush left in field
Blank if zero	Does not print output if field contents contains zero
(Negative)	Negative numbers are enclosed in parentheses
Edit SET date	Prints data as date that follows the current SET DATE format
British Date	Prints data following the British (European) date format
CR if positive	CR (for Credit) appears after a number if the number is positive
DB if negative	DB (for Debit) appears after a number if the number is negative

TABLE 7-1. Formatting Options

Option	Result
Leading zero	Leading zeros are printed
Currency	Values are printed in Currency format
Scientific	Values are printed using scientific notation
For date data	
Edit SET date	Prints data as date that follows the current SET DATE format
British Date	Prints data following the British (European) date format

TABLE 7-1.   Formatting Options (*continued*)

then selecting OK; you can choose more than one option at a time. (Your printer must support the chosen options.)

The Stretch Vertically option of the Report Expression dialog box lets you stretch the contents of a long character field or a memo field vertically. This permits the wrapping of text past more than one line in the report, making the option quite useful with memo fields. If you do not select this option, a memo field placed in a report will not take more than one line per record printed; any excess text gets cut off when the field ends at the width you specified. If you select the Stretch Vertically option, FoxPro will use as many lines as are necessary to print the complete contents of the memo or character field.

The Totaling option, when chosen, reveals a choice of totals. This option allows you to define a numeric summary field. Once you check the Totaling box, FoxPro allows you to select whether the total will be a count of the number of records, the sum of the numeric data, an average, the lowest value in any of the records, or the highest value in any of the records.

Also shown when you select the Totaling option is a Reset option, which determines when the totaling field will be reset. Tab to this menu and press ENTER, and you are provided with reset choices of End of Report, End of Page, or the name of the field or expression you are using (in other words, each time the value of that field or expression changes, the total will be printed).

The Suppress Repeated Values option of the Report Expression dialog box will tell FoxPro not to print repeated values within the report. If this option is selected and the field value is the same for more than one consecutive record, the value is printed for the first record but not for successive records.

Once you have chosen the desired options within the Report Expression dialog box, select OK. The dialog box will close, revealing the report specification underneath. You can modify the formatting and style settings for an existing field at any time: just place the cursor anywhere in the field and press ENTER. Doing so will redisplay the Report Expression dialog box. You can make the desired modifications to the formatting and style options, and then choose OK to implement the changes.

Adding Text or Lines And Overlaying Objects

The Text option of the Report menu can be used to add text at the cursor location. Choose the Text option, and then begin typing your desired text. Complete the entry by pressing ENTER. Note that you do not need this menu option to enter text; if you move to any blank area in the report specification and begin typing, FoxPro will assume that you want to enter text.

The Add Line and Remove Line options of the Report menu are used to add or delete lines (rows) from the report specification. To add a line, place the cursor anywhere in the desired row location and choose Add Line from the menu; the new line will be inserted at the cursor location. To remove a line, place the cursor anywhere in the unwanted line and choose Remove Line from the Report menu. Note that there are shortcut keys for these options; you can use CTRL-N for Add Line and CTRL-M for Remove Line.

The Bring to Back, Send to Front, and Center options of the Report menu are used when, for one reason or another, you choose to overlay one object (such as a box) with another object (such as a field). For example, it is possible to drag a field so it partially covers a box or a title you have entered as text. If you then select one of the objects (such as the text) with the TAB key and choose Bring to Front from the Report menu, the selected object appears over the object it partially covers. If you select Send to Back, the selected object is placed under the other object. You may find these options useful when you are combining text labels and boxes; you might, for example, type a few words as a descriptive label and later add a box whose position covers the label. By selecting the box and choosing Send to Back from the Report menu, the text would overlay the box. The Center option of the Report menu will center the selected object within the left and right edges of the report.

The Quick Report option provides an immediate report based on either a columnar or a form layout, as detailed earlier in this chapter.

Moving and Deleting Objects

You can move or delete existing objects (fields, boxes, or text) within a report. This can be particularly useful in modifying a quick report to serve as a customized report. To move an object to another location, place the cursor anywhere within the desired object, and press the spacebar to select the object. Once selected, the object will be highlighted. Use the cursor keys to move the object to its new location, and press ENTER to complete the movement. Mouse users can simply click and drag the desired object to its new location. To delete an object, first select the object as just described. Then open the Edit menu with ALT-E and choose Cut from the menu to delete the object.

Note that the Edit menu's Cut, Copy, and Paste options provide an alternative method for moving objects, as well as a method for duplicating objects in the report. You can select an object with the techniques just described, and choose Cut from the Edit menu to remove the object from its existing location. Then place the cursor at the new location and choose Paste from the Edit menu to insert that same object at the new location. (The Paste option always inserts whatever was deleted last with the Cut option.)

You can make duplicates of objects with the Copy option of the Edit menu. Just select the object using the methods described, and choose Copy from the Edit menu. Place the cursor where the duplicate of the object is to appear, and choose Paste from the Edit menu.

Saving and Running the Report

Once you have made your desired changes to the report design, press CTRL-W or choose Save from the File menu (and enter a name, if prompted for one, in the dialog box that appears). To run a report from the menus, choose Report from the Database menu and enter the report's name in the dialog box that appears. You can also run a report from the command level by entering the command

REPORT FORM *filename* TO PRINT

where *filename* is the name with which you saved the report. Omit the TO PRINT designation if you simply wish to view the report on the screen.

PRACTICE DESIGNING A CUSTOMIZED REPORT

As an example of the steps involved in creating a customized report, consider the case of the Generic Videos membership file. The company needs a report with the name, city, and state of each member, along with the phone number, expiration date, tape limit, and beta information. Below all of this data, a listing of the comments in the Preferences field should appear. They also want a title and the current date and time on the report. For now, the report will contain a single group of data; later, the report will be broken into separate groupings of members by state.

To begin designing the report, enter

USE MEMBERS
CREATE REPORT MEMBERS

The report specification will appear. Let's begin with the headings. The date and time need to appear in the upper-right corner of the first page, so these items need to be placed in the Page Header band. Move the cursor to row 1, column 50. You can tell the cursor location from the R and C designations shown in the upper-left corner of the report specification; mouse users can quickly move the cursor by clicking in the desired area of the screen.

Open the Report menu and choose Field. The Report Expression dialog box now appears (Figure 7-12). You could enter a field name here, but in this case a field isn't desired; the date is what's wanted. If you knew the syntax for the date function, you could type it in here; however, if you cannot recall the syntax, the Expression Builder can be used as an aid. If you tab over to the Expr heading in the dialog box and press ENTER or mouse-click

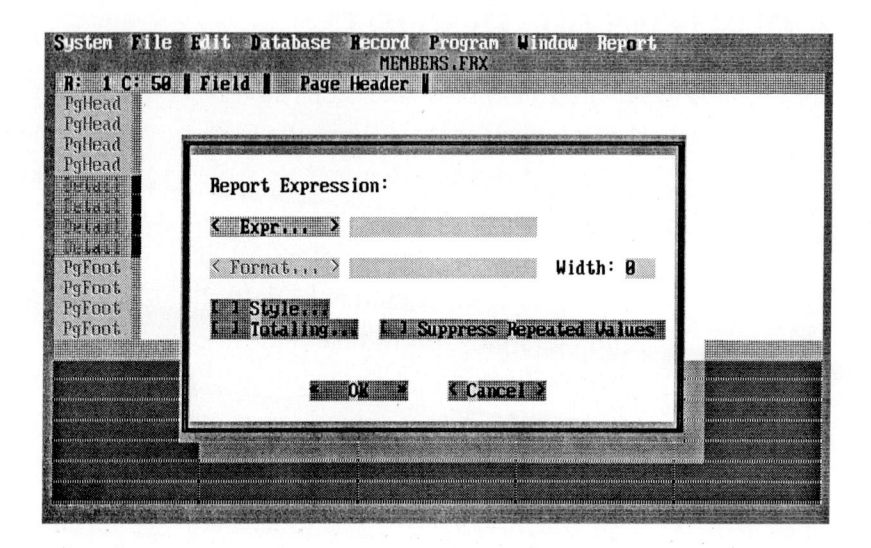

FIGURE 7-12. Report Expression dialog box

on the Expr heading, you will see the Expression Builder, as shown in Figure 7-13. Here you can select field names, functions, and math, string, or logical symbols to build a desired expression.

In this case, all that's needed is the appropriate function for the current date. Tab over to the Date menu box and press the spacebar to open the menu (or mouse-click on the Date box and drag down the menu of choices), and select DATE as the desired function. The DATE function, when used, provides the current date as read from the system clock.

Press CTRL-W (or choose OK from the dialog box), and then choose OK when the Report Expression dialog box reappears. You should see the DATE function, now located at row 1, column 50.

Move the cursor down to row 2, column 50; the time function will be inserted here, to provide the time when the report is run. Open the Report menu and choose Field. This time when the

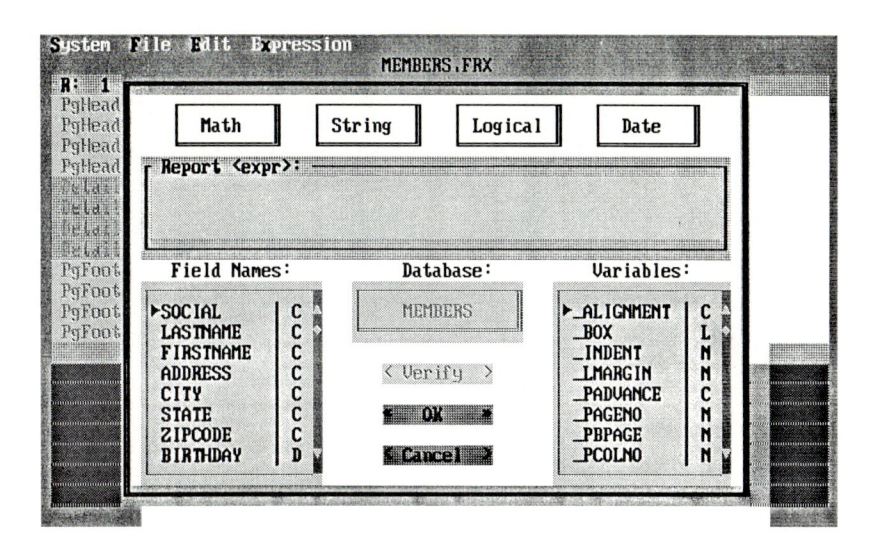

FIGURE 7-13. Expression Builder

Report Expression dialog box appears, use the shorter method of entering the function directly. Tab to the Expr window, and enter

TIME( )

Then choose OK from the dialog box. The TIME function will appear in the report specification immediately below the DATE function.

Press HOME to get back to the left margin, and move the cursor down to row 4, the first line in the Detail band. Type

Name:

and press ENTER to complete the entry of text, and then move the cursor over to column 6. Open the Report menu with ALT-O, choose Field, and enter **LASTNAME** in the window as the desired field name. Select OK from the dialog box to complete the placement of the Lastname field.

Move the cursor two spaces to the right, to row 4, column 22. As a shortcut to using the Field choice of the Report menu, you might want to try the CTRL-F key combination this time. Press CTRL-F, and the Report Expression dialog box will again appear. Tab to the window, enter **FIRSTNAME**, and then select OK from the dialog box to place the field.

Move the cursor four spaces to the right, to row 4, column 40. Enter

Phone:

Press ENTER to complete the entry of text. Move the cursor one space to the right of the colon, and press CTRL-F to open the dialog box. Tab to the window, enter **PHONE** as the field name, and select OK to place the field.

Move the cursor to the start of row 5 and enter

City & State:

as the heading. Press ENTER to complete the entry of text. Move the cursor to row 5, column 16, open the dialog box with CTRL-F, tab to the window, and enter **CITY**. Then select OK to place the field.

Move the cursor two spaces to the right, to row 5, column 32. Press CTRL-F, and enter **STATE** as the field name; then select OK to place the field.

Move the cursor four spaces to the right, to row 5, column 37. Enter

Exp. date:

Then press ENTER to complete the entry of the text. Move the cursor to row 5, column 48. Press CTRL-F, and enter **EXPIREDATE** as the field name; then select OK to place the field.

Move the cursor to the start of row 6, and enter

Tape limit:

Press ENTER to complete the entry of the text. Move the cursor to column 12. Press CTRL-F and enter **TAPELIMIT** as the field name; then select OK to place the field.

Move the cursor to row 6, column 20, enter

Uses Beta?

and press ENTER to complete the entry of the text. Move the cursor to column 31. Press CTRL-F and enter **BETA** as the field name; then select OK to place the field.

For this report, a blank line is desired between the contents of the Preference field and the next row of data. To accomplish this, you will need to add another line to the Detail band. Move the cursor down to the start of row 7. Open the Report menu and choose Add Line to add a new line. Next, enter the label

Preferences:

Then press Enter to complete the entry of the text. Move the cursor to column 13. Press CTRL-F and enter **PREFERENCE** as the field name. Since this is a memo field, you can use the Stretch Vertically option, which allows long text entries to use up as much vertical space as is needed. Tab over to the Stretch Vertically option and press the spacebar to select it. Then select OK to place the field. At this point, your screen should resemble the one shown in Figure 7-14.

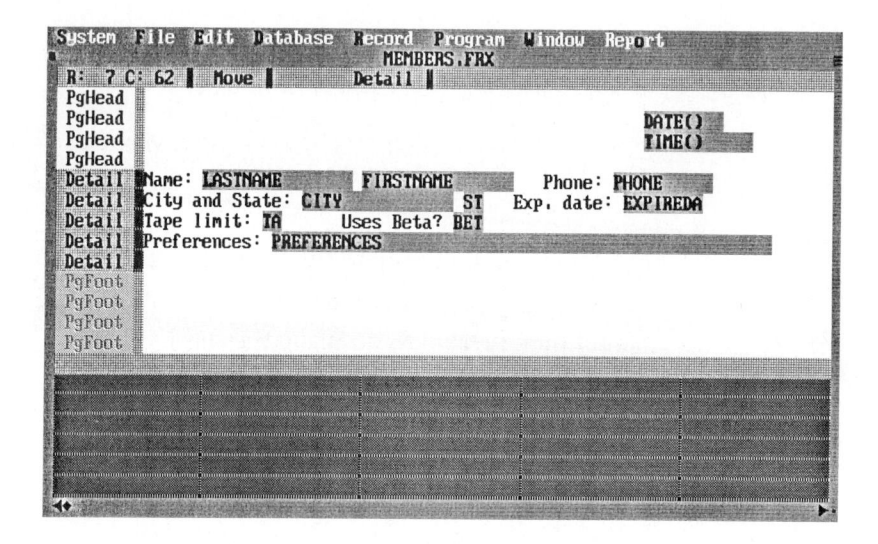

FIGURE 7-14. Report Specification with fields added

To enable more data to fit on each page, the staff has decided that the default of four lines for a Page Footer band isn't really necessary. Move the cursor to row 9 (the first line in the Page Footer band) and choose Remove Line from the Report menu. Choose the same option two more times, which will leave one line remaining in the Page Footer band.

The staff has decided that a summary field showing the number of members in the video club would be a nice addition; for this, you will need a summary field based on a count of records (members) in the database. Open the Report menu and choose Title/Summary. From the dialog box that appears, choose Summary Band by highlighting the option and pressing the spacebar. Then choose OK from the dialog box.

This step adds the Summary band at the bottom of the report specification; you must still add any desired text or fields in the

Introducing Reports   255

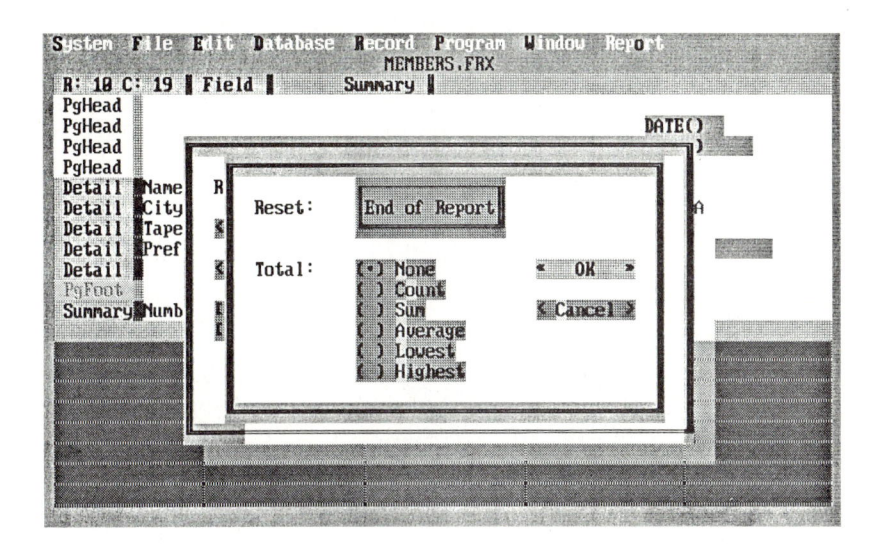

[screenshot of Total dialog box overlaying the MEMBERS.FRX report designer]

FIGURE 7-15. Total dialog box

Summary band. At the start of the Summary Band, type the heading

Number of Members:

and press ENTER to complete the text entry. Move the cursor over to column 19, and press CTRL-F to open the Report Expression dialog box. Because you will request a total count of the number of entries, you could use any field that would always have an entry. Since the Social field will always contain an entry for each record, enter SOCIAL as the field name. Then tab to the Totaling option and press the spacebar to select it (or mouse-click on the entry).

You will see the dialog box shown in Figure 7-15. This dialog box lets you base the contents of a summary field on a count of records, a numeric sum, an average, or a lowest or highest value. The last four options will apply only to numeric fields, while the Count option can count the occurrences in any type of field. Select Count by tabbing to it and pressing the spacebar or by using the mouse. Then select OK within the dialog box. When the Report Expression dialog box reappears, change the Width entry to 3. (This will prevent a count of 8 members appearing as 8.000000000 in the Summary Band.) Finally, select OK from the dialog box to complete the placement of the field.

Save the report by pressing CTRL-W. When you are back at the command level, enter

REPORT FORM MEMBERS

or, if your printer is connected and turned on, you might want to instead try

REPORT FORM MEMBERS TO PRINT

You should see (or print) a report similar to the example shown here:

```
                                              08/28/89
                                              10:56:20 pm

Name: Miller         Karen            Phone: 301-555-66
City and State: Chevy Chase     MD    Exp. date: 07/25/92
Tape limit:    6      Uses Beta? .F.
Preferences: Prefers science fiction, horror movies.  Fan of
             Star Trek films.

Name: Martin         William          Phone: 301-555-29
City and State: Silver Spring   MD    Exp. date: 07/04/91
Tape limit:    4      Uses Beta? .F.
Preferences: Enjoys Clint Eastwood, John Wayne films.
```

Name: Robinson   Carol   Phone: 703-555-87
City and State: Falls Church   VA   Exp. date: 09/05/93
Tape limit: 6   Uses Beta? .F.
Preferences: Likes comedy, drama films.

Name: Kramer   Harry   Phone: 703-555-68
City and State: Arlington   VA   Exp. date: 12/22/90
Tape limit: 4   Uses Beta? .T.
Preferences: Big fan of Eddie Murphy. Also enjoys westerns.

Name: Moore   Ellen   Phone: 301-555-02
City and State: Takoma Park   MD   Exp. date: 11/17/94
Tape limit: 6   Uses Beta? .F.
Preferences: drama, comedy.

Name: Zachman   David   Phone: 703-555-54
City and State: Falls Church   VA   Exp. date: 09/19/90
Tape limit: 4   Uses Beta? .T.
Preferences: science fiction, drama.

Name: Robinson   Benjamin   Phone: 202-555-45
City and State: Washington   DC   Exp. date: 09/17/91
Tape limit: 2   Uses Beta? .F.
Preferences: westerns, comedy. Clint Eastwood fan.

Name: Hart   Wendy   Phone: 703-555-12
City and State: Fairfax   VA   Exp. date: 10/19/92
Tape limit: 2   Uses Beta? .T.
Preferences: drama, adventure. Likes spy movies, including all
            in 'James Bond' series.

Number of Members: 8.0

USING THE GROUP MENU OPTIONS

You can use the various group options of the Report menu to work with groupings of records within a report. You will probably need

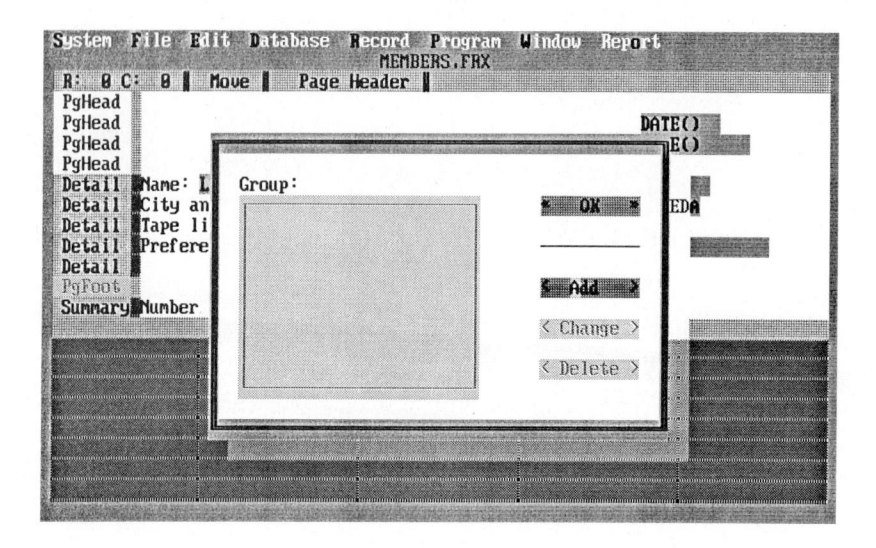

FIGURE 7-16. Group dialog box

to arrange reports broken down by groups. For example, you might need to see all members divided into groups by state of residence. Using the Data Grouping option of the Report menu, you can define multiple levels of grouping.

While many more than three levels of groups may seem like overkill to some, it is nice to know that FoxPro is accommodating when you must base a complex report on a large number of subgroups. Multiple groupings can be quite common in business applications. In something as simple as a national mailing list, for example, you might need to see records by groups of states, and within each state group by city, and within each city group by ZIP code. That represents three levels of grouping alone. Cut the data in the table more specifically—by other categories like income levels, for example—and you can quickly come to appreciate FoxPro's ability to perform effective grouping.

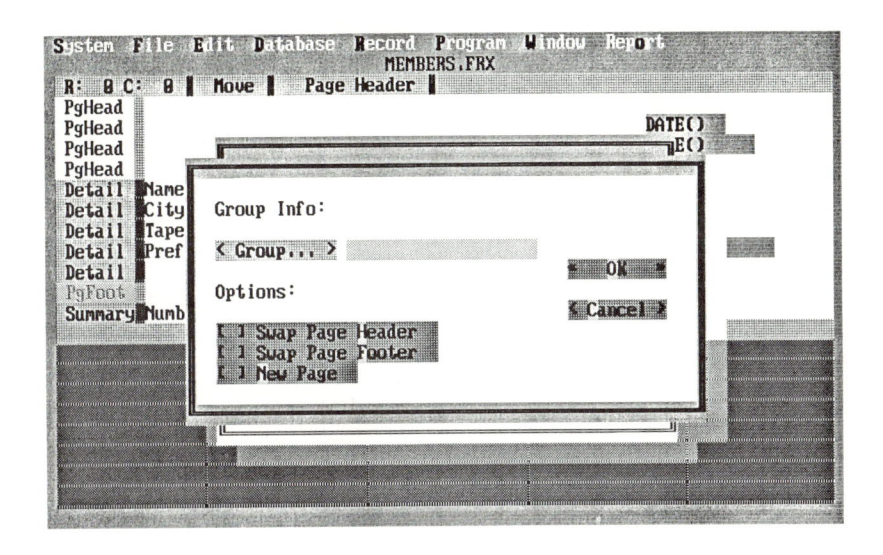

FIGURE 7-17. Group info box

When you choose the Data Grouping option from the Report menu while designing a report, the Group dialog box shown in Figure 7-16 is displayed. You use the Add, Change, or Delete buttons to add, change, or delete Group bands from a report. When you choose Add, you see the Group Info dialog box (Figure 7-17). You can use this dialog box to enter a field name (or other expression) to base your group on.

If you want to establish the group by field (as in groups of records from the same state or with the same assignment), you would enter the name of that field. You can also group records based upon a valid FoxPro expression. For example, if you were using an index based on a combination of Lastname + Firstname to control the order of the records, you could enter the expression LASTNAME + FIRSTNAME to define the grouping. Once you add a Group band, you can then enter text or fields into that band within the report specification. After selecting the desired type of grouping, FoxPro will insert a new starting Group band and a new ending Group band for the group. Group bands must fall outside of the Detail bands.

The Swap Page Header option tells FoxPro to place group headers instead of page headers on all pages where the group header appears. The Swap Page Footer option does the same for footers; when chosen, each page containing a group footer prints the group footer at the bottom of the page in place of the page footer.

Once you've placed the desired group, you can check to see if the results are what you desire by pressing ALT-O for the Report menu and choosing Page Preview. The resulting report will be divided by group. Note that the file must be sorted or indexed on the field you are grouping by to get the records in the proper group order; you may need to save the report, index or sort the file from the menus or command level, and then run the report. When you are satisfied with the results, save the report specification by pressing CTRL-W.

ADDING GROUPING BY STATE TO THE MEMBERSHIP REPORT

Try adding a group by state to the existing membership report you created earlier in the chapter. From the command level, you can enter **MODIFY REPORT MEMBERS**. The report specification for the report you designed earlier will appear.

To add the group to the report, first place the cursor on the line above the Detail band. Next, open the Report menu with ALT-O, and choose Data Grouping to insert a new group. The Group dialog box appears. There are no existing groups in the report, so the list box is empty. Select Add from the dialog box to add a group. Doing so will reveal the Group Info dialog box, shown in Figure 7-18.

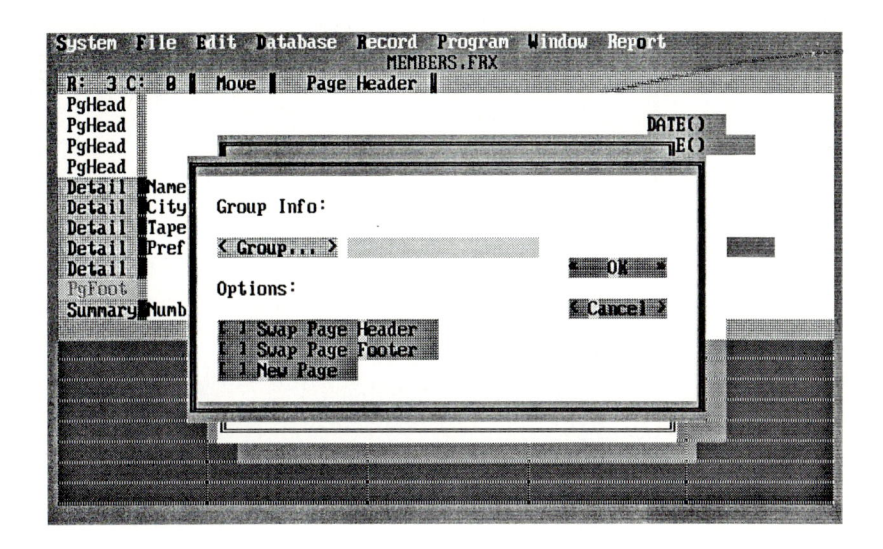

FIGURE 7-18. Group Info dialog box

In the Group box, you enter the field name or expression that will control the grouping. (When you can't remember the name of a field, you can tab to or click on the Group heading and use the Expression Builder to select field names or parts of expressions.) In this case, enter

STATE

in the text box, and then select OK. When you choose OK, you'll see the Group dialog box uncovered; note that it now contains the designation

1: State

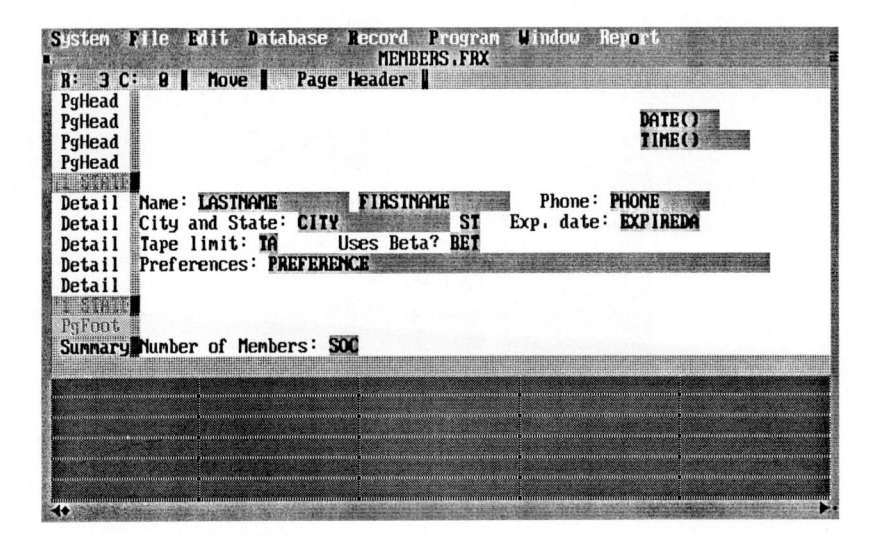

```
System File Edit Database Record Program Window Report
                            MEMBERS.FRX
R: 3 C: 0 | Move | Page Header |
PgHead
PgHead                                                    DATE()
PgHead                                                    TIME()
PgHead

Detail  Name: LASTNAME         FIRSTNAME      Phone: PHONE
Detail  City and State: CITY              ST   Exp. date: EXPIREDA
Detail  Tape limit: TA      Uses Beta? BET
Detail  Preferences: PREFERENCE
Detail

PgFoot
Summary Number of Members: SOC
```

FIGURE 7-19. Report Specification with single level of grouping added

in the list box, showing that there is one level of grouping based on the State field. Again, select OK from the dialog box. The new Group bands will appear in the report specification, as shown in Figure 7-19.

Save the report by pressing CTRL-W. Then create an index file that will control the order of the grouping by entering the following command:

INDEX ON STATE TO STATES

The file will be indexed in the order needed to provide the groups within the report. Next, turn on your printer and enter the command

REPORT FORM MEMBERS TO PRINT

The report will be printed and should resemble the following listing:

08/28/89
11:13:38 pm

Name: Robinson   Benjamin   Phone: 202-555-45
City and State: Washington   DC   Exp. date: 09/17/91
Tape limit: 2   Uses Beta? .F.
Preferences: westerns, comedy. Clint Eastwood fan.

Name: Miller   Karen   Phone: 301-555-66
City and State: Chevy Chase   MD   Exp. date: 07/25/92
Tape limit: 6   Uses Beta? .F.
Preferences: Prefers science fiction, horror movies. Fan of
             Star Trek films.

Name: Martin   William   Phone: 301-555-29
City and State: Silver Spring   MD   Exp. date: 07/04/91
Tape limit: 4   Uses Beta? .F.
Preferences: Enjoys Clint Eastwood, John Wayne films.

Name: Moore   Ellen   Phone: 301-555-02
City and State: Takoma Park   MD   Exp. date: 11/17/94
Tape limit: 6   Uses Beta? .F.
Preferences: drama, comedy.

Name: Robinson   Carol   Phone: 703-555-87
City and State: Falls Church   VA   Exp. date: 09/05/93
Tape limit: 6   Uses Beta? .F.
Preferences: Likes comedy, drama films.

Name: Kramer   Harry   Phone: 703-555-68
City and State: Arlington   VA   Exp. date: 12/22/90
Tape limit: 4   Uses Beta? .T.
Preferences: Big fan of Eddie Murphy. Also enjoys westerns.

```
Name: Zachman      David               Phone: 703-555-54
City and State: Falls Church      VA   Exp. date: 09/19/90
Tape limit:    4      Uses Beta? .T.
Preferences: science fiction, drama.


Name: Hart         Wendy               Phone: 703-555-12
City and State: Fairfax           VA   Exp. date: 10/19/92
Tape limit:    2      Uses Beta? .T.
Preferences: drama, adventure.  Likes spy movies, including all
             in 'James Bond' series.
```

Number of Members: 8.0

And if you are observant, you will immediately notice a problem here. The actual contents of the State field do not appear with each group, so the meaning of the grouping is not obvious. To add a heading indicating the grouping, you'll need to place the field where you want it to appear. You can place the field used to control the group within the Group band, and it will then print once for each occurrence of that group. To see how this works, enter

MODIFY REPORT MEMBERS

to get back into the report specification. Place the cursor inside the starting Group band for the State field. At the far left margin, type the heading

For State:

and press ENTER to complete the entry of the text. Then move the cursor to the right two spaces (to column 11). Press CTRL-F to get to the Report Expression dialog box, enter

STATE

as the expression, and select OK from the dialog box. A field template representing the State field will appear in the Group band.

Place the cursor at the start of the ending Group band (row 10). A count of members per group would be desirable here, so enter the text

Members per State:

and press ENTER. Move the cursor over to column 19 and press CTRL-F. Tab into the Expr window, and enter **SOCIAL** as the field to base the count upon. Tab down to the Totaling option, and press the spacebar to select the option.

At the next dialog box that appears, tab over to the Count option and press the spacebar to select it. Tab back up to the Reset menu, and press ENTER to open the menu. Select State from the menu. This tells FoxPro to reset the member count for each state group.

Choose OK in the dialog box. In the Report Expression dialog box that reappears, tab over to the Width box and enter **3**. Finally, choose OK from the Report Expression dialog box.

Save the report by pressing CTRL-W. To see the results, enter

SET INDEX TO STATES
REPORT FORM MEMBERS TO PRINT

The report will appear or be printed, and this time the contents for the State field will appear along with each group:

```
                                                            08/28/89
                                                         11:12:00 pm

For State: DC
Name: Robinson        Benjamin              Phone: 202-555-45
City and State: Washington        DC        Exp. date: 09/17/91
Tape limit:    2      Uses Beta? .F.
Preferences: westerns, comedy. Clint Eastwood fan.
```

Members Per State: 1.0
For State: MD
Name: Miller   Karen   Phone: 301-555-66
City and State: Chevy Chase   MD   Exp. date: 07/25/92
Tape limit: 6   Uses Beta? .F.
Preferences: Prefers science fiction, horror movies. Fan of
             Star Trek films.

Name: Martin   William   Phone: 301-555-29
City and State: Silver Spring   MD   Exp. date: 07/04/91
Tape limit: 4   Uses Beta? .F.
Preferences: Enjoys Clint Eastwood, John Wayne films.

Name: Moore   Ellen   Phone: 301-555-02
City and State: Takoma Park   MD   Exp. date: 11/17/94
Tape limit: 6   Uses Beta? .F.
Preferences: drama, comedy.

Members Per State: 3.0
For State: VA
Name: Robinson   Carol   Phone: 703-555-87
City and State: Falls Church   VA   Exp. date: 09/05/93
Tape limit: 6   Uses Beta? .F.
Preferences: Likes comedy, drama films.

Name: Kramer   Harry   Phone: 703-555-68
City and State: Arlington   VA   Exp. date: 12/22/90
Tape limit: 4   Uses Beta? .T.
Preferences: Big fan of Eddie Murphy. Also enjoys westerns.

Name: Zachman   David   Phone: 703-555-54
City and State: Falls Church   VA   Exp. date: 09/19/90
Tape limit: 4   Uses Beta? .T.
Preferences: science fiction, drama.

Name: Hart   Wendy   Phone: 703-555-12
City and State: Fairfax   VA   Exp. date: 10/19/92
Tape limit: 2   Uses Beta? .T.
Preferences: drama, adventure. Likes spy movies, including all
              in 'James Bond' series.

Members Per State: 4.0
Number of Members: 8.0

CREATING A REPORT WITH MULTIPLE GROUPS

You can insert additional groups to further define your groups. As an example, consider the RENTALS database, which contains records of the tapes rented by the members. If what is needed is a report grouped by the name of the movie, and by the rental date within each group of movie names, you must create a report containing more than one group.

Enter **USE RENTALS** to open the RENTALS database. Next, enter **CREATE REPORT RENTS** to begin a new report. Open the Report menu, choose Quick Report, and leave the Column Layout option selected as the desired layout. Select OK from the dialog box to create a standard columnar report. The standard report format will do for this example.

In this case, what is wanted is a report grouped by movie name, and within each movie name, by groups of rental dates. Place the cursor at the start of the last Page Header band, just above the Detail band. Press ALT-O to get to the Report menu, and choose Data Grouping to insert a new group; from the dialog box that appears, choose Add. In the next dialog box, enter **TITLE** as the field name, and then select OK.

To add a second level of grouping, you simply select Add from the Group dialog box again. Choose Add now, and the Group Info dialog box will again appear. The field controlling the second level of grouping is the Dayrented field, so enter DAYRENTED as the field name and select OK. Once you select OK, the "DAYRENTED" field name appears under "TITLE" in the list box. Choose OK in the Group dialog box to get back to the report specification.

Press HOME to move the cursor to the left margin, and move down into the first Group band (labeled "1- Title"). Choose Add Line from the Report menu to add another line; this will provide blank space when the report is produced. Move the cursor down one line and type the heading

Movie name:

Press ENTER to complete the text entry, and then press the RIGHT ARROW key twice. Press CTRL-F to open the Report Expression dialog box, and enter **TITLE** as the field name. Then choose OK.

Move the cursor down one line and press HOME to get back to the left margin of the second Group band (labeled "2-dayre," short for "day rented"). Again, choose Add Line from the Report menu, and then move the cursor down one line. Type the heading

Rental date:

and press ENTER to complete the text entry, and press the RIGHT ARROW key twice. Press CTRL-F to open the Report Expression dialog box, and enter **DAYRENTED** as the field name. Then choose OK.

Since the movie title will appear as a group heading in the first Group band, it is not needed in the Detail band. Place the cursor anywhere in the Title field that is inside the Detail band (*not* the one in the 1st Group band), and press the DEL key.

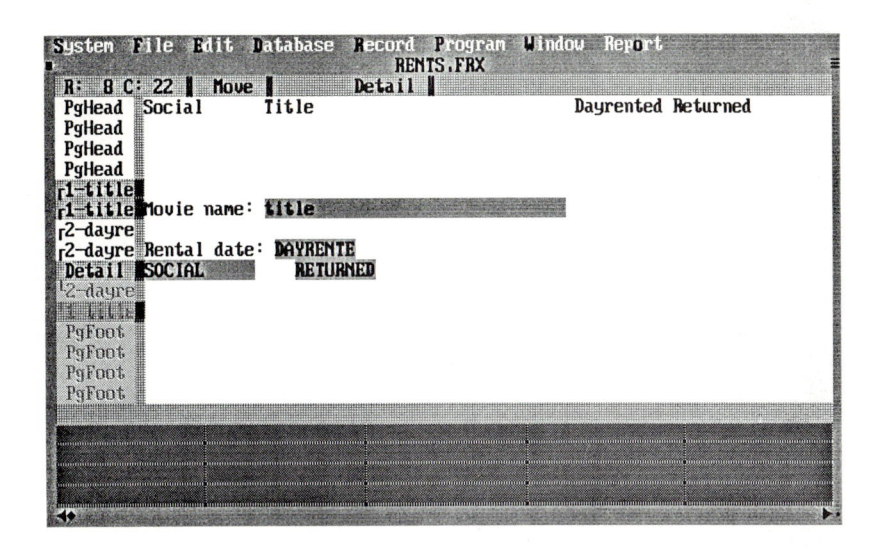

FIGURE 7-20. Report Specification containing multiple groups

The Dayrented field is also in a Group band, so it is not needed in the Detail band. Place the cursor anywhere in the Dayrented field that is inside the Detail band (*not* the one in the 2nd Group band), and press the DEL key. Then move over to the Returned field and press DEL again. Move the cursor back to column 15 (just to the right of the Social field), press CTRL-F, tab into the window, and enter **RETURNED** as the field name; then choose OK from the dialog box. Your screen should resemble the one shown in Figure 7-20.

Because the report will be grouped by movie title and then by rental date, the database must be sorted or indexed on a combination of the Title and Dayrented fields for the groupings to appear in the correct order. Save the report by choosing Save As from the File menu; use RENTS2 as a report name. Choose Close from the File menu to exit the Report Generator. Then enter the following command:

INDEX ON TITLE + DTOS(DAYRENTED) TO DAYFILE

The file will be indexed in the order needed to provide the groups within the report. As you may recall from Chapter 6, the DTOS function allows indexing on two fields of different types when one of the fields is a date field.

To see the results, enter

REPORT FORM RENTS2 TO PRINT

The report will be printed and should resemble the following:

SOCIAL   TITLE   DAYRENTED RETURNED

Movie name: Beverly Hills Cop II

Rental date: 03/04/90
901-77-3456   03/05/90

Movie name: Coming To America

Rental date: 03/14/90
901-77-3456   03/18/90

Movie name: Dirty Rotten Scoundrels

Rental date: 03/01/90
121-90-5432   03/06/90

Movie name: Friday 13th Part XXVII

Rental date: 03/14/90
123-44-8976   03/16/90

Movie name: Lethal Weapon II

Rental date: 03/02/90
121-33-9876   03/06/90

Rental date: 03/07/90
876-54-3210   03/08/90

Movie name: Licence To Kill

Rental date: 03/15/90
121-33-9876   03/17/90

Rental date: 03/16/90
876-54-3210   03/18/90

Movie name: Star Trek IV

Rental date: 03/05/90
123-44-8976   03/06/90

Movie name: Star Trek V

Rental date: 03/18/90
495-00-3456   03/18/90

Movie name: When Harry Met Sally

Rental date: 03/06/90
343-55-9821   03/12/90

Rental date: 03/16/90
121-90-5432   03/17/90

Rental date: 03/17/90
232-55-1234   03/19/90

Movie name: Who Framed Roger Rabbit

Rental date: 03/06/90
232-55-1234   03/09/90

Movie name: Young Einstein

Rental date: 03/04/90
495-00-3456   03/09/90

Rental date: 03/19/90
343-55-9821   03/20/90

REPORT DESIGN

Before you start to design your custom reports, you should plan the design of the report. This may mean asking the other users of the database what information will actually be needed from the report. In the case of Generic Videos, you would consider what information the managers need from the report, and how the report should look.

In many cases, you'll find it advantageous to outline the report contents and format on paper. Once the report has been designed on paper, your outline should resemble the actual report that is produced by FoxPro. You may also find it helpful to print a list of fields from the database structure, particularly if you are designing a report that contains a large number of fields. This can be done with the LIST STRUCTURE TO PRINT command.

8

MANAGING YOUR FILES

Using the Filer
Commands for Managing Files

This chapter's topic is file operations—copying, renaming, and erasing files, and using more than one database file at a time. Although some file operations usually are performed from your operating system (DOS or OS/2), these operations can also be performed without leaving FoxPro.

In addition to performing file operations without returning to the operating system, you can also transfer information between database files. You can transfer all the data in a file, or selected data. You can also open and work with more than one file at once. The use of multiple files is common in a relational database manager like FoxPro, and you will find it a virtual necessity for performing some types of tasks, such as inventory and complex accounting functions.

USING THE FILER

Various options for managing files are available through the Filer option of the System menu. If you open the System menu and choose Filer, the Filer appears, as shown in Figure 8-1. Its list box shows all files in the current directory. Also shown at the bottom of the Filer are options such as Find, Copy, Move, and so forth. These options can be selected (by typing the highlighted letter within the option or by mouse-clicking on the option) to perform various file operations. At the upper-right side of the Filer are two menus for your disk drives and directories. You can tab to either menu and press ENTER to display an additional menu that lists available disk drives or directories. Using these menus, you can navigate within other drives and directories.

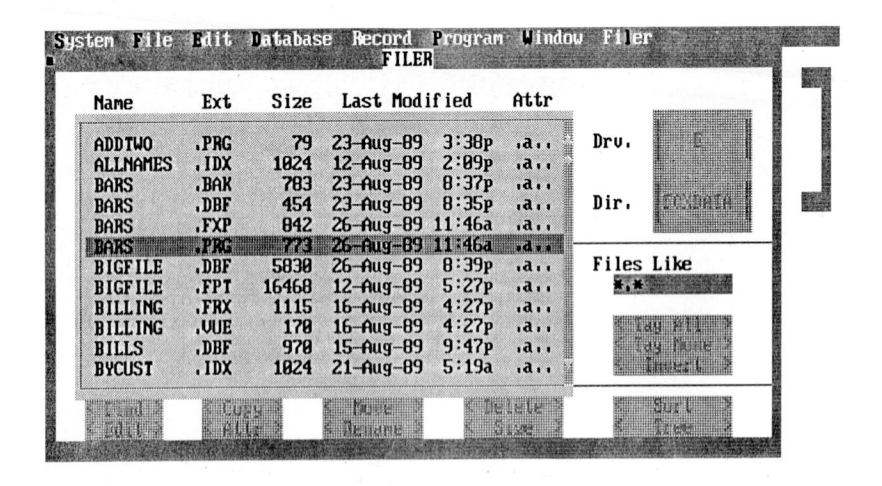

FIGURE 8-1. The Filer

Underneath the menus is the Files Like entry box. You can enter filenames or DOS wildcards here, to restrict the types of files displayed in the list box. For example, entering *.**DBF** in the Files Like box would restrict the files shown to database files only.

The list box is divided into five columns: Name, Ext, Size, Last Modified, and Attr (for Attribute). The Name and Ext columns show the filename and extension (if any) of the file. Directories and subdirectories are displayed within brackets; in the figure, the filename [..] at the top of the list denotes the parent directory, E:\FOXPRO.

The Size column shows the size of each file in bytes, and the Last Modified column shows the DOS date and time stamp on the file. The Attr column shows the attributes of the file, as determined by your operating system. Up to four letters can appear in this column: A, for archive; H, for hidden; R, for read-only; and S, for system. More information about file attributes can be found in your DOS manual.

Moving Around the Files List

You can use the UP ARROW and DOWN ARROW keys and the PGUP and PGDN keys to move the cursor within the files list. Try PGDN and your DOWN ARROW key now to see the effect. As you highlight a particular file, you can press ENTER to *tag* (place a marker) beside the file. Once a file has been tagged, you can use the options at the bottom of the Filer to perform a desired operation (such as copying or erasing) on the tagged file.

Note the Tag All, Tag None, and Invert options at the right side of the Filer. You can select Tag All to tag all files, and you can select Tag None to remove all tags from files. Selecting Invert reverses the order of existing tags; all tagged files are untagged, and all untagged files are tagged. You may find that using the Tag All option along with the Files Like entry box is useful for selecting groups of files of the same type. For example, you could delete all backup (.BAK) files by entering ***.BAK** in the Files Like box, selecting Tag All, and then selecting Delete.

You are not limited to working within the current directory. By tabbing to the Dir menu at the right side of the Filer and pressing ENTER, you can display directories above the current one. Highlight the desired directory and press ENTER to switch to that directory, or highlight the drive letter to switch to the root directory. When you do this, the files list box shows the directory you have switched to. You can highlight any directory in the Files List and press ENTER to switch to that directory.

After experimenting with moving around, be sure to get back to the subdirectory that contains your working files (it will probably be FOXPRO\FOXDATA, unless you set up your hard disk differently at the start of this book). If you somehow get lost and can't find your way back, just exit the Filer by pressing ESC and restart the Filer by choosing Filer from the System menu. FoxPro will automatically put you back in the working directory. You can exit the Filer at any time by pressing the ESC key or by mouse-clicking on the close box in the upper-left corner of the window.

Deleting Files

You can delete files by tagging the files (highlighting the file and pressing ENTER to tag it) and then choosing the Delete option. When you do this, a dialog box will warn you that the file will be deleted. You must then choose Delete from the dialog box to delete the file.

Renaming Files

You can rename a file by tagging the file and choosing the Rename option. When you do this, a dialog box will display the old name and ask you for the new name. Enter the new name and choose Rename from the dialog box to rename the file.

Finding Files

You can find a file in the current directory by choosing the Find option. When you choose this option, you are prompted for a filename. Enter the filename, and the highlight within the files list box will move to the desired file.

Editing Files

You can edit a file with the Edit option. (This should only be attempted with text files, such as programs you write in FoxPro; you should not attempt to load nontext files, such as databases or indexes, into the Editor.) To edit a file, highlight the desired file in the list box and choose Edit. The uses of the Editor are covered in more detail in Chapter 12.

Moving and Copying Files

You can copy files with the Copy option. To copy a file, highlight its name in the list box and choose Copy. You will be prompted for a name for the copied file. Enter the name, and the file will be copied to the new file. With the Move option, you can move a file from one directory to another. Highlight the desired file in the list box and choose Move. You will be prompted for the destination directory for the file (you can include a drive name, if desired). The Move operation moves the file by copying it to the new location and deleting it from the existing location.

Changing File Attributes

You can change the DOS attributes of a file with the Attr option. When you tag a file and then select Attr, a dialog box appears with the four attribute choices: Archived, Hidden file, Read-Only, or

System. The check boxes for the choices will already be selected or unselected, depending on the file's current status; for example, if you have tagged a read-only file, the Read- Only check box will be filled in with an X. You can press the highlighted letters of your choice or click on the check boxes with the mouse to change any file attributes as desired.

Warning: You should not change file attributes without being aware of possible consequences, particularly with files that are part of the program or the operating system. If you were to change the attributes of files that make up the actual FoxPro program or of your system (DOS) files, the results could be disastrous. Your computer could fail to operate normally.

Using Size and Tree

Use the Size option to display statistics on the size of a file. To use the option, select the desired file in the list box and choose Size. A dialog box containing information on the size of the file will appear. Use the Tree option to display a files tree (a visual representation of the layout of files within your directories). Choose Tree, and the visual representation of your files and directories will appear.

Using Sort

Use the Sort option to sort the files in the files list. When you choose the Sort option, a dialog box lets you select the sort criteria. You can choose to sort by name, extension, size, date, or file attributes. You can also choose whether the list will be sorted in ascending or descending order. After choosing the desired options from the dialog box, choose OK, and the files in the list box will be sorted. This in no way affects the order of the files on the disk; only the appearance of the files in the list box is affected.

COMMANDS FOR MANAGING FILES

If you prefer to stick with commands, you can use a number of different commands for file management. You can even run a DOS command from the command level within FoxPro. You can also perform selective copying of records within a database file to another file.

The RUN Command

To exit FoxPro temporarily and run a DOS command, use the RUN command. The syntax for this command is

RUN *DOS command or program name*

It causes FoxPro to suspend itself temporarily in memory and exit to DOS. Note that a substantial portion of FoxPro remains in memory when you do this. On a 640K machine, between 128K and 256K of memory will be available (the exact amount varies with your version of DOS and hardware configuration). So while you can technically run other programs, you will probably find few programs that will fit in the available memory.

The RUN command is primarily useful for executing DOS commands you may be familiar with, such as COPY, DIR, and RENAME. To see how this works, enter the following command:

RUN DIR/P

You will see the current directory displayed just as if you had entered **DIR/P** at the DOS prompt. When the command completes, you will be returned to the Command window within FoxPro.

Note that you should never attempt to run a program that will modify your PC's memory with the RUN command. All memory-resident programs fall into this category, as does the PRINT command in DOS.

The COPY FILE Command

You can use the COPY FILE command as an equivalent to the COPY command in DOS to make copies of entire files. The format for this command is

COPY FILE *source-filename* TO *destination-filename*

You must include any extensions when using this command. As an example, if you wanted to make a copy of a file named LETTER1.TXT and the copy was to be named MYFILE.TXT, you could use the following command:

COPY FILE LETTER1.TXT TO MYFILE.TXT

Drive identifiers and path names are optional and can be included before the filenames.

Note that if you use this method to copy a database file, be sure to also copy any .FPT (memo field) file that may accompany the database. Remember, whenever a database contains memo fields, it is made up of two files, one with a .DBF extension and another with a .FPT extension.

The COPY Command

The COPY command copies all or parts of a database file. Its format is

COPY TO *filename*

where *filename* is the name of the new file that you want the records copied to. You must first use the USE command to open the file that you want to copy from. For example, if you enter

USE MEMBERS
COPY TO FILE1
USE FILE1
LIST

all of the records in the MEMBERS database will be copied to the new file, FILE1.

One advantage of the COPY command is that you need not worry about copying the memo field (.FPT) file; it is copied automatically. A disadvantage of COPY is that with large databases, it is much slower than the COPY FILE command.

The COPY command offers significant flexibility when you choose to copy specific fields. To select the fields to be copied, use the format

COPY TO *filename* FIELDS *fieldlist*

By adding the word "FIELDS" after the filename and then adding a list of fields, you tell FoxPro to copy only the fields that you place in the list to the new database. As an example, you can copy just the Lastname, Firstname, City, and State fields in FILE1 by entering

COPY TO FILE2 FIELDS LASTNAME, FIRSTNAME, CITY, STATE
USE FILE2
LIST

The listing shows that only the fields you specified by name in FILE1 are copied to FILE2.

You can also use a FOR clause to copy specific data from a database. When used with the COPY command, the optional FOR clause limits the records that will be copied to the new file; only the records meeting the condition specified by the FOR clause will be copied. The format for the COPY command when used with the FOR clause is

COPY TO *filename* FIELDS *fieldlist* FOR *condition*

Using the FOR clause as part of the COPY command, you can copy the Lastname and Tapelimit fields from FILE1 for all records in which the Tapelimit field contains a value greater than 3. To do this, enter

```
USE FILE1
COPY TO FILE3 FIELDS LASTNAME, TAPELIMIT FOR TAPELIMIT
> 3
```

The FOR condition specified before the Tapelimit field resulted in the new file, FILE3, containing only those members with a tape limit of more than 3. To see the results, enter

```
USE FILE3
LIST
```

You can perform this type of copying from the menus, if desired, by choosing the Copy To option of the Database menu. The dialog box that appears when you choose this option lets you specify a For or While condition to limit the records copied, as well as a scope or a list of fields to be copied to the new database.

Work Areas and Active Files

FoxPro can access any database file that is open, up to a limit of ten database files at the same time. Opening a database file is equivalent to telling FoxPro, "I am ready to work with a database file that is stored on disk; now go get it." FoxPro can read any information in the database from an open database file. However, if you want to change, add, or delete any information in a database, the database file must not only be open, but it must be active as well. Commands like CHANGE or EDIT, APPEND, and DELETE normally operate on active database files. FoxPro allows only one active database at a time, so out of a possible ten open files, only one can be active.

Opening a database file from disk requires that it be assigned to a *work area*. No database file can be open unless it resides in a work area. As you might have guessed, there are ten work areas in FoxPro, numbered from 1 to 10. Assigning a database file to a work area, or opening a database file, is a two-step process. You tell FoxPro what work area you want the file opened in, and you open the file in that work area. The SELECT command enables you to choose the work area, and the USE command opens the file. For example, if you wanted to open the MEMBERS file in work area 2, you could first select the work area by entering

SELECT 2

To load the MEMBERS file into the current work area, you would enter

USE MEMBERS

As an alternative, you could perform both steps— specifying the work area and opening the file—on a single command line by using the IN clause along with the USE command. For example, the following command tells FoxPro to open MEMBERS in work area 2:

USE MEMBERS IN 2

If you had specified a different filename—for example, RENTALS instead of MEMBERS—that file (RENTALS) would have been loaded into work area 2. In fact, any database file that you now load with the USE command will be loaded in work area 2 until you use the SELECT command to choose a different work area. Note that the USE *filename* IN *work-area* syntax of the USE command does *not* select a work area; it only loads the file in the named work area. If the current work area happened to be work area 1 and you entered **USE MEMBERS IN 2**, the MEMBERS file would be loaded in work area 2, but you would still be using work area 1.

The current work area is always the last area you chose with the SELECT command. The active database file is the last database file you loaded into the current work area. For an example, open the RENTALS file in work area 1 and the MEMBERS file in work area 2 by entering the following commands:

SELECT 1
USE RENTALS
SELECT 2
USE MEMBERS

MEMBERS is now the active database, because work area 2 was the last work area selected; thus, FoxPro is pointed to MEMBERS. FoxPro can now change or access any information in the MEMBERS file but can only access information from the RENTALS file. If you wanted RENTALS to be the active file, you would enter **SELECT 1** after opening both databases. The active database would switch from MEMBERS to RENTALS, although MEMBERS would remain open.

When you start a session, FoxPro selects work area 1 as the default work area. Also, when you open a file using the Open option of the File menu, it is opened in work area 1 by default. This is why in the other chapters you did not have to use the SELECT command first in order to load the MEMBERS file. Note that you could also select a file and work area by specifying the alias after the SELECT command. (The term "alias" will be explained shortly.) For example, once MEMBERS is open in work area 1, entering **SELECT MEMBERS** would switch to work area 1, making MEMBERS the active file.

Until now, you've worked with only one database file at a time, so when you referenced a field you didn't need to include the filename; whatever file you were working with was the active file. If you need information from a neighboring open database file, however, it is necessary to include the filename with the field. For example, enter the following:

SELECT 2
LIST

You will see from the listing that MEMBERS, open in work area 2, is the active file. To inspect the Dayrented field in the RENTALS file in work area 1 while MEMBERS is active in work area 2, enter

LIST RENTALS->DAYRENTED

The hyphen and the greater-than sign are combined to form a pointer for the field name. If you want to list the Title, Dayrented, and Returned fields from the RENTALS database, include the filename and pointer for all three:

LIST RENTALS->TITLE, RENTALS->DAYRENTED, RENTALS->RETURNED

Listing the filename while referencing a neighboring work area can be tedious, especially if the filename is long or difficult to remember. To alleviate part of the problem, you can give a shorter or more descriptive *alias* to a file when you assign it to a work area. An alias is any name that you specify to substitute for the filename. If you are dissatisfied with a default filename, you can name your own alias when you load a database file into a work area by including the ALIAS option with the USE command. The syntax for assigning an alias is

USE *filename* ALIAS *aliasname*

The same naming conventions for a filename apply to *aliasname,* but the .DBF extension is not included with an alias name. For example, the following command will give the alias MEM to the MEMBERS database file open in work area 2:

SELECT 2
USE MEMBERS ALIAS MEM

FoxPro assigns default names of A to work area 1, B to work area 2, C to work area 3, and so on. You can also choose to use these names when referring to work areas. As an example, instead of entering LIST RENTALS->DAYRENTED, you can enter **LIST A->DAYRENTED** and the same result will appear.

The CLOSE DATABASES Command

Another command that you will use often is the CLOSE DATABASES command. It closes all database and index files and returns FoxPro to work area 1. Enter

CLOSE DATABASES

to close all of the database files that you have opened earlier.

Combining Files

FoxPro lets you transfer records from one database file to another by using a variation of the APPEND command that you have used to add records to a database. However, the format of the command is somewhat different when it is used for transferring records from another database. Instead of simply entering **APPEND**, you must enter the command in the format

APPEND FROM *filename*

where *filename* is the name of the file from which you wish to transfer records. The file to which you are adding the records must be the active database file.

As an example, to transfer records from the newly created FILE3 database to the FILE2 database, you should first activate FILE2. Enter

USE FILE2

You can append the records to FILE2 with

APPEND FROM FILE3

When you list the database to see the appended records, your display should resemble this:

Record#	LASTNAME	FIRSTNAME	CITY	STATE
1	Miller	Karen	Chevy Chase	MD
2	Martin	William	Silver Spring	MD
3	Robinson	Carol	Falls Church	VA
4	Kramer	Harry	Arlington	VA
5	Moore	Ellen	Takoma Park	MD
6	Zachman	David	Falls Church	VA
7	Robinson	Benjamin	Washington	DC
8	Hart	Wendy	Fairfax	VA
9	Miller			
10	Martin			
11	Robinson			
12	Kramer			
13	Moore			
14	Zachman			

One characteristic of the APPEND FROM command becomes apparent when you examine the list: only fields having the same names in both databases are appended. Remember, you gave different structures to these files as a result of the selective use of the COPY command. FILE2 contains the Lastname, Firstname, City, and State fields, while FILE3 contains the Lastname and Tapelimit fields. When you appended from FILE3 to FILE2, FoxPro found just one field in common between the two files: Lastname.

Even if the field name is the same, FoxPro may or may not append the field if the data type is different. If FoxPro can make sense of the transfer, it will append the data. For example, a numeric field will transfer to a character field of another database, with data appearing in the character field as numbers. A character field, if it contains only numbers, will transfer to a numeric field. A memo field will not transfer to any other type of field. In addition, if the field being copied has a field size larger than the field receiving the record, character data will be truncated and asterisks will be entered for numeric data that does not fit within the new field size.

The file that you appended from does not have to be a FoxPro database file. The APPEND FROM command is also commonly used to transfer data from other programs like spreadsheets or word processors. This aspect of using FoxPro are discussed in more detail in Chapter 15.

Copying a Database Structure

Another helpful FoxPro command, COPY STRUCTURE, lets you make an identical copy of the database structure (in effect, an empty database). You can use COPY STRUCTURE to create empty copies of a database, on multiple floppy disks, which others can use at their machines (provided they have FoxPro) to add records. Later, the records can be combined at a single site with the APPEND FROM command.

To use this command, first open the database you want to copy the structure from with the USE command. Then use the command

COPY STRUCTURE TO *filename*

where *filename* is the desired name of the file. You can precede the filename with a path or a drive identifier if desired. As an example, the commands

USE MEMBERS
COPY STRUCTURE TO A:REMOTE

would copy an empty database containing the structure of MEMBERS to a file called REMOTE.DBF on the disk in drive A. If the file contains memo fields, both a .DBF and an .FPT file will be copied under the new name.

9

AUTOMATING YOUR WORK WITH MACROS

Creating Macros
Saving Macros
Command-Level Use and Macros
Macro Menu Options
Adding to Existing Macros
Rules and Limitations of Macros

FoxPro provides *macros,* which are combinations of keystrokes that can automate many of the tasks you normally perform while within FoxPro. Macros let you record a sequence of characters in a single key combination. You can save the macro and later use it to play back those key sequences by pressing the same single key combination. When the macro is played back, FoxPro performs as if you had manually performed the actions contained within the macro.

Using macros, a single key combination can hold a complex series of menu choices or commands. You can store frequently used phrases, names, or complete paragraphs of text in a macro. And you are not limited to one key combination; you can use various combinations of letter and function keys for macros. If you must print daily reports or perform similar repetitive tasks, you can save many keystrokes by using macros.

If you use commercially available keyboard enhancers like Superkey and ProKey, you are familiar with the advantages of automating your work with macros. Users of other keyboard enhancers may wonder whether they should simply continue to use such products instead of using FoxPro's macro capability. The advantage of using the macro capability within FoxPro is twofold. First, you will not consume additional memory that could be used by the program because you have loaded a memory-resident keyboard enhancer. FoxPro requires a minimum of 512K of RAM. Unless your memory-resident keyboard enhancer can use extended or expanded memory, you may run into "insufficient memory" messages when trying to use it with FoxPro. Second, you will avoid any possible conflicts between the operation of FoxPro and the memory-resident keyboard enhancer. Memory-resident programs have, in the past, been known to conflict with other software such as FoxPro. During the writing of this book, Borland's Sidekick did at times conflict with FoxPro, depending on the number of Sidekick features loaded simultaneously with FoxPro.

CREATING MACROS

To create a macro, follow these four steps:

1. Press SHIFT-F10 to display the Macro Key definition dialog box. (An alternate method for this step is to choose the Macros option of the System menu, and then choose New from the dialog box that appears.)

2. Press the CTRL or ALT key with the letter key or function key that is to be assigned to the macro. You can use CTRL or ALT plus any of the 26 letters or 10 function keys. (Note that if you

use ALT with a letter key that normally opens a menu, the key combination will override the menu choice. For example, if you assign ALT-F to a macro, you will not be able to use ALT-F to open the File menu while that macro is loaded.)

3. Enter the keystrokes that will make up the macro. If you make an error, press SHIFT-F10 and choose Discard from the dialog box to end the recording, and start again.

4. Once all the keystrokes have been entered, press SHIFT- F10, and then select OK to stop the macro recording.

Once the macro has been recorded, you can press the CTRL- or ALT-key combination to play back the macro at any time.

For a quick example of what macros can do for you, consider editing within the MEMBERS database. Perhaps you regularly update records by splitting a Browse window just past the three leftmost fields and performing a forward search in the Lastname field for a desired last name. A macro would automate much of this process.

Press SHIFT-F10 and then press CTRL-A to designate that key combination for the macro. Select OK. In the message that appears you will see

Recording CTRL_A. Shift-F10 stops.

indicating that FoxPro is now recording each of your keystrokes in the form of a macro. Enter **USE MEMBERS** to open the file, and enter **BROWSE** to enter Browse mode. Press ALT-B to open the Browse menu, and press R to choose the Resize Partitions option. Press the RIGHT ARROW key repeatedly until the window is split just past the Firstname field. Then press ENTER to complete the resizing. Press CTRL-H to move the cursor to the left partition of the Browse window. Press CTRL-F10 to zoom the Browse window to full size.

Open the Record menu with ALT-R and choose Locate. From the dialog box that appears, choose For. In the Expression window, enter the following (note the pair of quotes is not a misprint):

LASTNAME = ""

Then press the LEFT ARROW key once so the cursor is between the quotes. Press SHIFT-F10, and choose OK from the dialog box to stop the recording of the macro.

To try the macro, first press ESC and choose Yes from the dialog box. Then press ESC twice to twice the menus and exit Browse mode. Assuming that you now want to open the file, enter Browse mode, split the window past the first three fields, and search for a particular name, you could use the macro to carry out all steps except the final ones of entering the name to search for, choosing OK from the dialog box and then choosing Locate. Press CTRL-A now to play back the macro. All the keystrokes are entered from the macro, and you are presented with the prompt for a last name to search for.

Go ahead and enter any last name in the database. Then choose OK and choose Locate from the next dialog box to appear. When the search is complete, press ESC to exit Browse mode.

SAVING MACROS

Macros that you create are saved in temporary memory, not permanently on the disk. If you want to keep a permanent record of your macros, you must use the Save option, which appears in the Keyboard Macros dialog box when you choose Macros from the System menu. Open the System menu now with ALT-S and choose Macros. From the dialog box that appears, choose Save.

FoxPro will ask you to name the macro file; enter **MYMACROS** as the filename. Then choose Save from the dialog box.

Once the file has been saved, you can exit FoxPro. When you return to the program, you can reload the macros you saved by choosing Macros from the System menu and then selecting Restore from the Keyboard Macros dialog box.

Note: While recording this macro, the ALT- key shortcuts to menu choices were used on purpose. You could have used the cursor keys and the ENTER key to choose menu options, but when you are building macros it is a good idea to get into the habit of avoiding the cursor keys whenever possible. Not only does this use less overall keystrokes in the macro, but there is also less chance of an error during playback due to a list of available options being different than it was during recording. This can be a particular problem when choosing filenames from a pick list, because the list changes as files are added to or deleted from your directory.

COMMAND-LEVEL USE AND MACROS

Macros can also be used to repeat a series of commands, but this is not the speediest way to carry out a series of commands. You could start a macro with SHIFT-F10, assign a key to the macro, and enter a series of commands at the command level and then stop the recording and save the macro. When you played back the macro, all of those commands would be repeated just as if you had typed them. However, FoxPro will execute a series of commands much faster if they are stored in a command file or program. Details on creating programs begin with Chapter 12.

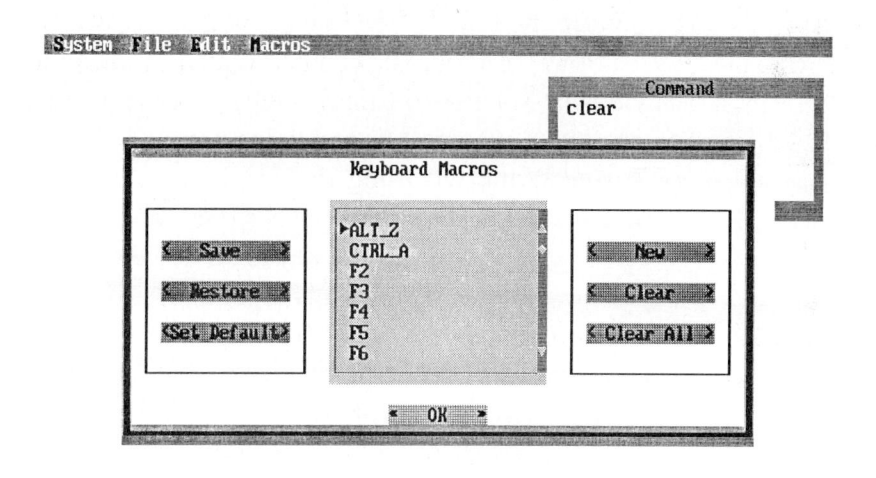

FIGURE 9-1. Keyboard Macros dialog box

MACRO MENU OPTIONS

When you choose the Macros option of the System menu, a dialog box called Keyboard Macros appears (Figure 9-1). In the center of this box is a list containing all macros currently in memory and the keys assigned to those macros. The upper portion of the list displays the macros that are assigned to the letter keys, and the lower portion shows the macros that are assigned to the function keys.

The Save and Restore options let you load a set of macros into memory or save the current macros in memory to a macro file. The command-level equivalents for these options are RESTORE MACROS FROM *macro-filename*, which loads the macro file, and SAVE MACROS TO *macro-filename*, which saves the current macros to the named file. The Set Default option stores the macros currently in memory to a startup macro file. The macros stored in this manner will be loaded automatically into memory whenever FoxPro is started.

The New option begins the creation of a new macro; selecting this option is equivalent to pressing SHIFT-F10 and causes the dialog box requesting the key combination for the new macro to appear. To record a macro, press the combination of ALT or CTRL and function or letter key you want to assign to the macro. If that key was used earlier, FoxPro will ask for confirmation before overwriting the old macro in memory. After pressing the desired key, you can proceed to perform the actions desired in the macro. When you are done, press SHIFT-F10, and then choose OK to stop the recording.

The Clear option clears the highlighted macro from memory. To use this option, first highlight the unwanted macro in the list box. Then choose Clear to clear the macro. The Clear All option clears all existing macros from memory.

Since you can save different sets of macros under different filenames, you can have an unlimited number of macros. One helpful hint in keeping track of your macro files is to give them the same name as the associated database file. Macros are saved to a file with an extension of .FKY.

ADDING TO EXISTING MACROS

You can add to the end of an existing macro by pressing SHIFT-F10 to start a macro and then pressing the same key combination as the existing macro. For example, if you have already defined CTRL-A as a macro and want to add more keystrokes to the end of it, you can press SHIFT-F10, which reveals the macro-key definition box. Press CTRL-A as the key to define, and choose OK. The dialog box shown in Figure 9-2 appears.

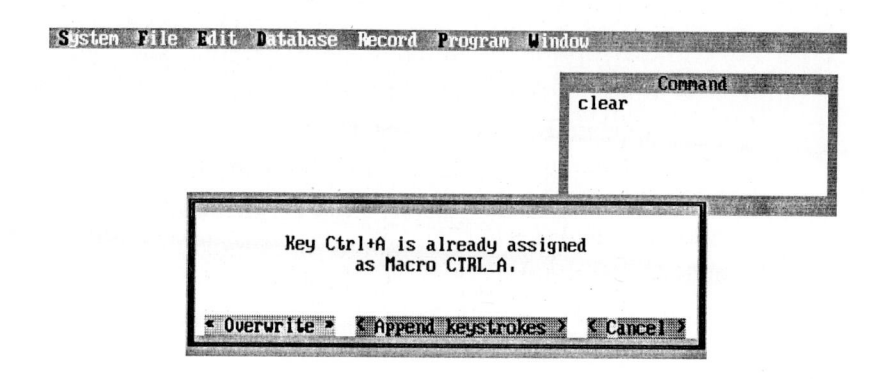

FIGURE 9-2. Overwrite Macro dialog box

The dialog box presents you with three options: Overwrite, Append Keystrokes, or Cancel. You can now choose Append Keystrokes to add your keystrokes to the end of the existing macro. Selecting Overwrite clears the old macro and assigns the key combination you picked to a new macro; Cancel exits the macro definition without adding any changes.

Adding Pauses to Macros

FoxPro lets you add pauses to a macro. This is useful for allowing a user to enter an item that will change from day to day. A good example is the macro you created earlier, which searches for a record based on a last name. A pause could be added to let the user enter a last name in the dialog box; then the macro could perform the final steps of selecting OK from the dialog box and selecting

Locate from the next dialog box to appear. To try this now, you need to be at the spot where the search process ends; you can easily get there by replaying the macro. Press CTRL-A to replay the macro. When the macro ends, you should be in the dialog box for the search expression, with the cursor flashing between the double quotes.

Press SHIFT-F10. When the macro-key definition box appears, press CTRL-A to add to the existing macro. Next, choose OK from the dialog box. From the next dialog box to appear, choose Append Keystrokes. You will see the message "Recording CTRL_A" in the upper-right corner of the screen.

Press SHIFT-F10 again to display the Stop Recording dialog box. Choose Insert Pause from the dialog box. It will vanish, leaving the Expression Builder still visible underneath. Choose OK from the Expression Builder dialog box. From the next visible dialog box choose Locate. Then press SHIFT-F10 and choose OK from the next dialog box to stop recording the macro. Press ESC to exit Browse mode.

Try playing the macro by pressing CTRL-A. When the macro pauses, enter any last name in the database, and then press SHIFT-F10 to continue the macro. This time the macro will complete the search process by locating the record.

RULES AND LIMITATIONS OF MACROS

A macro should never be made a part of itself. (For example, if a macro can be called with the Macro menu's Play option followed by the letter "J," you cannot call up the Macros menu, choose Play, and enter the letter "J" within the macro.) Such a technique would set up an anomaly known in programming as a *recursive loop*, where the program chases its own tail. FoxPro will let you get away with this, but only to a point. The macro will repeat itself until an internal limit is reached, and an error message will then result.

Allowable key combinations for assigning macros are ALT or CTRL plus the function keys F1 through F9, or the alphabetic keys. Any attempt to assign a macro to other keys will be ignored.

10
ADVANCED REPORT TOPICS

Using Expressions and Functions
Designing Form Letters
Designing Invoices
Creating and Printing Mailing Labels
An Example Label
Modifying Existing Labels

Chapter 7 began the process of covering how FoxPro can meet your reporting needs by allowing you to create quick reports and customized reports. This chapter continues with that topic, describing the use of form letters, labels, and other report topics in detail.

USING EXPRESSIONS AND FUNCTIONS

Much flexibility can be coaxed out of your reports and labels by using various expressions within the entry window of the Expression Builder. You usually enter a field in this window, but you can use any valid expression, including memory variables, field names, fields with alias names for related database files (see Chapter 11), and combinations of fields with or without spaces added.

Combinations of character fields are routinely used. As an example, consider a database with fields called Lastname, Firstname, and Midname (it contains the middle name of a person). With such a database, the expression

TRIM(FIRSTNAME)+" "+LEFT(MIDNAME,1)+". "+TRIM(LASTNAME)

would yield a name like Thomas A. Harris. This expression uses the LEFT function to get the leftmost character of a field and the TRIM function to trim excess spaces from the Firstname and Lastname fields. In this example if there were no entry in the middle initial field, you would get an unwanted space and a period. However, this can be cured by including the IIF function in the Expr window, a topic that is covered later in this chapter. Combine names like this to save space in the report; if you can safely assume that 25 characters is enough for any reasonable combination, you can set the Width entry within the Report Expression dialog box to 25, regardless of the actual field widths. If 25 characters turns out to be too small for a given name, the Report Generator will drop the excess characters.

You can also combine various expressions of different types by converting the noncharacter portions of the expressions to characters with string functions (discussed in detail in Chapter 12). For example, you could enter an expression like

STR(AMOUNT) + " " + DTOC(DATESOLD)

to combine a numeric amount and a date field into the contents of a single column. This example uses the STR function, which converts a numeric value into a string of characters, along with the DTOC function, which converts a valid date into a string of characters.

Using the IIF Function In Expressions

The Immediate IF Function, IIF, is also quite useful as a part of an expression within reports or labels when you want to display one set of data if a condition is true and another set if a condition is false. In a personnel report, you may want to indicate the number of weeks of vacation that an employee gets; the company gives two weeks for employees with fewer than five years employment, and three weeks for all others. Assuming five years is equivalent to 365 days multiplied by 5 plus 1 day for at least one leap year, this means that any employee who has over 1826 days with the firm from the hire date to the date on the computer's clock gets three weeks' vacation. This is simple enough to calculate; for a given record in the personnel database with a date field called Hire_date, the expression

IIF((DATE()–HIRE_DATE) < 1826, "two weeks", "three weeks")

would return the character string "two weeks" if less than 1826 days have passed since the date of hire, and "three weeks" if 1826 or more days have passed since the date of hire. You could place the entire expression into the Expression Builder window for a field within the report, and the report would display the appropriate number of weeks of vacation for that employee.

As an example of another use of the IIF function, recall that an earlier example of the combination of fields in a report expression had the problem of an unwanted period if no name was entered into the middle-name field. To cure such a deficiency, you could use an expression like the following:

TRIM(FIRSTNAME) +" " + IIF(LEFT(MIDNAME) = " ",
(LEFT(MIDNAME,1))+". ","") + TRIM(LASTNAME)

If the leftmost character of the Midname field is a space (indicating no middle name), a space appears instead of the middle initial and a period.

Yet another common use for the IIF function within a report is to blank out numeric amounts that are equivalent to zero. For example, to display hyphens in place of zero if a numeric field called Balance in a sales database contains a zero, you could use the following expression:

IIF(BALANCE=0," ---",STR(BALANCE,7,2))

The results are shown in this sample report:

```
              Credit Sales
              Account Report
Customer Name  Cust.    High       Account
               Number   Credit     Balance
Smith, A.      1001     2000.00     788.50
Johnson, L.    1002     1200.00     675.00
Jones, C.      1003      900.00     350.00
Jones, J.L.    1004     2000.00    1850.00
Allen, L.      1005     2000.00     312.00
Walker, B.     1006     1300.00    1167.00
Keemis, M.     1007     2000.00       ---
Artis, K.      1008     1200.00       ---
Smith, A.M.    1009     2000.00     220.00
Williams, E.   1010     2000.00       ---
Jones, J.      1011     2000.00     875.00
```

Again, if the precise syntax for these functions is unfamiliar, you can consult the material on the use of functions contained in Chapter 12.

Other Useful Functions

Always remember the availability of functions within reports and labels. A few additional functions and one system variable that may come in handy are shown here; see Chapter 12 for more details on these.

PAGENO_ This is a special system memory variable that Fox-Pro interprets as the current page number. It is most useful at the top or bottom of each page of a report's design to add page numbering to the report. If you want page numbering, simply place the cursor in the Page Header band (for page numbers at the top of the page) or in the Page Footer band (for page numbers at the bottom of the page). Then press CTRL-F to open the Expression Builder, tab to the entry window, and enter **PAGENO_** in the window. Select OK from the dialog box to place the page numbers in the report.

DATE
TIME These functions place the current date or the current time, respectively. Place them anywhere within a report or label by placing the cursor at the desired location, pressing CTRL- F (in reports) or CTRL-E (in labels), and typing **DATE()** or **TIME()** as desired.

CMONTH
DAY
YEAR These functions can be combined with the DATE function to produce the current month, day, or year as determined by the PC's clock. For example, the expression

CMONTH(DATE())

will produce the name of the current month spelled out, while the expression

YEAR(DATE())

will produce the current year. (Note that the YEAR function yields a number, so you must use it along with the STR function to combine it with character data.) You can place these functions as expressions within text in a report to produce the current date in a spelled-out fashion.

DESIGNING FORM LETTERS

Designing a report in the format of a form letter lets you generate form letters for names and addresses within a database. Another way to do this is to export a file for use with a word processor (as described in Chapter 16), but the following method has the advantage of letting you create the form letters without leaving FoxPro.

The basic process in designing a report to serve as a form letter is to expand the size of the Detail band, and place the text of the form letter within the expanded Detail band along with the necessary fields for the name and address. Add fields as desired at appropriate locations within the letter. Add a Summary band at the bottom of the report and turn on the New Page option for the Summary band, so that each record in the report prints on a separate page. You can see how this works by using the following steps as an example along with the MEMBERS database.

Open the database with **USE MEMBERS**, and create a new report by entering **CREATE REPORT LETTER**. If you examine the Report menu by pressing ALT-O, you will note that the Add Line option has a shortcut key, CTRL-N, and the Remove Line option also has a shortcut key, CTRL-M. Move the cursor down to the first row of the Page Footer band, and press CTRL-M three times to remove three lines from the Page Footer band. (You will not be able to remove the last line; every report must have at least one line in the Page Footer band.)

Move the cursor back into the Detail band, and press CTRL-N ten times to add ten new lines to the Detail band. The number of lines you will want in your own applications will vary, depending on the amount of text that is needed in the form letter. In your applications, you may choose to type text into the Detail band and add needed new lines as you go along.

Place the cursor at row 4, column 40. (Remember, the row and column locations appear at the upper-left corner of the report specification.) Enter

March 1, 1990

and press ENTER to complete the entry. Use HOME to get back to the left margin, and place the cursor two lines down, at the start of row 6. Press CTRL-F to open the Report Expression dialog box. Tab into the Expr window, and enter

TRIM(FIRSTNAME) + " " + LASTNAME

This expression will cause the contents of the Firstname field (trimmed of extra blanks) to appear, followed by one space and the contents of the Lastname field. This combination of names will require sufficient room, so after you enter the expression, tab over to the Width box and enter **40** as the maximum width. Then select OK from the dialog box to place the expression in the report.

Move the cursor to the start of line 7. Press CTRL-F, tab into the Expr window, and enter **ADDRESS**. Then choose OK to place the field.

Move the cursor to the start of line 8. Press CTRL-F, tab into the Expr window, and enter the following expression:

TRIM(CITY) + ", " + STATE + " " + ZIPCODE

Then tab over to the Width box and enter **35** as the maximum width. Select OK from the dialog box to place the expression in the report.

To fill in the rest of the Detail band, you simply type the text of the form letter. You are not using a word processor, so you must complete each line by pressing ENTER, and use the HOME and DOWN ARROW keys to move the cursor to the start of the next line. Use this technique to enter the following text on the lines as shown:

Line	**Text**
10	Dear Member:
11	We have been pleased to have you as a member of Generic
12	Videos movie club during the past year. As a valued member,
13	we would like to extend to you the chance to renew your video
14	membership now at a special reduced rate. By returning the
15	enclosed form, you will save an additional 33% off the regular
16	membership renewal rate.

Note that you could intermix fields within the text of the form letter. Although it is not necessary in this case, you might find such a technique helpful in your applications. For example, if you had a database with a numeric field of a customer's past-due amounts, you could have the past-due amount appear within a sentence in the letter. To do this, you would press CTRL-F at the point in the letter where the field is to appear, enter the field name in the Expr window, and choose OK to place the field.

If you are inserting numeric fields into the body of your form letters, you will want to get rid of leading blanks. You can do this by converting the numeric value into a character string and using the LTRIM function to trim leading blanks. For example, if you wanted to insert the Tapelimit field into the text of the letter and trim the leading blanks, you could place the cursor at the desired location, press CTRL-F, and enter an expression like

```
LTRIM(STR(TAPELIMIT))
```

to accomplish such a task.

One item is still needed: a Group band containing a New Page option must be added so that each record will print on a separate page. Open the Report menu with ALT-O and choose the Data Grouping option. Choose ADD, tab into the Group entry box, and enter SOCIAL. Turn on the New Page option by tabbing to it and pressing the spacebar. Finally, select OK from the dialog box to place the Group band in the report. Choose OK from the next dialog box to appear. At this point, your screen should resemble the example shown in Figure 10-1.

This completes the letter for this example, so save the report by pressing CTRL-W. You can use the command

REPORT FORM LETTER TO PRINT

to print a letter for every record in the database. Or, in the interests of saving paper, you may want to try a more limited scope, such as

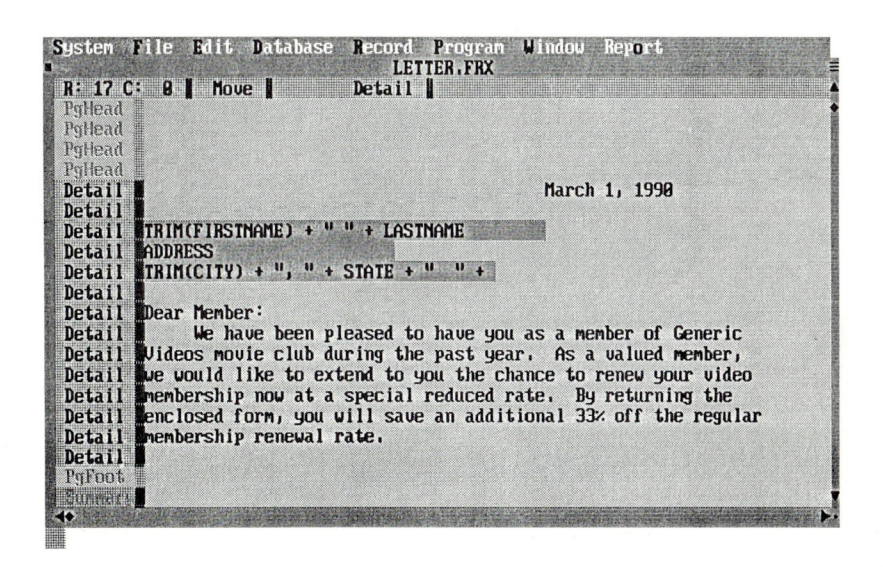

FIGURE 10-1. Report specification for form letters

REPORT FORM LETTER NEXT 3 TO PRINT

The results should resemble this sample:

March 1, 1990

Carol Robinson
4102 Valley Lane
Falls Church, VA 22043-1234

Dear Member:
   We have been pleased to have you as a member of Generic Videos movie club during the past year. As a valued member, we would like to extend to you the chance to renew your video membership now at a special reduced rate. By returning the enclosed form, you will save an additional 33% off the regular membership renewal rate.

You could add more text by placing as many additional Detail lines as you needed; in this example, a closing salutation could have been added in the lines following the paragraph of the form letter. You are not limited by the screen size in the number of Detail bands you place in the report; as you reach the bottom of the screen, additional lines added to the Detail band can be reached by moving the cursor down, which will cause the top of the report specification to scroll off the screen as more of the bottom comes into view. In practice, a maximum of 64 lines in the Detail band, one line in the Page Header band, and one line in the Page Footer band would use up a full 11-inch sheet of paper. Fortunately, few form letters will require 64 lines of text.

DESIGNING INVOICES

If your printer supports the drawing of lines and boxes, you can use the capabilities of FoxPro's Report Generator to design invoices that imitate printed forms. Consider the standard invoice

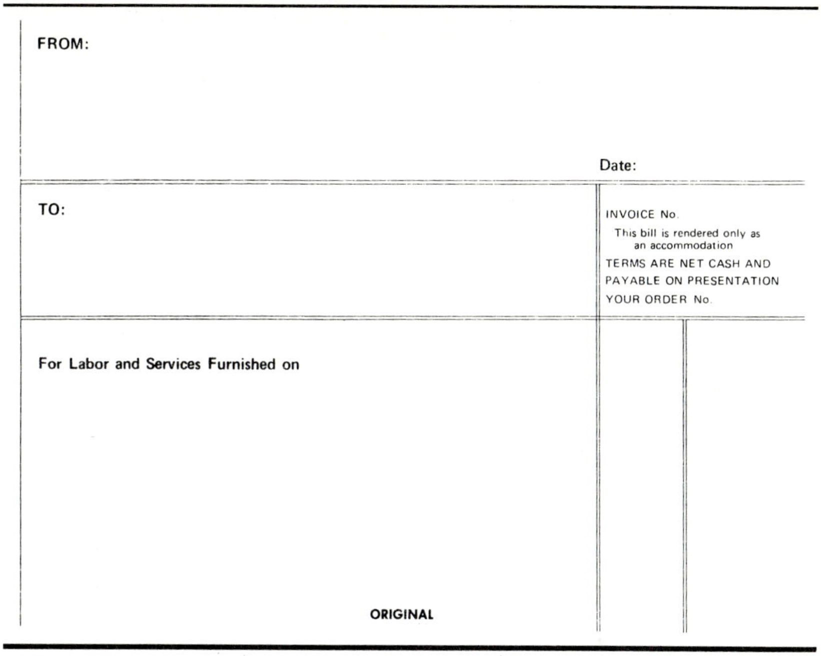
FROM:

Date:

TO:

INVOICE No.

This bill is rendered only as an accommodation

TERMS ARE NET CASH AND PAYABLE ON PRESENTATION

YOUR ORDER No.

For Labor and Services Furnished on

ORIGINAL

FIGURE 10-2. Common invoice

form, available from most office supply stores, as shown in Figure 10-2.

To follow this example, another database with a numeric field containing a billing amount would be appropriate. You can quickly create one by entering the following commands:

```
USE MEMBERS
COPY TO BILLS FIELDS LASTNAME, FIRSTNAME, ADDRESS,
CITY, STATE, ZIPCODE
USE BILLS
MODIFY STRUCTURE
```

When the Database Structure window appears, add a new field at the end of the database; call the field Amountdue. Make it a numeric field, with a width of 6 and 2 decimal places. Save the modified structure with CTRL-W. Then use BROWSE to add sample amounts of your choosing to the new Amountdue fields of each record.

With the database ready for use, you can begin creating the report. Enter **CREATE REPORT BILLING** to display the report specification of a new report. With the cursor at the top of the Page Header band, press CTRL-M three times to remove three lines from the band. More lines will be needed in the Detail band to duplicate the form. Place the cursor in the first row of the Detail band, and press CTRL-N 20 times to add 20 new lines.

You will first need to place the "From" and "Date" information, as shown in Figure 10-2, so enter the following text at the positions described:

Row 1, column 2:   Generic Sales Company
Row 2, column 2:   121 West Main Street
Row 3, column 2:   Houston, TX 75202

Move the cursor to row 4, column 45. Enter the text

Date:

and press ENTER. Then move the cursor over to column 51. Press CTRL-F to bring up the Report Expression dialog box, and tab over to the window. Enter

DATE()

The DATE function will cause the current date, according to the PC's clock, to be displayed in this location of the report. Choose OK from the dialog box to place the expression in the report.

Place the cursor at row 6, column 1. Open the Report menu with ALT-O, and choose Box. Using the spacebar followed by the arrow keys or the mouse, stretch the box across and down to row 20, column 65. As you stretch downwards, you may not be able to see the end of the line beyond the bottom of the screen; however, you can use the row and column indicators in the upper-left corner of the report specification to tell the cursor location.

Place the cursor at row 10, column 2. Again, choose Box from the Report menu. Using the same technique, stretch the line directly across to row 10, column 64. Because you stretched across and remained on the same line, a solid line will be drawn instead of a box. Place the cursor at row 11, column 50. Again, choose Box from the Report menu. This time, stretch the box directly down to row 19, column 50.

Place the cursor at row 7, column 3. Enter

To:

and complete the entry with ENTER. Then move the cursor over to column 7 of the same line. Press CTRL-F, tab over to the Expr window of the dialog box, and enter the following expression:

TRIM(FIRSTNAME) + " " + LASTNAME

This will cause the first and last names to appear, separated by one space. Tab over to the Width entry, and change the width to **40**, then choose OK from the dialog box to place the expression in the report.

Move the cursor to row 8, column 7. Press CTRL-F, tab over to the window, enter **ADDRESS**, and select OK from the dialog box to place the field.

Move the cursor to row 9, column 7. Press CTRL-F, tab to the window, and enter the following expression:

TRIM(CITY) + ", " + STATE + " " + ZIPCODE

Then tab over to the Width box and enter **35** as the maximum width. Select OK from the dialog box to place the expression in the report.

At row 8, column 46, enter the following text:

Terms are net cash

At row 9, column 46, enter the following text:

payable on receipt

At row 12, column 4, enter the following text:

Our records show the amount at the right

At row 13, column 4, enter the following text:

is PAST DUE. Please remit this amount.

Place the cursor at row 12, column 52. Press CTRL-F, tab to the window, and enter **AMOUNTDUE**. Select OK from the dialog box to place the Amountdue field at this location in the report.

A Group band containing a New Page option is needed so that each record will be printed as a separate invoice on its own page. Open the Report menu with ALT-O and choose the Data Grouping option. Choose ADD, tab into the Group entry box, and enter LASTNAME + FIRSTNAME. Turn on the New Page option by tabbing to it and pressing the spacebar. Finally, select OK from the dialog box to place the Group band in the report. (The Group band will not be visible unless you use the PGDN or DOWN ARROW key, but it has been placed at the bottom of the report.) Choose OK from the next dialog box to appear.

At this point, your screen should resemble the example shown in Figure 10-3. In this case, the report was laid out in imitation of

Advanced Report Topics   315

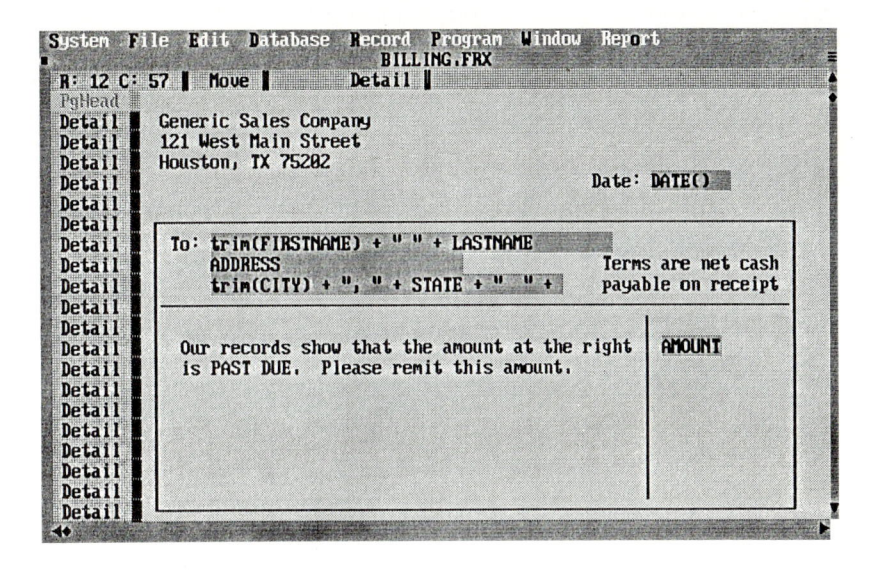

```
 System  File  Edit  Database  Record  Program  Window  Report
                             BILLING.FRX
 R: 12 C: 57   Move            Detail
 PgHead
 Detail    Generic Sales Company
 Detail    121 West Main Street
 Detail    Houston, TX 75282
 Detail                                           Date: DATE()
 Detail
 Detail
 Detail    To: trim(FIRSTNAME) + " " + LASTNAME
 Detail        ADDRESS                            Terms are net cash
 Detail        trim(CITY) + ", " + STATE + " " +  payable on receipt
 Detail
 Detail
 Detail    Our records show that the amount at the right   AMOUNT
 Detail    is PAST DUE.  Please remit this amount.
 Detail
 Detail
 Detail
 Detail
 Detail
 Detail
```

FIGURE 10-3.   Report specification for invoices

the form shown in Figure 10-2. In your applications, you can use the box-drawing capabilities of the Report Generator to imitate the forms commonly used in your office. Save the report with CTRL-W, and try the report by entering

REPORT FORM BILLING TO PRINT

Note that whether the lines appear as lines depends on whether your printer has the capability to print the IBM graphic character set. Some printers will not handle graphics, and on such printers the lines may appear as symbols or letters, or not appear at all.

CREATING AND PRINTING MAILING LABELS

FoxPro provides a facility for designing mailing labels. You can enter various dimension parameters that will allow you to use different label sizes. And you can print labels in the common three-across or four-across formats, where the labels are placed on the label sheets in rows of three or four labels each. Label designs are stored on the disk with an .LBX extension.

Creating the Label

To create a mailing label from the menus, you choose New from the File menu and select Label from the dialog box that appears. From the command level, you can enter

CREATE LABEL *filename*

where *filename* is the name assigned to the label file. When you do so, the label design screen appears, as shown in Figure 10-4.

The label design screen contains six parameters that control the overall dimensions of the labels: Margin, Number Across, Width, Height, Spaces Between, and Lines Between. In the center of the window is a label design area representing the contents of the label. In this area, you place the field names or expressions that will provide the data when the labels are printed. At the top of the screen is a Remarks window, which can contain an optional description of the label. When you create a new label, the window contains the designation shown in Figure 10-4 as a default; this is the most commonly used size and matches standard peel-and-stick labels available in office supply stores. As with other design screens in FoxPro, you can use the TAB key or the mouse to move between the various parameters and the label design area.

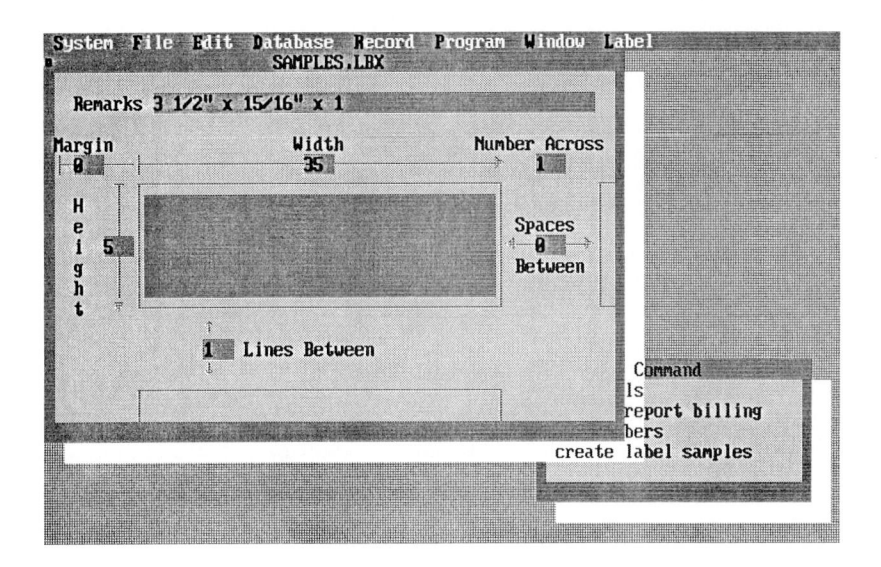

FIGURE 10-4. Label design screen

Figure 10-5 shows the relationship between the various parameters that make up the label dimensions. The Margin parameter controls the distance between the start of the leftmost label and the left edge of the sheet of labels. By default this is zero, since many labels are attached to the underlying paper at the left edge of the label sheet. Height and Width control the height and width of the label, respectively. The default values of 35 characters for the width and 5 rows for the height will match the standard 3 1/2-inch by 15/16-inch label size (assuming you are printing at the standard of 10 characters per inch and 6 lines per inch). The Number Across parameter controls the number of labels printed across a sheet of labels. With roll-fed labels, this is usually one, but with the popular sheets of three-across labels used in laser printers this value would be set to 3. The Spaces Between parameter controls the number of spaces between the labels. This value matters only when the

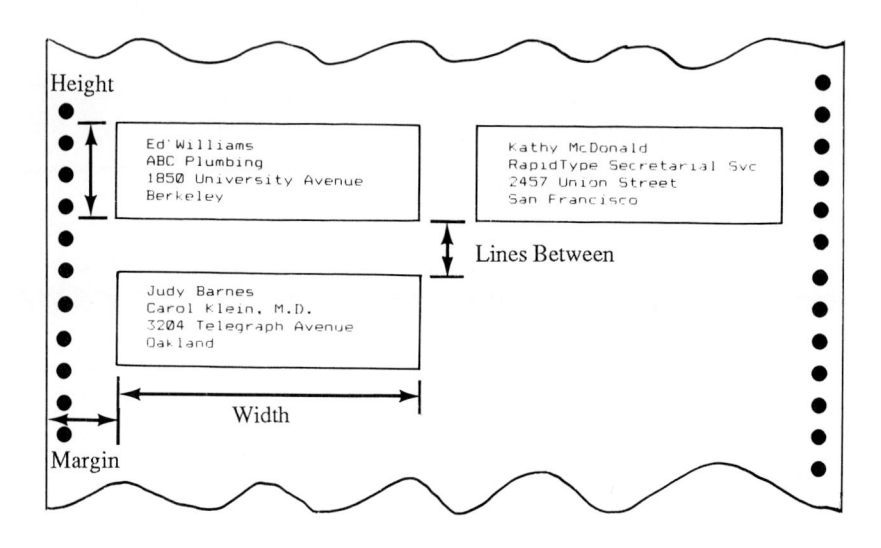

FIGURE 10-5. Label dimensions

Number Across value is set at more than 1. Finally, the Lines Between parameter controls the number of blank lines between labels. Depending on your labels, you may need to play with this option to prevent data from printing across the breaks in the labels. Table 10-1 gives some suggested settings for common label sizes.

Note that these sizes assume a standard printing character size of 10 characters per inch and printer line spacing of 6 lines per inch, matching that of most standard printers including Epson-compatible dot-matrix and Hewlett-Packard or compatible lasers. If your printer is set to a different character size (such as compressed print) or has an unusual line spacing, you will need to experiment with different values to discover the right settings for the dimensions of your labels.

Type of Label	Width	Height	Across	Margin	Line	Spaces
3 1/2 by 15/16 by 1 across	35	5	1	0	1	0
3 1/2 by 15/16 by 2 across	35	5	2	0	1	2
3 1/2 by 15/16 by 3 across	35	5	3	0	1	2
4 inch by 1-7/16 inch	40	8	1	0	1	0
1 7/16 by 5 by 1 across	50	8	1	0	1	0
Xerox Cheshire labels	32	5	3	0	1	2
Rolodex 3 inch by 5 inch	50	14	1	0	4	0
Rolodex 2-1/4 inch by 4 inch	40	10	1	0	1	0
No. 7 envelope	65	14	1	0	8	0
No. 10 envelope	78	17	1	0	8	0

TABLE 10-1. Settings for Common Label Sizes

Adding Fields to the Design Area

When the dimensions of the label are set, you can add fields in the design area of the screen. To do so, place the cursor at the desired location and choose Expression from the Label menu (or press CTRL-E). With either method, the Expression Builder appears, as shown in Figure 10-6.

Enter the desired field name in the window, or enter an expression (such as a combination of field names). You can combine two name fields with an expression as you do with reports; for example, an expression such as

TRIM(FIRSTNAME) + " " + LASTNAME

would cause the first name to be printed without any blank spaces at the end, followed by a space, followed by the last name. You

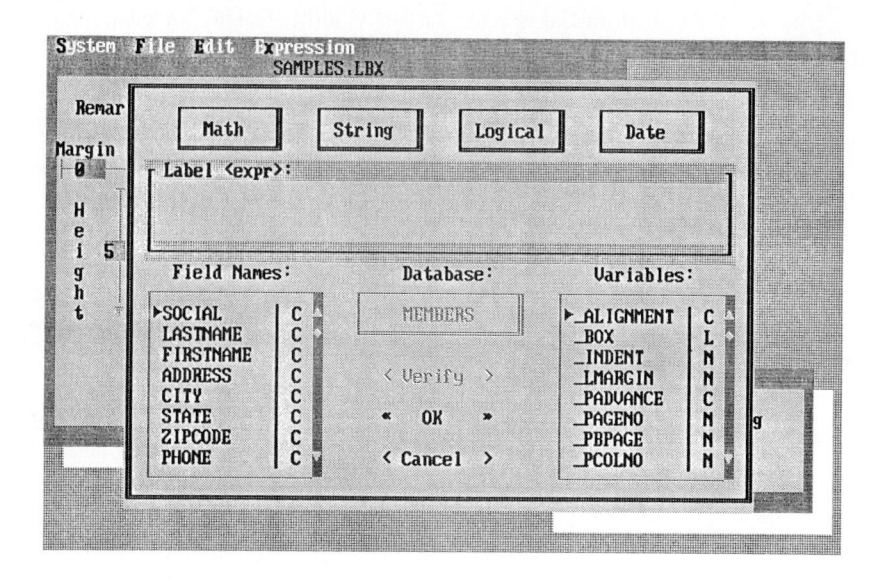

FIGURE 10-6. Expression Builder

can also use calculations you create based on fields. With a numeric field called Salescost, you could enter the expression

SALESCOST * .06

to calculate a charge that is 6% of the amount contained in the Salescost field. And you can use functions, such as DATE() to produce the current date.

You can check the design of the label as you go along by opening the Label menu with ALT-L and choosing Page Preview. When you choose this option, a visual representation of the label appears, as shown in Figure 10-7.

Choose More to see additional labels, or choose Done when you are finished with the Page Preview option. The shortcut key CTRL-P can be used to call up the Page Preview option.

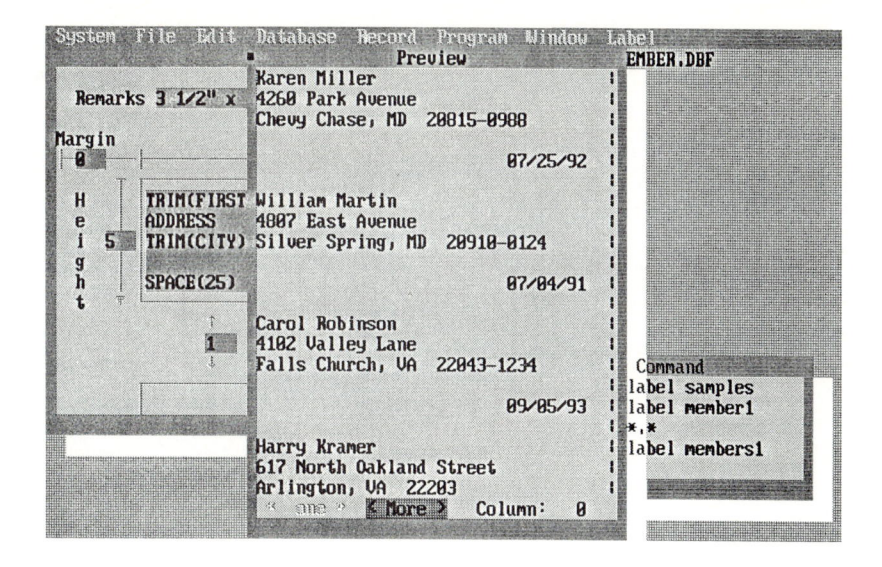

FIGURE 10-7. Use of Page Preview

Saving the Label Design

Once you have placed the desired fields or expressions in the label, you can save the label by choosing Save from the File menu or by pressing CTRL-W. If you did not enter a name when you started the process, you will be prompted for a filename for the label, and then you will be returned to the command level.

Printing Labels

Once the label design has been saved, you can print labels by choosing Label from the Database menu or by using the LABEL FORM command. If you choose Label from the Database menu, the dialog box shown in Figure 10-8 appears.

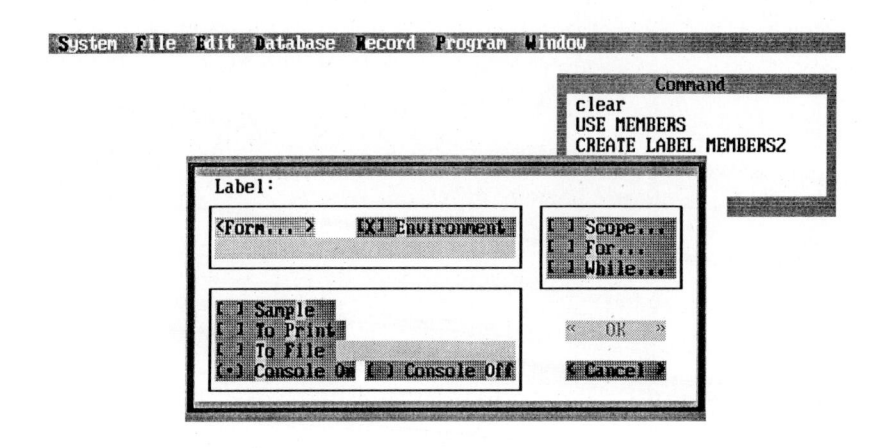

FIGURE 10-8. Label dialog box

Enter the name of the label in the Form window. You can select Scope, For, or While to limit the number of records that appear as labels; see Chapter 6 for a discussion of these options. Turn on the Sample option if you want to print a sample label (containing rows of X's) before the actual printing of data begins. This is often helpful for aligning labels in your printer before printing. Turn on the To Print option to route the labels to the printer; otherwise, they only appear on the screen. The To File option can be selected to store the output in an ASCII text file. If you choose this option, enter a name for the file in the window beside the To File option. When you are done selecting the options, choose OK to begin producing the labels.

From the command level, you use the command

LABEL FORM *filename* [SCOPE] [FOR *condition*] [WHILE *condition*] [SAMPLE] [TO PRINT] [TO FILE *filename*]

and as with other commands, all clauses within the brackets are optional. The SCOPE, FOR, and WHILE clauses are used to limit the records printed, as detailed in Chapter 6. Add the SAMPLE clause to print a sample label (composed of rows of X's) before you print the data. Add the TO PRINT clause to route the output to the printer, and add TO FILE followed by a filename to store the output as an ASCII text file.

If you want the labels printed in a certain order, simply index or sort the database first and then use the LABEL FORM command (or the Label option of the Database menu). It is usually wise to print a test run of labels on plain paper first and to visually align the printout with a sheet of blank labels. If the alignment looks correct, you can proceed to print on the labels themselves.

To print labels selectively, you can use the SET FILTER or INDEX ON...FOR commands, or you can apply view files (as detailed in Chapter 6) that will specify a group of records for which you want to print labels. From the command level, you can combine conditional FOR clauses to print labels for specific records, just as you did with reports. For example, assuming the use of a label file based on the MEMBERS database, the command

LABEL FORM MEMBER1 FOR STATE = "VA" TO PRINT

will print mailing labels for members in Virginia. The command

LABEL FORM MEMBER1 FOR YEAR(EXPIREDATE) = 1991 TO PRINT

will print mailing labels for only those members whose membership expires in 1991.

AN EXAMPLE LABEL

To try creating a label for use with the MEMBERS database, enter the commands

USE MEMBERS
CREATE LABEL MEMBERS1

The label design screen shown earlier in Figure 10-4 appears. For this example, the default parameters will suffice. With the cursor on the first line of the design area, press CTRL-E to open the Expression Builder. The first line should contain a combination of first and last names, separated by a space. Enter the following expression in the window to accomplish this:

TRIM(FIRSTNAME) + " " + LASTNAME

Then choose OK from the dialog box to place the expression. The expression will appear on the first line. Move the cursor down to the second line of the design area.

Press CTRL-E again, and enter **ADDRESS** in the window of the Expression Builder. Select OK from the dialog box to place the expression, and move the cursor down to the third line. Open the Expression Builder with CTRL-E, and enter the following expression:

TRIM(CITY) + ", " + STATE + " " + ZIPCODE

Then select OK from the dialog box, and move the cursor down to the last line of the label.

Press CTRL-E again, and this time enter the following expression:

SPACE(25) + DTOC(EXPIREDATE)

This particular expression uses the SPACE function to insert 25 blank spaces, followed by the DTOC function to convert the contents of the Expiredate field to a character expression. The end result will be 25 blank spaces, followed by the member's expiration date, appearing at the bottom of the label. Choose OK from the dialog box when done to place the expression.

Save the label with CTRL-W. Try the labels by entering the command

LABEL FORM MEMBERS1

and add the TO PRINT option at the end of the command if you want to see a printed version. Your results should resemble these shown below.

Karen Miller
4260 Park Avenue
Chevy Chase, MD 20815-0988

07/25/92

William Martin
4807 East Avenue
Silver Spring, MD 20910-0124

07/04/91

Carol Robinson
4102 Valley Lane
Falls Church, VA 22043-1234

09/05/93

Harry Kramer
617 North Oakland Street
Arlington, VA 22203

12/22/90

MODIFYING EXISTING LABELS

To change an existing label, use

MODIFY LABEL *filename*

at the command level, where *filename* is the name of the label you wish to change. Or you can choose open from the File menu, and from the Type menu in the dialog box that appears choose Label. Then select the desired label by name from the list box. With either method, the label design screen appears, as shown earlier in Figure 10-4.

Keep in mind that you can make changes to existing fields by placing the cursor in the field and pressing ENTER to display the Expression Builder. When the changes are completed, press CTRL-W or choose Save from the File menu to save the changes.

11

USING FOXPRO'S RELATIONAL POWERS

How to Relate Files
Creating Relational Reports
Getting Selective Data from Related Files
Relating More Than Two Database Files
Analyzing Types of Relationships

FoxPro is a relational database manager, which means that it offers you the ability to use more than one database file at a time and to define relationships between two or more database files. This chapter will describe a number of ways you can take advantage of the relational capabilities of FoxPro. By using the SET RELATION command, you can link multiple database files by means of a common field that exists in each database file. The examples in this chapter will make extensive use of the MEMBERS and RENTALS databases created in Chapters 2 and 5. If you did not create those database files as outlined earlier, do so now before proceeding.

Consider the MEMBERS and RENTALS files. The RENTALS file contains records of the videotapes rented by each member.

Last Name	First Name	Title	Day Rented	Day Returned
Miller	Karen	Star Trek IV	3/5/90	3/6/90
Martin	William	Lethal Weapon II	3/2/90	3/6/90
Robinson	Carol	Who Framed Roger Rabbit	3/6/90	3/9/90

FIGURE 11-1. Desired relational report

However, it does not contain the names of the members. The MEMBERS file, on the other hand, contains the full names of each member but no record of the tapes that were rented.

The purchasing manager at Generic Videos needs a report in a format illustrated by Figure 11-1. A report with this kind of information is a *relational report* because it draws its information from more than one file. The MEMBERS file contains the Lastname and Firstname fields. The RENTALS file contains the Title, Dayrented, and Returned fields. In order to produce a report based on these fields, you can establish a relationship that will permit the retrieval of data from both files. The data provided through the link can then be used to produce the desired report.

The key to retrieving data from a relational database is to link the desired records on some sort of matching, or common, field. In this context, the term *common field* is used to indicate a field that is common to both database files. Consider an example of two files; one contains records of computer parts, and the other contains purchasers who have ordered certain parts. These files (in this example, called PARTS and ORDERS) are typical examples of database files that benefit from the use of relational commands.

The PARTS file contains part numbers, descriptions, and the costs of each part:

Field Name	Type
PARTNO	Numeric
DESCRIPT	Character
COST	Numeric

The ORDERS file, on the other hand, contains the names and customer numbers of the customers who order computer parts, as well as the part numbers and quantities of the parts that have been ordered:

Field Name	Type
Custno	Numeric
Custname	Character
Partno	Numeric
Quantity	Numeric

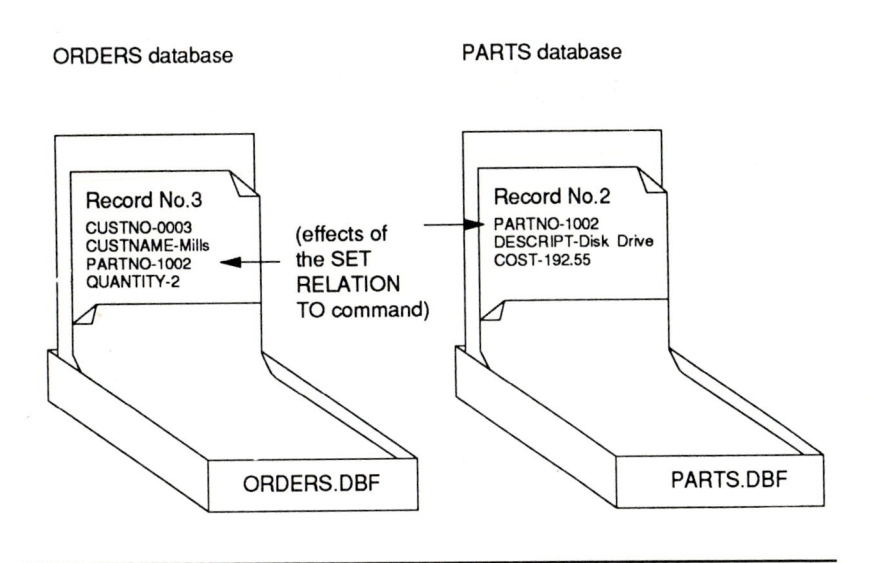

ORDERS database   PARTS database

Record No. 3
CUSTNO-0003
CUSTNAME-Mills
PARTNO-1002
QUANTITY-2

(effects of the SET RELATION TO command)

Record No. 2
PARTNO-1002
DESCRIPT-Disk Drive
COST-192.55

ORDERS.DBF   PARTS.DBF

FIGURE 11-2. Concept of relational database

Record#	SOCIAL	LASTNAME	FIRSTNAME	CITY	STATE
1	123-44-8976	Miller	Karen	Chevy Chase	MD
2	121-33-9876	Martin	William	Silver Spring	MD
3	232-55-1234	Robinson	Carol	Falls Church	VA
4	901-77-3456	Kramer	Harry	Arlington	VA
5	121-90-5432	Moore	Ellen	Takoma Park	MD
6	495-00-3456	Zachman	David	Falls Church	VA
7	343-55-9821	Robinzon	Benjamin	Washington	DC
8	876-54-3210	Hart	Wendy	Fairfax	VA

Record#	SOCIAL	TITLE	DAYRENTED	RETURNED
1	123-44-8976	Star Trek IV	03/05/90	03/06/90
2	121-33-9876	Lethal Weapon II	03/02/90	03/06/90
3	232-55-1234	Who Framed Roger Rabbit	03/06/90	03/09/90
4	901-77-3456	Beverly Hills Cop II	03/04/90	03/05/90
5	121-90-5432	Dirty Rotten Scoundrels	03/01/90	03/05/90
6	495-00-3456	Young Einstein	03/04/90	03/09/90
7	343-55-9821	When Harry Met Sally	03/06/90	03/12/90
8	876-54-3210	Lethal Weapon II	03/07/90	03/08/90
9	123-44-8976	Friday 13th Part XXVII	03/14/90	03/16/90
10	121-33-9876	Licence to Kill	03/15/90	03/17/90
11	232-55-1234	When Harry Met Sally	03/17/90	03/19/90
12	901-77-3456	Coming To America	03/14/90	03/18/90
13	121-90-5432	When Harry Met Sally	03/16/90	03/17/90
14	495-00-3456	Star Trek V	03/18/90	03/18/90
15	343-55-9821	Young Einstein	03/19/90	03/20/90
16	876-54-3210	Licence To Kill	03/16/90	03/18/90

FIGURE 11-3. RENTALS, MEMBERS database files

If you had a single database file with all of the fields present in these two files, each time one customer ordered a part number that had been previously ordered by another customer, you would have to duplicate the part description and part cost. To avoid such duplication, you can use two files and link the files together based upon the contents of the common Partno field, as illustrated in Figure 11-2.

With all relational databases, establishing a link between common fields allows you to match a particular record in one file with a corresponding record in another file. Take Generic Videos' problem of the rental tapes again. If you needed to know which tapes Carol Robinson rented, you could do this visually by looking at the data from the two files, shown in Figure 11-3. To find the answer manually, you would first look at the listing from the MEMBERS file, and find the social security number for Ms. Robinson, which is 232-55-1234. You would then refer to the listing of the RENTALS file, and look for all the records with the matching social security number. The process of matching social security numbers between the files could be repeated for every member in the database.

The important point to realize is that without a field that contains matching data in each of the database files, such a relational link is not possible. This is one reason that designing complex, relational databases is not a process to be taken lightly. Unless you include matching fields in the files you want to link, you will find it impossible to access multiple files in the desired manner. As Figure 11-3 illustrates, the Social field makes it possible to access data simultaneously from both files. While relational links are usually established by using a single field, it is possible to establish such links based on a combination of fields.

HOW TO RELATE FILES

The relational powers provided by FoxPro are easily implemented from the command level. You can link databases together with the SET RELATION command. It will link the files together by means of a common field. In our example, you will draw a relation between the RENTALS database and the MEMBERS database by linking the common Social field. Then, whenever you move to a record in the RENTALS database, the record pointer in the MEMBERS database will move to the record that contains the same social security number as is contained in the record in the RENTALS database. As you will see shortly, this link allows you to display matching data from two files with a LIST command. You can also take advantage of a relational link within the reports or labels you create.

The format of the SET RELATION command is

SET RELATION TO (*key-expression*) INTO (*alias*) [ADDITIVE]

The key expression is the common field present in both databases. The alias is usually the name of the other database that the active database is to be linked to. Note that ADDITIVE is an optional clause, needed only when you are setting a relation in more than one file at a time.

The overall process of linking two databases using a common field involves the following steps:

1. Open the file from which you want to establish the relation in one work area.

2. In another work area, open the file you wish to link to the first file.

3. Activate an index file based on the field (or expression) that is the basis of the relationship.

4. Use the SET RELATION command to establish the link.

Once the link has been established, any movement of the record pointer in the active file will result in a corresponding movement of the pointer in the related file. The nature of such a relationship can be seen in the example shown in the following paragraphs.

One important requirement of the SET RELATION command is that you must index the related file on the common field. In our case, the MEMBERS database must be indexed on the Social field.

Enter the following commands now to create an index file for the MEMBERS database, based on the social security field:

```
USE MEMBERS
INDEX ON SOCIAL TO SOCIALS
```

To work with multiple database files, you will need to open more than one database file at a time. As mentioned in Chapter 8, you do this by using different work areas, which contain the database files. You choose the work area with the SELECT command; for example, entering **SELECT 2** at the command level would choose work area 2. (If no SELECT command is used, work area 1 is chosen by default.)

Open the RENTALS and MEMBERS database files by using the following commands:

```
CLOSE DATABASES
SELECT 1
USE RENTALS
USE MEMBERS IN 2 INDEX SOCIALS
```

An explanation of the last command is in order. The USE MEMBERS IN 2 portion of the command line tells FoxPro to open the database file MEMBERS, but to open it in work area 2 without actually switching work areas (hence the "in 2" designation). The INDEX SOCIALS option tells FoxPro to open the SOCIALS index file you just created.

It is now possible to link the files by the Social field, with the SET RELATION TO command. The RENTALS database is the active database, so you will link the MEMBERS database to the RENTALS database. Enter

```
SET RELATION TO SOCIAL INTO MEMBERS
```

No changes are immediately visible, but FoxPro has linked the files. To see the effects, enter the commands,

GO 3
DISPLAY

and you will see the third record in the RENTALS database. The record indicates that a member having the social security number of 232-55-1234 rented *Who Framed Roger Rabbit.* To see just who this member is, enter these commands

SELECT 2
DISPLAY

The MEMBERS database (open in work area 2) will become the active database. The record pointer will be at record 3 (the record containing the social security number 232-55-1234), showing that the member in question is Carol Robinson.

Get back to the RENTALS database with these commands:

SELECT 1
GO 2
DISPLAY

Again, you can see that because of the relation, FoxPro has automatically found a matching social security number in the MEMBERS database by entering these commands:

SELECT 2
DISPLAY

Wherever you move in the RENTALS database, FoxPro will try to move the record pointer to a matching social security number in the MEMBERS database. If FoxPro cannot find a match according to the relation that you have specified, the record pointer will be positioned at the end of the database. (At the end of a file, all fields are blank. You can use this fact to test for failures to find a match by listing key fields from both databases.)

You can retrieve data in the related file by including the alias name and pointer (*filename->*) along with the field name. In the expression

MEMBERS->FIRSTNAME

the filename MEMBERS is the alias, while FIRSTNAME is the field name. The combination of the hyphen and greater-than symbol make up the pointer. To see how this works, try the following commands:

SELECT 1
LIST MEMBERS->LASTNAME, TITLE, DAYRENTED, RETURNED

the results are shown here:

Record#	MEMBERS->LASTNAME	TITLE	DAYRENTED	RETURNED
1	Miller	Star Trek IV	03/05/90	03/06/90
2	Martin	Lethal Weapon II	03/02/90	03/06/90
3	Robinson	Who Framed Roger Rabbit	03/06/90	03/09/90
4	Kramer	Beverly Hills Cop II	03/04/90	03/05/90
5	Moore	Dirty Rotten Scoundrels	03/01/90	03/06/90
6	Zachman	Young Einstein	03/04/90	03/09/90
7	Robinson	When Harry Met Sally	03/06/90	03/12/90
8	Hart	Lethal Weapon II	03/07/90	03/08/90
9	Miller	Friday 13th Part XXVII	03/14/90	03/16/90
10	Martin	Licence To Kill	03/15/90	03/17/90
11	Robinson	When Harry Met Sally	03/17/90	03/19/90
12	Kramer	Coming To America	03/14/90	03/18/90
13	Moore	When Harry Met Sally	03/16/90	03/17/90
14	Zachman	Star Trek V	03/18/90	03/18/90
15	Robinson	Young Einstein	03/19/90	03/20/90
16	Hart	Licence To Kill	03/16/90	03/18/90

This shows that such use of the SET RELATION command to establish the relational link, combined with the use of the alias and pointer, can be a powerful tool for obtaining data of a relational nature. You could add the TO PRINT option at the end of the LIST command to generate a printed list like this one.

When working with related files in this manner, keep in mind that you can test for mismatched records (such as an entry in the RENTALS file with no matching social security number) by listing the common field from each of the related files. For example, the command

```
LIST RENTALS->SOCIAL, MEMBERS->SOCIAL,
MEMBERS->LASTNAME
```

should produce a listing with a matching member for each entry in the RENTALS file. If a member name and social security number turns up blank next to an entry in the RENTALS listing, it is clear that a mismatch exists. Such a mismatch could be caused by a social security number entered incorrectly in the RENTALS file.

A Warning About Index Files

When you are working with related files, it is completely up to you to make sure your indexes that allow the use of the SET RELATION command are kept updated. If you or another user opens a database without using an accompanying index file and adds or edits records, the resulting incomplete index files can cause incorrect results when you are trying to establish relationships or generate relational reports. If in doubt, use REINDEX to rebuild any indexes you are using.

Using View Files to Store Relations

If you are going to establish relationships from the command level (as opposed to creating them by running a program), keep in mind the use of the CREATE VIEW FROM ENVIRONMENT command. This command, introduced in Chapter 6, stores a record of all open databases, index files, and any existing relationships. You can save much repetitive typing by saving the relationship as part of a view file, and then using the SET VIEW command to open the database files and index files and establish the relationship at the same time. You save the environment, including the relational link, by entering the command

CREATE VIEW *filename* FROM ENVIRONMENT

where *filename* is the name you assign to the view file. Later, you open the databases, index files, and the relational link by entering the command

SET VIEW TO *filename*

where *filename* is the name that you gave to the view file earlier. If you followed the prior example in establishing a relational link between MEMBERS and RENTALS, you can save that information in a view file now. Enter the following command:

CREATE VIEW RELATE1 FROM ENVIRONMENT

Then enter **CLOSE DATABASES** to close all the open files. If you now enter the commands

USE RENTALS
LIST MEMBERS->LASTNAME, TITLE, DAYRENTED

you get an "Alias not found" error message, because the RENTALS file is not open and no relationship exists. Enter **CLOSE DATABASES** again to close the open file and start from scratch.

(This is not a requirement, but doing so makes it clear that the SET VIEW command will be all you need to open all files and reestablish the link.) Enter the command

SET VIEW TO RELATE1

Then retry the earlier command:

LIST MEMBERS->LASTNAME, TITLE, DAYRENTED

The results show that the files are open and the relationship has been reestablished. You can verify this in another way with the DISPLAY STATUS command. Enter **DISPLAY STATUS** now. The display you see should resemble the following:

```
Processor is INTEL 80386
Currently Selected Database:
Select area: 1, Database in Use: E:\FOXPRO\FOXDATA\RENTALS.DBF
Alias: RENTALS
            Related into:    MEMBERS
               Relation:     SOCIAL
Select area: 2, Database in Use: E:\FOXPRO\FOXDATA\MEMBERS.DBF
Alias: MEMBERS
       Master index file:   E:\FOXPRO\FOXDATA\SOCIALS.IDX  Key: SOCIAL
             Memo file:     E:\FOXPRO\FOXDATA\MEMBERS.FPT
```

The first few lines of the listing show the names of the open databases, the index files in use, and the relationship between the files.

CREATING RELATIONAL REPORTS

As shown earlier, you can use the LIST...TO PRINT command to generate simple listings of relational data; you must include the filename and pointer when you are retrieving data that is in the related file. The same technique can be used for designing relational reports. When you enter a field name or an expression into the Expr window during the creation of the report, you must again include the filename and pointer symbols to indicate a field that is in a related database.

As an example, consider a report similar to the one shown in Figure 11-1, but using a form-oriented format. You could quickly construct such a report by opening the files, establishing the relationship, creating a new report, and adding the Lastname and Firstname fields to the report design along with the filename and pointer.

To try this, the relationship described in the prior example should still be in effect (if not, use the SET VIEW TO RELATE1 command). Enter

CREATE REPORT RELATE1

to start a new report. Open the Report menu with ALT-O, and choose Quick Report. Select the Form Layout option, and then choose OK from the dialog box. The report appearing on the screen resembles the one shown in Figure 11-4.

Because the RENTALS file is the active database, the quick report placed all fields from that database into the report specification. Using the filename and pointer combination, you can replace the rather ambiguous social security field with the actual name of the member from the related MEMBERS file. Move the cursor to the word, "SOCIAL" and press the DEL key to delete it; then move the cursor into the Social field and press DEL to remove the field.

Press HOME to get back to the left margin, and enter this text:

Member

Then press ENTER to complete the text entry. Move the cursor over to column 11 and press CTRL-F to add an expression. Press ENTER

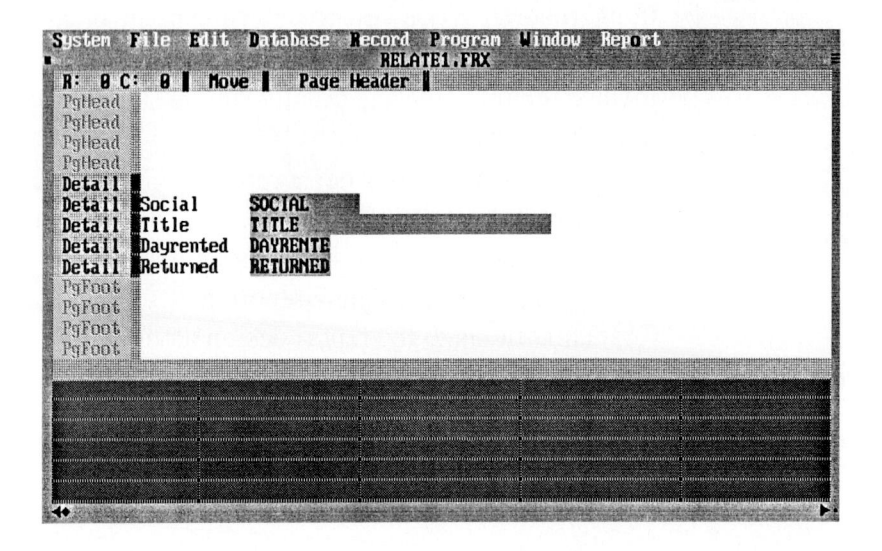

FIGURE 11-4. Quick report based on RENTALS file

to bring up the Expression Builder. (This will provide room to enter and view a long expression.) In the window, enter the following:

TRIM(MEMBERS->FIRSTNAME) + " " + MEMBERS->LASTNAME

Choose OK from the dialog box to close the Expression Builder. Tab over to the Width box and change the width to **25** (this should provide ample width for a combination of last and first names). Choose OK from the dialog box to complete the entry.

For aesthetics' sake, you may want to change the field heading "Dayrented" to two words, "Day rented." Move the cursor to the Dayrented label and press the DEL key. Then type in the text

Day Rented

Press ENTER to complete the entry. Next, save the report with CTRL-W, and enter

REPORT FORM RELATE1

to see the results. They should resemble those shown here:

Member   Karen Miller
Title   Star Trek IV
Day rented 03/05/90
Returned   03/06/90

Member   William Martin
Title   Lethal Weapon II
Day rented 03/02/90
Returned   03/06/90

Member   Carol Robinson
Title   Who Framed Roger Rabbit
Day rented 03/06/90
Returned   03/09/90

Member   Harry Kramer
Title   Beverly Hills Cop II
Day rented 03/04/90
Returned   03/05/90

Member   Ellen Moore
Title   Dirty Rotten Scoundrels
Day rented 03/01/90
Returned   03/06/90

Member   David Zachman
Title   Young Einstein
Day rented 03/04/90
Returned   03/09/90

Member   Benjamin Robinson
Title   When Harry Met Sally
Day rented 03/06/90
Returned   03/12/90

Member   Wendy Hart
Title   Lethal Weapon II
Day rented 03/07/90
Returned   03/08/90

Member   Karen Miller
Title   Friday 13th Part XXVII
Day rented 03/14/90
Returned   03/16/90

Member   William Martin
Title   Licence To Kill
Day rented 03/15/90
Returned   03/17/90

Member   Carol Robinson
Title   When Harry Met Sally
Day rented 03/17/90
Returned   03/19/90

Member   Harry Kramer
Title   Coming To America
Day rented 03/14/90
Returned   03/18/90

Member   Ellen Moore
Title   When Harry Met Sally
Day rented 03/16/90
Returned   03/17/90

Member   David Zachman
Title   Star Trek V
Day rented 03/18/90
Returned   03/18/90

Member   Benjamin Robinson
Title   Young Einstein
Day rented 03/19/90
Returned   03/20/90

Member   Wendy Hart
Title   Licence To Kill
Day rented 03/16/90
Returned   03/18/90

If desired, you could improve a report like this one by adding grouping to the report, as described in Chapter 7. You could index the RENTALS file on the Social field and then group the report on the Social field, using the member name in the group heading. You can use this same technique with labels, if desired. Just include the filename and pointer whenever you are referencing a field that is not in the active database.

Remember that all needed files must be open and the relationship established before you can generate a relational report or label. If, for example, you now enter **CLOSE DATABASES** and then open just one database, such as MEMBERS, and try to print this same report, you will get an "Alias not found" error message. This indicates that because the related file has not been opened and the relationship established, the report cannot locate the data it needs.

The use of SET VIEW combined with stored reports provides you with a powerful capability for generating relational reports when needed. You can continue to add and edit data within the databases; and whenever a relational report is needed, you could use commands like

SET VIEW TO RELATE1
REPORT FORM RELATE1 TO PRINT

to generate the needed data. Note that there is no need to name your view files and your reports with the same name, but it often is helpful in keeping track of which files are used with which reports. Also, when you save your report, a view file with the same name as the report is automatically created. This lets you use the ENVIRONMENT clause along with the REPORT FORM command. If you enter

REPORT FORM RELATE1 TO PRINT ENVIRONMENT

the ENVIRONMENT clause at the end of the command tells FoxPro to look for the view file with the same name as the report. That view file is put into effect automatically before the report is generated.

Because a view file is automatically created when you save the report, you should make sure any desired relationships exist *before* you create a relational report. It is possible to create and save a relational report without having established the relationships by manually entering the filenames and pointers in your expressions. But if you do this, the saved view file won't contain the relationships, and the REPORT FORM...ENVIRONMENT command will result in an error message.

A Warning About SET FIELDS and dBASE

Those who are familiar with Ashton-Tate's dBASE products may be aware of the use of the SET FIELDS command to eliminate the need for filenames and pointers. In dBASE III Plus or dBASE IV, you can use SET FIELDS to establish fields from related files once; from then on, you can drop the filename and pointer prefix, and dBASE will still find the data. As a brief example, using the same databases that have been used throughout this text, you could enter the following commands in dBASE IV:

```
SELECT 1
USE RENTALS
USE MEMBERS IN 2 INDEX SOCIAL
SET RELATION TO SOCIAL INTO MEMBERS
SET FIELDS TO MEMBERS->LASTNAME,
MEMBERS->FIRSTNAME, TITLE, DAYRENTED
```

You could then access the Lastname, Firstname, Title, or Dayrented fields without using any filenames or pointers in the case of the Lastname and Firstname fields. You could also create reports without using the filename and pointer in the report expressions.

What's important to note is that FoxPro and its predecessor, FoxBase Plus do *not* support this relational use of the SET FIELDS command. You can enter the SET FIELDS command as just shown in FoxPro, and you will not get an error message. However, if you try to access the fields without the prefix of filename and pointer, you will not be able to do so. If you plan to use dBASE programs that contain such use of the SET FIELDS command, you will need to make changes to those programs so that they use the filename and pointer method instead.

GETTING SELECTIVE DATA FROM RELATED FILES

You can use the same techniques covered in Chapter 6—the SET FILTER, FOR, and WHILE clauses, and the INDEX ON...FOR command—to retrieve selective data from multiple files. One of the biggest challenges in working with multiple files at the same time is in keeping track of where you are. This is particularly true when you want to retrieve specific data, because the commands you use will apply to the active file unless you include filenames and pointers as a prefix. If, for example, you use the commands

```
SELECT 1
USE RENTALS
USE MEMBERS IN 2 INDEX SOCIALS
SET RELATION TO SOCIAL INTO MEMBERS
```

to establish a relationship, and you then apply a filter with a command like

```
SET FILTER TO TITLE = "Beverly Hills Cop II"
```

you can then list or report on selective data, based on a condition you applied to the active file (RENTALS).

If you wanted to instead apply a filter to the MEMBERS file, you would need to do things a little differently. You would have to apply a filter condition within that work area. To do this, include a filename and pointer in the filter condition. For example, while the RENTALS file is active, you could enter the commands

```
SET FILTER TO MEMBERS->LASTNAME = "Kramer"
GO TOP
```

followed by a LIST command to limit rentals retrieved to only those for Mr. Kramer.

Keep in mind that a filter condition is only saved along with a view if it was established from the active work area. If you establish a filter condition with SET FILTER, switch work areas, and then save the environment to a view file, the filter condition will not be saved in the view.

RELATING MORE THAN TWO DATABASE FILES

As many database files as you need (up to the limit of ten possible open database files) can be linked to provide you with the results that you need in FoxPro. One common example of the type of application requiring more than two files is the tracking of customers, sales, and product inventory. A complete sales-tracking system is commonly built around at least three database files: one containing customer data such as names and addresses, one containing product data such as descriptions and prices, and a third containing a record of each item purchased by a customer. The three database structures shown here contain the fields necessary, at a minimum, to accomplish such a task:

ITEMS.DBF	ORDERS.DBF	CUSTOMER.DBF
Stockno	Custno	Custno
Descript	Stockno	Name
Cost	Quantity	Address
	Date	City
		State
		Zip

Such a database system, properly designed, could meet a variety of needs. Inventory could be tracked using the ITEMS file; reports summarizing total sales could be generated using the ITEMS and ORDERS files; mass mailings to customers could be handled with the CUSTOMER file. The task of generating customer invoices is a prime example of a relational application demanding the use of three files; the data listed in an invoice would need to come from three different databases, as illustrated in Figure 11-5.

An example of the needed relationships can be demonstrated if you duplicate the following database structures and the sample data contained in the files. The structure of ITEMS.DBF is as follows:

Field Name	Type	Width	Decimals
STOCKNO	character	4	
DESCRIPT	character	25	
COST	numeric	7	2

Add this data to it:

STOCKNO	DESCRIPT	COST
2001	leather handbag, black	89.95
2002	attache case	139.95
2003	suitcase, overnighter	159.95
2004	carry on bag, leather	69.95

The structure of ORDERS.DBF is shown here:

Field Name	Type	Width	Decimals
CUSTNO	character	4	
STOCKNO	character	4	
QUANTITY	numeric	2	0
DATE	date		

Add this data to it:

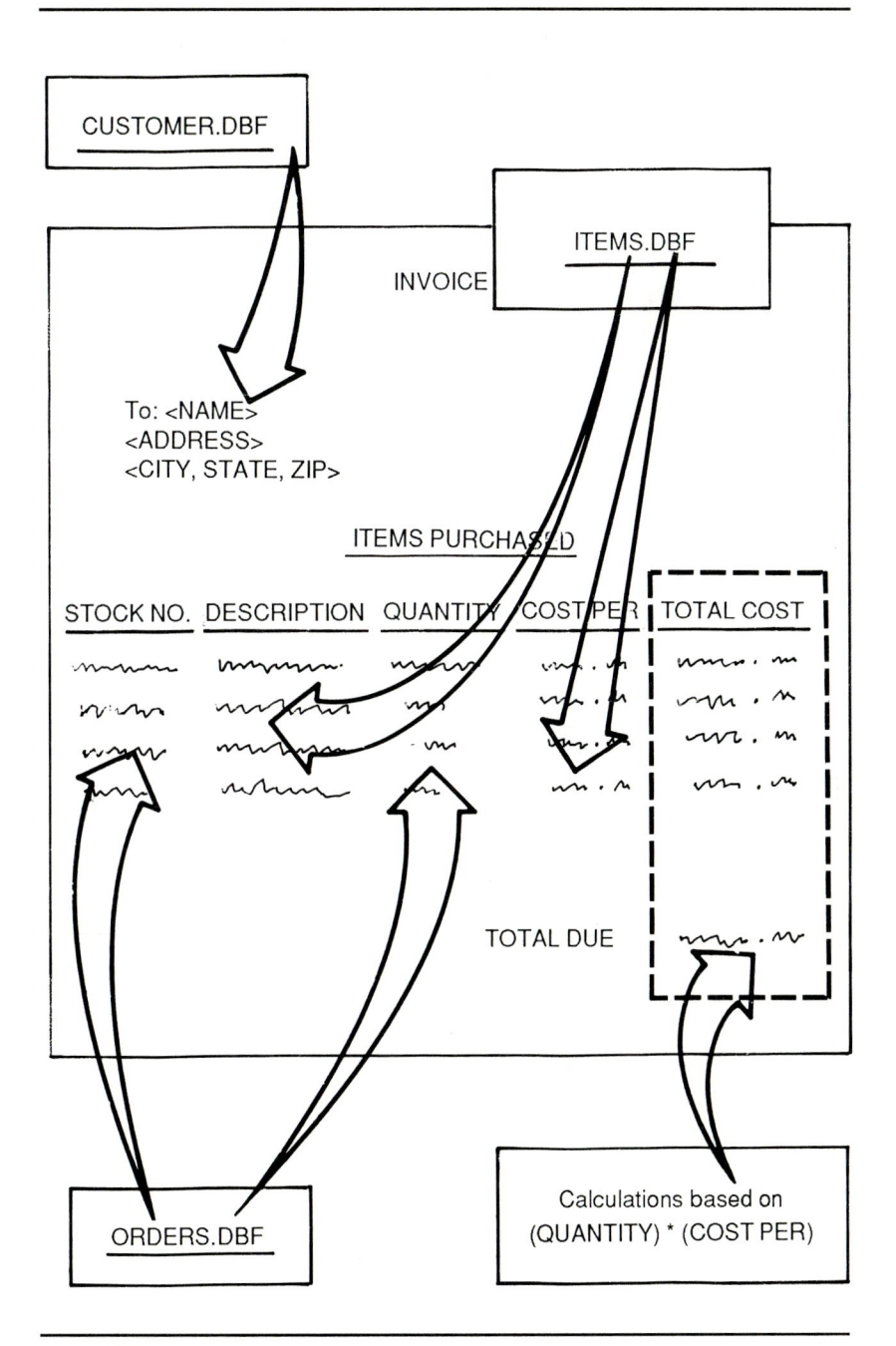

FIGURE 11-5. Invoice and supporting databases

CUSTNO	STOCKNO	QUANTITY	DATE
9001	2001	1	03/05/90
9001	2004	1	03/05/90
9002	2002	2	03/06/90
9004	2004	1	03/04/90
9003	2001	1	03/05/90
9001	2002	1	03/05/90
9003	2003	1	03/04/90
9005	2002	1	03/06/90
9002	2004	2	03/06/90

CUSTOMER.DBF has this structure:

Field Name	Type	Width
LASTNAME	character	15
FIRSTNAME	character	15
ADDRESS	character	25
CITY	character	15
STATE	character	2
ZIPCODE	character	10
CUSTNO	character	4

To quickly duplicate the example CUSTOMER.DBF file, you can copy existing data from the MEMBERS file with the following commands:

CLOSE DATABASES

USE MEMBERS

COPY TO CUSTOMER NEXT 5 FIELDS LASTNAME, FIRSTNAME, ADDRESS, CITY, STATE, ZIPCODE

USE CUSTOMER
MODIFY STRUCTURE

When the Database Structure dialog box appears, add a new field:

CUSTNO   character   4

and then save the structure. Then enter

BROWSE FIELDS CUSTNO, LASTNAME, FIRSTNAME FREEZE CUSTNO

to add customer numbers to the existing records, as shown below:

CUSTNO	NAME
9001	Miller, Karen
9002	Martin, William
9003	Robinson, Carol
9004	Kramer, Harry
9005	Moore, Ellen

Once the databases like these exist, the entry of day-to-day sales, new customers, and changes to inventory can be performed on each file individually. Screens can be created, as detailed in Chapter 5, for adding and editing data. The ability of FoxPro to display data in multiple windows can come in handy here. If, for example, you enter

SELECT 1
USE ITEMS
BROWSE

and then open the Window menu and choose Command (or just press CTRL-F2) to switch back to the Command window, you can next enter

SELECT 2
USE ORDERS
CHANGE

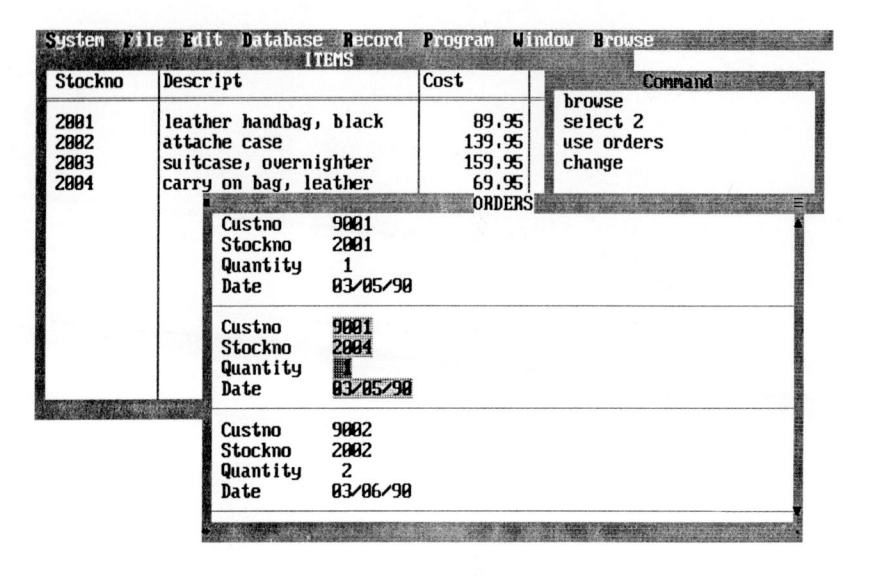

```
┌─────────────────────────────────────────────────────────────┐
│ System File Edit Database Record Program Window Browse      │
│           ITEMS                                             │
│ Stockno  Descript              Cost          Command        │
│                                              browse         │
│  2001    leather handbag, black   89.95      select 2       │
│  2002    attache case            139.95      use orders     │
│  2003    suitcase, overnighter   159.95      change         │
│  2004    carry on bag, leather    69.95                     │
│                                     ORDERS                  │
│            Custno    9001                                   │
│            Stockno   2001                                   │
│            Quantity     1                                   │
│            Date      03/05/90                               │
│                                                             │
│            Custno    9001                                   │
│            Stockno   2004                                   │
│            Quantity                                         │
│            Date      03/05/90                               │
│                                                             │
│            Custno    9002                                   │
│            Stockno   2002                                   │
│            Quantity     2                                   │
│            Date      03/06/90                               │
└─────────────────────────────────────────────────────────────┘
```

FIGURE 11-6.   Display of data in multiple windows

You then can move the windows and add new orders while viewing the descriptions in the inventory database, as shown in Figure 11-6. When done, remember that you can close a window by selecting the window by name from the Window menu, and then pressing ESC once you are in the window.

Most reports generated from this type of database will be of a relational nature. A visual representation of the needed links appears in Figure 11-7.

```
                STOCKNO  ←┐   CUSTNO  ←────→ CUSTNO
                DESCRIPT  └→ STOCKNO          NAME
```

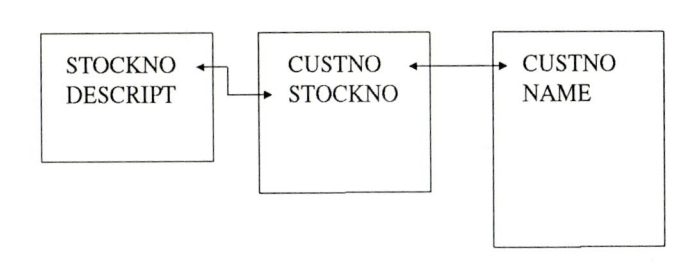

FIGURE 11-7. Map of relationships

Assuming you are retrieving order data for reports or invoices, you could establish the relational links with these commands:

```
CLOSE DATABASES
SELECT 1
USE ITEMS
INDEX ON STOCKNO TO BYSTOCK
SELECT 2
USE ORDERS
INDEX ON CUSTNO TO BYCUST
SELECT 3
USE CUSTOMER
INDEX ON CUSTNO TO CUSTOM
SELECT 2
SET RELATION TO CUSTNO INTO CUSTOMER
SET RELATION TO STOCKNO INTO ITEMS ADDITIVE
```

Note the use of the ADDITIVE clause for the second SET RELATION command. Once a relation exists out of an active file, the ADDITIVE clause must be used to establish a second relation. Without the clause, the second SET RELATION command would simply override the first.

At this point, the ORDERS file is the active file. For any record located in the ORDERS file, the corresponding customer name and address can be retrieved from the CUSTOMER file, and the corresponding item cost and description can be retrieved from the ITEMS file. You can obtain a columnar listing of sales with a command like the one shown here. The OFF option turns off the record numbers, so each record will still fit on one line.

LIST CUSTOMER->LASTNAME, DATE, QUANTITY, ITEMS->DESCRIPT, ITEMS->COST OFF

CUSTOMER->LASTNAME	DATE	QUANTITY ITEMS->DESCRIPT	ITEMS->COST
Miller	03/05/90	1 leather handbag, black	89.95
Miller	03/05/90	1 carry on bag, leather	69.95
Miller	03/05/90	1 attache case	139.95
Martin	03/06/90	2 attache case	139.95
Martin	03/06/90	2 carry on bag, leather	69.95
Robinson	03/05/90	1 leather handbag, black	89.95
Robinson	03/04/90	1 suitcase, overnighter	159.95
Kramer	03/04/90	1 carry on bag, leather	69.95
Moore	03/06/90	1 attache case	139.95

An alternative is to lay out all desired fields in an invoice, including filenames and pointers where necessary, to refer to the related files. Since the ORDERS database is the active file, any report would include one group of orders for each customer (unless you applied some type of filter first). As an example, you can create an invoice for each customer. To try this, enter **CREATE REPORT SALESINV** to start a new report. Then perform the following steps.

With the cursor in row 0, press CTRL-M three times to get rid of three lines in the Page Header band. Open the Report menu with ALT-O, and choose Data Grouping to add a Group band. Select

Add, and then enter **CUSTNO** in the Group window as the field to group the report on. This will provide a group of purchases printed for each individual customer.

Turn on the New Page option in the Group Info dialog box. Choose OK from the dialog box, and then choose OK again from the remaining dialog box.

Move the cursor into the Group band (anywhere on row 1) and press CTRL-N four times to add four lines to the starting Group band. The customer name and address data will need to be placed here, since it should only print once for each invoice.

Move to row 1, column 1. Press CTRL-F and ENTER to open the Expression Builder. Enter the expression

TRIM(CUSTOMER->FIRSTNAME) + " " + CUSTOMER->LASTNAME

and choose OK from the dialog box. When the Report Expression dialog box reappears, change the width to **30**, and choose OK.

Move to row 2, column 1. Press CTRL-F and then ENTER to open the Expression Builder. Enter the expression

CUSTOMER->ADDRESS

and choose OK from the dialog box. When the Report Expression dialog box reappears, choose OK again to close the box.

Move to row 3, column 1. Press CTRL-F, and then ENTER to open the Expression Builder. Enter

TRIM(CUSTOMER->CITY) + ", " + CUSTOMER->STATE + " " + CUSTOMER->ZIPCODE

and choose OK from the dialog box. When the Report Expression dialog box reappears, change the width to **35**, and choose OK.

At row 5 column 1, enter these words

Stock no Description

Press ENTER to complete the entry, and move over to column 40. Enter these words, with three spaces between them

Quantity Cost

Press ENTER to complete the entry. Move over to column 60, and enter

Total

Again, press ENTER to complete the entry.

Move to row 6 column 1, the first line in the Detail band. Add fields to the report by performing the following steps. Be sure to press ENTER after entering each expression, and choose OK from the dialog box after each entry:

Location	Keypress	Text Entry
Row 6, column 1	CTRL-F then TAB	STOCKNO
Row 6, column 10	CTRL-F then TAB	ITEMS->DESCRIPT
Row 6, column 40	CTRL-F then TAB	QUANTITY
Row 6, column 50	CTRL-F then TAB	ITEMS->COST
Row 6, column 60	CTRL-F then TAB	ITEMS->COST*QUANTITY

Move the cursor down into row 7, and press CTRL-M twice to delete two of the blank lines in the Detail band. If not removed, these would appear as blank lines in the invoice between each purchase for a customer.

Save the report with CTRL-W, turn on your printer, and enter

REPORT FORM SALESINV TO PRINT

to see the results. An invoice for a single customer should be printed on each page, resembling the following:

Karen Miller
4260 Park Avenue
Chevy Chase, MD 20815-0988

Stock no	Description	Quantity	Cost	Total
2001	leather handbag, black	1	89.95	89.95
2004	carry on bag, leather	1	69.95	69.95
2002	attache case	1	139.95	139.95

One minor point is worth noting. The commands used to establish the links also included these commands:

```
USE ORDERS
INDEX ON CUSTNO TO BYCUST
```

They constructed an index on ORDERS, the active file. This was not needed for the SET RELATION command; only the files into which the relations are set need to be indexed (in this case, CUSTOMER.DBF and ITEMS.DBF). The indexing of the ORDERS file was done only to support grouping, based on the customer number (Custno) field. Without the grouping, an invoice would be printed for each item ordered, and customers ordering more than one item would receive multiple invoices as a result.

Of more significance is the overall complexity that the day-to-day management a system of this nature involves. Adding and updating all three files as needed from the command level will require all users of such a system to be familiar with FoxPro commands. With the staff turnover typical in today's workplace, this could be a problem. Also, there is virtually no referential integrity in a relational system maintained entirely from the command level. In a nutshell, this means that there is nothing to protect users from entering corrupt data, such as an incorrect social security number that will not support the relationship. The same problem applies to edits of existing data. For example, if a user of the system deletes a customer from the CUSTOMER file while orders still exist for that customer in the ORDERS file, later invoices will contain orders for which no matching customer name can be found.

The answer to these problems lies in programming, the subject of the chapters to follow. With programming techniques, you can build applications that will guard against mistakes such as deleting customers who have existing orders. Such applications can also present menu choices to novice users, shielding them from the complexity of FoxPro commands.

ANALYZING TYPES OF RELATIONSHIPS

Before you delve deeply into working with relationships between multiple files, you may find it necessary to do some analysis on paper and determine the relationships that need to be drawn between the fields. The different types of possible relationships mean you may want to establish your links in different ways.

Relationships can be one-to-one, one-to-many, or many-to-many. When one field in one record of a database relates in a unique manner to a field in another record in a different database, you have a *one-to-one* relationship. An example may exist in a personnel system that contains medical and benefit information in one file and salary information in another file. Each database contains one record per employee, meaning that for every record in the medical file there is a corresponding record for the same employee in the salary file. The relationship between the files is a one-to-one relationship. Figure 11-8 shows two such databases and the relationship between them. In such a case, things are relatively simple; you use the SET RELATION command to link on the common field used between the two files (in this example, a unique patient ID number).

EMPLOYEEID	LASTNAME	FIRSTNAME	SALARY	GRADE	HIRED
X288	Anderson	Terence	750.55	8	03/17/69
X289	Smith	Linda	890.00	10	06/25/75
G343	Robinson	James	790.40	6	08/19/86

EMPLOYEEID	HEALTHNAME	HEALTHCOST	DENTALNAME	DENTALCOST
G343	Blue Cross	95.50	Prudential	33.00
X288	Kaiser	62.00	Kaiser	27.00
X289	Prudential	55.00	Kaiser	27.00

FIGURE 11-8. One-to-one relationship

When relating files, it is often advantageous to have a field that will always contain unique data for each record such as this one; unless an incorrect entry is made, no two members ever have the same employee ID number. Customer numbers, social security numbers, and stock numbers are other types of data commonly used for the same purpose of unique identification.

In some cases, a single field with unique data may not be available; for example, you may have a list of customers, but your company may not assign customer numbers as a practice. If you can't convince management to change the way it tracks customers, you have the alternative of creating a link based on more than one field. In the case of customers, you could index on a combination of Lastname + Firstname + Address and establish the relation on the expression with a command like

SET RELATION TO (LASTNAME+FIRSTNAME+ADDRESS) INTO MYFILE

This would work, assuming you never have two customers with the same name living at the same address.

By comparison, if one field of one record in the first file relates to a field in one or more records in the second file, you have a *one-to-many* relationship. An example is the relationship between

SOCIAL	LASTNAME	FIRSTNAME	CITY	STATE
123-44-8976	Miller	Karen	Chevy Chase	MD
121-33-9876	Martin	William	Silver Spring	MD
→232-55-1234	Robinson	Carol	Falls Church	VA
901-77-3456	Kramer	Harry	Arlington	VA
121-90-5432	Moore	Ellen	Takoma Park	MD
495-00-3456	Zachman	David	Falls Church	VA
343-55-9821	Robinson	Benjamin	Washington	DC
876-54-3210	Hart	Wendy	Fairfax	VA

SOCIAL	TITLE	DAYRENTED	RETURNED
123-44-8976	Star Trek IV	03/05/90	03/06/90
121-33-9876	Lethal Weapon II	03/02/90	03/06/90
→232-55-1234	Who Framed Roger Rabbit	03/06/90	03/09/90
901-77-3456	Beverly Hills Cop II	03/04/90	03/05/90
121-90-5432	Dirty Rotten Scoundrels	03/01/90	03/06/90
495-00-3456	Young Einstein	03/04/90	03/09/90
343-55-9821	When Harry Met Sally	03/06/90	03/12/90
876-54-3210	Lethal Weapon II	03/07/90	03/08/90
123-44-8976	Friday 13th Part XXVII	03/14/90	03/16/90
121-33-9876	Licence To Kill	03/15/90	03/17/90
→232-55-1234	When Harry Met Sally	03/17/90	03/19/90
901-77-3456	Coming To America	03/14/90	03/18/90
121-90-5432	When Harry Met Sally	03/16/90	03/17/90
495-00-3456	Star Trek V	03/18/90	03/18/90
343-55-9821	Young Einstein	03/19/90	03/20/90
876-54-3210	Licence To Kill	03/16/90	03/18/90

FIGURE 11-9. One-to-many relationship

the Generic Videos MEMBERS and RENTALS database files, as illustrated in Figure 11-9. For every member in the MEMBERS file, there are a number of records in the RENTALS file corresponding to a different rental of a videotape by that member. Again, SET RELATION is used to establish the link, as was demonstrated earlier in the chapter with the video database. However, things do get more complex with one-to-many relationships, because you must keep track of where you are when performing data retrieval operations.

In this example, the MEMBERS file is the "one" file, and the RENTALS file is the "many" file. When a listing of all video rentals was needed, the RENTALS file had to be the active file, and the relation had to be set out of that file because it contained the "many" data. If the MEMBERS file had been the active file and a relation had been set out of MEMBERS into RENTALS, you could have retrieved only those rentals associated with a particular member. Depending on your needs at the time, this might be exactly what you wanted. The point is to keep in mind the nature of the one-to-many relationship, and plan your relationships accordingly.

Finally, a type of relationship that is not as common as the first two but occasionally arises is the *many-to-many* relationship. This relationship exists when a field in several records in one database will relate to a field in several records in another database. A classic example of a many-to-many relationship is that of student tracking at a high school or college, where many students are assigned to many different classes. To set up this or any many-to-many relationship under FoxPro, you will need at least three database files. The third file serves as an intermediate or "linking" file between the other two files, which contain the "many" data.

Using the example of students and classes, a student file can be created with the names of each student, along with a unique student ID number (for simplicity's sake, social security numbers are used in this example). A database containing a unique class ID number for each class, the class name, room number, and teacher name is also created. Finally, a schedule file containing a record for each student's enrollment in a class is also created. Figure 11-10 shows the databases and illustrates the relationships between the files. You can duplicate the files and the data shown if you want to try the examples that follow. If you decide to duplicate the example, you can easily create the STUDENTS database by copying the first five records from the MEMBERS file and including only the Social, Lastname, and Firstname fields in the copy.

Once the databases are created, you can use the SET RELATION command to link the SCHEDULE file to both the STU-

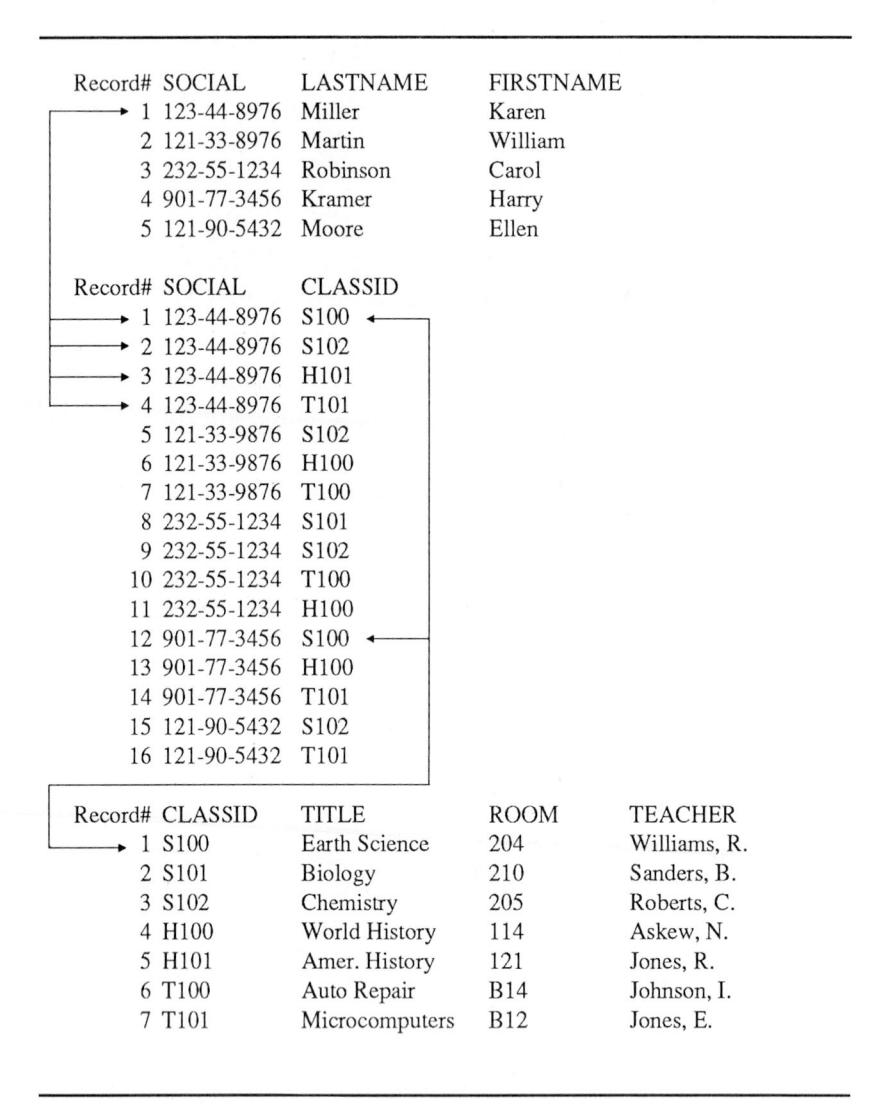

Record#	SOCIAL	LASTNAME	FIRSTNAME
1	123-44-8976	Miller	Karen
2	121-33-8976	Martin	William
3	232-55-1234	Robinson	Carol
4	901-77-3456	Kramer	Harry
5	121-90-5432	Moore	Ellen

Record#	SOCIAL	CLASSID
1	123-44-8976	S100
2	123-44-8976	S102
3	123-44-8976	H101
4	123-44-8976	T101
5	121-33-9876	S102
6	121-33-9876	H100
7	121-33-9876	T100
8	232-55-1234	S101
9	232-55-1234	S102
10	232-55-1234	T100
11	232-55-1234	H100
12	901-77-3456	S100
13	901-77-3456	H100
14	901-77-3456	T101
15	121-90-5432	S102
16	121-90-5432	T101

Record#	CLASSID	TITLE	ROOM	TEACHER
1	S100	Earth Science	204	Williams, R.
2	S101	Biology	210	Sanders, B.
3	S102	Chemistry	205	Roberts, C.
4	H100	World History	114	Askew, N.
5	H101	Amer. History	121	Jones, R.
6	T100	Auto Repair	B14	Johnson, I.
7	T101	Microcomputers	B12	Jones, E.

FIGURE 11-10. Many-to-many relationship

DENTS file and the CLASSES file. Depending on the data you need, you could use various LIST commands or design different reports to produce the desired results. If you duplicated the above files, you could try these commands:

```
SELECT 1
USE STUDENTS
INDEX ON SOCIAL TO STUDENTS
SELECT 2
USE SCHEDULE
SELECT 3
USE CLASSES
INDEX ON CLASSID TO CLASSES
SELECT 2
SET RELATION TO SOCIAL INTO STUDENTS
SET RELATION TO CLASSID INTO CLASSES ADDITIVE
```

If you wanted to use this relationship at a later date, it would be wise to save it with a command like

```
CREATE VIEW SCHOOL FROM ENVIRONMENT
```

You could then proceed to retrieve the needed data. As an example, a cross-list of student names and instructor names could be produced with a command like

```
LIST CLASSES->TEACHER, STUDENTS->LASTNAME,
STUDENTS->FIRSTNAME
```

The results would resemble this:

Record#	CLASSES->TEACHER	STUDENTS->LASTNAME	STUDENTS->FIRSTNAME
1	Williams, R.	Miller	Karen
2	Roberts, C.	Miller	Karen
3	Jones, R.	Miller	Karen
4	Jones, E.	Miller	Karen
5	Roberts, C.	Martin	William
6	Askew, N.	Martin	William
7	Johnson, I.	Martin	William
8	Sanders, B.	Robinson	Carol
9	Roberts, C.	Robinson	Carol
10	Johnson, I.	Robinson	Carol
11	Askew, N.	Robinson	Carol

12	Williams, R.	Kramer	Harry
13	Askew, N.	Kramer	Harry
14	Jones, E.	Kramer	Harry
15	Roberts, C.	Moore	Ellen
16	Jones, E.	Moore	Ellen

If you needed a course list for all students, you could use a command like

LIST STUDENTS->LASTNAME, STUDENTS->FIRSTNAME, CLASSID, CLASSES- >TITLE

and the results would resemble this:

Record#	STUDENTS->LASTNAME	STUDENTS->FIRSTNAME	CLASSID	CLASSES->TITLE
1	Miller	Karen	S100	Earth Science
2	Miller	Karen	S102	Chemistry
3	Miller	Karen	H101	Amer. History
4	Miller	Karen	T101	Microcomputers
5	Martin	William	S102	Chemistry
6	Martin	William	H100	World History
7	Martin	William	T100	Auto Repair
8	Robinson	Carol	S101	Biology
9	Robinson	Carol	S102	Chemistry
10	Robinson	Carol	T100	Auto Repair
11	Robinson	Carol	H100	World History
12	Kramer	Harry	S100	Earth Science
13	Kramer	Harry	H100	World History
14	Kramer	Harry	T101	Microcomputers
15	Moore	Ellen	S102	Chemistry
16	Moore	Ellen	T101	Microcomputers

If you wanted a list of classes for a single student, you could include a FOR clause, as in the following example:

LIST STUDENTS->LASTNAME, STUDENTS->FIRSTNAME, CLASSID,
CLASSES->TITLE FOR STUDENTS->LASTNAME = "Kramer"

The results would include only the classes for the student named:

Record#	STUDENTS->LASTNAME	STUDENTS->FIRSTNAME	CLASSID	CLASSES->TITLE
12	Kramer	Harry	S100	Earth Science
13	Kramer	Harry	H100	World History
14	Kramer	Harry	T101	Microcomputers

You could use similar techniques to obtain listings of all students for a given teacher, as shown in this example:

```
LIST STUDENTS->LASTNAME, STUDENTS->FIRSTNAME, CLASSID,
CLASSES->TITLE FOR CLASSES->TEACHER = "Roberts, C."
```

Record#	STUDENTS->LASTNAME	STUDENTS->FIRSTNAME	CLASSID	CLASSES->TITLE
2	Miller	Karen	S102	Chemistry
5	Martin	William	S102	Chemistry
9	Robinson	Carol	S102	Chemistry
15	Moore	Ellen	S102	Chemistry

While the management of a many-to-many application like this one gets fairly complex, it also demonstrates the power and usefulness of a well-planned relational database system. To manage this data in a single database file would call for an enormous amount of redundant data entry; student names and teacher names would be repeated needlessly dozens or hundreds of times in such a file. In spite of this, database users create single files to manage tasks like this all too often either to avoid learning the necessary relational commands or because the student data-entry labor is cheap.

12
INTRODUCTION TO FOXPRO PROGRAMMING

Creating Command Files
Constants
Memory Variables
Expressions
Operators
Functions
Commands Used in Command Files
Overview of a Program Design

Although you may not have purchased FoxPro with the intent of becoming a computer programmer, you'll find that programming with FoxPro is not as difficult as you might expect. As you will see in this chapter, you program in FoxPro through the use of command files. Using programs that automate the way FoxPro works for you is well worth the effort spent in designing and writing command files. For the most part, FoxPro is command-compatible with dBASE IV and with dBASE III Plus, so you can use programs written for them with FoxPro. dBASE IV users should note that there are a few dBASE IV commands and functions, such as SET SKIP, which are not supported by FoxPro. If in doubt, compare the command listing from your dBASE IV documentation with the command listing in this book (or in your FoxPro documentation).

Any computer *program* is simply a series of instructions to a computer. These instructions are commands that cause the computer to perform specific tasks. The commands are written in a file contained on a disk, and they are performed each time the file is retrieved from the disk.

A FoxPro *command file* is made up of FoxPro commands. Each time you use a command file, FoxPro will execute the list of commands in sequential order, unless you request otherwise.

Let's look at an example using the Generic Videos database. If a Generic Videos manager wanted a printed listing of members' last names, cities, states, and expiration dates, that manager could enter commands, like those you have learned to use, to produce the listing. This may not seem like a complex task; in fact, it could be done with the following two commands:

USE MEMBERS
LIST LASTNAME, FIRSTNAME, CITY, STATE, EXPIREDATE

If, however, the manager needed to reprint this list frequently, typing the same commands over and over would be a waste of time. Instead, he could place them inside of a command file, and then he would only type one short command to execute all the commands in the file.

Two characteristics of command files make them a powerful feature of FoxPro:

- Any series of FoxPro commands entered from the command level can be stored in a command file. When the command file is run, the FoxPro commands present in the file are executed just as if they had been entered from the keyboard.

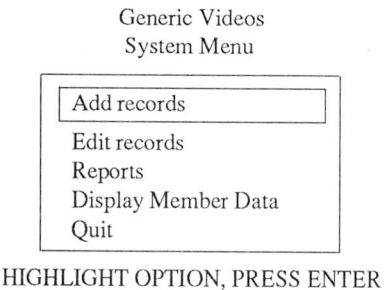

```
                    Generic Videos
                    System Menu
            ┌─────────────────────────┐
            │ Add records             │
            ├─────────────────────────┤
            │ Edit records            │
            │ Reports                 │
            │ Display Member Data     │
            │ Quit                    │
            └─────────────────────────┘
        HIGHLIGHT OPTION, PRESS ENTER
```

FIGURE 12-1. Sample menu for Generic Videos

- One command file can call and execute another command file. Information can be transferred between command files. This means that complex systems can be designed efficiently through creating a series of smaller command files for individual tasks.

Using command files, you can create a system that provides the user with one or more menus of options. An example of a menu screen is shown in Figure 12-1. Rather than using individual commands, the user simply makes choices from the menu to retrieve and manipulate information in the database. Such a menu-driven system can easily be used by people unfamiliar with FoxPro commands.

CREATING COMMAND FILES

You create command files with the MODIFY COMMAND command, using the form

MODIFY COMMAND *filename*

Key	Action
UP ARROW	Moves cursor up one line
DOWN ARROW	Moves cursor down one line
LEFT ARROW	Moves cursor left one character
RIGHT ARROW	Moves cursor right one character
ENTER	Inserts a new line
INS	Turns Insert mode on or off
DEL	Deletes character at the cursor position
BACKSPACE	Deletes character to the left of cursor
PGUP	Scrolls screen upwards
PGDN	Scrolls screen downwards
CTRL-W	Saves file on disk
ESC	Exits Editor without saving

TABLE 12-1. Editing Keys in the FoxPro Editor

Entering **MODIFY COMMAND** along with a filename brings up the FoxPro Editor. You then use the Editor to type the commands that will be stored as a command file. When you use MODIFY COMMAND, the file you create will have an extension of .PRG (for Program) unless you enter a different extension. If the filename you enter already exists on the disk, it will be recalled to the screen. If the filename does not exist, a blank screen within the Editor window is displayed. You can also create command files from the menus by opening the File menu, choosing New, and then choosing Program from the dialog box that appears.

To try a simple example of a command file now, enter

MODIFY COMMAND TEST

The FoxPro Editor appears. At this point, the screen is like a blank sheet of paper. You type the commands that you wish to place in your command file, pressing ENTER as you complete each line. If you make any mistakes, you can correct them with the arrow keys and the BACKSPACE or DEL key. The editing keys available in the Editor are listed in Table 12-1. When you use the Editor, any characters you type will push any existing characters in the same position to the right unless you are in Overwrite mode. You can get out of Insert mode and into Overwrite by pressing INS. When you are in Insert mode, the cursor takes the shape of a thin line, and any characters to the right of the cursor will be pushed to the right as you type new characters. When you are in Overwrite mode, the cursor is shaped like a block, and any characters you type overwrite existing characters.

One ability of the Editor that comes in handy for programming is its ability to delete, move, and copy blocks of text. You can mark a block of text for deletion in the Editor by placing the cursor at the beginning of the text, holding down the SHIFT key, and moving the cursor to the end of the block of text while continuing to hold the SHIFT key down. The marked text will appear in a different shade. You can then delete the marked text by pressing the DEL key.

To move or copy text, you mark the block of text in the same manner, but you then use the Cut, Copy, or Paste option of the Edit menu. To copy a block of text to another location, first place the cursor at the start of the text, hold down the SHIFT key, and move the cursor to the end of the text. Open the Edit menu and choose Copy. Move the cursor to where the copied text should appear, open the Edit menu, and choose Paste. The copied text will appear in the new location.

To move a block of text to another location, first place the cursor at the start of the text, hold down the SHIFT key, and move the cursor to the end of the text. Open the Edit menu and choose Cut. Move the cursor to where the text is to be moved, open the Edit menu, and choose Paste. The copied text will appear in the new location.

Type the following series of commands now, pressing ENTER after you complete each line; only one command should appear on each line. (If you don't have a printer on your system, omit the SET PRINT ON, SET PRINT OFF, and EJECT commands.)

```
USE MEMBERS
SET PRINT ON
LIST LASTNAME, FIRSTNAME, CITY, TAPELIMIT FOR STATE = "MD"
LIST LASTNAME, FIRSTNAME, CITY, TAPELIMIT FOR STATE = "VA"
LIST LASTNAME, FIRSTNAME, CITY, TAPELIMIT FOR STATE = "DC"
SET PRINT OFF
EJECT
```

Whenever you finish editing with the FoxPro Editor, choose Save from the File menu (or press CTRL-W) to save the command file. (If you want to leave the Editor without saving the file, you can press ESC and then answer No in the dialog box that appears.)

The simple command file that you have created will print a listing of each employee, grouped by state, including employee names, city names, and salary amounts. Make sure that your printer is turned on; then, to see the results of your work, enter

DO TEST

The commands in the file will be carried out in sequential order, just as if you had entered them individually:

Record#	LASTNAME	FIRSTNAME	CITY	TAPELIMIT
1	Miller	Karen	Chevy Chase	6
2	Martin	William	Silver Spring	4
5	Moore	Ellen	Takoma Park	6

Record#	LASTNAME	FIRSTNAME	CITY	TAPELIMIT
3	Robinson	Carol	Falls Church	6
4	Kramer	Harry	Arlington	4
6	Zachman	David	Falls Church	4
8	Hart	Wendy	Fairfax	2

Record#	LASTNAME	FIRSTNAME	CITY	TAPELIMIT
7	Robinson	Benjamin	Washington	6

You can also create a command file by using other word processing programs. Although the FoxPro Editor is convenient and quite powerful, you may prefer to use your favorite word processing program. (If you do use your own editor, be sure to see "Compiling" following this paragraph.) Any word processor that can save files as ASCII text (text without any control codes) can be used to create a FoxPro command file. This includes the programs WordPerfect, MultiMate, WordStar, as well as Microsoft Word. In WordPerfect, save the file with the CTRL-F5 then 1 key combination. In WordStar, save the file in the Nondocument mode. In Microsoft Word, save the file as Unformatted. The important points to remember are to save the file as ASCII and to use the .PRG extension when naming the file; otherwise, FoxPro won't recognize the file as a command file unless you include the extension when calling the program with the DO command.

Compiling

Foxpro uses a compiler to run programs on a compiled basis rather than an interpreted basis. (*Interpreters* convert each line of a program into machine language each time the program runs; *compilers* translate the entire program into what is known as *object code* once, and each time the program runs, it runs using the object code.) A compiler offers significant speed over an interpreter. Earlier versions of Ashton-Tate's dBASE, including dBASE II, dBASE III, and dBASE III Plus, were based on interpreters. By comparison, FoxPro, FoxBase, and dBASE IV all use compilers.

When you run a FoxPro program with the DO *filename* command, FoxPro looks for a compiled object-code file with an extension of .FXP. If FoxPro finds the file, it runs the program using the already compiled object code. If FoxPro can't find the file, it looks for a "source file"—an ASCII text file of commands with a .PRG extension. FoxPro compiles this file, creating an object-code file of the same name, and then runs the program.

It is important to know this if you use your own editor to modify existing programs. When you change an existing program with the FoxPro Editor, FoxPro recompiles to a new object file when you run the program. If you use your own editor to change a program and the existing object-code file is not erased, using DO *filename* will cause the old version of the program to be run.

When making changes with your editor, you must erase the old object-code (.FXP) version of the program, or you must use the SET DEVELOPMENT ON command when you start your FoxPro session. Entering **SET DEVELOPMENT ON** will tell FoxPro to compare creation dates and times between source (.PRG) and object (.FXP) files; if they differ, FoxPro will recompile the program before running it.

There are various concepts associated with programming that you should know about before delving into the topic of FoxPro command files: constants, variables, expressions, operators, and functions.

CONSTANTS

A *constant* is an item of fixed data, or data that does not change. Unlike fields (whose values change, depending on the position of the record pointer), a constant's value is dependent on nothing; once established, the constant remains the same. There are numeric, character, date, and logical constants. For example, 5.05 might be a numeric constant, while the letter "a" might be a character constant. All character constants must be surrounded by quotes. Date constants must be surrounded by curly braces, and logical constants must be surrounded by periods.

MEMORY VARIABLES

A *memory variable* (or simply *variable* for short) is a memory location within the computer that is used to store data. Memory variables are referred to by their assigned names. A variable name must be ten or fewer characters. It must consist of letters, numbers, and underscores only, and it must start with a letter. You cannot use the names of commands, and it is best not to use field names. Because the contents of a memory variable are stored apart from the contents of a database, memory variables are useful for the temporary processing of values and data within a FoxPro program. Data can be stored in the form of memory variables and then be recalled for use by the program at a later time.

The STORE command is commonly used to assign data to a variable. The format is

STORE *expression* TO *variable-name*

An alternate way of assigning data to a variable is to use the "variable = X" format, as shown here:

variable-name = *expression*

FoxPro allows four types of variables: character, numeric, date, and logical variables. Character variables store strings of characters, which can be letters, numbers, or a combination of both. Numbers in a character variable are treated as characters. Numeric variables contain whole or decimal numbers. Date variables contain dates written in date format (for example, 12/16/84). Logical variables contain a logical value of T (true) or F (false), or Y (yes) or N (no).

You do not have to designate the type when creating a variable—just assign the value you will be using. Use a descriptive name to help you remember what is stored in the variable. For example, the following STORE command assigns a numeric value of 18 to the variable LEGALAGE:

STORE 18 TO LEGALAGE

If you preferred the alternate format, you could accomplish the same result with the statement,

LEGALAGE = 18

You can change the value by using the STORE command again.

STORE 21 TO LEGALAGE

The contents of a field can be stored to a memory variable. As an example, the command STORE LASTNAME TO ROSTER would store the contents of the Lastname field to a memory variable named ROSTER. When a list of characters is stored in a variable, the list of characters, known as *character string*, must be surrounded by single or double quotation marks. For example, the command

STORE "BILL ROBERTS" TO NAME

would store the character string BILL ROBERTS in the variable NAME.

Surround the logical variable T, F, Y, and N with periods to distinguish them from regular characters: while .T. has a logical value of true, "T" is simply the letter T. Logical values can also be stored in variables with the STORE command. The following command would assign a logical value of false to the variable CHOICE:

STORE .F. TO CHOICE

To initialize a date variable, surround the date with curly braces. As an example, the statement

STORE {11/01/88} TO MYDAY

would store the date 11/01/88 in a date variable named MYDAY.

In addition to STORE, other commands assign values to variables. These commands will be discussed in later chapters. To display a list of the variables you have used and their values, enter the command DISPLAY MEMORY.

You can use memory variables in direct commands and in command files. However, memory variables are only temporary: as soon as you turn off the computer, they vanish. You can make a memory variable permanent by storing the variable to a memory file on disk. As you might expect, when the values are stored on disk, they can be recalled by a FoxPro program. Each memory variable is assigned a different name.

Try entering the following:

STORE 25 TO QUANTITY
STORE "Jefferson" TO NAMES
STORE TIME() TO CLOCK
? QUANTITY, NAMES, CLOCK

The previous example displayed the values stored in memory with the STORE command. However, you can use the DISPLAY MEMORY command to take a look at all variables that have been defined in memory. Enter

DISPLAY MEMORY

to display a listing of variables, a letter designating the type of variable, and what each variable contains. The letter "C" indicates a character variable, "N" a numeric variable, "D" a date variable, and "L" a logical variable. The designation "Pub" beside each variable indicates that these are public variables, available to all parts of FoxPro. Variables can be public or private; the difference is explained in detail in Chapter 16. For now, you needn't be concerned about this designation. Along with the memory variables you created, you will see information on print system memory variables that FoxPro uses; you can ignore these.

You should keep two guidelines in mind. First, it's a good idea not to name variables after a field. If a program encounters a name that can be either a variable or a field, the field name will take precedence over the memory variable. If you must give a variable the same name as a field, use the M-> prefix ahead of the variable name so that FoxPro knows when you are referring to the variable. For example, if MEMBERS were in use, LASTNAME would refer to the Lastname field, while M->LASTNAME would refer to a variable called LASTNAME.

Second, note that you must store a value to a memory variable before you start using it in a program. This must be done because of FoxPro's firm rule that some type of value, even if it is a worthless one, must be stored to a FoxPro variable before you can begin using the variable. If you attempt to use variables in a program before defining them with the STORE command, FoxPro will respond with a "Variable not found" error message.

To save variables on disk, use the SAVE TO command. The format of this command is

SAVE TO *filename*

where *filename* is the name of the file that you want the variables saved under. The .MEM extension will automatically be added to the filename.

Right now, you have at least four memory variables defined from the previous examples—WORDS, QUANTITY, NAMES, and CLOCK. (You may also have other variables created from prior examples.) To save the variables currently in memory, enter the following:

SAVE TO FASTFILE

Once the variables have been stored, you can clear the memory of variables with the RELEASE ALL command. Enter the following:

RELEASE ALL
DISPLAY MEMORY

You'll see that the memory variables no longer exist in memory. To get the memory variables back from FASTFILE, use the RESTORE FROM *filename* command. This command will restore variables from filename to memory. You do not have to include the file extension .MEM. Enter

RESTORE FROM FASTFILE

Then enter **DISPLAY MEMORY**. The variables are again in the system, ready for further use.

When you use the RESTORE FROM *filename* command, all variables currently in memory will be removed to accommodate variables from the file. If you want to keep existing variables in memory while loading additional variables that were saved to a disk file, use the RESTORE FROM *filename* ADDITIVE variation of the command.

Getting back to RELEASE ALL, you can select specific variables to remove from memory by including either the EXCEPT or the LIKE option. RELEASE ALL with EXCEPT eliminates all variables except those that you list after EXCEPT. RELEASE ALL with LIKE, on the other hand, removes the variables that you list after LIKE, the opposite of EXCEPT. As an example, the command

RELEASE ALL LIKE N*

would cause all memory variables starting with the letter "N" to be erased from memory.

You can use LIKE to erase some memory variables and leave other variables untouched. Try this:

RESTORE FROM FASTFILE
RELEASE ALL LIKE Q*
DISPLAY MEMORY

This causes all memory variables beginning with the letter "Q," including the memory variable QUANTITY, to be erased from memory (the others will be untouched). Note that you can use the same LIKE and ALL options in a similar manner with the SAVE command. For example, you could enter the command

SAVE ALL LIKE Q* TO QFILE

to save all memory variables starting with the letter "Q."

```
                    Expression
           ⎴⎴⎴⎴⎴⎴⎴⎴⎴⎴⎴⎴⎴⎴⎴⎴⎴
           (RENTAMT  *  MONTHS)  *  0.95
                ↑           ↑          ↑
            Field   Memory variable  Constant
```

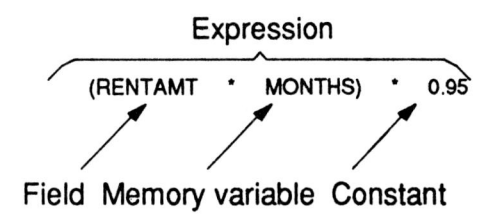

FIGURE 12-2.   An example of an expression

EXPRESSIONS

An *expression* can be a combination of one or more fields, functions, operators, memory variables, or constants. Figure 12-2 shows a statement combining a field, a memory variable, and a constant to form a single expression. This statement calculates total rent over a period of months, deducting 5% for estimated utilities (water, garbage, and so on). Each part of an expression, whether that part is a constant, a field, or a memory variable, is considered an element of the expression. All elements of an expression must be of the same type. You cannot, for example, mix character and date fields within the same expression unless you use functions to convert the dates to characters. If you try to mix different types of fields within an expression, FoxPro will display an "Operator/operand type mismatch" error message.

The most common type of expression found in FoxPro programs is the math expression. Math expressions contain the elements of an expression (constants, fields, memory variables, or functions), usually linked by one or more math operators (+, −, *, /). Examples of math expressions include

HOURLYRATE - SALARY

COST + (COST * .05)

HOURLYRATE * 40

637.5/HOURLYRATE

82

Character expressions are also quite common in FoxPro programs. Character expressions are used to manipulate character strings or groups of characters. Examples of character expressions include the following:

"Bob Smith"

"Mr." + FIRSTNAME + " " + LASTNAME + " is behind in payments."

OPERATORS

Operators, which are represented by symbols, work on related values to produce a single value. Operators that work on two values are called *binary* operators; operators that work on one value are called *unary* operators. Most of FoxPro's operators are binary operators, but there are a couple of unary operators. FoxPro has four kinds of operators: mathematical, relational, logical, and string operators.

Mathematical Operators

Mathematical operators are used to produce numeric results. Besides addition, subtraction, multiplication, and division, FoxPro has operators for exponentiation and unary minus (assigning a negative value to a number, as in −47). The symbols for math operators are as follows:

Operation	Symbol
Unary minus	−
Exponentiation	** or ^
Division	/
Multiplication	*
Subtraction	−
Addition	+

If an expression contains more than one math operator, FoxPro executes the operations in a prescribed order, known as the *order of precedence*. Unary minus will be performed first, followed by exponentiation; then multiplication or division is calculated, and then addition or subtraction. In the case of operators with equal precedence—division and multiplication, subtraction and addition—calculation will be from left to right. In the case of logical operators, the order is .NOT., then .AND., and then .OR. When different types of operators are in a single expression, any math and string operators are handled first, and then any relational operators, and then any logical operators.

You can alter the order of operations by grouping them with matched pairs of parentheses. For example, the parentheses in (3 + 6) * 5 forces FoxPro to add 3 + 6 first and then multiply the sum by 5. You can group operations within operations with nested parentheses. FoxPro begins with the innermost group and calculates outward, as in the case of $((3 + 5) * 6) \wedge 3$, where $3 + 5$ is added first, multiplied by 6, and then raised to the power of 3.

Relational Operators

Relational operators are used to compare character strings with character strings, date values with date values, and numbers with numbers. The values you compare can be constants or variables. The relational operators are as follows:

Operation	Symbol
Less than	<
Greater than	>
Equal to	=
Not equal to	< > or #
Less than or equal to	<=
Greater than or equal to	>=

Any comparison of values results in a logical value of true or false. The simple comparison 6 < 7 would result in .T. The result of 6 < NUMBER depends on the value of NUMBER.

You can also compare such character strings as "canine" < "feline" because FoxPro orders letters and words as in a dictionary. However, uppercase letters come before lowercase letters, so "Z" < "a" even though "a" comes before "Z" in the alphabet.

Logical Operators

Logical operators compare values of the same type to produce a logical true, false, yes, or no. The logical operators are .AND., .OR., and .NOT. Table 12-2 lists all possible values produced by

First Value	Operator	Second Value	Result
.T.	.AND.	.T.	.T.
.T.	.AND.	.F.	.F.
.F.	.AND.	.T.	.F.
.F.	.AND.	.F.	.F.
.T.	.OR.	.T.	.T.
.T.	.OR.	.F.	.T.
.F.	.OR.	.T.	.T.
.F.	.OR.	.F.	.F.
.T.	.NOT.	N.A.	.F.
.F.	.NOT.	N.A.	.T.

TABLE 12-2. Truth Table for Logical Operators .AND., .OR., and .NOT.

the three logical operators. .AND. and .OR. are binary operators, and .NOT. is a unary operator.

String Operators

The string operator you will commonly use in FoxPro is the plus sign (+). It is used to combine two or more character strings, which is known as *concatenation*. For example, "Orange" + "Fox" would be combined as "OrangeFox" (remember, a blank is a character). Strings inside variables can also be concatenated; for example, if ANIMAL = "Fox" and COLOR = "Orange", then COLOR+ANIMAL would result in "OrangeFox".

FUNCTIONS

Functions are used in FoxPro to perform special operations that supplement the normal FoxPro commands. FoxPro has a number of different functions that perform operations ranging from calculating the square root of a number to finding the time.

Every function statement contains the function name, followed by a set of parentheses. Most functions require one or more arguments inside the parentheses. A complete list of functions can be found in Appendix B. For now, it will help to know about some functions that are commonly used in command files.

EOF

The EOF function indicates when the FoxPro record pointer has reached the end of a database file. The normal format of the function is simply EOF(). To see how EOF() is set to true when the pointer is past the last record, enter

GO BOTTOM

This moves the pointer to the last record. Now enter

DISPLAY

and you will see that you are at record 8, the final record in the database. Next, enter

? EOF( )

to display the value of the EOF function. FoxPro returns .F. (false), meaning that the value of the EOF function is false because you are not yet at the end of the file.

The SKIP command, discussed shortly, can be used to move the FoxPro record pointer. Enter

SKIP

to move the pointer past the last record. Next, enter

? EOF( )

The .T. (true) value shows that the pointer is now at the end of the file.

BOF

The BOF function is the opposite of the EOF function. The value of BOF is set to true when the beginning of a database file is reached. The format is BOF(). To see how BOF operates, enter

GO TOP

The pointer moves to the first record. Now enter

DISPLAY

and the first record in the database is displayed. Next, enter

? BOF( )

to display the value of the BOF function, which is .F. (false) because the pointer is at the first record and not at the beginning of the file. Enter

SKIP −1

to move the pointer above record 1. Then enter

? BOF( )

The .T. (true) value shows that the pointer is at the beginning of the file.

DATE and TIME

The DATE and TIME functions are used to provide the current date and time, respectively. FoxPro provides the date and time by means of a clock built into your computer. For this reason, if the date and time set with your computer's DOS are incorrect, the date and time functions of FoxPro will also be incorrect.

The format for DATE is DATE(), and it provides the current date in the form MM/DD/YY. Dates follow the American date format, month followed by day followed by year, unless you use the PICTURE option (Chapter 14) or the SET DATE command to tell FoxPro otherwise. The TIME format of the function is TIME(), and it provides the current time in HH:MM:SS format. Note that for either function you do not need to supply anything between the parentheses, since they only serve to identify TIME and DATE as functions.

From the command level, you could display the current date and time by entering

```
? DATE()
? TIME()
```

The output of the DATE and TIME functions can be stored as a variable for use within a program, as in the example shown here:

```
? "Today's date is: "
?? DATE()
STORE TIME() TO BEGIN
?
LIST LASTNAME, FIRSTNAME, TAPELIMIT, EXPIREDATE
?
```

```
? "Starting time was: "
?? BEGIN
? "Ending time is: "
?? TIME()
```

UPPER

The UPPER function converts lowercase letters to uppercase letters. This function is especially useful when you want to search for a character string and you are not sure whether it was entered in all capital letters or initial caps. UPPER can thus be used to display text and variables in a uniform format if consistency is desired. It may be used with a character field, a character string, a constant, or a memory variable that contains a character string. Here is an example:

```
? UPPER ("This is not really uppercase")
THIS IS NOT REALLY UPPERCASE

STORE "not uppercase" TO WORDS
? UPPER(WORDS)
NOT UPPERCASE

? WORDS
not uppercase
```

As shown from the example, the UPPER function displays characters in the uppercase/lowercase format but does not actually alter the data.

You can use the UPPER function to compare data when you are not sure whether the data was entered as all uppercase or in initial caps only. For example, a command like

```
LIST FOR UPPER(LASTNAME) = "SMITH"
```

would find a record whether the last name was entered as Smith or SMITH.

LOWER

The LOWER function is the reverse of UPPER; it will convert uppercase characters to lowercase characters, as in the following example. As with the UPPER function, the LOWER function does not convert the actual data; it only changes the appearance of the data.

```
STORE "NOT CAPS" TO WORDS
? LOWER(WORDS)
not caps
```

CTOD and DTOC

CTOD and DTOC are the Character-To-Date and Date-To-Character functions, respectively. CTOD converts a string of characters to a value that is recognized as a date by FoxPro. DTOC performs the opposite function, converting a date into a string of characters.

Acceptable characters that can be converted to dates range from 1/1/100 to 12/31/9999. The full century is optional. Usually, you only specify the last two digits of the year, unless the date falls in a century other than the current one. Any character strings having values that fall outside of these values will produce an empty date value if the CTOD function is used.

As an example of the CTOD function, the following command might be used within a program to convert a string of characters to a value that could be stored within a date field:

```
MYEAR = YEAR(DATE())
STORE CTOD("01/01/" + LTRIM(STR(MYEAR))) TO JAN1
```

As an example of the DTOC function, the following command would combine a text string along with a date converted to a text string:

? "The expiration date is: " + DTOC(EXPIREDATE)

DTOS

The DTOS function converts a date to a character string that follows the YYYYMMDD format. For example, the DTOS function would convert a date of 12/03/1986 to the character string, 19861203. This function is very useful when building indexes based on dates, so that any dates spanning multiple years will appear in the correct chronological order. (If you were to use the DTOC function to build the index instead, dates only appear in true chronological order if they all occurred within a single year.) As an example, the command

INDEX ON DTOS(EXPIREDATE) TO BYDAYS

creates an index in chronological order, with records arranged by order of the hire date.

SPACE

The SPACE function creates a string of blank spaces, up to a maximum length of 254 spaces. As an example, the following commands make use of a variable called BLANKS, which contains ten spaces (the variable was created with the SPACE function):

STORE SPACE(10) TO BLANKS
LIST LASTNAME + BLANKS + CITY + BLANKS + STATE

TRIM

The TRIM function removes trailing blanks, or spaces that follow characters, from a character string. You have already used this function in expressions for reports and labels. The expression

TRIM(CITY) + ". " + STATE + " " + ZIPCODE

for example, was used to print the contents of the City and State fields, separated by one space.

The TRIM function also is useful as part of an expression, when displaying information with LIST or DISPLAY, to close large gaps of space that often occur between fields. For example, the commands

```
USE MEMBERS
GO 2
SET PRINT ON
? FIRSTNAME, LASTNAME, ADDRESS
```

result in an unattractive printout that looks like this:

William   Martin   4807 East Avenue

With the TRIM function, the large gaps between the fields can be eliminated, as shown here:

```
USE MEMBERS
GO 2
SET PRINT ON
? TRIM(FIRSTNAME), TRIM(LASTNAME), ADDRESS
```

William Martin 4807 East Avenue

Note that you should *not* use the TRIM function as part of an indexing expression, such as INDEX ON TRIM(LASTNAME) + FIRSTNAME TO NAMES. Such an index would result in variable-length index keys, which can cause problems in searching for data.

LTRIM

The LTRIM function performs an operation similar to that of the TRIM function, but it trims leading spaces (spaces at the start of the expression) rather than trailing spaces. The following example shows the effect of the LTRIM function:

```
STORE "          ten leading spaces here." TO TEXT
? TEXT
          ten leading spaces here.
? LTRIM(TEXT)
ten leading spaces here.
```

STR

The STR function is used to convert a numeric value into a character string. This type of conversion lets you mix numeric values with characters within displays and reports. As an example of the STR function, the command

? "Name is " + LASTNAME + " and limit is " + TAPELIMIT

will produce an "Operator/operand type mismatch" error message, because Tapelimit is a numeric field and the rest of the expression contains character values. The STR function can be used to convert the numeric value into a character value as follows:

? "Name is " + LASTNAME + " and limit is " + STR(TAPELIMIT)

COMMANDS USED IN COMMAND FILES

Some FoxPro commands are often used within command files but are rarely used elsewhere. You will be using command files with increasing regularity through the rest of this book, so these commands deserve a closer look. At the end of this chapter, you will begin using the commands to design a program.

SET TALK

SET TALK ON displays on-screen execution of the commands within a command file. When SET TALK OFF is executed within a command file, visual responses to the FoxPro commands will halt until a SET TALK ON command is encountered. You can use SET TALK OFF to stop the display of messages such as the "% of file indexed" message during indexing or the record number displayed after a GO TO or LOCATE command. When you begin a session with FoxPro, SET TALK is on.

SKIP

The SKIP command moves the record pointer forward or backward. The format of the command is

SKIP [+/−*integer*]

The integer specified with SKIP will move the pointer forward or backward by that number of records. For example, entering **SKIP 4** moves the record pointer forward by four records. Entering **SKIP − 2** moves the record pointer backward by two records. Entering **SKIP** without an expression moves the pointer one record forward.

The values can be stored in a memory variable, which can then be used as part of SKIP. For example, entering **STORE 4 TO JUMP** assigns 4 to JUMP; then the SKIP JUMP command moves the record pointer forward by four records. If you attempt to move the record pointer beyond the end of the file or above the beginning of the file, a "Beginning of file encountered" or an "End of file encountered" error message will result.

RETURN

The RETURN command is used to halt the execution of a command file. When a RETURN command is encountered, FoxPro will leave the program and return to the command level. If the RETURN command is encountered from within a command file that has been called by another command file, FoxPro will return to the command file that called the file containing the RETURN command.

ACCEPT and INPUT

Two FoxPro commands display a string of characters and wait for the user to enter a response that is then stored in a variable. These commands are ACCEPT and INPUT. The ACCEPT command stores characters; the INPUT command stores values of any data type. The format for ACCEPT is

ACCEPT "prompt" TO *variablename*

For INPUT the format is

INPUT "prompt" TO *variablename*

 The order of the commands is the same whether you are dealing with characters or numbers. You enter the command, followed by the question or message that is to appear on the screen (it must be enclosed in single or double quotes), followed by the word "TO," followed by the memory variable you want to store the response in. For example, let's use this format with the ACCEPT statement to store a name in a memory variable. Enter the following:

ACCEPT "What is your last name? " TO LNAME

When you press ENTER, you'll see the message "What is your last name?" appear on the screen. FoxPro is waiting for your response, so enter your last name. When the cursor reappears in the Command window, enter the following:

? LNAME

(The ? command, as you may recall from earlier use, displays the contents of the expression following the question mark.) You'll see that FoxPro has indeed stored your last name as a character string within the memory variable LNAME.

The same operation is used for numbers, but you use the INPUT statement instead. For example, enter

INPUT "How old are you? " TO AGE

and in response to the prompt, enter your age. Next, enter

? AGE

You'll see that the memory variable AGE now contains your response.

COUNT

The COUNT command is used to count the number of occurrences of a condition within a database. One condition might be to count the number of occurrences of the name Robinson in a file, another to find out how many members live in Washington. The general format is

COUNT FOR *condition* TO *variablename*

The condition often takes the form of {*fieldname*} = {*value*}. It can also take the form of {*fieldname*} > {*value*}, or {*fieldname*} > {*value*} .AND. {*fieldname*} < {*value2*}. Or, in the case of logical fields, the condition can simply take the form {*fieldname*}. The value to which you compare the field must be of the same data type as the field. The entire logical expression constitutes the condition. Every condition can eventually be evaluated as true or false.

The number of occurrences of the condition will be stored in *variablename*. The variable can then be used in another part of the program for calculations or for printing. For example, the command

COUNT FOR LASTNAME = "Robinson" TO NAMECOUNT

would count the occurrences of the last name Robinson in the Lastname field of MEMBERS. That count would then be stored as a memory variable, NAMECOUNT. The FOR clause used in this example is optional. You could accomplish the same type of selective counting by setting a filter with the SET FILTER command and then simply entering the COUNT command.

SUM

The SUM command calculates the total for any numeric field. The basic format of the command is

SUM [*scope*] [*fieldlist*] [FOR *condition*] [WHILE *condition*] TO [*variablelist*]

SUM can be used with or without conditions in a number of ways. The scope identifies the magnitude of the summation; that is, if *scope* is absent, all records will be checked; if *scope* is NEXT followed by an integer, then only the specified number of records will be summed, or if *scope* is ALL, all records are summed, which is the same as when no scope is specified. The record pointer is considered to be at the beginning of the current record, so a command like SUM NEXT 5 sums the current record plus the next four records. If *scope* is REST, all records from the current record will be summed. If the clause RECORD <*n*> is used as a scope, only the single record designated by <*n*> will be summed (which is rather ridiculous, since there is nothing to add). The *fieldlist* parameter is a list of the numeric fields to be summed by the SUM command. Entering **SUM** without a field list will cause FoxPro to add and display the totals of all the numeric fields within the database. Note that SUM always displays its results unless SET TALK is off. You may also want to store the results in memory variables so that you can redisplay them later or use them in calculations.

The memory variable list (*variablelist*) assigns the memory variables that the values produced by SUM will be stored in. The SUM TAPELIMIT TO TOTAL command will store the total of the Tapelimit field in a memory variable called TOTAL. SUM TAPELIMIT, HOURLYRATE TO C,D stores the total of the Tapelimit field in variable C and the total of the Hourlyrate field in variable D. SUM TAPELIMIT FOR LASTNAME = "Robinson" TO E would store salary amounts for the name Robinson in variable E.

The WHILE clause, which is optional, is used with indexed files to sum the records while (or as long as) a particular condition is true. For example, in a file indexed by last names, you could find the first occurrence of the name Smith and then use a command like

SUM WHILE LASTNAME = "Smith"

to obtain the sum of any numeric fields for all the persons named Smith. You can use the FOR clause to accomplish the same task, but in a large database, using WHILE is considerably faster.

AVERAGE

The AVERAGE command calculates the average value of a numeric field. The basic format is

AVERAGE [FOR *fieldname*, ...] [WHILE *fieldname=condition*] [TO *variable*, ...]

Here, *fieldname* must be a numeric field (there can be more than one field name). If you include a TO clause, the average of each field named will be stored in variable.

The command AVERAGE TAPELIMIT TO F would store the average value of the Tapelimit field in variable F.

@, ?, ??, and TEXT

Four commands are commonly used to display or print text: @, ?, ??, and TEXT. The ? and ?? commands display a single line of text at a time. If ? is used, a linefeed and carriage return occur before the display. A ?? command does not include a linefeed and carriage return before the display, so the subsequent value is displayed on the current line.

If the ? or ?? command is preceded by a SET PRINT ON command, output is also routed to the printer. An example is shown in the following command file:

```
SET PRINT ON
? "The last name is: "
?? LASTNAME
?
? "The salary per 40-hour week is: "
?? SALARY * 40
SET PRINT OFF
```

You can also add the optional AT clause and a column position to the ? or ?? commands to control where on the line the data appears. For example, the command

```
? "Lastname:" AT 26
```

prints "Lastname:" starting at column 26 on the current line.

For more selective printing or display, the @ command will move the cursor to a specific location on the screen or page and, when combined with SAY, will display the information there. FoxPro divides the screen into 24 rows and 80 columns. The top left coordinate is 0,0, and the bottom right coordinate is 23,79. The general format of the @ command is

@ row,column [SAY *character-string*]

Omitting the SAY clause clears the designated row from the column position to column 79.

To try the use of the @ command, enter

```
CLEAR
@ 12, 20 SAY "This is a display"
```

Using the @ command with the SAY option, you can generate report headings or statements at any required location. Screen formatting with the @ command will be covered in greater detail in Chapter 14.

The TEXT command is useful for displaying large amounts of text. TEXT is commonly used to display operator warnings, menu displays, and notes that appear during various operations of the program. TEXT is followed by the text to be displayed, and then ended with ENDTEXT. The text does not need to be surrounded by quotes. Everything between TEXT and ENDTEXT is displayed. The following example will erase the screen with CLEAR and then display a copyright message:

```
CLEAR
TEXT
****************************************************************
          FoxPro Copyright (C) 1989 Fox Software
Personnel Director Copyright (C) 1987 J Systems, Inc.
For technical support, phone our offices at 555-5555
****************************************************************
ENDTEXT
WAIT
```

In this example, the WAIT command at the end of the program causes FoxPro to display a "press any key" message and pause until the user presses a key.

The TEXT command must be used from within a command file. Any attempt to use TEXT as a direct command will result in an error message.

OVERVIEW OF A PROGRAM DESIGN

How do you start to write a program, and after it is operational, how do you determine whether the program is efficient? Unfortunately, there is no one correct way to write a program or determine when it is efficient or good. However, most programmers have a natural tendency to follow five steps in the design of a program:

1. Defining the problem

2. Designing the program

3. Writing the program

4. Verifying the program

5. Documenting the program

As these steps imply, the process of good programming is more than just writing a series of commands to be used in a particular command file. Programming requires careful planning of the code and rigorous testing afterward.

If you are programming, you are probably building *applications,* which are a group of programs that perform a general task. Designing an application is somewhat similar to the process of designing a database (outlined in Chapter 1) in that careful planning is required. However, because you are designing an application and not a database, you must think about how the application will use information in the source database, how the application will produce reports, and how the application can be designed so that it is easy to use. Once these design steps have been clearly defined, you can proceed to design and create the programs that will make up the application.

Defining the Problem

The first step is to define the problem that the program is intended to solve. This step is too often skipped, even by professional programmers, in the rush to create a program. The problem may be as simple as wanting to automate a task; but in the process of defining it, you should query the people who will be using the program and find out just what they expect the program to do. Even if you will be the only user, you should stop to outline what the program must provide before you begin writing it.

Output Requirements

Output, the information the application must produce, should be considered. Output is often useful in the form of a printed report, so defining what type of output is needed is often similar to the process of defining what is needed in a report. What types of output must the application produce? What responses to queries do the users expect? What must the reports look like? Sample screen displays or reports should be presented to the users for suggestions and approval. This may sound like a time-consuming process (and it often is), but the time saved from unnecessary rewrites of an inadequate program is worth the initial effort.

In the case of Generic Videos, asking the staff to list the kinds of reports they needed revealed two specific output needs. The first is a printed summary report that shows all outstanding rented tapes by state. The second is a way to find and display all of the information about a particular member. You want to be able to display information so that it appears organized and is easy to read and visually pleasing.

Input Requirements

Input, the ways in which the application will facilitate the collection of the data, also should be considered during the problem definition process. How will the information used by the application be entered and manipulated? A logical method for getting all of the information into the computer must be devised, and once the information is in the computer, you'll need efficient ways to change the data. For example, someone must key in all of the information for an inventory that is being placed on the computer system for the first time. It's easy to think, "Why not just use the APPEND command to enter a record, and let personnel type in all the data they might ever need?" Data integrity is the reason against such an approach; if the data-entry screens aren't easy to understand and logically designed, and if verification of the data isn't performed, chances are you'll have a database full of errors. Good design comes from using program control to make the data-entry process clear and straightforward.

Most database applications must encompass two specific input needs. The first is a way to add new records to the database. You will do this by using not only the APPEND command, but also other commands that will make the screen display visually appealing and easy to read. The second is a way to select and edit or delete a particular record in the database. If you outline the output and input requirements of Generic Videos, the list might look like Figure 12-3.

```
Generic Videos
Database System

Output Operations
    1. Print summary report
    2. Display member data
Input Operations
    1. Add new records
    2. Edit existing records
```

FIGURE 12-3. Input and output operations for Generic Videos database system

Accounting Program

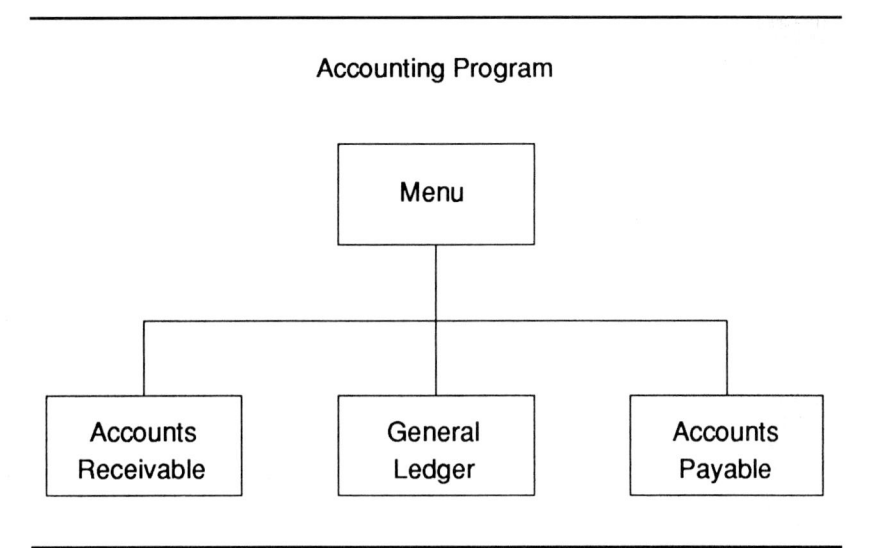

```
                    ┌──────────┐
                    │   Menu   │
                    └──────────┘
         ┌───────────────┼───────────────┐
  ┌──────────┐    ┌──────────┐    ┌──────────┐
  │ Accounts │    │ General  │    │ Accounts │
  │Receivable│    │  Ledger  │    │ Payable  │
  └──────────┘    └──────────┘    └──────────┘
```

FIGURE 12-4. Modules of an accounting program

Designing the Program

Well-designed applications are a collection of smaller programs, often referred to as *modules,* each performing a specific function. For example, a payroll accounting application is thought of as one program, but most such applications consist of at least three smaller modules. One module handles accounts receivable, the process of tracking incoming funds; the second module handles accounts payable, the process of paying the bills; and the third module handles the general ledger, a financial balance sheet that shows the funds on hand (see Figure 12-4).

Small modules help you tackle large programming tasks in small steps, which is an important principle of good program design. Many tasks worth performing with a database management system are too large in scope to be done in one simple operation. An inventory system is an excellent example. At first glance, such a system may appear to be just a way of keeping track of the items on hand in a warehouse. Scratch the surface, though, and you'll find that there are numerous modules in such a system. The first module in the system adds items to the inventory as they are received; a second module subtracts inventory items as they are shipped; a third module monitors inventory levels; and if the quantity of an item falls below a specific point, a fourth module alerts the user by printing a message on the screen. Modules will interact and exchange information with other modules in the system, but they share one pool of information: the database itself. In addition, finding errors in the program is easier if the program is divided into modules, since the problem can be traced to the modules performing the tasks that may be in error.

It is during the design phase that the general and subsidiary functions of the program are outlined in detail. Remember: Any program worth writing is worth outlining on paper. The designer should resist the urge to begin writing programs at the keyboard without first outlining the steps of the program. The outline will help ensure that the intended program design is followed and that no steps are accidentally left out. Outlines are of great help in identifying the smaller tasks to be done by your system.

You'll find that it's best to list the general steps first and then break the general steps into smaller, more precise steps. Let's use the Generic Videos database system as an example. The system should perform these tasks:

1. Allow new members and new rentals to be added

2. Allow existing records to be changed (edited)

3. Display data from a record

4. Produce reports on all rentals or members

This simple outline shows what is basically required of the database management system. You then add more detail to the outline, as in Figure 12-5.

Outline of Program Design

1. Allow new entries to be added—APPEND

2. Change (edit) existing entries
    —Show all record numbers and names on the screen
    —Ask the user for number of the record to edit
    —Edit the selected record

3. Display data regarding a chosen entry
    —Ask the user for name of member
    —Search for that name in the database
    —If name is found, print the information contained in all fields of the record

4. Produce reports of all rentals or all members
    —Use the REPORT FORM *filename* command to produce a report

FIGURE 12-5. Outline of database management system

For purposes of simplicity, a specific requirement for the deleting of records has been omitted from this design. In a complete database system, you would also want to include a specific process for deleting records, as well as for performing file maintenance (such as rebuilding index files and performing a PACK from time to time).

With so much to think about during the process of designing a program, you can easily overlook how the user will use it. Good program design considers users by including menus. Menus provide the user with a simple way of selecting what he or she would like to do. In a way, they are like a road map of the system; they guide the user through the steps in performing a task. For that reason, menus should be easy to follow, and there should always be a way out of a selection if the user changes his or her mind. In addition, the program should not operate abnormally or crash (stop running) in the event that the user makes an error when entering data.

Writing the Program

Now it's time to write the program. Most applications begin with a menu of choices, so the menu module should be written first. Each selection within the menu should then lead to the part of the program that performs the appropriate function. For example, a "Run Report" choice on a menu could result in a REPORT FORM command being issued to print a report. An "Add New Entries" choice could result in an APPEND command that adds data to the database. When you design your own systems, you'll find it helpful to design the menu first and then use it as a starting point for the other modules in the program. In this example, however, you will design the menu module of the program in the next chapter, because it will use various commands that will be explained there.

It often helps, particularly if you are new to designing programs, to use *pseudocode*. Writing pseudocode means writing out all the steps of an operation in English. You write the program in pseudocode and then convert it into actual code. For instance, the process that would allow users to display a list of names and edit a particular name would look like this in pseudocode:

1. Open the MEMBERS database.

2. Clear screen.

3. List all names in the database.

4. Ask user for number of record to be edited, and store that number as a variable.

5. Edit specified record.

6. Return to main menu.

When you know what steps are needed to perform the task, you store the corresponding commands in a command file. As an example, enter

MODIFY COMMAND EDITMEMB

to create a new command file called EDITMEMB.PRG. When the Editor appears, enter the following commands and then press CTRL- W to save the command file:

```
USE MEMBERS
CLEAR
LIST LASTNAME, FIRSTNAME
INPUT "Edit what record? " TO RECNO
CHANGE RECNO
RETURN
```

Verifying the Program

Any errors in the program are corrected during this step. You also examine the program to see if the needs of all the users have indeed been met; if not, you may need to make changes or additions to some modules. In addition, you should now make any improvements that can speed up the system or minimize user confusion.

The best way to find errors in a program is to use the program, so verify the program's operation by entering

DO EDITMEMB

The program will display a list of all member names. The corresponding record numbers will be shown to the left of the names:

Record#	LASTNAME	FIRSTNAME
1	Miller	Karen
2	Martin	William
3	Robinson	Carol
4	Kramer	Harry
5	Moore	Ellen
6	Zachman	David
7	Robinson	Benjamin
8	Hart	Wendy

Edit what record?

The program now asks for the number of the record that you wish to edit. In response to the prompt, enter **8** (for record 8). If the program works as designed, the edit screen for record 8 should appear. Change the phone number for Wendy Hart to 555-3456, and save the change by pressing CTRL-W. (Later, as a convenience for users unfamiliar with FoxPro, you may want to display a message explaining how to save changes.)

You should return to the command level, and for now, that is all that is expected of the program. In later chapters, you'll add commands that will use more attractive designs, like the data-entry screen you created in Chapter 5, to view and edit data.

Documenting the Program

Documentation of a program takes one of two forms: written directions (like a manual) explaining how the program operates, and comments within the program itself about how the program is designed. The use of clear and simple menus and instructions within the program can help minimize the need for written documentation. A few sentences on how to start FoxPro and run the command file that displays the menu may be sufficient. As for directions and remarks within the program, FoxPro lets you put comments, in the form of text, at any location in a command file. Comments are preceded by an asterisk (*) or by the NOTE command. You can also use the double ampersand (&&) to add comments to the right of a command. When FoxPro sees a line beginning with an asterisk or the word "NOTE," no action is taken by the program. And when FoxPro sees a double ampersand at the end of a command line, FoxPro ignores everything that follows it on that line.

Comments are simply an aid to you or any other person who modifies your command files. As an example, this short command file documents the program with NOTE and the asterisk (*):

```
CLEAR
NOTE Display the employees' names
LIST LASTNAME, FIRSTNAME
NOTE Ask for a record number and store it.
INPUT "Edit what record?" TO RECNO
*Edit the record.
EDIT RECNO
RETURN
```

This file may seem to have an overabundance of comments because it does not need elaboration. If a command file consists of dozens of commands, however, comments become more necessary. Not only do they make the program easier to understand, but if any other person must make changes to your FoxPro program, the task will be much easier.

13

PROGRAM CONTROL

Going in Circles
SCAN and ENDSCAN
IF, ELSE, and ENDIF
Using CASE to Evaluate Multiple Choices
EXIT
CANCEL
WAIT
ZAP
Using Programming Macros

Using command files to automate the storing and retrieving of records provides you even more flexibility when you use decision-making conditions to provide control of the program. A program can prompt the user for a response, and the user's response determines what the program does next. To program a condition, you'll need a way to evaluate user responses and, based on those responses, cause FoxPro to perform certain actions. Similarly, a program can read through a database file and perform different actions, depending on the values stored in individual records. In this chapter you'll use the IF, ELSE, ENDIF, DO

WHILE, and ENDDO commands to perform these operations within a program. A number of other commands involved in the control process, such as CANCEL, EXIT, and WAIT, are also covered in this chapter.

GOING IN CIRCLES

There will be many times when your program will need to perform the same task repeatedly. FoxPro has two commands, DO WHILE and ENDDO, that are used as a matched pair to repeat a series of commands for as long as necessary. The commands that you want to repeat are enclosed between the DO WHILE and the ENDDO commands.

The DO WHILE command always begins the loop, and the ENDDO command normally ends it. The series of commands contained within the DO WHILE loop will continue to execute until the condition, specified immediately next to the DO WHILE command, is no longer true. You determine when the loop should stop by specifying the condition; otherwise, the loop could go on indefinitely. The format is

DO WHILE *condition*
        [*commands...*]
ENDDO

As long as the condition within the DO WHILE command is true, the commands between the DO WHILE and the ENDDO commands are executed. Whenever ENDDO is reached, FoxPro returns to the top of the loop and reevaluates the condition. If the condition is true, FoxPro executes the commands within the loop again; if the condition is not true, FoxPro jumps to the command following the ENDDO command. If the condition is false when the DO WHILE command is first encountered, none of the commands in the loop are executed, and the program proceeds to the first command that follows the ENDDO command.

You could use the DO WHILE and ENDDO commands in a command file that will print the names and addresses in the Generic Videos database with triple line spacing between them. Get to the command level and open a command file. Name it TRIPLE by entering

MODIFY COMMAND TRIPLE

When the FoxPro Editor comes up, you should enter the following command file

```
SET TALK OFF
USE MEMBERS
SET PRINT ON
DO WHILE .NOT. EOF()
    ? FIRSTNAME + LASTNAME
    ? ADDRESS
    ? CITY + STATE + " " + ZIPCODE
    ?
    ?
    ?
    SKIP
ENDDO
? "Triple report completed."
SET PRINT OFF
EJECT
```

Before you save this command file, take a brief look at its design. After such preliminaries as activating the MEMBERS file and routing the output to the printer, the program begins the DO WHILE loop. The condition for DO WHILE is .NOT. EOF(), which simply means, "As long as the end of the file—EOF()—is not reached, continue the DO WHILE loop." The first three statements in the loop print the name and address from the current record. The next three question marks print the three blank lines between each name and address. SKIP moves the pointer down a record each time the body of the DO WHILE loop is executed. If this command were absent, the pointer would never reach the end of the file, the condition would never be false, and the program would never leave the loop. The ENDDO command is then reached, so FoxPro returns to the DO WHILE statement to evaluate the condition. If the pointer hasn't reached the end of file, the loop is repeated. Once the end of file has been reached, FoxPro proceeds past the ENDDO command. The final two commands in the program are executed, and you are returned to the command level.

Indenting the commands between DO WHILE and ENDDO will help you identify the body of the loop. This is especially helpful if you have *nested* DO WHILE loops—a DO WHILE loop within a DO WHILE loop.

After entering the commands in the file, press CTRL-W to save the command file to disk; then make sure your printer is on, and enter **DO TRIPLE**. The command file will print the names and addresses, triple line spacing each, on your printer.

SCAN AND ENDSCAN

Another set of commands you may encounter in working with FoxPro programs are the SCAN and ENDSCAN commands. These commands, like DO WHILE and ENDDO, are a matched pair. Also like DO WHILE and ENDDO, the SCAN and ENDSCAN commands let you create a repetitive loop in which operations are performed for a group of records in a database. The syntax for these commands is

SCAN [*scope*] [FOR *condition*] [WHILE *condition*]
    [*commands...*]
ENDSCAN

The SCAN and ENDSCAN commands are simpler alternatives to the DO WHILE and ENDDO commands. If you simply wish to use DO WHILE and ENDDO to perform repetitive processing, you can often use SCAN and ENDSCAN instead, and use slightly fewer lines of programming code.

As an example, perhaps you wanted to write a program that, using a DO WHILE loop, would print the name and tape limit for every person in the database who has a tape limit of more than three. You could accomplish the task with a program like this:

```
USE MEMBERS
SET PRINT ON
DO WHILE .NOT. EOF()
      IF TAPELIMIT > 3
          ? LASTNAME, FIRSTNAME
          ?? TAPELIMIT
      ENDIF
      SKIP
ENDDO
```

By comparison, you could use the SCAN and ENDSCAN commands to accomplish the same task. An example of the program code using SCAN and ENDSCAN is shown here:

```
USE MEMBERS
SET PRINT ON
SCAN FOR TAPELIMIT > 3
      ? LASTNAME, FIRSTNAME
      ?? TAPELIMIT
ENDSCAN
```

Because you combined FOR and WHILE clauses with the SCAN command to specify the condition (a tape limit greater than three), the IF and ENDIF conditions are not needed, so fewer lines of program code accomplish the same task.

FoxPro automatically skips to the next successive record when it encounters ENDSCAN unless you are at the end of the file. Once the end of the file is reached, program control drops out of the loop and moves on to the next command. Note that program control may exit from the loop before the end of the file is reached if you include a WHILE clause as a part of the SCAN statement.

IF, ELSE, AND ENDIF

In many command files, FoxPro will need to perform different operations depending on a user's response to an option, a previous calculation or operation, or different values encountered in a database. For example, if the user has a choice of editing or printing a record in a main menu, the program must be able to perform the chosen operation. FoxPro uses the IF, ELSE, and ENDIF commands to branch to the part of the program where the chosen operation is performed. Much like the DO WHILE- ENDDO loop, the IF and ENDIF commands are used as a matched pair enclosing a number of commands. The ELSE command is optional and is used within the body of IF-ENDIF as another decision step. The IF command along with the ENDIF command can be used to decide between actions in a program.

The format of the command is

IF *condition*
    [*commands...*]
ELSE
    [*commands...*]
ENDIF

This decision-making command must always start with IF and end with ENDIF. The commands that you place between the IF and

ENDIF commands determine exactly what will occur if the condition is true, unless an ELSE is encountered. (Again, indenting the commands within the body of IF-ENDIF will made the flow of the program easier to follow.) If an ELSE is encountered and the condition specified by ELSE is true, the commands that follow ELSE are carried out.

A good way to write IF and ELSE commands is to write them in pseudocode first and then compare them:

Pseudocode	FoxPro
If last name is Cooke, then display last name.	IF LASTNAME = "Cooke" ? LASTNAME ENDIF
If monthly rent is less than $300, then display "Reasonably priced."	IF RENTMONTH < 300 ? "Reasonably priced" ENDIF

Using IF and ENDIF alone will work fine for making a single decision, but if you wish to add an alternative choice, you'll need the ELSE statement:

Pseudocode	FoxPro

If last name is Cooke, then print last name; or else print "There is no one by that name in this database."	IF LASTNAME = "Cooke"
	   ? LASTNAME
	ELSE
	   ? "There is no one by that name in this database."
	ENDIF

FoxPro will evaluate the condition following the IF command to see if any action should be taken. If no action is necessary, FoxPro will simply move on to the next command after the ENDIF command. In this example if SALARY is not 10, the STORE command will not be executed and FoxPro will proceed to the command following ENDIF:

```
IF SALARY = 10
      STORE SALARY TO MATCH
ENDIF
```

You can also use multiple IF-ENDIF commands if you need to have the program make more than one decision. Consider this example:

```
? "Enter 1 to print mailing labels or 2 to edit."
INPUT "What is your choice?" TO CHOICE
IF CHOICE = 1
      DO TRIPLE
ENDIF
IF CHOICE = 2
       DO CHANGES
ENDIF
```

The answer that the user types will be stored in a variable called CHOICE. One of three things can happen then, depending on the user's types a 1 or a 2 in response to the question. If CHOICE equals 1, the TRIPLE program will be run from disk. If CHOICE equals 2, the CHANGES program will be run. If CHOICE does not equal 1 or 2, the program will proceed to the next command after the ENDIF command.

Nesting IF-ENDIFs

You can use nested IF-ENDIF statements, which are IF-ENDIF statements placed inside of other IF-ENDIF statements. For the innermost IF-ENDIF statement to be processed, the condition tested by the outermost IF-ENDIF statement must be true. The following demonstrates an example of a nested IF-ENDIF statement:

```
INPUT "Display report on (S)creen or (P)rinter?" TO ANS
IF UPPER(ANS) = "P"
     INPUT "Ready printer, press Enter, or type C then;
     press ENTER to cancel report." TO ANS2
     IF UPPER(ANS2) = "C"
          *user cancelled print run.
          RETURN
     ENDIF
     REPORT FORM MEMBERS TO PRINT
     EJECT
ENDIF
```

In this example, whether the innermost IF-ENDIF is ever processed is determined by the response supplied to the outermost IF-ENDIF statement. If the user does not type P for printer, dBASE skips ahead to the outermost ENDIF statement. If the user does respond with P for printer, dBASE displays the "Ready printer" message, and the innermost IF-ENDIF tests for a response and takes appropriate action.

The Immediate IF Function

Within programs, you may want to make use of the IIF (Immediate IF) function, detailed in Chapter 10. The syntax for the function is

IIF(*condition, expression1, expression2*)

If the condition specified is true, FoxPro returns the first expression; if the condition is false, FoxPro returns the second expression. As an example, the statement

CREDITOK = IIF(INCOME>=15000, "yes", "no")

would, when processed in a program, store a character expression of "yes" to the CREDITOK variable if the amount in INCOME was equal to or greater than 15,000. In effect, this statement performs the same task as the following commands:

```
IF INCOME >= 15000
     CREDITOK = "yes"
ELSE
     CREDITOK = "no"
ENDIF
```

The advantage of the Immediate IF function is that it takes less lines of code to accomplish the same task, and it is executed slightly faster.

You can use the IF-ENDIF statement in a command file to search for and display the data regarding a specific entry in the database. If you want to find a member named Zachman, you can use the ACCEPT and IF-ENDIF commands to search for the record. (This operation can be done faster with SEEK, but for demonstration purposes, a combination of IF and DO WHILE will be used here.)

First let's use pseudocode to outline what needs to be done:

USE MEMBERS database

ACCEPT the last name

BEGIN the DO-WHILE loop

IF the Lastname field = the ACCEPT variable;

PRINT (on the screen) name, address, tape limit, and expiration date

END the IF test

SKIP forward one record

END the DO-WHILE loop

RETURN to the command level

Now create a command file by entering

MODIFY COMMAND SHOWMEMB

When the FoxPro Editor appears, enter the following command file:

```
*This program finds and shows data in the members file.
USE MEMBERS
SET TALK OFF
CLEAR
*Begin loop that contains commands to display record.
ACCEPT "Search for what last name? " TO SNAME
```

```
DO WHILE .NOT. EOF()
     IF LASTNAME = SNAME
          ? "Last name is: "
          ?? LASTNAME
          ? "First name is: "
          ?? FIRSTNAME
          ? "Address is: "
          ?? ADDRESS
          ? CITY + STATE + " " + ZIPCODE
          ?
          ? "Tape limit is: "
          ?? TAPELIMIT
          ? "Expiration Date is: "
          ?? EXPIREDATE
          ?
     ENDIF
     SKIP
ENDDO
WAIT
RETURN
```

After saving the file with CTRL-W, try the program by entering **DO SHOWMEMB**. In response to the last-name prompt that appears on the screen, enter **Zachman**, and FoxPro will search the database for the record containing Zachman. Run the program again and enter **Robinson**. You will see both records for the two Robinsons displayed.

In this search you used the ACCEPT, IF, and ENDIF commands. The ACCEPT command stored the name that you entered into the memory variable SNAME. The IF loop began a decision-making process that stated the condition, "If the memory variable SNAME contains the same name as the Lastname field, then execute the commands that follow the IF command."

There is no limit to the number of commands that you can place between IF and ENDIF in the loop. You can also link multiple IF-ENDIF and ELSE commands if multiple choices are needed within a program.

USING CASE TO EVALUATE MULTIPLE CHOICES

Your program may need to make more than two or three decisions from a single response. A series of IF-ENDIF statements could do the job, but using more than three IF-ENDIFs to test the value of one field or memory variable is unwieldy. There is an easier way: the CASE statement. With the CASE statement, the IF-ENDIF tests are made into cases, and FoxPro then chooses the first case, the second case, or another case.

The CASE statement is a matched pair of DO CASE and ENDCASE. All choices are declared between DO CASE and ENDCASE. OTHERWISE is treated exactly like the ELSE in an IF-ENDIF statement. The general format is

```
DO CASE
    CASE condition
    [commands...]
    [CASE condition...]
    [commands...]
    [OTHERWISE]
    [commands...]
ENDCASE
```

Whenever FoxPro encounters a DO CASE command, it will examine each case until it finds a condition that is true; then it will execute the commands below CASE until it encounters the next CASE statement or ENDCASE, whichever comes first.

If you want to create a menu that offers to display a record, print labels, edit a record, or add a record, you could create a command file like this:

```
CLEAR
? "1. Display a membership record"
?
? "2. Print the membership database"
?
? "3. Change a membership record"
?
INPUT "Choose a selection " TO SELECT
DO CASE
     CASE SELECT = 1
          DO SHOWMEMB
     CASE SELECT = 2
          DO TRIPLE
     CASE SELECT = 3
          DO EDITMEMB
ENDCASE
```

In this example, FoxPro will query the user for a selection with the INPUT statement (the SHOWMEMB file for the first selection was created in the last chapter). When the user enters the choice, it is stored in the SELECT variable. Then, in the DO CASE series, FoxPro examines the SELECT variable for each CASE until it finds one that matches the value of SELECT. Once a match has been found, no other CASE statement will be evaluated. If no match is found, FoxPro proceeds to the next statement after the ENDCASE command. Like IF-ENDIF, the DO CASE and END-CASE commands are used in pairs. You must always end a CASE series with an ENDCASE command.

You should use DO CASE to process menu selections if you have more than three choices. For example, if you wanted to offer the same three selections from the last program using IF-ENDIF and ELSE, the command file might look like this:

```
CLEAR
? "1. Display a membership record"
?
? "2. Print the membership database"
?
? "3. Change a membership record"
?
INPUT "Choose a selection" TO SELECT
IF SELECT = 1
     DO SHOWMEMB
ENDIF
IF SELECT = 2
     DO TRIPLE
ENDIF
IF SELECT = 3
     DO EDITMEMB
ENDIF
```

Using IF-ENDIF is more complex than DO CASE as the number of choices increases.

Let's use a CASE statement to create a main menu for the users of the Generic Videos database. Enter **MODIFY COMMAND MENU1**, and when the FoxPro Editor appears enter the following command file:

```
USE MEMBERS
SET TALK OFF
STORE 0 TO CHOICE
DO WHILE CHOICE < > 5
 CLEAR
 * Display the menu.
 ? "Generic Videos Membership System Menu"
 ?
```

```
? " 1. Add a new entry to the database."
? " 2. Change an existing entry."
? " 3. Produce the membership report."
? " 4. Display data regarding a particular member."
? " 5. Exit this program."
INPUT "Enter selection: " TO CHOICE
DO CASE
        CASE CHOICE=1
            APPEND
        CASE CHOICE=2
            DO EDITMEMB
        CASE CHOICE=3
            REPORT FORM SAMPLE
        CASE CHOICE=4
            DO SHOWMEMB
        CASE CHOICE=5
            CLOSE DATABASES
            SET TALK ON
            RETURN
    ENDCASE
ENDDO
```

There are five choices, and the INPUT command stores the response in the corresponding CHOICE variable. When FoxPro finds a matching choice, it executes the command or commands that follow that choice.

Save this command file by pressing CTRL-W. When the prompt reappears, enter **DO MENU1**. Try some of the menu choices on your own to see how the system operates.

EXIT

The EXIT command is used when you are within a DO WHILE programming loop. EXIT lets FoxPro exit from a DO WHILE-ENDDO loop to the first command below ENDDO. An EXIT command arbitrarily placed within a DO WHILE loop will prevent FoxPro from ever reaching the commands below EXIT to

ENDDO; thus, EXIT only makes sense if it is executed conditionally. For this reason, you will frequently find EXIT commands with IF-ENDIF and CASE statements.

Consider the following example, in a program that lists a name based on a desired address. The same task could be done with a LOCATE command, but to demonstrate the EXIT command this program uses a DO WHILE loop.

```
USE MEMBERS
SET TALK OFF
GO TOP
ACCEPT "What is the address- " TO CHOICE
DO WHILE .NOT. EOF()
        IF ADDRESS = CHOICE
                ? LASTNAME, FIRSTNAME
                EXIT
        ENDIF
        SKIP
ENDDO
```

If the contents of Address, a field, match CHOICE, a variable, the EXIT command will cause the DO WHILE loop to terminate. If no match is found, the commands below the IF statement will be executed and finally will drop from the loop when the last record is accessed.

Use EXIT commands conservatively: a program that is always jumping out of loops—and around the program, for that matter—is difficult to follow and debug and is contrary to good program design. Most DO WHILEs that have EXITs can be redesigned without them.

CANCEL

The CANCEL command will exit a FoxPro command file and return you to the command level. It can be useful when you are testing various commands and program files. However, using CANCEL in a completed FoxPro program may be unwise. CANCEL will drop the user at the command level, and the inexperienced user may not know how to exit FoxPro to DOS or return to the program. QUIT is used more often to exit programs and return to the DOS prompt. You can add a selection at the main menu that allows the user to get out of FoxPro and back to the computer's operating system when the work is completed.

WAIT

The WAIT command halts execution of a FoxPro program until a key is pressed. WAIT can also display a message or prompt and store the value of the key pressed as a character variable. The normal format of the command is

WAIT [*prompt*] [TO *memory-variable*]

Both the prompt and the memory-variable are optional. If a prompt is not specified, FoxPro supplies the message "Press any key to continue..." as a default prompt. As an example, to display a message halt execution of a program until a key is pressed, and store that key as a variable named ANSWER. You could use the following command:

WAIT "Enter Y to begin processing transactions, any other key to continue:" TO ANSWER

You could then use an IF-ELSE-ENDIF structure to test the value of ANSWER and take different actions depending on the result.

ZAP

The ZAP command is a one-step command for erasing all records from a database while leaving the structure of the database intact. Using ZAP is functionally equivalent to entering **DELETE ALL** and then entering **PACK**. However, ZAP operates considerably faster than a DELETE ALL command followed by a PACK command.

If you include ZAP in a program, you may want to include a SET SAFETY OFF command near the start of the program; this tells FoxPro not to ask for confirmation before erasing all records from the file.

USING PROGRAMMING MACROS

FoxPro has a handy macro-substitution function. It is used specifically within programs and is not to be confused with the types of macros covered in Chapter 9. Macro substitution works like this: an ampersand (&) is placed in front of a memory variable name, and the combination of ampersand and variable name becomes the FoxPro macro. Then, whenever FoxPro sees the macro, it replaces it with the contents of the memory variable.

If, for example, you had a memory variable called NAME, you could store names of people in variables at different times during a program. When you prefix NAME with an ampersand (&), it becomes a macro. Each time FoxPro encounters &NAME, it references the value of &NAME instead of the name of the variable. Try a macro operation by entering the following commands from the command level:

```
USE MEMBERS
INDEX ON LASTNAME TO NAME
STORE "Zachman" TO TEST
FIND &TEST
DISPLAY
```

Commands that use literal values require macros if they are to treat the value as a variable. One such command is FIND. With the FIND command, you are normally required to enter the literal value, or the actual name of the item to be found. With the macro function, however, you are able to substitute a variable for the actual name. In the example just shown, you could have easily specified the contents of the variable instead of creating the variable to use as a macro; using macros saves time in programming, since the variable will probably have been declared.

You can use macro substitution in response to a user's query to search a database selectively for information, and once you have found the item you can edit or delete it. An example of these techniques will be used in a routine for editing records discussed in the following chapter.

14

PROGRAMMING FOR DATA ENTRY AND EDITING

Putting Information on the Screen
Customizing a Data-Entry Screen
Using Format Files
Using Windows
Designing Light-Bar Menus with @-PROMPT and MENU TO
Editing Records Under Program Control
Data Entry and Editing with Memory Variables
Deleting Records Under Program Control
Helpful Hints on Screen Design

FoxPro can help you design screen displays that won't confuse the people who use your database management system. The appearance of screen displays may at first seem like a minor point of importance, but if you were a new FoxPro system user, which

Generic Video Membership System
1. Add new entries
2. Change an entry
3. Print reports
4. Display member data
5. Exit system

Generic Videos Membership Data System
Add Members
Edit Members
Print Reports
Display Member Data
Exit System

FIGURE 14-1. Two screen displays

of the following two screen displays would be easier to use: the top screen in Figure 14-1 or the bottom screen? Obviously, the bottom screen will make more sense to the novice FoxPro user; it is clearer and less cluttered than the top screen.

As you will see in this chapter, you can easily create well-designed screens by storing various screen-display commands within a FoxPro command file. You'll use the @ command and the SAY and GET options to place prompts and information at selected locations on the screen, and the READ option to allow responses to the prompts displayed by the system. You can use the PROMPT and MENU TO commands to create, with relative ease, pop-up menus similar to those used by FoxPro. You'll also examine how the forms design screen can provide most of the commands needed for the formatting of screens.

PUTTING INFORMATION ON THE SCREEN

The @ command (commonly referred to as the "AT" command) tells FoxPro where to place the cursor on the screen. The FoxPro screen is divided into 25 lines and 80 columns as shown in Figure 14-2. Rows are numbered from 0 to 24, and columns are numbered

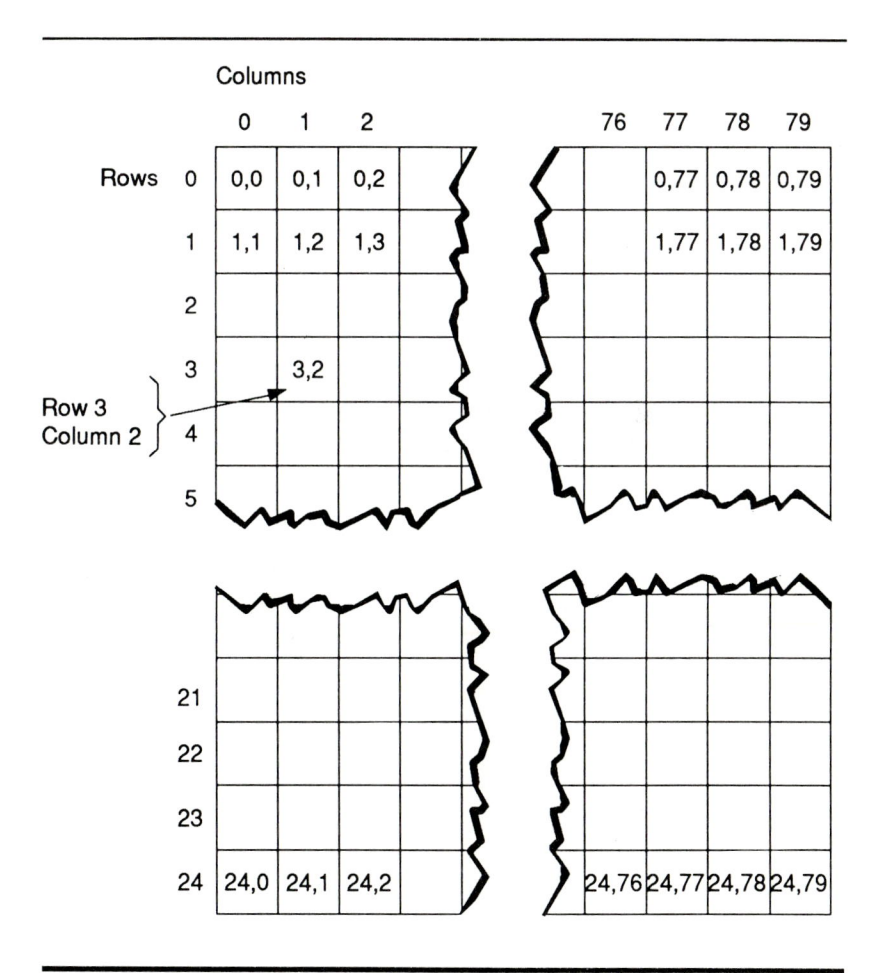

FIGURE 14-2. FoxPro screen

from 0 to 79. Row 0, column 0 is in the upper-left corner of the screen; row 24, column 79 is in the lower-right corner. The cursor can be placed in any screen position.

Once the cursor has been placed in the proper position with the @ command, you can print a message with the SAY option. The SAY option causes the text or the contents of a string variable that follows the command to appear on the screen. The SAY option can be used, along with the @ command, in one of these two possible ways:

@ *row,column* SAY *"message"*
@ *row,column* SAY *varname*

In the first format, SAY is followed by one or more characters, which must be enclosed by double or single quotes. (You should use double quotes whenever there is an apostrophe in the message itself.) The characters will be displayed on the screen exactly as they appear between the quotes. In the second format, *varname* is a variable name. Any value that your program stores in that variable will be displayed.

To try the first format, let's display a message beginning at row 12, column 40 on the screen. Get to the command level, and then enter

CLEAR
@ 12,40 SAY "Enter name."

This displays the prompt "Enter name." beginning at row 12, column 40 on the screen.

You can try the second format by entering this:

STORE 1200.57 TO AMOUNT
@ 6,30 SAY AMOUNT

This stores 1200.57 in the AMOUNT variable and then displays the value at row 6, column 30.

Keep in mind when you use the @ command and SAY option to design screen displays that the coordinates for the edges of the screen may or may not actually be displayed at your screen's edges. Some monitors cut off the edges, so to be safe you may want to stay away from the outer edges of the screen.

You can erase any part of the screen with the @ command and CLEAR option. The format is

@ *row,column* CLEAR

The screen beginning at *row,column* will be erased to the lower-right corner. You use the @ command and CLEAR option in a manner similar to the @ command and SAY option, but don't enter any prompts or variables after the word "CLEAR." For example, the command

@ 9,7 CLEAR

would erase the screen beginning at 9,7 to the lower-right corner.

Using GET and READ With @ and SAY

Now that you know how to display information at selected places on the screen, you need a way to store responses to screen prompts. This is done with the GET and READ options, which in combination display existing variables or field names and the field length of the record being referenced by the pointer, and store the typed replies to screen messages and prompts. There are two formats:

@ *row,column* SAY "*prompt*" GET *varname*... READ
@ *row,column* SAY "*prompt*" GET *fieldname*... READ

The GET option tells FoxPro to get ready to accept information. The information displayed with GET can be either an existing memory variable or any field in the database in use. The READ option then tells FoxPro to enter Edit mode, which, much like Append mode, allows the user to move the cursor around the screen; to accept responses from the keyboard for any of the preceding GET options; and to store the responses in memory. In addition, the READ option lets you edit the displayed information. A READ command applies to all GET statements between the READ option any any previous use of the READ option, or the start of the program, whichever is closest.

A GET option does not have to be immediately followed by a READ option; it can be the last command in a series of GET statements. But if you use GET without READ, you cannot enter any responses from the keyboard. READ options are only used following GET options.

You could, for example, create a command file like this one:

```
@ 5,10 SAY "Enter name." GET LASTNAME
@ 7,10 SAY "Enter address." GET ADDRESS
@ 9,10 SAY "Enter city." GET CITY
@ 11,10 SAY "Enter state." GET STATE
READ
```

If you were to use the database containing the field names and run this command file, FoxPro would provide a screen display that would prompt you for the desired information. The prompts would appear at the screen locations identified by the @ command and SAY option. Once the READ option was encountered, full-screen Edit mode would be entered, and the cursor would be placed at the start of the first area identified by a GET option. As data is entered, FoxPro stores all of the entries in memory under the field names or variable names used. The name would be stored in Lastname, the address in Address, the city in City, and so on. Once a READ occurs, data entered under the field names is written to the database file itself.

You could also use the INPUT command along with a prompt to place information on the screen and store a response, but with INPUT, it is not easy to specify where on the screen the information appears. The example that follows will combine the use of the @ command and the SAY, GET, and READ options along with the PROMPT and MENU TO commands to produce a clear, well-designed menu screen.

Working with Memo Fields

Although you can use the name of a memo field along with the @-SAY-GET commands like those just shown, you will probably want to take advantage of better ways to enter and edit data in memo fields. If you include a memo field in a command file, as in

@ 12, 5 SAY "Preferences? " GET PREFERENCE

the field will appear in a small box containing the word "memo," and you will have to use the same editing techniques discussed earlier to enter and exit the memo field. If you instead make use of the MODIFY MEMO command, you can automatically open a window for the editing of a memo field. The syntax for the command is

MODIFY MEMO *field1* [,*field2*...] [NOWAIT]

When processed in a program, the command will automatically open a window for each of the named memo fields. The contents of the memo field for the current record will appear in the window, and the window(s) remain open until closed with the usual methods for closing windows.

The MODIFY MEMO command can be entered from the command level or within a program to modify the contents of a memo field; the NOWAIT option is used only within programs. Normally, a program halts while the window is open and continues when the window is closed. You can add the NOWAIT option to tell FoxPro to open the window and continue execution of the program.

In the case of the MEMBERS database, a program specifically designed to edit the contents of the Preference field might resemble the following:

```
*EditMemo.PRG edits memo field.
USE MEMBERS
INPUT "Which record number? " TO FINDIT
GOTO FINDIT
CLEAR
@ 22, 5 SAY "Member: " + TRIM(FIRSTNAME) + " " + LASTNAME
MODIFY MEMO PREFERENCE
RETURN
```

Your programs will probably use a more detailed method to search for the desired record, but this simple example demonstrates the use of the MODIFY MEMO command. Once the desired record number has been entered, the member name appears near the bottom of the screen and the memo field opens within a window. Editing of the memo field can be performed, and the window can be moved or resized as desired. When the window is closed, the RETURN statement in the program exits this routine.

CUSTOMIZING A DATA-ENTRY SCREEN

One area of the system that could stand improvement is in the adding of data. Currently, the system relies on the APPEND command. With the @ command and the SAY, GET, and READ options, you can display the prompts more neatly than you could with the APPEND command, and you can store the data in the fields of the database.

Let's create a new command file called ADDER that will be used whenever you want to add a record to the database. Enter **MODIFY COMMAND ADDER**, and enter the following as the command file:

```
USE MEMBERS
CLEAR
APPEND BLANK
@ 1,0 SAY "      Social Sec."  GET SOCIAL
@ 2,0 SAY "       Lastname:"   GET LASTNAME
@ 3,0 SAY "      Firstname:"   GET FIRSTNAME
@ 4,0 SAY "        Address:"   GET ADDRESS
@ 5,0 SAY "           City:"   GET CITY
@ 6,0 SAY "          State:"   GET STATE
@ 7,0 SAY "       ZIP Code:"   GET ZIPCODE
@ 8,0 SAY "      Telephone:"   GET PHONE
@ 9,0 SAY "     Birth date:"   GET BIRTHDAY
@ 10,0 SAY " Expiration Date:" GET EXPIREDATE
@ 11,0 SAY "     Tape limit:"  GET TAPELIMIT
@ 12,0 SAY "          Beta?:"  GET BETA
READ
MODIFY MEMO PREFERENCE
RETURN
```

Examine this command file before saving it. After opening the file with USE and clearing the screen, you then use the BLANK option of the APPEND command. Whenever FoxPro sees APPEND BLANK as a command, it adds a blank record to the end of the database, and the record pointer is positioned at the last record. Each @ command and SAY option prints a query, such as "Birth Date:". The GET option not only displays the contents of each field listed, but it displays them in reverse video in the dimensions of the field width. Since the record pointer is referencing the last record, which is empty, only the reverse video will be displayed. The READ command toward the bottom of the file activates the full-screen entry and editing specified by the GET options. When data entry or editing has been completed for the last field, you return to the main menu section of the program.

Press CTRL-W to save the command file. Now you'll need to make one change in the main-menu command file to integrate the new ADDER command file into the system. Enter **MODIFY COMMAND MENU1** to change the program. Delete the USE MEMBERS line directly underneath CASE CHOICE = 1, and change APPEND in the command file to **DO ADDER**. Then, press CTRL-W to save the file.

Try out the new command file by entering **DO MENU1**. Choose the first option on the menu, and try entering a new member of your own choosing.

Using PICTURE

The PICTURE option is used with the @ command to format data. Using PICTURE, you can display dollar amounts with both commas and decimal places, or you can display dates in American or European date formats. PICTURE restricts the way data can be entered into the system. You can accept numbers only, for dollar amounts, or a date only, rejecting any other characters.

The PICTURE option is divided into function and template symbols (see Table 14-1). The format is

@ *row,column* SAY *expression* PICTURE *"clause"*

You use the PICTURE option by adding the word "PICTURE" and then the letters or symbols that specify the function or template. The functions or templates in the clause are surrounded by quotes. An @ symbol must appear as the first character in a function.

Symbol	Meaning
	FUNCTIONS
A	Displays alphabetic characters only
B	Left-justifies numeric data
C	Displays "CR" for credit, after a positive number
D	Displays American date format
E	Displays European date format
X	Displays "DB" for debit, after a negative number
Z	Displays any zeros as blanks
!	Displays capital letters only
(	Surrounds negative numbers with parentheses
	TEMPLATES
9	Allows only digits for character data, or digits and signs for numeric data
#	Allows only digits, blanks, and signs
A	Allows only letters
L	Allows only logical data (.T. or .F.; .Y. or .N.)
N	Allows only letters and digits
X	Allows any characters
!	Converts letters to uppercase
$	Displays dollar signs in place of leading zeros
*	Displays asterisks in place of leading zeros
.	Specifies a decimal position
,	Displays a comma if there are any numbers to the left of the comma

TABLE 14-1. Functions and Templates Used with PICTURE

Two examples of the PICTURE option are shown here:

@ 12,40 SAY "Enter effective date-" GET PICTURE "@E"
@ 14,20 SAY "Customer name is: "LASTNAME PICTURE"!!!!!!!!!!!!!!!"

In the first example, the @ symbol after the word "PICTURE" defines the clause as a function. The letter "E" defines the function as European date format. A template is used in the second example.

The exclamation points in the template will result in a display of uppercase letters, regardless of how the letters were stored in the database.

Some of the functions used with PICTURE apply only to certain kinds of data. The C, X, B, (, and Z functions apply only to numeric data. The @ and ! functions apply to character data only, but the D and E functions apply to date, character, and numeric data.

You can combine function symbols for multiple functions. For example, the function symbols BZ align numeric data at the left side of the field and display any zero values as blanks.

You can get a better idea of how the PICTURE option is used if you try a few examples. First let's try the X and C functions. The X function will display "DB," for debit, after a negative number, and the C function will display "CR," for credit, after a positive number. Try the following commands to illustrate these functions:

```
CLEAR
STORE -1650.32 TO A
STORE 795 TO B
@5,0 SAY A PICTURE "@X"
@10,0 SAY B PICTURE "@C"
```

The results are as follows:

1650.32 DB

795 CR

This is useful in accounting.

The ! template is useful when you want character displays to appear in all uppercase letters. Try this:

```
CLEAR
STORE "small words" TO WORDS
@10,10 SAY WORDS PICTURE "@!"
```

The # template reserves space for digits, blanks, or signs, and the comma template specifies where the comma should appear in numeric data. Try these templates with the following example:

STORE 1234.56 TO A
@16,0 SAY A PICTURE "#,###.##"

1,234.56

When you are using templates, you must use a symbol for each character that is to be displayed with SAY or GET. To display a character field that is ten characters wide in uppercase, for example, you would need ten exclamation points in the template. The template would look like this:

@20,10 SAY "Name is--"+NAME PICTURE "!!!!!!!!!!"

Let's try a PICTURE option in the command file for adding a record. Enter **MODIFY COMMAND ADDER**. Change the line of the program that reads

@ 1,0 SAY "Social Sec.: " GET SOCIAL

to this:

@ 1,0 SAY "Social Sec.: " GET SOCIAL PICTURE "999-99-9999"

Note the use of the hyphens in this example. Any characters that are not valid template symbols will be displayed as literal data; hence, they are called "literals." In this picture template, the hyphens are literals, while the 9's are valid template symbols.

Save the program with CTRL-W, and then run the system with **DO MENU1**. Choose the "Add new entries" option and enter another record. You'll see the new format caused by the PICTURE specification as you enter the social security number; the hyphens will automatically be added. You can get out of the system without making changes to the database by pressing the ESC key and then choosing the Exit System option to return to the command level.

Note that when you use functions and templates along with a GET command, as you did in this example, the data is stored in the specified format, and is not just displayed that way (as with the SAY command). The use of functions and templates along with GET commands can be very useful for forcing data entries into uppercase.

USING FORMAT FILES

Let's say that you wanted to enter only last names, first names, and membership expiration dates without being required to step through all of the other fields that normally appear on the screen—addresses, phone numbers, birth dates, and so on. You can limit the amount of information shown on a screen in either Append mode or Change mode by using a *format file*. A format file is a special file with the extension .FMT that contains an @ command and SAY and GET options that will display messages and prompts according to your arrangements. Once you have created the format file, you can implement it with the SET FORMAT TO command. For an example, create a format file with the Editor by entering

MODIFY COMMAND QUICKIE.FMT

This will create a file called QUICKIE with the format extension .FMT. Now enter the following commands:

@ 10,10 SAY "The last name is: " GET LASTNAME
@ 12,10 SAY "The first name is: " GET FIRSTNAME
@ 14,10 SAY "The expiration date is: " GET EXPIREDATE

Press CTRL-W to save the format file. When the prompt reappears, enter

USE MEMBERS
GO TOP
CHANGE

Notice that what you see is the normal editing screen with all of its fields. Press ESC to get back to the command level.

To use the format file, you must use the SET FORMAT TO *filename* command (you don't have to supply the .FMT extension). Enter

SET FORMAT TO QUICKIE

Now enter **APPEND**. With the new format file in effect, only the specified fields are shown. Press ESC to leave APPEND without making changes.

Now enter **GOTO 5**. This will move the pointer to record 5. Enter **CHANGE**. Instead of the normal editing screen, you get just those fields specified in the format file that apply to record 5. Press ESC to get out of Edit mode without making any changes. To disable a format file when you finish using it, simply enter **CLOSE FORMAT** without specifying a filename (because only one format file may be opened at a time).

Format files can come in handy when you want to use the same screen format many times in different parts of a program. You can include SET FORMAT TO *filename* anywhere in a FoxPro command file, and the resulting format file will take effect for any appending or editing until you use CLOSE FORMAT.

An Easier Way

Now that you've learned how to write @-SAY-GET commands to place information on the screen and prompt the user for a response, let's consider why you shouldn't bother writing such files—at least in some circumstances, such as for common data-entry screens. The Forms View mode, discussed in Chapter 5, automatically creates format files with all the @-SAY-GET commands you may ever need.

To summarize what was covered in Chapter 5, Forms View mode is a feature of FoxView that creates data-entry screens, complete with descriptive titles and borders, when desired. The information used within FoxView to design a particular screen is stored in a table, which is assigned the .FV extension. Forms View mode can also create a format file with an .FMT extension. This file contains the @-SAY-GET commands that would be required if you were to write a command file that would display the same information in the same format as the screen form created in Forms View mode.

For example, in Chapter 5 you created an entry form called MEMBERS. To see the effects of that form, enter these commands:

```
USE MEMBERS
SET FORMAT TO MEMBERS
CHANGE
```

The screen that appears is the entry form created with the aid of FoxView. Press ESC to leave Change mode, and enter this command:

```
DIR *.FMT
```

This use of the Directory command will cause FoxPro to display a list of all format files currently on your disk. Among those files, you will see one named MEMBERS.FMT, the file created by FoxView for the Generic Videos form.

To see the contents of the file, you can use the TYPE command. (The TYPE command is a command that will cause the contents of any text file to be "typed," or displayed, on the screen.) Enter

TYPE MEMBERS.FMT

and you will see a file similar to the following:

```
* Program.: MEMBERS.FMT
* Author..: Edward Jones
* Date....: 08/23/89
* Notice..: Copyright (c) 1989, JEJA Software
* Version.: FoxPro, revision 1.0
* Notes...: Format file for MEMBERS.DBF
*
SET COLOR TO R/N
@  6,15 SAY "Social    "
@ 4,6 TO 20,71 DOUBLE
@  7,15 SAY "Lastname  "
@  8,15 SAY "Firstname "
@  9,15 SAY "Address   "
@ 10,15 SAY "City      "
@ 10,43 SAY "State     "
@ 11,15 SAY "Zip       "
@ 13,15 SAY "Birth date  "
@ 14,15 SAY "Date of Expiration "
@ 15,15 SAY "Beta      "
@ 17,10 SAY "Preference "
@ 17,30 SAY "ENTER to change data; CTRL-W saves."
*
SET COLOR TO ,N/W
@  6,25 GET Social
SET COLOR TO ,N/BG
@  7,25 GET Lastname
@  8,25 GET Firstname
SET COLOR TO ,N/W
@  9,25 GET Address
```

@ 10,25 GET City
@ 10,53 GET State
@ 11,25 GET Zipcode
@ 13,27 GET Birthday
@ 14,34 GET Expiredate
@ 15,25 GET Beta
@ 17,21 GET Preference
*
* EOF: MEMBERS.FMT

There are some SET COLOR TO commands in the file that have not yet been covered, but you can see that most of the file is made up of the @-SAY-GET commands that display information on the screen and ask for the user responses. If you wanted to manually create a format file that would display the information in the Generic Videos database in the same manner as the MEMBERS format file, you would be faced with writing a format file that contained these commands. Obviously, in many cases, it can be advantageous and time-saving to use the commands generated by Forms View instead of writing format files from scratch.

A direct example of the time that can be saved is evident if you compare this format file to the manual commands entered previously in the ADDER command file. Enter the command

TYPE ADDER.PRG

and the command file that you created earlier to display new records appears. This command file uses 20 lines of programming code to accomplish its task. Now create another command file by entering the command

MODIFY COMMAND ADDTWO

You will create another program for adding records. Enter the following commands in this program:

```
USE MEMBERS
SET FORMAT TO MEMBERS
APPEND BLANK
READ
SET FORMAT TO
RETURN
```

Save this program with CTRL-W, and then enter **DO ADDTWO** to try the program. With six lines of programming code, this program has accomplished a function similar to the ADDER program, which uses nearly four times as many lines of programming.

That's not to say that the first method of creating format files is necessarily wrong. In some cases, you may want to display just one or two pieces of information. It would be overkill to use Forms View to create an entry form for a single variable that's displayed somewhere in a program. The two methods of creating format files described in this chapter can be likened to the difference between manual and automatic transmission in a car. Neither is necessarily correct; it is up to the driver (in this case, you) to determine the appropriate method.

FORMS VIEW AND FORMAT FILES If you use the Forms View mode of FoxView to create forms, and you save the table and generate a format file, you will update both the table (.FV) file and the format (.FMT) file. If you use the format files along with your programs, and you make any changes manually to the format file using the Editor, you should rename the file with a name different from the corresponding table. This will prevent the format file from being accidentally overwritten if you later use Forms View to make changes to the screen. If you do use the Editor to make changes manually to a format file, remember that the corresponding table is not updated. To update the table, you must make your changes within Forms View.

USING WINDOWS

One of FoxPro's greatest assets, which you should not ignore when designing programs, is its ability to display information within windows. From the prior use of commands like BROWSE and EDIT, it is obvious that FoxPro lets you add and edit data within windows, and it should also be clear by now that you can open multiple windows at the same time and place them at various locations on the screen. What may not be obvious is that you can use certain window-related commands within programs to display or edit data inside of windows.

There are three often-used commands that relate to window management within FoxPro.

- *DEFINE WINDOW windowname* is used to define the screen coordinates (location) and the display attributes for a window.

- *ACTIVATE WINDOW windowname [ALL]* is used to activate a window that has been defined. Once activated, all screen output appears in the window until another window is activated or until the current window is deactivated. The ALL option, when used, activates all previously defined windows, and current screen output appears in the last window to be defined.

- *DEACTIVATE WINDOW windowname [ALL]* is used to deactivate, or turn off, an active window. The ALL option, when used, deactivates all active windows.

To use windows in your program, you first use the DEFINE WINDOW command to define as many windows as will be needed (one DEFINE WINDOW command is used for each window). Window names can be up to ten characters in length. Then, as you need to display data in a window, you use the ACTIVATE WINDOW command to make the window active. When you are done with the window, you use the DEACTIVATE WINDOW command to deactivate the window.

Defining the Window

A number of options can be used with the DEFINE WINDOW command to control the appearance and colors of the window. All of the options are covered in detail in Appendix A; for now, some of them are detailed along with this command:

DEFINE WINDOW *windowname* FROM *row1,col1* TO *row2,col2* [TITLE *character-expression*] [DOUBLE/PANEL/NONE] [SHADOW/NOSHADOW] [COLOR *standard/enhanced*[*,border*]] [COLOR SCHEME *n*]

The *row1,col1* coordinates indicate the row and column number for the upper-left corner of the window. The *row2,col2* coordinates indicate the row and column number of the lower-right corner of the window. The TITLE option, followed by a character expression, defines an optional title. If used, the expression appears as a title at the top of the window.

The DOUBLE, PANEL, and NONE options can be used to define a different border for the window. The default border, if no option is specified, is a single-line box. DOUBLE causes the window to have a double-line box. PANEL gives the window a panel border like that used by FoxPro for editing and browsing. NONE specifies no border.

The SHADOW and NOSHADOW options specify whether or not a shadow will appear beneath the window. You must have used a SET SHADOWS ON command earlier in the program before any shadows you define will take effect.

The COLOR option lets you define color attributes for the window. The appropriate letters separated by a slash indicate standard and enhanced colors; separate the standard color pair from the enhanced color pair with a comma. The first letter in the pair is the foreground, and the second letter is the background. The color codes are as follows:

Black N	Yellow GR+
Cyan BG	Blue B
White W	Magenta RB
Blank X	Brown GR
Green G	Red R

For example, you could define the window as having the standard colors of a black-on-white background, and the enhanced colors of a blue-on-red background, by adding an option like this one to the DEFINE WINDOW command:

COLOR N/W, B/R

You can also use the COLOR SCHEME option to define the window colors. Use COLOR SCHEME followed by a number from 1 to 11 to set the window to one of the standard FoxPro color schemes. (See SET COLOR in Appendix A for more details on the color schemes.) For example, the standard user menus in FoxPro use Color Scheme 2, while the default Browse window uses Color Scheme 10. Hence, if you were to add the optional clause

COLOR SCHEME 10

to a DEFINE WINDOW command, the window would use the same default colors as the FoxPro Browse window. (Note that if you don't like the colors in a color scheme, you can use the Colors option of the Window menu to change them.)

You can use as many optional clauses as you need with the exception of both SET COLOR and COLOR SCHEME (it would make sense to use either SET COLOR or COLOR SCHEME to define the colors, but not both options at the same time). Here is an example of a window definition:

DEFINE WINDOW members1 FROM 8,8 TO 22,75 PANEL SHADOW COLOR SCHEME 2

This defines a window with a panel border and a shadow underneath, with its upper-left corner at row 8, column 8 of the screen. The window's lower-right corner is at row 22, column 75 of the screen. The window colors are the same as those of Color Scheme 2, which is used by the FoxPro user menus.

Activating and Using the Window

Once you have defined the window with the DEFINE WINDOW command, use the ACTIVATE WINDOW *windowname* command to activate, or turn on, the window. When you activate a window, all screen output appears inside of that window. When you use @-SAY commands to place data inside a window, it is important to realize that the coordinates are now *relative* to the window. This means that row 0, column 0 is no longer the upper-left corner of the screen; it is now the upper-left corner of the window. It will remain that way until you stop using the window with a DEACTIVATE WINDOW command. It is important to grasp this point to avoid errors in your program. If, for example, you activate a window that is only 5 rows deep in size and you then try to display data at row 15, your program will halt with a "Position is off the screen" error message because the window you are using has no row 15.

You can use the LIST or DISPLAY command to display data without worrying about screen locations, and the data will be contained completely within the window. If the data wraps around lines in an unattractive fashion, you can either change the size of the window to fit more data or include less fields in the LIST or

DISPLAY command. And you can activate a window and then use a BROWSE, CHANGE, or EDIT command to allow changes inside the window (although this is not generally necessary, since BROWSE, CHANGE, and EDIT cause windows to open on their own). You might find such a technique useful if for some reason you wanted a Browse or Edit window of a specific size to appear at a specific screen location.

Deactivating the Window

Once you are done with the window, use the DEACTIVATE WINDOW *windowname* command to turn off the window. Screen output is then restored to the normal screen. If you have activated a number of windows, you can use the ALL clause in place of a window name with the command, and all the windows will be deactivated.

An Example of the Window Use

Assuming you've created the MEMBERS and RENTALS files in earlier chapters, you can try the following program to see how multiple windows can be used to visually highlight your application. Perhaps Generic Videos would like a program that asks for a user's name, displays the corresponding tape limit and membership expiration date, and then displays all tapes rented by that member. The program shown here presents the information inside of multiple windows, using shadows and different colors.

```
*windows.prg shows off window use.*
STORE SPACE(15) TO MLAST
SET SHADOWS ON
DEFINE WINDOW members1 FROM 5,5 TO 9,50 PANEL SHADOW COLOR SCHEME 1
DEFINE WINDOW rentals1 FROM 8,8 TO 22,75 PANEL SHADOW COLOR SCHEME 2
DEFINE WINDOW askthem FROM 3,15 TO 6,45 PANEL SHADOW COLOR SCHEME 3
USE MEMBERS INDEX NAME
ACTIVATE WINDOW askthem
```

```
@ 1,1 SAY "Last name? " GET MLAST
READ
SEEK MLAST
IF .NOT. FOUND()
    @ 1,1 SAY "NAME NOT FOUND IN DATABASE!"
    WAIT
    DEACTIVATE WINDOW askthem
    CLOSE DATABASES
    RETURN
ENDIF
STORE SOCIAL TO FINDER
ACTIVATE WINDOW members1
@ 1,2 SAY "Name: " + TRIM(FIRSTNAME) + " " + LASTNAME
@ 2,2 SAY "Exp. date:"
@ 2,15 SAY EXPIRFDATE
@ 2,25 SAY "Tape limit:"
@ 2,38 SAY TAPELIMIT
WAIT "Press a key to see rentals..."
SET ESCAPE OFF
ACTIVATE WINDOW rentals1
SELECT 2
USE RENTALS
DISPLAY ALL OFF FOR SOCIAL = FINDER
WAIT "Press a key when done viewing..."
DEACTIVATE WINDOW ALL
CLOSE DATABASES
SET ESCAPE ON
RETURN
```

Early in the program, the SET SHADOWS ON command permits the display of shadows when called for by a SHADOW clause along with the DEFINE WINDOW command. Next, three DEFINE WINDOW commands are used to define three different windows for later use. After opening a database and index file, the program activates the window called Askthem and displays a prompt for a last name within that window.

Once the user responds with a last name, a SEEK command finds the name in the index, and the window called Members1 is activated. The tape limit and expiration date, along with the member's full name, are displayed in this window, and the user is asked to press a key to see the tape rentals. Once the user presses a key, the window called Rentals1 is activated, and all tapes rented by that member are shown in it. At the end of the program, all of the windows are deactivated and the files are closed.

You may notice the addition of the SET ESCAPE OFF command just before the final window is opened. This is used to prevent a user from halting the program in midstream by pressing the ESC key. You may prefer to use the SET ESCAPE OFF command early on in most of your programs so users cannot interrupt a program by pressing ESC.

DESIGNING LIGHT-BAR MENUS WITH @-PROMPT AND MENU TO

You now have a main-menu system for the Generic Videos database, but it uses ? and INPUT commands that do not provide much flexibility when it comes to placing the information on the screen. You can replace these commands with the @-PROMPT and MENU TO commands. Using @-PROMPT and MENU TO, you can create light-bar menus similar to those used by FoxPro.

A series of @-PROMPT commands are first used to display the desired menu options at specific positions on the screen. The format for this command is

row, column PROMPT "*expression*" [MESSAGE "*expression*"]

where the character expression that follows the PROMPT clause appears in a bar at the specified row and column position. The MESSAGE clause is optional. If it is used, the character expression that follows MESSAGE will appear in the message area of the screen whenever that particular menu option is highlighted.

A series of @-PROMPT commands are followed by a MENU TO command. The format of this command is

MENU TO *memory-variable*

It activates the menu choices defined with the PROMPT commands and waits for a user response. The user can highlight the desired menu option and press ENTER, at which time a numeric value representing the chosen menu option gets passed on to the memory variable specified in the MENU TO command. For example, if the user highlights the first menu option and presses ENTER, 1 gets stored to the variable. If the user highlights the fourth menu option and presses ENTER, 4 gets stored to the variable.

To use these commands in the Generic Videos menu, you must get into the FoxPro Editor and edit the command file used to display the menu. Enter this:

MODIFY COMMAND MENU1

When the FoxPro Editor appears, the menu command file you developed in Chapter 13 will appear along with it. Change the file so it looks like the one shown next.

Note: You can delete a series of lines at once by placing the cursor at the start of the first unwanted line, holding down the SHIFT key, and moving the cursor down to the last unwanted line. With all the unwanted lines highlighted, press the DEL key to remove the lines. You can use ENTER to add new blank lines between existing lines.

```
USE MEMBERS
SET TALK OFF
STORE 0 TO CHOICE
DO WHILE CHOICE < 5
        CLEAR
        *Display main menu.
        @ 5, 5 SAY "Generic Videos Database System Menu"
        @ 6, 4 SAY "Highlight selection, and press Enter:"
        @ 8,10 PROMPT "Add Members      "
        @ 9,10 PROMPT "Edit Members     "
        @ 10,10 PROMPT "Print Report    "
        @ 11,10 PROMPT "Display Member"
        @ 12,10 PROMPT "Exit System     "
```

```
        @ 7, 8 TO 13,25 DOUBLE
        * above line draws double line box around menu.*
        MENU TO CHOICE
        DO CASE
            CASE CHOICE = 1
                APPEND
            CASE CHOICE = 2
                DO EDITMEMB
            CASE CHOICE = 3
                REPORT FORM SAMPLE
            CASE CHOICE = 4
                DO SHOWMEMB
            CASE CHOICE = 5
                RETURN
        ENDCASE
ENDDO
```

When you are finished changing the command file, press CTRL-W to save it. You then might want to try using the system; start it by entering **DO MENU1**. Choose the menu choice for adding a record, and while you are watching the system's operation, you might want to think about ways to improve further on the system design. Perhaps you can modify the command files used by your system so that other choices from the menu provide easy-to-understand screen displays. When you are finished using the system, CTRL-W will get you out of any of the Edit or Append functions and back to the system menu.

EDITING RECORDS UNDER PROGRAM CONTROL

You know that you can edit records with the CHANGE or EDIT command or by using @-SAY-GET and READ commands, but first you must get to the record before you can change it. Let's use macro substitution for the editing functions of the Generic Videos database system. If you remember where you left that section of the system, the Editor program (EDITMEMB.PRG) displays all records in the database. The system then asks you for the record number to be edited, and the EDIT command is used to edit that record. If the database has grown beyond a screenful of members, however, you won't be able to see all of the records on a screen at once. Obviously, a better method of editing is needed.

The employees of Generic Videos have agreed that it would be best if they could enter the last name of a member to have FoxPro search for the record. When you first think about what must be done, you might draw up this list:

1. Ask for the last name of the member whose record is to be edited.

2. Store the name to a variable.

3. Using the macro function, find the name in the database.

4. Edit the record whose number corresponds to that name.

Let's change the EDITOR command file so that it does this task. Enter

MODIFY COMMAND EDITMEMB

Change the program so it looks like this:

```
CLEAR
STORE SPACE(15) TO TEST
USE MEMBERS
SET INDEX TO NAME
@ 5,10 SAY "Editing a record."
@ 7,10 SAY "Enter the last name of the member."
@ 10,10 SAY "Last name: " GET TEST
READ
IF TEST = " "
```

```
            RETURN
ENDIF
FIND &TEST
IF .NOT. FOUND()
        CLEAR
        @5,10 SAY "There is no such name in the database."
        WAIT
        *wait command causes a pause.
        RETURN
ENDIF
CHANGE
RETURN
```

Press CTRL-W to save the file. Try the system again by entering **DO MENU1**, and choose the "Edit" menu selection. Try entering the name **Miller**. If all went well, the selected record will appear on the screen. FIND &TEST is the key to the solution; whatever name is entered with the ACCEPT command will be substituted for the macro when the FIND command is executed. The SEEK command, which accepts a memory variable directly, could be used in place of FIND and a macro. In this example, FIND was used instead to demonstrate the use of the macro (&) function.

One obvious flaw in this program's design is that the search routine is based on the last name only. If two persons have the same last name, such a design may not find the name you want. However, you can apply the same logic to combinations of fields if you use an index file built on that same combination of fields to perform the search. You could, for example, build the NAME index file on a combination of Lastname and Firstname with commands like

```
USE MEMBERS
INDEX ON LASTNAME + FIRSTNAME TO NAME
```

and then the search routine could be rewritten to prompt for both the last and the first names. The responses could be combined with the plus symbol, which combines (concantenates) text strings. The combined expression could then be used as the search term. As an example, the modified search routine shown here would work if the index was built on a combination of last and first names:

```
CLEAR
STORE SPACE(15) TO TESTLAST
STORE SPACE(15) TO TESTFIRST
USE MEMBERS
SET INDEX TO NAME
@ 5,10 SAY "Editing a record."
@ 7,10 SAY "Enter the last name of the member."
@ 8,10 SAY "Last name: " GET TESTLAST
@ 10,10 SAY "Enter the first name of the member."
@ 11,10 SAY "First name: " GET TESTFIRST
READ
STORE TESTLAST + TESTFIRST TO TEST
IF TEST = " "
      RETURN
ENDIF
FIND &TEST
IF .NOT. FOUND()
      CLEAR
      @5,10 SAY "There is no such name in the database."
      WAIT
      *wait command causes a pause.
      RETURN
ENDIF
CHANGE
RETURN
```

DATA ENTRY AND EDITING WITH MEMORY VARIABLES

Another common method of writing programs for data entry and editing makes use of memory variables for the temporary storage of data. This method has not been used for any of the examples in this book up to this point. However, it is popular with many programmers, you may want to consider it in designing your own programs. This programming approach moves data from memory variables to fields. The program resembles the following:

```
*create memory variables.
CLEAR
MLAST = SPACE(15)
MFIRST = SPACE(15)
MADDRESS = SPACE(25)
MCITY  = SPACE(15)
MSTATE = SPACE(2)
MZIP = SPACE(10)
*display prompts, store data to variables.
@ 3, 5 SAY " LAST NAME:" GET MLAST
@ 4, 5 SAY "FIRST NAME:" GET MFIRST
@ 8, 5 SAY "ADDRESS:" GET MADDRESS
@ 10, 5 SAY "   CITY:" GET MCITY
@ 10, 35 SAY "STATE:" GET MSTATE
@ 10, 45 SAY "ZIP CODE:" GET MZIP
READ
*open database, make new record, store variables.
USE NAMES INDEX NAMES
APPEND BLANK
REPLACE LASTNAME WITH MLAST, FIRSTNAME WITH MFIRST;
ADDRESS WITH MADDRESS, CITY WITH MCITY;
STATE WITH MSTATE, ZIP WITH MZIP
RETURN
```

Such a command file has three main parts. The first consists of a series of commands that create memory variables; the memory variables precisely match the field types and field lengths. The second portion of the file uses @-SAY-GET commands to display prompts at the desired screen locations, along with data-entry fields for the desired data. The final portion of the file opens the database, uses an APPEND BLANK command to add one blank record to the end of the database, and uses the REPLACE command to move the data from the variables into the database fields. Once all of the required records have been added, the database can be closed. The code just described is often enclosed within a DO WHILE .T. loop, with a conditional prompt added just before the ENDDO that matches the DO WHILE command, as in the following example:

```
WAIT "Add another record? Y/N:" TO ANSWER
IF UPPER(ANSWER) = "N"
     CLOSE DATABASES
     EXIT
ENDIF
```

If the data-entry person presses N in response to the prompt, the program ends.

For this method to be as popular as it is with programmers, it clearly has advantages. One significant one is *database integrity;* the database is open only during the append process and not necessarily throughout the entire application, minimizing chances of damage. Another is ease of validation; since the data is stored in memory variables and later moved to the fields of the actual database, you can add other lines to the program to see if the data is valid before moving it to the database. And you can make it easier on the data-entry operators by storing default values in the memory variables. As an example, if 80% of the addresses that get stored in an order database are in San Diego, you could store the text string "San Diego", along with the required number of spaces following the string to fill the field, to the memory variable for the City field. It will then appear by default in the entry screen, and the users can overtype the entry to enter something else.

Now, the disadvantages: This approach involves a lot of programming, like it or not. Anyone who has written an entry routine like this one for a 60-field database will tell you that it is no fun typing all the lines of program code; you'll spend two pages just creating the variables! The effort involved in writing such a program is enough to make you wonder whether database integrity is all that important, or whether you can get by with a format file and a CHANGE or EDIT command.

DELETING RECORDS UNDER PROGRAM CONTROL

If you're going to be writing your own applications, you should add a routine for deleting unwanted records. This is too often left out of a system's design, as if users want to add but never want to delete records from a database. The logic is very similar to a search-and-edit program, because for both the editing and deleting you have to find the record first.

For deleting a record, your program-design pseudocode might look like this:

```
open database, index files
prompt user for variables to search by
FIND variable in index file
IF NOT FOUND
     show error message, exit routine
ELSE
     show record to user with @-SAY commands
     ask user for confirmation to delete record
     IF confirmation is given
          DELETE the record
     ELSE
          move to next record to see if it is same name
          ask user for confirmation to delete record
     ENDIF
ENDIF
```

The fastest way to build such a routine is probably to copy your "edit" routine, remove the lines of code that allow for changing the fields, and add lines of code that ask for confirmation and proceed to delete the record. Here is an example that uses a modified version of the program shown earlier for editing records based on a last and first name:

```
CLEAR
STORE SPACE(15) TO TESTLAST
STORE SPACE(15) TO TESTFIRST
USE MEMBERS
SET INDEX TO NAME
*name.idx is indexed on lastname + firstname.*
@ 5,10 SAY "DELETING a record."
@ 7,10 SAY "Enter the last name of the member."
@ 8,10 SAY "Last name: " GET TESTLAST
@ 10,10 SAY "Enter the first name of the member."
@ 11,10 SAY "First name: " GET TESTFIRST
READ
STORE TESTLAST + TESTFIRST TO TEST
FIND &TEST
IF .NOT. FOUND()
      CLEAR
      @5,10 SAY "There is no such name in the database."
      WAIT
      *wait command causes a pause.
      RETURN
ENDIF
DO WHILE .NOT. EOF()
      STORE "N" TO DOIT
      @ 5, 5 SAY " Lastname:"
      @ 5,15 SAY LASTNAME
      @ 6, 5 SAY "Firstname:"
      @ 6,15 SAY FIRSTNAME
      @ 7, 5 SAY "  Address:"
      @ 7,15 SAY ADDRESS
      @ 8,15 SAY TRIM(CITY) + " " + STATE + " " + ZIPCODE
      @ 12, 20 SAY "DELETE THIS MEMBER? Y/N or C to CANCEL: "
      @ 12, 62 GET DOIT
      READ
      DO CASE
         CASE UPPER(DOIT) = "Y"
         DELETE
         RETURN
         CASE UPPER(DOIT) = "N"
         SKIP
         CASE UPPER(DOIT) = "C"
         RETURN
```

```
        ENDCASE
ENDDO
RETURN
```

The advantage of placing the portion of the program that displays the member and asks for confirmation in a DO-WHILE loop is that if two members have the same last and first names, the user can press N for No to automatically view the next member. Once the user views the desired member to delete and presses Y for Yes, the record is deleted. Note also that this routine does not perform a PACK, because packing a database can be time-consuming (particularly with larger databases). Most systems provide the user with an option to pack the file at some point in time. It probably isn't wise to do this all too often, nor is it necessary, since you can place a SET DELETED ON statement near the start of the program to hide the deleted records. Given that a PACK is going to be time-consuming with all but the smallest of databases, this should be an option that is performed at the users' discretion.

Many systems provide a PACK option in the form of a question that the user sees just before exiting the system. This can be done with a program like the one shown here:

```
CLEAR
ACCEPT "  ==PACK database now? Y/N: " TO PACKANS
IF UPPER(PACKANS) = "Y"
      CLEAR
      @ 5,5 SAY "Please wait... do NOT interrupt!"
      SET TALK ON
      USE MEMBERS INDEX NAME
      PACK
      SET TALK OFF
ENDIF
QUIT
```

The user of your application, who may not want to spend the time at that particular instant, now has the option of performing or not performing the pack.

HELPFUL HINTS
ON SCREEN DESIGN

Think about these aspects of screen design when you are designing a FoxPro system:

- Use menus as often as necessary. They should clearly say what choices are available to the person using the system.

- Avoid overly cluttered menus or data-entry screens. It may be better to break the entry screen in half, input half of the information, clear the screen with CLEAR, and then input the other half of the information rather than trying to fit a large number of fields on one data-entry screen. You can apply the same tactic to a menu by grouping a number of choices in a second menu—a reports menu, for example—that can be reached by a single choice on the main menu.

- Give users a way out—that is, a way of changing their minds after making a choice from a menu or selecting a particular entry screen. Many application designers handle this need by making the last option on any menu serve as an "exit" back to the previous menu with a RETURN statement.

- Finally, never leave the screen blank for any noticeable period of time. Few things are as unnerving to a computer user as a blank screen. A simple message that states that the computer is doing something (sorting, indexing, or whatever) is reassuring to the user.

15

PROGRAMMING FOR DATA RETRIEVAL

Generating Reprots from Stored Report Forms
Users' Choice: Reporting to the Screen or Printer
Writing Reports with Program Code
Creating Columnar Listings
Controlling Your Printer

This chapter covers ways to retrieve data, in the form of reports, from within your programs. You should already be familiar with the use of the Report Generator, as detailed in Chapters 7 and 10, for designing reports. The stored reports created by the Report Generator can be called from within a program to produce a variety of reports. You can also write programs that produce reports, although the flexibility of the Report Generator makes this task necessary only on the rarest of occasions.

GENERATING REPORTS FROM STORED REPORT FORMS

If you have designed your reports using the Report Generator, all that is needed is to place the REPORT FORM command, detailed in Chapter 7, at the appropriate place in your program to generate a report. You may also want to build selective indexes or set some sort of filter before generating the report, and it is a good idea to give users a way to cancel the report just before it starts.

A simple report-producing program called from one of the options in the main menu might resemble the following:

```
*REPORTER.PRG produces the membership report.*
CLEAR
TEXT
**************************************************************
This menu option prints the membership report.
Make sure that the printer is turned on, and that
paper is loaded.

Press C to CANCEL, any other key to start printing.
**************************************************************
ENDTEXT
WAIT TO DOIT
IF UPPER(DOIT) = "C"
        *user cancelled option, so...
        RETURN
ENDIF
REPORT FORM MEMBERS TO PRINT
RETURN
```

Using stored reports like the one used by this program is by far the easiest way to generate reports within a program. You can add more lines to the program to limit the records that are printed with an INDEX ON-FOR command or with a SET FILTER command. With SET FILTER, for example, you could offer various menu options that select different filter conditions, and then print the same stored report. As an example, one user might want to see the members in the video database restricted by a specific ZIP code, while another user might want to see all members who lived in a specific state. You could provide menu options in a simple reporting program like the one shown here to handle this task:

```
*REPORTER.PRG produces the membership report.*
CLEAR
@ 5, 5 PROMPT "All members    "
@ 6, 5 PROMPT "By State       "
@ 7, 5 PROMPT "By ZIP code range"
@ 4, 4 TO 8, 23 DOUBLE
MENU TO CHOICE
DO CASE
        CASE CHOICE = 1
        WAIT "All members chosen. Press a key."
        CASE CHOICE = 2
        STORE SPACE(2) TO MSTATE
        @ 12,10 SAY "For which state? " GET MSTATE
        READ
        SET FILTER TO UPPER(STATE) = UPPER(MSTATE)
        GO TOP
        CASE CHOICE = 3
        STORE SPACE(10) TO STARTZIPS
        STORE SPACE(10) TO ENDZIPS
        @ 12,10 SAY "Starting ZIP code? " GET STARTZIPS
        @ 13,10 SAY "  Ending ZIP code? " GET ENDZIPS
        @ 15,10 SAY "(enter same ZIP code for a single ZIP.)"
        READ
        SET FILTER TO ZIPCODE >= STARTZIPS .AND. ZIPCODE <= ENDZIPS
        GO TOP
ENDCASE
CLEAR
TEXT
***************************************************************
Ready to print the membership report. Make sure that
the printer is turned on, and that paper is loaded.

Press C to CANCEL, any other key to start printing.
***************************************************************
ENDTEXT
WAIT TO DOIT
IF UPPER(DOIT) = "C"
        *user cancelled option, so...
```

```
            SET FILTER TO
            *above line needed to clear effects of filter.*
            RETURN
ENDIF
REPORT FORM MEMBERS TO PRINT
SET FILTER TO
*above line needed to clear effects of filter.*
RETURN
```

In this example, depending on the menu choice selected, one of two filters may be set to limit the records printed. Note the inclusion of the SET FILTER TO statement near the end of the program to clear any existing filter. If a filter is set and not cleared after the report is done, it may cause havoc in other parts of your program when records suddenly appear to be "missing" from the database.

USERS' CHOICE: REPORTING TO THE SCREEN OR PRINTER

Often, a report is needed for both screen and printer. A program may need to display a report on the screen, or optionally send the output to the printer. Anyone who has designed a single report to try to meet the two different needs of screen and printer has discovered that the two tasks are similar but not identical. The screen limitation of 24 lines puts a severe constraint on the amount of information you can display at once; the program must prompt for each display, or the data scrolls by so fast as to be useless. With a printer, however, there is no need to stop every 24 lines, but page ejects must be taken into consideration.

One way to handle such a need is to use a program like the one shown here:

```
PRINANS = "S"
@ 5, 5 SAY 'Screen (S) or Printer (P)?" GET PRINANS
READ
IF UPPER(PRINANS) = "P"
    REPORT FORM MEMBERS TO PRINT
ELSE
    GO TOP
    CLEAR
    WAIT "Press C to CANCEL, any other key to view members."
    CLEAR
    DO WHILE .NOT. EOF( )
        REPORT FORM MEMBERS NEXT 20
        WAIT TO KEEPGOING
        IF UPPER(KEEPGOING) = "C"
            RETURN
        ENDIF
    ENDDO
ENDIF
RETURN
```

This lets the same stored report form work for both the screen and the printer. If the user answers the prompt with S for screen, the DO WHILE loop causes the REPORT FORM MEMBERS NEXT 20 statement to repeat over and over until the end of the file is reached. The scope of NEXT 20 limits the report to 20 records, which fit on a screen, and the WAIT command pauses the screen, allowing the user to view the records. In your application, you could change NEXT 20 to whatever number of records will fit on your screen at one time.

WRITING REPORTS WITH PROGRAM CODE

Before proceeding with this topic, you should know that producing stored reports with the Report Generator will be far easier than the following methods of writing reports manually with program code. The methods are described here primarily because you may run into FoxPro applications written by other programmers who chose to use these methods. This was often due to the limitations in earlier versions of FoxBase. The Report Generator in FoxBase did not let you create form-oriented reports with ease, so many programmers wrote report programs to accomplish the task. It may help to be familiar with these methods of programming, in case you ever want to modify another programmer's work, but if at all possible, you should avoid these techniques in favor of writing your reporting programs with stored reports created by the Report Generator.

There are about as many ways to design a reporting program as there are to build data-entry screens. About the only thing such programs have in common are one or more repetitive (DO WHILE) loops, which print selected contents of a record for each record within a group of records. Beyond this, the commands you will need vary with the complexity of the reports, the levels of grouping, whether or not the report is relational, and numerous other factors. However, many reports written in program code do follow a common methodology, which is something like this:

OPEN Database and Index files
FIND first record in desired group, or SET FILTER and go top
Initialize any memory variables for page and line counters
Route output to the printer
Print report headings
DO WHILE not at the end of the file or the desired data group
    Print the desired fields or expressions for one record
    Update counter for page position
    IF form feed counter exceeds max lines per page
        Print footers, if any
        EJECT the paper
        Print headers, if any

                ENDIF
                SKIP to the next record in logical sequence
    ENDDO

There are two ways to route the data to the printer: by using SET PRINT ON and a series of ? statements or by using SET DEVICE TO PRINT followed by a series of @-SAY statements. As an example, the two simple programs that are shown here use both approaches within the design framework just shown:

```
*MEMLIST.PRG prints membership roster.*
CLEAR
STORE 1 TO LINES
STORE 1 TO PAGES
USE MEMBERS INDEX NAMES
SET PRINT ON
? "*********************************************"
? "    Membership Address and Phone Roster"
? "*********************************************"
DO WHILE .NOT. EOF( )
        ? "Name: " + TRIM(FIRSTNAME) + " " + LASTNAME
        ? "Phone: " + PHONE
        ?? "Expiration Date: " + DTOC(EXPIREDATE)
        ? "Home address: " + ADDRESS
        ? SPACE(15) + TRIM(CITY) + " " + STATE + " " + ZIPCODE
        ? "******************************"
        STORE LINES+ 5 TO LINES
        IF LINES > 55
            ?
            ? SPACE(40) + "Page" + LTRIM(STR(PAGES))
            EJECT
            STORE 1 + PAGES TO PAGES
            STORE 1 TO LINES
            ? "*********************************************"
            ? "    Membership Address and Phone Roster"
            ? "*********************************************"
```

```
            ENDIF
            SKIP
ENDDO
IF LINES > 1
      EJECT
ENDIF
SET PRINT OFF
RETURN
```

SET PRINT ON and the ? statements get the job done, but they don't offer precise control over where the data appears in the report. For more precision, you can use the other method of printing in a program, which is to use SET DEVICE TO PRINT to reroute screen output to the printer, combined with @-SAY commands to position the data on the printed page. The following example of a printing program creates a simple tabular report with custom headers and footers using this approach:

```
CLEAR
STORE 5 TO LINES
STORE 1 TO PAGES
USE MEMBERS INDEX NAMES
SET DEVICE TO PRINT
@ 2, 15 SAY "MEMBERSHIP EXPIRATION DATES REPORT"
@ 3, 10 SAY "*******************************************"
@ 4, 10 SAY "Name          City"
@ 4, 50 SAY "Tape Limit   Exp.Date"
DO WHILE .NOT. EOF( )
      @ LINES, 5 SAY TRIM(FIRSTNAME) + " " + LASTNAME
      @ LINES, 30 SAY CITY
      @ LINES, 50 SAY TAPELIMIT
      @ LINES, 60 SAY EXPIREDATE
      STORE LINES + 1 TO LINES
      IF LINES > 50
            @ LINES + 2, 40 SAY "PAGE " + TRIM(STR(PAGES))
            EJECT
            STORE PAGES + 1 TO PAGES
            STORE 5 TO LINES
            @ 2, 15 SAY "MEMBERSHIP EXPIRATION DATES REPORT"
            @ 3, 10 SAY "*******************************************"
            @ 4, 10 SAY "Name          City"
            @ 4, 50 SAY "Tape Limit   Exp.Date"
```

```
        ENDIF
        SKIP
ENDDO
IF LINES > 5
        EJECT
ENDIF
SET DEVICE TO SCREEN
RETURN
```

Whichever approach best suits you can be modified to handle any complex reporting need. Multiple file reporting, for example, is simple to implement by selecting appropriate work areas and including filenames and pointers, as discussed in Chapter 11, to find the related data. In one-to-many relationships, where one record in the controlling database may have dozens or hundreds of records in a related file, you can add program code to monitor the page count and line count and to eject pages and print new headings when appropriate.

Note that both of these examples of report code use memory variables incremented by the program to keep track of page numbers and the line counts. This approach was also common in FoxBase+ and other earlier dBASE-compatible languages. In Fox-Pro, however, system memory variables (discussed shortly in "Controlling Your Printer") can be used to keep track of page numbers and line postions. These system memory variables work with the stored reports, and you may want to consider using them if you need reports that begin with a specific page number other than 1.

CREATING COLUMNAR LISTINGS

Sometimes what you need is a report with data in a two-across or three-across fashion. You can spend an inordinate amount of time writing a program to handle this need, or you can use the LABEL FORM command as a part of your report. This works well when the data you need follows a format like this one:

Page 1
10/06/89

      Employee Address Roster
           ABC Company

Marcia Morse	Carol Levy	David Jackson
4260 Park Avenue	1207 5th Street	4102 Valley Lane
Chevy Chase, MD	Washington, DC	Falls Church, VA

This use of the LABEL FORM command is similar to earlier described uses of the REPORT FORM command within a program. Create a label form using the CREATE LABEL command, and choose 3- across or 2-across as desired from the Label menu. Decide how many records you want to appear on each page, and use the command

LABEL FORM *filename* NEXT *no.-of-recs-per-page* TO PRINT

within your program. The following program shows how this can be handled:

```
SET TALK OFF
USE MEMBERS INDEX NAMES
STORE 1 TO PAGES
SET DEVICE TO PRINT
DO WHILE .NOT. EOF( )
        @ 3, 50 SAY "Page: " + LTRIM(STR(PAGES))
        @ 4, 50 SAY DATE( )
        @ 5, 20 SAY "Generic Videos Membership Address Roster"
        @ 7, 0
        LABEL FORM MEMBERS NEXT 20 TO PRINT
        STORE PAGES + 1 TO PAGES
        EJECT
ENDDO
SET DEVICE TO SCREEN
```

This will give you a report fashioned after the example previously shown, with a minimum amount of programming. You will need to decide how many records can appear on each page, based on the size of the paper and the position of your headers and footers, and adjust the number that you use along with the NEXT scope in the LABEL FORM command accordingly.

CONTROLLING YOUR PRINTER

By changing the printer memory variables, you can control the various print settings that are used when stored report forms are generated with the REPORT FORM command. Printer memory variables are special memory variables that FoxPro uses to control the output produced when a REPORT FORM command is directed to the printer. They affect settings like page length, page offset from the left margin, the number of pages printed within a report, and line spacing. You can change the values of these memory variables by storing different values to the variables before running the report with the REPORT FORM command.

If you perform a LIST MEMORY command, you will see the printer memory variables, similar to the example shown here. The names of printer memory variables start with "_P."

```
LIST MEMORY

    0 variables defined,      0 bytes used
  256 variables available,  6000 bytes available

Print System Memory Variables

_ALIGNMENT    Pub   C    "LEFT"
_BOX          Pub   L    .T.
_INDENT       Pub   N             0 (    0.00000000)
_LMARGIN      Pub   N             0 (    0.00000000)
_PADVANCE     Pub   C    "FORMFEED"
_PAGENO       Pub   N             1 (    1.00000000)
```

_PBPAGE	Pub	N	1 (	1.00000000)
_PCOLNO	Pub	N	55 (	55.00000000)
_PCOPIES	Pub	N	1 (	1.00000000)
_PDRIVER	Pub	C ""		
_PECODE	Pub	C ""		
_PEJECT	Pub	C "BEFORE"		
_PEPAGE	Pub	N	1 (	1.00000000)
_PFORM	Pub	C ""		
_PLENGTH	Pub	N	66 (	66.00000000)
_PLINENO	Pub	N	52 (	52.00000000)
_PLOFFSET	Pub	N	0 (	0.00000000)
_PPITCH	Pub	C "DEFAULT"		
_PQUALITY	Pub	L .F.		
_PSCODE	Pub	C ""		
_PSPACING	Pub	N	1 (	1.00000000)
_PWAIT	Pub	L .F.		
_RMARGIN	Pub	N	80 (	80.00000000)
_TABS	Pub	C ""		
_WRAP	Pub	L .F.		

The variables have the following meanings:

_PADVANCE contains a character expression of either LINE-FEED or FORMFEED. Depending on the value of the expression, new pages are generated either with multiple linefeeds or with form feeds.

_PAGENO indicates the page number to use on the first page of a report. The default is 1, but you can enter any value from 1 to 32,767.

_PBPAGE indicates the beginning page of a report when you don't want to print the entire report.

_PCOLNO indicates a new starting column position. This repositions the printer at the specified cursor location before the report begins.

_PCOPIES indicates the number of copies of a report desired; default is 1.

_PDRIVER contains a character expression that is the name of the printer driver in use, such as EPSONFX (for Epson FX series) or HPLAS1 (for Hewlett-Packard LaserJet 1). If no printer has been chosen with the Printer Setup option, the default will be a null string ("").

_PECODE contains any ending escape codes you want to send to the printer after the report is completed.

_PEJECT contains the character expression NONE, BEFORE, AFTER, or BOTH. NONE indicates no form feed is needed (other than those that naturally occur inside the report); BEFORE indicates a form feed should occur at the start of printing; AFTER indicates a form feed should occur at the end of printing; and BOTH indicates a form feed is needed both before and after printing.

_PEPAGE indicates the ending page of a report when you don't want to print the entire report.

_PFORM contains a character expression that evaluates to the name of a stored report-form file.

_PLENGTH indicates the page length for the printed page. The default of 66 matches standard 11-inch (U.S.) paper; you can store 84 to this value if using 14-inch (U.S. legal-size) paper.

_PLINENO indicates a new starting line number. This repositions the printer at the specifed row location before the report begins.

_PLOFFSET indicates the left offset (distance from left edge) where printing will begin. Enter a desired numeric value, such as 15 for a left offset of 15 spaces.

_PPITCH contains a character expression that selects the printing typestyle. Valid choices are PICA, ELITE, COMPRESSED, or

DEFAULT. Note that a printer driver must be installed, and your printer must support the option, for the desired typestyle to be used successfully.

_PQUALITY indicates whether quality printing mode will be used. A logical false stored to this variable turns off quality printing, and a logical true turns on quality printing. Note that a printer driver must be installed, and your printer must support quality printing for this variable to have an effect.

_PSCODE contains any starting escape codes you want to send to the printer before the report begins printing.

_PSSPACING contains a numeric value of 1, 2, or 3, indicating the line spacing to be used within a report. The default value for this is 1.

_PWAIT indicates whether printer should pause between each page. A logical value of false indicates no pause, and a logical value of true indicates a pause.

Most of these parameters can be controlled in other ways, such as through the various selections you make when designing or printing a report or when you enter other commands such as SET MARGIN TO (the command equivalent of the left offset variable). However, these variables can be quite useful if you want to offer your users multiple options for report printing while under program control. Depending on the user's response to various menu options, you could store certain values to different printer variables and then print the report with the REPORT FORM command.

Sending Escape Codes to the Printer

In its default mode, FoxPro treats the printer as a simple device capable of receiving ASCII, and sends that ASCII information. This saves you the worry of trying to get a particular printer to match the output of FoxPro, but it also means that FoxPro will not by default use any special effects that your printer has to offer. You can take advantage of your printer's special effects by sending escape codes to the printer by using the CHR function to send the applicable code. As an example, the code for compressed print for Epson-compatible printers is the ASCII value of 27 followed by the ASCII value of 15. You can, therefore, switch an Epson-compatible printer into Compressed mode with commands like

```
SET PRINT ON
??? CHR(27) + CHR(15)
SET PRINT OFF
```

The printer will remain in this mode until you send another escape code that clears the prior one or selects a different font or until you manually reset the printer. (Note the use of the ??? command, which is ideal for sending data to the printer. Unlike the ? command, the ??? does not add a carriage return or linefeed code.)

Consult your printer manual for a listing of your escape codes. The popular escape codes for Epson-compatible printers are listed in Table 15-1.

Code	Meaning
CHR(27) + CHR(4)	Italics On
CHR(27) + CHR(5)	Italics Off
CHR(27) + CHR(15)	Compressed On
CHR(27) + CHR(18)	Compressed Off
CHR(27) + CHR(45)	Emphasized On
CHR(27) + CHR(46)	Emphasized Off
CHR(27) + CHR(47)	Bold On
CHR(27) + CHR(48)	Bold Off

TABLE 15-1. Epson Printer Codes

If you use the escape codes to select different print styles often, consider storing them as memory variables and then saving those variables as a part of a configuration file. When escape codes are stored as variables, you can use them wherever they are appropriate in your various printer routines by using a SET PRINT ON statement followed by a ? *varname* command, where *varname* is the memory variable that contains the escape code. As an example, you can store an escape code to a variable with a command like

BOLD = CHR(27) + CHR(47)

Within your printer routines, you can start printing with commands like

```
WAIT "Press a key to begin printing report..."
SET PRINT ON
? BOLD
<more commands to print report...>
```

If you are using the Hewlett-Packard LaserJet or another laser printer compatible with the HP description language, you can use similar escape codes to select fonts, assuming they are available with your particular printer. The following simple menu program uses the approach of storing the escape codes for the HP LaserJet to a series of memory variables; then, depending on the chosen selection, the escape codes are routed to the printer to select the desired fonts.

```
*Fonts.PRG for HP Laserjet and compatibles.*
STORE CHR(27)+"(0U"+CHR(27)+"(s 1p 10v 1s 0b 5T" to TmsRoman
STORE CHR(27)+"(0U"+CHR(27)+"(s 1p 10v 0s 3b 5T" to TmsRomanB
STORE CHR(27)+"(0U"+CHR(27)+"(s –1p 10v 0s 0b 5T" to TmsRomanC
STORE CHR(27)+"(0U"+CHR(27)+"(s 1p 10v 1s 0b 5T" to TmsRomanI
STORE CHR(27)+"(8U"+CHR(27)+"(s 0p 10h 12v 1s 0b 3T" to CourierI
STORE CHR(27)+"(8U"+CHR(27)+"(s 0p 10h 12v 1s 3b 3T" to CourierB
STORE CHR(27)+"(0U"+CHR(27)+"(s 1p 10h 14.4v 0s 3b 4T" to HelvBold
CLEAR
@ 3, 25 SAY [SELECT A PRINTER FONT]
```

```
@ 5, 15 SAY [ 1. Times Roman]
@ 7, 15 SAY [ 2. Times Roman Italic]
@ 9, 15 SAY [ 3. Times Roman Bold]
@ 11, 15 SAY [ 4. Times Roman Compressed]
@ 13, 15 SAY [ 5. Courier Italic]
@ 14, 15 SAY [ 5. Courier Bold]
@ 15, 15 SAY [ 6. Helvetica Bold]
@ 17, 28 SAY [0. EXIT]
STORE 0 TO SELECTNUM
@ 19, 10 SAY " YOUR CHOICE?" GET SELECTNUM PICTURE '9'
READ
SET PRINT ON
DO CASE
        CASE SELECTNUM = 1
        ??? TmsRoman
        CASE SELECTNUM = 2
        ??? TmsRomanI
        CASE SELECTNUM = 3
        ??? TmsRomanB
        CASE SELECTNUM = 4
        ??? TmsRomanC
        CASE SELECTNUM = 5
        ??? CourierI
        CASE SELECTNUM = 6
        ??? CourierB
        CASE SELECTNUM = 7
        ??? HelvBold
ENDCASE
SET PRINT OFF
RETURN
```

If you are using an HP-compatible laser, you may want to experiment with the various fonts before using them in an appli-

```
J.E. Jones Associates           Reston           VA     22094
The Software Bar, Inc.          Herndon          VA     22070
Computers R Us                  Pasadena         CA     90556
Chapel Hill Life & Casualty     Carrboro         NC     27805
Sun City Transit Corporation    El Paso          TX     78809
Osborne-McGraw Hill             Berkeley         CA     94710
```

FIGURE 15-1.   Results of list with Courier Italic font

```
J.E. Jones Associates          Reston        VA    22094
The Software Bar, Inc.         Herndon       VA    22070
Computers R Us                 Pasadena      CA    90556
Chapel Hill Life & Casualty    Carrboro      NC    27805
Sun City Transit Corporation   El Paso       TX    78809
Osborne-McGraw Hill            Berkeley      CA    94710
```

FIGURE 15-2.   Results of list with Helvetica Bold font

cation. Because FoxPro assumes a standard character width for each printed character, the proportionally spaced fonts generated by a laser printer may or may not appear where you would like to see them. Figure 15-1 shows the results of a LIST command using the Courier Italic font of the HP LaserJet, and Figure 15-2 shows the results of the same LIST command with the HP LaserJet set to the Helvetica Bold font. Without the ability to incrementally space characters on the printed page, it becomes impossible to maintain proper character spacing with the laser's proportional fonts. This limits the use of the proportional fonts to items like headings and cover pages.

16
ADVANCED PROGRAMMING TOPICS

Speeding Up Your Programs with Procedures
Hiding and Showing Variables
Debugging Techniques
Customizing FoxPro with SET Commands
Using User-Defined Functions
Enhancing FoxPro Power with LOAD and CALL
Drawing Bar Graphs
Using Modular Programming

This chapter describes additional commands and programming techniques that are useful for creating more intricate command files to automate your work with FoxPro.

SPEEDING UP YOUR PROGRAMS WITH PROCEDURES

Throughout the development of the Generic Videos database system, you've used separate command files, each of which performs a specific operation. To perform an operation, the user selects it from the listing on the main menu. This is the recommended way to develop your system for an important reason: It is far easier to design, implement, and debug individual command files that perform one function or a small group of functions than it is to create and debug one large program that performs dozens of functions. But once your program is well tested and thoroughly debugged, it makes sense to combine the individual program files into a large file.

Special sections of a program, called *Procedures,* can be used for this purpose. Procedures are also useful for repeating such often-used tasks as printing a report header or displaying a commonly used error message. You can store repetitive tasks (any programming task you perform at more than one place in the program) in a procedure. Then, rather than duplicate that program code in multiple places within the program, you can use the procedure.

Procedures are groups of commands, identified by different group names, that are stored in a single command file. To see how procedures can be used, consider the four command files currently in the Generic Videos system: MENU1, ADDER, EDITMEMB, and SHOWMEMB. MENU1 contains the commands that display the menu and call (transfer program execution to) one of the other command files. ADDER contains the commands necessary for adding records to the membership database, EDITMEMB contains the commands for editing records, and SHOWMEMB contains the commands for displaying a member. Each time the user makes a choice from the menu that requires the execution of one of the command files, FoxPro must load the command file from disk and then execute the commands in it. When the commands in that command file have been executed, FoxPro exits the file and returns to the MENU command file.

With small files, the delays may not be obvoius because FoxPro will store as much of the program as will fit into available memory. With large programs, however, the use of multiple command files creates noticeable delays (not to mention wear and tear on your disk drives). However, it's not necessary to rewrite the entire set of programs to function as a single program; instead, you can perform a two-step process.

In the first step you combine the individual command files into a single command file. Each command file in the new combined file is then enclosed, or bracketed, with a procedure name and the RETURN command. (The RETURN command is not essential, although it makes the program easier to read.) Next, a SET PROCEDURE statement must be added to the file that called the command files. Figure 16-1 illustrates the design of command files that use procedures.

The second step is to tell the main file (in this case, MENU1) that the command files are now located in one file as procedures. The command that does this is SET PROCEDURE. SET PROCEDURE *filename* tells FoxPro what file will contain all of the procedures. Once you have opened a procedure file, FoxPro will look there first when it encounters a DO command. If it does not find a procedure with that name, it will look for a separate command file. When the program encounters a DO command-file statement, such as DO ADDER, instead of accessing the ADDER command file, FoxPro will first jump to the procedure file named in SET PROCEDURE. There is no required placement of the SET PROCEDURE command in the main file other than it be positioned where it will be executed before encountering a DO statement that calls the procedure. No modifications to the DO command-file statements in the main file are necessary.

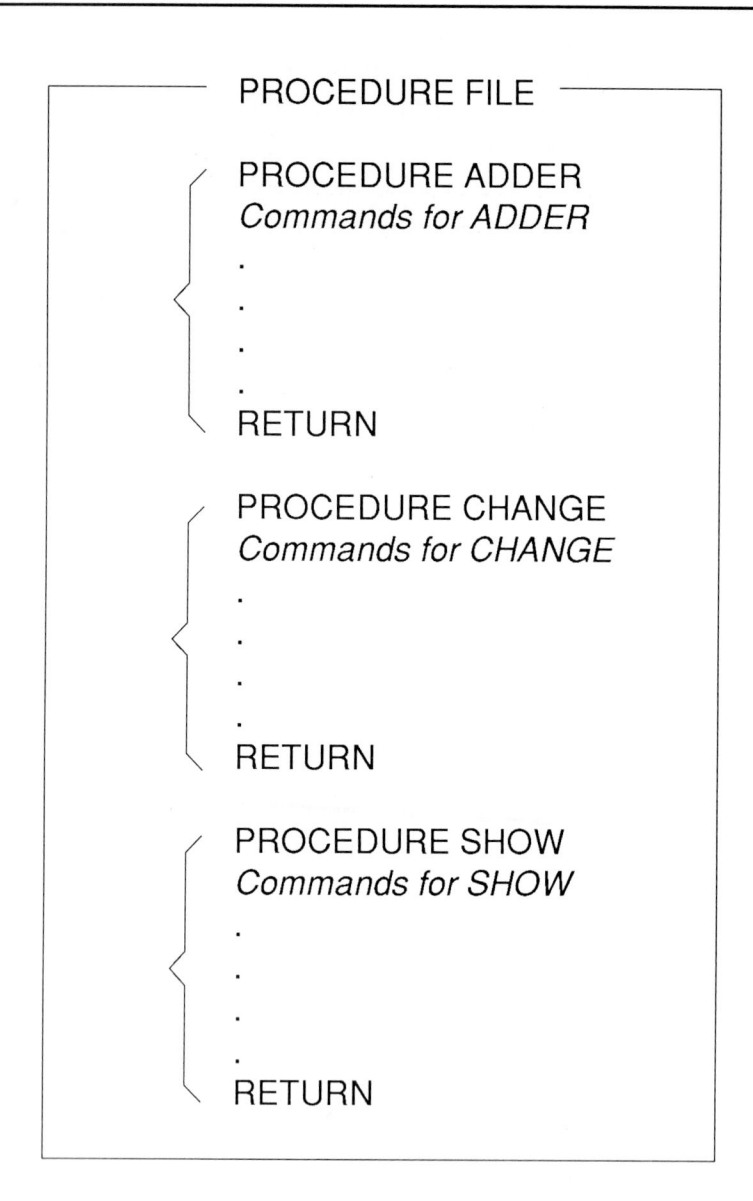

```
┌─────────── PROCEDURE FILE ───────────┐
│                                      │
│    ⎧ PROCEDURE ADDER                 │
│    ⎪  Commands for ADDER             │
│    ⎪   .                             │
│    ⎨   .                             │
│    ⎪   .                             │
│    ⎪   .                             │
│    ⎩ RETURN                          │
│                                      │
│    ⎧ PROCEDURE CHANGE                │
│    ⎪  Commands for CHANGE            │
│    ⎪   .                             │
│    ⎨   .                             │
│    ⎪   .                             │
│    ⎪   .                             │
│    ⎩ RETURN                          │
│                                      │
│    ⎧ PROCEDURE SHOW                  │
│    ⎪  Commands for SHOW              │
│    ⎪   .                             │
│    ⎨   .                             │
│    ⎪   .                             │
│    ⎪   .                             │
│    ⎩ RETURN                          │
│                                      │
└──────────────────────────────────────┘
```

FIGURE 16-1.   Model of a procedure file

Applying this logic to the Generic Videos system, you would have to create a procedure file (in the example that follows, MYFILE.PRG) that will contain all command files referenced by MENU1, the main program. With all of the command files combined into a single procedure file, the MYFILE.PRG file is read from disk just once. FoxPro stores the contents of the procedure file in memory. From that point on, FoxPro can instantaneously access any procedure in the procedure file rather than having to find the commands in another disk file.

If you want to try speeding up the Generic Videos system with procedures, you'll need to combine the files and then load them into the Editor. You can combine the files at the DOS level with the COPY command. By using the RUN command, you can do this without leaving FoxPro. Enter the following command now:

RUN COPY ADDER.PRG + EDITMEMB.PRG + SHOWMEMB.PRG MYFILE.PRG

Then enter

MODIFY COMMAND MYFILE

to begin editing the combined file with the Editor. You must now separate the programs into three groups by adding a PROCEDURE *name* command at the beginning of each group (Figure 16-1). Then add a new procedure at the end of the file:

PROCEDURE REPORTER
REPORT FORM SAMPLE TO PRINT
RETURN

This procedure prints the membership report for Generic Videos. When you are done, the MYFILE.PRG file should look like this:

```
PROCEDURE ADDER
USE MEMBERS
CLEAR
APPEND BLANK
@ 1,0 SAY "      Social Sec."  GET SOCIAL PICTURE "999-99-9999"
@ 2,0 SAY "       Lastname:"  GET LASTNAME
@ 3,0 SAY "      Firstname:"  GET FIRSTNAME
@ 4,0 SAY "        Address:"  GET ADDRESS
@ 5,0 SAY "           City:"  GET CITY
@ 6,0 SAY "          State:"  GET STATE
@ 7,0 SAY "       ZIP Code:"  GET ZIPCODE
@ 8,0 SAY "      Telephone:"  GET PHONE
@ 9,0 SAY "     Birth date:"  GET BIRTHDAY
@ 10,0 SAY " Expiration date:"  GET EXPIREDATE
@ 11,0 SAY "      Tape limit:"  GET TAPELIMIT
@ 12,0 SAY "          Beta?:"  GET BETA
READ
MODIFY MEMO PREFERENCE
RETURN

PROCEDURE EDITMEMB
CLEAR
STORE SPACE(20) TO TEST
USE MEMBERS
SET INDEX TO NAME
@ 5,10 SAY "Editing a record."
@ 7,10 SAY "Enter the last name of the member."
@ 10,10 SAY "Last name: " GET TEST
READ
FIND &TEST
IF EOF( )
        CLEAR
        @5,10 SAY "There is no such name in the database."
        WAIT
        *wait command causes a pause.
        RETURN
ENDIF
CHANGE
RETURN

PROCEDURE SHOWMEMB
```

```
USE MEMBERS
SET TALK OFF
CLEAR
ACCEPT " Search for what last name? " TO SNAME
DO WHILE .NOT. EOF( )
      IF LASTNAME = SNAME
      ? "Lastname is: "
      ?? LASTNAME
      ? "Firstname is: "
      ?? FIRSTNAME
      ? "Address is: "
      ?? ADDRESS
      ? CITY + STATE + " " + ZIPCODE
      ?
      ? "Tape limit is: "
      ?? TAPELIMIT
      ? "Expiration date is: "
      ?? EXPIREDATE
      ?
      ENDIF
      SKIP
ENDDO
WAIT
RETURN

PROCEDURE REPORTER
REPORT FORM SAMPLE TO PRINT
RETURN
```

Now save the file, and enter

MODIFY COMMAND MENU1

to edit the MENU.PRG command file. Add one line at the beginning of the file that reads

SET PROCEDURE TO MYFILE

and change the line that reads REPORT FORM SAMPLE to

DO REPORTER

Save the modified command file. Turn on your printer, and enter **DO MENU1**. Try using various menu choices to move around to different parts of the system. With the small command files used by this system, the speed increase may not be apparent, but with larger systems the improvement in speed will be well worth your efforts.

HIDING AND SHOWING VARIABLES

FoxPro offers two commands, PRIVATE and PUBLIC, that are used to classify memory variables. The terms *private* and *public* refer to how the individual programs within a large FoxPro program will treat variables. Private variables are available only to the program in which they are created and to all programs called by that program. Variables that you create in one program are considered private by default; if you do not use the PUBLIC command, FoxPro will assume that all the variables you create are private variables. This means that if you create a variable in a program that is called by another program and then transfer control back to the calling program with the RETURN command, the contents of that memory variable will be lost. You may or may not want those contents to be discarded, so you can use the PRIVATE and PUBLIC commands to specifically tell FoxPro how to handle your variables.

The PUBLIC command tells FoxPro that a memory variable is to be made available to all programs, regardless of where the memory variable is created. The PRIVATE command tells FoxPro that the variable will be available only to the program that created the variable and all programs that are called by that specific program. Declaring a variable public requires two steps: using the PUBLIC command in the format PUBLIC *variablename* and declaring the actual variable with the STORE command or with an assignment symbol (=). Here is an example:

PUBLIC YearsRents
STORE rentamt * 12 to YearsRents

In this example, the variable YearsRents will be available to all parts of the program, even if program control returns from the part of the program containing these commands to a higher-level (calling) program.

There is normally little need to declare a memory variable private, since FoxPro sets all memory variables to private by default. However, there may be times that you want to declare a variable that was previously declared public as private. To do this, you can use the PRIVATE command in the format PRIVATE *variablename* in a similar manner to the way you use the PUBLIC command. An example is

PRIVATE Staffer
STORE LASTNAME + FIRSTNAME to Staffer

As an example of the problems that can occur if variables are not declared private or public, consider the following programs. The first program, FIRST.PRG, passes control to the second program, SECOND.PRG. The second program declares a variable (NAME) and then passes control back to the calling program, FIRST.PRG. The calling program then tries to display the contents of the memory variable NAME.

```
*FIRST.PRG is first program
CLEAR
? "This program will call the second program."
WAIT
DO SECOND
CLEAR
? "Control has returned to first program."
```

? "The name is: " + NAME
? "End of first program."

*SECOND.PRG is second program
CLEAR
STORE "Smith" to name
? "The name is: " + NAME
WAIT "Press any key to return to first program."
RETURN

When the program is run with DO FIRST, an error message results after program control returns from the second program. FoxPro reports an error because the NAME variable was private to the second program. When control was passed back to the first program, the contents of the variable were lost. This problem can be solved by declaring the variable public, as shown in the following example:

*SECOND.PRG is second program
CLEAR
PUBLIC NAME
STORE "Smith" to name
? "The name is: " + NAME
WAIT "Press any key to return to first program."
RETURN

When the FIRST program is run after the change is made, the program completes successfully without an error.

You can use the ALL, LIKE, and EXCEPT options with PRIVATE to cover more than one variable at a time. Here are some examples of the use of the ALL, LIKE, and EXCEPT options with PRIVATE:

PRIVATE ALL EXCEPT ???names
PRIVATE ALL LIKE *rent
PRIVATE ALL EXCEPT YearsRents

You can use the accepted DOS wildcards, the asterisk (*), and question mark (?) as a part of the variable names. The asterisk represents any sequence of characters, and the question mark represents any single character.

DEBUGGING TECHNIQUES

Debugging is the process of finding out why a program does not operate the way it was designed. Debugging can range from correcting a spelling error to rewriting the entire program. Some program bugs are relatively easy to find and solve, such as a misspelled command, which results in a "Syntax error" message displayed on the screen when the command is executed. Other program bugs may cause problems that don't surface until you reach a different part of the program, and these can be far more difficult to solve. But remember that it is truly a rare experience for a program of any complexity, written for the first time, to operate without any bugs.

FoxPro helps you find bugs by placing you at or near the source of the problem. When an error in a program causes the program to halt, the Editor automatically opens in a window, and the highlighted line is where the program halted. This line often (but not always) contains the cause of the error.

The bugs that you are likely to see most often in FoxPro are as follows:

- Misspelled variable names and commands. The message "Syntax error" is usually displayed for misspelled commands. The message "Variable not found" is usually displayed for misspelled variables.

- Missing ENDIF, ENDDO, ENDCASE, or ENDSCAN commands. Every DO WHILE loop must end with an ENDDO statement, every IF statement must be matched by an ENDIF statement, DO CASE statements must have matching END-CASE statements, and SCAN statements must have matching ENDSCAN statements. FoxPro will wander off in the wrong direction if you leave out an ending statement.

- Errors in loops. To avoid this major cause of program bugs, verify on paper that your program loops are properly designed to begin with. An example of an improperly designed DO WHILE loop is

```
STORE 0 TO CHOICE
DO WHILE CHOICE < 3
     INPUT "Enter selection:" TO CHOICE
     IF CHOICE = 1
          IF .NOT. EOF( )
               SKIP
          ENDIF
          DELETE
     ELSE
          IF .NOT. EOF( )
               SKIP
          ENDIF
          ? NAME, CITY, STATE
ENDDO
STORE RECNO( ) TO LOCATION
ENDIF
(rest of program...)
```

The flaw in this example is that the IF statement begins within the DO WHILE loop but ends outside of it. Whenever an IF-ENDIF statement is used inside a DO WHILE loop, the IF statement must terminate within the DO WHILE loop. The same is true for the other programming structures with matching statements—ENDSCAN, ENDDO, and ENDCASE. In this example, the properly designed loop would look like this:

```
STORE 0 TO CHOICE
DO WHILE CHOICE < 3
    INPUT "Enter selection:" TO CHOICE
    IF CHOICE = 1
        SKIP
        DELETE
    ELSE
        IF .NOT. EOF( )
            SKIP
        ENDIF
        ? NAME, CITY, STATE
    ENDIF
ENDDO
STORE RECNO( ) TO LOCATION
(rest of program...)
```

- Improper mixing of data types, such as character strings mixed with numeric variables or date strings mixed with logical expressions. If you tell FoxPro to store the value 3 to a variable and to store the character string "3" to another variable, the two items are interpreted in entirely different ways. FoxPro recognizes the first entry as a numeric value of 3. The second entry is stored as a string of characters—in this case, the character 3. If you apply a string option to the numeric variable or you try to use the string variable in a calculation, you will get all sorts of errors in your program. Different types of variables cannot be used interchangeably unless you use functions (like ASC, DTOC, and VAL) to convert the type.

FoxPro provides you with debugging tools to help you track down hard-to-find bugs in your programs. These tools take the form of several SET commands: SET TALK, SET ECHO, SET DEBUG, SET STEP, and SET ALTERNATE.

Using SET TALK

You have routinely used the SET TALK command in previous examples. If SET TALK is activated (which it is by default), FoxPro displays responses to its commands that perform calculations or display record numbers (like LOCATE). This extra information isn't all that necessary during daily operation of the program, but in debugging it is useful to display results as the command file is being executed. To see this "talk" on the screen, tack on the SET TALK ON command at the beginning of the command file. You can then watch the screen as the program is run for hints that will help you find the errors in the program. Using SET TALK OFF will turn off the screen display of processing results. Note that turning on either SET TALK or SET ECHO (detailed next) will slow down program execution.

Using SET ECHO

SET ECHO is similar to SET TALK. The SET ECHO command will cause each command line to be printed on the screen as it is executed. This will let you follow the flow of the program. Since SET ECHO is normally deactivated, enter a SET ECHO ON command before running the program. Entering a SET ECHO OFF command will disable the display.

Using SET STEP

FoxPro programs often execute with such speed that it is difficult to pace the flow of the program. If you use the SET STEP ON command, FoxPro will pause after the execution of each command line and display the program inside of a Trace window. Two options that appear at the bottom of the window are Cancel and

Resume. Choose Resume to continue stepping through the program, or choose Cancel to halt program execution.

Using SET ALTERNATE

For problems that occur only when you are not around and some one else is using the program, you can use the SET ALTERNATE commands to save a record of operations to a disk file. SET ALTERNATE TO *filename* creates a file that will store any keyboard entries and most screen displays. The file will have the extension .TXT. When the SET ALTERNATE ON command is used, everything that appears on your screen, with the exception of full- screen editing operations, will be stored in the text file in ASCII format. When you no longer want the information to be stored in the file, you use the SET ALTERNATE OFF command. You can continue to use SET ALTERNATE ON and SET ALTERNATE OFF as many times as desired to add more text to the file. When you are finished with the process altogether, you can close the file with the CLOSE ALTERNATE command.

You can later examine the contents of the text file to see what replies to the program were typed and what program responses occurred as a result. Obviously, using these commands may quickly consume disk space, so consider available disk space before using the SET ALTERNATE commands for an extended period of time.

CUSTOMIZING FOXPRO WITH SET COMMANDS

Other SET commands can be used to customize your program and take advantage of various FoxPro features. The list presented here is not a complete list, but it does include the most commonly used SET commands.

SET BELL

The SET BELL ON command activates the beep that sounds during data entry. The beep is normally on and will sound when you fill a field with data or enter incorrect data into a field (such as character data into a numeric field). SET BELL OFF will deactivate the beep.

SET CARRY

When you use APPEND, the record that appears on the screen is normally blank. Entering a SET CARRY ON command causes FoxPro to copy the entries in the fields of the previous record to the new record when you issue an APPEND command. SET CARRY OFF disables this feature.

SET COLOR

The SET COLOR command sets color for screen display for a color monitor and sets screen highlighting for a monochrome monitor. The normal format of the command is

SET COLOR TO *standard, enhanced, border*

where *standard, enhanced,* and *border* are pairs of letters, separated by a slash, that represent the desired foreground and back-

Color	Code
Black	N
Blue	B
Green	G
Cyan	BG
Red	R
Magenta	BR
Brown	GR
White	W
Blank (secure)	X

TABLE 16-1. Color Code for SET COLOR

ground colors or screen highlighting. The values are shown in Table 16-1. If you have a color monitor, try the following:

```
SET COLOR TO B/W, R/GR, BR
CLEAR
LIST STATUS
```

This results in a standard display of blue letters on a white background, an enhanced (reverse-video) display of red letters on a brown background, and a border color of magenta. On monochrome monitors, acceptable values are white, black, and the letter "U" (for underline), which causes all characters on the screen to be underlined.

SET CONSOLE

The SET CONSOLE command turns screen displays on or off. SET CONSOLE is normally on, but once a SET CONSOLE OFF command is encountered, no information is displayed on the screen, although commands will still be executed. Not until a SET CONSOLE ON is executed will information again be displayed. Using SET CONSOLE is like turning the monitor screen on or off.

SET DATE

The SET DATE command sets the desired format for date values and expressions. FoxPro offers any one of ten date formats: American (MM/DD/YY), ANSI (YY.MM.DD), British/French (DD/MM/YY), Italian (DD-MM-YY), Japan (YY/MM/DD), USA (MM-DD-YY), German (DD.MM.YY), MDY (MM/DD/YY), DMY (DD/MM/YY), and YMD (YY/MM/DD). Unless told otherwise, FoxPro sets the default value of the date format to American. The format of the command is SET DATE *format,* where *format* is American, ANSI, British, Italian, French, German, Japan, USA, MDY, DMY, or YMD.

SET DECIMALS

This command sets the number of decimal places that are displayed during calculations. The format of the command is SET DECIMALS to *expression,* where *expression* is an integer value limiting the decimal places. Thus, if SET DECIMALS is assigned to 4, then 4 decimal places will be displayed until another SET DECIMAL command is executed. The default is 2 digits. Numbers are rounded off as necessary to match the settings of SET DECIMALS.

SET ESCAPE

The SET ESCAPE command disables the ability of the ESC key to interrupt a program. To disable the ESC key, you enter the SET ESCAPE OFF command. SET ESCAPE ON turns the ESC key back on. In most cases, the use of SET ESCAPE OFF within a program is recommended. You probably do not want novice users pressing the ESC key and seeing the dialog box with the Cancel, Ignore, and Suspend choices appearing. Most novice users would have no idea what to do at such a point. Simply add a SET ESCAPE OFF statement near the start of your program to disable the use of the ESC key.

SET EXACT

The SET EXACT command is used to tell FoxPro to perform (or not to perform) exact comparisons between character strings. The format of the command is SET EXACT ON/OFF. For example, assuming that SET EXACT is off, the commands

```
USE MEMBERS
LIST FOR LASTNAME = "Rob"
```

will find all records with Robinson in the Lastname field, because FoxPro will only compare as many characters as are contained in the string to the right of the operator (in this case, three characters). When SET EXACT is off, FoxPro will only compare as many characters as there are in the shorter string, so in the previous example FoxPro only looks at the first three characters because there are only three characters in "Rob." By comparison, the commands

```
SET EXACT ON
USE MEMBERS
LIST FOR LASTNAME = "Rob"
```

will not find any records in the MEMBERS database that apply, because Rob is not an exact match of Robinson.

SET NEAR

The SET NEAR command tells FoxPro to position the record pointer at the nearest record if a FIND or SEEK operation is unsuccessful. If SET NEAR is off (which is the default) and you perform a FIND or SEEK command that is not successful, the record pointer is placed at the end of the database, and the EOF function returns a logical true. You can use the SET NEAR ON command to tell FoxPro to get as close as possible if a search of the index is not successful. This can be useful when you are searching for the beginning of a range of data.

SET FUNCTION

This command changes the performance of the function keys. Each function key is assigned to a FoxPro command. When pressed the keys execute the commands shown in Table 16-2 (the semicolons following the commands produce carriage returns). You can

Function Key	FoxPro Command
F1	HELP;
F2	SET;
F3	LIST;
F4	DIR;
F5	DISPLAY STRUCTURE;
F6	DISPLAY STATUS;
F7	DISPLAY MEMORY;
F8	DISPLAY;
F9	APPEND;

TABLE 16-2. Model of a procedure file

change the function keys, with the exception of F1 and F10, to any character expression of 79 characters or fewer by entering

SET FUNCTION *integer-expression* TO *"character- string"*

The F1 key is reserved for the Help key, and the F10 key is reserved for the FoxPro menus.

The character string must be enclosed in quotes. For example, to change F7 from DISPLAY MEMORY to BROWSE, enter

SET FUNCTION "7" TO "BROWSE;"

Remember to include the semicolon to produce a return.

The SET FUNCTION command can be quite useful for reducing the number of repetitive steps during the data-entry process. As an example, if you include the following SET FUNCTION commands within the MENU.PRG program for Generic Videos, the function keys would be redefined to enter the names of various cities and states:

```
SET FUNCTION "2" TO "Silver Spring"
SET FUNCTION "3" TO "Rockville"
SET FUNCTION "4" TO "Columbia"
SET FUNCTION "5" TO "Washington"
SET FUNCTION "6" TO "Alexandria"
SET FUNCTION "7" TO "Falls Church"
SET FUNCTION "8" TO "Alexandria"
SET FUNCTION "9" TO "Springfield"
```

When the commands shown in this example have been executed, users can press the respective function keys during the APPEND or CHANGE process to enter the names without typing the actual keystrokes. You can also assign a sequence of commands to a function key, providing you separate commands with a semicolon and do not exceed the 79-character limit. During large data-entry jobs, reassigning the function keys in this manner can save hours of time in entering records.

SET INTENSITY

This command turns on or off the reverse-video display of fields during full-screen operations such as APPEND. To activate reverse video, use SET INTENSITY ON; to deactivate reverse video, use SET INTENSITY OFF. In general, you only use SET INTENSITY OFF if you use the SET DELIMITERS command to change the default delimiters. Otherwise, you won't be able to gauge the limits of the data-entry areas. SET INTENSITY is normally on, but you can find out the current state of SET INTENSITY or the status of any SET command by entering

DISPLAY STATUS

The status of the SET commands along with the function key designations will then be displayed. Here is an example:

```
LIST STATUS
Processor is INTEL 80386
File search path:
Default disk drive: E:
Print file/device: PRN:
Work area =   1
Margin   =   0
Decimals =   2
Memowidth = 50
Typeahead = 20
History  = 20

Date format: American
```

Alternate	- off	Console	- on	Exact	- off	Safety	- on
Bell	- on	Debug	- off	Fields	- off	Scoreboard	- off
Carry	- off	Deleted	- off	Fixed	- off	Space	- on
Catalog	- off	Delimiters	- off	Heading	- on	Status	- off
Century	- off	Device	- scrn	Help	- on		Step-off
Clear	- on	Dohistory	- off	History	- on	Talk	- on
Color	- on	Echo	- off	Intensity	- on	Title	- off
Compatible	- off	Ems	- on	Menu	- on	Unique	- off
Confirm	- off	Escape	- on	Print	- off		

SET MEMOWIDTH TO

The SET MEMOWIDTH TO command is used to control the width of a memo field when it is displayed with a LIST or DISPLAY command. The default value is 50 characters wide. Using SET MEMOWIDTH TO to narrow the default width of a memo field can result in a more pleasing display of information. As an example, the commands

USE MEMBERS
LIST LASTNAME, FIRSTNAME, PREFERENCE

result in this display:

Record#   LASTNAME FIRSTNAME   PREFERENCE

       1   Miller   Karen   Prefers science fiction,
horror movies. Fan of Star Trek films.

       2   Martin   William   Enjoys Clint Eastwood,
John Wayne films.

       3   Robinson Carol   Likes comedy, drama
films.
       4   Kramer   Harry   Big fan of Eddie Murphy.
Also enjoys westerns.

The display is an unattractive one because the words in the memo field wrap around the screen at the right-hand margin. The commands

```
SET MEMOWIDTH TO 20
USE MEMBERS
LIST LASTNAME, FIRSTNAME, PREFERENCE
```

provide a much more attractive format for the display of the memo field, as shown here:

Record#	LASTNAME	FIRSTNAME	PREFERENCE
1	Miller	Karen	Prefers science fiction, horror movies. Fan of Star Trek films.
2	Martin	William	Enjoys Clint Eastwood, John Wayne films.
3	Robinson	Carol	Likes comedy, drama films.
4	Kramer	Harry	Big fan of Eddie Murphy. Also enjoys westerns.

SET MESSAGE TO

The SET MESSAGE TO command is used to display an optional message at a specific line, and it is used to determine which line the message will appear on. For messages to appear, SET STATUS must also be on. First you enter SET MESSAGE TO *n,* where *n* is a number representing the line on the screen where the message should appear. Next, you use the command SET MESSAGE TO *character-string,* where *character-string* is the text you want included in the message. The message will appear whenever menus are displayed using the MENU TO command. The commands

SET MESSAGE TO 24
SET MESSAGE TO "Generic Videos Database System - F1 for HELP"

causes the message to be displayed at the bottom of the screen if SET STATUS was on and a menu was being displayed.

SET SAFETY

The SET SAFETY command lets you specify whether a prompt will warn you when FoxPro is about to overwrite an existing file. When SET SAFETY is on and any command will result in the overwriting of an existing file (such as rebuilding an index or sorting to a file with the same name as an existing file), FoxPro will display a warning message within a pop-up menu, and you must confirm the desire to overwrite the file by choosing Overwrite from the menu. SET SAFETY is normally on with FoxPro. This can result in unwanted messages and interruptions within your programs when you intentionally want to overwrite a file. In such cases, you can include a SET SAFETY OFF command in your program, and FoxPro will not stop to ask for confirmation before overwriting a file. If you use SET SAFETY OFF in a program, it is a good idea to turn it on again before returning the user to the command level.

USING USER-DEFINED FUNCTIONS

User-defined functions (UDFs) are functions that you design, and like the standard functions in FoxPro, they can be provided with values and they return values. You can use UDFs to accomplish specialized tasks that are outside the range of the standard functions provided with FoxPro.

You place functions within a procedure file, along with any other procedures your program may be using. All UDFs start with the FUNCTION command, and they contain the commands and parameters needed to return the desired values. The names given to UDFs must be eight characters or less. The syntax of a UDF is shown here:

FUNCTION *UDFname*
PARAMETERS *list-of-parameters*
    commands....
RETURN *value-or-variable*

where *list-of-parameters* is a list of one or more memory variable names representing the values you will supply to the function. As an example, perhaps you often need to convert temperature readings in centigrade stored in a scientific database to Fahrenheit. You could define the following function for this purpose:

FUNCTION FARENHT
PARAMETERS ctemp
ftemp = 9/5 * (ctemp+32)
RETURN ftemp

Then, at any location in the program, you would call the function just as you would any other function. If the database field containing the temperature readings was named TEMP, you could use a statement like

? FARENHT(TEMP)

and the FARENHT function would return the value contained in the Temp field, converted to Fahrenheit.

You can also specify that UDFs return a true or false value, depending on how the commands within your UDF evaluate a particular condition. An example of this technique appears in the sample UDF shown here, which checks to see if a two-letter code for a state entered by a user is actually a valid state:

```
FUNCTION ValState
PARAMETERS State
IF UPPER(state) $ "AK AL AR AZ CA CO CT DC DE FL GA + ;
HI IA ID IL IN KA KY LA MA MD ME MI MN MO MS MT NB + ;
NC ND NH NJ NM NY OH OK OR PA RI SC SD TN TX UT VA + ;
VT WA WI WV WY"
        RETURN .T.
ENDIF
RETURN .F.
```

A portion of a data-entry program could use the function to verify for proper entries, as shown here:

```
@ 7, 5 SAY "State: " GET MSTATE
READ
IF .NOT. ValState(MSTATE)
        WAIT "Error in State code."
        LOOP
ENDIF
<...rest of program...>
```

If the user's response did not match one of the two-letter codes defined in the function, the function would return a value of false, causing the error message to appear.

ENHANCING FOXPRO POWER WITH LOAD AND CALL

Two FoxPro commands that do much towards tapping power not normally present in FoxPro are the LOAD and CALL commands, which are used to access assembly language programs written in binary (.BIN) format. You can transfer control to an assembly language routine, and assuming the program is written to move data, you can pass data from the routine back to FoxPro.

The LOAD command is used to tell FoxPro that the assembly language routine exists and needs to be loaded into memory for future use. The syntax for the command is

LOAD *binary-filename.ext*

The extension is optional; if omitted, it is assumed to be .BIN. Up to five binary files can be loaded into memory at once, and each can be up to 32K in size. (Unneeded modules that have been loaded into memory can be released with the RELEASE MODULE *module-name* command.)

Once the binary file has been loaded into memory, it can be executed at any time with the CALL command, which has the syntax of

CALL *module-name* [WITH *expression/memory- variable*]

where *module-name* is the name of the binary file (the extension is omitted). The optional WITH clause lets you specify a character expression or a memory variable that is passed to the assembly language routine. When your FoxPro program processes the CALL command, control is passed to the binary routine, and execution begins at the first byte of the routine. Once control passes to the routine, the data segment (DS and BX registers) will contain the address for the first byte of the memory variable or character expression that was passed from FoxPro.

FoxPro treats binary files loaded and executed with the LOAD and CALL commands differently than external program files executed with RUN. When you use RUN, FoxPro creates a DOS shell and transfers control over to the program called with RUN. Because you are building a duplicate of COMMAND.COM in memory and loading the external program, this can eat up significant amounts of memory. By comparison, with LOAD and CALL, FoxPro treats the binary files as subroutines or *modules,* and not as external programs. As a result, FoxPro needs considerably less additional memory to use LOAD and CALL. You may encounter problems on a 512K machine, but any system with 640K or more should allow FoxPro and your external assembly language routines to coexist without difficulty.

An Example of Using LOAD and CALL

A simple example can demonstrate the ease with which LOAD and CALL can be used. For this simple example you will need nothing more than your DOS disks and FoxPro. Find your DOS Supplemental disk, and copy the DEBUG.COM program onto your working disk, into a directory accessible through your PATH commands or into your FoxPro directory.

This binary routine, which changes the shape of the cursor, can easily be created with a copy of DEBUG. To try creating the program, get to the DOS prompt and enter **DEBUG**. The Debug prompt (a hyphen) will appear. Enter the following:

```
A              (press ENTER)
MOV CX,[BX]    (press ENTER)
MOV AH,1       (press ENTER)
INT 10         (press ENTER)
```

RETF	(press ENTER)
	(press ENTER again; hyphen will appear)
RCX	(press ENTER; colon will appear)
7	(press ENTER; hyphen will appear)
NCURSOR.BIN	(press ENTER)
W	(press ENTER; file will be saved to disk)
Q	(press ENTER to get back to DOS)

This book is not meant to serve as an introduction to assembler; there are enough well-done texts on the market for that purpose. Suffice to say that these commands used the mini-assembler built into DEBUG to create a binary assembly language routine.

With the program, CURSOR.BIN, saved on disk, get into FoxPro, and at the command level enter

LOAD CURSOR

to load the .BIN file into memory. Then enter

CALL CURSOR WITH CHR(18)

to change the shape of the cursor to a flashing block.

This simple example performs an admittedly simple function, but all binary routines, no matter how complex, can be accessed from within FoxPro in the same manner.

Sources of Assembler Routines

If you are thinking "This is just fine for those assembly language hackers, but I have no intention of writing code in assembler," the good news is you don't have to if you don't wish to. There is no shortage of assembly language .BIN files on publicly available disks from software vendors, user groups, and computer bulletin boards. Many of the utilities provided in commercial products such as dBASE Tools for C and the Tom Rettig Library are .BIN files, executable with the LOAD and CALL commands. Listings of products like these can often be found in the pages of magazines like *DBMS* and *Databased Advisor*.

Assembler Guidelines And a Warning

Certain guidelines must be followed if you are designing your own binary files to be accessed from FoxPro with the LOAD and CALL commands. If you do write your own binary files, the guidelines that follow will make sense. If you don't, the guidelines become someone else's problem; however, that person should be aware of these rules.

1. Your binary routine must begin (ORG) its first executable instruction at offset zero.

2. Leave the stack pointer and the contents of the stack *alone*. Violating this rule is a sure way to wreak havoc when you attempt to return from the binary routine back to FoxPro. At worst, you will crash your system, requiring a complete reboot. If you must play around with the stack within your routine, you should restore both the stack segment (SS) and code segment (CS) registers to their original states before returning control to FoxPro.

3. Do not design routines that consume additional RAM beyond the size of the program. The LOAD command uses the file size to allocate memory, and you may overwrite portions of FoxPro in RAM if the program dynamically increases its memory needs.

4. Make sure that the binary routine ends with a FAR RETURN. This ensures that program control will return to the address that was pushed onto the stack before the routine began its execution. If someone else is writing a BIN routine for use in FoxPro for you, this is an important point to stress. Many binary routines are written to end with an EXIT, rather than a FAR RETURN. Assembly language programs that end with EXIT should be assembled into fully executable files and called with RUN, rather than with LOAD and CALL.

Finally, a warning: If you commonly use both binary routines accessed with LOAD and CALL and external programs accessed with RUN, you can paint yourself into a corner with memory allocation conflicts that are very, very difficult to debug. If you use LOAD to load a series of binary files and then use RUN to run an external program before you get around to using the binary files with CALL commands, you may overwrite the binary files in memory with the effects of the RUN command. Then your program later tries a CALL command and jumps to a point in memory where the expected routine no longer exists. To avoid the bizarre results of this problem, remove unneeded binary files from memory with the RELEASE *binary-module-name* command before running external programs with the RUN command.

DRAWING BAR GRAPHS

Bar graphs can be drawn by using the CHR and REPLICATE functions to plot representative columns on the screen. If your printer supports the extended character set, you can route the output to the printer and achieve similar results. Given a database containing the data shown here,

Record#	SALESREP	REPNUMB	AMTSOLD
1	Jones, C.	1003	350.00
2	Artis, K.	1008	110.00
3	Johnson, L.	1002	675.00
4	Walker, B.	1006	1167.00
5	Keemis, M.	1007	47.00
6	Williams, E.	1010	256.00
7	Smith, A.M.	1009	220.00
8	Allen, L.	1005	312.00
9	Smith, A.	1001	788.50
10	Jones, J.	1011	875.00
11	Shepard, F.	1004	1850.00
12	Robertson, C.	1013	985.50

plotting the data with the following program results in the display shown in Figure 16-2.

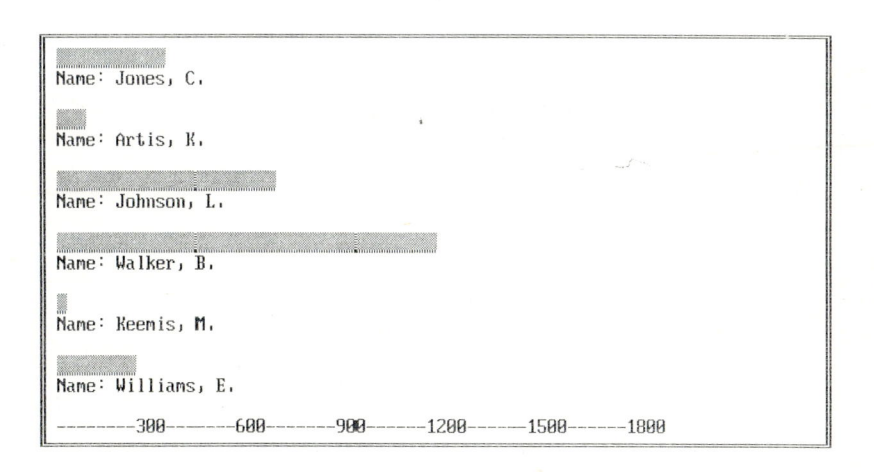

FIGURE 16-2. Bar graph

```
*Bars.PRG is bar graph program.
SET TALK OFF
Divisor = 30
*See note in text on calculating Divisor.
*AmtSold is field in database to be graphed.
CLEAR
USE SALES
@ 2, 1
*above line positions cursor at row 2, col 1.
DO WHILE .NOT. EOF( )
        BarLength = INT(AMTSOLD/DIVISOR)
        @ ROW( ), 2 SAY REPLICATE(CHR(177),BarLength)
        @ ROW( )+1, 2 SAY "Name: " + SALESREP
        @ ROW( ) + 2, 0
        IF ROW( ) > 18
                @ 20, 2 SAY "--------300-------600-------900--" +;
                "----1200------1500------1800"
                @ 1, 0 TO 21, 79 DOUBLE
                WAIT "Press a key for next screen..."
                CLEAR
                @ 2, 1
        ENDIF
        SKIP
ENDDO
IF ROW( ) > 2
        @ 20, 2 SAY "--------300-------600-------900--" +;
        "----1200------1500------1800"
        @ 1, 0 TO 21, 79 DOUBLE
        WAIT
ENDIF
RETURN
```

The program takes the contents of a field that is to be graphed (in this case, Amtsold), divides it by a set amount (Divisor), and uses the INT function to return an integer based on that figure. This number, stored to the memory variable BarLength, is then used as an argument in the REPLICATE function to determine the length of the bar. The ROW function, which returns the current row in which the cursor is located, is used at various locations in the program to place data on the screen.

The calculation of the best value for Divisor is a simple matter. Assuming you want to use nearly a complete screen width for the longest bar, the value of Divisor must be no less than the value of the highest amount to be graphed, divided by the available screen width. In this example, the highest sales amount ($1850) divided by a screen width of 76 (which leaves room for the starting position and the borders) suggests a value of no less than 24. The example used a value of 30, partly to make the scale simple to construct and partly to leave room for increased sales performance. You will need to adjust the scope of your scale accordingly.

USING MODULAR PROGRAMMING

Don't get the impression that this section is going to take you through a textbook discussion of the benefits of system analysis and modular design. You can find that kind of a discussion in more than enough basic programming textbooks. What this section will demonstrate are ways to design FoxPro applications in modular form so that you can easily utilize the same code repeatedly.

Assuming you write programs in FoxPro (and if you didn't, you probably would not be reading this chapter), chances are you're spending time on the development of more than one program. If all your FoxPro work centers around a single application (like that monster of a sales-tracking system that keeps tabs on things at your office), then writing very modular programs may not help you much except as an aid in debugging and providing a warm feeling for having developed efficient code. But if you have to develop or maintain a number of different applications at your work location or for others, you will save a lot of time by writing programs in modules and reusing the modules (with appropriate modifications) for different tasks.

The first step in adopting a system of modular FoxPro coding is to recognize that tasks in most FoxPro applications fall into the same common groups. Applications provide a main menu, leading to other choices stored in individual programs or as procedures. Among those other tasks handled within the submodules, or individual procedures of the FoxPro application, are the tasks of adding records, editing records, and deleting unwanted records. You can further break many of the subtasks down into common parts.

As an example, consider the task of editing records in a database. Well-written routines for editing records are faced with at least six tasks within the editing module:

1. Find the desired record to edit.

2. Store the contents of the fields into memory variables.

3. Display the prompts and memory variables on the screen.

4. Allow editing of the memory variables with GET statements.

5. Perform any data validation desired, and allow corrections when necessary.

6. Move the validated data into the database.

Most programs written to perform a task like this one are written as one complete submodule that handles all these steps. But if you are going to use and reuse your code for multiple applications, strict adherence to the concepts behind modular programming suggest that you take it a step further and create individual modules for the individual steps. This may seem like a lot of work, but the first time you need to use the existing code in another application, you'll be glad that you chose this method of design.

A general approach you can consider following in designing highly modular code for a FoxPro application is to write the following routines for each database file and then enclose the routines within a procedure file that can be accessed through the SET PROCEDURE TO *filename* command:

- A "display" procedure for adding borders and graphic designs in a consistent format

- A "makevars" procedure for creating memory variables

- A "fillvars" routine for moving the contents of a field into a memory variable

- A "sayer" routine to display the prompts and memory variables

- A "getter" routine for getting memory variables

- A "validate" routine for performing any desired data validation

- A "movevars" routine to move the contents of the memory variables into the database fields

- A "finder" routine to locate records based on FIND or SEEK commands using available index files

As an example, consider the procedures described within a procedure file:

```
*Procedrs.PRG
Procedure Border
@ 0, 0 TO 19, 79 DOUBLE
@ 0, 1 TO 4, 78 DOUBLE
Draw = 1
Do While Draw < 4
     @ Draw, 2 SAY REPLICATE(chr(176),76)
     Draw = Draw + 1
Enddo
Return
**************************
```

```
Procedure Finder
DO MAKEVARS
@ 3, 5 SAY "Enter BLANKS to EXIT."
@ 5, 5 SAY "Last name? " GET M_LAST
@ 6, 5 SAY "First name? " GET M_FIRST
READ
STORE M_LAST + M_FIRST TO FINDIT
SEEK FINDIT
RETURN
***************************
Procedure Sayer
@ 5, 10 SAY "Last Name:"
@ 5, 22 SAY M_LAST
@ 6, 10 SAY "First name:"
@ 6, 22 SAY M_FIRST
@ 7, 10 SAY "Address:"
@ 7, 22 SAY M_ADDRESS
@ 8, 15 SAY "City:"
@ 8, 22 SAY M_CITY
@ 9, 15 SAY "State:"
@ 9, 22 SAY M_STATE
@ 10, 15 SAY "Zip:"
@ 10, 22 SAY M_ZIP
RETURN
***************************
Procedure Getter
@ 5, 22 GET M_LAST
@ 6, 22 GET M_FIRST
@ 7, 22 GET M_ADDRESS
@ 8, 22 GET M_CITY
@ 9, 22 GET M_STATE
@ 10, 22 GET M_ZIP
RETURN
***************************
Procedure MakeVars
PUBLIC M_LAST, M_FIRST, M_ADDRESS, M_CITY,;
M_STATE, M_ZIP
M_LAST = space(15)
```

```
M_FIRST = space(15)
M_ADDRESS = space(25)
M_CITY = space(15)
M_STATE = space(2)
M_ZIP = space(10)
RETURN
***************************
Procedure FillVars
M_LAST = LASTNAME
M_FIRST = FIRSTNAME
M_ADDRESS = ADDRESS
M_CITY = CITY
M_STATE = STATE
M_ZIP = ZIPCODE
RETURN
***************************
Procedure MoveVars
REPLACE LASTNAME WITH M_LAST, FIRSTNAME WITH M_FIRST,;
ADDRESS WITH M_ADDRESS, CITY WITH M_CITY,;
STATE WITH M_STATE, ZIPCODE WITH M_ZIP
RETURN
***************************
Procedure Validate
IF M_LAST = SPACE(15)
   WAIT " Name required!"
   VALID = .F.
ENDIF
RETURN
```

By putting all of these tasks in a procedure file and using DO commands to call the procedures from your add, edit, and delete subroutines, you can repeatedly use the same procedures in all of the routines. A program for adding records utilizing these procedures can be visually laid out in a block diagram, as shown in Figure 16-3. The resultant code that might be used as follows:

```
*Adder.PRG adds records*
VALID = .T.
DO WHILE .T.
   DO MAKEVARS
   CLEAR
   DO BORDER
   @ 3, 10 SAY "DATA ENTRY SCREEN ADD NEW RECORDS"
   DO SAYER
   DO GETTER
   READ
   DO VALIDATE
   IF .NOT. VALID
      LOOP
   ENDIF
   APPEND BLANK
   DO MOVEVARS
   ACCEPT "Add another record? Y/N:" TO ANS
   IF UPPER(ANS) = "N"
      EXIT
   ENDIF
ENDDO
```

The beauty of taking program modularization down to this level is that you can get away with the same code that is already in the procedures for the edit and delete routines. An editing routine,

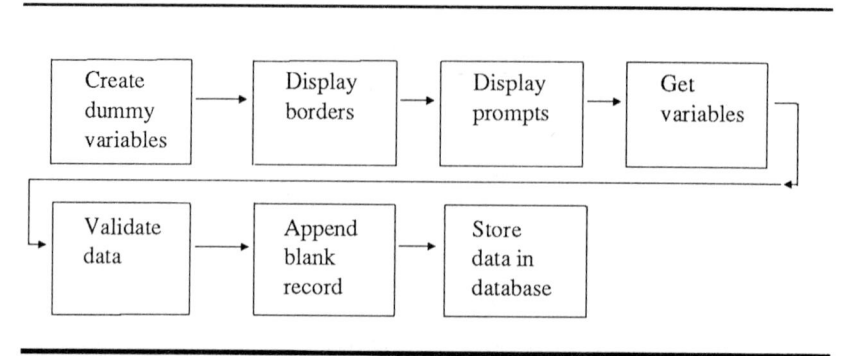

FIGURE 16-3. Block diagram of add routine

Advanced Programming Topics 529

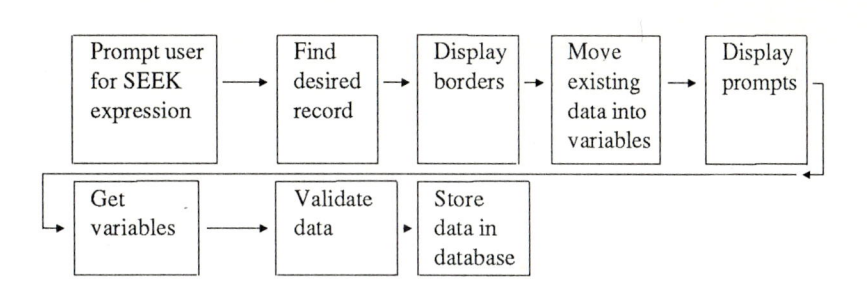

```
┌─────────────┐   ┌─────────┐   ┌─────────┐   ┌──────────┐   ┌─────────┐
│ Prompt user │   │ Find    │   │ Display │   │ Move     │   │ Display │
│ for SEEK    │──▶│ desired │──▶│ borders │──▶│ existing │──▶│ prompts │
│ expression  │   │ record  │   │         │   │ data into│   │         │
│             │   │         │   │         │   │ variables│   │         │
└─────────────┘   └─────────┘   └─────────┘   └──────────┘   └─────────┘
   ┌─────────┐   ┌─────────┐   ┌─────────┐
   │ Get     │   │ Validate│   │ Store   │
 ─▶│variables│──▶│ data    │──▶│ data in │
   │         │   │         │   │ database│
   └─────────┘   └─────────┘   └─────────┘
```

FIGURE 16-4. Block diagram of edit routine

assuming the database is indexed on a combination of last and first names, is illustrated in the block diagram shown in Figure 16-4. The resultant code that might be used is shown here:

```
*Editor.PRG edits records
SET INDEX TO NAMES
DO WHILE .T.
        CLEAR
        DO MAKEVARS
        DO FINDER
        VALID = .T.
        IF FOUND( )
           CLEAR
           DO BORDER
           DO FILLVARS
           DO SAYER
           DO GETTER
           READ
           DO VALIDATE
           IF .NOT. VALID
             EXIT
           ENDIF
           DO MOVEVARS
           CLEAR
           ACCEPT "Edit another? Y/N " TO ANS
```

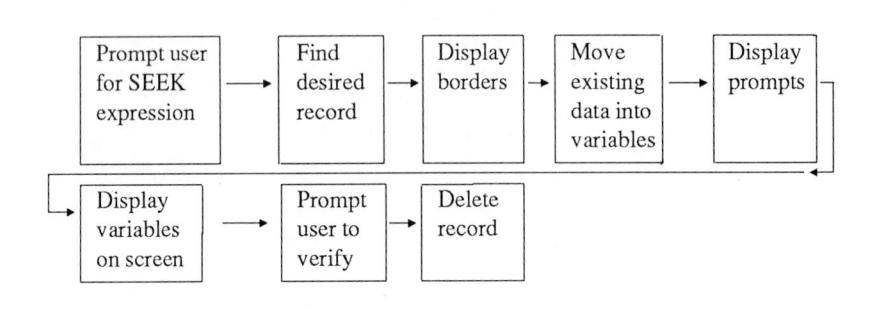

```
                Prompt user     Find           Display        Move            Display
                for SEEK    →   desired    →   borders    →   existing    →   prompts
                expression      record                        data into
                                                              variables

         ┌───── Display         Prompt         Delete
         │      variables   →   user to    →   record
                on screen       verify
```

FIGURE 16-5. Block diagram of delete routine

```
            IF UPPER(ANS) = "N"
                  EXIT
            ENDIF
      ELSE
            CLEAR
            @ 5, 5 SAY "No record by that name!"
            WAIT
            EXIT
      ENDIF
ENDDO
```

Your routine for deleting records would use much of the same code, like that illustrated in Figure 16-5, and shown in this code:

```
*Eraser.PRG deletes records
SET INDEX TO NAMES
DO WHILE .T.
      CLEAR
      STORE "Y" TO ANS
      DO MAKEVARS
      DO FINDER
      IF FOUND( )
            CLEAR
            DO BORDER
            DO FILLVARS
```

```
            DO SAYER
            @ 20, 5 SAY "Delete record, are you SURE? Y/N:"
            @ 20,40 GET ANS
            READ
            IF UPPER(ANS) = "Y"
                DELETE
            ENDIF
        ELSE
            CLEAR
            @ 5, 5 SAY "No record by that name!"
            WAIT
            EXIT
        ENDIF
ENDDO
```

Since the routines that perform the adding, editing, and deleting of records are generic routines (containing few or no specifics to that particular application), when you need to rewrite an application for a different database design, you'll need to make most changes only in the procedure file.

When do you modularize? It's easy to get carried away and modularize virtually every task in an application, but this probably won't buy you visible benefits in every case. A major objective of this approach is to save you the time it takes to duplicate program code in more than one location, so a general rule to follow is obvious: If the task is likely to be repeated at more than one place in your application, code that task as a procedure and call it from the procedure file. If the task will only be performed once, you may want to leave it as program code integral to that particular program, since calling it as a procedure won't provide you with any visible benefits.

17

CREATING APPLICATIONS WITH FOXVIEW

Applications
Creating a Simple Application
Creating a More Complex Application
Creating an Advanced Application
About FoxPro Templates

If you've followed this book closely, you should have a good knowledge of how you can put FoxPro to work. You have created different database files, used menu options or commands for getting information from those database files, designed custom reports, and used macros to automate your work. If you've covered the last five chapters, you've also been introduced to writing programs made up of command files in FoxPro. This chapter covers the use of an additional tool, FoxView, which is useful for creating menu-driven applications. Chapter 5 detailed the use of FoxView to create screen forms; this chapter shows how you can

533

use additional menu options within FoxView to create complete applications.

APPLICATIONS

First, why are applications so important to database users? In a nutshell, an application makes things easier on the average user by combining a series of building blocks—such as database files, forms, reports, and labels—into a complete system. An application is what makes an accounts receivable system different from a database containing accounts receivable information. Both deal with the same kinds of information: dollar amounts and bills to recipients containing breakdowns of those amounts. But the accounts receivable database can only store the data, while the accounts receivable system has the database and all the other files (indexes, forms, reports, and programs) needed to solve a particular business problem.

Besides helping you meet the needs of a specific task, an application binds together the building blocks of a database system. If you consider the parts of a database system—one or more database files, the indexes, the forms, labels, and the reports—to be building blocks of a sort, the application can be thought of as a kind of glue that binds them into a complete unit. Applications are nothing new in the computer world, and there is a good chance that you have already used some types of specialized applications based on a database of some sort. Programs to handle mailing lists, inventory, sales tracking, and accounting are all specialized applications that make use of databases. To use these types of applications, however, you had to buy a software package designed for the application or pay a programmer to write it, and then you were often stuck with something that did most but not all of what you wanted. By using your programming skills along with tools such as FoxView, you can build custom applications designed to do precisely what you want.

To further illustrate how an application can make things easier, consider the work you've done, if you have followed the examples throughout this book, to create a system for Generic Videos. You have database files for tracking both members and rental tapes checked out by members, and you have custom forms and custom reports. With your familiarity with FoxPro, if you want to add or edit data or generate reports, you can load FoxPro and use various menu options or commands to accomplish the desired results.

But what happens when you want to show someone else in the office how to add or edit data or how to produce reports? That person must go through the same kind of learning curve and become familiar enough with the FoxPro menus or commands to accomplish the same kind of results that you can manage. If your office has the usual moderate-to-high staff turnover common in today's business world, you could be faced with having to show others how to use FoxPro for the same tasks, year in and year out. The answer to this sort of dilemma, as proven by thousands of programmers year after year, is to build custom applications with menu choices that casual users will need no specialized training to understand.

Since the applications templates used to build applications are part of FoxView, you must get into FoxView to create an application. You can start FoxView by choosing FoxView from the Program menu or by entering **FOXVIEW** at the command level. Once you press ENTER to get past the entry screen, you are at the FoxView shell. You can then either load an existing screen form on which the application will be based, or you can open a database with the USE command and design a screen form around that database, as detailed in Chapter 5.

Once the screen form has been designed, you select a template that instructs FoxPro to build a complete application. You do this by opening the Gen menu and choosing the Select From Template List option. When this option is selected, another dialog box listing all possible templates appears. The template you choose controls what type of code is generated by FoxView. You used the Format File Generator template option in Chapter 5 to create format files for use in adding and editing data. For complete applications, you can use the FoxPro Advanced Application template, the File-Maintenance Application template, or the Simple Database Application template option. Each of these options will cause FoxView to generate complete applications based on your screen design.

The FoxPro Advanced Application option generates a complete application that is the most advanced of the three types. When produced, the application will provide a number of menu choices for moving around a database, adding or editing records, and performing various utility options such as reindexing and packing the database. The File-Maintenance Application option generates an application of moderate complexity; the application has menu options for adding or editing records, for generating labels or reports, for viewing or editing in Browse mode, and for performing a PACK on the database. The Simple Database Application template creates the least complex application, one which always displays a record on the screen along with a menu of choices below the record. The choices let you add records, edit or delete records, and move around within the database.

CREATING A SIMPLE APPLICATION

As an example, perhaps all that is needed is a quick way to add and edit records within the RENTALS database. Get into FoxView by entering **FOXVIEW** at the command level or choosing FoxView from the Program menu. Since no screen has yet been created for the RENTALS file, you must open the RENTALS file now. At the FoxView shell, enter the command

USE RENTALS

After the "4 field(s) loaded" message appears on the screen, press F10 to get to Forms View. Press F6 (Extend Select), press the DOWN

ARROW key three times, and then press ENTER to select all the fields. Press F3 (Drag) and move the block of fields four lines down and ten spaces to the right. Press ENTER to complete the movement.

Open the Box menu with CTRL-B, choose Double-Line, and move the box that appears one line up and two spaces to the left. Press ENTER to anchor the box, press F4 (Size), and use the arrow keys to stretch the box until all fields fit within the box with room to spare. Press ENTER when done to complete the resizing.

With the form designed, you are ready to tell FoxView to build a complete application. Press ESC to open the Gen menu, and choose Select From Template List from the menu. The list of templates will appear on the screen (Figure 17-1).

The first choice, FoxPro Advanced Application, generates the most complex type of application. The second choice, File Maintenance Application, generates the moderately complex type of

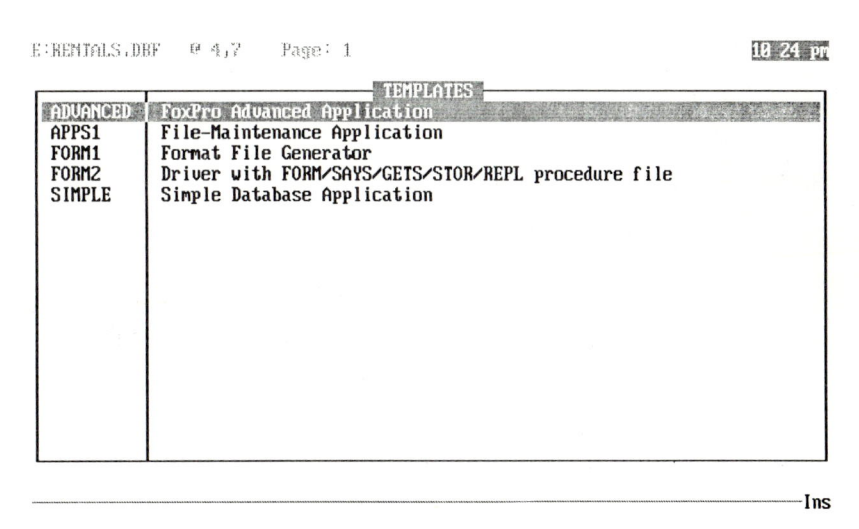

FIGURE 17-1. List of templates

application. (Both these types of applications will be demonstrated later in the chapter). The third option, Format File Generator, was demonstrated for building screen forms in Chapter 5. The fourth option, Driver with FORM/SAYS/GETS/STOR/REPL Procedure File, creates a program for displaying and editing a record. When run, the program displays the current record on the screen; you can press E (for Edit) to make changes to the record, or you can press ENTER to leave the program. The program created by this option is designed for use as part of a larger program that you may be writing; it would be the responsibility of your program to first locate the desired record for editing.

The last option, Simple Database Application, generates a simple application for use with the chosen database. Highlight this last option and press ENTER. A blank window will appear, and at the bottom of the screen FoxView will ask for a filename for the application. (This filename will contain a program, which you will later run with the DO command to start the application.) Enter

RENTS

as the name for the program file. You will next be asked to enter the name of the procedure file to generate. The application uses this name to build a procedure file, containing additional parts of the application. Enter

RENTS2

as the name for the procedure file. These names are up to you and need not be related in any way. However, you cannot use the same name for both files, because they will both be stored with a .PRG extension. It is helpful to keep track of the names for both the program and the procedure files in case you ever want to make changes to these programs with the Editor.

Once you enter the name for the procedure file, you will see program code generated by FoxView within the window. When the application is complete, you will see a "Press any key to continue" message at the bottom of the screen.

Press a key. The window will close, and the FoxView menu will reappear. Since this is a new screen design, you should save it also in case you want to modify it at a later time. Open the Load menu and choose Save Table; call the table RENTALS. Then open the Disk menu and select Quit FoxView to exit FoxView.

Once back in FoxPro, you can run the program with the DO command. Enter **DO RENTS** to start the program. In a moment, you will see a record shown through the screen form with the application choices in the form of a menu below the form as in Figure 17-2.

Each of the menu choices are selected by pressing the first letter of the choice. For example, pressing A for Append brings up a blank screen, and you can add a new record, finishing with CTRL-W. Pressing E for Edit lets you edit a record; again, pressing CTRL-W stores the changes and puts you back at the menu. Pressing D for Delete deletes the current record. This key acts as a toggle; if a record has been previously deleted, pressing D again will undelete the record.

The Next-Prev-Top-Bottom option moves you around in the database according to the letter that corresponds to your choice. Pressing N takes you to the next record, and P takes you to the previous one. Pressing T takes you to the top of the file, and pressing B takes you to the bottom of the file. The final choice, Q, will quit the system, taking you back to the FoxPro command level.

As designed, this application is suited for simple file management and little else; nevertheless, it does provide a clean, bug-free application that will let you add and edit records in a file. Perhaps more importantly, it provides an application that is relatively easy to modify to suit your tastes. You can use the Editor to view the program or make any changes you desire. If you examine the programs created, RENTS.PRG and RENTS2.PRG, you may note some similarities between these programs and those developed in Chapters 12 through 16. You can enter **MODIFY COMMAND**

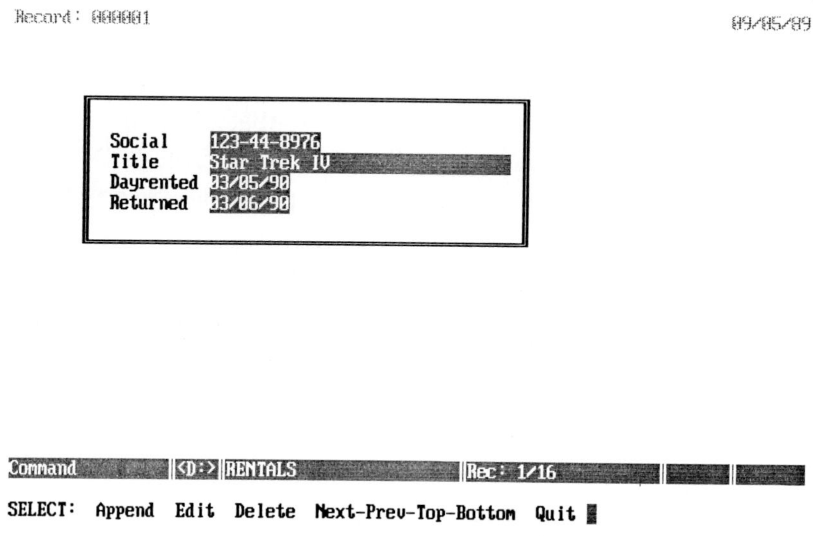

```
Record: 000001                                              09/05/89


       ┌─────────────────────────────────┐
       │ Social   123-44-8976            │
       │ Title    Star Trek IV           │
       │ Dayrented 03/05/90              │
       │ Returned  03/06/90              │
       └─────────────────────────────────┘




 Command          <D:> RENTALS        Rec: 1/16
SELECT:  Append  Edit  Delete  Next-Prev-Top-Bottom  Quit
```

FIGURE 17-2. Simple application using RENTALS file

RENTS or **MODIFY COMMAND RENTS2** to view the programs through the Editor. Or you may wish to produce a hardcopy by turning on your printer and entering these commands:

TYPE RENTS.PRG TO PRINT
EJECT
TYPE RENTS2.PRG TO PRINT

EJECT

The programs produced by the Simple Database Application template are shown here:

```
* Program.: RENTS.PRG
* Author..: Edward Jones
* Date....: 09/03/89
* Notice..: Copyright (c) 1989, JEJA Software, All Rights Reserved *
Notes...: Simple database application.
*
* ---Set environment.
SET TALK OFF
SET BELL OFF
SET SCOREBOARD OFF
* ---Open procedure file.
SET PROCEDURE TO RENTS2
*
* ---Initialize database file.
SELECT 1
USE RENTALS
*
* ---Declare PUBLIC memvars to store field values.
PUBLIC mSocial
PUBLIC mTitle
PUBLIC mDayrented
PUBLIC mReturned
*
* ---Display screen format.
DO DispForm
*
* ---Main execution loop.
```

```
DO WHILE .T.
    * ---Display record.
    DO DispRec
    * ---Display simple menu.
    choice = " "
    SET COLOR TO GR+/N,N/W
    @ 24,0 SAY "SELECT: Append  Edit  Delete  Next-Prev-Top-Bottom  Quit";
        GET choice PICTURE "!" VALID(choice $ "AEDNPTBQ")
READ
    DO CASE
    CASE choice ='Q'
        EXIT
    CASE choice ='A'
        * ---Append record.
        DO AddRec
    CASE choice ='E'
        * ---Edit record.
        DO EditRec
    CASE choice ='D'
        * ---Delete record.
        IF .NOT. DELETED( )
            DELETE
        ELSE
            RECALL
        ENDIF
    CASE choice ='N'
        * ---Next record.
        SKIP
        IF EOF( )
            GOTO BOTTOM
        ENDIF
    CASE choice ='P'
        * ---Previous record.
        SKIP -1
        IF BOF( )
            GOTO TOP
        ENDIF
    CASE choice ='T'
        * ---Top record.
        GOTO TOP
```

```
        CASE choice ='B'
            * ---Bottom record.
            GOTO BOTTOM
        ENDCASE
ENDDO
*
* ---Closing operations.
SET COLOR TO R+/N,N/W
CLEAR
SET SCOREBOARD ON
SET BELL ON
SET TALK ON
RETURN
* EOF: RENTS.PRG


* Program.: RENTS2.PRG
* Author..: Edward Jones
* Date....: 09/03/89
* Notice..: Copyright (c) 1989, JEJA Software, All Rights Reserved
* Notes...: Procedures for simple database application.
*

PROCEDURE DispForm
    CLEAR
    SET COLOR TO BU/N,N/W
    @ 0, 0 SAY SPACE(80)
    @ 0,72 SAY DATE( )
    SET COLOR TO R+/N,N/W
    @ 6,10 SAY "Social    "
    @ 4,7,11,48 BOX " Ï Ï"
    @ 7,10 SAY "Title     "
    @ 8,10 SAY "Dayrented "
    @ 9,10 SAY "Returned  "
RETURN

PROCEDURE DispRec
    SET COLOR TO BU/N,N/W
    @ 0, 0 SAY "Record: "+SUBSTR(STR(RECNO( )+1000000,7),2)
    IF DELETED( )
        @ 0,50 SAY "*DELETED*"
```

```
            ELSE
                @ 0,50 SAY "      "
            ENDIF
            SET COLOR TO R+/N,N/W
            @ 6,20 GET Social
            @ 7,20 GET Title
            @ 8,20 GET Dayrented
            @ 9,20 GET Returned
            CLEAR GETS
RETURN

PROCEDURE EditRec
            @ 6,20 GET Social
            @ 7,20 GET Title
            @ 8,20 GET Dayrented
            @ 9,20 GET Returned
            READ
RETURN

PROCEDURE BlankRec
        mSocial = SPACE( 11 )
        mTitle = SPACE( 25 )
        mDayrented = DATE( )
        mReturned = DATE( )
RETURN

PROCEDURE ReplRec
        REPLACE Social WITH mSocial
        REPLACE Title WITH mTitle
        REPLACE Dayrented WITH mDayrented
        REPLACE Returned WITH mReturned
RETURN

PROCEDURE AddRec
        * ---Initialize memvars.
        DO BlankRec
        @ 24,0
        @ 24,0 SAY "Press {Ctrl-W} to Exit"
```

```
    * ---Read into memvars.
    SET COLOR TO R+/N,N/W
    @ 6,20 GET mSocial
    @ 7,20 GET mTitle
    @ 8,20 GET mDayrented
    @ 9,20 GET mReturned
    READ
    * ---Confirm that user wants to append this record.
choice = " "
    SET COLOR TO GR+/N,N/W
    @ 24,0
    @ 24,0 SAY "SELECT: {A}ccept {I}gnore";
        GET choice PICTURE "!" VALID( choice $ "AI" )
READ
    IF choice = "A"
        * ---Add the new record.
        APPEND BLANK
        * ---Replace from memvars.
        DO ReplRec
    ENDIF
RETURN

* EOF: RENTS2.PRG
```

Note that the program is highly proceduralized, using the modular programming techniques described in Chapter 16. The main program (called RENTS.PRG) uses an @-SAY command to place the menu options on line 24 of the screen and uses a DO CASE-END CASE statement to respond to whichever letter is typed by the user. Depending on the letter typed, a program routine from the procedure file is run. The procedure file, RENTS2.PRG, contains different procedures for displaying a form, displaying a record in the form, adding a record, or editing a record.

Once you have studied the program, you can probably think of places where improvements can be made. You may want to try adding changes of your own design to the program, using the programming techniques you learned about in previous chapters.

CREATING A MORE COMPLEX APPLICATION

By comparison, another template designed for applications building, called the File-Maintenance Application template, can be used to produce an application with a bit more versatility than the simple example just shown. Before starting FoxView, note that you will need an index file based on the Lastname field of the MEMBERS file. This file, called NAMES, should have been created by the examples in Chapter 4. You can verify that the file exists by entering the command

DIR NAMES.IDX

You should see the filename as a directory of one file that appears on the screen. If you instead see a "None" message indicating that the file does not exist, enter these commands before proceeding:

USE MEMBERS
INDEX ON LASTNAME TO NAMES

Get into FoxView by entering **FOXVIEW** at the command level or choosing FoxView from the Program menu. Assuming you followed the exercise outlined in Chapter 5, a screen already exists for the MEMBERS file. Load that file now by entering the command

LOAD MEMBERS

and you will see the "15 field(s) loaded" message appear on the screen.

As you may recall, you changed the screen form to convert last names to all uppercase in Chapter 5. You will need to undo that change here, or it will cause problems in trying to find existing records in the application. Press F10 until you are in Table View.

Move the cursor down to the Lastname field, tab over to the Picture column, and delete the !@ entry from the column.

Adding Index-File Information To the Application

In order to make use of a "search" option that is provided as part of this application, you will need to make use of an index file. In prior chapters, an index file called NAMES was built on the Lastname field. You can use this index file to search for records in the application.

To tell FoxView that the index file exists, you must use the alias screen accessible from within FoxView by pressing F9. Press F9 now, and you will see the database files screen shown in Figure 17-3. This screen shows the name of the database file in use as part of the screen form design; in this case, MEMBERS appears as the

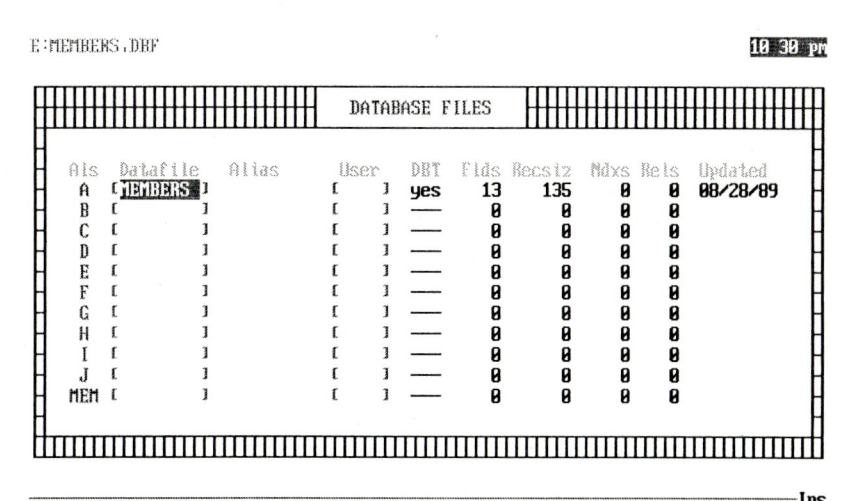

FIGURE 17-3. Database files screen

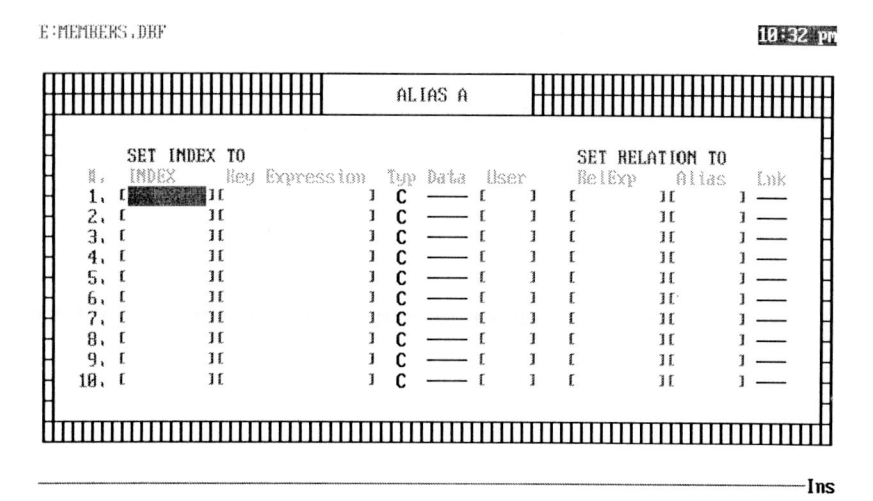

```
E:MEMBERS.DBF                                                    10:32 pm

                                    ALIAS A

            SET INDEX TO                         SET RELATION TO
    N.    INDEX     Key Expression  Typ Data  User     RelExp    Alias    Lnk
    1.  [        ][             ]    C  ——— [     ]  [       ][        ]  ———
    2.  [        ][             ]    C  ——— [     ]  [       ][        ]  ———
    3.  [        ][             ]    C  ——— [     ]  [       ][        ]  ———
    4.  [        ][             ]    C  ——— [     ]  [       ][        ]  ———
    5.  [        ][             ]    C  ——— [     ]  [       ][        ]  ———
    6.  [        ][             ]    C  ——— [     ]  [       ][        ]  ———
    7.  [        ][             ]    C  ——— [     ]  [       ][        ]  ———
    8.  [        ][             ]    C  ——— [     ]  [       ][        ]  ———
    9.  [        ][             ]    C  ——— [     ]  [       ][        ]  ———
   10.  [        ][             ]    C  ——— [     ]  [       ][        ]  ———

                                                                          Ins

                             FoxPro index file
```

FIGURE 17-4. Alias screen

filename. The remaining columns indicate whether memo fields are present (indicated by a "yes" in the DBT column), the number of fields in the file, the size of each record, number of indexes or relations specified, and date of the last update for the file. (The User column is used by advanced programmers when modifying the actual templates that create the programs; it will not be detailed here.)

To specify indexes or relations for use, you press F9 again to get to the alias screen. Press F9 now, and you will see the alias screen (Figure 17-4). Here, you can add the name of the index file you want to use in the INDEX column. Once you enter the name, FoxView will automatically add the key expression on which the index is based in the Key Expression column.

With the cursor in the INDEX column, enter **NAMES** as the index-file name. Once you press ENTER to complete the entry, "LASTNAME" will appear in the Key Expression column. In this case, this is all that is needed. Note that you can switch between the database files screen and the alias screen by repeatedly pressing F9. You can also press F10 at any time to switch to Forms View or Table View, and you can press SCROLL LOCK to get back to the FoxView shell. The alias screen is labelled Alias A, corresponding to work area A. Which alias screen appears depends on where the cursor is in the database files screen. You can enter the names of additional database files in the database files screen, and when you place the cursor on the desired file and press F9, you are shown the alias screen for that particular database and work area. This feature is intended for working with multiple files when designing an application.

The alias screen lets you enter a relational expression in the RelExp column to relate files, but there is a severe limit to how useful this will be in practice. As designed, the application built by FoxView will work with relational files that depend on a one-to-one relationship (see Chapter 12 for details on types of relationships). To create such an application, you would load two different files at the start of the screen design and the appropriate letter indicating the work area would be placed in the Alias column when in Table View. If your relationship is anything other than a one-to-one relationship, the screen form that appears when adding and editing records will not properly handle the relationship. You will need to write program code of your own design to handle one-to-many and many-to-many relationships.

If you decide to experiment with the use of relational applications built with FoxView, note that you can enter the remainder of the expression that normally follows the "SET RELATION TO" command words in the RelExp column (see Chapter 12 for details on the SET RELATION command). Be sure to also add any additional index names in the INDEX column, and add the name of the related file in the database files screen, accessible by pressing the F9 key.

Press ESC now to open the Gen menu, and choose Select From Template List from the menu. When the list of templates appears, highlight File-Maintenance Application and press ENTER. A blank window will appear, and at the bottom of the screen FoxView will ask for a filename for the application. (Again, this filename will contain a program that you will later run with the DO command to start the application.) Enter

MEMBERS

as the name for the program file. You will next be asked

Do you want Special Features (Y/N)?

This option will not be needed for this example. However, when chosen, Special Features lets you decide whether to place all fields in a query table (which means including all fields in a conditions screen used by the program to select records), whether to include a Label/Report option in the Append and Edit routines of the program, and whether to include an optional Browse feature using the Rettig Library (an add-on program that must be purchased separately).
   Answer N for No to the Special Features prompt, and you will next be asked

Generate specific modules? (y/n)

Here, FoxView is asking if it should generate specific modules, or subroutines of the application, as opposed to the entire application. Type N for No, to tell FoxView to generate the entire application.
   You are next given a choice of a simple menu or a light-bar menu. A simple menu is a numbered-choice menu, and a light-bar menu designs the menu of the application around a highlighted bar that can be moved with the cursor keys. For this example, choose Simple as your choice.
   You are next asked which style is desired for the submenus: parenthesis, bracketed, or lite-bars. Choosing Parenthesis results in submenus in which each option is surrounded by (parentheses),

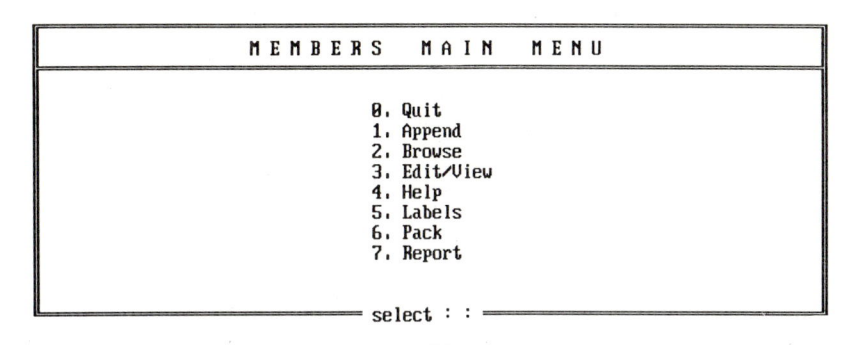

```
                MEMBERS   MAIN   MENU

                      0. Quit
                      1. Append
                      2. Browse
                      3. Edit/View
                      4. Help
                      5. Labels
                      6. Pack
                      7. Report

                    select : :
```

FIGURE 17-5. File-maintenance application using MEMBERS file

and choosing Bracketed results in menus in which each option is surrounded by {brackets}. The Lite-bar choice causes submenus to use lite-bars, or highlighted bars movable with the cursor keys. Choose Lite-bar from the menu.

Once you make your choice, the code for the application will be generated and appear in the window as it is written by FoxView. Once the program generation is complete, the FoxView menu will reappear. Open the Disk menu and choose Quit FoxView to get back to FoxPro. Since you added information about indexes to the FoxView table, you will be asked whether you want to save the screen design and overwrite the existing table file. Answer Y to both prompts that appear.

Once you are back in FoxPro, you can run the program with the DO command. Enter **DO MEMBERS** to start the program. In a moment, you will see the application choices in the form of a menu, as shown in Figure 17-5.

The application provides choices for adding records (Append), for using Browse mode, for editing or viewing records, for generating labels or reports, for removing all records marked for deletion with a PACK operation, and for getting help. If you try the Help option, you will see the pictorial breakdown of the menu options shown in Figure 17-6.

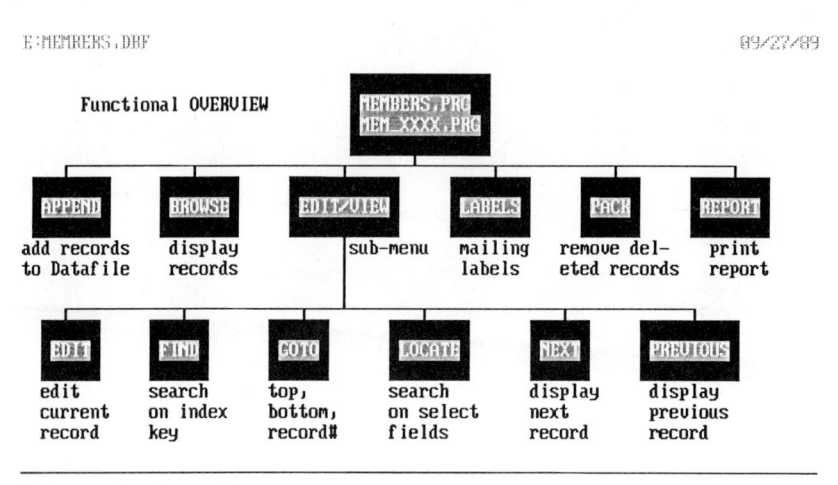

```
E:MEMBERS.DBF                                                    09/27/89

              Functional OVERVIEW       MEMBERS.PRG
                                        MEM_XXXX.PRG
            ┌──────┬──────────┬─────────┼─────────┬──────────┬──────┐
          APPEND  BROWSE   EDIT/VIEW  LABELS     PACK      REPORT
          add records display   sub-menu  mailing  remove del-  print
          to Datafile records             labels   eted records report
                       ┌───────┬─────────┼─────────┬─────────┐
                     EDIT    FIND      GOTO     LOCATE     NEXT    PREVIOUS
                     edit    search   top,     search    display   display
                     current on index bottom,  on select next      previous
                     record  key      record#  fields    record    record

Press any key to continue ...
```

FIGURE 17-6. Application help screen

Note that in order to use the Report or Labels option, you must first create a stored report and a stored label form using the techniques detailed in Chapters 7 and 10. The first four characters in the name of the report form must be MEM_ and the last one to four characters in the name can be of your choosing. (The letters "MEM" in the filename are taken from the first three letters of the application name, MEMBERS.) The same rule applies to the label form you create for use with the application. This is necessary because, as written, the application searches for all filenames beginning with MEM_ when you select the Report or Labels option.

You may want to try the various options of the application now to see how the more complex application differs in design from the simpler one. If you take the time to examine the program code behind the application, you will find it to be considerably more complex in design than the earlier example. Space limitations prevent the display of the program code here, but you can examine it using the Editor, or you can use the TYPE *filename* TO PRINT command to generate a hardcopy of the programs with your printer. Assuming you used the name MEMBERS for the main program file, FoxView has generated these files for the application:

MEM_MENU.PRG	MEM_PROC.PRG	MEMBERS.PRG
MEM_OPEN.PRG	MEM_EDIT.PRG	MEM_APPE.PRG
MEM_BROW.PRG	MEM_EXPR.PRG	MEM_COND.PRG
MEM_DISP.PRG	MEM_PHRA.PRG	MEM_HELP.PRG
MEM_LABE.PRG	MEM_PACK.PRG	MEM_APAC.PRG
MEM_REPO.PRG		

As indicated by this list, the names of all subroutines in the application begin with the first three letters of the main program filename followed by an underscore. The following list details the overall purpose of each subroutine:

Subroutine	Description
MEMBERS.PRG	Main program
MEM_PROC.PRG	Procedure file containing assorted procedures
MEM_MENU.PRG	Displays main menu
MEM_HELP.PRG	Displays Help screen
MEM_OPEN.PRG	Opens files, initializes memory variables
MEM_APPE.PRG	Used to add records to file
MEM_EDIT.PRG	Used to edit records
MEM_BROW.PRG	Used to display or edit records while in Browse mode
MEM_EXPR.PRG	Sets query (conditions) for selected records
MEM_COND.PRG	Displays conditions for selected records
MEM_DISP.PRG	Displays records for Browse subroutine

MEM_PHRA.PRG   Builds phrase used by MEM_EXPR routine
MEM_LABE.PRG   Prints mailing labels using stored label file
MEM_REPO.PRG   Prints reports using stored report file
MEM_PACK.PRG   Used by the MEM_APAC routine
MEM_APAC.PRG   Used to pack database

CREATING AN ADVANCED APPLICATION

The first option on FoxView's template list, FoxPro Advanced Application, provides a database application that makes detailed use of many FoxPro features, including windows, shadows, and light-bar menus. Like the Simple Database Application template, it displays a record on the screen while offering a number of different menu options. However, the choices are much more varied with a FoxPro advanced application, because each menu option displays a pull-down menu with additional choices.

If you would like to see how the FoxPro Advanced Application template works, you can quickly build an application, again using the MEMBERS screen you created with FoxView in Chapter 5. Enter **FOXVIEW** at the command level, and when in FoxView enter **LOAD MEMBERS** to load the existing table. Open the Gen menu with ESC, and choose Select From Template List. This time, choose the first option, FoxPro Advanced Application. When prompted for a program name at the bottom of the screen, enter **MEM2** as a filename.

The complete application will be generated. When the application is complete, a message indicating its completion will appear at the bottom of the screen. Press a key, and the menus will reappear. Open the Disk menu, and choose Quit FoxView to get back into FoxPro.

To try the application, enter **DO MEM2**. The program code will take a few moments to completely compile and load. Once it does, a record in the database will appear, along with pull-down menus

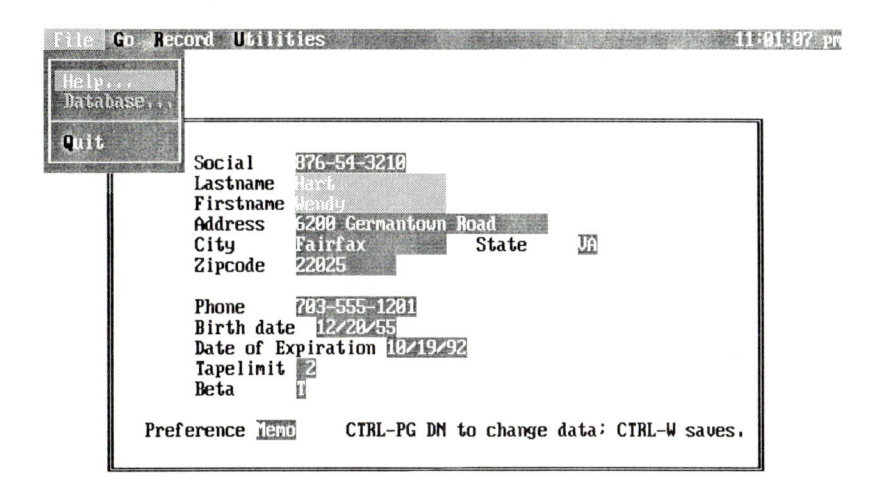

Creating Applications with FoxView   555

```
 File  Go  Record  Utilities                              11:01:07 pm
┌──────┐
│Help..│
│Databa│se..
│Quit  │ Social    876-54-3210
└──────┘ Lastname  Hart
         Firstname Wendy
         Address   6200 Germantown Road
         City      Fairfax          State    VA
         Zipcode   22025

         Phone          703-555-1201
         Birth date     12/20/55
         Date of Expiration 10/19/92
         Tapelimit      2
         Beta           T

         Preference Memo     CTRL-PG DN to change data; CTRL-W saves.


Database: MEMBERS.DBF
```

FIGURE 17-7. Advanced applications

offering choices named File, Go, Record, and Utilities, as shown in Figure 17-7.

Try using the LEFT and RIGHT ARROW keys to view the different menu choices, and you will see that each main menu option displays a pull-down menu of additional choices relating to that topic. If you try selecting the Help option of the File menu, you will see a window that provides more details on the various options of the application. One note of warning: The way the application is written, choosing the Seek option of the Go menu brings up the Expression Builder. Because the application searches for records using a Seek instead of a Find, you must enclose the last name with quotation marks or the Expression Builder will display an error message when you choose OK to begin the search. Try the various menu options to get a feel for the design of the advanced pplication. When done, you can choose Quit from the File menu to leave the application.

ABOUT FOXPRO TEMPLATES

From the examples in this chapter, it should be evident that the applications templates provided with FoxView can save time in helping you to create applications. However, this does not mean that the programming topics covered in the previous chapters are not necessary if you use FoxView to generate applications. The templates provided with FoxView generate applications that follow a standard design. As you desire applications that are different in nature than these, you will need to be familiar with the programming language used by FoxPro to create such applications. Keep in mind that studying the programs generated by FoxView is an excellent way to learn to write your own programs.

This chapter is meant to provide a brief overview of FoxView's capability to produce applications. There are additional features of FoxView that can be used to produce parts of applications. You can also modify the templates used to generate applications so that the applications produced by the templates are more in line with your way of doing things. More details on the use of FoxView can be found in your FoxPro documentation.

18

USING FOXPRO WITH OTHER SOFTWARE

File Formats
Data Sharing with the APPEND and COPY Commands
Examples of Transferring Files

The ability to exchange information with other programs enhances the power of FoxPro. FoxPro allows you to transfer files between it and most popular software available for the PC. There is just one condition to FoxPro's ability to transfer information: The other programs must be able to transfer information in a format acceptable to FoxPro.

FILE FORMATS

You can transfer information between FoxPro and another program in various formats. These include Delimited format (ASCII text in a predefined format, with fields separated by characters or blanks), System Data format (SDF), and DBMEMO3/FOXPLUS format (files with memo fields in dBASE III/III Plus and FoxBase

Plus format). As described shortly, delimited and SDF files are composed of ASCII text in a special format.

ASCII Format

The term *ASCII format* refers to files that are composed of characters and spaces not necessarily arranged in any particular order. ASCII stands for the American Standard Code for Information Interchange, an international method of representing information in computers. Text files created by most word processors can be stored as ASCII text. You'll use ASCII files if you need to merge the contents of a database with a document created by a word processor. If, for example, your database contains a list of names, you can save those names to a text file in ASCII format. You can then use your word processor to call up the text file and use it as part of a document.

Delimited Format

Delimited-format ASCII files are composed of records in which the fields are *delimited*, or separated by a specific character or a space. If the character fields are surrounded by a certain character (such as a quotation mark) and fields are separated by commas, the format is called Character-Delimited. If the fields are separated by a single space, the format is called Blank-Delimited.

Character-delimited files can use any character as the delimiter, but the most commonly used format surrounds the data in each character field with quotation marks and separates each field from other fields by commas. Each record ends in a carriage return, so each record occupies a separate line. The following example shows a character-delimited file using this common format:

```
"Miller","Karen","4260 Park Avenue","Chevy Chase","MD","20815- 0988"
"Martin","William","4807 East Avenue","Silver Spring","MD","20910-0124"
"Robinson","Carol","4102 Valley Lane","Falls Church","VA","22043-1234"
"Kramer","Harry","617 North Oakland Street","Arlington","VA","22203"
"Moore","Ellen","270 Browning Ave #2A","Takoma Park","MD","20912"
"Zachman","David","1617 Arlington Blvd","Falls Church","VA","22043"
"Robinson","Benjamin","1607 21st Street, NW","Washington","DC","20009"
"Hart","Wendy","6200 Germantown Road","Fairfax","VA","22025"
```

As an example, WordStar's MailMerge option uses this Character-Delimited format for storing information.

SDF Format

Like delimited files, files in SDF format store each record as an individual line, so the records are separated from each other by carriage returns. However, the fields in an SDF file are a preset width, regardless of the data stored in a particular record. All records are therefore identical in length. (The term SDF was popularized by Ashton-Tate, makers of dBASE; many other vendors call the same type of file flat files, fixed-length files, or DOS text files.) FoxPro has the ability to store files in SDF format for use by other programs. Many spreadsheets can store data on a disk in SDF. FoxPro can then read those files, using an SDF option of the APPEND command (which will be discussed shortly).

The following example shows a file in SDF format created by FoxPro using the Lastname, City, Expiredate, and Tapelimit fields of the Generic Videos database. Note that dates are stored in a year-month-day format in the file.

```
Miller      Chevy Chase    19920725  6
Martin      Silver Spring  19910704  4
Robinson    Falls Church   19930905  6
```

```
Kramer     Arlington        19901222  4
Moore      Takoma Park      19941117  6
Zachman    Falls Church     19900919  4
Robinson   Washington       19910917  6
Hart       Fairfax          19921019  2
```

The SDF format uses a fixed number of spaces for each field, regardless of the actual size of the information in the field. Information that is too long to fit in an SDF file will be truncated.

DBMEMO3 or FOXPLUS Format

The DBMEMO3 and FOXPLUS formats create files in dBASE III/III Plus and FoxPlus file format. Using either format, FOXPLUS or DBMEMO3, results in the creation of the same type of file. FoxPro provides these options to aid in the transferring of database files containing memo fields. FoxPro stores memo field data in a manner that is more efficient than but not compatible with most other dBASE-language products. As a result, trying to open a FoxPro database file containing memo fields will cause error messages with products that normally accept dBASE files, such as Lotus 1-2-3, Excel, FoxBase and Foxbase Plus, dBASE III Plus, and dBASE IV. To get around this problem, you can use the DBMEMO3 or FOXPLUS format when working with files with memo fields. Either format results in the creation of a file in the older FoxBase Plus/dBASE III Plus format. That file can then be read by other products that have the ability to read dBASE files. You will need the DBMEMO3/FOXPLUS format even when transferring data to dBASE IV, because FoxPro and dBASE IV use different methods of storing memo-field data.

Note that DBMEMO3/FOXPLUS format is not needed if your database has no memo fields. (Using it won't hurt, but it won't provide any benefits, either.) Database files without memo fields can be used "as is" in any other product that can read a file in dBASE format.

Brand	Type of Package	File Type
WordPerfect	Word processor	Delimited or SDF
WordStar	Word processor	Delimited or SDF
MailMerge	Option of WordStar	Delimited
Microsoft Word	Word processor	Delimited or SDF
MultiMate	Word processor	Delimited or SDF*
Lotus 1-2-3	Spreadsheet	dBASE or SDF**
Microsoft Excel	Spreadsheet	dBASE
dBASE III/IV	Database manager	dBASE
Paradox	Database manager	dBASE
PC-File III	Database manager	Delimited
R:base	Database manager	Delimited or dBASE***

*Newer versions of Multimate can read FoxPro databases without memo fields directly, and can read FoxPro databases with memo fields copied with the DBMEMO3/FOXPLUS type option.

**Very early versions of Lotus may require the use of SDF. Most versions should use the Translate option to import and export files in dBASE format.

***R:base 5000, R:base System 5, and R:base for DOS or OS/2 can all read FoxPro files directly (with memo fields, use the DBMEMO3 or FOXPLUS type option). Earlier versions of R:base can read delimited files.

TABLE 18-1. Software Interchange Formats

When transferring data out of FoxPro, you must decide what format you wish to use. A list of some of the better-known programs and the types of data they can exchange is shown in Table 18-1. As a general rule, most word processors will transfer in ASCII, Delimited, or SDF format. You will generally use the Delimited format for mailmerge files. Many spreadsheets will transfer data in SDF format, and most database managers will transfer data in Delimited format. Most versions of Lotus 1-2-3 and Symphony can read and write files in the dBASE file format.

If it isn't obvious which format your software package uses, check the owner's manual.

DATA SHARING WITH THE APPEND AND COPY COMMANDS

Many exchanges of data between FoxPro and other programs will be accomplished with the aid of certain Type options within the COPY and APPEND commands. Using COPY, you can copy data from FoxPro to another program; using APPEND, you can append, or transfer, data from another program into a FoxPro database. The normal format for these commands, when used with a Type option, is as follows:

COPY TO *filename* [SCOPE] [FIELDS *fieldlist*]TYPE *type*

APPEND FROM *filename* [FIELDS *fieldlist*] TYPE *type*

In this case, *filename* is the name of the file to be transferred between FoxPro and the other program, and *type* is one of the acceptable types. The acceptable types options are DELIMITED [WITH *character*], SDF, and DBMEMO3/FOXPLUS. The WITH parameter of the DELIMITED option lets you specify a character to use as the field delimiter in place of the default quotation marks.

As a brief example, to copy the Generic Videos database into a dBASE III file that could be read by Lotus 1-2-3, you might use this command:

COPY TO 123FILE TYPE DBMEMO3

You might use the following command to transfer a file from Supercalc 3 to FoxPro:

APPEND FROM SCFILE TYPE SDF

Because the MEMBERS database contains memo fields, the DBMEMO3 option is used in the previous example. If you wanted to use a file without memo fields (such as RENTALS), you could load the file in 1-2-3 using the 1-2-3 Translate utility, without any special preparation while in FoxPro.

You can add other options, such as a scope (ALL, NEXT, or a record number) or a list of fields to the COPY command when transferring data to other programs. You can also use the FOR condition to specify records that will be transferred. Note that you can include a FOR clause when importing data from foreign files with APPEND, but a scope is not allowed when importing foreign files.

EXAMPLES OF TRANSFERRING FILES

The rest of this chapter will provide working examples of transferring files. Since you may not be using the software packages described here, you may not be able to follow along with the examples. If you have the software package mentioned or a similar software package with the ability to use the file formats acceptable to FoxPro, try using the examples with your software.

Transferring from FoxPro to WordStar And Other Word Processors

Most word processors work with ASCII format, so let's try it first. Suppose you needed to pull names and salary amounts from the database to provide a memo to the company president containing all employees' salary amounts. You can use the TO FILE option of the LIST command to help you perform this task. When you enter the LIST command (along with any preferred fields) followed by TO FILE and a filename, the data displayed with LIST is also stored as ASCII text in the file you named within the command.

Try using the TO FILE option of the LIST command by entering the following:

```
USE MEMBERS
LIST LASTNAME, FIRSTNAME, EXPIREDATE TO FILE PEOPLE.TXT
```

Now exit FoxPro and load your word processor. Enter the command normally used by your word processor to read an ASCII file. When your word processor asks you for the filename to load, enter the drive and path of your FoxPro data directory, followed by the filename **PEOPLE.TXT**. The file should then appear on your screen. Figure 18-1 shows an example of the file loaded into Microsoft Word.

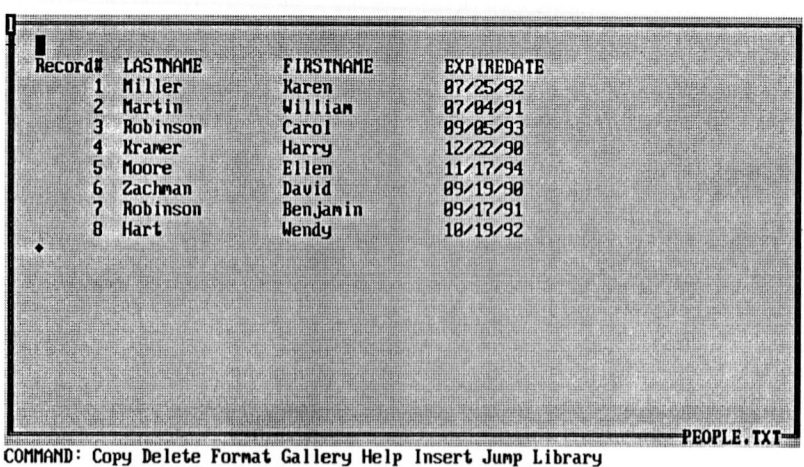

FIGURE 18-1. File transfer from FoxPro to Microsoft

You can also store the output of a report in a file by adding the TO FILE option at the end of a REPORT FORM command. As an example, the command

REPORT FORM SAMPLE TO FILE REPS.TXT

would create a file named REPS.TXT containing the data in the report format generated by the stored report SAMPLE.

Note: At the bottom of the file that was transferred with FoxPro, there may be a left-pointing arrow or a similar graphics character (whether or not there is one depends on what word processor you are using). If you are using WordStar, you may see one or more control-at symbols (^@) at the end of the file. This character represents an end-of-file marker that FoxPro produced when it was finished writing to the file. You can use the BACKSPACE key or a DELETE command to erase this unwanted character. Different word processors interpret this end-of-file marker in different ways, so you may see a character other than ^@ or a left-pointing arrow.

Get out of your word processor in the usual manner, and reload FoxPro now.

Transferring from FoxPro to MailMerge And Other Database Managers

Delimited formats are used by the merge-print options of many word processors and by some other database managers. If you need to transfer data to another database manager, first check your documentation to see if the database manager will accept files in dBASE format. If it can, use the file directly (if no memo fields are present), or use the DBMEMO3/FOXPLUS format instead of the Delimited format. If you need data in Delimited format, you'll use the DELIMITED option of the COPY command.

To create the delimited file, copy the fields from the active database to a separate file used by the other program. The format of the COPY command with the Delimited option is

COPY TO *filename* [SCOPE] [FIELDS *fieldlist*] TYPE DELIMITED

where *filename* is the name of the file that will contain the fields. You can limit which records to copy by including the scope, specified by ALL, NEXT, or RECORD. Fields can be limited by the FIELDS *fieldlist* option. When you specify the DELIMITED option, the .TXT extension is automatically appended to *filename*.

As an example, let's say that you need to transfer a list of the names, addresses, and cities from MEMBERS to a file named DATAFILE that will be used by another database manager. Enter the following commands:

```
USE MEMBERS
COPY TO DATAFILE FIELDS LASTNAME, FIRSTNAME, ADDRESS, CITY STATE, TYPE DELIMITED
```

The DATAFILE.TXT file created by COPY TO will contain one line for each record that was copied from MEMBERS. Each record includes the member's last name, first name, address, and city. Each field is enclosed by quotation marks, and each field is separated by a comma. FoxPro automatically adds the .TXT extension unless you specify otherwise.

The TYPE command can be used to list on the screen the contents of any disk file. Let's examine DATAFILE with the TYPE command to see the Delimited file format. With the TYPE command you are required to supply the file extension (in this case, .TXT). Enter the command

```
TYPE DATAFILE.TXT
```

and your display will resemble the following:

"Miller","Karen","4260 Park Avenue","Chevy Chase","MD"
"Martin","William","4807 East Avenue","Silver Spring","MD"
"Robinson","Carol","4102 Valley Lane","Falls Church","VA"
"Kramer","Harry","617 North Oakland Street","Arlington","VA"
"Moore","Ellen","270 Browning Ave #3C","Takoma Park","MD"
"Zachman","David","1617 Arlington Blvd","Falls Church","VA"
"Robinson","Benjamin","1607 21st Street, NW","Washington","DC"
"Hart","Wendy","6200 Germantown Road","Fairfax","VA"

This file can be used by many other database managers, including PC-File and R:base, or it can be used by WordStar's Mail-Merge option to create a form letter. (More detailed explanations of using FoxPro data for a WordStar, Microsoft Word, or Word Perfect mailmerge appear in the next section.) In such cases, you must use the appropriate commands of the particular database manager or MailMerge to import a file in the Delimited format.

Remember that when you import data into FoxPro with the APPEND command, the database structure must match the structure of the records within the file that contains the data. In other words, the fields must be in the same order, and the fields in the FoxPro database should be wide enough to accommodate the incoming data. As an example, if you had a file of names and addresses in WordStar laid out in this format,

Lastname   (longest name: 12 characters)
Firstname   (longest name: 10 characters)
Salary   (dollar amounts not larger than 999.99)
Hired   (a date)

and you wanted to transfer data in such a format to a FoxPro database, you would need to create a database structure like the one shown here:

Fieldname	Field Type	Width	Decimal
LASTNAME	character	12	
FIRSTNAME	character	10	
SALARY	numeric	6	2
HIRED	date	8	

In such a case, the field names would not matter. What is important is that the fields in the matching database structure are in the same order as the structure of the records in the incoming file.

Creating Files for Use With MailMerge Options

If your word processor supports some type of mailmerge or merge-print operation, you may prefer to create a foreign file and use that file with your word processor to generate form letters. The precise approach differs from word processor to word processor, so some of the more popular approaches are covered in detail here.

WordStar

If you are using WordStar and its companion product, MailMerge, create a delimited file using the default delimiters. For example, use commands like these to create the following foreign file:

```
USE MEMBERS
COPY NEXT 5 TO WSFILE FIELDS LAST, FIRST, ADDRESS,;
CITY, STATE, ZIPCODE TYPE DELIMITED
```

"Miller","Karen","4260 Park Avenue","Chevy Chase","MD","20815-0988"
"Martin","William","4807 East Avenue","Silver Spring","MD","20910-0124"
"Robinson","Carol","4102 Valley Lane","Falls Church","VA","22043-1234"
"Kramer","Harry","617 North Oakland Street","Arlington","VA","22203"
"Moore","Ellen","270 Browning Ave #2A","Takoma Park","MD","20912"

You can then proceed to create a form letter within WordStar with two lines of text at the top of the file. These lines of text will denote the name of the foreign file that will provide the data and the names that should be assigned to the fields when in WordStar. As an example, a WordStar letter designed to use the foreign file just shown might resemble the following:

.df wsfile.txt
.rv last,first,address,city,state,zip

     Johnson, Johnson,
     Fennerson & Smith
     303 Broadway South
     Norfolk, VA 56008

&first& &last&
&address&
&city&, &state& &zip&

Dear &first& &last&:

  In response to your letter received, we are pleased to enclose a catalog of our latest products. If we can answer any questions, please do not hesitate to call.

Sincerely,

Mike Rowe
Sales Manager

 The field names assigned to the fields in WordStar are independent of those used in FoxPro; WordStar uses the text that follows the .rv command to assign the names to the fields in the order they appear in the foreign file. The line of the WordStar document that starts with .df tells WordStar the name of the foreign file containing the data.

Microsoft Word

With Microsoft Word, the process is very similar to that used with WordStar. Again, you can create a delimited file with the default delimiters. Microsoft Word, however, does not expect to see the names of the fields defined within the form letter; instead, it expects the names of the fields to appear as the very first line of text in the foreign file, with the fields separated by commas. Using the prior example again, the foreign file that Microsoft Word would need to use would resemble this:

```
last,first,address,city,state,zip
"Miller","Karen","4260 Park Avenue","Chevy Chase","MD","20815-0988"
"Martin","William","4807 East Avenue","Silver Spring","MD","20910-0124"
"Robinson","Carol","4102 Valley Lane","Falls Church","VA","22043-1234"
"Kramer","Harry","617 North Oakland Street","Arlington","VA","22203"
"Moore","Ellen","270 Browning Ave #2A","Takoma Park","MD","20912"
```

A quick and painless way to do this is to build a file that contains the heading, and then use the DOS COPY command to combine the heading file with the foreign file to produce a file ready for use by Microsoft Word. This could be done entirely within FoxPro with commands like these:

```
SET TALK OFF
SET ALTERNATE TO HEADS
SET ALTERNATE ON
? "Last,First,Address,City,State,Zip"
?
CLOSE ALTERNATE
COPY TO WFILE FIELDS LAST, FIRST, ADDRESS,;
 CITY, STATE, ZIPCODE TYPE DELIMITED
RUN COPY HEADS.TXT + WFILE.TXT WORDFILE.TXT
```

The resultant file, called WORDFILE.TXT in this case, would resemble the foreign file shown earlier, with the header containing the field names for use by Microsoft Word as the first line in the foreign file.

When designing a form letter from within Microsoft Word, use CTRL- [to mark the start of each field and CTRL-] to mark the end of each field. The CTRL-[key combination actually produces a symbol that resembles a double less-than sign, and pressing CTRL-] produces a symbol resembling a double greater-than sign. Using these characters, you can create a form letter like this example:

<<data wordfile.txt>>

        Johnson, Johnson
        Fennerson & Smith
        303 Broadway South
        Norfolk, VA 56008

<<first>> <<last>>
<<address>>
<<city>>, <<state>> <<zip>>

Dear <<first>> <<last>>:

    In response to your letter received, we are pleased to enclose a catalog of our latest products. If we can answer any questions, please do not hesitate to call.

Sincerely,

Mike Rowe
Sales Manager

You could generate the form letters using the Print Merge command from within Microsoft Word. (See your Microsoft Word documentation for details, if needed.)

An Export Program for WordPerfect

If you wish to use the Mailing Merge feature of WordPerfect, you must do things a little differently than with most other software. WordPerfect expects to see data on individual lines, all flush left, with the ends of fields marked by a Control-R followed by a carriage return. The end of a record is indicated by a Control-E followed by a return. A data file when loaded within WordPerfect would resemble the following:

```
Jerry^R
Sampson^R
1412 Wyldewood Way^R
Pheonix^R
AZ^R
78009^R
^E
Paris^R
Williamson^R
P.O. Box 1834^R
Herndon^R
VA^R
22070^R
^E
Mary^R
Smith^R
37 Mill Way^R
Great Neck^R
NY^R
12134^R
```

Unfortunately, you cannot create a file like this with something as simple as a COPY command. You can, however, write a short program to accomplish this task. To generate such a file, simply write each desired field out to a line of a file, and end that line with a Control-R (ASCII 18). After the last field of the record, write a line containing only Control-E (ASCII 5). You can use the SET ALTERNATE TO and SET ALTERNATE ON commands to turn on the output to a foreign text file, and write each desired line until done; then close the foreign file with the CLOSE ALTERNATE command.

As an example, the following program would perform such a task. You could enter the command MODIFY COMMAND *filename* (where *filename* is the name you want to give the program) and enter the program as shown next, saving it with CTRL-W. Substitute your field names and database filename for the ones used in this example.

```
*CREATES Word Perfect MAIL MERGE FILES.*
USE MEMBERS
SET TALK OFF
STORE CHR(18) TO ENDFIELD
STORE CHR(5) TO ENDREC
SET ALTERNATE TO PERFECT
SET ALTERNATE ON
GO TOP
DO WHILE .NOT. EOF( )
   ? TRIM(FIRSTNAME) + ENDFIELD
   ? TRIM(LASTNAME) + ENDFIELD
   ? TRIM(ADDRESS) + ENDFIELD
   ? TRIM(CITY) + ENDFIELD
   ? STATE + ENDFIELD
   ? ZIPCODE + ENDFIELD
   ? ENDREC
   SKIP
ENDDO
CLOSE ALTERNATE
RETURN
```

When you run the program with the DO command, the result would be a foreign file similar to the one just shown, with each field on a separate line terminated by the ASCII character Control-R, with Control-E on lines between the records. To use the files in a WordPerfect form-letter document, first make note of the order of the fields as output by your program (the first field after an end-of-record indicator is field 1, the next is field 2, and so on). In WordPerfect, when creating the form letter, use the ALT-F9 key combination to define the field numbers desired. For example, when you press ALT-F9 and enter **F** followed by **3** (to indicate field #3), and then press the ENTER key, WordPerfect will enter a symbol (^F3^), which indicates that the contents of the third field in the sequence will appear in that position when the form letters are generated. Our WordPerfect form letter might resemble the following:

                        Johnson, Johnson
                        Fennerson & Smith
                        303 Broadway South
                        Norfolk, VA 56008

^F1^ ^F2^
^F3^
^F4^, ^F5^ ^F6^

Dear ^F1^ ^F2^:

     In response to your letter received, we are pleased to enclose a catalog of our latest products. If we can answer any questions, please do not hesitate to call.

Sincerely,

Mike Rowe
Sales Manager

Save the letter using the usual save commands for WordPerfect. To generate the form letters in WordPerfect, first use CTRL-F5 to import the FoxPro file, select 1 from the menu (DOS Text File), and then select 2 (Retrieve). Eliminate any blank lines at the top of the document, and save the file with F10 under a new name. Use F7 to exit the document and get to a blank screen. Then press CTRL-F9, choose Merge, enter the name of the form letter, and then enter the name of the file containing the data. WordPerfect will proceed to create the letters, which can then be printed in the usual manner.

Two programs that this section did not deal with are IBM's DisplayWrite software and Ashton-Tate's MultiMate. IBM's DisplayWrite uses a complex data tranfer language called DCA (Document Content Architecture). This format does not transfer simply between any of the available FoxPro formats, so if you are faced with trying to do a mailmerge of sorts and DisplayWrite is your word processor of choice, consider creating the form letter completely in FoxPro with the Report Generator (see Chapter 10). MultiMate users who are using later versions of the software should refer to the MultiMate documentation; recent versions of MultiMate can directly read dBASE files, so you can use the FoxPro database directly or use the DBMEMO3/FOXPLUS type option if memo fields are in the file.

Transferring Between FoxPro And Lotus 1-2-3 or Symphony

Exchanging data between Lotus 1-2-3 or Symphony and FoxPro is a simple matter. FoxPro has the ability to read and write files in dBASE III format. And all but the earliest versions of Lotus and Symphony can read and write data in dBASE III file format.

To transfer data to Lotus 1-2-3 or Symphony, you will use the COPY command with the DBMEMO3/FOXPLUS file type where memo fields exist as shown here:

COPY TO LOTUSFIL TYPE DBMEMO3

The COPY TO command will copy the contents of an existing database to a file that can be read by Lotus 1-2-3 or Symphony. When in Lotus 1-2-3, you must use the Translate option to convert the file into 1-2-3 file format (see your Lotus documentation for details on the Translate option).

To transfer spreadsheet data from Lotus 1-2-3 or Symphony to FoxPro, use the Translate option in 1-2-3 or Symphony to save the file in dBASE format. Then you can load the file directly in FoxPro; since the file is in dBASE format, no APPEND command is needed.

If you have Lotus 1-2-3, try the following commands to create a file for conversion to a 1-2-3 spreadsheet:

USE RENTALS

COPY TO 123FILE

Enter **QUIT** to leave FoxPro and return to the DOS prompt. If your copy of 1-2-3 is in a different subdirectory of a hard disk, then use the DOS COPY command to copy the file, 123FILE.DBF, to that directory.

Load Lotus 1-2-3 in your usual manner. When the Lotus Access menu appears, choose Translate to get into the Translate utility. (Note that you can also get into the Translate utility directly from DOS by entering **TRANS** at the DOS prompt.) You are first asked which format you wish to translate from; choose dBASE III. The next screen asks which format you wish to translate to; select your version of 1-2-3 or Symphony as appropriate. A screen with some notes regarding dBASE files will appear, and you can press ESC to continue.

Enter the filename of the incoming file, 123FILE.DBF (or select it from the list of files), and accept the default name for the

```
A1: (F0) 'SOCIAL                                                              READY

         A                    B                      C            D
 1  SOCIAL           TITLE                      DAYRENTED    RETURNED
 2  123-44-8976      Star Trek IV               05-Mar-90    06-Mar-90
 3  121-33-9876      Lethal Weapon II           02-Mar-90    06-Mar-90
 4  232-55-1234      Who Framed Roger Rabbit    06-Mar-90    09-Mar-90
 5  901-77-3456      Beverly Hills Cop II       04-Mar-90    05-Mar-90
 6  121-90-5432      Dirty Rotten Scoundrels    01-Mar-90    06-Mar-90
 7  495-00-3456      Young Einstien             04-Mar-90    09-Mar-90
 8  343-55-9821      When Harry Met Sally       06-Mar-90    12-Mar-90
 9  876-54-3210      Lethal Weapon II           07-Mar-90    08-Mar-90
10  123-44-8976      Friday 13th Part XXVII     14-Mar-90    16-Mar-90
11  121-33-9876      Licence To Kill            15-Mar-90    17-Mar-90
12  232-55-1234      When Harry Met Sally       17-Mar-90    19-Mar-90
13  901-77-3456      Coming To America          14-Mar-90    18-Mar-90
14  121-90-5432      When Harry Met Sally       16-Mar-90    17-Mar-90
15  495-00-3456      Star Trek V                18-Mar-90    18-Mar-90
16  343-55-9821      Young Einstien             19-Mar-90    20-Mar-90
17  876-54-3210      Licence To Kill            16-Mar-90    18-Mar-90
18
19
20
```

FIGURE 18-2. Lotus 1-2-3 spreadsheet

converted file (123FILE.WKS or 123FILE.WK1, depending on your version of 1-2-3). Select Yes to proceed with the translation.

Once the file has been translated, you can use the usual file-load commands in 1-2-3 or Symphony to load the spreadsheet. In the example in Figure 18-2, the Set Column-Width command in Lotus 1-2-3 was used to widen the columns, to allow for a full display of the Socialsec, Title, Dayrented, and Returned fields.

Spreadsheet users should keep in mind that nearly all spreadsheets are limited in size by the available memory of the computer, while FoxPro files are limited in practice by available disk space. It is possible to export a file so large that it cannot be loaded into your spreadsheet. When creating files for spreadsheets from large databases, you may find it necessary to export small portions of the file. You can use the FOR condition with the commands, or you can set a filter with the SET FILTER command before exporting the data to the spreadsheet file. Also, when transferring spreadsheet data to FoxPro, you should only export the database section of the spreadsheet (excluding any titles, macro references, or explanatory text).

Note: When you translate logical fields from a dBASE file, Lotus 1-2-3 only recognizes T (true) and F (false). It will not recognize Y (yes) and N (no), even though these are acceptable logical values in FoxPro.

Transferring from FoxPro To Non-dBASE-Compatible Spreadsheets

If you need to save a file in SDF format, you use the SDF option of the COPY command. The SDF format is used for transferring data from FoxPro to spreadsheets that cannot read dBASE files. (This format is also useful for exchanging data with mainframe computers.) Try this variation of the COPY command to create an SDF file:

```
USE MEMBERS
COPY TO CALCFILE FIELDS LASTNAME, CITY, EXPIREDATE TYPE SDF
```

The CALCFILE file created by this command will contain one line for each record, with each record containing Lastname, City, and Expiredate fields. Instead of being surrounded by quotes and separated by commas, each field is allotted space according to its width. To see the file in SDF format, enter

```
TYPE CALCFILE.TXT
```

and the following will be displayed on your screen:

Miller	Chevy Chase	19920725
Martin	Silver Spring	19910704
Robinson	Falls Church	19930905
Kramer	Arlington	19901222
Moore	Takoma Park	19941117
Zachman	Falls Church	19900919
Robinson	Washington	19910917
Hart	Fairfax	19921019

How you will load the file into your spreadsheet will depend on what spreadsheet you are using. It would be impossible to explain the file-loading commands for all spreadsheets, but in most cases you will need to use an appropriate load command that lets your spreadsheet receive files in the SDF format. Your spreadsheet documentation should contain details on how you can do this.

Transferring from Other Spreadsheets to FoxPro

An increasing number of spreadsheets (including Microsoft Excel, Twin, and VP-Planner) can work with the popular dBASE III file format. Check your spreadsheet owner's manual to see if your spreadsheet can save files in dBASE III file format. Most spreadsheets that cannot write dBASE-compatible files do provide an option for printing a file onto disk, and the resulting disk file matches the SDF format. Different spreadsheets use different commands to create such files, so check your spreadsheet manual for instructions. In most cases, the way to get a spreadsheet into SDF format is to use the "print to disk" option of the particular spreadsheet. Figure 18-3 lists methods for creating FoxPro-compatible files with some of the more popular spreadsheets.

Before transferring an SDF file into a database, be sure that the database field types and field widths match the SDF format pre-

Lotus 1-2-3 Users:
1. From the Lotus Access menu, choose Translate.
2. At the first screen to appear, choose your version of 1-2-3.
3. At the second screen to appear, choose dBASE III. Read the next screen to appear, and press ENTER or ESC.
4. Enter the name for the 1-2-3 file when prompted.
5. Enter the name for the dBASE file when prompted.
6. Choose between Worksheet and Range when prompted. If you choose Range, enter the name of the worksheet range.
7. Open the file in FoxPro in the usual manner.

Microsoft Excel Users:
1. Highlight a range of data to export.
2. Choose Set Database from the Data menu.
3. Choose Save As from the File menu.
4. Select the Options button in the dialog box.
5. Choose DBF3 from the available formats.
6. Choose OK to create the file.
7. Open the file in FoxPro in the usual manner.

Multiplan Users:
1. Press ESC to highlight Multiplan commands.
2. Press P (for Print).
3. Press F (for File).
4. Specify a name for the file you will create; include the .TXT extension.
5. Create a matching database structure and APPEND the file as TYPE SDF.

Note: Multiplan will append additional carriage returns to the file when saving it. These will appear as blank records in FoxPro. You can delete the extra records and PACK the database.

SuperCalc 2 and 3 Users:
1. Press the slash key (/) to display SuperCalc commands.
2. Press O (for Output).
3. Press D (for Display Option).
4. Specify a range of the spreadsheet to be transferred to the file.
5. Press D (for Disk).
6. Specify a name for the SDF file.
7. Create a matching database structure and APPEND the file as TYPE SDF.

Note: SuperCalc saves all non-SuperCalc files with an extension of .PRN. You must include this extension when naming the file in the FoxPro APPEND TO command. Users of later versions of SuperCalc may be able to save the files in dBASE III format; see your SuperCalc manual for details.

FIGURE 18-3. Procedures for creating FoxPro-compatible files for Lotus 1-2-3, Excel, Multiplan, and SuperCalc 2 and 3

cisely. You can use the APPEND FROM command with the SDF option to transfer the data into FoxPro. The format of APPEND FROM with the SDF option is

APPEND FROM *filename* TYPE SDF

(Note that you can't use a scope with APPEND when appending from non-FoxPro files.) The APPEND FROM with TYPE SDF operates exactly like APPEND FROM with TYPE DELIMITED. The filename is the name of the file that will be transferred and appended to the active database file.

The fields in the database must be exactly as wide as the fields in the SDF file. An alternative method for transferring data from a spreadsheet is to convert the SDF file to a delimited file. This is done by using your word processor to edit the file, removing extra spaces between fields, and adding commas and quotation marks to separate the fields. You can then transfer the data with the DELIMITED option of the APPEND FROM command, but this time you need not be concerned that the field widths precisely match the width of the SDF files. If the database fields are narrower, the incoming data will be truncated to fit the field.

Transferring from WordStar And Other Word Processors to FoxPro

Transferring data from other programs into a FoxPro database may take just a little more work than the process of sending FoxPro data to other programs (particularly to word processors). This is because files brought into a FoxPro database must follow a precise format, such as an SDF or Delimited format. Thus, when you send data from your word processor to a FoxPro database, you must edit the file from your word processor until it matches the format of a delimited or an SDF file.

WordPerfect users should note that it is possible to create a delimited file in WordPerfect, which can then be easily read into FoxPro. To do so, you must merge a secondary file (a file containing data) with a primary file (a merge document containing only quotes, commas, and field markers). See your WordPerfect manual for additional details.

After your word processor creates a file in Delimited or SDF format, you can use the APPEND command of FoxPro to load the file. At first glance it may seem easier to use SDF format instead of Delimited format because you don't have to type all of the quotes and commas. But if you choose the SDF format, you must keep track of the size of each field; each field must have the same width as the database field in which you will be transferring data. For this reason, it is sometimes easier to use Delimited format.

When transferring files created by your word processor (or any other program) to FoxPro, you must also create or use a FoxPro database with a structure that matches the design of the files you wish to transfer. For purposes of simplicity, the following examples assume that the files created by other software match the structure of the Generic Videos database.

Let's try a transfer using a delimited file. Suppose you have created a mailing list with a word processor and you now want to use that mailing list with FoxPro. If you have a word processor that can create files in ASCII text, follow along.

Use your word processor to create the following delimited file and give it the name MAIL2.TXT. (*Note:* If you are using WordStar, press N from the No-File or Opening menu to create a document that does not contain WordStar formatting codes. If you are using Microsoft Word, WordPerfect, or IBM DisplayWrite, save the file as ASCII text.)

```
"123-80-7654","Johnson","Larry","4209 Vienna Way","Asheville","NC","27995"
"191-23-5566","Mills","Jeanette","13 Shannon Manor","Phoenix","AZ","87506"
"909-88-7654","Simpson","Charles","421 Park Avenue","New York","NY","10023"
```

Save the file as ASCII text with your word processor's save commands. Now load FoxPro. You'll use the DELIMITED option of the APPEND FROM command to append the file to MEMBERS. The format of the APPEND command when used to import a Delimited file is

APPEND FROM *filename* DELIMITED.

To transfer MAIL2.TXT to FoxPro, enter the following commands:

USE MEMBERS
APPEND FROM MAIL2.TXT TYPE DELIMITED

FoxPro will respond with the message "3 records added." To examine the database, enter **GO TOP** and then **LIST**, and at the bottom of the database you will see that the names and addresses from the mailing list have been added to the database.

In this example, fields are in order of last name, first name, address, city, state, and ZIP code. Fortunately, this is the same order as the fields in MEMBERS. In real life, though, things may not be as simple. When the fields in the database used by the other program do not match the database used by FoxPro, you will need to perform whatever work is necessary to make them match. You can do this in one of two ways: either change the order of the data in the other file, or design a new database in FoxPro that matches the order of the data in the other file. In most cases, it is easiest to first create a matching file structure in FoxPro and then append the data from the other file. After the data has been appended to FoxPro, either modify the structure of the file or copy the data into a second file that has the fields in the desired order (in which case, FoxPro will match fields by the field names).

Notes About FoxPro
And Other dBASE Compatibles

Files from FoxBase and FoxBase Plus can be used in FoxPro without your having to perform any changes. You can also use FoxPro database files within FoxBase and FoxBase Plus. However, because of differences in the way memo-field text is stored, FoxBase or FoxBase Plus will not open a FoxPro database that contains memo fields. You must convert the database, by using the COPY TO *filename* command with the TYPE DBMEMO3 or TYPE FOXPLUS option. The copied file can then be opened by FoxBase or FoxBase Plus.

You should use the same DBMEMO3/FOXPLUS type option if exporting a file containing memo fields for use with other dBASE compatibles. This includes dBASE III Plus, dBASE IV, PC-File DB, and Clipper. FoxPro files without memo fields can be used with no changes in these products.

A

GLOSSARY OF FOXPRO COMMANDS

Glossary Symbols and Conventions
List of Commands

This appendix contains a listing of FoxPro commands. Each command name is followed by the syntax of the command and a description of how the command works. Examples of applications are provided for some commands. You will recognize most commands from the tutorial section; others will be introduced here.

GLOSSARY SYMBOLS AND CONVENTIONS

1. All commands are printed in UPPERCASE, although you can enter them in either upper- or lowercase letters.

2. All parameters of the command are listed in *italics*.

3. Any part of a command or parameter that is surrounded by left and right [ ] brackets is optional.

4. When a slash separates two choices in a command, as in ON/OFF, you specify one choice but not both.

5. Ellipses (...) following a parameter or command mean that the parameter or command can be repeated "infinitely"—that is, until you exhaust the memory of the computer.

6. The *scope* parameter, which is always an option, can have four different meanings, depending on the command: ALL for all records; NEXT *n* for *n* number of records beginning at the current position of the record pointer; REST for all records from the pointer position to the end of the file; and RECORD *n* for record number *n*.

7. The term *expC* indicates a character expression, *expN* indicates a numeric expression, and *expL* indicates a logical expression. Where data type does not matter, the term *expression* is used.

LIST OF COMMANDS

? or ??

Syntax

? / ?? [*expression*] [PICTURE "*clause*"] [FUNCTION "*function-list*"] [AT *expN*]

The ? command displays the value of a FoxPro expression. If a single question mark (?) is used, the cursor executes a carriage return and linefeed, and then the value of the expression is displayed. If the double question mark (??) is used, the cursor is not moved before the value of the expression is displayed. The PICTURE and FUNCTION options may be used to customize the appearance of the displayed information. The AT option may be used to place the expression at a specific column location.

???

Syntax

??? expC

The ??? command sends characters to the printer without changing the current row and column positions. Use this command to send control codes or escape sequences to the printer. To specify control codes, enclose the ASCII code in curly braces.

@

Syntax

@ *row,col* [SAY *expression*] [PICTURE *expression*] [FUNCTION *list*] [GET *variable*] [PICTURE *expression*] [FUNCTION *list*] [RANGE *low, high*] [VALID *condition*] [ERROR *expC*] [COLOR *std/enhanced*] [COLOR SCHEME *expN*] [WHEN expC] [DEFAULT excC] [OPEN WINDOW none]

The @ command places the cursor at a specific screen location, which is identified by *row,col*. The @ command can be used with one or more of the named options. The SAY option displays the value of the expression following the word "SAY." The GET option allows editing of the variable (which can be a field). The PICTURE option allows the use of templates, which specify the way data will be displayed or accepted in response to the GET option. The RANGE option is used with the GET option to specify a range of acceptable entries. The VALID option specifies acceptable entries for GET using a condition. ERROR displays a custom error message if VALID is not met. COLOR defines new color settings for the @-SAY-GET command. COLOR SCHEME is a numeric value from 1 to 11, denoting colors based on the corresponding color scheme (see SET COLOR OF SCHEME). Note that a READ command must follow the use of GET commands to achieve full-screen editing. WHEN is a logical expression that permits or prevents editing in the GET. DEFAULT provides a default value for the GET. OPEN WINDOW is used with memo fields, to open a predefined window for the field.

Example

To place the message "Enter shareholder name:" at screen location 12,2 and to allow full-screen editing of the value contained in the variable SHN, enter

@ 12, 2 SAY "Enter shareholder name:" GET SHN

@-TO

Syntax

@ *row,col* TO *row,col* [DOUBLE / PANEL / *border- string*] [COLOR*standard* [,*enhanced*]] [COLOR SCHEME *expN*]

This variation of the @ command draws a line or a rectangular border (box) on the screen. The first value represents the upper-left screen coordinate, and the second value represents the lower-right screen coordinate. If both coordinates share a horizontal or vertical coordinate, a line is drawn; otherwise, a rectangular border is drawn. When used with the DOUBLE options, the @ command draws double lines or borders (or a combination) on the screen. COLOR *standard* [,*enhanced*] denotes a color-pair combination for the foreground and background colors for the line or box. COLOR SCHEME is a numeric value from 1 to 11, denoting colors based on the corresponding color scheme (see SET COLOR OF SCHEME).

Example

To draw a single line from row 3, column 5 to row 3, column 50, enter the following:

@ 3, 5 TO 3,50

To draw a double-line box with the upper-left corner at row 4, column 1 and the lower-right corner at row 18, column 70, enter

@ 4,1 TO 18,70 DOUBLE

@-CLEAR TO

Syntax

@ *row,col* CLEAR / CLEAR TO *row,col*

This variation of the @ command clears a portion of the screen. If @ *row,col* CLEAR is used, the screen is cleared to the right and below the coordinates provided. If @ *row,col* CLEAR TO *row,col* is used, the screen is cleared within a rectangular area, with the first coordinate indicating the upper-left corner and the second coordinate indicating the lower-right corner.

Example

To erase a rectangular area from row 4, column 5 to row 12, column 70 while leaving the remainder of the screen unchanged, enter

@ 4,5 CLEAR TO 12,70

@-BOX

Syntax

@ *row1,col1,row2,col2* BOX *expC*

This command draws a box between the specified coordinates. (Note that this command is compatible with FoxBase Plus. If compatibility with dBASE IV is desired, use the @ *row,col* TO *row,col* variation of the command.) An optional character expression containing up to 9 different characters may be specified, in which case those characters are used to construct the box. The first 4 characters define the 4 corners, starting from the upper-left corner and moving clockwise. The next 4 characters define the 4 sides, starting from the top and moving clockwise. The last character, if specified, is used as the background. If no character expression is provided, a single-line box is drawn.

Example

To draw a single-line box with the upper-left corner at row 4, column 1 and the lower-right corner at row 18, column 70, enter

@ 4,1,18,70 BOX

@-FILL TO

Syntax

@ *row1,col1* FILL TO *row2,col2* [COLOR *std. /enhanced*] [COLOR SCHEME *expN*]

The @-FILL command changes the color of the screen within the defined area. The *std/enhanced* is *x/y,* where *x* is the code for the standard color and *y* is the code for the enhanced color. If the COLOR option is omitted, the screen is cleared within the defined area. COLOR SCHEME is a numeric value from 1 to 11, denoting a color based on the corresponding color scheme (see SET COLOR OF SCHEME).

Example

@ 5,5 FILL TO 10,40 COLOR B/R

@-MENU

Syntax

@ *row,col* MENU *array,expN1*[,*expN2*] [TITLE *expC*]

This command creates a pop-up menu. Note that the DEFINE BAR and DEFINE POPUP commands can accomplish the same result; DEFINE BAR and DEFINE POPUP are compatible with dBASE IV programs, while @ *row,col* MENU is compatible with Fox-Base Plus programs. The row and column locations specify the left corner location of the menu; *array* contains a one-dimensional array that contains the menu items. *expN1* is the number of items in the menu; and *expN2* is an optional number of menu items to be displayed on the screen at one time, to a maximum of 17 items. TITLE is an optional menu title that appears at the top of the menu window.

@-PROMPT

Syntax

@ *row,col* PROMPT *expC* [MESSAGE *expC*]

This command, along with the MENU TO command, is used to create light-bar menus. (These commands for menu design are compatible with FoxBase Plus and Clipper; if compatibility with dBASE IV is desired, use the DEFINE POPUP and DEFINE BAR commands instead.) A series of PROMPT commands are used to display the options on the screen at the positions indicated by the *row,col* coordinates. The MENU TO command invokes the light-bar menu, and the user response is controlled by the cursor keys. A maximum of 128 prompts can be displayed on the screen at a time. If an optional message is included, the message appears at the row defined with the SET MESSAGE TO command when that particular option is highlighted in the menu.

Example

```
@ 5,5 PROMPT "1. Add records   "
@ 6,5 PROMPT "2. Edit records  "
@ 7,5 PROMPT "3. Delete records"
@ 8,5 PROMPT "4. Print records "
@ 9,5 PROMPT "5. Quit System   "
MENU TO Mychoice
DO CASE
        CASE Mychoice = 1
                DO ADDER
        CASE Mychoice = 2
                DO EDITOR
        CASE Mychoice = 3
                DO ERASER
        CASE Mychoice = 4
                DO REPORTER
        CASE Mychoice = 5
                QUIT
ENDCASE
```

ACCEPT

Syntax

ACCEPT [*expC*] TO *memvar*

The ACCEPT command stores a character string to the memory variable *memvar*. ACCEPT can be followed by an optional character expression. If this expression is included, its contents will appear on the screen when the ACCEPT command is executed.

Example

To display the prompt "Enter owner name:" and store to the memory variable OWNER the character string that the user enters in response to the prompt, enter

ACCEPT "Enter owner name:" TO OWNER

ACTIVATE MENU

Syntax

ACTIVATE MENU *menuname* [PAD *padname*]

The ACTIVATE MENU command activates a predefined menu and displays that menu on the screen. If the PAD option is specified, the highlight bar appears at the named pad; otherwise, the first pad in the menu is highlighted.

Example

ACTIVATE MENU MainMenu PAD Add A Record

ACTIVATE POPUP

Syntax

ACTIVATE POPUP *Popup Name*

The ACTIVATE POPUP command activates a predefined pop-up menu and displays it on the screen.

Example

ACTIVATE POPUP Printer

ACTIVATE SCREEN

Syntax

ACTIVATE SCREEN

The ACTIVATE SCREEN command redirects output to the screen instead of to a predefined window.

Example

ACTIVATE SCREEN

ACTIVATE WINDOW

Syntax

ACTIVATE WINDOW *windowname- list* / ALL [BOTTOM / TOP / SAME] [NOSHOW]

The ACTIVATE WINDOW command activates a predefined window from memory. After the ACTIVATE WINDOW command is used, all screen output is directed to that window. If the ALL option is used, all defined windows in memory are displayed in the order in which they were defined. Use BOTTOM or TOP to place a window at the bottom or top of a stack of existing windows. The SAME option applies only to windows previously hidden with

DEACTIVATE WINDOW or HIDE WINDOW. Use SAME to put the previously hidden window back in the same position it occupied earlier. Use the NOSHOW option to send output to a window without changing the window's status (for example, if it was hidden, output goes to the window but it remains hidden).

Example

ACTIVATE WINDOW MyWindow

APPEND

Syntax

APPEND [BLANK]

The APPEND command appends records to a database. When the APPEND command is executed, a blank record is displayed, and FoxPro enters full-screen editing mode. If the BLANK option is used, a blank record is added to the end of the database, but full-screen editing mode is not entered.

APPEND FROM

Syntax

APPEND FROM *filename* [FIELDS *fieldlist*] [FOR *condition*] [TYPE *filetype*] [DELIMITED [WITH *delimiter* / BLANK / TAB]]

APPEND FROM copies records from *filename* and appends them to the active database. The FOR/WHILE option specifies a condition that must be met before any records will be copied. If the filename containing the data to be copied is not a FoxPro database, an acceptable type option must be used. Valid type options are

DELIMITED, DELIMITED WITH BLANK, DELIMITED WITH TAB, DELIMITED WITH "*specified-character*," or SDF.

APPEND FROM ARRAY

Syntax

APPEND FROM ARRAY *arrayname* FOR *condition*

The APPEND FROM ARRAY command appends records to a database file from a named array. (Note that APPEND FROM ARRAY is compatible with dBASE IV; if you need compatibility with FoxBase Plus, use the GATHER FROM command instead.) The contents of each row in the array are transferred to a new record in the database file. The first column in the array becomes the first field, the second column in the array becomes the second field, and so on. If there are more elements in the array than fields in the database, the extra elements are ignored. If there are more fields in the database than there are elements in the array, the extra fields remain empty. The FOR clause, which is optional, lets you define a condition that must be met before data in the array will be added to a new record. An array must exist (be defined with DECLARE, and filled with data using STORE) before you can successfully use the APPEND FROM ARRAY command.

Example

APPEND FROM ARRAY TempData FOR Dues = "paid"

APPEND MEMO

Syntax

APPEND MEMO *memofield- name* FROM *filename* [OVERWRITE]

The APPEND MEMO command imports a file into a memo field. The contents of the file are normally added to the end of any existing text in the memo field. If the OVERWRITE option is used, the contents of the file will overwrite any existing text in the memo field. FoxPro assumes that the file has an extension of .TXT. If this is not the case, the extension must be specified along with the filename. If the file has no extension, include a period at the end of the filename.

Example

APPEND MEMO comments FROM letter.doc

AVERAGE

Syntax

AVERAGE *fieldlist* [*scope*][FOR *condition*] [WHILE *condition*] [TO *memvarlist* / TO ARRAY *arrayname*]

The AVERAGE command computes an average of the specified numeric field listed in *fieldlist*. If the TO option is not used, the average is displayed on screen. If TO is used, the average of the first field is assigned to the first memory variable, the average of the second field to the second memory variable, and so on down the list; and the average is stored as the memory variable specified. If the *scope* option is not used, the quantifier of ALL is assumed, meaning all records in the database will be averaged unless you use the FOR or WHILE option. The FOR option can be used to specify a condition that must be met for the fields to be averaged. If you use the WHILE option, records will be averaged until the condition is no longer true.

BROWSE

Syntax

BROWSE FIELDS [*fieldlist*] [FORMAT] [FREEZE *field*] [LAST]
[NOAPPEND] [NOCLEAR] [NODELETE] [NOEDIT / NOMODIFY]
[NOMENU] [NOFOLLOW] [NORMAL] [NOWAIT] [SAVE] [WIDTH
expN] [WINDOW *windowname*] [PREFERENCE *expC*]
[COLOR[*standard*][,*enhanced*][,*border*]] / [COLOR SCHEME *expN*]

The BROWSE command displays up to 20 records from a database on screen. If the database contains too many fields to fit on the screen, BROWSE displays only the fields that fit. More fields can be viewed by scrolling to the left or right with the mouse or the TAB key. The contents of any field can be edited while in Browse mode. To save changes made during Browse press CTRL- W; to exit Browse, press ESC. The FIELDS option will display only the fields listed in *fieldlist*. FORMAT tells the Browse window to assume any settings of an active format file. FREEZE *field* freezes the cursor within the named field. LAST tells FoxPro to use the most recent configuration (window size, column sizes) of Browse, as stored in the FoxUser configuration file. NORMAL causes the Browse window to assume normal color attributes rather than those of a previously defined window.

If NOFOLLOW is included, changes to a field that is part of an index expression will not cause the Browse display to follow the record to its new location in the database. The NOWAIT option is used within programs; when included, program control continues immediately after the Browse window is opened, rather than waiting for the user to exit Browse mode. The SAVE option is also used only in programs; it keeps both the Browse window and any memo field window that is active open after editing is completed.

The NOAPPEND, NOEDIT, and NODELETE options restrict the use of appending, editing, or deleting when in Browse mode. The WIDTH option lets you adjust the width of columns. The

WINDOW option causes the Browse display to appear in a previously defined window. PREFERENCE, when used initially, states the Browse settings under the name provided to the FoxUser file. When used with a previously-stored name, PREFERENCE causes the Browse settings stored with that name to take effect. NOMENU prevents user access to the Browse menu. NOCLEAR leaves the Browse window visible on the screen after Browse mode is exited. The COLOR or COLOR SCHEME options may be used to specify colors for the Browse window.

CALCULATE

Syntax

CALCULATE [*scope*] *options* [FOR *condition*] [WHILE *condition*][TO *memvarlist*/TO ARRAY *arrayname*]

The CALCULATE command calculates amounts, using standard financial and statistical functions. The functions are defined as part of the options list shown here. All records are processed until the scope is completed or the condition is no longer true. The following financial and statistical functions can be used within the options list:

AVG(*expN*) calculates the numerical average of value *expN*. CNT() counts the records in a database file. If a condition has been specified with the FOR clause, the condition must be met before the record will be counted.
MAX(*exp*) determines the maximum value in a field; *exp* is usually a field name or an expression that translates to a field name.
MIN(*exp*) determines the minimum value in a field; *exp* is usually a field name or an expression that translates to a field name.
NPV(*rate,flows,initial*) calculates the net present value where *rate* is the discount rate, *flows* is a series of signed periodic cash-flow values, and *initial* is the initial investment.

STD(*exp*) determines the standard deviation of values stored in a database field; *exp* is usually a field name or an expression that translates to a field name.

SUM(*exp*) determines the sum of the values in a database field; *exp* is usually a field name or an expression that translates to a field name.

VAR(*exp*) determines the variance of the values in a database field; *exp* is usually a field name or an expression that translates to a field name. The value supplied by VAR(*exp*) is a floating-point number.

Example

```
USE PERSONNL
SET TALK ON
CALCULATE MAX(SALARY), MIN(SALARY), AVG(SALARY)
```

CALL

Syntax

CALL *module name* [WITH *expC* / *memvar*]

The CALL command executes a binary (assembly-language) program that was previously loaded into memory with the LOAD command (see LOAD). The WITH option is used to pass the value of the expression or memory variable to the binary program. The CALL command should only be used with external programs designed as binary modules. Normal executable programs should be accessed with the RUN / ! command.

CANCEL

Syntax

CANCEL

The CANCEL command halts execution of a command file and returns FoxPro to the Command window.

CHANGE

Syntax

CHANGE [*scope*][FIELDS *fieldlist*][FOR *condition*] [WHILE *condition*] [NOAPPEND] [NOCLEAR] [NOEDIT] [NODELETE] [NOMENU]

The CHANGE command permits editing of fields listed in *fieldlist*. If the *scope* option is absent, the quantifier ALL is assumed. The FOR/WHILE option allows editing to only those records satisfying the condition. The NOAPPEND, NOEDIT, and NODELETE options restrict the appending, editing, or deleting of records. The NOCLEAR option leaves the display on the screen after the user exits the CHANGE process. NOMENU prevents the menu display.

Example

To edit the Tapelimit and Expiredate fields in the MEMBERS database, enter

CHANGE FIELDS TAPELIMIT, EXPIREDATE

CLEAR

Syntax

CLEAR

The CLEAR command erases the screen. CLEAR can also be used as an option of the @ command to clear the screen below and to the right of the location specified by the @ command.

Examples

To erase the entire screen, enter

CLEAR

To erase the screen below and to the right of the cursor at 12,20, enter

@ 12, 20 CLEAR

CLEAR ALL

Syntax

CLEAR ALL

The CLEAR ALL command closes all open database, memo, index, and format files, and resets the current work area to 1.

CLEAR FIELDS

Syntax

CLEAR FIELDS

The CLEAR FIELDS command clears the list of fields specified by the SET FIELDS command. The CLEAR FIELDS command has no effect if SET FIELDS was not previously used to specify fields (see SET FIELDS).

CLEAR GETS

Syntax

CLEAR GETS

The CLEAR GETS command clears all pending GET statements, or all GET that have not yet been accessed by a READ command. Use CLEAR GETS to prevent the next READ command in the program from invoking full-screen editing of the fields or variables named in the previous GET.

Example

```
ACCEPT "Enter Y to store entries, N to delete" TO ANS
IF ANS = "N"
    CLEAR GETS
ELSE
    READ
ENDIF
```

CLEAR MEMORY

Syntax

CLEAR MEMORY

The CLEAR MEMORY command erases all current memory variables.

CLEAR MENUS

Syntax

CLEAR MENUS

The CLEAR MENUS command clears all menus from the screen, and erases all menus from memory.

CLEAR POPUPS

Syntax

CLEAR POPUPS

The CLEAR POPUPS command clears all pop-up menus from the screen and erases all pop-up menus from memory.

CLEAR PROGRAM

Syntax

CLEAR PROGRAM

The CLEAR PROGRAM command clears the buffer of any compiled program.

CLEAR PROMPTS

Syntax

CLEAR PROMPTS

The CLEAR PROMPTS command releases all menu prompts created with the @-PROMPT command from a screen or a window.

CLEAR TYPEAHEAD

Syntax

CLEAR TYPEAHEAD

The CLEAR TYPEAHEAD command clears the contents of the typeahead buffer (see SET TYPEAHEAD).

CLEAR WINDOWS

Syntax

CLEAR WINDOWS

The CLEAR WINDOWS command clears all active windows from the screen and erases all windows from memory (see DEFINE WINDOW).

CLOSE [ALL]

Syntax

CLOSE *filetype* / ALL

The CLOSE command closes all file types listed in *filetype,* which can be ALTERNATE, DATABASES, FORMAT, INDEX, or PROCEDURE. If the ALL option is used, all open files are closed, including any that may have been opened using low-level file functions of FoxPro.

CLOSE MEMO

Syntax

CLOSE MEMO memo field [ALL]

The CLOSE MEMO command closes an open memo-field window. The ALL option clases all open memo windows.

COMPILE

Syntax

COMPILE *filename / skeleton*

The COMPILE command reads a FoxPro program or command file and creates an object (.DBO) file, which is an execute-only FoxPro program file. A skeleton composed of wildcards can be used in place of the filename; for example, COMPILE M∗.PRG would compile all .PRG files beginning with the letter "M."

Example

COMPILE mailer.prg

CONTINUE

Syntax

CONTINUE

The CONTINUE command resumes a search started by LOCATE. After LOCATE finds the record matching the criteria specified in the command, you can find additional records that meet the same criteria by entering CONTINUE (see LOCATE).

COPY

Syntax

COPY TO *filename* [*scope*] [FIELDS *fieldlist*] [FOR *condition*] [WHILE *condition*] [TYPE SDF/DBMEMO3/FOXPLUS/DELIMITED [WITH *delimiter/blank/tab*]]

The COPY command copies all or part of the active database to *filename. If scope* is not listed, ALL is assumed. The FIELDS option is used to pinpoint the fields to be copied. The FOR option copies only those records meeting the condition. The WHILE option copies records as long as the condition is true. Specifying SDF will copy the file in SDF format; specifying DELIMITED will copy the file in Delimited format. The DBMEMO3 or FOXPLUS type is used when databases with memo fields must be copied out to dBASE III/III Plus or FoxBase file format.

Example

To copy Lastname, Firstname and City fields from the active database MEMBERS to TOWNS, enter

COPY TO TOWNS LASTNAME, FIRSTNAME, CITY

COPY FILE

Syntax

COPY FILE *source-file* TO *destination-file*

The COPY FILE command creates an identical copy of a file. You must supply the extension in both *source-file* and *destination-file*. Note that you can include a drive and path designation along with the destination if desired.

Example

To copy a file named REPORTER.FRX to a new file named TESTER.FRX, enter

COPY FILE REPORTER.FRX TO TESTER.FRX

COPY MEMO

Syntax

COPY MEMO *memofield-name* TO *filename* [ADDITIVE]

The COPY MEMO command is used to copy the contents of a memo field to a text file. A drive name and path can be included as a part of the filename. If the ADDITIVE option is used, the text of the memo field will be added to the end of an existing filename; if the ADDITIVE option is omitted, any existing file with the same name will be overwritten.

Example

```
USE MEMBERS
GO 4
COPY MEMO preference TO A:COMMENTS.TXT
```

COPY STRUCTURE

Syntax

COPY STRUCTURE TO *filename* [FIELDS *fieldlist*]

The COPY STRUCTURE command copies the structure of an active database to *filename*, creating a new, empty database file. Specifying FIELDS with *fieldlist* will copy only those fields to the new structure.

COPY STRUCTURE EXTENDED

Syntax

COPY TO *filename* STRUCTURE EXTENDED

The COPY STRUCTURE EXTENDED command creates a new database with records that contain information about the fields of the old database. The new database contains the fields FIELD_NAME, FIELD_TYPE, FIELD_LEN, and FIELD_DEC. One record in the new database is added for each field in the old database.

COPY TO ARRAY

Syntax

COPY TO ARRAY *arrayname* [FIELDS *fieldlist*] [SCOPE] [FOR *condition*] [WHILE *condition*]

The COPY TO ARRAY comand copies data from the fields of a database into an array. (Note that the COPY TO ARRAY command is compatible with dBASE IV; if you need compatibility with FoxBase Plus, use the SCATTER command instead.) For each record in the database, the first field is stored in the first element of the array, the second field in the second element, and so on. (You must first declare the array with the DECLARE command.) If the database has more fields than the array has elements, the contents of extra fields are not stored to the array. If the array has more elements than the database has fields, the extra elements in the array are not changed. Note that memo fields are not copied into the array.

Example

```
USE HOURS
DECLARE ThisWeek [6,5]
COPY TO ARRAY ThisWeek NEXT 5
```

COUNT

Syntax

COUNT [*scope*] [FOR *condition*] [WHILE *condition*] [TO *memvar*]

The COUNT command counts the number of records in the active database that meet a specific condition. The *scope* option quantifies the records to be counted. The FOR option can be used to specify a condition that must be met before a record will be counted. If you use the WHILE option, counting will take place until the condition is no longer true. The TO option can be used to store the count to the memory variable *memvar*.

Example

To count the number of records containing the letters "MD" in the State field and to store that count as the memory variable MTEMP, enter

COUNT FOR STATE = "MD" TO MTEMP

CREATE

Syntax

CREATE *filename*

The CREATE command creates a new database file and defines its structure. If CREATE is entered without a filename, FoxPro will prompt you for one when the structure is saved. If CREATE is followed by a filename, a database with that filename will be created. The file name extension .DBF is added automatically to the filename unless you specify otherwise.

CREATE FROM

Syntax

CREATE *file1* FROM *file2*

The CREATE FROM command creates a new database, with its structure based on a file created earlier with the COPY STRUCTURE EXTENDED command (see COPY STRUCTURE EXTENDED).

CREATE LABEL

Syntax

CREATE LABEL [*filename*]

The CREATE LABEL command creates a label form file. This file can be used with the LABEL FORM command to produce mailing labels.

CREATE VIEW [FROM ENVIRONMENT]

Syntax

CREATE VIEW [FROM ENVIRONMENT]

The CREATE VIEW command saves the current environment to a view file. The command operates in the same manner, whether or not the FROM ENVIRONMENT clause is specified. The optional clause is supported for compatibility with dBASE.

CREATE REPORT

Syntax

CREATE REPORT [*filename*]

The CREATE REPORT (or, as an alternative, MODIFY REPORT) command creates or allows the user to modify a report form file for producing reports. Once the report has been outlined with the CREATE REPORT command, the report can be displayed or printed with the REPORT FORM command. As with CREATE LABEL, if you omit a filename, FoxPro will ask for one when you save the report.

DEACTIVATE MENU

Syntax

DEACTIVATE MENU

The DEACTIVATE MENU command deactivates the active menu and clears the menu from the screen. The menu remains in memory and can be recalled with the ACTIVATE MENU command.

Example

DEACTIVATE MENU

DEACTIVATE POPUP

Syntax

DEACTIVATE POPUP

The DEACTIVATE POPUP command deactivates the active pop-up menu and erases it from the screen. The pop-up menu remains in memory and can be recalled to the screen with the ACTIVATE POPUP command.

Example

DEACTIVATE POPUP

DEACTIVATE WINDOW

Syntax

DEACTIVATE WINDOW *windowname* / ALL

The DEACTIVATE WINDOW command deactivates the window or windows named within the command and erases them from the screen. The windows remain in memory, and can be restored to the screen with the ACTIVATE WINDOW command. If the ALL option is not used, the most recently activated window is deactivated. If a window is underlying the most recent window, it becomes the active window. If the ALL option is included, all active windows are deactivated.

Example

DEACTIVATE WINDOW output

DECLARE

Syntax

DECLARE *arrayname 1* [*no.-of-rows, no.-of-cols*] [*arrayname2*][*no. of rows, no. of cols*]

The DECLARE command creates an array. (Note that the DECLARE command is compatible with dBASE IV. If you desire compatibility with FoxBase Plus, use the DIMENSION command instead.) In the definition list, you enter the array name and the dimensions of the array. Array names may be up to 10 characters in length. Array dimensions consist of the row and column numbers. If a column number is omitted, FoxPro creates a one-dimensional array. If row and column numbers are used, they must be separated by a comma, and FoxPro creates a two-dimensional array. Arrays declared within programs are private unless declared public with the PUBLIC command.

Examples

To declare a private array, enter

DECLARE ARRAY Finance[10,4]

To declare an array as public within a program, enter

PUBLIC ARRAY Finance[10,4]

Note that these examples both declare an array and makes it public. You can make a previously declared array public with the syntax, PUBLIC *arrayname*.

DEFINE BAR

Syntax

DEFINE BAR *line-number* OF *popupname* PROMPT *expC*
[MESSAGE *expC*] [SKIP [FOR *condition*]]

The DEFINE BAR command defines one bar option within a pop-up menu. The *popupname* must have been previously defined with the DEFINE POPUP command. The line number specifies the line number within the pop-up menu; line 1 appears on the first line of the pop-up, line 2 on the second line of the pop-up, and so on. The text specified with PROMPT appears as text in the bar of the menu. The MESSAGE option can be used to specify text that will appear at the bottom of the screen when the specified menu bar is highlighted. The SKIP option causes the bar to appear, but the bar will not be selectable within the menu.

Example

```
DEFINE BAR MainMenu FROM 3,10 TO 10,30
DEFINE BAR 1 OF MainMenu PROMPT "Add records"
DEFINE BAR 2 OF MainMenu PROMPT "Edit records"
DEFINE BAR 3 OF MainMenu PROMPT "Delete records"
DEFINE BAR 4 OF MainMenu PROMPT "Print reports"
DEFINE BAR 5 OF MainMenu PROMPT "Exit system"
```

DEFINE BOX

Syntax

DEFINE BOX FROM *print- column* TO *print- column* HEIGHT *exp* [AT LINE *print-line*] [SINGLE/DOUBLE / *border-definition-string*]

The DEFINE BOX command lets you define a box that appears around printed text. Use the specified options in the command to define the starting column on the left, the ending column on the right, the height of the box, and the starting line for the top of the box. The *border-definition-string* option lets you specify a character that will be used as the box border; the default, if this option is omitted, is a single line.

Example

DEFINE BOX FROM 4 TO 76 HEIGHT 45 AT LINE 5

DEFINE MENU

Syntax

DEFINE MENU *menuname* [MESSAGE *expC*]

The DEFINE MENU command defines a bar menu. If the MESSAGE option is added, the text of the message appears at the bottom of the screen when the menu is displayed. (See ACTIVATE MENU.)

Example

DEFINE MENU MainMenu

DEFINE PAD

Syntax

DEFINE PAD *padname* OF *menuname* PROMPT *expC* [AT *row,col*] [MESSAGE *expC*]

The DEFINE PAD command defines one pad of a bar menu. Use a separate statement containing this command for each desired pad within the menu. The text specified with PROMPT appears inside the menu pad. If the AT *row,col* option is omitted, the first pad appears at the far left, and each successive pad appears one space to the right of the previous pad. Any text that accompanies the MESSAGE option appears on the message line (see SET MESSAGE TO) when that pad is highlighted within the menu.

Example

```
DEFINE MENU MainMenu
DEFINE PAD Adder OF MainMenu PROMPT "Add" MESSAGE "Add new records"
DEFINE PAD Editor OF MainMenu PROMPT "Edit" MESSAGE "Edit records"
DEFINE PAD Eraser OF MainMenu PROMPT "Delete" MESSAGE "Delete records"
DEFINE PAD Printer OF MainMenu PROMPT "Print" MESSAGE "Print reports"
DEFINE PAD Quit OF MainMenu PROMPT "Exit" MESSAGE "leave application"
```

DEFINE POPUP

Syntax

DEFINE POPUP *popupname* FROM *row1,col1* [TO *row2,col2*] [PROMPT FIELD *fieldname*/PROMPT FILES [LIKE *skeleton*]/PROMPT STRUCTURE] [MESSAGE *expC*] [COLOR *std* [*,enhanced*] / [COLOR SCHEME *expN*] [SHADOW]

Use the DEFINE POPUP command to define a pop-up menu. The FROM and TO row and column coordinates define the upper-left and lower-right corners of the pop-up. If the TO coordinate is omitted, FoxPro will make the menu as large as needed to contain the prompts within the menu. The PROMPT FIELD, PROMPT FILE, and PROMPT STRUCTURE clauses are optional. These allow you to display selection lists of field contents, filenames, or field names from a database structure. The COLOR or COLOR SCHEME option may be used to specify colors for the pop-up. By default, pop-ups take on the colors of color scheme 2. If the optional SHADOW clause is included, a shadow appears beneath the pop-up.

Example

DEFINE POPUP MainMenu FROM 5,5 TO 14,40
DEFINE POPUP PrintMen FROM 15,12 TO 30,17

DEFINE WINDOW

Syntax

DEFINE WINDOW *windowname* FROM *row1,col1* TO *row2,col2* [DOUBLE/PANEL/NONE/*border- definition-string*] [TITLE *expC*] [CLOSE/NOCLOSE] [SHADOW] [GROW/NOGROW] [FLOAT/NOFLOAT] [ZOOM/NOZOOM] [COLOR [*standard*] [*,enhanced*] [*,border*]] / [COLOR SCHEME *expN*]

The DEFINE WINDOW comand defines display attributes and screen coordinates for a window. The FROM and TO coordinates define the upper-left and lower-right corners of the window. The default border is a single-line box; you can use the DOUBLE, PANEL, NONE, or *border-definition-character* options to specify a different border for the window. (Use ASCII codes for the border definition option.) By default, windows take on the colors of color scheme 1. The expression named with TITLE appears at the top of the window

The CLOSE/NOCLOSE option specifies whether the window may be closed with the System menu or by mouse-clicking on the close box. If the option is omitted or NOCLOSE is specified, the window may not be closed (other than by deactivating it). The SHADOW option causes a shadow to appear beneath the window. By default, windows do not have shadows. The FLOAT/NOFLOAT and ZOOM/NOZOOM options determine whether the window can be moved (in the case of FLOAT) or zoomed (in the case of ZOOM). If the options are omitted or if the NOFLOAT or NOZOOM options are specified, the window may not be moved or zoomed. The GROW/NOGROW options specify whether the user will be permitted to resize the window. If GROW is included, the user can resize the window; if NOGROW is included, the user cannot.

Example

DEFINE WINDOW MyWindow FROM 5,5 TO 7,52 DOUBLE COLOR B/W
ACTIVATE WINDOW MyWindow
@ 1, 6 SAY "Are you SURE you want to do this?"

DELETE

Syntax

DELETE [*scope*] [FOR *condition*] [WHILE *condition*]

The DELETE command marks specific records for deletion. If DELETE is used without a record number, the current record is marked for deletion. The *scope* option is used to identify the records to be deleted. The FOR option can be used to specify a condition that must be met before a record will be deleted. If you use the WHILE option, records will be deleted until the condition is no longer true. DELETE marks a record for deletion; the PACK command actually removes the record.

Example

To mark records within the next 24 records for deletion, beginning with the current record and specifying that they have an entry of VA in the State field in order to be deleted, enter

DELETE NEXT 24 FOR STATE = "VA"

DELETE FILE

Syntax

DELETE FILE *filename.ext* / [?]

The DELETE FILE command deletes a file from the disk. If an extension is present, it must be specified. If the optional question mark is used in place of a filename, a list box of all files in the current directory appears. The user can then select the file to be deleted from the list box.

DIMENSION

Syntax

DIMENSION *arrayname 1* [*no.-of-rows,no.-of-cols*] [*arrayname2*][*no. of rows,no. of columns*]...[*arraynamex*][*no.-of-rows,no.-of- cols*]

The DIMENSION command creates an array. (Note that the DIMENSION command is compatible with FoxBase Plus. If you desire compatibility with dBASE IV, use the DECLARE command instead.) In the definition list, you enter the array name and the dimensions of the array. Array names may be up to 10 characters in length. Array dimensions consist of the row and column numbers. If a column number is omitted, FoxPro creates a one-dimensional array. If row and column numbers are used, they must be separated by a comma, and FoxPro creates a two-dimensional array.

Example

DIMENSION ARRAY Finance[10,4]

DIR

Syntax

DIR [*drive:*][*filename*] [*skeleton*] [TO PRINT/TO FILE *filename*]

The DIR command displays the directory of all database files or files of a specific type if a file extension is specified. *Drive* is the drive designator, and *filename* is the name of a file with or without an extension. Skeletons composed of wildcards, which are asterisks or question marks, can be used as part of or as a replacement for *filename*. In the case of database files, the display produced by DIR includes the number of records contained in the database, the date of the last update, and the size of the file in bytes. The TO PRINT and TO FILE options may be used to route the directory display to the printer or to a filename.

Example

To display all index files from the current default drive, enter

DIR *.IDX

DISPLAY

Syntax

DISPLAY [*scope*] [*fieldlist*] [FOR *condition*] [WHILE *condition*] [OFF] [TO PRINT / TO FILE *filename*]

The DISPLAY command displays a record from the active database. You can display more records by including the *scope* option. The FOR option limits the display of records to those satisfying the condition. If you use the WHILE option, records will be displayed until the condition is no longer true. Only the fields listed in *fieldlist* will be displayed; if *fieldlist* is absent, all fields will be displayed. The OFF option will prevent the record number from being displayed. The TO PRINT and TO FILE options may be used to route the display to the printer or to a file called *filename*. Note that when the TO FILE option is used, the default extension for the file is .TXT.

Example

To display the Lastname, Firstname, City, and State fields for 10 records beginning with the current record, enter

DISPLAY NEXT 10 LASTNAME, FIRSTNAME, CITY, STATE

DISPLAY MEMORY

Syntax

DISPLAY MEMORY [LIKE *skeleton*] [TO PRINT / TO FILE *filename*]

The DISPLAY MEMORY command displays all active memory variables, their sizes, and their contents. The numbers of active variables and available variables are listed along with the numbers of bytes consumed and bytes available. Wildcards may be used as skeletons; for example, DISPLAY MEMORY LIKE MEM* would display all variables beginning with the letters "MEM." The TO PRINT and TO FILE options may be used to route the display to the printer or to a filename. Note that when the TO FILE option is used, the default extension for the file is .TXT.

DISPLAY STATUS

Syntax

DISPLAY STATUS [TO PRINT / TO FILE *filename*]

The DISPLAY STATUS command displays, for every active work area, the name and alias of the currently open database, any filter condition currently in effect, and the expressions used in any open index files. The current drive designator, function-key settings, and settings of SET commands are also displayed. The TO PRINT and TO FILE options may be used to route the display to the printer or to a filename. Note that when the TO FILE option is used, the default extension for the file is .TXT.

DISPLAY STRUCTURE

Syntax

DISPLAY STRUCTURE [IN *alias*] [TO PRINT / TO FILE *filename*]

The DISPLAY STRUCTURE command displays the structure of the active database, unless the IN *alias* option is used. The complete filename, along with the current drive designator, number of records, date of last update, and name of fields, including their statistics (type, length, and decimal places), are listed. If you have established a fields list with SET FIELDS, a > symbol appears to the left of the selected fields in the structure list. The IN alias option causes the structure of a file open in another work area (as specified by the alias) to be displayed. The TO PRINT and TO FILE options may be used to route the display to the printer or to a filename. Note that when the TO FILE option is used, the default extension for the file is .TXT.

DO

Syntax

DO *filename* [WITH *parameter-list*]

The DO command starts execution of a FoxPro command file. The filename extension of .PRG or .DBO is assumed unless otherwise specified. If the WITH option is specified and followed by a list of parameters in *parameter-list,* those parameters are transferred to the command file.

DO CASE

Syntax

```
DO CASE
   CASE condition
      commands...
   [CASE condition]
      [commands...]
   [OTHERWISE]
      [commands...]
ENDCASE
```

The DO CASE command selects one course of action from a number of choices. The conditions following the CASE statements are evaluated until one of the conditions is found to be true. When a condition is true, the commands between the CASE statement and the next CASE, or OTHERWISE and ENDCASE, will be executed. FoxPro then executes the command following the END-CASE statement. If none of the conditions in the CASE statements are found to be true, any commands following the optional OTHERWISE statement will be executed. If the OTHERWISE statement is not used and no conditions are found to be true, FoxPro proceeds to the command following the ENDCASE statement.

Example

In the following DO CASE commands, FoxPro chooses from among three possible alternatives: (1) executing a command file named MENU, (2) appending records to the database, or (3) exiting from FoxPro.

```
DO CASE
 CASE SELECT = 1
 DO MENU
 CASE SELECT = 2
 APPEND
 CASE SELECT = 3
 QUIT
ENDCASE
```

DO WHILE

Syntax

```
DO WHILE condition
    commands...
ENDDO
```

The DO WHILE command repeatedly executes commands between DO WHILE and ENDDO as long as *condition* is true. When FoxPro encounters a DO WHILE command, the condition in that command statement is evaluated: if the condition is false, FoxPro proceeds to the command following the ENDDO command; but if it is true, FoxPro executes the commands following the DO WHILE command until the ENDDO command is reached. When the ENDDO command is reached, the condition in the DO WHILE statement is again evaluated. If it is still true, the commands between DO WHILE and ENDDO are again executed. If the condition is false, FoxPro proceeds to the command below the ENDDO command.

Example

To display Lastname, Firstname, City, and State fields for each record until the end of the database, you could use the following program:

```
DO WHILE .NOT. EOF()
    ? LASTNAME, FIRSTNAME, CITY, STATE
    SKIP
ENDDO
```

EDIT

Syntax

EDIT [*scope*] [NOAPPEND] [NOCLEAR] [NOEDIT] [NODELETE] [NOMENU] [FIELDS *list*] [FOR *condition*] [WHILE *condition*]

The EDIT command invokes the FoxPro full-screen Editor. If no record number is specified in the scope, the current record, which is identified by the current position of the record pointer, will be displayed for editing.

The FIELDS option will display only the fields listed in field list. The NOCLEAR option causes the edit display to remain on the screen after the changes are completed. The NOAPPEND, NOEDIT, and NODELETE options restrict the use of appending, editing, or deleting when in Edit mode. The NOMENU option prevents access to the Edit menu. The FOR and WHILE options let you specify conditions that must be met before a record will appear in the edit screen.

EJECT

Syntax

EJECT

The EJECT command causes the printer to perform a formfeed.

EJECT PAGE

Syntax

EJECT PAGE

The EJECT PAGE command causes the printer to perform a formfeed. Use the EJECT PAGE command along with the ON PAGE command to handle page ejects for printed reports. The EJECT PAGE command invokes any end-of-page routines you have established with the ON PAGE command, and it increments _PAGENO and resets _PLINENO to zero. Note that the output of the EJECT PAGE command is made available to a disk file or screen, if output is being sent to a disk file or screen instead of to the printer.

ERASE

Syntax

ERASE *filename.ext* / [?]

The ERASE command erases the named file from the directory. The name must include the file extension. You can also use the command DELETE FILE *filename.ext* to erase a file. If the file is on a disk that is not in the default drive, you must include the drive designator. If the optional question mark is used in place of a filename, a list box appears. The user can select the file to be deleted from the list box.

EXIT

Syntax

EXIT

The EXIT command exits a DO WHILE, FOR, or SCAN loop and proceeds to the first command following the end of the loop (that is, the command after the ENDDO, ENDFOR, or ENDSCAN command).

Example

The following command-file portion uses EXIT to exit the DO WHILE loop if a part number of 9999 is entered:

```
DO WHILE .T.
     ? "Enter part number to add to inventory."
     ? "Enter 9999 to exit."
```

```
        INPUT TO PARTNO
        IF PARTNO = 9999
            EXIT
        ENDIF
        APPEND BLANK
        REPLACE PARTNUMB WITH PARTNO
        EDIT
ENDDO
```

FILER

Syntax

FILER [LIKE *skeleton*] [NOWAIT]

The FILER command displays the FoxPro file maintenance utility. Use the LIKE option with a skeleton to display a specific type of file. The NOWAIT option, when used, causes program execution to continue after the Filer utility appears.

FIND

Syntax

FIND *character-string*

The FIND command positions the record pointer at the first record containing an index key that matches *character-string*. If there are leading blanks in *character-string, character-string* must be surrounded by single or double quotes; otherwise, no quotes are necessary. If the specific character string cannot be found, the EOF value is set to true and a NO FIND message is displayed on the screen (if FoxPro is not executing a command file). An index file must be open before you use the FIND command.

FLUSH

Syntax

FLUSH

The FLUSH command flushes all active buffers to disk, without closing the files.

FOR

Syntax

FOR *memvar* = *expN1* TO *expN2* [STEP *expN3*]
    commands...
ENDFOR

The FOR and accompanying ENDFOR statements set up a repetitive loop that repeats a set number of times, as defined by the numeric expressions. The value of *expN1* marks the starting point, and the value of *expN2* marks the ending point. The loop repeats the number of times specified between *expN1* and *expN2*, unless an incremental value other than 1 is specified with the optional STEP clause. Once the set number of repetitions has been accomplished, FoxPro proceeds to the command below the ENDFOR command. If a STEP clause is used, *memvar* is incremented or, if the value of STEP is negative, decremented every time the ENDFOR is encountered until *memvar* equals or exceeds *expN2*.

Example

To use the FOR-ENDFOR commands to print Lastname, Firstname, City, and State fields for a specified number of records, you could use the following program:

```
USE MEMBERS
INPUT "Print how many records? " TO COUNTERS
STORE 1 TO BEGIN
FOR BEGIN = 1 TO COUNTERS
    ? LASTNAME, FIRSTNAME, CITY, STATE
    SKIP
ENDFOR
```

FUNCTION

Syntax

FUNCTION *procedurename*

The FUNCTION command identifies a procedure that serves as a user-defined function.

Example

```
FUNCTION StateTax
PARAMETERS SaleCost, TaxRate
Gross = SaleCost + (SaleCost * TaxRate)
RETURN(Gross)
```

GATHER FROM

Syntax

GATHER memory variable FROM *array* [FIELDS *fieldlist*]

The GATHER FROM command is used to move data from a set of variables, or an array of memory variables into a database file. (Note that GATHER FROM is compatible with FoxBase Plus; if you need compatibility with dBASE IV, use APPEND FROM

ARRAY instead.) The elements of the array are transferred, beginning with the first element of the array, into the corresponding records of the database file. If there are more elements in the array than fields in the database, the extra elements are ignored. If there are more fields in the database than there are elements in the array, the extra fields remain empty. The FOR clause, which is optional, lets you define a condition that must be met before data in the array will be added to a new record. Note that memo fields are ignored during the data transfer process, as there is no memo-type memory variable.

GETEXPR

Syntax

GETEXPR [*expC*] TO *memvar*

The GETEXPR command brings up the Expression Builder. The expression constructed by the user with the Expression Builder is then stored to the memory variable specified as part of the GETEXPR command. The GETEXPR command can be used within a program to allow the user to define selection criteria for printing a report or a set of labels.

GO or GOTO

Syntax

GO or GOTO BOTTOM/TOP/*ExpN* [IN *alias*]

The GO and GOTO commands position the record pointer at a record. GO TOP will move the pointer to the beginning of a database, and GO BOTTOM will move it to the end of a database. If a numeric value is provided, the pointer moves to that record number. The IN *alias* clause can be used to move the record pointer in a database that is open in another work area; *alias* can be either the file alias or a work area number.

HELP

Syntax

HELP [*command name-or-functionname*]

The HELP command provides instructions on using FoxPro commands and functions, as well as other information. If you enter HELP without specifying a command or function, a menu-driven system of help screens allows you to request information on various subjects. If HELP is followed by a command or function, information about that command or function will be displayed.

HIDE MENU

Syntax

HIDE MENU [[*name1*][,*name2*...]] / [ALL] [SAVE]

The HIDE MENU command hides a current menu bar, while retaining the menu bar in memory. If the ALL option is used, all current menu bars are hidden. Use the SAVE option to place an image of the menu bar on the screen or in a window. This option can prove useful when developing or testing programs.

HIDE POPUP

Syntax

HIDE POPUP [[*name1*][,*name2*...]] / [ALL] [SAVE]

The HIDE POPUP command hides a current pop-up menu, while retaining the pop-up in memory. If the ALL option is used, all current pop-ups are hidden. Use the SAVE option to place an image of the menu bar on the screen or in a window. This option can prove useful when developing or testing programs.

HIDE WINDOW

Syntax

HIDE WINDOW [[*name1*[,*name2*...]] / [ALL]

The HIDE WINDOW command hides a current window while retaining the window in memory. If the ALL option is used, all current windows are hidden.

IF

Syntax

IF *condition*
    commands...
[ELSE]
    commands...
ENDIF

IF is a decision-making command that will execute commands when certain conditions are true. If the condition for the IF statement is true, the commands between IF and ENDIF will be executed. Should the condition be false and there is an ELSE, the commands between ELSE and ENDIF will be executed. On the other hand, if the condition for IF is not true and there is no ELSE, FoxPro will drop to the ENDIF statement without executing any commands.

INDEX

Syntax

INDEX ON *ExpC* TO *filename* [FOR expC] [UNIQUE] [DESCENDING]

The INDEX command creates an index file based on an expression (which is usually a field name or a combination of fields) from the active database. Depending on the field, the index file will be indexed alphabetically, numerically, chronologically, or logically. If the index based on the first field has duplicate entries, the duplicates are indexed according to additional fields in *fieldlist*, provided additional fields have been listed. When the UNIQUE option is used, duplicate entries are omitted from the index. The indexing occurs in ascending order unless you add the DESCENDING option. Use the FOR option to limit records included in the index.

Example

To create an index file called TOWNS based on the values in a field named City, enter

INDEX ON CITY TO TOWNS

INPUT

Syntax

INPUT [*expC*] [TO *memvar*]

The INPUT command stores an entry that is entered by the user to a memory variable. An optional character expression can display a message to the user during keyboard entry. The expression can be a memory variable or a character string.

Example

To display the prompt "Enter name to search for:" and store the response to the memory variable NEWNAME, enter

INPUT "Enter name to search for:" TO NEWNAME

INSERT

Syntax

INSERT [BLANK][BEFORE]

The INSERT command adds a new record below the record pointer's position and renumbers the records below the insertion. Specifying BEFORE causes the record to be inserted at the record pointer; thus, if the pointer is at record 3, the new record will be 3 and the records below it renumbered. If the BLANK option is omitted, FoxPro allows immediate editing of the new record; otherwise, the record will be blank, but Edit mode will not be entered.

Example

To insert a new record at position 10 in the active database, enter

GO 10
INSERT BEFORE

JOIN

Syntax

JOIN WITH *alias* TO *filename* FOR *condition* [FIELDS *fieldlist*] [FOR *condition*]

The JOIN command creates a new database by combining specific records and fields from the active database and the database listed as *alias*. The combined database is stored in *filename*. You can limit the choice of records from the active database by specifying a FOR condition. All fields from both files will be copied if you do not include a field list; but if you do, only those fields specified in the field list will be copied. Specify fields from the nonactive database by supplying *filename -> field name*.

KEYBOARD

Syntax

KEYBOARD expC

The KEYBOARD command stuffs the keyboard buffer with the character expression supplied as expC. The data stays in the keyboard buffer until FoxPro looks for input, at which time the buffer is read.

LABEL FORM

Syntax

LABEL FORM *label- filename* / ? [*scope*] [SAMPLE] [FOR *condition*] [WHILE *condition*] [TO PRINT] [TO FILE *filename*] [ENVIRONMENT] [OFF]

The LABEL FORM command is used to print mailing labels from a label form file (extension .LBX). The SAMPLE option allows a sample label to be printed. The FOR option can be used to specify a condition that must be met before a label for a record will be printed. If you use the WHILE option, records will be printed until the condition is no longer true. The TO PRINT option sends output to the printer, and the TO FILE option sends output to a named disk file. The ENVIRONMENT option causes a view file with the same name as the label file to be used before printing begins. If the question mark is substituted in place of a filename, a box containing a list of all label files appears. The user may then select the label to print from the list. The OFF option causes the display of labels on the screen to be suppressed while the labels are printed or sent to a file.

Example

To print mailing labels using a label form named MAILERS for records with State fields containing NM, and to restrict printing to the next 25 records beginning at the current record-pointer position, enter

LABEL FORM MAILERS NEXT 25 FOR STATE = "NM" TO PRINT

LIST

Syntax

LIST [OFF][*scope*][*fieldlist*][FOR *condition*] [WHILE *condition*][TO PRINT / TO FILE *filename*]

The LIST command provides a list of database contents. The *scope option* is used to quantify the records to be listed. If *scope* is absent, ALL is assumed. The FOR option specifies a condition that must be met before a record will be listed. If you use the WHILE option, records will be listed until the condition is no longer true. The OFF option will prevent the record number from being listed. If the TO PRINT option is used, the listing will be printed on the printer. TO FILE directs the list to a disk file.

LIST FILES

Syntax

LIST FILES [ON *drive/dir* [LIKE *skeleton*] [TO PRINT/TO FILE *filename*]

The LIST FILES command displays a list of disk files. Use the ON option to specify a drive and/or directory. Wildcards may be used as skeletons; for example, LIST FILES LIKE *.IDX would display all files with the extension of .IDX. The TO PRINT and TO FILE options may be used to route the list to the printer or to the named disk file.

LIST MEMORY

Syntax

LIST MEMORY [LIKE *skeleton*] [TO PRINT / TO FILE *filename*]

The LIST MEMORY command lists the names, sizes, and types of memory variables. Wildcards may be used to define filename skeletons; for example, LIST MEMORY LIKE MEM* would display all variables beginning with the letters "MEM." If the TO PRINT option is used, the listing will be printed on the printer. If the TO FILE option is used, the listing will be directed to the named disk file.

LIST STATUS

Syntax

LIST STATUS [TO PRINT / TO FILE *filename*]

The LIST STATUS command lists information on currently open work areas, the active file, and system settings. All open files and open index filenames are displayed, along with work area numbers, any expressions used in index files, the default disk drive, function-key settings, and settings of the SET commands. If the TO PRINT option is used, the listing will be printed on the printer. LIST STATUS does not pause during the listing, which is the only difference between LIST STATUS and DISPLAY STATUS.

LIST STRUCTURE

Syntax

LIST STRUCTURE [TO PRINT / TO FILE *filename*] [IN ALIAS *alias*]

The LIST STRUCTURE command lists the structure of the database in use, including the name, number of records, all names of fields, and the date of the last update. If the TO PRINT option is used, the listing will be printed on the printer. The TO FILE option may be specified to redirect the output to a file. LIST STRUCTURE does not pause during the listing, which is the only difference between LIST STRUCTURE and DISPLAY STRUCTURE. The IN ALIAS option may be used to list the structure of a file in another work area; *alias* may be either an alias name or a work area number.

LOAD

Syntax

LOAD *binary-filename*

The LOAD command is used to load binary (assembly language) programs into memory for future use. An extension is optional; if omitted, it is assumed to be .BIN.

LOCATE

Syntax

LOCATE [*scope*] [FOR *condition*] [WHILE *condition*]

The LOCATE command finds the first record that matches *condition*. The *scope* option can be used to limit the number of records that will be searched, but if *scope* is omitted, ALL is assumed. The LOCATE command ends when a record-matching condition is found, after which FoxPro displays the location of the record but not the record itself. Use the CONTINUE command after a LOCATE command to locate additional records meeting the same condition (see CONTINUE). The FOR option specifies a condition that must be met before a record will be located. If you use the WHILE option, a record will be located until the condition is no longer true.

Example

To locate a record containing the character string Smith in the Lastname field, enter

LOCATE FOR LASTNAME = "Smith"

LOOP

Syntax

LOOP

The LOOP command causes a jump back to the start of a DO WHILE loop. The LOOP command is normally executed conditionally within an IF statement.

MENU

Syntax

MENU BAR *array1,expN1*
MENU *expN2,array2,expN3* [,*expN4*]
READ MENU BAR TO *var1,var2* [SAVE]

The MENU BAR, MENU, and READ MENU BAR TO commands are used to create a menu bar system, where the menu bar appears in a horizontal format across the top of the screen and each option of the menu when chosen displays a list of associated choices in a pop-up menu. (Before creating a menu bar, you must use the DIMENSION command to initialize an array for each list of menu options.) Use the MENU BAR command to insert the character expressions contained in *array1* into the menu bar; *array1* is a two-dimensional array of character strings. $Array1(i,1)$ becomes the menu pad that is displayed on the menu bar at position i. $Array1(i,2)$ can be used to define an optional message that will appear at the SET MESSAGE TO location when the pad is selected. *ExpN1* defines the number of pads that appear on the menu bar.

Use the MENU command to insert menu pop-ups into a menu bar. *ExpN2* defines the position on the menu bar where the pop-up being defined will appear; *expN3* defines the number of options on the pop-up menu. *ExpN4*, which is optional, limits the number of menu options shown on the screen at any time. If there are more options in the menu than this limit, the options scroll within the pop-up menu. *Array2* is a one-dimensional array containing the character strings that are used as menu options. Use a backslash (\) as the first character to make an option nonselectable. Use a backslash followed by a hyphen (\-) to draw a graphics bar in place of a menu item.

Use the READ MENU BAR TO command to activate the menu bar defined by the prior commands. Use *var1* and *var2* to control which menu bar pad and menu options are selected by default when the menu is initially displayed. Once a selection has been made by the user, *var1* and *var2* will contain values that correspond to the menu selection. These values may then be acted on by the program. Use the optional SAVE clause to cause the menu bar to remain on the screen after a menu option has been chosen.

Example

```
*Mainmenu.PRG displays main menu.*
SET TALK OFF
SET MESSAGE TO 24 CENTER
*Initialize arrays used for menu bar.
DIMENSION TOPBAR(3,2)
TOPBAR(1,1) = ' ADD '
TOPBAR(2,1) = ' EDIT '
TOPBAR(3,1) = ' PRINT '
TOPBAR(1,2) = 'Add data to file'
TOPBAR(2,2) = 'Edit data in file'
TOPBAR(3,2) = 'Print data in file'
*Initialize array used for Add pop-up.
DIMENSION Adder(4)
Adder(1) = 'Add Members  '
Adder(2) = 'Add Rentals  '
Adder(3) = 'Add Purchases '
Adder(4) = 'Exit this menu'
*Initialize array used for Edit pop-up.
DIMENSION Edits(4)
Edits(1) = 'Edit Members  '
Edits(2) = 'Edit Rentals  '
Edits(3) = 'Edit Purchases '
Edits(4) = 'Exit this menu'
*Initialize array used for Print pop-up.
DIMENSION Print(4)
Print(1) = 'Print Members  '
```

```
Print(2) = 'Print Rentals  '
Print(3) = 'Print Purchases '
Print(4) = 'Exit this menu'
*Insert the pop-ups into the menu bar.
MENU BAR TOPBAR,3
MENU 1,Adder,4
MENU 2,Edits,4
MENU 3,Print,4
*Activate the menu system.
READ MENU BAR TO 1,1
```

MENU TO

Syntax

MENU TO *memvar*

The MENU TO command is used along with the @-PROMPT command to implement light-bar menus. See @-PROMPT for a complete explanation of the use of the MENU TO command.

MODIFY COMMAND / MODIFY FILE

Syntax

MODIFY COMMAND/FILE *filename* [*skeleton*] [NOEDIT] [NOWAIT] [RANGE *expN1*[,*expN2*]] [WINDOW *windowname*] [SAVE]

MODIFY COMMAND or MODIFY FILE starts the FoxPro Editor, which can be used for editing command files or ASCII text files. If MODIFY COMMAND is used, the filename will be given the extension .PRG unless a different extension is named. If MODIFY FILE is used, no extension is added unless one is specified in the filename. The WINDOW option may be used to open the file in a previously defined window. The *skeleton* option may be used to open windows for all files that match the file skeleton supplied. The NOEDIT option causes the text to be displayed, but editing is not allowed. The NOWAIT option causes program execution to continue as soon as the window is opened. The RANGE option may be used to open an editing window with a range of characters selected for editing. The characters selected begin with the position specified in *expN1*, and continue for *expN2* characters. If *expN2* is omitted, editing begins at the character position specifed by *expN1*. The SAVE option causes the window to remain visible after editing is completed.

MODIFY LABEL

Syntax

MODIFY LABEL *filename* / ? [SAVE]

The MODIFY LABELS command creates or allows editing of a label form file. This file can be used with the LABEL FORM command to produce mailing labels. The filename will be given the extension .LBX. If the question mark is used in place of a filename, FoxPro displays a list of all label files in the current directory. The user may then select a label file for editing from the list. The SAVE option causes the label design window to remain visible after changes to the label are completed.

MODIFY MEMO

Syntax

MODIFY MEMO *memofield1* [,*memofield 2*...] [NOEDIT] [NOWAIT] [RANGE *expN1*[,*expN2*]] [WINDOW *windowname*] [SAVE]

MODIFY MEMO places the contents of a memo field in the FoxPro Editor. The WINDOW option may be used to open the memo field in a previously defined window. The NOEDIT option causes the text to be displayed, but editing is not allowed. The NOWAIT option causes program execution to continue as soon as the window is opened. The RANGE option may be used to edit a memo field with a range of characters selected for editing. The characters selected begin with the position specified in *expN1* and continue for *expN2* characters. If *expN2* is omitted, editing begins at the character position specifed by *expN1*. The SAVE option causes memo window to remain visible after editing is completed.

MODIFY REPORT

Syntax:

MODIFY REPORT filename / ? [SAVE]

The MODIFY REPORT command allows you to use the Report Generator to create or modify a report form file for producing reports. The filenames produced will be given the extension .FRX. If the question mark is used in place of a filename, FoxPro displays a list of all report form files in the current directory. The user may then select a report file for editing from the list. The SAVE option causes the report design to remain visible after changes to the report are completed.

MODIFY STRUCTURE

Syntax

MODIFY STRUCTURE

The MODIFY STRUCTURE command allows you to alter the structure of the active database. After the structure has been modified, a backup copy containing the original data remains on disk with the same filename but with a different extension of .BAK.

MOVE WINDOW

Syntax

MOVE WINDOW *windowname* TO *row,col* /BY *delta-row,delta-col*

The MOVE WINDOW command moves a predefined window to a new location on the screen.

Examples

To move the window to the starting position of row 15, column 20, enter

MOVE WINDOW MyWindow TO 15,20

To move the window 6 lines down and 4 lines to the right, enter

MOVE WINDOW MyWindow BY 6,4

NOTE or * or &&

Syntax

NOTE or * or &&

The NOTE or * or && command is used to insert comments in a command file. Use && to add a comment at the end of an existing statement. Use NOTE or * at the beginning of a line when the entire line is to be a comment. Text after the * or the && or the word NOTE in a command file will be ignored by FoxPro.

ON

Syntax

ON ERROR *command*
ON ESCAPE *command*
ON KEY *command*

This command causes a branch within a command file, specified by *command,* to be carried out when the condition identified by ON (an error, pressing the ESC key, or pressing any key) is met. If more than one ON condition is specified, the order of precedence is ON ERROR, ON ESCAPE, and then ON KEY. All ON conditions remain in effect until another ON condition is specified to clear the previous condition. To clear an ON condition without specifying another condition, enter ON ERROR, ON ESCAPE, or ON KEY without adding a command.

Examples

To cause program control to transfer to another program called ERRTRAP if an error occurs, enter

ON ERROR DO ERRTRAP

To cause the program to display a customized error message if an error occurs, use the following form:

ON ERROR ? "A serious error has occurred. Call J.E.J.A. Tech Support for instructions."

To cause the program to call another program named HELPER.PRG containing customized help screens if the ESC key is pressed, enter

ON ESCAPE DO HELPER

To halt processing within a program and transfer program control to a program named HALTED.PRG if any key is pressed, enter

ON KEY DO HALTED

Use of the ON KEY syntax of the command will result in the key that is pressed being stored in the keyboard buffer. The routine that is called by the ON KEY command should use a READ command or INKEY function to clear the buffer.

ON KEY =

Syntax

ON KEY = *expN* [*command*]

The ON KEY = *expN* command branches to a subroutine when the user presses the key that has the ASCII code indicated by the expression.

ON KEY-LABEL

Syntax

ON KEY [LABEL *key-label*] [*command*]

The ON KEY-LABEL command branches to a subroutine based on the pressing of a specific key as identified by the key label.

ON PAD

Syntax

ON PAD *padname* OF *menuname*
[ACTIVATE POPUP *popupname*]

The ON PAD command ties a given pad within a bar menu to a specific pop-up menu. When the named pad is selected from the menu, the associated pop-up menu appears.

Example

ON PAD Add OF MainMenu ACTIVATE POPUP AddRecs
ON PAD Edit OF MainMenu ACTIVATE POPUP EditRecs
ON PAD Print OF MainMenu ACTIVATE POPUP PrintRec

ON PAGE

Syntax

ON PAGE [AT LINE *expN command*]

The ON PAGE command executes the command named after the ON PAGE command whenever FoxPro reaches the designated line number or encounters an EJECT PAGE command. The ON PAGE command is generally used to call a procedure that prints a footer, ejects a page, and prints a header. Using ON PAGE without any clauses will cancel the effects of the previous ON PAGE command.

Example

ON PAGE AT LINE 58 DO FOOTERS
SET PRINT ON
LIST LASTNAME, FIRSTNAME, SALARY, HIREDATE

(...more commands...)

```
PROCEDURE FOOTERS
?
? " Salary listing- for personnel use only."
EJECT PAGE
? " SALARY LISTING "
?
? DATE()
RETURN
```

ON READERROR

Syntax

ON READERROR [*command*]

The ON READERROR command runs a program or executes a named command or procedure after testing for an error in input. The ON READERROR command is called in response to invalid dates, improper responses to a VALID clause, or improper entries when a RANGE clause is in effect. ON READERROR without the *command* clause is used to cancel the previous ON READERROR command.

ON SELECTION PAD

Syntax

ON SELECTION PAD *padname* OF *menuname* [*command*]

The ON SELECTION PAD command links a program, procedure, or command to a specific pad of a bar menu. When the named pad is chosen from the menu, the command, procedure, or program named within the ON SELECTION statement will be executed.

ON SELECTION PAD without the *padname* clause is used to cancel the previous ON SELECTION PAD command.

Example

ON SELECTION PAD Print OF MainMenu DO REPORTER

ON SELECTION POPUP

Syntax

ON SELECTION POPUP *popupname* /ALL [*command*]

The ON SELECTION POPUP command names a program, procedure, or command that executes when a selection is made from a pop-up menu. If no command or procedure is named, the active pop-up is deactivated. If the ALL option is used, the command or procedure applies to all pop-ups. ON SELECTION POPUP without the *popupname* clause is used to cancel the previous ON SELECTION POPUP command.

Example

ON SELECTION POPUP Print DO Reporter

PACK

Syntax

PACK

The PACK command removes records that have been marked for deletion by the DELETE command and rebuilds any open index files. Because the command involves recopying much of the active database, it can be time-consuming with large files.

PARAMETERS

Syntax

PARAMETERS *parameter- list*

The PARAMETERS command is used within a command file to assign variable names to data items that are received from another command file with the DO command. The PARAMETERS command must be the first command in a command file. The number, order, and data types of the items in the parameter list must match the list of parameters included with the WITH option of the DO command that called the command file.

Example

The following portion of a command file shows the use of the PARAMETERS command to receive a location for displaying an error message, along with the contents of the message:

```
PROCEDURE ErrMessage
PARAMETERS Row, Message
@ Row, 36-(LEN(TEXT)/2) SAY Text
RETURN
```

PLAY MACRO

Syntax

PLAY MACRO *macroname*

The PLAY MACRO command plays a previously stored macro.

PRINT JOB/ENDPRINTJOB

Syntax

PRINTJOB
commands
ENDPRINTJOB

The PRINTJOB command places stored print-related settings into effect for the duration of a printing job. Desired values must be stored to print-system memory variables before the PRINTJOB command is encountered. When PRINTJOB is executed, starting codes stored to _pscodes are sent to the printer; a form feed is sent if _peject contains BEFORE or BOTH; _pcolno is initialized to zero; and _plineno and ON PAGE are activated. When the printing process is complete and the ENDPRINTJOB command is encountered, any ending print codes stored to _pecodes are sent to the printer; a form feed is sent if _peject contains AFTER or BOTH; FoxPro returns to the PRINTJOB command if the _pcopies variable contains more than 1 (set to more than one copy of the report); and _plineno and ON PAGE are deactivated.

Example

```
*sets compressed print on for Epson with ESC code 018.
*does page eject after end of each report.
*spools two copies of report to printer.
STORE 018 to _pecodes
STORE "AFTER" to _peject
STORE 2 to _pcopies
PRINTJOB
REPORT FORM Payroll TO PRINT
END PRINTJOB
```

PRIVATE

Syntax

PRIVATE ALL [LIKE/EXCEPT *skeleton*] / *memvarlist* / ARRAY *array-definition- list*]

This command sets specified variables to private, hiding values of those variables from all higher-level parts of a program. Skeletons are filename patterns that include the acceptable DOS wildcards of asterisk (*) and question mark (?). Memory variables are private by default.

Examples

To hide all variables, excluding BILLPAY, from higher-level parts of the program, enter

PRIVATE ALL EXCEPT BILLPAY

To hide all variables with 8-character names that end in TEST from higher-level parts of the program, enter

PRIVATE ALL LIKE ????TEST

To hide only the variable named PAYOUT from higher-level parts of the program, enter

PRIVATE PAYOUT

PROCEDURE

Syntax

PROCEDURE procedure-name

The PROCEDURE command identifies the start of each separate procedure within a procedure file.

Although using a one-line procedure is inefficient (procedures should be at least two lines long), the following example demonstrates a simple procedure.

Example

```
PROCEDURE ERROR1
@ 2, 10 SAY "That is not a valid answer. Try again."
RETURN
```

PUBLIC

Syntax

PUBLIC *memvarlist* / ARRAY *array-definition-list*

This command sets named variables or arrays to public, making the values of those variables or arrays available to all levels of a program.

Example

To make the variables named BILLPAY, DUEDATE, and AMOUNT available to all modules of a program, enter

```
PUBLIC BILLPAY, DUEDATE, AMOUNT
```

QUIT

Syntax

```
QUIT
```

The QUIT command closes all open files, leaves FoxPro, and returns you to the operating system prompt.

READ

Syntax

READ [SAVE]

The READ command allows entry from an @ command with a GET option. Normally, a READ command clears all GETs when all data entry or editing is completed. The SAVE option is used to avoid clearing all GETs after completion of data entry or editing.

READ MENU

Syntax

READ MENU TO memory-variable [SAVE]

The READ MENU TO command activates a popup menu defined with the @...MENU command. (See @...MENU) The SAVE option causes the menu to remain visible after a menu selection has been made.

RECALL

Syntax

RECALL [*scope*] [FOR *condition*] [WHILE *condition*]

The RECALL command unmarks records that have been marked for deletion. If *scope* is not listed, ALL is assumed. The FOR option can be used to specify a condition that must be met before a record will be recalled. If you use the WHILE option, deleted records will be recalled until the condition is no longer true.

REINDEX

Syntax

REINDEX

The REINDEX command rebuilds all open index files in the current work area. If any changes have been made to the database while its index file was closed, you can update the index file with REINDEX.

RELEASE

Syntax

RELEASE *memvarlist* / ALL [LIKE/EXCEPT *wildcards*]
RELEASE MODULE *modulename* / MENUS *menuname-list* / POPUP *popupname-list* / WINDOW *windowname-list*

The RELEASE command removes all or specified memory variables from memory. Wildcards, which are asterisks or question marks, are used with the LIKE and EXCEPT options. The asterisk can be used to represent one or more characters, the question mark to represent one character. The RELEASE MENUS, RELEASE POPUP, and RELEASE WINDOW variations of the command release the named objects from active memory. The RELEASE MODULE command releases any binary files loaded with the LOAD command from memory.

Example

To release all memory variables except those ending with the characters TAX, enter

RELEASE ALL EXCEPT ???TAX

RENAME

Syntax

RENAME *filename.ext* TO *new-filename.ext*

The RENAME command changes the name of a file. The name must include the file extension. If the file is on a disk that is not in the default drive, the drive designator must be included in *filename.ext*.

REPLACE

Syntax

REPLACE [*scope*] *field* WITH *expression* [...*field2* WITH *expression2*...] [FOR *condition*] [WHILE *condition*] [ADDITIVE]

The REPLACE command replaces the contents of a specified field with new values. You can replace values in more than one field by listing more than one *field* WITH *expression;* be sure to separate each field replacement with a comma. The FOR option can be used to specify a condition that must be met before a field in a record will be replaced. If you use the WHILE option, records will be replaced until the condition is no longer true. If the *scope* or FOR or WHILE options are not used, the current record (at the current record-pointer location) will be the only record replaced. The ADDITIVE option can be used when replacing a memo field to add the expression to the existing text in the field. FoxPro will automatically insert a carraige return between the old text and the new.

Example

To replace the contents of a field called Salary at the current record with a new amount equal to the old amount multiplied by 1.05, enter

REPLACE SALARY WITH SALARY * 1.05

REPORT FORM

Syntax

REPORT FORM *filename* / ? [*scope*] [FOR *condition*] [WHILE *condition*] [PLAIN] [HEADING *character-string*] [SUMMARY] [NOEJECT] [TO PRINT / TO FILE *filename*] [OFF]

The REPORT FORM command uses a report form file (previously created with the CREATE REPORT command) to produce a report. A filename with the extension .FRX is assumed unless otherwise specified. The FOR option can be used to specify a condition to be met before a record will be printed. If you use the WHILE option, records will be printed until the condition is no longer true. If *scope* is not included, ALL is assumed. The PLAIN option omits page headings. The HEADING option (followed by a character string) provides a header in addition to any header that was specified when the report was created with CREATE REPORT. The NOEJECT option cancels the initial formfeed. The

SUMMARY option causes a summary report to be printed. TO PRINT directs output to the screen and the printer, while TO FILE directs output to a disk file. If the question mark is substituted in place of a filename, a list of all report files appears. The user may then select the report to print from the list. The optional OFF clause, when used, turns off the normal screen output while the report is being printed.

RESTORE

Syntax

RESTORE FROM *filename* / MEMO *memofield* [ADDITIVE]

The RESTORE command reads memory variables into memory from a memory variable file, or from a memo field. When used with files RESTORE FROM assumes that *filename* ends with .MEM; if it does not, you should include the extension. If the ADDITIVE option is used, current memory variables will not be deleted.

RESTORE MACROS

Syntax

RESTORE MACROS FROM *macro-filename* / MEMO *memofield*

The RESTORE MACROS command restores macros that were saved in a macro file or in a memo field to memory. If the MEMO clause is used, the macros are restored from a memo field. Any macros existing in memory that are assigned to the same keys when you use this command will be overwritten.

RESTORE SCREEN

Syntax

RESTORE SCREEN [FROM *memvar*]

The RESTORE SCREEN command restores a screen from the buffer or from the named memory variable (see SAVE SCREEN).

RESTORE WINDOW

Syntax

RESTORE WINDOW *windowname- list* / ALL FROM *filename* / MEMO *memofield*

The RESTORE WINDOW command restores window definitions that were saved in a file or in a memo field with the SAVE WINDOW command. If the MEMO clause is used, the windows are restored from a memo field.

RESUME

Syntax

RESUME

The RESUME command is a companion to the SUSPEND command. RESUME causes program execution to continue at the line following the line at which program operation was suspended (see also SUSPEND).

RETRY

Syntax

RETRY

The RETRY command returns control to a calling program and executes the same line that called the program containing the RETRY command. The function of RETRY is similar to the function of the RETURN command; however, where RETURN executes the next successive line of the calling program, RETRY executes the same line of the calling program. RETRY can be useful in error recovery situations, where an action can be taken to clear the cause of an error and the command repeated.

Example

```
*printing program includes error recovery.*
WAIT "Press a key to start the report."
ON ERROR DO PROBLEMS
REPORT FORM MyFile TO PRINT
ON ERROR
RETURN
*...more commands...*

*PROBLEMS.PRG*
*error trapping for printer program.*
CLEAR
? "Printer is NOT READY."
? "Take corrective action, then press any key."
WAIT
RETRY
RETURN
```

RETURN

Syntax

RETURN [TO MASTER / *expression* / TO *procedurename*]

The RETURN command ends execution of a command file or procedure. If the command file was called by another command file, program control returns to the other command file. If the command file was not called by another command file, control returns to the *command level*. If the TO MASTER option is used, control returns to the highest-level command file. If the TO *procedurename* option is used, control returns to the named procedure. The *expression* option is used to return the value in a user-defined function to another procedure or command file.

RUN or !

Syntax

RUN [/N] *filename* or ! [/N] *filename*

The RUN command executes a non-FoxPro program from within the FoxPro environment, provided there is enough available memory. The program must be an executable file (having an extension of .COM, .EXE, or .BAT). When the program completes its execution, control is passed back to FoxPro. You can also execute DOS commands with RUN. The exclamation point (!) can be substituted for the word RUN. The */N* option can be used to specify an amount of memory to be freed, where *N* is a numeric value. If *N* is omitted, RUN frees a standard amount of memory (which varies, depending on your system). If *N* is 0, RUN frees as much memory as possible, swapping large portions of FoxPro out to disk.

Any value other than 0 is interpreted as memory needed in kilobytes, and as much of FoxPro as is needed is swapped out to disk to provide the memory.

SAVE

Syntax

SAVE TO *filename* / MEMO *memofield-name* [ALL LIKE/EXCEPT *skeleton*]

The SAVE command copies memory variables to a disk file or to the contents of a memo field. Wildcards, which are asterisks or question marks, are used with parts of filenames as skeletons along with the LIKE and EXCEPT options. The asterisk can be used to represent one or more characters, the question mark to represent one character.

Example

To save all existing 6-letter memory variables ending in the letters "TAX" to a disk file named FIGURES, enter

SAVE TO FIGURES ALL LIKE ???TAX

SAVE MACROS

Syntax

SAVE MACROS TO *macro-filename* / MEMO *memofield*

The SAVE MACROS command saves macros currently in memory to a macro file. If the MEMO option is used, the macros are saved to the named memo field of the current record.

SAVE SCREEN

Syntax

SAVE SCREEN [TO *memvar*]

The SAVE SCREEN command saves the current screen image to the buffer. If the TO clause is included along with a variable name, the screen image is saved to the named memory variable. You can later use RESTORE SCREEN to redisplay the screen.

SAVE WINDOW

Syntax

SAVE WINDOW *windowname- list* / ALL TO *window- filename* / MEMO *memofield*

The SAVE WINDOW command saves the windows named in the list to a disk file. If the ALL option is used, all windows in memory are saved to a file. If the MEMO option is used, the windows are saved to the named memo field of the current record. The windows can be restored to memory using the RESTORE WINDOW command.

SCAN

Syntax

```
SCAN [scope] [FOR condition] [WHILE condition]
  + [commands...]
    [LOOP]
    [commands]
    [EXIT]
ENDSCAN
```

The SCAN and ENDSCAN commands are simplified alternatives to the DO WHILE and ENDDO commands. The SCAN-ENDSCAN commands cause the file in use to be scanned, processing all records that meet the specified conditions.

Example

```
USE MEMBERS
SCAN FOR EXPIREDATE <= DATE()+60
    SET PRINT ON
    ? "Dear: "
    ?? trim(FIRSTNAME) + " " + LASTNAME
    ?
    ? "Your membership expires within the next 60 days."
    ? "Please call 555-1212 to renew your membership."
    EJECT
    SET PRINT OFF
ENDSCAN
```

SCATTER TO

Syntax

SCATTER memory variable [FIELDS *fieldlist*] TO *array*

The SCATTER TO command is used to move data from the current record of a database file or from memory variables into an array. (Note that SCATTER TO is compatible with FoxBase Plus; if you need compatibility with dBASE IV, use COPY TO ARRAY instead.) The fields of the current record are transferred, beginning with the first field of the record, into the corresponding elements of the array. If the database has more fields than the array has elements, the contents of extra fields are not stored to the array. If the array has more elements than the database has fields, the extra elements in the array are not changed. Note that memo fields are ignored during the data transfer process.

SCROLL

Syntax

SCROLL *row1,col1,row2,col2,expN*

The SCROLL command causes a rectangular portion of the screen to scroll. The upper-left corner of the portion is designated by *row1,col1* and the lower-right corner is designated by *row2,col2*. The numeric expression indicates the number of lines of the area to scroll. A negative number forces a scroll downwards, and a positive number forces a scroll upwards.

SEEK

Syntax

SEEK *expression*

The SEEK command searches for the first record in an indexed file whose field matches a specific expression. If *expression* is a character string, it must be surrounded by single or double quotes. If expression cannot be found and FoxPro is not executing a command file, the EOF value is set to true and a "No find" message is displayed on the screen. An index file must be open before you can use the SEEK command. Also note the use of two related commands, SET EXACT and SET NEAR. Use SET EXACT to tell FoxPro to find a precise match. Use SET NEAR to tell FoxPro that if a match cannot be found, the record pointer should be positioned at the closest record rather than the end of the file.

SELECT

Syntax

SELECT *n* or SELECT *alias*

The SELECT command chooses from among 10 possible work areas for database files. When FoxPro is first loaded into the computer, it defaults to work area 1. To use multiple files at once, you can select other work areas with the SELECT command; other files can then be opened in those areas. Acceptable work areas are the numbers 1 through 10.

Example

To open a file named TAXES in work area 5, enter

```
SELECT 5
USE TAXES
```

SET

Syntax

SET

This command causes the View window to be displayed. The View window options (at the left edge of the window) can then be used to view and modify most available SET parameters within FoxPro.

SET ALTERNATE

Syntax

SET ALTERNATE ON/OFF and SET ALTERNATE TO *filename* [ADDITIVE]

The SET ALTERNATE TO command creates a text file with the extension .TXT, and when activated by SET ALTERNATE ON stores all keyboard entries and screen displays to the file. The SET ALTERNATE OFF command halts the process, after which CLOSE ALTERNATE is used to close the file. (You can SET ALTERNATE OFF temporarily, and turn it on again later before using CLOSE ALTERNATE, to resume sending output to the file.) If the ADDITIVE option is used, SET ALTERNATE appends to the end of any existing file.

Example

To store the actions of the LIST command to a text file, enter

```
SET ALTERNATE TO CAPTURE
SET ALTERNATE ON
LIST LASTNAME, FIRSTNAME
SET ALTERNATE OFF
CLOSE ALTERNATE
```

SET AUTOSAVE

Syntax

SET AUTOSAVE ON/OFF

The SET AUTOSAVE command, when turned on, causes FoxPro to save changes to disk after each I/O operation. This reduces the chances of data loss due to power or hardware failure. The default for SET AUTOSAVE is OFF.

SET BELL

Syntax

SET BELL ON/OFF

The SET BELL command controls whether audible warnings will be issued during certain operations. SET BELL ON enables the bell, and SET BELL OFF disables the bell.

SET BELL TO

Syntax

SET BELL TO *frequency/duration*

The SET BELL TO command controls the frequency and duration of the bell. The frequency is the desired tone in hertz, and each unit of duration is approximately .0549 seconds. Available frequency is from 19 to 10,000 and available duration is from 1 to 19.

SET BLINK

Syntax

SET BLINK ON/OFF

The SET BLINK command determines whether screen elements (borders, shadows, text) can be made to blink on EGA or VGA monitors. SET BLINK ON enables blinking of selected elements. Use the Color option of the Window menu or the SET COLOR command to change the actual elements to blinking.

SET BLOCKSIZE

Syntax

SET BLOCKSIZE TO expN

The SET BLOCKSIZE command defines the size of blocks used to store memo fields on disk. Each block is 512 bytes, and expN can be a value from 1 to 32. If expN is greater than 32, disk space for memo fields is allocated in bytes rather than in 512-byte blocks. The default value for SET BLOCKSIZE is 64.

SET BORDER

Syntax

SET BORDER TO [SINGLE/DOUBLE/PANEL/NONE/ *border-definition-string1*] [,*border-definition-string2*]

The SET BORDER command redefines the border, which is a single line. The SINGLE option defines a single line; the DOUBLE option defines a double line; the PANEL option defines a panel built with the ASCII 219 character; and NONE defines no border. The *border-definition-string* option may contain up to 8 ASCII values separated by commas. Value 1 defines the top of the border; value 2 the bottom; values 3 and 4 the left and right edges; and values 5, 6, 7, and 8 the upper-left, upper-right, lower-left, and lower-right corners, respectively. By default, *border-definition-string1* is also used for the active window. The optional *border-definition-string2* defines the appearance of the border if the window is not active.

SET CARRY

Syntax

SET CARRY ON/OFF

The SET CARRY command controls whether data will be copied from the prior record into a new record when APPEND or INSERT is used. By default, SET CARRY is OFF.

SET CENTURY

Syntax

SET CENTURY ON/OFF

This command causes or does not cause the century to be visible in the display of dates. For example, a date that appears as 12/30/86 will appear as 12/30/1986 after the SET CENTURY ON command is used.

SET CLOCK

Syntax

SET CLOCK ON/OFF

The SET CLOCK command defines whether the system clock will appear. SET CLOCK ON displays the clock, and SET CLOCK OFF hides the clock.

SET CLEAR

Syntax

SET CLEAR ON/OFF

The SET CLEAR command determines whether the screen will be cleared after a SET FORMAT TO or a QUIT command. If SET CLEAR is OFF, the screen will not be cleared upon execution of SET FORMAT TO or QUIT. The default for SET CLEAR is ON.

SET CLOCK TO

Syntax

SET CLOCK TO *row,col*

The SET CLOCK TO command defines the location of the system clock, as defined by the row and column coordinates provided.

SET COLOR OF

Syntax

SET COLOR OF NORMAL / MESSAGES / TITLES / BOX / HIGHLIGHT / INFORMATION / FIELDS TO [*color-pairs-list*]

The SET COLOR OF command can be used to define colors for standard items, such as messages, titles, boxes, and highlights. *Color-pairs-list* is 1 to 10 color pairs, with foreground and background values separated by a slash and each color pair separated by commas.

SET COLOR OF SCHEME

Syntax

SET COLOR OF SCHEME *expN* TO [*color-pairs- list*]

The SET COLOR OF SCHEME command sets the colors of the numbered scheme to the colors list identified in *color-pairs-list;* *expN* is a numeric expression from 1 to 11 or from 17 to 24. (Schemes 12 through 16 are reserved by FoxPro.) Schemes 17 through 24 can be user-defined. Schemes 1 through 11 apply to the following objects:

Scheme 1   User windows
Scheme 2   User menus
Scheme 3   Menu bar
Scheme 4   Pop-up menus
Scheme 5   Dialog boxes
Scheme 6   Dialog popups
Scheme 7   Alert boxes
Scheme 8   Windows
Scheme 9   Window pop-ups
Scheme 10 Browse window
Scheme 11 Report Layout window

The color pairs list is 1 to 10 color pairs, with foreground and background values separated by a slash and each color pair separated by commas.

SET COLOR OF SCHEME TO

Syntax

SET COLOR OF SCHEME *expN1* TO [SCHEME *expN2*]

The SET COLOR OF SCHEME TO command copies the colors of the first color scheme to the second color scheme. The *expN* is a numeric expression from 1 to 11 or from 17 to 24. (Schemes 12 through 16 are reserved by FoxPro.) Schemes 17 through 24 can be user-defined. If SCHEME expN2 is omitted, colors will be copied from the last named color set.

SET COLOR ON/OFF

Syntax

SET COLOR ON/OFF

The SET COLOR ON/OFF command is used to change between color and monochrome monitors. SET COLOR ON turns on color mode, and SET COLOR OFF turns on monochrome mode.

SET COLOR SET TO

Syntax

SET COLOR SET TO [*colorset-name*]

The SET COLOR SET TO command loads a color set that was defined and saved previously. Use the Color option of the Window menu to define and save a color set.

SET COLOR TO

Syntax

SET COLOR TO *color-pairs-list*

The SET COLOR command is used to select screen colors and display attributes. *Color-pairs-list* is 1 to 10 color pairs, with foreground and background values separated by a slash and each color pair separated by commas.

SET COMPATIBLE

Syntax

SET COMPATIBLE ON/OFF

The SET COMPATIBLE command turns on or off compatibility with FoxBase Plus. When SET COMPATIBLE is OFF, FoxBase Plus programs run in FoxPro without modification.

SET CONFIRM

Syntax

SET CONFIRM ON/OFF

The SET CONFIRM command controls the behavior of the cursor during editing. When SET CONFIRM is ON, the ENTER key must be pressed to move from one field to another when editing in a highlighted field, even if you completely fill the field. When CONFIRM is OFF, the cursor automatically advances when you fill a field.

SET CONSOLE

Syntax

SET CONSOLE ON/OFF

The SET CONSOLE command turns output to the screen on or off. SET CONSOLE does not control output to the printer. Use SET CONSOLE within a program when you want to hide any screen display while leaving the keyboard active (during the typing of a user's password, for example).

SET CURRENCY

Syntax

SET CURRENCY TO [*expC*]

The SET CURRENCY command changes the symbol used for currency. A character expression containing up to 9 characters may be used as the currency symbol.

SET CURRENCY LEFT/RIGHT

Syntax

SET CURRENCY LEFT/RIGHT

The SET CURRENCY LEFT/RIGHT command changes the placement of the currency symbol, allowing the symbol to appear to the left or the right of the value.

SET DATE

Syntax

SET DATE AMERICAN/ANSI/BRITISH/ITALIAN/FRENCH/GERMAN /JAPAN/USA/MDY/DMY/YMD

This command sets the display format for the appearance of dates. American displays as MM/DD/YY; ANSI displays as YY.MM.DD; British displays as DD/MM/YY; Italian displays as DD-MM-YY; French displays as DD/MM/YY; German displays as DD.MM.YY; Japan displays as YY/MM/DD; USA displays as MM-DD-YY; MDY displays as MM/DD/YY; DMY displays as

DD/MM/YY; and YMD displays as YY/MM/DD. The default value is American.

SET DECIMALS

Syntax

SET DECIMALS TO *expN*

The SET DECIMALS command changes the number of decimal places that are normally displayed during calculations.

SET DEFAULT

Syntax

SET DEFAULT TO *drive: directory*

This command changes the default drive and/or directory used in file operations.

SET DELETED

Syntax

SET DELETED ON/OFF

With SET DELETED set OFF (as it is by default), all records marked for deletion will be displayed when commands such as LIST and REPORT FORM are used. With SET DELETED set to ON, deleted records are omitted from the output of LIST, DISPLAY, LABEL FORM, and REPORT FORM commands. They are also omitted from the Edit and Browse displays, unless you explicitly move the record pointer to a deleted record with a GOTO command before issuing the EDIT or BROWSE command.

SET DEVELOPMENT

Syntax

SET DEVELOPMENT ON/OFF

The SET DEVELOPMENT command, when ON, tells FoxPro to compare creation dates of .PRG files and compiled .DBO files, so that when a program is run, an outdated .DBO file will not be used. The FoxPro Editor automatically deletes old .DBO files as programs are updated, so the SET DEVELOPMENT command is not needed if you use the FoxPro Editor. If you use another editor to create and modify program files, add a SET DEVELOPMENT ON statement at the start of your programs.

SET DEVICE

Syntax

SET DEVICE TO PRINTER/SCREEN/FILE *filename*

The SET DEVICE command controls whether @ commands are sent to the screen or printer. SET DEVICE is normally set to SCREEN, but if PRINTER is specified output will be directed to the printer. The FILE option directs output to the named disk file.

SET DISPLAY TO

Syntax

SET DISPLAY TO
MONO/COLOR/CGA/EGA25/EGA43/MONO43/VGA25/VGA43/VGA50

The SET DISPLAY command chooses a monitor type and sets the number of lines displayed. For the number of lines option to have effect, the graphics hardware must support the type chosen within the SET DISPLAY command.

SET DOHISTORY

Syntax

SET DOHISTORY ON/OFF

The SET DOHISTORY command turns on or off the storage of commands from command files in the Command window. When DOHISTORY is ON, program file commands are stored in the Command window as they are executed. You can later edit and reexecute those commands as if they had been entered at the command level.

SET ECHO

Syntax

SET ECHO ON/OFF

The SET ECHO command determines whether instructions from command files will be displayed or printed during program execution. Setting ECHO to ON can be useful when debugging pro-grams. The default for SET ECHO is OFF.

SET ESCAPE

Syntax

SET ESCAPE ON/OFF

The SET ESCAPE command determines whether the ESC key will interrupt a program during execution. The default for SET ESCAPE is ON.

SET EXACT

Syntax

SET EXACT ON/OFF

The SET EXACT command determines how precisely two character strings will be compared. With SET EXACT OFF, which is the default case, comparison is not strict: a string on the left of the test is equal to its substring on the right if the substring acts as a prefix of the larger string. Thus, "turnbull" = "turn" is true even though it is clearly not. SET EXACT ON corrects for this lack of precision. Note that SET EXACT determines whether you can FIND or SEEK the first part of an index key. If SET EXACT is OFF, you can search for the first part of the key; if SET EXACT is ON, you must search for the entire key expression.

SET FIELDS

Syntax

SET FIELDS ON/OFF

This command respects or overrides a list of fields specified by the SET FIELDS TO command.

SET FIELDS TO

Syntax

SET FIELDS TO [*fieldlist* / ALL [LIKE/EXCEPT *skeleton*]] [ADDITIVE]

This command sets a specified list of fields that will be available for use. The ALL option causes all fields present in the active database to be made available. The LIKE/EXCEPT *skeleton* options select fields that match or do not match the skeleton. The ADDITIVE option adds the fields to a prior list of fields.

SET FILTER

Syntax

SET FILTER TO [*condition*]

The SET FILTER command displays only those records in a database that meet a specific condition.

Example

To display only those records in a database that contain the name "Main St." in the Address field during a DISPLAY or LIST command, enter

SET FILTER TO "Main St." $ ADDRESS

SET FIXED

Syntax

SET FIXED ON/OFF

The SET FIXED command sets the number of decimal places used within a numeric display.

SET FORMAT

Syntax

SET FORMAT TO *filename* /?

The SET FORMAT command lets you activate a format file called *filename* to control the format of the screen display used during EDIT, CHANGE, and APPEND operations. If *filename* has the extension .FMT, you need not supply the extension. The SET FORMAT command without a specified filename cancels the effects of the previous SET FORMAT command. The question mark, if used, causes a list of format files to appear.

SET FULLPATH

Syntax

SET FULLPATH ON/OFF

The SET FULLPATH command specifies whether full pathnames appear with filenames returned by the DBF and NDX functions.

If SET FULLPATH is OFF, only the drive designator and filename are returned by the functions. If SET FULLPATH is ON, the drive designator, pathname, and filename are returned by the functions.

SET FUNCTION

Syntax

SET FUNCTION *expN / key-label* TO *character-string*

The SET FUNCTION command resets a function key to a command or sequence of commands of your choice. The maximum width of a command sequence is 75 characters. You can view the current settings with the DISPLAY STATUS command.

Example

To change the function of the F5 key to open a file named MEMBERS and enter Append mode, enter

SET FUNCTION "5" TO "USE MEMBERS;APPEND;"

The semicolon (;) represents a carriage return.

SET HEADING

Syntax

SET HEADING ON/OFF

The SET HEADING command determines whether column headings appear when the LIST, DISPLAY, CALCULATE, AVERAGE, or SUM command is used.

SET HELP

Syntax

SET HELP ON/OFF or SET HELP TO *filename*

The SET HELP command turns on or off the FoxPro on-line help facility. When SET HELP is ON, pressing F1 or entering HELP as a command displays the Help window. When SET HELP is OFF, the Help window is not available.

All help commands are stored in a database file named FOXHELP.DBF. You can use the SET HELP TO *filename* command to specify a different database file. This can be useful if you are designing your own custom help system for an application.

SET HOURS

Syntax

SET HOURS TO [12/24]

The SET HOURS command changes the time display to the desired format, 12 or 24 hours. If you choose the 12-hour clock, AM or PM is displayed along with the time.

SET INDEX

Syntax

SET INDEX TO *filename* / ?

The SET INDEX command opens the index file *filename*. If your file has the .IDX extension, you do not need to include the extension in the command. If the question mark is substituted in place of a filename, a list of all index files appears. The user may then select the index file to activate from the list.

SET INTENSITY

Syntax

SET INTENSITY ON/OFF

The SET INTENSITY command determines whether reverse video is on or off during full-screen operations. SET INTENSITY is ON when you begin a session with FoxPro. If you SET INTENSITY to OFF, you should generally turn on the delimiters to mark the boundaries of the data entry area for each field.

SET LOGERRORS

Syntax

SET LOGERRORS ON/OFF

The SET LOGERRORS command determines whether FoxPro stores compilation errors in a file.

SET MARGIN

Syntax

SET MARGIN TO *expN*

The SET MARGIN command resets the left printer margin from the default of 0.

SET MARK

Syntax

SET MARK TO *expC*

The SET MARK command specifies the delimiter used to separate the month, day, and year of a date. The character expression must be a single character, surrounded by quotes.

Example

SET MARK TO "#"

SET MEMOWIDTH

Syntax

SET MEMOWIDTH TO *expN*

SET MEMOWIDTH controls the width of columns containing the display or printed listings of contents of memo fields. The default value provided if this command is not used is 50.

SET MESSAGE

Syntax

SET MESSAGE TO *expC*

This variation of the SET MESSAGE command identifies a user-definable message that appears at the position specified earlier with SET MESSAGE TO (see the next command).

Example

To display the message "Press F1 for assistance." on the message line, enter

SET MESSAGE TO "Press F1 for assistance."

SET MESSAGE TO

Syntax

SET MESSAGE TO [*expN* / LEFT / CENTER / RIGHT]

This variation of the SET MESSAGE command is used to specify the screen or window line and the optional left, center, or right placement for screen messages when the MENU TO command is used.

SET MOUSE

Syntax

SET MOUSE TO *expN*

The SET MOUSE command adjusts the sensitivity of the mouse. Permissible values are from 1 to 10, with 1 being the least sensitive and 10 being the most sensitive. The default for the SET MOUSE command is 5.

SET NEAR

Syntax

SET NEAR ON / OFF

The SET NEAR command can be used to position the record pointer at the nearest record when a FIND or a SEEK is unsucessful. If SET NEAR is ON, the record pointer will be placed at the next record after the expression that could not be located. If SET NEAR is OFF, the record pointer is placed at the end of the file when the expression is not found.

SET ODOMETER

Syntax

SET ODOMETER TO [*expN*]

The SET ODOMETER command tells FoxPro how often commands that display a record count (such as APPEND and COPY) should update the screen display. The default value is 100, and the maximum value is 32,767. Setting ODOMETER to a higher value can speed up command execution slightly.

SET ORDER

Syntax

SET ORDER TO *expN*

This command makes the specified index file the active index without changing the open or closed status of other index files.

Example

If three index files, NAME, CITY, and STATE, have been opened in that order, and STATE is the active index, to change the active index to CITY, enter

SET ORDER TO 2

SET PATH

Syntax

SET PATH TO *pathname*

The PATH command identifies a search path that will be searched for files if a file is not found in the current directory. Note that the PATH command does not alter an existing DOS path; it merely specifies a search path for database and related FxoPro files.

Example

To change the path from the default path to a path named FoxPro on drive C, enter

SET PATH TO C:\FOXPRO

For more information on search paths, read your DOS manual (version 2.1 or later).

SET POINT

Syntax

SET POINT TO *expC*

The SET POINT command changes the character used as the decimal point. The specified expression can be any single character surrounded by quotes.

Example

SET POINT TO ","

SET PRINTER

Syntax

SET PRINTER ON/OFF

The SET PRINTER command directs output to the printer as well as the screen. The default for SET PRINTER is OFF. (The SET PRINT ON/OFF command is identical to this command.)

SET PRINTER TO

Syntax

SET PRINTER TO LPT1 / COM1 / COM2 / *other-DOS-device* / *filename*

SET PRINTER TO reroutes printer output to the device or disk file specified.

SET PROCEDURE

Syntax

SET PROCEDURE TO *procedure-filename*

The SET PROCEDURE command opens a procedure file. SET PROCEDURE is placed in the command file that will reference the procedures in a procedure file, or in its calling program.

SET RELATION

Syntax

SET RELATION TO [*expression1* INTO *alias*] [ADDITIVE]
[[,*expression2* INTO *alias*] [ADDITIVE]...]

The SET RELATION command links the active database to an open database in another area. If the key-expression option is used, the active file must contain that key, and the other file must be indexed on that key. The ADDITIVE option may be used to specify multiple relations out of a single work area.

Example

To set a relation between the active database and a database named PARTS using a key field named CUSTNO, enter

SET RELATION TO CUSTNO INTO PARTS

SET RELATION OFF

Syntax

SET RELATION OFF INTO *alias*

The SET RELATION OFF command breaks an existing relation between two databases. The parent database must be the currently selected database, and *alias* indicates the related (child) database; *alias* may be the alias name or a work area number.

SET RESOURCE

Syntax

SET RESOURCE ON/OFF

The SET RESOURCE command tells FoxPro whether to save any changes made to the FoxPro environment when exiting the program. Changes are saved to the resource file (FOXUSER.DBF). If SET RESOURCE is OFF, changes will not be saved upon exiting FoxPro.

SET RESOURCE TO

Syntax

SET RESOURCE TO *filename*

The SET RESOURCE TO command tells FoxPro to use a different file as the resource file. By default, the resource file is a database named FOXUSER.DBF. You can provide another filename along with the SET RESOURCE TO command to cause that file to be used as the resource file.

SET SAFETY

Syntax

SET SAFETY ON/OFF

The SET SAFETY command determines whether a confirmation message will be provided before existing files are overwritten by commands such as SORT or COPY, or before a ZAP command is executed. SET SAFETY is normally set to ON.

SET SEPARATOR

Syntax

SET SEPARATOR TO *expC*

The SET SEPARATOR command specifies the symbol that should be used to separate hundreds in numeric amounts. The default is the comma, which is standard in U.S. currency. The expression may be any single character surrounded by quotes.

Example

SET SEPARATOR TO "."

SET SHADOWS

Syntax

SET SHADOWS ON/OFF

The SET SHADOWS command enables or disables shadows underneath windows.

SET SPACE

Syntax

SET SPACE ON/OFF

The SET SPACE command, when ON, tells FoxPro to add a space between expressions printed with the ? and ?? commands. The default for SET SPACE is ON.

Example

```
SET SPACE ON
USE ABCSTAFF
GO 1
? LASTNAME, FIRSTNAME
Morse Marcia
SET SPACE OFF
? LASTNAME, FIRSTNAME
MorseMarcia
```

SET STATUS

Syntax

SET STATUS ON/OFF

The SET STATUS command turns on or off the status display at the bottom of the screen.

SET STEP

Syntax

SET STEP ON/OFF

This is a debugging command that determines whether processing will stop each time a command in a command file is executed. The default of SET STEP is OFF.

SET STICKY

Syntax

SET STICKY ON/OFF

The SET STICKY command affects the operation of menu pads and menu pop-ups when the mouse is used. When SET STICKY is ON and a menu pad is selected with the mouse, the associated menu pop-up remains open on the screen until an option is selected (or ESC is pressed). When SET STICKY is OFF and a menu pad is selected with the mouse, the associated menu pop-up closes as soon as the mouse button is released.

SET TALK

Syntax

SET TALK ON/OFF

The SET TALK command determines whether results of FoxPro commands (such as the current record number after a SKIP or LOCATE, or the results of a SUM or AVERAGE command) are displayed on the screen. The default for SET TALK is ON.

SET TOPIC

Syntax

SET TOPIC TO [expC / *expL*]

The SET TOPIC command determines how help topics are displayed. When help is selected, a list of available topics is normally displayed. By entering SET TOPIC TO *expC* where *expC* is the name of a help topic, that particular topic will be displayed whenever help is selected. The logical expression *expL* is used when creating a user-defined help system.

SET TYPEAHEAD

Syntax

SET TYPEAHEAD TO *numeric-expression*

This command sets the size, in number of keystrokes, of the typeahead buffer. The default value is 20. The size of the typeahead buffer can be increased to prevent fast typists from outrunning the keyboard. An acceptable value is any number between 0 and 32,000.

SET UNIQUE

Syntax

SET UNIQUE ON/OFF

This command is used with the INDEX command to create lists of items with no duplicates. The list may not be indexed adequately if there are duplicates. When you build an index with UNIQUE set ON, there is only one index entry for each unique index key. (Note that an alternate way to achieve the same effect is to add the UNIQUE clause to the INDEX ON command.) The default setting for SET UNIQUE is OFF.

SET VIEW

Syntax

SET VIEW ON/OFF

The SET VIEW command enables or disables the View window.

SET VIEW TO

Syntax

SET VIEW TO *filename*

The SET VIEW TO command activates the named view file, placing all settings in that view file (open databases, indexes, relations, and filters) into effect.

SET WINDOW OF MEMO

Syntax

SET WINDOW OF MEMO TO *windowname*

The SET WINDOW command sets a window for use when editing the contents of memo fields. The window listed as windowname must have been previously defined with the DEFINE WINDOW command.

SHOW MENU

Syntax

SHOW MENU *menuname* / ALL [PAD *padname*] [SAVE]

The SHOW MENU command displays a menu without activating the menu. The command is primarily used in the program design process to check the visual appearance of a menu. The ALL option causes all menus to be shown. The SAVE option is used to place images of menus on the screen. This option is normally used testing and debugging programs.

SHOW POPUP

Syntax

SHOW POPUP *popupname* / ALL [SAVE]

The SHOW POPUP command displays a pop-up menu without activating the menu. The command is primarily used in the program design process to check the visual appearance of a menu. The ALL option causes all pop-ups to be shown. The SAVE option is used to place images of pop-ups on the screen. This option is normally used for testing and debugging programs.

SHOW WINDOW

Syntax

SHOW WINDOW *windowname* / ALL [SAVE] [TOP/BOTTOM/SAME]

The SHOW WINDOW command displays a window without activating the window. The command is primarily used in the program design process to check the visual appearance of a window. The ALL option causes all windows to be shown. Use BOTTOM or TOP to place a window at the bottom or top of a stack of existing windows. The SAME option applies only to windows previously hidden with DEACTIVATE WINDOW or HIDE WINDOW. Use SAME to put the previously hidden window back in the same position it occupied earlier. The SAVE option is used to place images of the window on the screen. This option is normally used for testing and debugging programs.

SKIP

Syntax

SKIP *expN* [IN *aliasname*]

The SKIP command moves the record pointer. SKIP moves one record forward if no value is specified. Values can be expressed as memory variables or as constants. The IN *aliasname* option can be used to move the record pointer within a file in another work area.

Example

To skip two records back, enter

SKIP -2

SORT

Syntax

SORT TO *filename* ON *field1* [/A][/C][/D] [,*field2* [/A][/C][/D]...] [ASCENDING/DESCENDING] [*scope*] [FOR *condition*] [WHILE *condition*] [FIELDS <Mlfieldlist>]

The SORT command creates a rearranged copy of a database. The order of the new database depends on the fields and options specified. The /C option creates a sorted file in dictionary order, where there is no differentiation between upper- and lowercase. Use /A for ascending order on a specific field, /D for descending order on a specific field. Use the ASCENDING or DESCENDING options to specify ascending or descending order for all fields. (The /A or /D option can be used with any field to override the effects of the ASCENDING or DESCENDING option.) The FIELDS option may be used to specify fields to be included in the sorted file; if omitted, all fields are included. You can sort up to 10 fields in a single sort; you cannot sort on memo fields or on logical fields.

Example

To sort a database on the Lastname and then Firstname fields, both in descending order, and output the sorted file to a file named NEWNAME, enter

SORT TO NEWNAME ON LASTNAME, FIRSTNAME DESCENDING

STORE

Syntax

STORE *expression* TO *memvarlist / array-element-list*

The STORE command creates a memory variable and stores a value to that variable or to the named array.

Example

To multiply a field called Salary for the current record by 1.05 and store it in the new memory variable named NEWAMT, enter

STORE SALARY * 1.05 TO NEWAMT

SUM

Syntax

SUM [*scope*] [*fieldlist*] [TO *memvarlist*] [TO ARRAY *arrayname*] [FOR *condition*] [WHILE *condition*]

The SUM command provides a sum total of *fieldlist* involving numeric fields. If the TO option is not used, the sum is displayed (assuming SET TALK is ON) but not stored in memory. If the TO option is used, the sum is displayed (assuming SET TALK is ON) and is stored as the specified memory variable. If the *scope* option is not used, ALL is assumed by FoxPro. The FOR option can be used to specify a condition that must be met before an entry in a field can be summed. If you use the WHILE option, records will be summed until the condition is no longer true. The TO ARRAY option stores the values summed to the elements of the named array.

Example

To total the contents of two specified fields (Salary and Taxes) and store those sums to the memory variables A and B, enter

SUM SALARY, TAXES TO A,B

SUSPEND

Syntax

SUSPEND

The SUSPEND command suspends execution of a command file or procedure and returns program control to the command level, while leaving current memory variables intact. Execution of the command file or procedure can be restarted where it was interrupted with the RESUME command.

TEXT

Syntax

TEXT
text to be displayed
ENDTEXT

The TEXT command displays blocks of text from a command file. If SET PRINT is ON, the text will be printed.

Example

TEXT
Press the RETURN key to run the payroll.
Or press the ESCAPE key to exit.
ENDTEXT

TOTAL

Syntax

TOTAL TO *filename* ON *key* [*scope*] [FIELDS *fieldlist*] [FOR *condition*] [WHILE *condition*]

The TOTAL command adds the numeric fields in a database and creates a new database containing the results. The file to be totaled must be indexed or sorted on the key field. If the FIELDS *fieldlist* option is used, fields totaled will be limited to those fields named in the list. If the *scope* option is not used, the quantifier of ALL is assumed, meaning all records in the database will be totaled unless you use the FOR or WHILE option. The FOR option can be used to specify a condition that must be met for the fields to be totaled. If you use the WHILE option, records will be totaled until the condition is no longer true.

Example

To total the Salary, Fedtax, Statetax, and Fica fields in a database named PAYROLL and store those totals to a second database named RECORDS, you could use commands like these:

```
USE PAYROLL
TOTAL TO NEWFIL ON FIELDS SALARY, FEDTAX, STATETAX, FICA
```

TYPE

Syntax

TYPE *filename.ext* [TO PRINT / TO FILE *filename*] [NUMBER]

The TYPE command displays the contents of a disk file on screen. If the TO PRINT option is used, the file will be printed. The TO FILE option directs the output of the TYPE command to a named disk file. The NUMBER option causes line numbers to be included.

UPDATE

Syntax

UPDATE [RANDOM] ON *keyfield* FROM *alias* REPLACE *field* WITH *expression* [,*field2* WITH *expression2*...]

The UPDATE command uses data from a specified database, *alias,* to make changes to the database in use. The value in the matching record in the file you are updating from is added to the value in the active file.

Example

To update the Rentamt field in a database named WORLDWIDE, based on the contents of the Rentamt field in a database named CURRENCY, enter

```
SELECT 2
USE CURRENCY
SELECT 1
USE WORLDWID INDEX LASTNAME
UPDATE ON LASTNAME FROM CURRENCY REPLACE RENTAMT
WITH CURRENCY- >RENTAMT RANDOM
```

Both files must be sorted or indexed on the key field unless RANDOM is included, in which case only alias need be indexed.

USE

Syntax

USE [*database-file* / ?] [IN *work-area-number*] [INDEX *index-file-list*] [ALIAS *aliasname*]

The USE command opens a database file and related index files in a work area. If the ? is used in place of the database filename, a list of available files appears. Use the INDEX option to specify index files that will be open or active. Use the ALIAS option to open the file in a different work area. Entering the USE command without specifying a filename will close the file that is currently open.

WAIT

Syntax

WAIT [*expC*] [TO *memvar*]

The WAIT command halts operation of a command file until a key is pressed. If a character expression is included, it will be displayed on the screen. If the TO option is used, the key pressed will be stored as a memory variable.

ZAP

Syntax

ZAP

The ZAP command removes all records from the active database file. The ZAP command is equivalent to a DELETE ALL command followed by a PACK command.

B

GLOSSARY OF FUNCTIONS

Glossary Symbols and Conventions
Summary of Functions

This appendix summarizes the FoxPro functions. Following the name of each function is the function's syntax and a description of its purpose. For a similar summary of FoxPro commands, see Appendix A.

GLOSSARY SYMBOLS AND CONVENTIONS

1. All functions are printed in UPPERCASE, although you can enter them in either upper- or lowercase letters.

2. The term *expC* indicates a character expression, *expN* indicates a numeric expression, and *expL* indicates a logical expression. Where data type does not matter, the term *expression* is used.

3. Whenever a function calls for or permits an *alias* argument, you can use the alias name (in quotes), or you can use the work-area number or letter.

4. Any part of a parameter that is surrounded by [ ] (left and right brackets) is optional.

5. Ellipses (...) following a parameter means that the parameter can be repeated infinitely; that is, until you exhaust the memory of the computer or reach the limit of 1024 characters on a single program line.

SUMMARY OF FUNCTIONS

ABS

Syntax

ABS(*expN*)

The ABS function returns the absolute (positive) value of the specified numeric expression.

ACOS

Syntax

ACOS(*expN*)

The ACOS function returns the arc cosine of *expN,* as measured in radians between zero and +pi (3.14159). Allowable values for *expN* are from +1 to −1.

ALIAS

Syntax

ALIAS([*expN*])

The ALIAS function returns the alias of the database open in the work area specified by *expN*. If *expN* is omitted, ALIAS returns the alias of the current work area.

ALLTRIM

Syntax

ALLTRIM(*expC*)

ALLTRIM returns the character expression *expC* minus any leading and trailing blanks.

ASC

Syntax

ASC(*expC*)

The ASC function returns the decimal ASCII code for the leftmost character in *expC*.

ASIN

Syntax

ASIN(*expN*)

The ASIN function returns the arc sine of *expN,* as measured in radians between −pi/2 and +pi/2 (−1.57079 to 1.57079). Acceptable values for *expN* are from +1 to −1.

AT

Syntax

AT(*expC1, expC2* [,*expN*])

The AT function finds *expC1* in *expC2*. (Note that *expC2* may be a memo field.) The function returns as an integer the starting position of *expC1*. If *expC1* is not found, the function returns a zero. If the optional *expN* is used, the *expN*th occurrence of *expC1* is searched for.

ATAN

Syntax

ATAN(*expN*)

The ATAN function returns the arctangent of *expN,* as measured in radians between −pi/2 and +pi/2 (−1.57079 to 1.57079). *ExpN* can be any value.

ATC

Syntax

ATC(*expC1, expC2* [,*expN*])

The ATC function searches a character string *expC1* for another character string *expC2*. If *expC1* is not found, the function returns a zero. If the optional *expN* is used, the *expN*th occurrence of *expC1* is searched for. The ATC function operates just like the AT function, but the ATC function is not case sensitive.

ATCLINE

Syntax

ATCLINE(*expC1, expC2*)

The ATCLINE function finds *expC1* within *expC2* and then returns the line number where it was found. *ExpC2* can be a memo field. If *expC1* is not found in *expC2*, the function returns a zero. ATCLINE is not case sensitive; the ATLINE function performs the same task, but is case sensitive. ATCLINE is usually used to locate text within a memo field and return the line number containing the desired text.

ATLINE

Syntax

ATLINE(*expC1, expC2*)

The ATLINE function finds *expC2* within *expC1* and then returns (as an integer) the line number where it was found. If *expC1* is not found in *expC2*, the function returns a zero.

ATN2

Syntax

ATN2(*expN1, expN2*)

The ATN2 function returns the arc-tangent angle (as measured in radians) for all four quadrants. You specify the X and Y coordinates (or sine and cosine of the angle) instead of specifying the tangent value as with the ATAN function. *ExpN1* is the X coordinate or sine of the angle, and *expN2* is the Y coordinate, or cosine of the angle.

BAR

Syntax

BAR( )

The BAR function returns the number of the option most recently selected from the active pop-up menu. Use the DEFINE BAR command to assign each menu item a number. If no pop-up menu is active, the BAR function returns a zero.

BETWEEN

Syntax

BETWEEN(*expr1, expr2, expr3*)

The BETWEEN function returns a logical true (.T.) if *expr1* is greater than or equal to *expr2* and less than or equal to *exp3;* otherwise, the function returns a logical false (.F.). The expressions used must be of the same type.

BOF

Syntax

BOF([*alias*])

The BOF function returns a logical true (.T.) if the record pointer is at the beginning of file (above the first record in the database file). Use the optional *alias* to test for the beginning of the file in a different work area.

CAPSLOCK

Syntax

CAPSLOCK([*expL*])

The CAPSLOCK function turns the CAPSLOCK keyboard mode on or off, or it returns the current state of CAPSLOCK. CAPSLOCK(.T.) turns the CAPSLOCK mode on, and CAPSLOCK(.F.) turns the CAPSLOCK mode off. If *expL* is omitted, the status of CAPSLOCK is returned without changing the state of the keyboard.

CDOW

Syntax

CDOW(*expD*)

The CDOW function returns the name of the day of the week for the given date expression.

CEILING

Syntax

CEILING(*expN*)

The CEILING function returns the nearest integer greater than or equal to *expN*. Positive numbers with decimals are rounded up to the next-highest number, and negative numbers with decimals are rounded up to the number next closest to zero.

CHR

Syntax

CHR(*expN*)

The CHR function returns the character whose decimal ASCII code is equivalent to *expN*.

CHRSAW

Syntax

CHRSAW([*expN*])

The CHRSAW function checks the keyboard buffer for the presence of a character and returns a logical true (.T.) if a character is found in the keyboard buffer. The optional *expN* specifies the number of seconds to wait for a keypress before returning the value.

CHRTRAN

Syntax

CHRTRAN(*expC1, expC2, expC3*)

The CHRTRAN function translates the characters of *expC1*. The strings in *expC2* and *expC3* are used as a translation table. Any occurrences of the first character in *expC2* are replaced by the first character in *expC3*, the second character in *expC2* by the second character in *expC3*, and so forth.

CMONTH

Syntax

CMONTH(*expD*)

The CMONTH function returns the name of the month that corresponds to the date expression.

COL

Syntax

COL( )

The COL function returns the current column location of the cursor.

COS

Syntax

COS(*expN*)

The COS function returns the cosine of *expN* as measured in radians. To convert an angle from degrees to radians, use the DTOR function.

CTOD

Syntax

CTOD(*expC*)

The CTOD function returns the date value that corresponds to *expC* in the default date format (generally MM/DD/YY). Use the SET DATE and SET CENTURY commands to change the default format.

CURDIR

Syntax

CURDIR([*expC*])

The CURDIR function returns the current DOS directory on the drive identified by *expC*. If no such drive exists, CURDIR returns a null string. If *expC* is omitted, the default drive is assumed.

DATE

Syntax

DATE( )

The DATE function returns the current system date.

DAY

Syntax

DAY(*expD*)

The DAY function returns the numeric day of the month that corresponds to the date expression.

DBF

Syntax

DBF([*alias*])

The DBF function returns the database filename for the file open in the specified work area. If no *alias* is specified, the DBF function returns the filename for the currently selected work area. If no file is open in the work area, the function returns a null string.

DELETED

Syntax

DELETED([*alias*])

The DELETED function returns a logical true (.T.) if the current record is marked for deletion; otherwise, it returns a logical false (.F.). Use the optional *alias* to test for deleted records in an unselected work area.

DIFFERENCE

Syntax

DIFFERENCE(*expC1*, *expC2*)

The DIFFERENCE function returns a numeric value between 0 and 4, representing the phonetic difference between two character strings, *expC1* and *expC2*. The DIFFERENCE function can be useful for searching databases when the precise spelling of an entry is not known.

DISKSPACE

Syntax

DISKSPACE( )

The DISKSPACE function returns the number of bytes available on the default drive.

DMY

Syntax

DMY(*expD*)

The DMY function returns a date expression in European format (DD-Month-YY) for the given date expression.

DOW

Syntax

DOW(*expD*)

The DOW function returns the numeric day of the week corresponding to the date expression. The value returned ranges from 1 (for Sunday) to 7 (for Saturday).

DTOC

Syntax

DTOC(*expD*[,1])

The DTOC function returns a character string containing the date that corresponds to the date expression. Use the SET DATE and the SET CENTURY commands to change the format of the string. The optional ,1 argument causes DTOC to return the string in the YYYYMMDD format, similar to the DTOS function.

DTOR

Syntax

DTOR(*expN*)

The DTOR function converts the angle specified by *expN* from degrees to radians.

DTOS

Syntax

DTOS(*expD*)

The DTOS function returns a character string in the format YYYYMMDD for the given date expression. This function is useful when indexing on a date field.

EMPTY

Syntax

EMPTY(*expr*)

The EMPTY function returns a logical true (.T.) if the expression *expr* is blank. The function will also return a value of true if the expression is a numeric expression with a value of zero or a logical expression with a value of false.

EOF

Syntax

EOF([*alias*])

The EOF function returns a logical true (.T.) if the end-of-file is reached (the record pointer passes the last record in the database, or a FIND, LOCATE, or SEEK command was unsuccessful). Use the optional *alias* to test for end-of-file in a different work area. Note that if you establish a relation with SET RELATION and the related file does not contain a record with the key matching the current record, the record pointer will be at the end-of-file in the related file.

ERROR

Syntax

ERROR( )

The ERROR function returns the number of the error causing the ON ERROR condition. An ON ERROR routine must be in effect for the ERROR function to return a value other than zero.

EXP

Syntax

EXP(*expN*)

The EXP function returns the value of e raised to *n*th power. *ExpN* is the exponent, *N*, in the equation e^*N*. The value of e is roughly 2.71828 (the base of natural logarithms).

FCLOSE

Syntax

FCLOSE(*expN*)

The FCLOSE function flushes the buffers for the file with the numeric file handle as specified by *expN* to disk and closes the file. Use the FCREATE or FOPEN function to assign a file handle to the file.

FCOUNT

Syntax

FCOUNT([*alias*])

The FCOUNT function returns the number of fields in a database. Use the [*alias*] option to return the number of fields in a database that is open in an unselected work area.

FCREATE

Syntax

FCREATE(*expC* [,*expN*])

The FCREATE function creates a new file named *expC* and opens the file for use. If a file with the name *expC* already exists, the existing file is overwritten. FCREATE also assigns the file a numeric "handle" to identify the file when other low-level file functions are used. By default, the file will have a DOS read/write attribute assigned. The optional numeric expression can be used to specify the attribute of the file created, using one of the following values:

0   Read/write (default)
1   Read-only
2   Hidden
3   Read-only/hidden
4   System
5   Read-only/system
6   System/hidden
7   Read-only/system/hidden

FEOF

Syntax

FEOF(*expN*)

The FEOF function returns a logical true (.T.) if the file pointer is positioned at the end of the file (EOF). *ExpN* indicates the numeric handle of the file that you wish to test for the end-of-file.

FERROR

Syntax

FERROR( )

The FERROR function is used to test whether a low-level file function has been successful. FERROR returns a zero if the last low-level function was successfully performed. If the last function was not successful, a value not equal to zero is returned.

FFLUSH

Syntax

FFLUSH(*expN*)

The FFLUSH function flushes the file whose handle is *expN*. If the file was written to, FFLUSH writes all data in the buffers to disk.

FGETS

Syntax

FGETS(*expN1* [,*expN2*])

The FGETS function returns a series of bytes from the file having the file handle specified by *expN1*. FGETS returns a series of bytes from a file until a carriage return is encountered. The optional numeric argument *expN2* can be used to specify the number of bytes that the function will return.

FIELD

Syntax

FIELD(*expN1*[, *alias*])

The FIELD function returns the name of the field in the active database that corresponds to the numeric position specified in the expression. If there is no corresponding field in the active database, FIELD returns a null string. Use the optional *alias* to return a field name from a database that is open in an unselected work area.

FILE

Syntax

FILE(*expC*)

The FILE function returns a logical true (.T.) if the character expression matches the name for an existing file in the default directory. If no such file can be found, the FILE function returns a logical false (.F.).

FILTER

Syntax

FILTER([*alias*])

The FILTER function returns the filter expression of the current work area. Use the optional *alias* to return a filter from an unselected work area. If no filter is in effect, a null string is returned.

FKLABEL

Syntax

FKLABEL(*expN*)

The FKLABEL function returns the name of the function key that corresponds to *expN*.

FKMAX

Syntax

FKMAX( )

The FKMAX function returns the number of programmable function keys available on your keyboard.

FLOOR

Syntax

FLOOR(*expN*)

The FLOOR function returns the nearest integer value less than or equal to the numeric expression. All positive numbers with a decimal will be rounded down to the next-lowest number, and all negative numbers with a decimal will be rounded down to the next number farther from zero.

FOPEN

Syntax

FOPEN(*expC* [,*expN*])

The FOPEN function opens the file named by *expC* for use. *ExpC* may include a full pathname for files on drives or in directories that are not in the current search path. The optional numeric expression can be used to specify an attribute of read-only, read/write, or write-only. Use 0 for read-only (the default), 1 for write-only, or 2 for read/write. If a file named by FOPEN is not found, the function returns a value of −1.

FOUND

Syntax

FOUND([*alias*])

The FOUND function returns a logical true (.T.) if the last CONTINUE, FIND, LOCATE, or SEEK command was successful. A logical false (.F.) is returned if the search command was unsuccessful. Note that if you have established a relation with SET RELATION and you specify the related file with *alias,* the function returns a logical true if the pointer is on a record with a key value matching that of the current record in the active database.

FPUTS

Syntax

FPUTS(*expN1, expC* [,*expN2*])

The FPUTS function writes the character string within *expC* to the file whose file handle is *expN1*. FPUTS is different from FWRITE in that FPUTS adds a carriage return and linefeed to the end of each line. The entire character string identified as *expC* is written, unless the optional numeric argument *expN2* is used; the value of *expN2* specifies the number of characters to write.

FREAD

Syntax

FREAD(*expN1*, *expN2*)

The FREAD function returns as a character string a specified number of bytes from a file whose file handle is *expN1*. The numeric value of *expN2* is the number of bytes to read, starting from the current position of the file pointer. (Use the FOPEN function to open the file.)

FSEEK

Syntax

FSEEK(*expN1*, *expN2* [, *expN3*])

The FSEEK function moves the file pointer within a file. *ExpN1* is the file's handle (returned from the FOPEN function), and *expN2* is the number of bytes the file pointer must be moved. If *expN2* is positive, the file pointer is moved toward the end of the file. If *expN2* is negative, the file pointer is moved toward the beginning of the file. The number of bytes moved is normally relative to the beginning of the file. The optional argument specified in *expN3* can be used to change this relative position. If *expN3* is 0, movement is relative to the start of the file (the default). If *expN3* is 1, movement is relative to the current position of the file pointer. If *expN3* is 2, movement is relative to the end of the file.

FSIZE

Syntax

FSIZE(*field* [, *alias*])

FSIZE returns the size of the specified *field* in bytes. Use the optional *alias* to select a field from a file in an unselected work area.

FULLPATH

Syntax

FULLPATH(*file* [, 1])

FULLPATH returns the full DOS pathname for the given *file*. If the file is not found in the default directory, FULLPATH will search the FoxPro path for the file. If the optional argument ,1 is added, the search will use the DOS path.

FV

Syntax

FV(*expN1, expN2, expN3*)

The FV function returns the future value of an investment. FV calculates the future value of a series of equal payments earning a fixed interest rate. The future value is the total of all payments plus the interest. *ExpN1* is the payment amount, *expN2* is the interest rate, and *expN3* is the number of periods. If the payments are compounded monthly and the interest rate is compounded yearly, divide the interest rate by 12 to get the proper results.

FWRITE

Syntax

FWRITE(*expN1, expC* [, *expN2*])

The FWRITE function lets you write to a file whose handle is *expN1*. The numeric value of *expN2* is the number of bytes to read, starting from the current position of the file pointer. (Use the FOPEN function to open the file and assign a handle.)

GETENV

Syntax

GETENV(*expC*)

The GETENV function returns a character string that contains the contents of the DOS environmental variable named as the character expression.

GETFILE

Syntax

GETFILE([*expC1*] [, *expC2*])

The GETFILE function causes the FoxPro Open File dialog box to be displayed. Using the dialog box, a file may be chosen. The function then returns the name of the chosen file. *ExpC1* is an optional extension; if used, only files with that extension will appear in the list box. *ExpC2* is an optional prompt that appears at the top of the Open File dialog box.

GOMONTH

Syntax

GOMONTH(*expD, expN*)

The GOMONTH function returns a date that is *expN* months before or after *expD*. If *expN* is positive, the date returned is *expN* months after *expD*. If *expN* is negative, the date returned is *expN* months before *expD*.

HEADER

Syntax

HEADER([*alias*])

The HEADER function returns the number of bytes in the header of the database open in the current work area. If no database is open in the specified work area, zero is returned. Use the optional *alias* to return the bytes in the header of a file open in an unselected work area.

IIF

Syntax

IIF(*expL, expr1, expr2*)

Glossary of Functions   733

The IIF function (Immediate IF) returns the value of *expr1* if the logical expression is true and returns the value of *expr2* if the logical expression is false. *Expr1* and *expr2* must be of the same data type.

INKEY

Syntax

INKEY([*expN*])

The INKEY function returns an integer value between 0 and 255. This value corresponds to the decimal ASCII code for the key that was pressed. A zero will be returned if no key has been pressed.

INLIST

Syntax

INLIST(*expr1*, *expr2* [, *expr3* ...])

The INLIST function determines if an expression is contained in a series of expressions. INLIST returns a logical true (.T.) if *exp1* is contained in the list of expressions *expr2*, *expr3*, and so on. The expressions must all be of the same data type.

INSMODE

Syntax

INSMODE([*expL*])

The INSMODE function changes the Insert/Overwrite mode based on *expL*. If *expL* is omitted, the function returns to the Insert mode setting.

INT

Syntax

INT(*expN*)

The INT function returns the integer portion of *expN*. No rounding occurs; any decimal values are simply dropped.

ISALPHA

Syntax

ISALPHA(*expC*)

The ISALPHA function returns a logical true (.T.) if the first character of *expC* is a-z or A-Z. A logical false (.F.) is returned if *expC* begins with a nonalphabetic or a numeric character.

ISCOLOR

Syntax

ISCOLOR( )

The ISCOLOR function returns a logical true (.T.) if the system has color capability (whether or not a color monitor is being used) and returns a logical false (.F.) if the system has monochrome capability.

ISDIGIT

Syntax

ISDIGIT(*expC*)

The ISDIGIT function returns a logical true (.T.) if the first character of *expC* is a digit (0-9).

ISLOWER

Syntax

ISLOWER(*expC*)

The ISLOWER function returns a logical true (.T.) if the first character in *expC* is a lowercase alphabetical character, or a logical false (.F.) if the first character is anything other than a lowercase alphabetical character.

ISUPPER

Syntax

ISUPPER(*expC*)

The ISUPPER function returns a logical true (.T.) if the first character in *expC* is an uppercase alphabetical character, and a logical false (.F.) if the first character is anything other than an uppercase alphabetical character.

KEY

Syntax

KEY(*expN* [, *alias*])

The KEY function returns the index expression of the specified index file. The numeric expression identifies the index file, where 1 is the first index file opened, 2 is the second index file opened, and so on. Use the *alias* option to return the key expression for an index file that is open in an unselected work area.

LASTKEY

Syntax

LASTKEY( )

The LASTKEY function returns the decimal ASCII value for the last key pressed. (The LASTKEY function returns the same ASCII values as the INKEY function.)

LEFT

Syntax

LEFT(*expC, expN*)

The LEFT function returns the leftmost number of characters specified in *expN* from the character expression *expC*, starting with the first or leftmost character.

LEN

Syntax

LEN(*expC*)

The LEN function returns the length of a character string expression specified in *expC*. *ExpC* can be a memo field name, in which case the length of the text stored within the memo field is returned. Note that in the case of character fields, LEN returns the length of the field, not the length of the text within the field. With character fields, you must add a TRIM function to get the length of the text stored in the field.

LIKE

Syntax

LIKE(*expC1, expC2*)

The LIKE function compares two character expressions and returns a logical true (.T.) if the character string in *expC2* contains the characters in *expC1*. The pattern can include the wildcard characters * (representing any sequence of characters) and ? (representing any single character).

LINENO

Syntax

LINENO( )

The LINENO function returns the line number of the next statement in the program that is currently running.

LOG

Syntax

LOG(*expN*)

The LOG function returns the natural logarithm of a number specified by *expN*. *ExpN* must be greater than zero. Use the SET DECIMALS command to specify the number of decimal places returned.

LOG10

Syntax

LOG10(*expN*)

The LOG10 function returns the common (base 10) logarithm of a number specified by *expN*. *ExpN* must be greater than zero. Use the SET DECIMALS command to specify the number of decimal places returned.

LOWER

Syntax

LOWER(*expC*)

The LOWER function converts all uppercase letters in *expC* to lowercase. The function will not affect nonalphabetic characters. The LOWER function does not change the way the data is stored unless you use it as part of a STORE or REPLACE command. The function is generally used for finding or comparing data, when you do not know what case the data was originally entered as.

LTRIM

Syntax

LTRIM(*expC*)

The LTRIM function trims all leading blanks from the character expression defined as *expC*.

LUPDATE

Syntax

LUPDATE(*alias*)

The LUPDATE function returns the last update of the active database. Use the optional *alias* to return the last update for a file open in an unselected work area.

MAX

Syntax

MAX(*expr1, expr2* [, *expr3* ...])

The MAX function returns the maximum value from the list of expressions. The expressions must all be of the same data type.

MDY

Syntax

MDY(*expD*)

The MDY function returns a Month DD, YY (or Month DD, YYYY) character string for a given date expression. The month is always spelled out, and the day always takes the DD format. If SET CENTURY is OFF, the year takes the YY format; otherwise, the year takes the YYYY format.

MEMLINES

Syntax

MEMLINES(*memofield*)

The MEMLINES function returns the number of lines in the named memo field for the current record. Note that the number of lines in the memo field will be affected by the current value of SET MEMOWIDTH.

MEMORY

Syntax

MEMORY( )

The MEMORY function returns the amount of free conventional memory as a numeric value in kilobytes.

MENU

Syntax

MENU( )

The MENU function returns the name of the currently active menu. If a menu is not active, MENU returns a null string.

MESSAGE

Syntax

MESSAGE([1])

The MESSAGE function returns the current error message, which is useful for situations in which FoxPro detects an error within a program. The MESSAGE function can be used along with the ON ERROR command for error-trapping and recovery purposes. The optional argument of (1) tells FoxPro to return the actual program code for the last line that caused the ON ERROR condition.

MIN

Syntax

MIN(*expr1, expr2* [, *expr3* ...])

The MIN function returns the minimum value expression from the list of expressions. The expressions must all be of the same data type.

MLINE

Syntax

MLINE(*memofield, expN*)

The MLINE function returns the specified line *expN* from the named memo field in the current record. Note that the value of SET MEMOWIDTH will affect the number of lines in a memo field.

MOD

Syntax

MOD(*expN1, expN2*)

The MOD function returns the remainder when *expN1* is divided by *expN2*. A positive number is returned if *expN2* is positive, and a negative number is returned if *expN2* is negative. If there is no remainder, a zero is returned.

MONTH

Syntax

MONTH(*expD*)

The MONTH function returns the numeric month (1 to 12) that corresponds to the date expression. The numbers 1 through 12 correspond to January through December.

NDX

Syntax

NDX(*expN*[, *alias*])

The NDX function returns the name of an open index file in the current work area. The numeric expression specifies the order of the index file, 1 being the first index file opened, 2 the second index file opened, and so on. Use the optional *alias* to return the name of an open index file in an unselected work area.

NUMLOCK

Syntax

NUMLOCK([*expL*])

The NUMLOCK function changes the NUMLOCK keyboard mode or returns the status of the NUMLOCK mode. NUMLOCK(.T.) turns on NUMLOCK, and NUMLOCK(.F.) turns off NUMLOCK. If the logical expression is omitted, NUMLOCK returns the status of the NUMLOCK mode.

OCCURS

Syntax

OCCURS(*expC1, expC2*)

The OCCURS function returns an integer that represents the number of times *expC1* occurs in *expC2*. If *expC1* is not found in *expC2,* the function returns a zero.

ORDER

Syntax

ORDER([*alias*])

ORDER returns the name of the master (or active) index file in the current work area. Use the optional *alias* to return the name of the active index in an unselected work area.

OS

Syntax

OS( )

The OS function returns the name and version of the operating system.

PAD

Syntax

PAD( )

The PAD function returns the name of the pad last chosen from the active menu bar. The function returns a null string if no menu is active.

PADC, PADL, PADR

Syntax

PADC(*expression, expN* [, *expC*])
PADL(*expression, expN* [, *expC*])
PADR(*expression, expN* [, *expC*])

These functions are used to pad the expression supplied as *expression* with a designated character on the left side, the right side, or on both sides. *ExpN* specifies the total length of the resultant string. The expression is padded with blanks unless an optional character is supplied as *expC;* if provided, the optional character is used to pad the expression. Use PADC to pad an expression on both sides; use PADL to pad an expression on the left side; and use PADR to pad an expression on the right side. You can pad character, date, or numeric expressions with these functions.

PARAMETERS

Syntax

PARAMETERS( )

The PARAMETERS function returns a numeric value indicating the number of parameters passed to the procedure most recently called.

PAYMENT

Syntax

PAYMENT(*expN1, expN2, expN3*)

The PAYMENT function returns the amount of a loan payment. PAYMENT assumes that the interest rate is constant and that payments are made at the end of each period. *ExpN1* is the principal amount, *expN2* is the interest rate, and *expN3* is the number of payments. If the payments are compounded monthly and the interest rate is compounded yearly, divide the interest rate by 12 to get the proper results.

PCOL

Syntax

PCOL( )

The PCOL function returns the current column position of the printer.

PI

Syntax

PI( )

The PI function returns the numeric constant pi (approximately 3.14159).

POPUP

Syntax

POPUP( )

The POPUP function returns the name of the active pop-up menu.

PRINTSTATUS

Syntax

PRINTSTATUS( )

The PRINTSTATUS function returns a logical true (.T.) if the printer is ready and a logical false (.F.) if it is not.

PROGRAM

Syntax

PROGRAM([*expN*])

The PROGRAM function returns the name of the program currently running or the program that was running when an error occurred. The optional numeric expression can be used for nesting programs (calling a program from a program). When used, the value of *expN* indicates how many levels back FoxPro should go to get the program name.

PROMPT

Syntax

PROMPT( )

The PROMPT function returns the prompt for the last option chosen from the active menu pad or pop-up menu. The function returns a null string if no pop-up menu is active.

PROPER

Syntax

PROPER(*expC*)

The PROPER function returns the character expression specified in *expC* with initial capitals. Each word in the character string has the first letter capitalized and the remaining letters in lowercase.

PROW

Syntax

PROW( )

The PROW function returns the current row position of the printer. Note that when an EJECT command is issued, PROW is reset to zero.

PUTFILE

Syntax

PUTFILE([expC1] [, expC2] [, expC3])

The PUTFILE function displays the Save As dialog box. The user can enter or choose a filename, and the filename is returned as a character expression by the function. The optional *expC1* argument is a prompt string that, if used, appears above the text box. The optional *expC2* argument is a default filename that appears in the text box. The optional *expC3* argument is a default file extension.

PV

Syntax

PV(expN1, expN2, expN3)

The PV function returns the present value of an investment, or the amount that must be invested to earn a known future value. *ExpN1* is the payment made each period, *expN2* is the interest rate, and *expN3* is the number of periods. If the payments are compounded monthly and the interest rate is yearly, divide the interest rate by 12 to get the proper results.

RAND

Syntax

RAND([*expN*])

The RAND function returns a random number between 0 and 1. The optional numeric expression can be used to provide a seed different than the default for generating the random number. A given seed will always produce the same sequence of random numbers; you can vary the sequence of random numbers by varying the seed. If *expN* is negative, the seed is taken from the system clock.

To obtain a random number in a particular range, multiply the result of the RAND function by a chosen value. For example, you could get a random number between 50 and 100 by using (RAND*50)+50.

RAT

Syntax

RAT(*expC1*, *expC2* [,*expN*])

The RAT function (Reverse AT) searches *expC2*, starting from the right, for the *expN*th occurrence of the character string *expC1*. The function returns as an integer the position where *expC1* is found. If *expC1* is not found in *expC2* the specified number of times, the function returns a zero. If *expN* is omitted, the default is 1.

RATLINE

Syntax

RATLINE(*expC1*, *expC2*)

The RATLINE function (Reverse ATLINE) searches *expC2* for the last occurrence of *expC1*. The function returns the line number of the line where *expC1* was found. If *expC1* is not found in *expC2*, the function returns a zero. Note that *expC2* can be a memo field.

READKEY

Syntax

READKEY( )

The READKEY function returns an integer value that indicates the key pressed when exiting from the editing commands APPEND, BROWSE, CHANGE, CREATE, EDIT, INSERT, MODIFY, and READ. READKEY provides a value between 0 and 36 if no changes were made to the data, or a value between 256 and 292 if changes were made to the data.

RECCOUNT

Syntax

RECCOUNT([*alias*])

The RECCOUNT function returns the number of records in the database open in the current work area. If no database is open, RECCOUNT returns a zero. Use the optional *alias* to return the number of records in a database open in an unselected work area.

RECNO

Syntax

RECNO([*alias*])

The RECNO function returns the current record number. Use the optional *alias* to return the current record number in a database open in an unselected work area. Note that RECNO(0) can follow an unsuccessful SEEK to determine what record number to return. If a SEEK is unsuccessful, the use of RECNO(0) immediately after the SEEK returns the record number of the closest matching record.

RECSIZE

Syntax

RECSIZE([*alias*])

The RECSIZE function returns the size of the database record in the current work area. Use the optional *alias* to return the size of the database record for a database open in an unselected work area. If no database is open, RECSIZE returns a zero.

RELATION

Syntax

RELATION(*expN* [, *alias*])

The RELATION function returns the relational expression for the *N*th relation of the work area identified by *alias*. Use the optional *alias* to specify an unselected work-area number, work-area letter, or alias name. If no relation exists, the function returns a null string.

REPLICATE

Syntax

REPLICATE(*expC, expN*)

The REPLICATE function returns a character string consisting of *expC* repeated *expN* times.

RIGHT

Syntax

RIGHT(*expC / memvar, expN*)

The RIGHT function returns the rightmost part of the character string *expC* or memory variable *memvar*. Use the numeric expression *expN* to specify the number of characters that will be returned.

ROUND

Syntax

ROUND(*expN1, expN2*)

The ROUND function rounds off the number supplied in *expN1*. Use *expN2* to specify the number of decimal places to round off to. If *expN2* is negative, the rounded number returned is a whole number.

ROW

Syntax

ROW( )

The ROW function returns the current row location of the cursor.

RTOD

Syntax

RTOD(*expN*)

The RTOD function converts radians to degrees. The numeric expression is the value in radians, and the value returned by the function is the equivalent value in degrees.

RTRIM

Syntax

RTRIM(*expC*)

The RTRIM function strips the trailing spaces from the named character string. The RTRIM function is identical to the TRIM function.

SCHEME

Syntax

SCHEME(*expN1*[, *expN2*])

The SCHEME function returns a color-pair list or a color pair from a color scheme. To return the complete color-pair listing for a color scheme, provide the color scheme number as *expN1*. To return a single pair listing from a color scheme, provide the optional argument *expN2*, which is the position of the color pair in the color-pair list.

SCOLS

Syntax

SCOLS( )

The SCOLS function returns the number of columns available on the display screen.

SECONDS

Syntax

SECONDS( )

The SECONDS function returns the value of the system clock, using a seconds.thousandths format.

SEEK

Syntax

SEEK(*expr* [, *alias*])

The SEEK function returns a logical true (.T.) if the search expression can be found in the active index. If the search expression is not found, the function returns a logical false (.F.), and the record pointer is placed at the end of the file. Use the optional *alias* to search an open index in an unselected work area.

SELECT

Syntax

SELECT( )

The SELECT function returns the number of the current work area (assuming SET COMPATIBLE is OFF). If SET COMPATIBLE is ON, the function returns the number of the highest unused work area.

SET

Syntax

SET(*expC* [,1])

The SET function returns the status of the various SET commands. The character expression contains the name of the desired SET command. Note that you need to use quotes around *expC* if it is a character string rather than a memory variable. Using SET without the optional argument returns the ON/OFF setting. Using SET with the optional argument ([,1]) returns the SET TO setting.

SIGN

Syntax

SIGN(*expN*)

SIGN returns a numeric value that represents the sign of the numeric expression. If *expN* is positive, SIGN returns a value of 1. If *expN* is negative, SIGN returns a value of –1. If *expN* is zero, SIGN returns a zero.

SIN

Syntax

SIN(*expN*)

The SIN function returns the sine of *expN*, where *expN* is an angle measured in radians. To convert degrees to radians, use the DTOR function.

SOUNDEX

Syntax

SOUNDEX(*expC*)

The SOUNDEX function returns a four-character string that represents the phonetic SOUNDEX code for the character expression *expC*. The four-character code returned by the SOUNDEX function can be useful for finding similar-sounding names or for building an index to perform lookups based on the sound of a word.

SPACE

Syntax

SPACE(*expN*)

The SPACE function returns a character string containing the specified number of blank spaces. The maximum number of spaces that can be specified by *expN* is 65,504.

SQRT

Syntax

SQRT(*expN*)

The SQRT function returns the square root of the numeric expression *expN*. The numeric expression must be a positive number.

SROWS

Syntax

SROWS( )

SROWS returns the number of rows available on the screen.

STR

Syntax

STR(*expN1* [, *expN2* [, *expN3*]])

The STR function converts a numeric expression to a character expression, where *expN1* is the numeric expression to be converted to a character string. Use the optional *expN2* to specify a length (including the decimal point and decimal places), and use the optional *expN3* to specify a number of decimal places.

STRTRAN

Syntax

STRTRAN(*expC1, expC2* [, *expC3*] [, *expN1*] [, *expN2*])

The STRTRAN function performs a search-and-replace operation on a character string. The function returns the given expression *expC1,* with occurrences of *expC2* replaced with *expC3.* Replacements start at the *expN1*th occurrence and continue for a total of *expN2* replacements.

STUFF

Syntax

STUFF(*expC1, expN1, expN2, expC2*)

The STUFF function inserts or removes characters from any part of a character string. *ExpC1* is the existing character string, *expN1* is the starting position in the string, *expN2* is the number of characters to remove, and *expC2* is the character string to insert.

SUBSTR

Syntax

SUBSTR(*expC, expN1* [, *expN2*])

The SUBSTR function extracts a portion of a string from a character expression. *ExpC* is the character expression to extract the string from, *expN1* is the starting position in the expression, and *expN2* is the number of characters to extract from the expression.

SYS

Syntax

SYS(*expN*)

The SYS functions return character-string values that contain various system data. *ExpN* is a numeric value that corresponds to the appropriate system function. The more commonly used system functions are shown here; consult your FoxPro documentation for a complete listing.

SYS(1)	Returns the current system date
SYS(2)	Returns the number of seconds since midnight
SYS(3)	Returns a unique legal filename
SYS(5)	Returns the current default device
SYS(6)	Returns the current print device
SYS(7)	Returns the name of the current format file
SYS(9)	Returns your FoxPro serial number
SYS(12)	Returns the amount of free memory
SYS(13)	Returns the printer status
SYS(23)	Returns the amount of EMS memory used by FoxPro
SYS(24)	Returns the EMS limit specified in CONFIG.FP
SYS(2003)	Returns the current directory name
SYS(2006)	Returns the type of graphics hardware in use

TAN

Syntax

TAN(*expN*)

The TAN function returns the tangent of *expN,* where *expN* is measured in radians. To convert degrees to radians, use the DTOR function.

TARGET

Syntax

TARGET(*expN* [, *expr*])

The TARGET function returns the alias of the work area that is the target of the *N*th relation from the work area specified by *expr*. Use the optional *expr* to specify another work area by alias, number, or letter. If *expr* is omitted, the current work area is used. If the relation specified by the function does not exist, a zero is returned.

TIME

Syntax

TIME([*expN*])

The TIME function returns the current system time in the format of HH:MM:SS (if SET HOURS is set to 24) or in the format of HH:MM:SS am/pm (if SET HOURS is set to 12). If you include the numeric argument *expN,* the function's result includes hundredths of a second. (Note, however, that maximum accuracy of the clock is about 1/18th of a second.)

TRANSFORM

Syntax

TRANSFORM(*expression, expC*)

The TRANSFORM function formats character strings or numbers with PICTURE options without using the @-SAY command. *Expression* is the variable or field to format; *expC* is a character expression that contains the PICTURE clause.

TRIM

Syntax

TRIM(*expC*)

The TRIM function trims trailing spaces from a character string. If the character string is composed entirely of spaces, TRIM returns a null string. The TRIM function is identical to the RTRIM function.

TYPE

Syntax

TYPE(*expC*)

The TYPE function returns a single character indicating the data type of the expression named in *expC*. The character C denotes character type, L denotes logical type, N denotes numeric type, D denotes date type, M denotes memo type, and U denotes an undefined type.

UPDATED

Syntax

UPDATED( )

The UPDATED function returns a logical true (.T.) if any data was changed in the associated GETs when the last READ command was processed.

UPPER

Syntax

UPPER(*expC*)

The UPPER function converts all alphabetic characters in *expC* to uppercase letters. The UPPER function does not change the way the data is stored unless you use the function as part of a STORE or REPLACE command. It is generally used for finding or comparing data when you do not know what case the data was originally entered as.

USED

Syntax

USED([*expression*])

The USED function returns a logical true (.T.) if a database is open in the current work area. Use the optional *expression* to identify a different work area by its alias, number, or letter. If no database is open in the specified work area, a logical false (.F.) is returned.

VAL

Syntax

VAL(*expC*)

The VAL function converts a character expression containing numbers into a numeric value. Starting at the leftmost character and ignoring leading blanks, VAL processes digits until a non-numeric character is encountered. If the first character of *expC* is not a number, VAL returns a value of zero.

VARREAD

Syntax

VARREAD( )

The VARREAD function returns the name of the field or variable currently being edited. The function can be useful when designing context-sensitive help systems, so that different help messages can appear for different fields.

VERSION

Syntax

VERSION( )

The VERSION function returns a character string indicating the version number of FoxPro.

WCOLS

Syntax

WCOLS([*expC*])

The WCOLS function returns the number of columns available in the active window. Use the optional *expC* to name a window other than the currently active window.

WEXIST

Syntax

WEXIST(*expC*)

The WEXIST function returns a logical true (.T.) if the window named in *expC* has been previously defined.

WONTOP

Syntax

WONTOP([*expC*])

The WONTOP function returns the name of the window that is frontmost on the screen. If the optional *expC* is used to name a window, the function returns a logical true (.T.) if the named window is frontmost.

WOUTPUT

Syntax

WOUTPUT([*expC*])

The WOUTPUT function returns the name of the window currently receiving output. If the optional *expC* is used to name a window, the function returns a logical true (.T.) if output is currently being directed to the window named in *expC*. If output is not being directed to a window, the function returns a null string.

WROWS

Syntax

WROWS([*expC*])

The WROWS function returns the number of rows available in the active window. Use the optional *expC* to return the number of rows available in the window named in *expC*.

WVISIBLE

Syntax

WVISIBLE(*expC*)

The WVISIBLE function returns a logical true (.T.) if the window named in *expC* has been activated and is not hidden. The function returns a logical false (.F.) if the window has not been activated, has been deactivated, or is hidden.

YEAR

Syntax

YEAR(*expD*)

The YEAR function returns the numeric year corresponding to the date expression.

C

DBASE COMMANDS NOT SUPPORTED BY FOXPRO

The following dBASE IV commands are not supported by FoxPro at the time of this writing. Note that some of the commands relating to using dBASE IV-style multiple-tag index files may be supported in later versions of FoxPro. If in doubt, check your FoxPro documentation.

ASSIST
BEGIN TRANSACTION
CONVERT
COPY INDEXES
COPY TAG
CREATE APPLICATION
CREATE QUERY
CREATE SCREEN
DEBUG
DELETE TAG
DISPLAY HISTORY

DISPLAY USERS
END TRANSACTION
EXPORT TO
IMPORT FROM
LOGOUT
MODIFY APPLICATION
MODIFY QUERY
MODIFY VIEW
MODIFY SCREEN
PROTECT
RESET
ROLLBACK
SET CATALOG ON/OFF
SET CATALOG TO
SET DEBUG
SET DELIMITERS
SET DESIGN
SET ENCRYPTION
SET HISTORY
SET INSTRUCT
SET MENU
SET PRECISION
SET REFRESH
SET REPROCESS
SET SCOREBOARD
SET SKIP
SET SQL
SET TITLE
SET TRAP
UNLOCK

TRADEMARKS

3Com®	3Com Corporation
3Plus Share®	3Com Corporation
Above™ Board	Intel Corporation
COMPAQ®	Compaq Computer Corporation
COMPAQ® DESKPRO 386®	Compaq Computer Corporation
COMPAQ® PORTABLE II®	Compaq Computer Corporation
COMPAQ® PORTABLE III®	Compaq Computer Corporation
dBASE II®	Ashton-Tate Corporation
dBASE III PLUS®	Ashton-Tate Corporation
dBASE IV™	Ashton-Tate Corporation
DisplayWrite™	International Business Machines Corporation
Epson®	Seiko Epson Corporation
FoxPro™	Fox Software
FoxBase™	Fox Software
IBM® AT®	International Business Machines Corporation
IBM® PC®	International Business Machines Corporation
IBM® PS/2®	International Business Machines Corporation
IBM® Token Ring® Network	International Business Machines Corporation
IBM® XT™	International Business Machines Corporation
Lotus® 1-2-3®	Lotus Development Corporation
Microsoft® Excel	Microsoft Corporation
Microsoft® Word	Microsoft Corporation
Multimate®	Ashton-Tate Corporation
Novell® SFT Netware®/286 TTS	Novell, Inc.

PC-File III®	ButtonWare, Inc.
ProKey™	RoseSoft, Inc.
RAMpage®	AST Research, Inc.
SideKick®	Borland International, Inc.
SuperCalc®	Lotus Development Corporation
Superkey®	Borland International, Inc.
Symphony®	Lotus Development Corporation
Twin®	Mosaic Software Inc.
VP-Planner®	Paperback Software International
WordPerfect®	WordPerfect Corporation
WordStar®	MicroPro International Corporation
Xerox®	Xerox Corporation

INDEX

? command, 586-587
??? command, 399-401, 587
@ command, 184, 187, 399-401, 435-437, 587
@-BOX command, (defined, 590)
@-CLEAR TO command, (defined, 589)
@ FILL TO command, (defined, 590)
@-MENU command, (defined, 591)
@-PROMPT commands, 458-459, (defined, 591)
@-SAY statement, 477
@-SAY-GET commands, 460, 464
@-TO command, (defined, 588)

A

ABS function, (defined, 710)
ACCEPT command, 395-396, (defined, 592-593)
ACCEPT and INPUT command, 395-396
Accessories, desktop, 42-43
Accounting program modules, (illus., 405)
ACOS function, (defined, 710-711)
ACTIVATE MENU command, (defined, 593)
ACTIVATE POPUP command, (defined, 593-594)
ACTIVATE SCREEN command, (defined, 594)
ACTIVATE WINDOW command, 452, 455, (defined, 594-595)
Active index, 130-132

Add Line option, 246, 306
ADDER command, 450-451
Adding lines, 307
ADDITIVE clause, 354
Address field, divisions of, 18
Addresses, 313
    using expressions to list, 307
Advanced applications, 555
ALIAS function, (defined, 711)
ALIAS option, 286
Alias screen, 549
Aliasname, 286
All Files check box, 41
All option, in Locate dialog box, 194
ALLTRIM command, (defined, 711)
Alphabetic sort, 108, 119-120
Alphabetical arrangement in database, 8
Alphabetizing names, in sort, 115
Als column, in Table View, 178
ALT-F, opening File menu with, 63
ALT-R, Records menu, 61
Append, 539
    command, 55, 287-288, 404, 441, 562-563, (defined, 595)
APPEND BLANK command, 441, 464
APPEND FROM command, (defined, 595-596)
APPEND FROM ARRAY command, (defined, 596)
APPEND MEMO command, (defined, 596-597)
Append mode, 55, 73
    exiting, 59, 104
Append option, 83

Append option, *continued*
    in Record menu, 55
Append Record option, (CTRL-P), 61, 80
Application, 534-536
    adding Index-File information, 547-553
    adding records, 404, 551
    creating an advanced, 554-555
    creating complex, 546-553
    creating simple, 536-545
    deleting records, 404
    editing records, 404
    help screen, 552
    options, (listed, 553-554)
    search option for, 547
    simple, (illus., 540)
    starting with DO command, 550
    using FoxView to create, 535
    using modular programming for, 545
Application program printing, 541-545
    viewing with Editor, 539
Application subroutines, (listed, 553-554)
Application template, 535, 556
Applications, 402-405
ARCHIVE.DBF file, 41
Arrow keys, 31
    changing box sizes with, 170-171
    choosing colors with, 174

771

Arrow keys, *continued*
    correcting errors with, 39
    highlighting fields with, 161
    in Calendar/Diary option, 43
    moving between fields with, 58
    moving Browse mode with, 60
    moving cursors with, 72-73
    moving fields with, 82
    moving in Filer with, 275
    resizing fields with, 82
    scrolling list box with, 41-42
    selecting menus with, 28
ASC function, (defined, 711)
    in indexing, 144
Ascending order
    selecting, 111
    sorting in, 108-110, 112, 114, 116
ASCII, 563
    characters, 43
    code, 144
    files, 323, 373, 558
    sorting in order, 109-110, 117
    storing output in, 322
    text, 225, 227, 233, 323
Ashton-Tate, 122, 559, 575
ASIN function, (defined, 712)
Assembler routines, sources of, 518-519
AST RAMPage memory board, 14
AT function, (defined, 712)
ATAN function, (defined, 712)
ATC function, (defined, 713)
ATCLINE function, (defined, 713)
ATLINE function, (defined, 713-714)
ATN2 function, (defined, 714)
Atr column, in Table View, 180

Attribute option, in resequencing, 184
Attributes, 17. *See also* Fields
    changing file in Filer, 277-278
Automated billing, databases in, 20
AVERAGE command, (defined, 399, 597)
    fieldname for, 399
    with the TO clause, 399

B

BACKSPACE key, 30, 73
    correcting errors with, 52, 57
Bands, report, 235-237
BAR function, defined, 714
Bar graphs, (illus., 521)
    drawing, 520-523
Batch files, 25-26
Beginning, database files, 387-388
BETWEEN function, defined, 714-715
Billing amount, creating numeric field for, 311-315
.BIN files, 518-519
Binary files, 517
    guidelines for, 519-520
Binary format, 516
Binary routines, accession of, 518
Blanks, using character strings to eliminate, 308
BOF function, defined, 387-388, 715
Boldface, 243
Borland SideKick, conflicting with FoxPro, 292
Bottom option, 192, 539
Bottom Margin option, 239
Box key, (CTRL-B), 169
Box option, 240-241, 312-313
Box-drawing capabilities, 315
Boxes, 178
    adding to report, 240
    changing sizes of, 170
    deleting, (CTRL-U), 171
    double-line, 170
    drawing on form, 169-172

Boxobject, designation in Table View, 178
Brackets, 551
Browse, 4, 59-62, 89-91, (illus., 4)
    command, 60, 89, 598-599
    defined, 60
    editing in, 78-88, (illus., 79)
    exiting from, 81, 88
    menu, 59, (illus., 82)
    options, 81-83
    viewing indexed file in, 125, 128
Browse mode display, 78
Browse window, 115
    changing size and contents of, 83-85
    default size of, 79
    exiting, 90
    simultaneous use with CHANGE, 352
Bugs, 499-501
Buttons, 40, 42
Bytes, 275
    limitation of number per record, 51, (illus., 52)

C

Calc column, in Table View, 182
CALCULATE command, (defined, 599-600)
Calculated fields, adding, 182
Calculations, field, 65, 182
Calculator option, 42
Calendar/Diary option, 43
CALL command, 516-520, (defined, 600)
CANCEL command, 429-430, (defined, 601)
CAP LOCKS function, (defined, 715)
CAP LOCKS key, 30
Capture option, 43
Case, standardizing, 144-146. *See also* Uppercase and Lowercase
Case-sensitive functions, 144-146
Categories of data. *See* Fields

Index

CDOW function, (defined, 715-716)
CEILING function, (defined, 716)
CHANGE command, 44, 72, 460, (illus., 72, defined), 601)
    as a global command, 96
Change mode, 72, 78. *See also* Edit mode
    editing records in, 73
    using PGUP and PGDN keys in, 73
Change option, 72
Change Partitions option, 81, 85
Changes, saving, (CTRL-W), 73, 78, 102-103
Character constant, 374
Character data type, 4
Character/dictionary sort, 117
Character expression, 382
Character fields, 49, 102, 302
    characteristics of, 48
    converting into, 128-129
    descending indexes on, 143-144
    storing numbers in, 149-150
Character formatting option, 242
Character keys, correcting errors with, 52
Character string, 385, 512-513, (defined, 376)
Character symbols, 445
Character-To-Date functions, 390
Character variable, 375-376, 378
Characters
    converting noncharacters to, 302
    storing, 395
Check boxes, 40
CHR function, 520, (defined, 716)
Chronological order
    storing values in, 147
    reverse, 148
Chronological sort, 120

CHRSAW function, (defined, 716)
CHRTRAN function, (defined, 717)
CLEAR command, 33-34, 401, 437, 469, (defined, 602)
    Help screen for, (illus., 34)
CLEAR commands, (defined, 602-605)
CLEARALL command, (defined, 602)
Clicking, mouse, 31
Clipper database, 584
Clock, computer, 43
CLOSE [ALL] command, (defined, 605-606)
CLOSE ALTERNATE command, 503
Close box, window, 36
CLOSE DATABASES command, 286-287, 343
CLOSE FORMAT command, 447
CLOSE INDEX command, 135, 137
CLOSE MEMO command, (defined, 606)
Close option, 35, 65
    in Browse mode, 81
Closing linked files, command for, 337
CMONTH function, (defined, 717)
Col column, in Table View, 179
COL function, (defined, 717)
Color
    background choice of, 173
    blinking, 180
    changing, 172-175
    code, (illus., 505)
    flashing display, 179
    foreground choice of, 173
    intensity, 180
    monitor, 172, 504
    option, 38, 454
    palette, 172-174, 179, 180, (illus., 173)
    steady display of, 179

Color, *continued*
    values of, 179, 180
COLOR SCHEME option, 454
Column Layout option, 64
Columnar
    layout, 222-223
    listings, 479-481
    reports, 234-248
Columns, 7, (illus., 8). *See also* Fields
    changing margin width in report, 224-225
    database, 7
    horizontal movement of, 80
Command files, 368-373
    AVERAGE, 399
    bracketed by procedures, 491
    characteristics of, 368-369
    combined in a procedure file, 493
    COUNT, 396-397
    from menus, 370
    halting, 395
    multiple, 491
    storing, 368
    SUM, 397-399
    TEXT, 399-401
    using modify command to create, 369-373
Command mode
    interactive, 38
    shifting to menus from, 33
Command option, (CTRL-F2), 38
Command window, 13, 27, 32, 35, 38-40, 46, 65, 67, 68, 78, 279, (illus., 27)
    hiding blind entries into, 39
    moving help window over, 37
    resizing, 39
    scrolling through, 39
Commands, 13, 585-707. *See also* specific commands
    abbreviated form of, 33

Commands, *continued*
   adding comments to, 411
   assigning sequences to function keys by, 510
   blind entry of, 39-40
   capacity of FoxPro for, 39
   dBase IV not supported by FoxPro, 767-768
   for managing files, 279-289
   FoxPro, 32-33
   glossary of, 585-707
   length of, 39
   on-screen execution of, 394
   order of, 395
   performing queries with, 206-214
   query, 191, 198-199
   repeating, 39
   results as menu options, 27
   sort, 116
   storing in command files, 409
   structure of, 32
   used in command files, 393-401
Comments, 411
Common field, 328
Compaq computers, 14
COMPILE command, (defined, 606)
Compiling programs, 373-374
Constants, 374
CONTINUE command, 78, 206, 207-208, 211-214, (defined, 606-607)
   comparing with FIND and SEEK, 211-214
Continue option, 77, 200-201
Conversion
   dates into string of characters, 303
   non-character fields into character fields, 128-129
   numeric values into string of characters, 302-303

COPY command, 280-282, (defined, 607)
   data sharing with, 562-563
Copy database structure, 289
Copy databases, 100
Copy Fields function (F8), 159
COPY command, 280, (defined, 607-608)
COPY MEMO command, (defined, 608)
Copy option, 248, 371
COPY STRUCTURE command, 289, (defined, 608-609)
COPY STRUCTURE EXTENDED command, (defined, 609)
Copy text, 371
COPY TO ARRAY command, (defined, 609-610)
Copyright message, 27
Corrections. *See* errors, correcting
COS function, (defined, 717-718)
COUNT command, 396-397, (defined, 610)
Counting occurrences in a database, 396-397
Courier Italic font, listing with, (illus., 487)
Crashing of program, 407
CREATE commands, (defined, 611-612)
CREATE LABEL command, 480, (defined, 611-612)
CREATE VIEW command, 218, (defined, 612)
CTOD function, 204, 390, (defined, 718)
CTRL-B (box key), 169
CTRL-H (Change Partition Key), 85
CTRL-P (adding and appending records), 60, 61
CTRL-W (closing windows and return to screen), 58, 59, 62
CURDIR function, (defined, 718)
Cursor indicator, 160

Cursor keys
   adding text with, 163
   correcting errors with, 39, 52
   inserting space with, 162
Cursor movement, 161, 435-436
   between fields in Browse mode, 60
   in Editor, 57
   in Forms View, 160
   in Search, 76
   through database screens, 80
   with arrow keys, 72-73
   with keys, 60
   with mouse, 60
Custom forms, data entry by, 5
Customized report, practice exercise in designing, 249-257
Customizing programs, using SET commands for, 503-513
Cut option, 248, 371
Cycle option (CTRL-F1), 37-38

D

Data, 16, 225
   assigned to a variable, 375
   categories of. *See* fields
   display of matching, 331
   establishing links in retrieving, 353
   listing selective, 346
   losing when converting between field types, 102
   moving from memory variables to field, 464
   refining, 17-19
   retrieving, 363
   retrieving with queries, 191-219
   searching for in files, 69

Index 775

Data, *continued*
    types, (listed, 4-5)
    unique, 359
Data definition, design steps in, 17-18
Data directory, 24
Data entry
    by custom forms, 5
    by on-screen forms, 5
    with memory variables, 463-465
Data fields, 4
Data formatting, 242
    using PICTURE option, 442-446
Data Grouping option, 240, 258, 260, 267, 309, 314
Database, 6-9, (illus., 6)
    adding a new field at end of, 311-312
    applications, 402, 404
    avoiding errors in design, 15
    benefits of computerized, 9
    changing, 71-105
    characteristics of relational, 10
    compared to file cards, 7-8, (illus., 7)
    counting occurrence in, 396-397
    creating, 45-55, (illus., 5)
    deleting records from, 407
    design, 15-23
    determining need for multiple, 20
    distinguished from file cabinets, 6-7
    editing, 72-78
    entering information into, 14
    integrity, 465
    limitations, 154
    linking an active, 332, 333
    linking with SET RELATION command, 331
    management system (DBMS), 9, (illus., 407)

Database, *continued*
    maximum number of linked, 347
    moving around with options, 539
    moving through, 83
    opening, 464
    option, 47
    parent, 121
    printing contents of, 14
    relational, 9-11, 20, 328, (illus., 13)
    relationship to user and software, 12-14
    saving, 53-55
    scrolling through, 79
    software, 12-14
    sorting, 107, 108-120
    supporting, 349, (illus., 349)
    system, 347, 534, (illus., 404)
    viewing, 66-68
Database display
    dot-prompt options for, 65-68
Database Fields list box, 111, 115
Database files, 534, (illus., 330). *See also* Files
    adding to screen, 182, 549
    avoiding duplication in, 330
    creating, 4, 103-105
    deleting, 114
    moving between alias and screen in, 549
    multiple, 333
    naming, 54
    opening with SET VIEW command, 337
    screen, (illus., 547)
    writing modular codes for, 524-527
Database menu
    opening (ALT-D), 65
Database structure
    duplicating, 348, 350
    modifying, 99-103, (illus., 101)

Database Structure
    dialog box, 46, 47, 205, (illus., 47)
    window, 104, 311
Database subsets
    sorting of, 118-119
Data-entry
    reducing steps for, 509
    screens, 448
Date
    characteristics of fields, 48
    constant, 374
    conversion to character string, 147
    data type, 4
    fields sorted in reverse chronological order, 108
    function for, 305, 312, 388-389, (defined, 718-719)
    indexing fields, 146-148
    information, 312
    placed in reports or labels, 305
    value, 232
    variable, 375, 377, 378
Date arithmetic, performing, 50
Date-to-Character string function, 390, 391
Date-to-String function (DTOS), 128
    converting date field with, 128-129
Day, expression for, 305-306
DAY function, (defined, 719)
dBASE
    compatibility with FoxPro, 367-368
    finding relational data in, 345
    language, 77
    speed, 373
dBASE IV
    commands not supported by FoxPro, (listed, 767-768)
    index files in, 122

dBASE IV, *continued*
    index style contrasted to FoxPro, 150-152
dBASE III, 6, 557, 559, 560, 561, 562, 575-576, 579, 584
    index files in, 122
DBF function, (defined, 719)
DBMEMO3 format, 557, 560-562, 584
DBMS (database management system), 9
DEACTIVATE MENU command, (defined, 613)
DEACTIVATE POPUP command, (defined, 613)
DEACTIVATE WINDOW command, 452, 455, 456, (defined, 614)
DEBUG command, 517-518
Debug option, 40
Debugging, 499-503
    using SET commands in, 501-502
    with SET ALTERNATE command, 503
    with SET TALK command, 502
Dec column, in Table View, 178
Decimal amounts, 51
Decimal places
    in numeric fields, 48, 50-51
    minimum field width of, 51
    number of, 178
DECLARE command, (defined, 614-615)
Default drive, changing, 25
Default form, data entry, 55, (illus., 56)
Default format, 48
DEFINE commands, (defined, 615-618)
DEFINE WINDOW command, 452, 453, 457, (defined, 618-619)
Defining windows, 453-455
DEL key, 30
Delete, 91, 530-531, 539
    files, 96, 276
    marking records to, 83, 91, 94-95

Delete, *continued*
    multiple records, 95
    objects, 247-248
    records, 406-408
    records in databases, 407
    text, 371
    toggle, 83
DELETE command, (defined, 619-620)
DELETE ALL command, 431
Delete dialog box, 91, (illus., 92)
DELETE FILE command, 95, (defined, 620)
Delete Line option, 246-247
DELETED function, (defined, 719)
Deleted records, hiding, 468
Delimited format, 557, 558-559, 565-567, 581-583
Delimiters, 558, 562, 565, 570-571
Descending order
    indexing dates by, 148
    indexing in, 142-144
    selecting, 111
    sorting in, 108, 110, 112, 113, 117
Design
    changing report, 238-242
    customized columnar report, 234-248
    customized reports, 249-257
    form letter, 306-310
    invoice, 310-315
    planning report, 272
Design area, adding files in, 319-320
Detail band, 236, 237, 240, 253, 260, 306, 307, 312, 356
    filling in the, 308
    maximum lines in, 310
Dialog boxes, 40-42, (illus., 41)
    for naming database file, 54, (illus., 54)
    new file, 46, (illus., 46)
DIFFERENCES function, (defined, 720)

DIMENSION command, (defined, 620-621)
DIR command, 39, (defined, 621-622)
    to determine remaining disk space, 23
Directory
    data, 24
    menu in Filer, 274, 276
    program, 24
Display
    in reverse video, 441
    report on screen, 474-475
    variable field name, 437
DISPLAY command, 66, 67, 511, (defined, 622)
DISPLAY MEMORY command, 377, 379, (defined, 622-623)
DISPLAY STATUS command, 132, 216, 338, (defined, 623)
DISPLAY STRUCTURE command, (defined, 623-624)
Disk, 14, 23-25
    installation, 23
Disk drives, 15
    menus, 274
Disk space, 23
    in sorting, 120
DISKSPACE function, (defined, 720)
DMY function, (defined, 720)
DO command, 539, 550, (defined, 624)
DO CASE command, 425-428. (defined, 624-625)
DO FIRST command, 498
DO MENU command, 460, 462
DO statement, 491
DO TRIPLE command, 416
DO WHILE command, 414-416, (defined, 625-626)
    loops, 476
Dollar amounts, entry of, 51
DOS
    commands, 279
    date, 275

Index 777

DOS, *continued*
  memory consumed by, 24
  prompt, 25-26
  running FoxView from, 190
  shell, 155
  version for operating FoxPro, 14, 15
DOS Compatibility Box (OS/2), 26
DOT-Prompt options for database display, 65-68
DOW function, (defined), 721
Drag key (F3), 159, 160, 169, 170
Dragging, mouse, 31
Drive menu, 40
Dropping excess characters, 302
DTOC function, 303, 390, (defined, 721)
DTOR function, (defined, 721)
DTOS function, 147, 391, (defined, 722)
Duplicate entries, ignoring in unique index, 123

E
EDIT command, 77, 460, (defined, 626-627)
Edit menu, 248, 371
Edit mode, 4, 85, 438. *See also* Change mode
Edit option, 81, 277
Editing
  database, 72-78
  in Browse mode, 85, (illus., 86)
  label, 162-163
  memo fields, 439-440
  record commands, 460
  records, 71, 80
  routine, 528-529
  specific information, 89, (illus., 90)
  with memory variables, 463-465
Editing keys, (illus., 370, listed, 53)
Editor, 43, 57, 277, 371, 539
  menu options in, 57

EJECT commands, (defined, 627)
ELSE command, 418-419
EMPTY function, (defined, 722)
End of database file, 386-387
END command, 425-428
ENDDO command, 414-416
ENDIF command, 418-420
ENDSCAN command, 416-418
ENDTEXT command, 401
ENTER key, 30, 33
Entries. *See* Expressions and Functions
Entry forms, 153-190
Environment
  check box, 226
  clause, 344
  option, 233-234
EOF function, 386-387, (defined, 722-723)
ERASE command, (defined, 628)
Erasing
  memory variables, 380
  records, 431
  the screen, 437
Error message, 93, 128, 498
Errors
  avoiding in design, 15
  correcting, 39, 52-53, 57, 409-410
  halting program due to, 499
ESC key, 28, 29
EXCEPT option, 380
EXIT command, (defined, 628-629)
Exiting
  ESC key in, 28
  Forms View, 156
  FoxView, 167
  from Append mode, 104
  from Browse mode, 81, 88
  from Browse window, 90
  Table View, 156
EXP function, (defined, 723)
Expression Builder, 204, 205, 227, 241-242, 249-250, 319, 355, 441, 555

defined, 301-302
entering fields in, 302
in index building, 123, 127
placing expression in, 303
using LEFT function in, 302
Expressions, 506, (illus., 381)
  combining, 302-303
  defined, 380-382
  mixing fields in, 382
  month, 306
  operating order in, 383
  parts of, 381
  placing in report, 308
Expressions and functions
  using, 301-303
Extend Select Key (F6), 159, 160-161
Extensions, 280
  automatic assigned, 54, 122

F
False value, 48
FCLOSE function, (defined, 723)
FCOUNT function, (defined, 724)
FCREATE function, (defined, 724)
FEOF function, (defined, 725)
FERROR function, (defined, 725)
FGETS function, (defined, 725-726)
Field column, 178
FIELD function, (defined, 726)
Field labels, changing, 162-163
Field names, 47, 97, 98, 178, 196, 203, 285
  list box, 127
  parameter, 98
Field option, 64, 89, 241
  dialog box, 111, 112, (illus., 242)
Field placement, customized, 65
Field size, 87-88
Field templates, 160

Field types
    choosing, 49-50
    menu of, 49
Field width, limitations of, 49
Fields, 7, 8, 16, 21, 178,
    (illus., 8)
    adding new to Table,
        182
    adding to reports, 240
    adding with MODIFY
        STRUCTURE
        command, 100
    calculated, 182
    changing character to
        numeric, 102
    changing limited with
        FREEZE option, 90
    changing to existing,
        326
    character, 48, 49, 302
    combination of character,
        302
    combining, 319
    common, 327, 328
    compiling lists of,
        17-18
    date, 50
    deleting from table, 183
    editing, 89, (illus., 90)
    eliminating unnecessary,
        20
    float, 48
    hidden, 180
    index based on, 123
    indexing different types
        of, 128-129
    intermixing, 308
    logical, 48
    matching, 331
    memo, 48, 57-59,
        439-440
    moving, 82, 88, 101,
        160-162, 179, 182-
        184, (illus., 88)
    naming, 47
    numeric, 48-49, 320
    picture, 49
    primary, in sort, 117
    relationships between,
        19-23
    renaming and changing
        locations of, 103
    resequencing order of,
        183-184

Fields, *continued*
    resizing, 82, 87-88,
        (illus., 87)
    searching within, 68-69
    secondary, in sort, 118
    selecting for inclusion in
        report, 64
    shifting left and right on
        screen, 80
    sorting, 114-118, 120,
        (illus., 116)
    sorting selected,
        119-120
    within a report, 303
File cards, compared to
    database, 7-8, (illus., 7)
File extensions, 370
File formats, 557-562
FILE function, (defined, 726)
File list, moving in, 275-276
File Maintenance
    Application, 537, (illus.,
        551)
        template, 536, 546
File managers, 10, 11
File menu, opening (ALT-F),
    27, 40, 46, 63, 65
File name dialog box, 128
File Open dialog box, 40
File size, determining, 278
Filename, 111, 337,
    specifying, 284-286
Filer, 42, 274-278, (illus.,
    274)
FILER command, (defined,
    629)
Files
    active, 283-286, 346,
        354, 357, 361
    adding information to,
        55-59
    automatic creating of
        view, 344
    changing attributes of,
        277-278
    combining, 287-289,
        490
    commands for managing,
        279-289
    copying, 277, 280-282
    creating batch, 25-26
    creating command,
        369-373
    deleting, 96, 276

Files, *continued*
    duplicating, 361-363
    editing, 277
    finding, 277
    index, 92, 120, 132-135,
        200, 332-333
    limitations of sorting,
        110
    linking, 331, 361
    managing, 273-289
    moving, 277
    multiple database, 333
    naming, 344
    opening, 55, 338, 441
    renaming, 276
    sorting, 108, 110,
        119-120, 278
    structures of, 288
    transferring between
        software packages,
        563-584
    tree display, 278
    viewing, 218-219, 449
FILTER function, (defined,
    726-727)
Filter option, 203, 215
Filters
    setting, 214-218, 219
FIND command, 146, 206,
    210-214, 432, 462, 508,
    (defined, 629)
    indexed file, 137-139
Firstname field, listing of, 307
FKLABEL function,
    (defined, 727)
FKMAX function, (defined),
    727)
Fld column, 180
Float fields, 48
Floating data type, 4
FLOOR function, (defined,
    727)
Floppy disk, 9, 14, 23
FLUSH command, (defined,
    630)
Footers, 65, 234, 260
FOPEN function, (defined,
    728)
FOR clause, 125, 323, 399,
    (defined, 630-631)
        dialog box, 75, (illus.,
            75, 198)
        window, 74, 75,
            195-196, 204

Index 779

For option, 74, 195, 197, 226, 227
Foreign characters, 43
Form feed, 233, 234
Form layout, 64, 223
Form Layout option, 64, 339
Form letters, 119, 306-310, 568-575, (illus., 309)
Form views, format files and, 451
Format
    columnar, 5
    dialog box, 242, (illus., 243)
Format File Generator option, 157, 536
Format files, 166, 447-451
    creating with Editor, 446
    extension, 446
Formats, 557-562
Formatting options, 242-246, (table, 244-245)
Forms, 154
    creating with Forms View, 157-160, 451
    custom, 5, (illus., 164)
    multiple-page, 179
    revising, 157
Forms View, 154-155, 157-160, 169, 189, 448, 450, (illus., 158)
    exiting, 156
    function keys for, 158, (listed, 159)
Formulas. *See* Expressions and Functions
FOUND function, (defined, 728)
FOXHELP.DBF file, 41
FOXPLUS format, 560-562
FoxPro
    Advanced Application, 536, 537, 554
    disk space requirements for, 23-24
    Editor. *See* Editor
    installing, 23-26
    memory required for, 24
    starting, 26-28
    versions of, 23
FOXUSER.DBF file, 41

FoxView, 154, 534, 547
    commands, 155-157, (listed, 156)
    creating applications with, 534-535
    entering, 155, 536, 546
    exiting, 167, 174, 189
    menu, 539
    running from DOS, 190
    shell, 168
FPUTS function, (defined, 728-729)
FREAD function, (defined, 729)
FREEZE option, 90
FSEEK function, (defined, 729-730)
FSIZE function, (defined, 730)
FULLPATH function, (defined), 730)
Function. *See also* by specific name
    BOF, 387-388
    command, 514, 631
    CTOD, 390-391
    DATE and TIME, 305, 388-389
    DTOC, 303
    EOF, 386-387
    IIF, 302, 303-304
    Lower, 390
    page number, 305
    SPACE, 391
    TRIM, 302
    UPPER, 389
Function keys, 29-30, (listed, 159)
    changing, 508-509
Functions, 303-306, 385-393, 442, 444, 446, 513-515. *See also* by specific name
    designed, 513-515
    glossary of, 709-765
    indexing combinations of fields by using, 128-129
    picture, 184-187
    string, 302-303
Functions and expressions, using, 301-303

FV function, (defined, 730-731)
FWRITE function, (defined, 731)

G

Games, puzzle, 43
GATHER FROM command, (defined, 631-632)
GET functions, (defined, 731-732)
GET option, 437-439, 441
GETEXPR command, (defined, 632)
GETFILE function, (defined, 731-732)
Global replacements, 96-99
GO command, 67, 69, 70
GO TO command, 394, 447, (defined, 632-633)
Go To option, 73, 77
    dialog box, 192-194, (illus., 193)
    in queries, 192-194
GO MONTH function, (defined, 732)
Graphic characters, 43
Graphic images, storage in Picture fields, 49
Graphs
    dividing the fields of, 522
    drawing bar, 520-523
Grid Off option, 81, 85
Grid On option, 85
Group bands, 237, 259-260, 262, 264-265, 268-269, 314, 355
    adding, 309
    placed in reports, 314
Group dialog box, 259, (illus., 258)
Group Info dialog box, 259-261, 268, 355, (illus., 261)
Group menu options, 257-260
Groupings, multiple, 258, 267-272, (illus., 262)
Groups
    adding to reports, 260-267
    multiple, 267-272

H

Hard disk, 14
    installing FoxPro on, 23-25
    cleaning up, 150
HEADER function, (defined, 732)
Headers, 234, 237, 260, 267
    customized, 65
    entering, 227
HEADING option, 227, 233, (illus., 228)
Height, label, 316, 317
Help, 33-34
    option, 28, 551
    screen, 186-187, (illus., 34, 186)
    screen for Range column, 187-189, (illus., 188)
    window, 28, 35, 39
HELP command, (defined, 633)
Helvetica Bold font, (illus., 488)
Hewlett-Packard LaserJet, 487, 488
HIDE MENU command, (defined, 633)
Hide option, 35
HIDE POPUP command, (defined, 633-634)
HIDE WINDOW command, (defined, 634)
Hiding variables, 496-499
Highlighted bars, 550, 551
Highlighting, field, 160
Horizontal movement, scroll bar used in, 80
Horizontal placement, text object, 180
Hue column, in Table View, 179
Hyphens, 49

I

IBM computers (AT, XT, PS/2), 14
IBM DisplayWrite, 575
IBM PC network, 15
Identification, in relational databases, 21
IF command, 418-419, (defined, 634)
IIF function (Immediate IF), 303-304, 421, (defined, 732-733)
    calculating spaces in names with, 304
    eliminating zero equivalents with, 304
    for true and false conditions, 303
    replacing zero with hyphen using, 304
Immediate IF function. *See* IIF function
Index
    activating, 133
    active, 130-132
    alphabetic reverse-order, 144
    avoiding use with filters, 217-218
    building selective, 122
    changing from dormant to active, 130-132
    date field, 146-148
    descending order, 142-144
    files, 357
    open files, 132-135
    unique, 122
    updating closed, 136
    While option with, 227
INDEX command, 121, 128, (defined, 635)
    distinguished from SORT command, 121-122
    format, 121-122, 129
    limitation, 128
    syntax, 125
    TAG variations of, 152
    using for multiple fields, 141
Index file, 120, 137-139, 151, 210-213, 547
    alphabetized, (illus., 121)
    automatic updating of, 135
    automatically opened with database opening, 151-152

Index file, *continued*
    creating, 121, 122-125, (illus., 121)
    deleting, 136
    incomplete, 336
    naming, 123
    opening, 130, 132
    opening with SET VIEW command, 337
    using for search, 210-213
    While clauses used in, 200
INDEX ON command, 124, 125, 323, 472
Index On dialog box, 123, 125, 127, (illus., 124)
Index option, 333
Indexing, 120-137
    from menus, 124-125
    groups in reports, 270
    in dBASE IV, 150-152
    in reverse chronological order, 148
    multiple fields, 126-129
    multiple fields from menus, 127-128
    parent database order unaffected by, 121
    routine maintenance, 150
    selective, 125
    tips, 139, 148-150
    using short keys in, 149
Indicator, scrolling, 79-80
Information
    accepting with GET option, 438
    displaying within windows, 452
    entering into database, 14
Information summary, 16
Init column, in Table View, 182
INKEY function, (defined, 733)
INLIST function, (defined, 733)
Input box, 111

Input command, 395-396, 439, (defined, 635-636)
INSERT command, 81, (defined, 636)
Insert mode, 53, 160, 371
Inserting
    characters, 53
INSMODE function, (defined, 733-734)
Installation, FoxPro, 23-26
    disk, 23
    on hard disk, 23-25
    program, 23
    steps, 25
INT function, (defined, 734)
Intel Above Board memory board, 14
Interpreters, 373
Invoices, (illus., 311)
    designing, 310-315
    designing line and box styles for, 310, 312-313
    report specification for, (illus., 315)
IS commands, (defined, 734-736)
Italics, 243

J
JOIN command, (defined, 636-637)

K
KEY function, (defined, 736)
Keyboard, 28-31
    IBM PC, 29, (illus., 29)
    enhanced IBM PC, (illus., 30)
    macro command entry at, 6
    macros, 294-295, (illus., 296)
KEYBOARD command, (defined, 637)
Keyfield, 97
Keyname, 97
Keypad, numeric, 31, 42
Keys
    editing, (listed, 53)
    for assigning macros, 300

Keys, *continued*
    function, 29-30
    location, 29
    numeric, 30

L
Label column, 178
Label design screen, 316, (illus., 317)
Label dialog box, 322
Label dimensions, 316, (illus., 318)
LABEL FORM command, 323, 479, 480, 481, (defined, 637-638)
Label menu, 319, 320
Label sizes, settings for, (illus., 319)
Labels, 315-326. *See also* Mailing labels
    adding fields to design area, 319-321
    aligning, 322
    changing, 162-163
    creating and printing, 315-323
    defaults, 317
    margins, 316, 317
    modifying, 326
    numbers across, 316-318
    option, 552
    printed in order, 323
    printing, 321-323
    relational link, 332
    saving the design for, 321
    stored on disks, 316
Laser printer, 231, 239
    proportionally spaced fonts, 488
Last Modified column, 275
LASTKEY function, (defined, 736)
Lastname field, listing of, 307
Layout, 222-223, 235. (illus., 235)
    options, 64
LEFT function, 302, (defined, 736)
LEN function, (defined, 737)
Length
    field, 52

Length, *continued*
    page, 238
    variable name, 375
Letters
    creating and printing form, 119, 306-307, 309-310
    typing text of form, 308
LIKE function, (defined, 737)
LIKE option, 380
LIM memory board specifications, 14
LINENO function, (defined, 737)
Lines
    adding, 246, 312
    between labels, 316, 318
    deleting, 246, 312
    drawing solid, 313
Link
    commands to establish, 357
    reestablishing with SET VIEW command, 338
Link Partitions option, 86-87
Linked files
    closing, 337
    commands to see, 334
Linking. *See also* Relating
    databases, 332
    files, 361
    multiple database files, 327
List box, 41
LIST command, 66, 205, 206, 331, 488, 511, (defined, 638)
    distinguished from DISPLAY, 67
    in printing data, 231
    indicating records to be deleted, 94-95
LIST FILES command, (defined, 639)
LIST MEMORY command, 481, (defined, 639)
LIST STATUS command, 132, 216, (defined, 639-640)
LIST STRUCTURE command, (defined, 640)

Lists of entries, 364. *See also*
    Expressions and Functions
Litebars, 551
Literal data, 445
LOAD command, 515-516,
    517-520, (defined,
    640-641)
Load menu, 166, 539
Locate button, 75
LOCATE command, 70, 78,
    93, 206, 207-209,
    211-214, (defined, 641)
    in indexed files, 138
Locate dialog box, 194-200
    options in, 194,
        (illus., 194)
Locate option, 73-74, 77
LOG function, (defined, 738)
Logical constant, 347
Logical data type, 4
Logical fields, 48, 49
    width of, 51
Logical formatting option,
    242
Logical operators, 384-385
Logical variable, 375, 378
LOG10 function, (defined,
    738)
LOOP command, (defined,
    641-642)
Loops, 414-418, 424
    enclosing codes in, 465
    leaving, 415, 418
    within a loop, 416
Lotus 1-2-3, 561, 562, (illus.,
    580)
    spreadsheet, 577,
        (illus., 577)
    transferring between
        FoxPro and,
        575-578
Lotus-Intel-Microsoft
    memory board
    specifications (LIM),14
LOWER function, 390,
    (defined, 738)
Lowercase letters, 139,
    144-146, 390
    in sorting, 109, 110, 111
LTRIM functions, 308, 393,
    (defined, 739)
LUPDATE function,
    (defined, 739)

M
Macros, 6, 291-300
    adding pauses to,
        298-299
    adding to existing,
        297-299
    advantages of FoxPro,
        292
    creating, 292-294
    limitations, 299-300
    menu options of,
        296-297
    repeating commands
        with, 295
    rules of, 299-300
    saving, 294-295
Mailing lists, 7, 13-14, (illus.,
    6)
    combined with
        customer-order
        invoice database,
        (illus., 12)
    creating with FoxPro,
        22
    relational database, 10,
        11, (illus., 11, 12)
    searching in, 213-214
Mailmerge, 561, 567
MailMerge, 568
    transferring FoxPro to,
        565-568
Manuals, FoxPro, 23
Margins, 224-225, 234
    changing, 224-225
    label, 316, 317
    setting, 224-225, 239
Matching records across
    files, 330
Math expressions, 382
Math pick list, opening, 127
Math symbols, 42
Mathematical operators,
    383-384
MAX function, (defined, 739)
MDY function, (defined,
    739-740)
MEMLINES function,
    (defined, 740)
Memo data type, 5
Memo fields, 48, 51,
    439-440, 548
    deleting, 114
    editing, 53

Memo fields, *continued*
    entering data in, 57-59
    text wrapping in, 245
Memo window, 57, 59
Memory
    modifying with RUN
        command, 280
    requirements for
        operating FoxPro,
        14
    using LOAD and
        CALL commands,
        517
Memory boards, 14
MEMORY function,
    (defined, 740)
Memory variables, 375-380,
    463-465
    data entry and editing
        with, 463-465
Memory-resident programs,
    avoiding when using
    FoxPro, 24
Menu bar, 27
MENU command, (defined,
    642-644)
MENU function, (defined,
    740-741)
Menu options, 13, 28, 31, 32
    Editor, 57
MENU TO commands,
    458-459, (defined, 644)
Menus
    cancelling, 28
    designing litebar,
        458-460
    FoxView, 164-165,
        (illus., 165)
    in dialog boxes, 40
    indexing from, 124-128
    opening, 27, 28, 40
    performing queries
        from, 192-205
    program, 407
    pull-down, defined, 28
    shifting from command
        mode to, 33
MESSAGE function,
    (defined, 741)
Messages, 512-513
Microsoft Excel, (illus., 580)
Microsoft Word, 567,
    570-572

Microsoft Word, *continued*
        creating command files with, 373
        file transfer from FoxPro to, 564, 567, (illus., 564)
MIN function, (defined, 741)
Mini-assembler, 518
Minus key, 30
Minus sign, 48
Mistakes. *See* Errors
MLINE function, (defined, 741-742)
MOD function, (defined, 742)
Modified data entry screen, (illus., 175)
Modify commands, 370-373, 539, 541, 644-645
MODIFY LABEL command, 326, (defined, 645)
MODIFY MEMO command, 439-440, (defined, 645-646)
MODIFY REPORT command, (defined, 646)
MODIFY STRUCTURE command, 99-100, 103, (defined, 646-647)
Modular coding, 523-524
Modular programming, 523-531, 545
Modules, 405-406
        writing programs in, 523
Monitors, color, 14, 172
Month, expression for, 305-306
MONTH function, (defined, 742)
Mouse, 14, 31-32, 80
        clicking, 31, 37
        cursor movement with, 60, 79
        deleting objects with, 247
        dragging, 31
        driver, 31
        opening menus with, 27
        optical sensor design, 32
        pad, 31-32
        pointer, 31
        scrolling with, 39

Mouse, *continued*
        split indicator for, 84
Mouse-clicking check box, 40, 42
Move Field option, 87, 88
Move fields, 160-162, 182-184
Move key (F7), 177
Move objects, 182-184, 247-248
Move option, in Filer, 277
Move text, 371
MOVE WINDOW command, (defined, 647)
Move windows, 36-37
MultiMate, 575
        creating command files with, 373
Multiplan, (illus., 580)
Multiple choices, evaluating, 425-428
Multiple fields
        indexing, 126-129
        sorting, 114-118, (illus., 116)
Multiple index file, 151

N

Name fields, combining, 319
Names
        entering without keystrokes, 509
        indexing, 126-127
        linking files with field, 21
        using expressions to list first and last, 302, 307
        using expressions to get, 313
        using expressions to select widths of, 302, 307-308
        using IIF function, 303-304
        view files and reports, 344
NDX function, (defined, 742-743)
Negative values, building index with, 142-143
Nested IF-ENDIF statements, 421

NETBIOS compatible network, 15
Networks, FoxPro used in, 14
New File dialog box, 63, (illus., 63)
New option, 4, 46
New Page option, 306, 309, 314, 355
Next option, 194-195, 539
Next statement, 475
No Eject option, 227
NOTE command, (defined, 647-648)
Novell Advanced NetWare, 15
Number column, 177
Numbers
        across labels, 316, 317, 318
        stored in character fields, 49
Numeric amounts, eliminating zero equivalents, 304
Numeric constant, 374
Numeric data type, 4
Numeric fields, 48-49, 320
        changing to character, 102
        multiple, 139-141
        searching in, 93
        specifying, 50
Numeric formatting option, 242
Numeric keypad, 30, 31, 42
Numeric sort, by indexing, 120
Numeric summary fields, defining, 245-246
Numeric value to character string, 393
Numeric variables, 375, 377, 378
Numerical order, sorting in, 108
NUMLOCK function, (defined, 743)
        key, 31

O

Objects
        moving in Table View, 182-184

Objects, *continued*
    overlaying, 246-247
OCCURS function, (defined, 743)
OFF option, 354
OK button, 53
ON commands, (defined, 648-652)
Open Report menu (ALT-O), 64
Operators, 382-385
    binary, 382, 385
    logical, 196-197, 208, 384-385
    mathematical, 383-384
    relational, 384
    string, 385
Optical sensor mouse, 32
Options, FoxPro, 12-13
ORDER function, 743
Orders, customers on databases, 10, (illus., 11, 12)
OS function, (defined, 744)
OS/2
    DOS Compatibility Box, 26
    version for operating FoxPro, 14, 15
Outlining, 406
Output box, 111
Overlaying objects, 246, 247
Overwrite, 53, 160, 371
    Macro dialog box, 297-298, (illus., 298)

P

PACK command, (defined, 652-653)
Pack operation, 551
Pack option, 91, 96, 468
    to make deletions permanent, 92-93
PAD functions, (defined, 744-745)
Page
    changing length of, 238
    column in Table View, 179
Page Footer band, 236, 254
    removing lines from, 306-307

Page Head band, 240
Page Header band, 236, 260, 267, 312
Page Layout dialog box, 238, (illus., 238)
Page Length option, 238
Page numbers, 305
Page preview, 240, 320, (illus., 321)
Palette key (CTRL-P), 172, 173
PARAMETERS command, (defined, 653)
PARAMETERS function, (defined, 745)
Parenthesis, 550
Partitions
    activating left (CTRL-H), 85
    changing sizes, 82
    switching between, 86
    unlinked, 86-87
Paste option, 248, 371
Paths, creating, 26
PAYMENT function, (defined, 745)
PC-File DB, 584
PCOL function, (defined, 745-746)
PGDN (Page Down) key, 80
PGUP (Page Up) key, 80
PI function, (defined, 746)
Pick list, 40, 41
Picture column, 181, 184-187
    functions, 184-187, (illus., 186)
    help for, 186
    templates, 184-187, (listed, 185)
Picture fields, 49
PICTURE functions, 184-187, (listed, 185)
    help screen for, (illus., 186)
    templates, 444, (illus., 443)
Picture option, 442-446
Picture templates, 184-187, (listed, 185)
Place column, in Table View, 180
Plain box, 227
Plain report, 233

PLAY MACRO command, (defined, 653)
Plus key, 30
Plus symbol, 140
    tying fields with, 127
Pointer, 69-70, 394
    movement in SET FILTER command, 216-217
    symbols, 335
POPUP function, (defined, 746)
Prev option, 539
Primary field, in sort, 117
PRINT commands, (defined, 654)
Print settings, 481
Print styles, 243
Print System Memory variables, 482-484, (listed, 481-482)
Printer, 206, 225, 231-232, 481-488
    character size settings, 318
    compressed mode, 485
    dot matrix, 239
    escape code for Hewlett Packard LaserJet, 486
    in default mode, 484
    memory variables, 481
    receiving and sending ASCII, 484-485
    routing data to, 477
    selecting print styles for, 486
    sending escape codes to, 484, 485
    sending reports to, 474-475
Printer Indent option, 239
Printing
    commands, 399-401
    data, 231-232
    database contents, 14
    form letters, 309-310
    from a loop, 415-416
    graphics, 315
    labels, 321-325
    reports, 65, 270
    text, 400
PRINTSTATUS function, (defined, 746)

PRIVATE commands, 496, (defined, 655)
PROCEDURE command, (defined, 655-656)
Procedure file, 527, 538, 545, (illus., 492, 508)
Procedures, 490
Program code, 538-539
    writing reports with, 475-479
Program control, 414-418
    repeating commands, 414-416
    using CANCEL command, 429-430
    using CASE statement, 425-428
    using EXIT command, 428-429
    using macros, 431-432
    using nested IF-ENDIF statements, 421
    using Immediate IF function, 421-424
    using WAIT command, 430
    using ZAP command, 431
Program design, 401-411. *See also* Design
Program errors, debugging, 499
PROGRAM function, (defined, 746-747)
Program menus, 407, 408
Program modules, 405-406
Program power
    assembler guidelines, 519-520
    enhancing, 515-520
Program routine, 545
Programming
    defined, 367-369
    using modular, 523-531
Programs
    crashing, 407
    halting, 430
    installing, 23
    loading FoxPro, 26
    speeding up, 490-496
ProKey, 292
PROMPT function, (defined, 747)

PROW function, (defined), 747-748
Pseudocodes, 408, 419, 423, 466
PUBLIC command, 496, (defined, 656)
Public variables, 378
Pull-down menu. *See* Menu
PUTFILE function, (defined, 748)
Puzzle option, 43
PV function, (defined, 748)

Q

Queries, 191-219
    performing from menus, 192-205
    performing with commands, 206-214
Question mark statement, 32, 477, 478
Quick Report dialog box, 64, (illus., 64)
Quick Report option, 5, 222, 224-225, 229, 247, 267, 339
Quick reports, 63-65
QUIT command, 70, 430, (defined, 656-657)
Quit FoxView, 167, 551
Quotes, used with SAY command, 436

R

RAM, retrieving data from, 174-175
RAND function, (defined, 749)
Range column, 181, 187-190, help screen for, 187-188, (illus., 188)
RAT function, (defined, 749)
RATLINE function, (defined, 750)
READ command, 442, 460, (defined, 657)
Read option, 437-439
READKEY function, (defined, 750)

RECALL command, 94-96, (defined, 657-658)
Recompiling, program, 374
Record menu (ALT-R), 28, 61, 77
    append option in, 55
    changing a database from, 73, 74
    delete option in, 91
Record number, 77
Record option, 192-193, 194, 195
Record pointer, 332, 334
Records, 7, (illus., 8). *See also* Rows
    adding new, 61, 80
    alphabetizing, 118
    default screen, 55
    deleting, 91-96, 466-468
    editing, 460-463
    hiding, 214
    limiting number in report, 226-227
    limiting printing of, 323
    marking for delete, 83, 94-95
    matching across files, 330
    moving between with Change mode, 73
    searching for, 77, 191-219
    testing for mismatched, 336
    tracking, 69-70
    updating, 89
RECSIZE function, 751
Recursive loop, 299
REINDEX command, 135-136, 137, 336, (defined, 658)
    from menus, 137
RELEASE ALL command, 380
RELEASE command, (defined, 658-659)
Related databases, 333, 347-358
Related fields, 346-347

Relating files, 332-336, 347-358
Relation
    overriding of commands, 354
    setting in multiple files, 332
Relational, 327-331. *See also* Link
    application using three files, 348
    capabilities of FoxPro, 5
    data in dBASE, 345
    data listed, 338
    databases, 9-11, 20, 328-330, (illus., 329)
    expression, 549
Relational files, 345
    error messages in, 337
    using a filter, 346
    using SET VIEW command in, 337
Relational link, 331-335, 337
Relational operators, 384, (listed, 384)
Relational reports, 328, 338-344, (illus., 328)
    designing, 339
    groups of orders in, 354-355
Relational use, 345
Relationships, 337-343, 351-365, (illus., 353, 359, 360, 362)
    analyzing types of, 358-365
    between fields, 19-23, 358
    from command level, 336-337
    verification of, 338
RELATION function, (defined, 751-752)
Remove Line option, 306
RENAME command, (defined, 659)
Renaming, files in Filer, 276
Repeating commands, 414-416, 475
REPLACE command, 98-99, 464, 659-660

REPLACE command, *continued*
    distinguished from CHANGE, 98, 99
Replacements, global, 96-99
REPLICATE function, 520, 522, (defined, 752)
Report band, 235
Report design screen, 63
Report dialog box, 65, 225-227, (illus., 226)
Report Expression dialog box, 243, 245-246, 250-252, 264-265, 307, 312, 355, (illus., 242, 250)
REPORT FORM command, 233, 344, 472, 480, 481, (defined, 660-661)
Report Generator, 5, 222, 224, 310, 472, 476-477
Report menu, 306, 237
Report option, 65, 552
Report specification, 235-237, 240, 312, (illus., 235, 236, 254)
Reports, 16, 221-272, 306, 312
    based on selected data, 205-206
    changing design of, 238-242
    columnar, 206, 222-223
    command for starting new, 339
    creating quick, 63-65
    creating relational, 338-344
    creating selective, 228-231
    custom, 222
    deleting objects from, 247-248
    designing customized columnar, 234-248
    generating from stored forms, 472-474
    generating with commands, 231-234
    indexing, 270
    moving objects in, 247-248
    plain without headings, 227, 233

Reports, *continued*
    printing, 231-233, 248, 256, 270
    quick, 222, 224-225, 229, (illus., 340)
    relational, 328, 332
    saving, 234, 248, 344
    viewing successive pages of, 240
    writing with program code, 475-479
Resequence (F5), 183-184
Resize function (F4), 159
Resize Partitions option, 84
Rest option, 194, 195
RESTORE commands, (defined, 661-662)
RESTORE FROM command, 379
Restoring memory variables, 379
RESUME command, (defined, 662)
RETURN command, 395, 496, (defined, 664)
Return key, 30
RETRY command, (defined, 663)
Reverse video, 180, 510
RIGHT function, (defined, 752)
Right Margin Column option, 239
ROUND function, (defined, 752)
Routines, 530-531, (illus., 528, 530)
Row column, 179
ROW function, 522-523, (defined, 753)
Rows, 7, (illus., 8). *See also* Records
RTOD function, (defined, 753)
RUN command, 279-280, (defined, 664-665)

S

Sample clause, 323
Sample menu screen, (illus., 369)

Index

Save As entry, 111
Save button, 54, 65
SAVE command, 372, 665
SAVE MACROS command, (defined, 665)
SAVE SCREEN command, (defined, 666)
Save Table option, 157, 166, 174
SAVE TO command, 378, 379
SAVE WINDOW command, (defined, 666)
Saving label designs, 321
Saving variables, 379
SAY command, 436, 437
SCAN command, 416-418, (defined, 666-667)
Scanning, 79
SCATTER TO command, (defined, 667)
SCHEME function, (defined, 753-754)
SCOLS function, (defined, 754)
Scope option, 92, 226, 323, 398
Scope parameter, 98
Screen
    alias, (illus., 548)
    calling text and string variables on, 436
    clearing, 32-33
    customizing, 440-446
    data entry, 57-58
    default, 55, (illus., 56)
    design hints, 434, 469
    display, 433-434, 437, 438, (illus., 434)
    displaying prompts on, 464
    erasing, 437
    form modifying, 168-169
    format, 4
    FoxPro, (illus., 435)
    putting information on, 435-440
    report design, 63
    saving in FoxPro, 164
Screen format files, 164, 167-168, 174, (illus., 168)
    saving, 164-167
Screen preview, (illus., 239)

Screen prompts, 437-439
Scroll bar, 39, 42, 61, 79, 80, 86
SCROLL command, (defined, 668)
SCROLL LOCK key, 156
Scrolling, 39, 67
SDF file, 579
SDF format, 581
Search, 193-194
    DISPLAY command to, 67-68
    index files, 137-139
    results, (illus., 76)
    sequential, 207-209
    with Locate option, 73
    within fields, 68-69
Search expression, 74
Search option, 547
Secondary field, in sort, 118
SECONDS function, (defined, 754)
SEEK command, 206, 210-214, 457, 462, 508, (defined, 668)
    comparing with Locate and Continue, 211-214
    in indexed files, 137-139
Seek function, (defined, 754-755)
Seek option, 193-194, 201-202
Select Box menu, 170, (illus., 171)
Select command, 333, (defined, 669)
Select From Template List option, 157, 165
Select function, (defined, 755)
Selected fields, sorting, 119-120
Selective reports, creating, 228-231
Sequential search, 217
SET BELL command, 204
SET CARRY command, 504
SET COLOR command, 504-505
SET COLOR TO command, 450
SET commands, 48, 504-513, (defined, 669-699)

SET CONSOLE command, 505-506
SET DATE command, 388, 506
SET DELETED command, 94-95, 468
SET DELIMITERS command, 510
SET DEVELOPMENT ON command, 374
SET DEVICE TO PRINT statement, 477, 478
SET EXACT command, 209, 507
SET ESCAPE command, 458, 506-507
SET FIELDS command, 225, 229-231, 345, (illus., 230)
SET FILTER command, 205, 214-218, 228, 323, 347, 472, 474
    in selective indexing, 125
Set Filter Expression window, 203-205, (illus., 204)
SET FORMAT TO command, 447
SET FUNCTION command, 508-510, 755
SET INDEX command, 130-132
SET INTENSITY command, 510
SET MARGIN command, 234
SET MEMOWIDTH TO command, 511-512
SET MESSAGE TO command, 512-513
SET NEAR command, 508
SET ORDER command, 133
SET PRINT ON command, 399-400, 471, 478, 486
SET PROCEDURE command, 491
SET RELATION command, 327, 333, 335-336, 354, 357, 549
SET SAFETY command, 431, 513
SET SHADOWS command, 457
SET STATUS command, 513

SET TALK command, 394
SET VIEW command, 337, 338, 344
Settings, width, 302
Setup dialog box, 203, (illus., 203)
SHIFT key, 29
SHIFT-TAB
    reversing movement through dialog choices, 40
    shifting fields right with, 80
SHOW MENU command, (defined, 699)
SHOW POPUP command, (defined, 700)
SHOW WINDOW command, (defined, 700)
Showing variables, 496-499
SideKick, memory consumed by, 24
SIGN function, (defined, 755-756)
Simple database application, 538
    template, 536, 554
SIN function, (defined, 756)
Size, changing window, 36-37
Size column, in Filer, 275
Size control dot, 37
Size Field option, 37, 82, 87, 278
SKIP command, 394-395, (defined, 701)
Skip option, 192
Social Security numbers
    as character fields, 49
    as database fields, 48
    use in relational databases, 21
Software packages, transferring files between, 563-584
Sort
    ASCII, 117
    character/dictionary, 117
SORT command, 108, 110, 117, 118, 119, 140-141, (defined, 701-702)
    conditional use of, 119
Sort dialog box, 111, (illus., 111)

Sort option, 108, 278
Sort Order box, 111, 115
Sorting
    adding records and, 120
    alphabetical, 108
    combinations of fields, 115
    database, 107, 108-120, (illus., 109)
    database subsets, 118-119
    disadvantages to, 120
    in ascending order, 108
    in descending order, 108
    multiple fields, 114-118, (illus., 116)
    new file creation while, 120
SOUNDEX function, (defined, 756)
Space, blank, 391
Space function, 391, 756-757
Spaces
    removing blank, 391-392
    removing leading, 393
Special Characters option, 43
Special features, 550
Speeding the program with Procedures, 490
Speeding up programs, 490-496
Split indicator, 84
Spreadsheets, 559, 561
    limitations as simple database managers, 10
    transferring from FoxPro to, 578-579
    transferring to FoxPro, 579-581
Square Root function (SQRT), 757
SROWS function, (defined, 757)
Storage, efficiency of database, 8
STORE command, 375, 702
Storing commands in command files, 409
Storing output in ASCII text files, 322

Storing responses to screen prompts, 437-439
Storing variables, 379
Stretch Vertically option, 245, 253
String function (STR), 128, 302-303, 393, (defined, 757)
    converting numeric field with, 128-129
String operators, 385
STRTRAN function, (defined, 758)
Structure
    copying database, 289
    dialog box, 102
Structure-Modify option, 100
STUFF function, (defined, 758)
Style option, 243, 245
Subdirectories
    changing, 25
    creating on hard disk with installation disk, 23
    data files in, 26
Submodule, 524
Subscript, 243
Subsets
    selecting, 202-205
    sorting database, 118-119
SUBSTR function, (defined, 758)
SUM command, 397-399, (defined, 703)
Summary bands, 236, 240, 254-256, 306
Summary option, 227
Summary records, 398, 399
SuperCalc, (illus., 580)
SuperKey, 292
    memory consumed by, 24
Superscript, 243
Suppress Repeated Values option, 246
SUSPEND command, (defined, 703-704)
Symphony, 561
    transferring between FoxPro and, 575-578
SYS function, (defined, 759)

Index 789

System Data format (SDF), 557, 559-560
System file, 369
System requirements for FoxPro, 14

T

Tab, 40-41, 54
TAB key, 29, 80
Table View, 156, 158, 169, 176-182, (illus., 177)
    advantages over Forms View, 176
    columns within, 177-182
    exiting, 156
    moving fields and objects in, 182-184
    switching to Forms View from, 176
Tables
    adding fields to, 182
    database, 7, 10
    deleting fields from, 183
    displaying information on, 59, (illus., 60)
    loading into FoxView, 169
    saving in FoxView, 164, 166, 169
Tabular format, 4
Tag options, 275-276
TAN function, (defined, 759-760)
TARGET function, (defined, 760)
Telephone directory, contrasted with database, 8-9
Telephone numbers
    adding to database, 22
    as character fields, 49
Templates, 165, 181, 443-446, 535, 548, 550, 554, 556, (illus., 166)
    application, 556
    field, 160
    FoxPro, 29
    list of, (illus., 537)
    picture, 184-187
    to build application, 545

Text
    adding, (CTRL-N), 163, 240
    adding to reports, 246-247
    display of, 401
    intermixing fields in, 308
    limitations in memo field, 57
    printing commands, 399-401
    storage of blocks, 48
Text command, 401, 704
    within a command file, 401
Text objects, 180
Text option, 246-247
Textobject designation, in TableView, 178
Time
    function for, 305, 760
    placed in reports or labels, 305
Title bands, 236, 240
Title bar, 37
Title option, 64
Title/Summary option, 240, (illus., 241)
To File clause, 323
To File option, 233, 322
To Print check box, 65
To Print command, 232, 323
To Print option, 206, 227, 322
Toggle, 37
Toggle Delete option, 83
Token Ring network, 15
Top Margin option, 239
Top option, 192, 539
TOTAL command, (defined, 704-705)
Total dialog box, 255-256, (illus., 256)
Totaling option, 245-246
Trace option, 40
TRANSFORM function, (defined, 760-761)
Tree option, 278
TRIM function, 302, 391-392, (defined, 761)
Triple spacing, 416
True/False data type, m 4-5.
    See also Logical data
True value, 48

Type column, in Database Structure dialog box, 49
Type column, in Table View, 178
TYPE command, 449, (defined, 705)
Type function, (defined, 761)

U

Underline, 243
Unlink Partitions option, 81, 86
UPDATE command, (defined, 705-706)
UPDATED function, (defined, 761-762)
UPPER function, 389, 762
Uppercase, 139, 389, 762
    letters, 144-146, 389
    letters in sorting, 109-111
USE command, 55, 77, (defined, 706, 707)
    choosing database file with, 65-66
    opening index files with, 130
USED function, (defined, 762)

V

VAL function, (defined, 762-763)
Valid column, 181
Value to Seek window, 201-202, (illus., 201)
Values, 513
    stored in memory, 394
    storing, 395
Variable names (Varname), 436
    length, 375
    storing occurences in, 397
    using DOS wildcards in, 499
Variables, 464, 497
    displaying lists of, 377-378
    erasing memory, 380
    hiding and showing, 496-499

Variables, *continued*
    losing memory, 496
    moving into database fields, 464
    naming, 378
    private, 496-497, 498
    problems with public and private, 497
    public, 378, 496-497
    restoring memory, 379
    saving, 378
    selecting specific, 380
    storing, 377, 378
    system memory, 479
    temporary storage of, 463
    types of, 375
VARREAD function, 763
Verify button, 197
VERSION function, 763
Vertical lines
    hiding with Grid Off option, 81
    removing with Grid Off option, 85
    restoring, 85
Vertical placement, text object, 180
View Files, 218-219, 323
VIEW FORMS command, 156
View option, 40

W

WAIT command, 401, 430
WCOLS function, 763-764
WEXIST function, 764)
While clause, 323, 398-399
    dialog box, 199-200
    window, 199-200
While option, 92, 199-200
    in Report dialog box, 226, 227
Wid column, in Table View, 178
Width
    column, 101
    changing field in Browse mode, 87-88

Width, *continued*
    determining field, 49-50
    entry area, 178
    label, 316, 317
    names, 302, 307-308
    limitations of field, 49
Width box, 243
Wildcards, 275
Window menu
    opening (ALT-W), 35, 67, (illus., 36)
Windows, 35-40
    active, 35, 38
    anchoring, 67
    Browse, 79, 456
    Change Partitions option and, 81
    changing sizes of, 37
    closing, (CTRL-W), 62
    color options for, 453-455
    deactivating, 456
    defining, 453-455
    displaying hidden, 38
    double option for, 453
    hiding, distinguished from closing, 35
    LIST commands in, 455
    manipulating, 83-85
    moving, 36-37
    multiple, 351
    opening, 439, 440
    resizing with mouse, 37
    restoring split back to single, 82
    shadow option for, 453
    splitting into partitions, 84-85
    title option for, 453
    unlinking portions of, 81
    using, 452-458
    using All option to activate, 452
WONTOP function, (defined, 764)
Word processing programs, 57
    organizing data with, 9-10

WordPerfect
    MailMerge feature, 572-575, 582
WordStar, 568-569
    creating command files with, 373
    MailMerge, 559
    to FoxPro from, 581-583
    transferring FoxPro to, 563-565, 567
Word-wrapping, 65
Work area, database file, 283
Work stations, memory required to run FoxPro in, 14
WOUTPUT function, (defined, 764-765)
Wrapping
    text, 245
    word, 65
WROWS function, (defined, 765)
WVISIBLE function, (defined, 765)

Y

Year,
    expression for, 305-306
    placed in reports, 305-306
YEAR function, (defined, 765)

Z

ZAP command, (defined, 707)
ZIP code, 8, 18, 50
    field, 50, 181
    indexed alphabetically, 132
    indexing, 127, 131
    replacing, 96-97
Zoom, window, 80
Zoom control,
    mouse-activated, 37
Zoom indicator, 83
Zoom option, 37, 83, (illus., 84)